HISTORY OF
THE SECOND WORLD WAR

UNITED KINGDOM MEDICAL SERIES

Editor-in-Chief:

Sir Arthur S. MacNalty, K.C.B., M.D., F.R.C.P., F.R.C.S.

THE EMERGENCY MEDICAL SERVICES

EDITED BY
Lieut. Colonel C. L. DUNN,
C.I.E., I.M.S. (ret.)

VOLUME II
Scotland, Northern Ireland and the Principal Air Raids on Industrial Centres in Great Britain

The Naval & Military Press Ltd

LONDON
HER MAJESTY'S STATIONERY OFFICE
1953

Published by

The Naval & Military Press Ltd
Unit 5 Riverside, Brambleside
Bellbrook Industrial Estate
Uckfield, East Sussex
TN22 1QQ England

Tel: +44 (0)1825 749494

www.naval-military-press.com
www.nmarchive.com

In reprinting in facsimile from the original, any imperfections are inevitably reproduced and the quality may fall short of modern type and cartographic standards.

EDITORIAL BOARD

Sir CYRIL FLOWER, C.B., F.S.A. (*Chairman*)

Sir WELDON DALRYMPLE-CHAMPNEYS, Bart., D.M., F.R.C.P.
Sir FRANCIS R. FRASER, M.D., F.R.C.P.
} *Ministry of Health*

Sir ANDREW DAVIDSON, M.D., F.R.C.P. Ed., F.R.C.S. Ed.
A. K. BOWMAN, M.B., Ch.B., F.R.F.P.S.
} *Department of Health for Scotland*

J. BOYD, M.D., F.R.C.P.I. — *Government of Northern Ireland*

Sir HAROLD HIMSWORTH, K.C.B., M.D., F.R.C.P.
JANET VAUGHAN, O.B.E., D.M., F.R.C.P.
} *Medical Research Council*

Surgeon Vice Admiral K. A. INGLEBY MACKENZIE, C.B., B.M., B.Ch., Q.H.P.
} *Admiralty*

Lt. General F. HARRIS, C.B., C.B.E., M.C., M.B., Q.H.S.
Brigadier H. T. FINDLAY, M.B., Ch.B.
} *War Office*

Air Marshal J. M. KILPATRICK, C.B. O.B.E., M.B., B.Ch., D.P.H., Q.H.P.
} *Air Ministry*

Brigadier H. B. LATHAM
A. B. ACHESON, ESQ., C.M.G.
} *Cabinet Office*

Editor-in-Chief: Sir ARTHUR S. MACNALTY, K.C.B., M.D., F.R.C.P., F.R.C.S.

Secretary: W. FRANKLIN MELLOR

The following persons served on the Editorial Board for varying periods: The Rt. Hon. R. A. Butler, P.C., M.A., F.R.G.S., M.P. (*Chairman*); Brigadier General Sir James E. Edmonds, C.B., C.M.G., D.Litt. (*Committee of Imperial Defence*); Surgeon Vice Admiral Sir Sheldon F. Dudley, K.C.B., O.B.E., M.D., F.R.C.P., F.R.C.S. Ed., F.R.S.; Surgeon Vice Admiral Sir Henry St. Clair Colson, K.C.B., C.B.E., F.R.C.P.; Surgeon Vice Admiral Sir Edward Greeson, K.B.E., C.B., M.D., Ch.B. (*Admiralty*); Lt. General Sir William P. MacArthur, K.C.B., D.S.O., O.B.E., M.D., B.Ch., D.Sc., F.R.C.P.; Lt. General Sir Alexander Hood, G.B.E., K.C.B., M.D., F.R.C.P., LL.D.; Lt. General Sir Neil Cantlie, K.C.B., K.B.E., C.B., M.C., M.B., F.R.C.S.; Major General H. M. J. Perry, C.B., O.B.E.; Major General L. T. Poole, C.B., D.S.O., M.C., M.B., Ch.B.; Brigadier J. S. K. Boyd, O.B.E., M.D., F.R.S. (*War Office*); Air Marshal Sir Harold E. Whittingham, K.C.B., K.B.E., M.B., Ch.B., F.R.C.P., F.R.C.S., LL.D.; Air Marshal Sir Andrew Grant, K.B.E., C.B., M.B., Ch.B., D.P.H.; Air Marshal Sir P. C. Livingston, K.B.E., C.B., A.F.C., F.R.C.S. (*Air Ministry*); Sir Edward Mellanby, G.B.E., K.C.B., M.D., F.R.C.P., F.R.S. (*Medical Research Council*); Professor J. M. Mackintosh, M.A., M.D., F.R.C.P. (*Department of Health for Scotland*); Lt. Colonel J. S. Yule, O.B.E., Philip Allen, Esq., G. Godfrey Phillips, Esq., M. T. Flett, Esq., A. M. R. Topham, Esq., D. F. Hubback, Esq. (*Cabinet Office*).

EDITORIAL COMMITTEE

Sir ARTHUR S. MACNALTY, K.C.B., M.D., F.R.C.P., F.R.C.S.
(*Chairman*)

Surgeon Commander J. L. S. COULTER, D.S.C., M.R.C.S., L.R.C.P. (Barrister at Law) } *Admiralty*

Professor F. A. E. CREW, D.Sc., M.D., F.R.C.P. Ed., F.R.S. } *War Office*

Squadron Leader S. C. REXFORD-WELCH, M.R.C.S., L.R.C.P. } *Air Ministry*

A. K. BOWMAN, M.B., Ch.B., F.R.F.P.S. { *Department of Health for Scotland*

J. BOYD, M.D., F.R.C.P.I. { *Government of Northern Ireland*

F. H. K. GREEN, C.B.E., M.D., F.R.C.P. — *Medical Research Council*

J. ALISON GLOVER, C.B.E., M.D., F.R.C.P. — *Ministry of Education*

A. SANDISON, O.B.E., M.D. — *Ministry of Pensions*

Lt. Colonel C. L. DUNN, C.I.E., I.M.S. (ret.)
V. ZACHARY COPE, B.A., M.D., M.S., F.R.C.S. } *Ministry of Health*

Secretary: W. FRANKLIN MELLOR

The following persons served on the Editorial Committee for varying periods:

Surgeon Commander J. J. Keevil, D.S.O., M.D.; Surgeon Lieutenant L. D. de Launay, M.B., B.S.; Surgeon Lieutenant Commander N. M. McArthur, M.D.; Surgeon Commander A. D. Sinclair, M.B., Ch.B. (*Admiralty*); Colonel S. Lyle Cummins, C.B., C.M.G., LL.D., M.D. (*War Office*); Wing Commander R. Oddie, M.B., B.Ch.; Wing Commander E. B. Davies, M.B., B.Ch.; Squadron Leader R. Mortimer, M.B., B.S.; Squadron Leader H. N. H. Genese, M.R.C.S., L.R.C.P. (*Air Ministry*); Charles E. Newman, M.D., F.R.C.P.; N. G. Horner, M.D., F.R.C.P., F.R.C.S. (*Ministry of Health*).

FOREWORD

This is the second Volume of the History of the Emergency Medical Services, the first of which was published in October 1952. It contains the history of these Services in Scotland and Northern Ireland, and the story of great air attacks on the chief Industrial Centres following the end of the Battle of Britain from September 1940, until June 1941. It also includes the 'Baedeker' raids in 1942.

The E.M.S. volumes of the Official Medical History of the war have been prepared under the direction of the Editorial Board appointed by H.M. Government; but the authors and editor are alone responsible for the method of presentation of the facts and the opinions expressed.

A.S.M.
Editor-in-Chief

PREFACE

PARTS I and II of this volume bring out the differences in the composition and administration of the Emergency Medical Services in Scotland and Northern Ireland which may be attributed chiefly to the differences in local authority administration and the topography of these countries. In Scotland, however, one of the chief differences was the central control of all *ad hoc* E.M.S. Hospitals, whether converted from existing buildings or newly constructed, and in the central control of the Auxiliary Hospital Services.

Although these areas of Britain did not experience such heavy attacks from the air as England and South Wales, their history shows that Scotland was subjected to a considerably greater number of air attacks than is generally known. Some of these were severe, such as those on Glasgow and Clydebank, and frequent, such as those on the North-East Coast.

In Northern Ireland there were very few enemy attacks outside Belfast, but during the second of the four raids on this city more people were killed in a raid lasting just over six hours than in any one day raid in England, outside London.

The stories of the raids in Part III are necessarily only samples, chosen in an endeavour to give a representative picture of the various E.M.S. services in action under the strain of heavy attacks, in the concerted enemy effort to disrupt the vital industrial organisation of the nation for war. It has truly been said that if the spirit of London had broken and had not stood up to the enemy as it did, the war would have been lost.

June 1952.
C. L. D.

CONTENTS

PART I: THE EMERGENCY MEDICAL SERVICES IN SCOTLAND

	PAGE
INTRODUCTION	3
CHAPTER 1: THE ORGANISATION OF THE CASUALTY SERVICES	5
CHAPTER 2: THE EMERGENCY HOSPITAL SERVICE	20
CHAPTER 3: THE ANCILLARY SERVICES:	
Personnel: Medical, Nursing and Lay Services	49
The Ancillary Hospital Services:	
The Emergency Laboratory Services	64
The Blood Transfusion Service	68
Rehabilitation	72
The Transport Services	76
The Civil Defence Casualty Services	79
CHAPTER 4: THE CLYDE ANCHORAGES	87
CHAPTER 5: THE EMERGENCY MEDICAL SERVICES IN ACTION	97
Hospital Occupancy Statistics	117
Conclusions	120
References	120
APPENDIX	121

PART II: THE EMERGENCY MEDICAL SERVICES IN NORTHERN IRELAND

INTRODUCTION	124
CHAPTER 1: EARLY STEPS TO CREATE A CASUALTY SERVICE IN THE PRE-WAR PERIOD	125
CHAPTER 2: EXPANSION AND WORK OF THE HOSPITALS FROM SEPTEMBER 1935 TO APRIL 1941	130
CHAPTER 3: WORK OF THE HOSPITALS FROM APRIL 1941 TO THE END OF THE WAR	142
CHAPTER 4: CIVIL DEFENCE AND AMBULANCE SERVICES	152
CHAPTER 5: MEDICAL AND NURSING PERSONNEL	163
CHAPTER 6: THE LABORATORY SERVICES	182

PART III: THE AIR RAIDS ON INDUSTRIAL CENTRES 1940–41 AND THE "BAEDEKER" RAIDS 1942

CHAPTER 1: LONDON	195
CHAPTER 2: MERSEYSIDE	317

	PAGE
CHAPTER 3: MANCHESTER GROUP	341
CHAPTER 4: BIRMINGHAM	358
CHAPTER 5: COVENTRY	370
CHAPTER 6: SOUTHAMPTON	383
CHAPTER 7: PORTSMOUTH	396
CHAPTER 8: PLYMOUTH	405
CHAPTER 9: BRISTOL	414
CHAPTER 10: SHEFFIELD	423
CHAPTER 11: HULL	433
CHAPTER 12: SOUTH WALES	443
CHAPTER 13: BELFAST	453
CHAPTER 14: THE 'BAEDEKER' RAIDS, 1942	461
INDEX	488

LIST OF PLATES

Page

London

London Regional Map 194

Plate   *Following page*

I. A Typical Example of Damage to a Hospital. Wrecked Wing of Mile End Hospital
II. Wreckage of St. Pancras Hospital . . . ⎫ 232
III. A Damaged Ward. The Middlesex Hospital . ⎭
IV. Casualties being Rescued in Bromley . . . ⎫ 236
V. A Typical Rescue Scene, Bromley . . . ⎭
VI. River Ambulance Service: Accommodation In Saloon . . . . . .
VII. River Ambulance: Service Stretcher Parties at Work
VIII. ,, ,, ,, ,, ,, ,, .
IX. ,, ,, ,, ,, ,, ,, .
X. Rescue Scene: Releasing Woman Trapped for Several Hours . . . . .
XI. Rescue Scene: Trapped Child being Saved by Rescue Workers . . . . .
XII. The Medical Services in Action: Doctor Waiting for Victims being Released from Debris . .
XIII. The Medical Services in Action: A Specialist Preparing Instruments for an Operation on Trapped Victim . . . . ⎬ 312
XIV. Rescue Scene: Victim being Carried Away after Operation . . . . . .
XV. The Medical Services in Action: Women Patients Evacuated from a Bombed Hospital to a School
XVI. The Medical Services in Action: Clothing for Casualties being got ready by Nurses, Guy's Hospital . . . . . .
XVII. Anglo-American Ambulance Corps in Action .

Merseyside

XVIII. The Wrecked Mill Road Hospital . . .
XIX. The Wrecked Operating Theatre, Mill Road Hospital, May 3-4, 1941 . . . .
XX. Burnt out Ward in the Maternity Hospital, Liverpool . . . . ⎬ 316
XXI. The Home of Professor McMurray, Professor of Orthopaedic Surgery, Liverpool University, May 4, 1941 . . . .

Plate *Following page*

XXII. A Wrecked Block, Birkenhead Municipal Hospital
XXIII. A Damaged First-Aid Post, Wallasey . . . } 316

BIRMINGHAM

XXIV. Ambulance Attendants Assisting in Rescue . .
XXV. Searching the Debris for Victims . . . } 360
XXVI. Mobile Canteen in Operation . . . .

COVENTRY

XXVII. A Typical First-Aid Post in a School . . .
XXVIII. Operating Theatre in Upgraded First-Aid Post .
XXIX. Coventry and Warwickshire Hospital, A Wrecked Wing, April 1941 . . . . . } 376
XXX. Coventry and Warwickshire Hospital, Scene Following Raid, April 1941 . . . .

PORTSMOUTH

XXXI. Scene Following the First Raid . . . .
XXXII. Salvaging after Raid which Damaged the Royal Portsmouth Hospital . . . . .

PLYMOUTH
} 404

XXXIII. City Hospital, Children and Nurse . . .
XXXIV. City Hospital, Bombed Wing, 32 Babies Killed .

BRISTOL

XXXV. A Damaged Ward of the Homœopathic Hospital .
XXXVI. Incident in Street. First-Aid Parties at Work . } 416

EXETER

XXXVII. The Wrecked City Hospital . . . .
XXXVIII.   ,,   ,,   ,,   ,, ...

NORWICH
} 472

XXXIX. The Woodlands Hospital, April 29, 1942 . .
XL. The Norfolk and Norwich Hospital on Fire, April 28, 1942 . . . . . .

PART I

The Emergency Medical Services in Scotland

FOREWORD
by the
Chief Medical Officer of the Department of Health for Scotland

THESE chapters, which describe the Emergency Medical Services in Scotland, were written by Dr. Alexander Bowman. They were compiled from official records and files, but the whole narrative is punctuated by evidence of his intimate personal knowledge of the events he describes. He was one of the Department's hospital officers from the beginning and served in that capacity throughout the war. I wish here to express my grateful acknowledgement of the work he has done in writing the account of a service in which he himself played a not inconsiderable part.

May 29, 1952   ANDREW DAVIDSON

INTRODUCTION

OF all the civilian medical interests which were associated, in Scotland, with the War of 1939-45, or which developed under the stimulus of war-time conditions, none exceeded in importance or potential permanent value that which was related to the Emergency Medical Services. The impulses which constituted its propelling force proceeded, in common with those which affected the nation as a whole, from the elementary necessity for a mechanism calculated to operate efficiently in the face of enemy action, and particularly of hostile aerial activity. All planning upon this subject had therefore to be orientated in accordance with what appeared to be the cardinal needs, although no one, of course, could venture to suggest in advance precisely what these needs might be. There were, however, certain broad strategic considerations which had to be kept constantly in mind and which permitted scheme-making upon what appeared to be a reasonable plan. The first of these considerations was the geography of the country, the second, concentrations of population and the third, lines of communication.

A historical review of the many factors which had to be taken into account in relation to medical preparations for a future war is contained in that part of the English narrative which deals with events between the years 1923 and 1935, and it is not proposed to consider here matters which have been dealt with in some detail elsewhere. A word may, nevertheless, be said about the strategic considerations which have been mentioned above, for it was upon these that much that was afterwards accomplished was to depend.

The two contingencies which appeared to have special relevance in the years which preceded the actual crisis were the possibility of invasion and the possibility—or rather probability, as it was generally believed—of savage and devastating attack from the air. It appeared, for example, that the open sea route from the German to the Scottish coast formed a more likely channel for invasion than the narrower waters of the southern reaches of the North Sea— for the possibility of the rapid elimination of France from a general struggle had scarcely been expected. The potential menace presented by a Scottish coast presumably favourable to some part of the enemy's intentions was thus responsible for much that followed. Fortunately, the general medical plan which suggested itself in response to the fear of invasion fitted in well with the second contingency; and thus, for the most part, medical schemes devised with invasion in mind were considered to be applicable also to conditions likely to be encountered under massive air attack.

The main concentrations of population in Scotland are those around the urban areas of Edinburgh, Aberdeen and Dundee, and—by far the most important—the area within a circle of 20 miles' radius with its centre in the City of Glasgow. This was a determining factor in the decisions which were made in connexion with new hospital building.

The simple provision of hospital accommodation and equipment was in itself no more than a means to an end, for of themselves these material assets form only the mechanism, which has to be co-ordinated and controlled by human agencies. The problem of medical, nursing and ancillary personnel must therefore be prominent in the narrative which follows; and an attempt is made to present the facts, a mere tabulation of which would be tedious to writer and reader alike, in a form at once concise and acceptable.

Compared with many other parts of the country, the occasions upon which the Scottish population came directly face to face with enemy activity were few. The greatest of them occurred during the spring of 1941, which was a testing time. These phases of major activity suggested that the plan upon which the hospital services had been built up was sound; and further testimony to this effect was presented by the facility with which casualties from the various fighting fronts, as well as service sick from the Home Commands, were absorbed and cared for by the organisation. The relative scarcity of wounded, moreover, during long periods of time, permitted the establishment of new medical services for the civilian population; and there was little doubt that the knowledge gained in connexion with these new services would be of significance in the development and administration of the national medical plans for the future.

CHAPTER 1
THE ORGANISATION OF THE CASUALTY SERVICES

ALTHOUGH the formal authority for the establishment of the Emergency Medical Services dated from 1939, the emergency planning of the Department of Health for Scotland may, for practical purposes, be said to have had its origin in the Report of a Sub-Committee of the Committee of Imperial Defence which, under the Chairmanship of Sir Arthur S. MacNalty, was charged with the duty of inquiring into the methods of casualty disposal likely to be most effective under the conditions which were expected (see Volume I, Chapter 2). One of the major difficulties encountered throughout the pre-war years was, of course, the uncertainty which existed as to the real potentialities of a situation which was new and had no counterpart in history from which the main features and probable developments could be deduced. It is true that there had been demonstrations of serious air raiding and of the effects of aerial bombardment during the War of 1914–18; and more recently the disquieting sequence of events, first in Abyssinia and then in Spain, had been graphically described. Yet the data which thus became available were significant only up to a point, for the lessons which could be gathered were hardly applicable to our own conditions of life, the concentrations of industry and of population, for example, as well as the types of building characteristic of the industrial age. Above all, the presumptive weight of the hostile air arm—the opposing force which was most dreaded from the civilian point of view—could not be accurately or even adequately assessed. It was, nevertheless, generally accepted that a situation of extreme gravity had to be faced; and it was commonly believed that the fate of the British nation might well depend upon the issue of a series of events which were likely to be devastating if not completely disastrous, although no one could foretell their probable effects.

ADMINISTRATIVE RESPONSIBILITY

All these considerations made it necessary that the Report of the MacNalty Committee, which was presented to and approved by the Government in October 1937, should be framed in general terms only. Through its agency, however, the following obligations containing medical connotations were laid upon the Secretary of State for Scotland:

(a) The organisation of an Emergency Hospital Service.
(b) The recruitment of medical, nursing and ancillary personnel.
(c) The review and development of ambulance services.

(d) The co-ordination of considerations relating to personnel, accommodation, supplies and equipment.

(e) The appointment of executive officers—the Hospital Officers—to deal with the operational needs of the casualty services in each of the five Civil Defence Districts into which the Scottish Region (Region No. 11) was to be divided on the outbreak of war.

With all these responsibilities in mind—and they were only part of an obligation which included the projected evacuation of population, the organisation of a system of emergency relief, the safeguarding of water supplies, the care of children and expectant mothers, the treatment and prevention of infectious diseases and so forth—it became clear that a radical reorientation and redistribution of the resources of the Scottish Department of Health was called for. Before the necessary changes could take place, however, it was essential that at least certain of the needs and problems which were likely to present themselves should be brought into focus and defined. It was not, therefore, until August 1938, that is, within two months of the Munich crisis, that the planning which had already taken place led to the formation of a Defence Section within the Establishment Division of the Department of Health. To this Defence Section, which was hardly more than nuclear, fell the important and urgent task of formulating and furthering immediate schemes for those aspects of Passive Civil Defence and Civilian Welfare which were war time functions of the Department. The Defence Section continued to expand, however, and it operated continuously until September 12, 1939. On this date, twelve days after the German invasion of Poland and nine days after the British declaration of war, the permanent war-time Divisions of the Department were established, and five of the eight Departmental Divisions were given responsibilities which were wholly associated with the war.

THE REGIONAL ORGANISATION

Long before these general administrative changes had taken place, however, the hospital organisation had come into being. In its earliest phase—the appointment of Hospital Officers for the South-eastern District (Headquarters, Edinburgh) and the Western District (Glasgow)—this new organisation, whose medical staff was recruited from the Regional Medical staff of the Department of Health, more or less coincided in its inception with the hospital survey, mentioned below, which was carried out in the spring of 1938 by a medical and an administrative member of the Department. In due time, Hospital Office organisations were also established in the remaining Districts—the Eastern (Dundee), the North-eastern (Aberdeen) and the Northern (Inverness). At the same time the Cabinet confirmed their earlier decision that the ordinary hospital resources of Scotland should, in the main and with few exceptions, be used for all special war-time needs, Service and civilian alike; and that a calculated expansion of hospital accommodation, both by new building, and by the adaptation of suitable properties, should be considered and carried out. The principle which dictated the provision of hospital facilities which were to be common to all was, of course, related to the fact that in the expected circumstances, it would be impossible under aerial bombardment to differentiate between classes of the population.

It is convenient at this point to indicate the component parts—that is, the Scheme-making Authorities for purposes of Passive Civil Defence—of the five Districts within the zone of the Scottish Region, together with the estimated population of these Districts.

Northern District: Population 226,500.
   Counties of Caithness, Sutherland, Ross and Cromarty, Inverness and Nairn; Islands of the Outer Hebrides and Skye; Burgh of Inverness.

North-eastern District: Population 455,400
   Counties of Aberdeen, Banff, Moray and Kincardine; Islands of Orkney and Shetland; Burgh of Aberdeen.

Eastern District: Population 684,500.
   Counties of Angus, Perth, Fife and Kinross; Burghs of Arbroath, Dundee, Dunfermline, Kirkcaldy and Perth.

South-eastern District: Population 802,900.
   Counties of Midlothian, West Lothian, East Lothian, Berwick, Peebles, Selkirk and Roxburgh; Burgh of Edinburgh.

Western District: Population 2,841,100
   Counties of Argyle, Stirling and Clackmannan, Dunbarton, Renfrew, Ayr, Lanark, Dumfries, Kirkcudbright and Wigtown; Western Island except those under the Northern District; Burghs of Airdrie, Ayr, Clydebank, Coatbridge, Dumfries, Dumbarton, Glasgow, Greenock, Kilmarnock, Hamilton, Motherwell and Wishaw, Paisley and Rutherglen.

Certain observations in relation to the respective vulnerability of the various Civil Defence Districts appear in the chapter dealing with the First-aid Post organisation; but it may be indicated here that, by reason of their operational functions, the Hospital Officers were located throughout the war at the Headquarters of the five District Commissioners for Civil Defence. Here also were situated the District Offices of the Ministry of Home Security. This arrangement made possible the intimate and continuous co-operation which was necessary for the efficient supervision and co-ordination of the medical services with the general A.R.P. organisations, which were designed to function through local authority mechanisms under the direction of the District Commissioners who were, in turn, responsible to the Regional Commissioner for the whole Scottish Region, whose Headquarters was in Edinburgh.

Thus, in pursuance of the planning remit from the Cabinet to the Secretary of State for Scotland which followed the adoption of the MacNalty Report, the formal administrative agencies concerned with planning came into operation in Scotland towards the end of 1937. The ground was rapidly prepared for the work which had to be undertaken, and which was got under way after a few months of preliminary deliberation. By the spring of 1938, sufficient definition had been achieved to permit the early phases in the creation of the Emergency Medical Services to begin.

THE PROVISION OF HOSPITAL ACCOMMODATION

It was clear from the outset that the potential urgency and danger of the national situation demanded that any hospital scheme designed to meet the needs of the expected air raid casualties, as well as of battle casualties among the Fighting Services, must be based upon and incorporate the existing hospital resources of the country. By a fortunate circumstance, there was in existence at the time of the outbreak of the Emergency, a full report upon the Scottish Health Services (1936). This report was catholic in scope and covered every aspect of the question. It pointed out that there had been a serious shortage of hospital facilities for a long time and that, even for the ordinary needs of the population at large, considerable extensions were necessary in order to provide adequate and reasonable coverage. It was, indeed, estimated that, on a basis of normal and legitimate peace-time requirements, there was a deficiency of not less than 3,600 beds. It became clear, therefore, that if new responsibilities in relation to air warfare were to be successfully encompassed, there could be no alternative to the building of new accommodation or to the elaboration of plans in respect of medical and nursing staffs. The only problem was to consider how much new construction should be undertaken, how it might best be obtained, where it should be located and—by no means least in importance—how it should be administered. In some respects the resolution of these difficulties was facilitated by the fact that plans were already in being for the formation of the five Civil Defence Districts within the frame of the Scottish (No. 11) Region. Four of these Districts were based upon the University Medical Schools at Glasgow, Edinburgh, Dundee and Aberdeen, and the fifth had its headquarters at Inverness. It could accordingly be taken for granted that such new building as was authorised by the Government should be distributed in relation to the presumptive needs of the five Districts concerned.

The situation at the end of 1937, might be described in general terms as follows: the greater part of the first-class hospital accommodation was located in the large voluntary hospitals—though some was in the municipal hospitals—in or closely adjacent to the four major Scottish cities, that is, in areas which were presumably highly vulnerable. Outside these areas there were a number of moderately sized district general hospitals—such as those at Greenock, Ayr, Dumfries, Perth and Inverness—and also several scattered institutions of the cottage hospital type. For the most part, all of these possessed only limited accommodation, staff, equipment and other resources; and in the main they all depended upon the appropriate city centres for the greater part of their specialist services. There were, however, a few country hospitals of larger size, such as local authority sanatoria with surgical facilities, or suitable for the installation of such facilities. In addition, it was considered that three or four mental hospitals could be cleared of ordinary patients and adapted for the needs of the emergency. Again, there were a number of convalescent homes, small infectious diseases hospitals, public assistance institutions and the like, which, though deficient in staff and equipment and unsuitable for any major works of adaptation, might nevertheless be pressed into service for convalescent work, and so reduce the pressure upon the first-line hospitals. By reason of the concentration of the latter in immediate proximity to the large towns, certain areas of the country, by no means inconsiderable in extent or lacking in population, were entirely devoid of local hospital facilities and even of resident surgeons. There was no reason to believe that those areas would remain undisturbed in face of the expected enemy action, particularly if the possibility of invasion had to be considered.

The Policy Adopted. In the urban areas, pre-war hospital accommodation was believed to be at least reasonably adequate—provided that certain adjustments were made in the qualifications for admission of the ordinary civilian sick—for the initial treatment of casualties within the limits of the communities concerned; but it was obvious that the services available in the country districts were far too meagre in volume and restricted in scope to permit the transfer of patients in any numbers from the city hospitals. A mechanism of transfer was, of course, necessary if a reserve of first-line casualty beds were to be maintained within the cities themselves. It was therefore decided that the principal units of new accommodation should be provided in the peripheral and rural areas, these units to consist either of completely new hospitals or of annexes to certain existing institutions. In order, however, to simplify the technical and constructional work involved, a standard type of building was devised by the Ministry of Health, the Department of Health for Scotland and (as it was then called) His Majesty's Office of Works. At the same time, two other important points were decided, namely, that, as has been previously indicated, all institutions included in the Emergency Hospital Scheme should be available both for Service and civilian use, and that, though annexes should be administered by the authorities controlling the parent institutions to which they were attached, the Central Department of Health should itself assume complete responsibility for the direct administration of the wholly new hospitals, as well as of the auxiliary hospitals to which reference will later be made (see Chapter 2). This was an important departure from established hospital practice in this country, and in the following chapter the experiment is dealt with in detail. The arrangements which were made for the treatment of infectious diseases among the Service population are also referred to later.

The Hospital Survey. The basic and most urgent problem which faced those responsible for the fabrication of the Emergency Hospital section of the general Emergency Medical Services was, of course, that which concerned the actual availability of beds which might immediately, by manipulation of resources, be employed for the reception of casualties. It was by no means sure that a serious blow might not fall before any appreciable extension of facilities could be made. An intensive survey of all the existing hospital resources in Scotland was thus called for; and in the spring of 1938, a rapid but exhaustive examination was carried out by the Department of Health. This investigation, which involved visits to most of the hospitals and kindred institutions throughout the country, was the foundation upon which the superstructure of the Emergency Hospital Scheme in Scotland was erected. In the course of the survey, beds to the following numbers came under review:

District	Centre	Number of hospitals			Number of beds		
		Local authority	Voluntary	Totals	Local authority	Voluntary	Totals
Northern	Inverness	22	18	40	666	501	1,167
North-eastern	Aberdeen	27	28	55	1,471	1,379	2,850
Eastern	Dundee	33	39	72	2,050	1,732	3,782
South-eastern	Edinburgh	48	44	92	3,985	3,319	7,304
Western	Glasgow	126	90	216	12,846	7,145	19,993
Totals		256	219	475	21,018*	14,076	35,096

* Comprising general hospitals and certain Poor Law institutions, mental hospitals, sanatoria and fever hospitals, and including only 4,361 beds in general medical and surgical wards.

THE SHORT-TERM POLICY

This survey was in no way an end in itself. In the first place, it could not be thought that anything remotely approximating to the total number of beds surveyed could, by any operational process, be pressed into effective hospital service, for, as is indicated by the footnote to the above table, many of them were quite unsuitable for the treatment of casualties. Again, the existing hospital accommodation was habitually occupied to saturation point by ordinary peace-time admissions. In many localities, indeed, beds were already at a premium; and in all areas more or less lengthy lists of patients awaiting hospital treatment had to be maintained.

Thus the only method by which beds could immediately or at short notice be made available for the reception of casualties was clearly one which involved, first, restricting ordinary admissions and, secondly, the discharge of many convalescent patients from hospital. Accordingly, while the hospital survey was still in progress, the Department of Health proceeded to set up its Hospital Office organisation in the respective Civil Defence Districts; and the Hospital Officers were instructed, in the spring of 1938, to prepare detailed plans (involving the clearance of hospitals and the associated discharge or transfer of patients as occasion might demand) for securing the availability of beds for civilian casualties. Thus, while strategic considerations were still under review in St. Andrew's House, the various Hospital Officers were already occupied with the tactical aspects of the problem in what was officially described as Stage I of its existence. At this period it resembled the "shadow" organisation which was set up in connexion with the potential aircraft factories; and, like the latter, it was operated substantially on the principle 'No expenditure in peace-time either by the Government or the local authorities'. The situation provided only for the restriction of admissions to hospital, sending home patients who were sufficiently far advanced in convalescence, and the transfer to less elaborately equipped institutions of patients who, while not fit for discharge, might properly be cared for in secondary or improvised accommodation. Apart from transport arrangements, which still remained nebulous and unsatisfactory, the first stage was virtually completed in August 1938, when it was estimated that, through the various processes of patient discharge and transfer, approximately 11,000 surgical beds could rapidly be pressed into commission throughout the five districts for the reception of air raid casualties. District by district, these beds were distributed as follows, the numbers shown being associated, for convenience, by the estimated population (1939) which they were designed to serve:

Northern District	300 beds	(226,500)
North-eastern District	600 ,,	(455,400)
Eastern District	900 ,,	(684,500)
South-eastern District	3,000 ,,	(802,900)
Western District	6,500 ,,	(2,841,100)

In addition to the beds which, at least on paper, would then exist and be suitable for the direct reception of casualties, there was also available a certain amount of scattered accommodation, indeterminate in quantity and doubtful in quality, but probably aggregating between 3,000 and 4,000 beds, for the reception of transferred patients from other hospitals, whose beds would thus be freed for more urgent use, and for the housing and treatment of victims of enemy action whose injuries or other disabilities were long-term, but for whom immediate major surgical care was not imperative or was no longer of the first importance.

The direction of thought which was stimulated by the 1938 hospital survey, and the local plans which were formulated by the Hospital

Officers, may thus be indicated. It was recognised in the first place that all forecasts of the possible trend of events must be regarded as tentative only and that they were subject to large margins of error and to radical change. It was inevitable that such should have been the case. When, however, the attempt was made to visualise the effects of powerful and continued attacks on Scotland by enemy aircraft—and this was the situation which the authorities were bound to contemplate—certain elementary propositions were clearly enough defined. It was, for example, reasonable to postulate that the main concentration of attack would be on the industrial areas, on the three great waterways—the Clyde, the Forth and the Tay—and on the capital city of Edinburgh. The presumptive vulnerability of the latter, and the still greater importance of Glasgow in this respect, immediately raised formidable problems, among which was the question of the propriety of increasing —or even of employing to any great extent—the supply of beds available within the congested areas. The objections to such employment were particularly the risk of duplicating casualties, the increased traffic difficulties incidental to casualty management in a populous centre, and the exposure to serious risks of a trained staff which could not be replaced. These objections, of course, became untenable when equated with the hospital position as it actually existed; but it followed from them that sites for new hospital accommodation should be sought outside the congested areas, and that hospital extensions within the populous centres should be discouraged. Further, since casualties were naturally to be expected in the greatest numbers from the vulnerable congested localities the new buildings which were contemplated should occupy strategic positions in relation to these localities. The survey specifically disclosed that certain areas, notably the counties of Lanark and Dunbarton, had general hospital facilities which were totally inadequate even for peacetime needs, the proximity of the resources of Glasgow being influential in this connexion. It was therefore clear that in its development the new hospital scheme should be orientated with special relation to these difficult areas, the existing position in which is represented by the following figures:

County	Year	Population	General hospital beds
Lanark	1938	508,112	187
Dunbarton	1938	155,243	197*

It is perhaps significant of the thinking of the time, and as such worthy of notice here, that early thought upon the subject of new hospital building tended to prescribe, as an underlying principle, that, in those areas in which permanent hospitals to serve peace-time needs were necessary, the erection of such hospitals should be encouraged in preference to temporary structures of the emergency type envisaged. In

---

* Including 120 beds in Canniesburn Hospital, the property of the Glasgow Royal Infirmary.

other words, it was suggested quite seriously that the secret of successful modern warfare consisted in a minimum of departure from the established ways of peace, and that schemes of hospital development which would give the best "civil" return for the money spent should be vigorously pursued with the assistance of exchequer grants. It is needless to say that such a policy was quite impracticable; but as an indication of failure to appreciate what is implied in the expression 'total warfare', this phase of thought was illuminating.

Another principle which was, however, sound and fundamental was formulated simultaneously in the words, 'Buildings are much less important than personnel'. Properly considered, a hospital under war conditions consists primarily of a team of skilled workers. This fact was readily perceived and appreciated by the authorities, although its recognition by the general body of the medical profession—at least in its relations to the possible development of battle-front conditions within these islands—was not quite so rapid or spontaneous. It was, of course, conceded that buildings and equipment were of great importance so long as they could be maintained; but in the last resort they could be replaced by the most primitive emergency apparatus provided that properly constituted teams of trained workers remained available to operate them. It will probably be conceded by all who had experience of them that the Scottish emergency hospitals, as they actually came to be, provided a happy medium between the refinements of the best peacetime hospitals and the makeshifts of the casualty clearing station, and that, on balance, they came in fact to bear a much greater resemblance to the former than to the latter. For the process of development which permitted this to be the case, the relative inactivity of the hostile air force over Scotland was, of course, responsible.

This happy circumstance connected with the fabric and equipment of the new hospitals had its counterpart on the personnel side also. In 1938, and for at least two years afterwards, it was believed that the problems of staffing might best be resolved (as seemed, indeed, almost inevitable) by the adoption of the 'Unit team' system, the projected details of which appear below; but in the event it became feasible, as will be seen in Chapter 3, to stabilise the professional staffs of the hospitals in a way which, in the early phases both of planning and of actual warfare, had scarcely been contemplated as a possibility. The 'Unit team' idea had much to commend it, and might, in fact, have been all important. So completely, indeed, was this realised that elaborate team arrangements remained in force throughout the war, though it was rarely necessary to use them.

The primary assumption was, therefore, that hospital organisation for war depended upon the construction of unit teams, the composition of which might vary but which would include surgeons, physicians, anaesthetists, sisters, trained nurses and V.A.Ds. on the medical side;

an administrator with clerical staff and auxiliary workers for wards, kitchens, laundries, etc.; and pathologists, radiologists, and other specialists whose services would be available part-time to a number of teams.

Among the advantages of the team system, the following points were considered material:

The selection of each team could be made beforehand, without expense. Each key member of the team would be instructed in his duties, and where they were to be carried out, in the event of an emergency.

The team system would permit the creation of reserve teams which would take over duty in the event of the primary team being put out of action. By this means, resources of personnel could be husbanded and used to best advantage.

The system would allow the movement of entire teams from one place to another at short notice, according to the needs of particular areas. Aberdeen Team No. 4 might, for example, be moved to Dundee to undertake necessary duties during a time of special stress.

The system would ensure mobility of personnel in the event of the destruction of a particular hospital, and the instructions given would provide for a transfer from place to place according to the needs of the situation.

Team wastages could be made good by new recruitment or by the transfer of members from one team to another under the instructions and general supervision of the Hospital Officers, who would also direct the teams operationally.

Ideally, the teams might have consisted of three surgeons, one physician and two anaesthetists, but man-power resources could hardly be stretched to this degree, and the standard composition thus came to be:

> 2 surgeons, one senior and one junior
> 1 physician
> 1 anaesthetist.

In certain cases, general practitioners and senior medical students were attached for general duties as they might arise; and arrangements were made with the hospitals to which the teams were allocated to provide the necessary nursing and ancillary personnel.

At this time, in the months before the Munich crisis, schemes for the setting up of special units for the treatment of specific types of injury—orthopaedic and ophthalmic and the like—had scarcely progressed beyond the phase of thought. Even the arrangements which had to be made for the provision of ambulance transport were indeterminate and nebulous. The necessity for urgent and intensive planning meant concentration on availability of beds and equipment for the bare essentials.

Upon the Hospital Officers, accordingly, fell the burden of practical organisation for the expected emergency. Their work had to be carried out at high pressure; and as the time apparently at their disposal shortened from weeks to days, and finally from days to hours and minutes, and as the shadows deepened over Berchtesgaden, the effort of their planning increased in intensity with the pressure of time. An equivalent effort was, indeed, hardly demanded from them at any later time. Thus, to take an individual example, in the Hospital Office in the Western District in Glasgow where, by reason of the density of population and the importance and profusion of military objectives, the situation was peculiarly difficult and complex, the hours of day and night were alike devoted to the buttressing, so far as possible, of what seemed at best to be a structure of meagre proportions and imperfect balance. Even at the last hour of this immediate crisis, the provisional organisation of the medical and surgical resources of the District was being anxiously completed.

The Munich crisis passed, and a respite—on the whole recognised to be no more than that, but a respite nevertheless—was at hand. An opportunity was thus afforded to consolidate Stage I plans, and a simultaneous beginning was made with Stage II, which involved long-term considerations. Rearmament now came to be the accepted policy of the Government, and the Treasury abandoned the restrictions associated with the 'shadow' policy to which reference has been made above. Since rearmament had its implications of attack and defence alike, the full development of the A.R.P. Scheme, including the programme of new hospital building, could therefore be proceeded with. The work to this end was carried on in an atmosphere of watchfulness in which the Stage I plans were maintained in readiness for operation should the occasion so require.

Immediately after the superficial easing of the international tension, the Cabinet Secretariat requested that a formal review of Service and civilian emergency preparations might be made, and consequently, on October 14, 1938, as part of the appropriate action taken by the Department of Health for Scotland, the Hospital Officers, in their capacity as the operational authority, were asked to make a critical report upon the problems connected with the Casualty Services. Two main questions were involved, namely, action taken during the actual emergency, and action still to be taken by the Department in order to extend and complete the defence structure.

An opportunity was thus given to the Hospital Officers, who, as the people on the spot in the various Districts, were most able to make an immediate and just assessment, to indicate to the Headquarters of the Department, comprehensively and without delay, the manner in which the emergency hours of 1938 had actually been met, and to make an analysis of the preliminary steps which had been taken and which, by one kind of improvisation or another, would have been progressively developed had the crisis merged at that time into actual warfare. Naturally, the action which could be taken was greatly restricted because of the immaturity of the plans involved and the meagre existing resources. In broad outline, it may be described as follows:

GENERAL ACTION TAKEN BY THE HOSPITAL OFFICERS

The Munich crisis week was spent in building up a series of improvised arrangements for hospital evacuation, transport services, co-ordination of surgical assistance, provision of equipment—consisting of beds and bedding and little more—and the like. These arrangements were as elaborate as circumstances allowed. It is doubtful indeed if they would have stood up to a single heavy bombardment from the air; and, this being well understood, little confidence was placed in them.

But, at the end of September 1938, the Hospital Officers kept themselves ready for action. Hospital authorities were instructed to be prepared to restrict the admission of patients and to accept only those who were urgently in need of care. They were further requested to maintain daily lists of patients who could, at short notice, be discharged to their own homes or to second-line institutions. Efforts were made to ensure that all the hospitals in each District had at least a four weeks' reserve of food, drugs and dressings, and other essential stores, over and above the reserves ordinarily carried. Arrangements were also made for the rapid distribution to hospitals of the important record forms which had been devised both by the Department of Health and by the Ministry of Pensions. The Ministry of Pensions forms related to claims for compensation for war injuries; the Department of Health forms were designed for returns by each hospital to the Hospital Officers, and by the Hospital Officers to Departmental Headquarters, and made it possible to determine the number of casualties received into hospital, and the number of beds available for further casualties. These forms were not actually issued to individual institutions, but the administrative authorities of all the principal hospitals were made familiar with them.

STORAGE AND PROJECTED PURCHASE OF HOSPITAL EQUIPMENT

The emergence of the crisis immediately brought into prominence the fact that deficiences of the most serious kind existed in the amount and nature of the equipment, mobile and stationary, which was necessary for the efficient handling and care of casualties. Even such elementary needs as beds and mattresses, blankets and stretchers were in short supply and consisted, indeed, only of those which were already in possession of the hospitals and local authorities and of the ambulance and other associations who were concerned with certain of these things as part of their ordinary running equipment. In a note originating in the Hospital Office of the Western District and sent to the District

Commissioner on October 3, 1938, it was stated that an inquiry had been undertaken into the possible sources of supply of stretchers, with special reference to the number which could be provided per week, the cost per stretcher, and the earliest date on which delivery could begin; and in a memorandum jointly prepared by the Hospital Officers of the Eastern and North-eastern Districts, and dated October 16, 1938, it was remarked that no stretchers of any pattern could be bought in these areas. These reports followed a fruitless attempt on the part of the Department of Health to buy, during September, and through the agency of the Ministry of Health, some 2,500 beds and mattresses, 10,000 blankets and 2,500 stretchers. This attempt represented the first of a long series of orders; but it was soon found that there was no prospect whatever of the early delivery of any of the equipment in question. Hospital Officers were thereupon instructed to make surveys of the stocks of suitable materials in the hands of manufacturers and retailers in their respective Districts, with a view to the requisitioning of these stocks, if necessary, by the Department. Action of this kind was, in fact, found to be unnecessary, because of the respite before the outbreak of war; but, since it was now certain that large volumes of equipment would now be required, the Hospital Officers were asked to make a special survey of hospitals in order to suggest suitable storage centres for the new materials as they became available. There was almost no limit to the anxiety of hospital authorities to assist in this connexion, even at the risk of overcrowding their already straitened storage accommodation. The first deliveries of new equipment—600 beds and mattresses to the Western District and 300 to the Eastern—occurred in November 1938; and from that date onwards a steady increment took place.

TRANSPORT ARRANGEMENTS

In 1938, no formal scheme for the transport of casualties had yet been adopted—nor, indeed, was any such scheme possible because of the shortage of vehicles and personnel. The Munich crisis, therefore, broke upon a situation which was a high state of unpreparedness. It is not to be assumed, however, that nothing had been done, or that the position presented a just cause for serious criticism. The problem had not been neglected, the necessary funds had not been provided and consequently more practical considerations had pressed it into the background. It was in any case—and possibly with some justification—assumed that, since motor fuel was not then rationed, and since an abundance of civilian motor transport of one kind or another would presumably be made available voluntarily on the occurrence of an emergency, it might safely be left to local effort and ingenuity for the time being to meet contingencies as they might arise. For the purposes of actual casualty movement the Hospital Officers in the five Districts were instructed so far as possible to obtain the promise of service from the owners of private and commercial vehicles, and the arrangements so made were probably as comprehensive as could be devised. Whether they would have worked with efficiency is another matter. At best, they were no more than provisional; and, since the probable reactions of a population under fire could not be assessed, they depended largely upon faith that the sense of public duty would overcome the sense of fear.

While the Hospital Officers of the Eastern and North-eastern Districts found themselves unable to assume that any ambulances whatever would be found at their disposal, they nevertheless made such representations to the owners of private motor vehicles that they satisfied themselves that they could, in one way or another, meet the immediate strain, at least, of any catastrophe. In the Western, South-eastern and Northern Districts, the hospitals themselves co-operated actively with the Hospital Officers in establishing contacts with car owners and securing promises of service. In all these areas, with the possible exception of the South-eastern District in which a greater volume of voluntary enthusiasm would have been welcome, schemes of a relatively satisfactory nature were evolved. The actual procedure adopted is illustrated by the following extract from a report (October 3, 1938) from the Western District, where, because of the congestion of the area, the transport problem was peculiarly difficult:

'From estimates which have been compiled, arrangements have been made which should, so far as can be foreseen, meet the travelling requirements involved in the transfer of patients from hospital, either to their own homes or to other hospitals ... and in the transference of patients from one institution to another during a state of continuing emergency. These arrangements have been discussed with the Secretary of the St. Andrew's Ambulance Association, and a census is about to be taken of all ambulances belonging to this Association, to the local authorities, to private firms, etc., in the Western District. In the information thus gained notes will be incorporated indicating the types of vehicle concerned, the carrying capacity, and the means of contact with the actual vehicles.

'So far as possible, each hospital is making its own arrangements in respect of the transference of 'sitting' cases. The hospitals are calling for voluntary transport (private cars, etc.) and are maintaining a list of the names and addresses of drivers.'

ACTION TO BE TAKEN BY THE DEPARTMENT

So far as 'action still to be taken' is concerned, it will be obvious that there was hardly any limit to the needs in this direction. Up to this period, only a rude skeleton had been constructed, and all the refinements of clothing and function had still to be provided and applied. In the main, the long-term planning associated with Stage II of the casualty arrangements now occupied first place in the minds of those involved, and the principal problems which presented themselves were those of the elaboration of the First-Aid Post Services with their ambulances, the plans for new hospital building and the provision of hospital annexes, the development of a chain of auxiliary hospitals, the provision of adequate equipment, the consolidation of the staffing position and the establishment of adequate inter-hospital transport services. Simultaneously, however, the short-term or Stage I plans had to be kept in being and improved upon in order to meet the possible emergence of another acute crisis in the immediate future. In the main, the continued short-term policy depended upon the factors which have already been indicated—the full use of the existing hospitals with good surgical facilities, and the various processes of discharge and transfer of patients. In addition, however, a policy of 'crowding' beds into existing accommodation was formulated in the later months of 1938; and as additional beds and bedding and other equipment became available allocations were made to the various institutions in accordance with their space and operative potentialities. Supplies of consumable stores and of non-expendable equipment were also sent to poorly equipped hospitals in order that they might be prepared to play a more active part in any emergency which might arise. The first step in this relation was to survey existing equipment and, with the advice of competent consultants, administrative and professional alike, to determine what extra supplies were needed and the amount which should be provided to individual institutions. Contact was established with the Scottish Branch of the British Red Cross Society and other voluntary organisations which were ready to co-operate in providing surgical dressings and other supplies. The distribution of medical man-power was worked out with assistance from the appropriate consultants, and the surgical team arrangements were consolidated. Several institutions which had been previously included in the category of casualty receiving or second-line hospitals were found, on further examination, to be virtually useless for the needs of the Emergency Medical Services, and these were accordingly eliminated from the scheme. At the time of the Declaration of War on September 3, 1939, the short-term plans were still in operation, but the long-continued quiet of the early phases of the war presented no opportunity for the testing of the arrangements which had been made. By the time of the actual emergence of active hostilities the long-term plans of Stage II were sufficiently advanced to take the strain.

CHAPTER 2

THE EMERGENCY HOSPITAL SERVICE

THE LONG-TERM POLICY

THE strategic considerations mentioned in the prefatory note on the Emergency Medical Services were influential in determining the trend of the new building which was to form the superstructure—and in time the virtual organisation itself—of the Emergency Hospital Scheme, the nucleus of which was represented by the existing hospitals, voluntary and local authority, which acted as the primary units in the scheme. Thus, while the concentrations of population in the Western District were served, in the first place, largely by the hospitals within the City of Glasgow itself, the situation rapidly changed through the construction of the large new hospitals at Ballochmyle (Ayrshire), Killearn (Stirlingshire), and Law Junction (Lanarkshire), and the addition of considerable annexes to various institutions on the periphery of the city, notably Gartloch and Robroyston (City of Glasgow), Mearnskirk (Renfrewshire), Hairmyres (Lanarkshire) and Lennox Castle (Stirlingshire). In the case of the last, the parent buildings were pressed into the service of the Emergency Hospital Scheme, and a hutted annexe was built for the continued care of the ordinary inmates, who were mental defectives. At the more distant hospitals at Larbert (Stirlingshire) and Stonehouse (Lanarkshire) important additions were also made. Similarly, in the East, the resources of Bangour Hospital (West Lothian) were much increased, and in the Border country, appropriate provision was furnished by new building at Peel Hospital. For the remainder of the country, the new hospitals at Bridge of Earn (Perthshire) and Stracathro (Angus) provided adequate coverage, and the needs of the northern counties were met by the building of Raigmore Hospital, Inverness. The details of the new building are given more fully below. Meantime, however, it is of interest to note how the new hospitals were fitted into the general strategic plan dictated by the geography of the country—a consideration which, in the nature of things, did not necessarily apply to the existing hospitals.

Thus Ballochmyle Hospital, situated just south of the town of Mauchline in central Ayrshire, was located on the main lines of road and rail which run northwards from Carlisle through Dumfries and Kilmarnock to Glasgow. The important aerodrome of Prestwick was only some twelve miles away. Excellent road and rail communications also ran from the populous Ayrshire seaboard north of Ayr, a district which contained important explosive factories. Greenock and the Clyde Anchorages were also within easy reach, and there were good cross-country communications with the congested industrial area of Lanark County.

The latter district, including the particularly important railway centre at Carstairs Junction was more specifically served by Law Junction Hospital, which was also located upon the trunk road from Aberdeen to Carlisle. Killearn Hospital covered the northern reaches of the Clyde Anchorages and the populous area of Dumbarton County. Bridge of Earn and Stracathro Hospitals had strategic relation to the great bridges over the Firths of Forth and Tay; and Raigmore Hospital had a specific function in connexion with the North Western Approaches and with Scapa Flow.

Before proceeding to a detailed examination of the new building and other arrangements which were made, it is desirable to indicate briefly the administrative plans upon which the operation of the Emergency Hospital Service depended. The various sections of this chapter are therefore dealt with under the following headings:

1. Administration
2. New building
3. Adaptation and protection
4. Equipment
5. Special units
6. Auxiliary hospitals
7. Shadow and crash hospitals

1. ADMINISTRATION

As in England and Wales, the survey of hospital accommodation made by the Department of Health for Scotland in the Spring of 1938 showed, on the one hand, that the firm distinction which, up till that time, had been made between casualty clearing and base hospitals was by no means practicable in the face of emergency conditions of a new pattern, and, on the other, that the plans to be prepared for the use of hospital resources in an emergency should contemplate the pooling of such resources over wide areas. Accordingly, from June 1, 1938, the Secretary of State for Scotland assumed responsibility for the whole of the Emergency Hospital Service, and, as has been seen, he laid upon the Department of Health the task of preparing and developing the necessary plans. This arrangement was dealt with in the first circulars (D.P. Circular Nos. 3 and 4) on the subject, which were issued to local authorities and voluntary hospitals on September 7, 1938.

The primary responsibility of the Department of Health was the formulation of a scheme for the effective employment of as much of the existing hospital accommodation as could be made available for the reception and treatment of casualties, reinforced as the occasion might require by additions to existing institutions and by the construction of new hospitals. The Department was consequently obliged to decide the general lines of the organisation, the hospitals which might suitably be included in it, and the functions which each unit should discharge within the general framework of the scheme. A further obligation relating to the provision of necessary or appropriate equipment was also laid upon the Department. It was, of course, clear from the outset that the Department was dependent upon the goodwill of the various hospital authorities for the satisfactory discharge of its duties, and it is significant of the spirit that prevailed that, throughout the whole course of the war, the powers of direction which were given by the Secretary of State to the Hospital Officers had not, on any occasion, to be exercised.

Subject to the general guidance given by the Department and its Hospital Officers as to the scale upon which—and the purpose for which —a civilian hospital was expected to operate, the Government desired that hospital authorities, voluntary and statutory, should retain throughout the emergency, full responsibility for the management of their hospitals and for the maintenance of the services which they provided. Each authority or institution was accordingly requested to adapt its internal mechanism so far as was necessary to the requirements of the part it was designed to play. For operational purposes, special channels of communication between the various hospitals and the Central Department were required, and every authority or institution was asked to nominate a particular officer who, with his deputies, would maintain contact with the Hospital Officers. In the main, medical superintendents or an equivalent officer, were so nominated.

Under the code, therefore, of the Emergency Hospital Scheme, it was understood that all existing hospitals, local authority and voluntary alike, should be carried on during the emergency by the ordinary agencies controlling them, subject, however, to direction by the Department of Health. Both the parent buildings and any annexes which might be added to them were included under this arrangement, which was accordingly equivalent to that in England and Wales throughout the war. But in the new hospitals which were about to be built, as well as in the auxiliary hospitals and certain other buildings which were to be adapted for hospital use, it was determined that an entirely new principle of management should be applied, and that the Department of Health itself should be the managing body. To this end, a Hospitals Division was set up within the Department of Health on September 12, 1939, and the activities of this and allied Divisions will be considered under the next and various other headings in this chapter. Meanwhile, however, the salient features of the organisation of the hospital services for casualty needs may be indicated.

Except in circumstances in which special medical considerations might arise, the majority of the hospitals included in the Emergency Hospital Scheme were expected to operate as follows: to carry on an essential minimum of their ordinary work and to provide emergency treatment for any casualties arising from air raids in their immediate vicinity. Civilians and Service personnel were alike covered by this arrangement. It was not proposed to abandon any particular hospitals, but those situated in the areas which appeared most likely to be attacked were, so far as possible, to be reserved for actual emergency use. Institutions located outside the more vulnerable areas were expected also to receive for further treatment both the casualties and the ordinary patients whom it might be necessary to transfer from the more dangerous districts.

The hospitals included in the casualty service might thus be regarded in three main groups. The first group consisted of those whose casualty work would be restricted, so far as circumstances permitted, to emergency treatment. The second included those hospitals which were not only expected, like all similar institutions, to treat any casualties occurring in their immediate vicinity, but which were so situated that they could give continued treatment not only to such local casualties, but also to those transferred at as early a stage as was practicable from hospitals situated in the more vulnerable areas. To some extent, therefore, this group could be regarded as base hospitals. The third group included those hospitals which were not equipped to undertake the initial reception of casualties—except in a dire local emergency—but which were nevertheless capable of dealing with convalescent and chronic patients as well as certain others for whose treatment no special facilities were required. They were thus designated for the reception not only of casualties in an advanced state of their treatment but also of ordinary patients transferred from other hospitals in order to free beds in the latter for the further victims of air attack. Lastly there were the auxiliary hospitals, established for the most part in large mansion houses in country districts, generously placed at the disposal of the Department of Health by their owners. The accommodation which they provided and of which a great deal came to be required, was in the first place regarded as supplementary to that in the third-group institutions. In 1941, the group definition was slightly amended and the standard hospital classification came to be set forth as follows:

Group I. Casualty Clearing Hospitals: that is, hospitals in areas most vulnerable to presumptive attack, which could give immediate surgical treatment to casualties occurring in their own localities.

Group II. Hospitals similar to those in Group I, but situated in areas believed to be less vulnerable and consequently suitable for continued as well as immediate treatment.

Group III. Base Hospitals: that is, hospitals in areas believed to be relatively safe and suitable for the immediate reception of patients in their own localities as well as for the continued treatment of casualties transferred from more dangerous areas.

Group IV. Hospitals which had no facilities for surgical treatment but which could receive patients who no longer required such facilities.

General administrative and operational considerations might therefore be summarised in this way, that the primary object of the Department of Health was to provide for the maximum use of existing accommodation and its rapid expansion by new building and other means. At the outset of the emergency it was recognised that beds would, of necessity, have to be made available through the adoption of a series of expediencies, namely:

(i) the drastic restriction of ordinary admissions;
(ii) the erection of beds which were ordinarily maintained in reserve;
(iii) the discharge of patients to their homes;
(iv) the introduction of additional beds to wards and other accommodation which could be employed for patient purposes; and
(v) by the transfer of patients from hospitals in Groups I and II.

The practicability even of these plans was dependent upon the appropriate distribution of personnel and equipment, but the problems connected with these matters will be discussed in their respective sections.

2. NEW BUILDING

In general, a standard plan was adopted for all new hospital building, designed to be applicable both at the sites of existing institutions and at such new locations as might be decided upon. Much thought was given to the many problems of the new building programme, the comprehensive scheme of which called for approximately 7,000 beds in new hospitals and over 8,000 in annexes. All these were to be strictly employed—in addition to an indeterminate number which might be provided by adapting premises such as hotels and the like—for general medical and surgical purposes. Convalescent needs, as has been shown, were to be met from the resources of certain secondary hospitals, largely supplemented by the commissioning of a number of private houses which were suitable for employment as auxiliary hospitals. The net result of the planning was upwards of 20,000 additional hospital beds—the new accommodation representing nearly 60 per cent. of the total number of beds previously available throughout the country. In summary, the actual figures of these new beds, ascertained at a stage when precise computation became possible, were as follows:

General hospitals		Auxiliary hospitals		Totals
New hospitals	7,038	Large country houses	3,426	10,464
Annexes	8,526	Miscellaneous	527	9,053
Converted hotels*	910			910
Other	100			100
Totals	16,574		3,953	20,527

* Gleneagles Hotel, Perthshire (610 beds) and Turnberry Hotel, Ayrshire (300 beds)—both the property of the L.M.S. Railway Co.

By midsummer 1939, co-operative effort by the Ministry of Health, Department of Health and His Majesty's Office of Works had resulted in the virtual completion of the plans for the new building both of independent hospitals and of hutted annexes. Sites had been chosen and other dispositions made, and the placing of contracts for the actual work of construction quickly followed. It is needless to pursue the various vicissitudes which beset the path of accomplishment, for the difficulties were industrial and had no immediate medical connotations. Fortunately, no impediments were imposed by direct enemy action, and thus, by the summer of 1941, the building programme had been substantially completed and much of the new accommodation had, indeed, already been employed for the reception and treatment of casualties resulting from the Clydeside air raiding of March and May of that year. The hospitals and annexes particularly concerned in the admission of casualties arising in these serious incidents were those at Killearn, Ballochmyle, Law Junction, Hairmyres, Mearnskirk, Lennox Castle and Larbert. With the commissioning of the whole scheme, some 30,000 beds became available in fully-equipped general hospitals; and of this total, the pre-war hospital accommodation amounted to only some 12,000 beds. This number, moreover, included additional beds in existing wards, beds in apartments not ordinarily employed as wards and beds which were kept unoccupied or which could be cleared at short notice.

The new base hospitals consisted of entirely new buildings, although in certain cases (as at Ballochmyle and Stracathro) there was an administrative nucleus in the form of an existing mansion within the grounds which were acquired. The sites chosen were at Ballochmyle, Ayrshire; Law Junction, Lanarkshire; Killearn, Stirlingshire—all those in the Western District; Bridge of Earn, Perthshire, and Stracathro, Angus (Eastern District); and Raigmore, Inverness-shire (Northern District). In addition, the hotels owned and operated by the London, Midland and Scottish Railway at Gleneagles, Perthshire and Turnberry, Ayrshire, were acquired and adapted for hospital use, but these, of course, were complementary only to the new hutted scheme. The individual institutions included in that scheme were all developed upon previously unbroken sites, in the centre of which the offices and main administrative buildings were situated.

As has already been indicated, the major part of the new building had been completed by 1941, by midsummer of which year appropriate provision had also been made for the accommodation in Military Wings of the Military Registrars and their staffs who were attached to all the base hospitals for the dual purpose of dealing with specialised military documents and of maintaining discipline. These wings consisted of the necessary offices, storage space and pack stores. In the appended summary appears the detail of the new accommodation provided by the Government between 1939 and 1941. The number of hospitals and the total bed complements of institutions in the Emergency Hospital Scheme are to be found in the Appendix at the end of Chapter 5.

3. ADAPTATION AND PROTECTION

Adaptation

Apart altogether from new building and the provision of annexes to many of the outlying hospitals, it was found necessary to prepare the Scottish hospitals for the impact of war by instituting an urgent and extensive process of adaptation of existing buildings. The actual work, which was spread over the period between the latter part of 1938 and the year 1942, involved strenuous planning which was shared in more or less equal proportions by the administrative, medical and technical staffs of the Department of Health; and the responsibility for the execution of the work (which was aided by a Treasury grant which varied from 50 to 100 per cent. of the total cost) was laid upon the hospital authorities concerned. No purpose would be served historically or otherwise, by attempting to follow in detail the progress of operations, which varied from hospital to hospital in accordance with the estimated needs or the obvious deficiencies of the individual institution. In general, the works of adaptation were utilitarian, and were designed specifically to augment the facilities available. They were roughly divided into three main categories, those, namely, which were intended to:

Increase the surgical potentialities of particular hospitals.

Convert existing institutions not suitable for casualties for the purposes of the emergency.

Upgrade second-line hospitals.

The principal adaptations carried out were consequently the extension of operating-room facilities, the elaboration of radiological resources, and the augmentation of sanitary provision. In certain of the large city hospitals, emergency electrical lighting supplies were installed; and in others, elevators were added. Alterations to certain out-patient departments, and to certain roads of access, were carried out in order to increase the potential volume of casualty traffic; and in general, the capabilities of the hospitals were materially increased.

Protection

Certain of the adaptations went hand-in-hand with works of protection. The latter were specifically planned with the objects of securing the maximum possible safety of medical and nursing staffs, ambulant and bed-fast patients, and essential equipment and administrative and domestic quarters. Vulnerable parts of lower floors were consequently reinforced by 14 in. brickwork applied to the windows, for example, of wards, operating theatres, X-ray departments, administrative offices and telephone exchanges. Underground premises which were free from steam and water pipes were in many cases strengthened as shelter quarters for staff and ambulant patients; and in other instances surface shelters conforming to the standard A.R.P. patterns had to be provided. The problem of the bed-fast patient was recognised to be well-nigh insoluble save by the institution of arrangements too elaborate to be practicable; and dependence had consequently to rest upon the simple protection of window glass by superficial applications. Although much glass was shattered in various hospitals in the vicinity of falling bombs, no serious damage was done, and no fatal casualties occurred within the hospitals themselves. It was, however, recognised that, under heavy bombardment from the air, no particular reliance was to be placed upon any protective devices which could have been adopted.

4. EQUIPMENT

Here also, no special purpose could be served by attempting to detail the process of equipment made necessary by the advent of war. The magnitude of the task is clear; and, though in the initial stage, various checks and difficulties were encountered, these were progressively overcome and by the year 1942 the mechanism of continuous supply had been generally established. It is important to understand that there was no type of equipment that was not required in large quantities, from the domestic articles necessary for wards and residential quarters to engineering, technical, medical and surgical materials of every description. In the early phases of the war, much had to be bought locally but as time passed, the advantages of central purchase became abundantly apparent. A whole Division of the Department of Health, with various subsections, was consequently established for mass buying. Close liaison was maintained with the Ministry of Health, and the combined resources of the two Departments did much to maintain the efficiency of the emergency hospitals.

5. SPECIAL UNITS

The Emergency Hospital Scheme was devised to care for the victims of enemy action. It was recognised that a considerable proportion of civilian injuries and Service wounds alike would involve bone damage, and the need to establish special facilities for the orthopaedic treatment of injuries immediately suggested itself. In this elementary way the whole system of special units for the therapeutic management of special types of disease was conceived; and within the first few months of war it became possible to create, and progressively to equip, special units for particular phases of medical and surgical work. These particular facilities were important as an immediate benefit to the patients and as a stimulus to professional enterprise; but they also influenced the trend of thought which had, despite the preoccupations of the war, to plan for the integration of hospital policy and hospital resources in the post-war years. The successful building up of the war-time organisation was in no small degree due to the fact that the establishment and distribution of the special units provided a mechanism for the interchange of patients which had never previously existed except upon a minor scale; and the comparative readiness with which the scheme was accepted was in itself an acknowledgement of the value of the method.

Before the special facilities which were established are summarised in a table, three incidental points are worthy of notice :

(i) A striking feature of the Emergency Hospital arrangements was the co-operative spirit engendered between the various interests concerned, both administrative and professional. In addition, a close association was maintained with the medical departments of the Fighting Services. Examples of co-operation—and of coincident friendliness and efficiency—were, for instance, to be seen at Turnberry Hospital in South Ayrshire where, throughout the year 1943 and part of 1944, an Army hospital unit was installed, mainly for training purposes; and at Bangour Hospital, in which the whole of East Fortune Sanatorium, displaced from its own site in East Lothian by certain needs of the Royal Air Force, was conveniently and acceptably installed and operated by its own Joint Board of local authorities. Further, the operation of the Emergency Medical Services was so flexible that it was possible to find accommodation at Gartloch and Larbert E.M.S. Hospitals (the peace-time function of which was the care and treatment of the insane) for some 200 mental patients displaced in 1941 from Smithston Institution, Greenock, by the Royal Canadian Navy, without embarrassment to the hospitals concerned; and again, by reason of the rise in the incidence of pulmonary tuberculosis, special units for the treatment of this disease were established for the benefit of certain local authorities at Law Junction and Bridge of Earn Hospitals, although the general administration in these instances remained with the Department of Health itself. These are but examples of a process which became widely prevalent and which will be noticed at various places in this chapter.

(ii) Although, as has already been pointed out, emergency hospital accommodation was specifically intended to meet the requirements of war casualties, both military and civilian, it early became possible to extend its use to the civilian population in general. In this connexion, the Waiting List Scheme and the Scottish Supplementary Medical Service is dealt with later. The point of immediate relevance is this, that the facilities of the orthopaedic units became available for the treatment of fractures occurring in war industry. A contribution of much moment was thus made to the prosecution of the war because of the fact that delays which must otherwise have occurred were almost entirely avoided.

(iii) A word should be said upon a specialised development of the special unit system in which the cardinal consideration was not clinical, but nationality. Thus in two E.M.S. hospitals—in addition to certain auxiliary accommodation—units were maintained for the treatment of our Polish and Norwegian allies. In those cases, immediate administration was delegated to the medical personnel of the countries concerned. The Polish Hospital developed in time into a fully constituted autonomous unit, the Paderewski Hospital, situated close to the Western General Hospital in Edinburgh. The clinical courses associated with the Medical School of the Polish University were pursued in both these institutions. Again, the Fighting French occupied two auxiliary hospitals in the Western District—Quothquhan and Knockderry—although in these the administrative direction remained in the hands of the Department of Health. In this general connexion it should also be recorded that special Navy and Royal Air Force units were maintained successfully at Mearnskirk and Gleneagles Hospitals respectively—always under direct E.M.S. auspices—and that Touch Auxiliary Hospital, near Stirling, was the exclusive preserve of the Women's Services. Smithston Hospital, a part of the institution of that name in Greenock, was vacated in favour of the Royal Canadian Navy, which used the buildings as Headquarters; and the chief hospital establishment of the United States Forces in Scotland was set up in the Glasgow Corporation hospital at Cowglen, near Glasgow.

The special units established by the Department of Health were as follows:

Special function	Number of centres	Number of beds
Orthopaedic	7	1,980
Plastic surgery	4	128
Psychoneurosis	3	262
Neurosurgery	2	160
Peripheral nerve and neurovascular	2	60
Effort syndrome	1	20
Thoracic	2	130
Eye injuries and ophthalmic disease	7	250
Gas casualties	7	280
	Total beds	3,270

Note: There were in addition two special amputation centres administered by Ministry of Pensions and one centre for miners' rehabilitation administered by the Department of Health, and associated with the Ministry of Fuel and Power and the Miners' Welfare agencies.

The establishment and operation of the orthopaedic special units, which were the first in the field, did much to awaken the professional consciousness to the desirability of employing the specialised services which were provided. Before the war, only one or two of the larger hospitals in Scotland had developed orthopaedic or even fracture departments. The outstanding pioneering enterprise in this relation was that of the Victoria Infirmary in Glasgow, which had already made material advances before 1939; but in 1940 an Orthopaedic and Rehabilitation Department was established in the Glasgow Royal Infirmary and a year later plans were formulated for the provision of special orthopaedic facilities in the Western Infirmary. In this case, the new department was associated with a Lectureship in Orthopaedics in the University of Glasgow. Steps of a similar nature were taken in 1945 and 1946 in Edinburgh, Dundee and Aberdeen, the Edinburgh arrangements being linked up with a projected Chair of Orthopaedic Surgery in the University there. In all the schemes which came to fruition or which were advanced, the claims and principles of rehabilitation were fully represented. A national orthopaedic scheme, of common interest to voluntary, local authority and central government agencies alike, had, in fact, progressively taken shape in the years since 1940; and this in itself was a substantial contribution to the evolution of surgical practice in Scotland.

It was scarcely to be expected that the system of treatment represented by the setting up of the special units would be enthusiastically accepted by all members of the medical and surgical staffs of the established hospitals. By custom and tradition, the functions of the general surgeon had been wide both in conception and in practice; and though the developments of the various specialties—gynaecology, ear, nose and throat, genito-urinary, ophthalmological and the like—had increasingly encroached upon the wide province of the surgeon at large, the latter (in many instances at least) regarded a number of the new special subjects—orthopaedics and so forth—as still within his territory. Nevertheless, it seemed proper to those who were ultimately responsible for the good of the patient that new technical advances and refinements of technique should be fully used in meeting the obligations which had been placed upon them. The official view upon the subject was formulated thus:

'It is a cardinal principle of the Emergency Hospital Scheme that specialised treatment should be secured at the earliest possible stage for patients whose condition requires it. To this end it is essential that every patient who is in need of treatment that cannot readily be given in the hospital to which he is first admitted should be transferred without avoidable delay either to a special unit appropriate to his condition or to another hospital where the necessary treatment is readily available. Medical Superintendents are expected to co-operate by arranging transfers of patients promptly for this purpose' (D.H.S. Circular No. 310/1941.)

It was, of course, pointed out that the arrangements for specialised treatment in appropriate units existed primarily for the benefit of those categories of patients for which the Government was financially responsible. Thus hospital authorities were instructed that transfers of ordinary civilian (i.e. non-Scheme) patients for specialised care should be made in accordance with normal peace-time practice. It frequently occurred, however, that beds had to be cleared, especially in city hospitals, in anticipation of casualty needs; and patients so transferred on the authority of the Hospital Officers became Scheme patients by reason of their transfer; and many ordinary civilians were in this way able to find beds in special units appropriate to their condition.

Orthopaedic Units: These units were staffed and equipped for specialised surgical treatment and for remedial and occupational therapy. They were intended to deal primarily with severe and multiple fractures requiring prolonged treatment; diseases, disabilities and derangements of the joints; and restoration of function in persons disabled by injury. By the time the new orthopaedic units had attained functional maturity —in the latter half of 1941—the patients entitled to treatment under the Emergency Hospital Scheme arrangements involved not only those included in the categories of civilian war injury, the Fighting Services, the Merchant Navy and the Civil Defence organisation, but also individuals engaged upon munition work, ship-building, ship-repairing, building, engineering, mining, agriculture, fishing and transport. These classes represented absolutely essential workers, and it was of the utmost moment that, when they became the victims of such injuries as fractures, they should be restored to work with the least possible delay and the maximum degree of functional recovery. In connexion, then, with this urgent problem, the treatment and disposal of fracture cases, an important memorandum was prepared at the request of the Department of Health by the late Professor (and Principal) Sir John Fraser, Bart., of Edinburgh University, who recommended the types of fracture which should be admitted with the least possible delay to one or other of the special orthopaedic units (D.H.S. Circular No. 311/1941).

Special arrangements were made for treatment of orthopaedic conditions in members of the Royal Air Force. After a survey of the facilities available in the autumn of 1941, the Air Ministry intimated that all R.A.F. orthopaedic cases in Scotland, including all fractures of the limbs and spine, should be transferred to one or other of the four special units at Larbert, Stracathro, Hairmyres or Raigmore. Such transfers were to be made as early as possible, and ordinarily during the first few days after injury. Immediate therapeutic methods—immobilisation and the like—employed during primary hospital treatment were to be such as would permit the early and reasonably safe transfer to one of the special units.

Royal Air Force orthopaedic patients treated in the four special units referred to above were usually transferred to R.A.F. Orthopaedic Rehabilitation Centres in England for the final phase of their treatment.

Amputations: It is appropriate that a note should be included here upon the subject of amputations. The Ministry of Pensions, undertook the responsibility for the supply of artificial limbs for service personnel, for civilians injured by enemy action, for members of the Civil Defence organisations and for members of the mercantile marine disabled by war service. It was recognised that the extent of the patient's ultimate ability to lead a normal life would depend materially upon the preparation of the stump and upon the careful fitting of the most suitable artificial limb, and it was therefore desirable that the Ministry of Pensions limb-fitting surgeons should be associated with the patients as early as possible; and appropriate arrangements to this end were made with the individual hospitals. All amputation (or re-amputation) cases were accordingly transferred at an early stage to Ministry of Pensions hospitals. So far, indeed, as it was practicable, patients were given into the care of the Ministry before amputation actually took place.

The Canadian Orthopaedic Unit: Certain points of particular interest must be noticed here. One of the most notable is the fact that, early in 1941, and as a result of the increasing threat of air raiding, it was felt in Canada that there might well be need of further provision for orthopaedic patients in Great Britain, and particularly in Scotland. Contact was therefore established between the Red Cross Society of Canada and the Scottish Department of Health, and arrangements were later completed for the installation in one of the Scottish orthopaedic hospitals of a fully equipped Canadian unit. Through selection committees, representative of the Red Cross Society and the Medical and Nursing Associations of Canada, eight surgeons, an anaesthetist, a matron and twenty-one nursing sisters were chosen. All of these were volunteers, who were drawn from almost every province of the Dominion, as well as the Yukon Territory. The group was financed and equipped through the resources of the Canadian Red Cross Society. After delays in the organisation of the party and the release of certain of its members from the Fighting Services, the unit was finally completed. Upon embarkation from a Canadian port it passed under the direction of the Department of Health for Scotland and arrived in Great Britain on Christmas Day, 1941. After brief consultations between the chiefs of the unit and the Department, Hairmyres Hospital in Lanarkshire was chosen as the base for the group.

In the view of the Canadian authorities, Hairmyres Hospital was peculiarly well equipped, especially in its treatment block, for the purpose in view, and few adjustments had to be made before work was begun. The equipment of the hospital was added to by gifts from the Relief Agency of the Canadian Red Cross Society. These included orthopaedic instruments, supplies of bandages, dressings, drugs and linen, and comforts for the patients.

During the early period of the unit's operation at Hairmyres, its Director was Mr. A. B. Le Mesurier of Toronto, who was supported by an assistant surgeon, two surgical registrars and four surgical house officers. This complement of surgeons was allotted a 400-bed unit in E.M.S. hutted wards. There were ten wards in all. Three of them were staffed by Canadian nursing sisters and seven by Civil Nursing Reserve personnel. The junior ward staff was composed of V.A.Ds and C.N.R. auxiliary nurses. After a period of six months, Mr. Le Mesurier returned to Canada and was progressively succeeded by orthopaedic surgeons representing the leading hospitals and universities in the Dominion of Canada. This circuit of personnel was of much advantage because of the experience gained in varying methods of treatment and technique. This, by some, may have been regarded as a disadvantage, but on the other hand it provided a clear demonstration and a broad view of different phases of Canadian orthopaedic surgery. All the surgical chiefs of the unit were members of the American Board of Orthopaedic Surgery.

Between January 1, 1942, and the middle of May 1945, when the unit prepared to return to Canada, some 11,000 patients had been treated in the wards and out-patients' department. These were in the first place representative of all the armed forces of the United Nations, and in the second place of other nationals, Scottish miners, shipyard workers from Clydeside and air raid victims. After 1944 a number of German prisoners-of-war were also dealt with. The work of the unit was, as was to be expected, primarily traumatic and reconstructive, and only a small part was corrective. Plastic surgery was practised in some degree, and for a time the unit had the services of a plastic surgeon who later joined the Royal Canadian Army Medical Corps. Much of the operative work of the unit showing the methods employed and the results of rehabilitation and occupational therapy, was recorded on Kodachrome film, thus making possible a review, at a later date in Canada, of some of the methods employed by the unit while abroad.

Maxillo-Facial and Plastic Units: The primary function of these units—situated at Ballochmyle, Bangour, Stracathro and Raigmore Hospitals—was the care of facial injuries and fractures of the jaw. It soon became apparent, however, that they could not be limited to a restricted field; and consequently, to emphasise the importance of the plastic surgery which was undertaken at the units, they were renamed, in December 1941, Plastic Surgery and Jaw Injury Units. Hospitals in the Emergency Hospital Scheme were accordingly notified that all cases, such as burns, which might require skin grafting, severe facial injuries, fractures of the jaw and like conditions should be transferred to the special units as early as possible. The units at Ballochmyle and Bangour were equipped and staffed for the treatment of every type of patient, including those in need of major plastic surgery. Major operations, however, were not ordinarily undertaken at the two secondary units, Stracathro and Raigmore, although in special circumstances in which it was considered desirable for clinical or operational reasons to retain a patient in one or other of these hospitals, a senior plastic surgeon could be made available. All general hospitals in the Emergency Scheme were equipped for the immediate treatment of burns, although the only special unit of this kind was the existing Burns Department of the Glasgow Royal Infirmary, some account of the work of which appears in Chapter 7 of the Volume of this series. Even the Royal Infirmary, however, was, for lack of space, unable to devote itself to major plastic surgery; and it was partly because of the amount of work originating in the Royal Infirmary and demanding continued treatment in a special unit that Ballochmyle emerged as the most important plastic unit in Scotland. Here every variety of plastic operation was carried out under conditions which involved the employment of progressive refinements in technique, and in the workshop which was established much effort was successfully expended upon the development of an efficient prosthetic service in which the acrylic resins were largely used.

A special note must be made on the dental service provided at the plastic units. Dental surgeons had, at the outbreak of war, been appointed to general hospitals at selected points throughout the country and these dentists, working in collaboration with the surgeons-in-charge, were available for inter-dental wiring or other immediate fixation. Ordinarily, their work was confined to such procedures as were necessary to permit comfortable and safe transport to a special unit, and sufficient equipment was supplied for the immediate needs. A consulting dental surgeon was available to all emergency hospitals in case of need.

At the four special units, specially selected dental teams were established, and these worked in close co-operation with the surgeons appointed to the plastic units. In conjunction with the Military Authorities, courses of instruction were arranged at Ballochmyle Hospital for Service dental officers, and these proved to be widely acceptable, popular and of the highest professional value. The instructional arrangements were in operation from June 1, 1942, until October 23, 1945. The ordinary or standard course covered a period of fourteen days and was taken by 211 Service dental surgeons; while nineteen officers were given a special long course of instruction which ran for two months or thereabouts. This teaching function was no doubt in part responsible for the fact that the centre at Ballochmyle became exceptionally strong in dentistry. The technique of immobilisation of fractured jaws was developed there to a degree which evoked wide commendation from all the recognised authorities who visited the unit, and its influence was felt in every part of the world into which the British Forces penetrated. Even in remote fields of action the workshop technique of Ballochmyle had valuable repercussions; and, although this hospital was in a specially favourable position because of its teaching facilities, it is to be noted that all four special units were equipped to manufacture dental splints and other appliances—not only for their own use but for use as might be required throughout the units of the Emergency Hospital Scheme as a whole.

Ophthalmic Units: These special units were equipped for what may be designated the more formal and deliberate type of eye surgery. They were thus designed to carry out the continuing surgical treatment of casualties and the treatment of such eye conditions as are ordinarily dealt with in the wards of a special eye hospital or in the eye department of a general hospital.

It is interesting to notice that the E.M.S. hospital which actually developed the most active ophthalmological department was one in which an eye unit had not originally been planned. This, however, was at Ballochmyle where the needs of the developing situation led to the formation of special eye facilities towards the end of 1940—soon after the commissioning of the hospital. In the initial stages, treatment was limited to Service cases and a few civilian patients whose casualties resulted from enemy action. The first considerable influx of patients came from the Clydeside raiding in March 1941, Ballochmyle serving as a base hospital to which the more serious cases from other E.M.S. hospitals were transferred. In the later war years the proportion under the waiting-list scheme increased. The total number of cases admitted by this unit until the end of 1945 was 307 of which 167 were service cases, while approximately 2,000 cases were treated as out-patients.

Brain Injuries: At the beginning of the war a special unit for the practice of neurosurgery was established at Bangour Hospital, West Lothian. It was staffed and equipped largely by personnel and material made available by Edinburgh Royal Infirmary. The resources of this unit were believed to be insufficient for the strain likely to be placed upon them, and a second unit of a similar kind was therefore projected for the Western District. Negotiations were accordingly entered into between the Department of Health on the one hand, and the Royal, Western and Victoria Infirmaries of Glasgow, in addition to the Public Health Department of Glasgow Corporation on the other, in order to determine what could be done in this way. Previously, a certain amount of neurosurgery had been carried on in the Victoria Infirmary and in Stobhill Hospital, the latter a local authority institution; but at neither of these centres were staff and equipment available for operations on a large scale. The result of the deliberations was the setting up of the neurosurgical unit at Killearn Hospital, in Stirlingshire. This enterprise, which was administered direct by the Department of Health, was in effect a confederation of the latter with the various bodies named above, each of which contributed in some measure to its staffing and equipment. Deficiencies were made good by the Central Department, which was aided in its administration by an Advisory Committee presided over by the Professor of Surgery in Glasgow University. The unit was opened on April 1, 1942, with 52 beds, a number which was later increased to 72.

Service patients, together with those categories of civilian patients for whom the Government were responsible, had, of course, priority rights to admission to the neurosurgical special units. Provided that beds remained available, ordinary civilian patients were also admitted for investigation and treatment; and the surgeons-in-charge were further permitted to admit certain private patients from whom they were authorised to collect limited professional fees. The private patients likewise contributed towards their maintenance in hospital.

So far as admissions to the unit are concerned, the number of patients steadily increased. Civilian figures showed a progressive rise, but Service figures fluctuated considerably, though their general trend was upwards. The periods before and after D-day, when compared, show some distinctive features. Early in 1942, a certain number of patients who had sustained head injuries during realistic training in battle schools began to arrive. Rather more numerous, however, were Service injuries resulting from motor accidents. In 1943, chronic battle casualties from North Africa arrived, followed by others from Sicily and Italy. In the winter of 1943–4, their numbers had so increased that further accommodation was necessary, and an additional male ward was made available for Service patients not in need of major surgical intervention. This provision eased a situation which was becoming difficult when, just before D-day, the admission of chronically ill civilian patients was suspended in order that arrangements might be made for the expected considerable influx of more acute battle casualties. At the request of the Director of Neurosurgical Services in the English E.M.S., Professor Sir Geoffrey Jefferson, who felt that it was necessary to be prepared for the evacuation of large numbers of battle casualties to hospitals within easy reach of the Normandy beaches, some of the members of the unit travelled south to Cardiff immediately after the start of the invasion. The team consisted of a neurosurgeon, one of the hospital anaesthetists, the senior neurosurgical resident and a theatre sister; and a quantity of instrumental equipment was carried. Fortunately, the casualties fell far short of the numbers expected, and the work of this 'sub-unit' during its stay of five weeks in Whitchurch Emergency Hospital, near Cardiff, was light, only a small number of battle casualties being evacuated to it.

Thoracic Units: The thoracic units were specially equipped to deal with such conditions as severe penetrating wounds of the chest and with patients in need of surgical treatment of the thoracic contents. Much successful endeavour was expended both at Hairmyres and Bangour Hospitals, and, wounds of the chest proving to be less frequent than had been expected, opportunities quickly became available for the material development of the peace-time type of thoracic surgery. Thus thoracoplasty and lobectomy in tuberculosis and bronchiectasis became almost commonplace, while operations on account of intrathoracic foreign bodies and malignant disease, cysts and the like, were frequently accomplished.

Psychoneurosis and other Mental Disorders: In 1940, formal provision for the treatment of psychoneurosis was made in special units at Gartloch Hospital, Glasgow (200 beds), Bangour Hospital, West Lothian (240 beds), and Oldmill Hospital, Aberdeen (22 beds). In the event, no more than a minimum of use was made of the facilities at Bangour, partly because of difficulty in obtaining specialised staff and partly because Gartloch Hospital was found to be capable of the greater number of admissions which were required. The beds set aside at Aberdeen were actively employed until the summer of 1944 when, with the increasing demand for casualty beds incidental to the Northern European offensive, the psychoneurotic patients were transferred to one of the neighbouring auxiliary hospitals.

These special units were specifically intended for the accommodation and treatment of civilian patients. It was expected that many victims of air attack would develop psychoneurotic syndromes, but no great difficulty of this kind was encountered and beds consequently remained available for the care of other civilian classes, including members of the Merchant Navy, pensioners for whom the Ministry of Pensions was responsible, and the ordinary sick. The waiting list scheme and the Scottish Supplementary Medical Service were frequent recruiting grounds for the psychoneurosis wards. It was emphatically urged upon the general hospital authorities that civilian cases of minor neurosis should not be retained in hospital but should be sent home as soon as possible after any necessary consultation with the neurologist or psychiatrist attached to the hospital. In cases in which continued institutional care was necessary or desirable, the transfer of patients to a special unit was enjoined.

No provision was made in the Emergency Hospital Scheme for the treatment of psychosis, which demanded reference to the mental hospitals in the usual way. So far as Service patients were concerned, the Royal Navy maintained beds for the purposes of psychoneurotic and psychotic needs at Kingseat Hospital, Aberdeen. The needs of the other Services were covered by the military hospitals at Bellsdyke (Larbert), Dumfries (officers only) and Carstairs.

When Gartloch Hospital reverted to the Corporation of Glasgow early in 1945, the psychoneurotic unit there was transferred to Law Hospital. Eighty beds were provided there. In 1945, the unit moved again to Lennox Castle Hospital, where 75 beds were available, and finally, in 1946, to Killearn Hospital, where, on account of staff shortages, only 30 beds could be maintained. At the last named hospital Army patients were also dealt with in the special unit because of the demobilisation of the military hospital at Bellsdyke.

The Effort Syndrome Unit was located at Bangour Hospital, West Lothian.

Peripheral Nerve Injury and Disease: Two special units were established for the treatment of affections of the peripheral nerves, including those resulting from wounding or other injury. The unit at Gogarburn Hospital received for the most part patients from all Districts except the Western, of which the needs were covered by the facilities at Killearn Hospital. Patients who were suffering from or threatened with trophic changes in the extremities (such as those associated with cold and exposure, frost-bite and the like) were also dealt with in the peripheral nerve units in order that the appropriate investigations on the peripheral nervous system might be carried out. This subject was an important one, and it had special reference to members of the Merchant Navy. The chief landing areas for survivors from enemy attack in the Atlantic were situated on the West Coast of Scotland, where the arrival of seamen suffering from various degrees of exposure was commonplace. All hospitals were accordingly advised that such patients, and others of a similar kind, should be transferred to the appropriate special unit as early as possible consistently with their general clinical state; and that the patients should be accompanied on transfer by a careful and complete statement of their condition immediately after their admission to the receiving hospital. For the guidance of hospital staffs in this matter, a document entitled "Notes on Peripheral Nerve Injuries" was prepared for and widely circulated by the Department of Health.

Gas Casualties: Lung Irritant Cases: For the treatment of casualties resulting from the possible use by the enemy of irritant gases, special oxygen wards were prepared in seven of the base hospitals administered by the Department of Health. Piping was installed and reservoirs of oxygen were maintained; and individual pieces of apparatus—flowmeters, B.L.B. masks, spectacle carriers and fine adjustment valves—were widely issued, not only to the specially equipped hospitals but to all casualty-receiving institutions in the emergency chain. The available resources were kept in a constant state of readiness, not only for use in a particular hospital but also as mobile equipment which could, in case of need, be speedily transported from place to place. In addition, a reserve of equipment was maintained by the Hospital Officers for issue in any emergency.

The desirability of placing patients suffering from the effects of irritant gases, such as phosgene, in institutions where continuous oxygen therapy could be carried out was impressed upon hospital and A.R.P. authorities alike; and the following general directions were issued for their guidance:

(*a*) It was pointed out that phosgene casualties should be moved by stretcher only—that is, completely recumbent, and by ambulance.

(b) Transfer, if necessary, was to be carried out within twelve hours and if possible within six hours of exposure to the gas. After twenty-four hours movement was dangerous, and consequently contra-indicated.

(c) Patients who were unfit to travel were to be retained in the casualty receiving hospitals, the equipment resources of which might be augmented where necessary on application to the Hospital Officers.

It follows from the fact that gas warfare did not happen that the formal provision thus made for the treatment of gas casualties was not employed for that purpose. Nevertheless, the arrangements made, and the equipment which was supplied, was used to good purpose by most of the general hospitals, which found that many of the casualties whom they received as well as many ordinary patients, were greatly assisted by the therapeutic agencies available.

As a concluding note to this section, the following table is appended. It indicates the numbers of patients who, year by year from 1940 until 1945 inclusive, were admitted to and treated in the special units:

Special units	1940 S	1940 C	1941 S	1941 C	1942 S	1942 C	1943 S	1943 C	1944 S	1944 C	1945 S	1945 C	Totals
Orthopaedic	912	1	2,732	745	6,076	1,802	6,241	2,250	8,592	2,121	7,239	2,215	40,926
Plastic surgery	9	—	130	52	353	204	286	234	595	226	622	270	2,981
Neurosurgical	125	96	300	210	522	577	642	630	767	579	632	993	6,073
Ophthalmic	14	—	73	46	106	5	112	38	221	26	230	15	886
Thoracic	34	—	117	33	185	83	217	132	259	106	166	139	1,471
Psychoneurosis	349	7	40	47	34	89	43	231	23	261	11	88	1,223
Effort syndrome	201	—	232	—	99	3	55	2	27	2	4	2	627
Peripheral nerve	—	—	110	56	172	73	411	165	898	358	834	303	3,380

Note: S = Service Cases. C = Civilian Cases.

6. AUXILIARY HOSPITALS

Before the outbreak of war, and while general hospital plans were under active discussion, it was appreciated that a considerable part of the hospital care and treatment which would be demanded by the needs of Service and civilian populations alike, would be during convalescence. The apparent absolute shortage of general surgical and medical beds at the initial period of planning, together with the fact that convalescent treatment in general hospitals was likely to be both uneconomical and inconvenient, determined the policy of the Department of Health in establishing Auxiliary Hospitals equipped, in the main, for convalescent patients only. For this purpose, some few existing institutions—such as the Grove Auxiliary Hospital at Dumfries and the Glen Coats Auxiliary Hospital at Paisley—were added to the Emergency Hospital Scheme; but accommodation of this kind was scanty, and thus the auxiliary hospital chain had to be fabricated, in the main, from other basic resources. The latter were found principally in large mansion houses offered to the Government for some purpose of the kind. From a Central Register of available premises which was maintained by H.M. Office of Works (afterwards the Ministry of Works and Buildings), a list of possible properties was made. To this list were added the names of other premises privately offered to the Department of Health, and individual houses were, in the first place, inspected in detail by the Hospital Officers. In the course of these inspections particular attention had to be paid to the availability of the various services—water, drainage, power and the like—as well as to general suitability and accessibility. As a result of the preliminary inspections, decisions were taken on further procedure in individual cases. Houses found to be satisfactory were appropriately modified in their structural design under the supervision of the Technical Officers of the Department of Health. In this way a remarkable chain of auxiliary hospitals was brought into being, the units of which were progressively commissioned throughout the years 1939 and 1940.

The auxiliary hospitals varied considerably in their accommodation. The smaller units were capable of housing only some thirty patients, while at the other end of the scale several buildings had a potential capacity of well over 100 patients. In order to meet a possible grave emergency in 1940, a rapid survey of all auxiliary hospitals was made by the Hospital Officers, immediately after the fall of France, to determine how many additional beds might reasonably be 'crowded' into each institution.

The auxiliary hospitals—with the exception of a small number of existing convalescent homes which remained under the control of their parent bodies—were administered directly by the Department of Health. For operational purposes, the hospitals were grouped around certain of the base hospitals, which were the principal but not the only source of convalescent patients, and which moreover, provided any necessary special services. Local administrative control was, until 1943, delegated to the medical superintendents of conveniently situated general hospitals but subsequently, this function was exercised by the Hospital Officers in person. A characteristic example of the grouping system—whereby, in addition to the foregoing, the Military Registrars at the base hospitals were responsible also for the observance of Service Regulations in the associated auxiliaries—was as follows:

Base hospital	Associated auxiliary hospitals
Ballochmyle	Auchendrane; Montgomerie; Hollybush; Paisley Convalescent Home, West Kilbride; Glenapp; Galloway House.

The total number of auxiliary hospitals in commission was 66, of which some 60 functioned actively throughout the greater part of the war. After the defeat of Germany, however, a rapid involution took place. By the end of 1945, the auxiliary hospital strength had been reduced by some two-thirds, and after the next six months few remained. At the period of maximum activity—that is, between the beginning of 1941 and the end of 1945—the following were in commission:

District	No. of hospitals	Standard beds	Crowded beds
Western	24	1,134	1,682
South-eastern	8	517	671
Eastern	14	901	1,283
North-eastern	14	663	1,107
Northern	6	342	481
Totals	66	3,557	5,224

For the most part, as has been seen, the auxiliary hospitals under the direct control of the Department of Health were private houses, the owners of which placed them at the disposal of the Government for the accommodation of casualties. In many cases, the owner, or wife of the owner, expressed a desire to give her services to the hospital, and where this was so the Department of Health agreed to her being designated Commandant. Since a matron had also to be appointed, the danger of this arrangement lay in the possibility of the clash of personalities, and it cannot be denied that in several instances the mutual relations of commandant and matron became seriously strained. This fact, together with the circumstances that, as the war progressed, greater and greater responsibilities became the lot of almost every individual, led to an attenuation of the ranks of the commandants, with the result that, by the end of the year 1943, only a few remained of what had previously been a considerable company.

The commandant was expected to act as the official correspondent of the hospital; to be responsible for housekeeping, heating and lighting, the ordering of supplies, the maintenance of records of expenditure and the supervision of the domestic staff not on duty in the wards. The matron, in turn, was wholly responsible for the nursing, discipline and welfare of the patients. So far as the medical treatment of patients was concerned, she was, of course, responsible to the medical officer appointed to the hospital; and the immediate assistance of the Military Registrar of the nearest base hospital was available to her for disciplinary control of Service patients. She was expected to maintain continuous contact with the Hospital Officer on all matters affecting her own position, the nursing staff and the welfare of the patients; and the Hospital Officer submitted to the Department every three months a report on matters dealt with on his frequent visits to the hospitals. The matron was further responsible—except where there was a resident medical officer—for keeping medical records and for maintaining a register showing the record and conditions of service of each member of her nursing staff.

It will be clear from what has been said that the management of the auxiliary hospitals demanded the exercise of much activity, and of no little administrative sense and sometimes ingenuity upon the part of the matrons. The employment of tact was no less important, for the nature of the relations between the auxiliary hospitals and the population of the surrounding districts—which were usually remote—was a matter of much importance in their successful operation. Thus the establishment and maintenance of a friendly enthusiasm for the work of the hospitals among the local Red Cross branches, the Women's Voluntary Services, the Women's Rural Institutes and kindred organisations was a matter of primary moment. A great deal was accomplished in this way, particularly when, in 1942, local welfare committees were set up for each auxiliary hospital, usually presided over by the Lord Lieutenant of the County in which they were located. As has been indicated above, the medical superintendents of the nearest base hospitals exercised for a time general supervision, but later this arrangement was terminated and the Hospital Officers still further augmented their relations with the hospitals. The nursing staff of all the auxiliary hospitals administered directly by the Department of Health was provided exclusively by the Civil Nursing Reserve. In the main, medical service was drawn from the resources of local civilian practice, nominations for the position of medical officer being made by the appropriate Local Medical War Committee. Consultants were available at the associated base hospitals, the ancillary services of which were also available to the auxiliaries. Occasional exceptions were made to the ordinary rule in respect of medical staff; and thus it was found to be not only desirable but actually necessary to appoint whole-time resident medical officers to three of the largest auxiliary hospitals in the Western District.

Equipment was supplied from the central resources of the Department of Health, and for the most part this was suitable for convalescent care only. Twelve of the auxiliaries were, however, supplied with surgical and other equipment suitable for the practice, should the necessity arise, of emergency operative surgery, and in these institutions rooms were set aside for use as operating theatres in case of need. To all intents and purposes, they were never so used; but in two of the hospitals in South-west Scotland—namely, Glenapp, Ayrshire and Galloway House, Wigtownshire—more elaborate arrangements were made. By adapting suitable rooms, formal operating departments with equipment suitable for major surgery were installed. Radiological services for both hospitals were carried out until 1943 at the Garrick Hospital, Stranraer; but at that time radiological quarters were set up and mobile X-ray units provided; so that, to all intents and purposes, Glenapp and Galloway House became small general hospitals in their own right. For upwards of three years, they both gave excellent service, and they remained continuously active in the surgical and medical fields alike. Glenapp covered the new port at Cairnryan and the many military units which underwent training among the hills of South Ayrshire and Galloway; and Galloway House was of the most material assistance to the Royal Air Force, which had large concentrations, training and otherwise, in the County of Wigtown. In addition, both hospitals accomplished much surgical work of a general emergency nature on behalf of the local civilian population, who were loosely regarded as potential members of the waiting lists of voluntary hospitals and so entitled to treatment under the waiting-list scheme. The voluntary hospitals were willing to accept the slight financial obligation which the treatment of these patients involved; and altogether the experiment was a happy one.

Other functions exercised by individual auxiliary hospitals were as follows:

(*a*) Rehabilitation Units, supervised by sergeant instructors supplied by the Army, operated at various times between 1941 and the end of the war at Blair Drummond, Montgomerie and Glenapp Hospitals. The facilities thus provided were acceptably and usefully employed for the rehabilitation of Service patients, merchant seamen and, on occasion, convalescent members of the general public. Admission of patients was effected through the agency of the associated base hospitals, at which suitable individuals were selected. The specialist surgical and medical staffs of the base hospitals prescribed the general line of treatment which it was desirable to follow. Equipment was provided by the Department of Health, and a general supervision was exercised by the military medical officer in charge of rehabilitation at Glencorse Camp, Midlothian. Before returning to their units, individual patients were ordinarily sent for a period of "hardening" either to Glencorse itself or to the associated convalescent depot at Hamilton.

(*b*) Women patients from all the Services, as well as those from civilian occupations, were dealt with at Touch Auxiliary Hospital, near Stirling, which was specially allocated for the purpose. This hospital also played a part in the care of patients with pleurisy mentioned under the Public Health Section of the present work. Dunira Hospital also was associated with this scheme.

(*c*) Ardgowan Hospital, Renfrewshire, had a special affiliation with the Naval Unit which was maintained under the E.M.S. auspices at Mearnskirk Hospital. It was therefore particularly influential in the care and treatment of convalescent ratings from the Royal Navy and members of ships' crews from the Merchant Navy.

(*d*) The accommodation of Knockderry Hospital, on the Firth of Clyde, was allocated for three years to the Fighting French Navy. The administration of the hospital was in the hands of the Department of Health, but the medical supervision was provided by the De Gaulle provisional government.

(e) Quothquhan Hospital, Lanarkshire, acted for a like period as a *maison de répos* for members of the Fighting French Services.

7. SHADOW AND CRASH HOSPITALS

The dramatic and disquieting situation in the spring and early summer of 1940 increased the anxieties of the Department of Health in the most material degree, for it then became apparent that the resources of the casualty organisation might well be strained up to or beyond the breaking point. Instructions were accordingly issued to the Hospital Officers to be prepared at short notice to mobilise every available bed for casualty reception. The initial clearance of hospital beds which took place at the outbreak of war was a drastic one; but the months of quiet and of freedom from air attack which succeeded the period of early activity had permitted the silting up, to some extent, of the accommodation in the existing hospitals. At this period, new construction had not proceeded far enough to permit of an expansion at the base hospitals; and it was therefore clearly evident that additional resources could only be obtained at short notice through a process of clearing beds afresh. Local authorities and voluntary hospital managements were accordingly notified, on May 18, 1940, that in view of the war situation it might become necessary for the Hospital Officers to issue an instruction by telegram bearing the words, 'Clear Hospital'. On the receipt of such a message it would be the duty of the medical superintendents to take action immediately:

(a) To send home all civilian patients for whom the continuance of in-patient treatment was no longer essential, except such patients as had no homes to which they could go at short notice.

(b) To inform the Hospital Officers by telephone when this action had been completed, and to state the total number of beds which were then available.

After any clearances of this kind, admissions to hospital were to be restricted to patients who were in urgent need of in-patient treatment.

Even so, it was recognised that the potential volume of casualties might be greatly in excess of that for which the Emergency Hospital Scheme as it then existed could possibly provide; and consequently it was considered necessary that immediate steps should be taken to make possible the early occupation of numerous buildings with large rooms—such as hotels or boarding schools—in which hospital accommodation for casualties could be improvised at short notice. These were first thoughts upon a subject which occasioned a great deal of work, and they were succeeded in June 1940, by the further thought, dictated by common prudence, that even the 39,000 beds which it was hoped to make available in the near future for the reception of casualties in Scotland might well be insufficient. The total of 39,000 comprised some 14,500 which could be found in hospitals as they existed in peace-time; 1,100 in converted hotels; 4,000 in other converted buildings; some 9,000 in hutted annexes; and approximately 6,400 in the new hutted hospitals. To this total of 35,000 were added some 4,250 beds in existing convalescent institutions and in the private houses which had been, or were in process of being, converted into auxiliary hospitals. The doubtful sufficiency of this provision stimulated the exertions of the Hospital Officers in the survey which was required before the approximate amount of additional accommodation suitable could be assessed. By this survey, which was completed by midsummer of 1940 and which covered the whole country, the 'Shadow' Hospital Scheme came into being. This scheme, which may be defined as an insurance against such contingencies as large masses of casualties, the destruction of various hospitals and the cutting-off of certain institutions by invasion, existed in shadow form only, for it would have been wasteful or extravagant to expand resources which had still to be proved insufficient. Nevertheless, it came in fact to be sufficiently developed to have made it a workable proposition had circumstances so demanded; and, apart from the actual survey, specific steps were taken to provide appropriate staff for each chosen property in the event of its being commissioned. Further, dumps of equipment, including medical and surgical supplies, were laid down at various strategic locations, so that, given the necessary transport improvised hospitals could have gone into operation at very short notice indeed—in some cases within twenty-four hours.

After the large series of inspections made by the Hospital Officers, two lists of shadow hospitals were prepared by the Department of Health—the first, a priority list of buildings which might have been called into immediate employment, and the second a list of reserve buildings. Since it was considered probable that, should invasion actually occur, the east coast would be untenable for all practical purposes, the priority list was composed of hotels, holiday homes and the like situated on or near the west coast and concentrated particularly in the area between the Firth of Lorne and the Solway Firth. The reserve list was wider in scope and gave substantial cover to the whole country. The gross details of the properties which formed the two units in the Shadow Hospital Scheme are:

A. *Priority List:*

Bed capacity		Existing beds	Beds required
Patients	Staff		
3,222	819	2,246	1,795

B. *Reserve List:*

	Bed capacity		Existing beds	Beds required
	Patients	Staff		
A	1,919	320	1,036	1,182
B	4,251	1,296	2,439	2,478
Totals	.	. .	3,475	3,660

A—Hotels. B—Schools.

From what has been said above, it will have been seen that the Shadow Hospital organisation remained a shadow only. None of the buildings which were included in it was brought into operation as a hospital; but many of them were in course of time requisitioned by the fighting services for uses of their own—some on the understanding that they would be placed at once at the disposal of the Department of Health had the necessity for their employment as hospitals actually arisen. The dumps of equipment were, however, maintained in readiness till the end of the German war, and after the middle of 1945 they were progressively withdrawn.

The object of the Shadow Scheme was, of course, to hold in reserve certain blocks of accommodation which could be used in a manner akin to that of base hospitals. In the urban areas themselves, particularly in the congested localities round the Clyde Basin in the Western District, a problem of another kind had to be met. It was recognised as being well within the bounds of possibility that one or more populous districts might suddenly be devastated by intensive air attacks, and that the hospital resources of such districts might share in the general catastrophe. In such circumstances, it would have become necessary to improvise as rapidly as possible such accommodation for casualties as could be found; and with this possible end in view another survey was made in the cities and towns of many blocks of property which, in emergency, could have been pressed into the service of the casualty organisations. The 'Crash' Hospital Scheme, which, in essence, was another 'shadow' structure, thus came into being. The buildings which would have been used in this connexion were for the most part local authority day schools, public halls, suitable places of entertainment and the like. Beyond the storage in these buildings of blankets and a few other elementary items of equipment, the physical resources of the crash hospitals were reduced to the barest minimum. They could, at best, have functioned only for a few days at a time, and as places of rest and shelter rather than hospitals. Even so, their occupation would have been possible only if certain essential services, such as water, remained available. The rudiments of medical and nursing care would have been furnished by surviving members of the staffs of adjacent hospitals which had been put out of action; and reinforcements of one kind or another would have been arranged by the Hospital Officers through such agencies as the British Red Cross Society, the Women's Voluntary Services and the like. For the feeding of patients and staff, the Hospital Officers made detailed arrangements for simple food, and the catering and transport contractors who would have been involved, assisted in the most efficient and enthusiastic way in the formulation of plans.

By the process thus described, a reserve of crash hospital accommodation was obtained, the bed capacity of which varied from about 18,000 on an ordinary estimate to a crowded figure of about 26,000. The ordinary functions of the buildings concerned were not interfered with, except that in many cases one apartment was set aside for the storage of blankets and other items of equipment.

Since the fear of invasion led to the establishment of the Shadow and Crash Hospital Organisations, and since *mobility* was the key note properly sounded, it is appropriate that a note should be included here upon the co-ordination of ambulance services which was an important feature of the operational arrangements to meet the threat of an enemy landing. In June 1940, this matter was discussed between the War Office, the Ministry of Health and the Department of Health for Scotland, and the following general principles were formulated.

All casualties, military or civilian, resulting from enemy attack were, in the first instance and as far as possible, to be treated in regimental aid posts or field ambulances if military casualties, and civilian casualties in the local first-aid posts of the civilian authorities, so long as they continued to function in the affected area. If necessary, however, all such establishments, civil and military, were to be prepared to treat civilian or military patients at any time and without discrimination. It seems likely that, had the need actually arisen, the latter course would have been followed in most instances. Casualties urgently in need of hospital treatment were, of course, to be admitted to the nearest hospital, irrespective of the status of the latter or of the patient.

Road transport for casualties was to be carried out from first-aid posts or regimental aid posts in vehicles under the control of civilian organisations or of military medical units, but again no discrimination was to be permitted unless circumstances happened to be favourable. That is to say, military ambulances could be employed for civilians, and civilian vehicles for military personnel. Administrative military medical officers of areas and formations were instructed to work in close co-operation with civilian administrative officers of the A.R.P. services, the Hospital Officers, and local officers of the British Red Cross Society and the St. Andrew's Ambulance Association in their areas. The prevailing situation could then be covered as comprehensively as possible by a fully co-ordinated service.

Generally speaking, except, probably, in the case of a landing from the sea, it was to be expected that local civilian organisations would continue to function alongside military units, even although the particular locality might be the object of an attack. It had, of course, to be appreciated that an attack might develop from any direction and that conditions which permitted the maintenance of a well-defined front—behind which were organised collecting, evacuating and distributing zones—were not likely to obtain in Home Defence warfare. Medical evacuation, therefore, had to be organised on an area basis rather than on the ordinary system in depth applicable to an expeditionary force in the field. In such areas of fighting, however, the medical arrangements to be made for Army formations was to be the responsibility of Commands, through corps or military areas as the case might be. These arrangements were to be based upon divisional medical units, motor ambulance convoys and ambulance car companies, or civil motor ambulance transport. Evacuation was to take place through military or civil hospitals, whether functioning as casualty clearing stations, as casualty receiving hospitals or as general hospitals, to such military or civil hospitals as were designated by the Hospital Officer. A general process of sorting out was to follow as soon as circumstances permitted.

CHAPTER 3

THE ANCILLARY SERVICES

MEDICAL, NURSING AND LAY SERVICES

BOTH the basic principles and the details of the staffing of the emergency hospitals have been covered so adequately in the English narrative that only certain aspects of the Scottish picture need be dealt with here. As an initial comment, it must be pointed out that the direct administration of the newly constructed general hospitals and of the chain of auxiliary hospitals by the Department of Health for Scotland dictated the direct appointment by the Department of a proportionately large number of medical, nursing and other staff.

The machine—the aggregate of buildings, beds and medical and surgical equipment—did not, of course, constitute the Emergency Medical Services, or even that specialised portion relating to the hospital expansion. The activator of the machine, man-power, was fundamental; and the many ramifications and responsibilities which developed at the call of war required, in view of the restricted personnel available, a judgment in their distribution which called for long and patient planning. Rightly or wrongly, it was determined before the outbreak of war that the three fighting services should maintain their own medical departments; and it was clear that, when the Navy, Army and Royal Air Force had met their increasing needs, considerable stringency would occur in the medical and associated man-power remaining at the disposal of the civil authorities. The necessary demands of the hospitals, of the Civil Defence organisations, of the Evacuation Scheme with its sickbays and hostels, of the industrial services and of ordinary civilian requirements had to be borne in mind; and it was increasingly impressed upon the authorities that the greatest possible economy would have to be exercised if all needs were to be met. A note on each of the following types of staffing in relation to the Emergency Hospital Scheme is given below, namely, medical, nursing, technical and domestic; and, while they are not specifically mentioned here, it is to be understood that the other emergency services received their due quota of such specialised personnel as was required.

MEDICAL

For some three years before the war, the British Medical Association had been officially concerned with a series of inquiries into the medical man-power resources of the country; and at the beginning of the war the Scottish Central Medical War Committee—a parent body associated with the various local Medical War Committees—was established to supervise and direct the allocation of doctors to the war-time services. So far as the Emergency Medical Services were concerned, rates of pay and terms of appointment were arranged by agreement between the Central Committee and the Department of Health for Scotland. The existing institutions which formed the major portion of the fabric of the Emergency Hospital Scheme had, of course, their own adequate staff resources for peace-time; and the reduction of these resources by the recruitment for the fighting services of certain members of their medical staffs necessitated no more than a re-allocation of accommodation and responsibility. In the new base hospitals, however, and in the hutted annexes, problems of staffing had to be dealt with from the beginning; and a similar problem, on a restricted scale, was met in the extensive chain of auxiliary hospitals which came into being.

In general terms, the obligations to be met in staffing the hospitals might be defined as follows: it became the duty of the Emergency Medical Services to provide skilled medical personnel for the treatment of patients within the scope of the Emergency Hospital Scheme to such hospitals whose permanent staff was insufficient for the efficient execution of essential war-time functions. In the earlier phases, when the whole situation was still fluid and uncertain, relatively few full-time senior appointments could be made; and in the new hospitals and most of the hutted annexes, physicians and surgeons-in-charge were generally appointed upon a visiting basis, the specialists in question being senior members of the staffs of the existing hospitals, who were prepared, in view of the urgency, to duplicate their ordinary commitments. Thus on June 30, 1941, the medical personnel of the Emergency Hospital Service in Scotland were divided into the following categories:

> 136 part-time visiting medical and surgical officers, who were mainly drawn from the senior specialist ranks of the voluntary hospitals;
>
> 161 whole-time resident medical and surgical officers; and
>
> 803 part-time officers attached to 'Surgical Teams' which could be called upon in emergency for service as units in the hospital or hospitals to which they were attached.

The leader of each team was a senior surgeon in established practice; but many of the team members had to be drawn from the ranks of already busy general practitioners. The willingness, and, indeed, anxiety of the latter to volunteer for this service was, in view of the other heavy duties to which they were committed, at once a striking and gratifying factor in the whole medical arrangements.

At this time, therefore, the general policy was to employ minimum whole-time staffs in the interests of the economical use of man-power, supplemented by the visiting specialists and by surgical team members as required. Medical and surgical advisers were appointed to the central offices of the Department of Health; and surgical directors were established in each of the five Civil Defence Districts. The function of the latter was to correlate and supervise the surgical work in their areas; and since, in the populous Western District, it early became apparent that the complexities of the situation there could not well be handled by one individual, three Sectoral surgical directors were appointed to supervise that area, to which a Director of Medical Services was also attached to integrate the activities of the various physicians.

With the increasing stabilisation of the new hospital service, it became apparent that what had been regarded as a minimum figure for residential appointments was, under the circumstances which prevailed, adequate for the performance (with such help from outside as might from time to time be required) of all likely routine duties. It became possible, indeed, at quite an early stage, to diminish the obligations which rested upon the visiting specialists, and at the same time to increase the number of senior appointments upon a residential and full-time basis. A slight shift therefore occurred in the ratio of visiting to resident appointments. As is shown above, the proportion in the middle of 1941 was 136 : 161. A year later, it was 114 : 156. This ratio was substantially maintained throughout the remainder of the war, and was, for example, 112 : 145 in June 1944; but these figures of themselves do not reflect the important fact that it became increasingly possible to lessen the calls which were made upon the visiting staffs, particularly in general medicine and surgery, and to increase the responsibilities of the resident physicians and surgeons. This alteration in emphasis made it possible for the former to devote themselves more fully to their ordinary duties in the existing hospitals.

In the year which ended in the summer of 1942, the problem of the supply of medical man-power to the Armed Forces became acute. A committee, known as The Medical Personnel (Priority) Committee, (see Volume I, Part II, Chapter 14), under the chairmanship of Sir Geoffrey Shakespeare, Bt., M.P., upon which there were two representatives from Scotland, was therefore appointed to secure economy in medical personnel in the Forces. This committee was requested to report from time to time on the allocation of medical man-power between the respective Services. It made a series of recommendations, to which effect was given, concerning co-operation between the Services, integration of resources, limitation of establishments and mobility of staffs. On one recommendation of the committee, a regional committee was set up under the chairmanship of the Regional Commissioner to secure the maximum co-operation between the Services.

The Shakespeare Committee was by no means solely concerned with the formally constituted medical services, both military and civilian, but was involved also with the medical man-power required to meet the ordinary needs of the civilian population. It was inevitable that the withdrawal of practitioners from their ordinary work should be heavy, and as early as 1942 the strains and stresses of civilian practice were already beginning to tell upon the attenuated band of doctors who continued to work in their accustomed environment. In some cases severe and prolonged anxieties were the lot of the civilian practitioner, but to the credit of the profession the additional individual burdens were shouldered successfully and uncomplainingly. From time to time the patients did experience unavoidable delays, but these delays were largely unimportant and acute illness could be depended upon to provoke the promptest possible response. The establishment of the waiting list scheme was undoubtedly of the most material assistance to the overburdened general practitioners of both urban and rural districts, for it dealt with a considerable number of patients who were legitimately in need of hospital care and correspondingly lightened the load of the family doctor. Although not formally incorporated in the Emergency Medical Services, the general practitioners in effect formed a part of it, and it is therefore proper that their part in the national effort should be noticed in this place.

As time went on, the supervisory responsibilities of the Central and the Local Medical War Committees attained a phase of maximum organisation and integration. The withdrawal of practitioners was controlled by the former body acting upon the advice of the local committees, which had the primary duty of considering the resources and needs of the various localities, and of the hospitals and other services, and of reporting in specific terms to the central body. So far as the public health services of the local authorities were concerned, the Department of Health undertook to advise the Scottish Central Medical War Committee how much rationalisation of these services was feasible. To this end, the local authorities were required to submit returns of their medical staffs and to notify to the Central Department any vacancies which might occur; and they were instructed that the consent of the Secretary of State must be obtained to any projected increase in their staffs and to the filling of any vacancy (including approval of any candidate selected).

Corresponding general arrangements to those indicated above were initiated in respect of dentists, pharmacists and opticians.

The year 1943 saw the problem of shortage of medical and associated man-power in its acutest form. It was a period in which there was serious continuous difficulty in meeting the demands—which were no more than equivalent to the needs—of the essential services; and it became increasingly apparent that economical utilisation of the work of every available doctor and dentist was of cardinal importance. The efficient discharge of the obligations of the Central and Local Committees, both medical and dental, involved, therefore, the circumvention of increasing difficulties; but the manner in which these bodies effected the solution of their problems was generally accepted. It is true that individual grievances were brought to light, but in the main these were transitory and could be discounted after adequate explanation was given.

The same year saw the initiation of important arrangements, which persisted throughout the remainder of the war, for a system of mutual aid between civilian doctors and those in the Armed Forces in times of special stress. This movement was of the utmost value and its effectiveness was, indeed, demonstrated both in hospital and general practice. When, for example, at the end of 1943 there was a serious threat of an influenza epidemic, Service medical officers gave assistance to overburdened civilian practitioners, and even replaced for the time being certain of the latter who were themselves victims of the infection.

During the years 1944 and 1945, additional emphasis was placed upon the same problems which had been encountered earlier. It may, indeed, be said, that no greater period of anxiety and stress has ever been encountered in this relation. At the beginning of 1945, 2,452 doctors out of a total of 7,245 on the register of the Scottish Central Medical War Committee were on actual service with the Armed Forces. The end of the fighting in Europe did not result in any immediate substantial relief; for, apart from the incidence of death and disability due to wounding and other causes, the release of doctors, and particularly of specialists, was made difficult by the relatively greater needs of the Forces in the Far East. The early end of widespread hostilities in the Orient could not then be foreseen; and, even apart from actual warfare, the size of the military effort in the East demanded the presence of adequate medical personnel. It was, nevertheless, apparent that the release of doctors from the Services on the basis of age and length of service was a matter of much moment; and to this end it was necessary—and also equitable— to continue the recruitment, after an initial period of experience, of almost all newly-qualified doctors who were medically fit. To enable specialists to be released with their proper groups, the Scottish Medical War Committee was requested to select others with suitable experience, ordinarily not older than 35 but in some cases up to 40 years of age, for recruitment as replacements. In the case of women graduates, compulsory recruitment for service with the Forces ceased in the earlier months of 1945, but suitable volunteers continued to be accepted. In the public health services, the increasing difficulties of 1945 compelled the Department of Health, after explanatory consultations with the Local Authority Associations and the Society of Medical Officers of Health, to extend the control exercised as a temporary war-time measure over the distribution of whole-time medical officers so employed by the local authorities. It was not until the early months of 1946 that it became possible to announce a reversion to ordinary working arrangements.

As a footnote to this outline of the mechanism by which medical manpower was controlled, a word of commendation and appreciation is proper. It is hard to escape the conclusion that, of all the many interests and professions which were involved in the essential labours of the war, no other body of men or women rendered more willing, efficient or important service with a greater measure of self-effacement. A common impulse dominated the whole of the medical profession, no matter how or where its members were employed; and it was clear that the special responsibilities which devolved upon it were discharged with cheerfulness, with life-saving effectiveness, and with supreme acceptability to friend and enemy alike. This absence of distinction between nation, race and creed was in itself a demonstration of what may be accomplished by single-minded recognition of an ideal of service; and as an augury for the future it is worth remembering.

NURSING

Like the medical departments of the Fighting Services, their nursing services remained distinct throughout the war. Thus, to the nuclei provided by the Queen Alexandra Naval Nursing Service, the Queen Alexandra Imperial Military Nursing Service, the Territorial Army Nursing Reserve and Princess Mary's Royal Air Force Nursing Service there had to be built up the considerable bodies of nurses so demanded by the expanding Armed Forces of the Crown. For this purpose, many trained nurses were withdrawn from civilian life. Nor was this all; for much of the V.A.D. resources of the British Red Cross Society were committed for service with the Forces. The problem, therefore—and it was a formidable one—of providing for the greatly extended civilian needs which were anticipated remained; and planning to meet these needs in Scotland became the joint responsibility of the Department of Health and the Scottish Central Emergency Committee for the Nursing Profession. The advice of various other bodies which were both interested and influential was obtained. In February 1939, the first formal steps were taken in the matter and these resulted in:

(*a*) preliminary arrangements for assessing resources in nursing staff throughout the country by medical officers of health in association with the Scottish Branch of the British Red Cross Society and the St. Andrew's Ambulance Association, which were also concerned with some questions of training;

(*b*) the establishment of local registers of volunteers for the projected Nursing Auxiliary Service; and

(*c*) the appointment of local Emergency Officers and Branch Secretaries of the College of Nursing.

In May 1939, it was announced that a Civil Nursing Reserve would be set up with the organisation of which would be associated machinery to register nurses and nursing auxiliaries and for continued recruitment, training and organisation. At that time it was fully recognised that in an emergency a large body of nurses would be required to supplement the nursing staffs of existing hospitals, to operate the projected new hospitals, to provide suitable personnel for the first-aid post organisation and to augment district nursing staffs in the areas named as Receiving Areas under the official Evacuation Scheme. It was estimated that approximately 300 first-aid posts might have been established on the outbreak of war, that as many as 10,000 additional beds might be commissioned (with increases in this number corresponding to the progress of the new hospital units), and that the number of evacuated women and children might be some 400,000. The size of the effort demanded in the recruitment of nurses was thus made clear; but happily the fears of massive enemy attacks early in the war proved unfounded and there was time for a more leisurely establishment of the Civil Nursing Reserve.

Originally, it was planned that the Reserve should comprise three groups, namely:

(a) trained nurses available for service who offered themselves for membership;

(b) assistant nurses—i.e. women who had undergone at least two years' training but who had not completed the requirements for State Registration; and

(c) nursing auxiliaries.

The recruitment of the first two classes was straightforward but that of the last class presented problems which were quite new. It was agreed, therefore, that nursing auxiliaries should be recruited from the following three sources:

(a) existing members of the St. Andrew's Ambulance Association;

(b) existing members of the British Red Cross Society (V.A.Ds); and

(c) untrained or partly trained women who offered themselves for national service in this capacity and who were prepared to undertake an appropriate course of instruction.

Entrance to the nursing auxiliary branch of the reserve might be made direct through one or other of the existing organisations mentioned above, which maintained close contact with the medical officers of health or through the agency of the medical officers of health themselves. Arrangements were made for courses of training, which were prescribed by the Department of Health and supervised by the Local Emergency Committee; and arrangements were set up for interviewing applicants by competent representatives of the profession. So far as the Central Department was concerned, a Chief Nursing Officer was appointed; and a little later Regional Nursing Officers were appointed to work with the Hospital Officers in the various Civil Defence Districts.

The prescribed course of training for nursing auxiliaries embodied the following particulars:

First Aid. This part of the course was based upon the scheme of training already provided by the British Red Cross Society and the St. Andrew's Ambulance Association, and it was required that the standard attained should be equivalent to that maintained by these bodies.

A.R.P. In this connexion the routine operation of the first-aid post services was emphasised.

Elements of Hospital Nursing. The primary object of this portion of the training was to instil into the candidates an elementary and necessarily much condensed knowledge of hospital routine and of the duties which the hospital nurse is expected or required to carry out. The existing conditions of emergency precluded the possibility of any elaborate training. It was decided, therefore, that formal instruction should extend over a period of not less than forty-eight hours; and it was suggested that the theoretical part of the training should be covered by twelve lectures of one hour each and that the remaining thirty-six hours should be devoted to practical work. For this purpose, every available hospital, both voluntary and municipal (with the exception of maternity and infectious diseases institutions) was asked to co-operate, and the response to this appeal was most gratifying. A synopsis of the scheme of training which was laid down contained the following main headings: Ward Hygiene; Beds and Bedding; Routine Care of the Patient; Diet; Surgical Technique; and Nursing.

In addition to the formal Civil Nursing Reserve organisation, there became available for service at first-aid posts a large number of people who were trained in first-aid only. These were recruited and trained by the local authorities and were not included, as such, in the ranks of the Civil Nursing Reserve. Many of them went further in course of time and underwent the training required for nursing auxiliaries; and thus they made themselves more efficient for their ordinary first-aid post service and at the same time became capable of a wide range of service.

Questions of uniform for the Civil Nursing Reserve presented certain difficulties in the early stages of its existence; but these were duly overcome. At the outset, also, it was felt to be desirable that members should be given the option of remaining in their own districts if they so desired. So many of them, however, chose this course that in 1941 the regulations governing the Reserve were altered, and from the early months of that year members became liable for service in any Scottish hospital included in the Emergency Hospital Scheme which was in need of nursing assistance. The amended regulations were, however, administered in the most sympathetic way, with the legitimate object of avoiding hardship on every possible occasion.

By the end of June 1941, whole-time members of the Civil Nursing Reserve employed in hospital numbered 1,274 trained nurses, 811 assistant nurses and 2,347 nursing auxiliaries. In addition, 261 whole-time members and 2,260 part-time members were at this time attached to first-aid posts. Active recruitment continued, but even at this time there were becoming apparent the first indications of the nursing shortage which was later to cause much anxiety. With the object of improving the standard of work among the nursing auxiliaries, and of giving them an opportunity to make themselves more familiar with the ideals of the profession, all applicants, from 1942 onwards, came to be interviewed by experienced matrons who placed themselves at the disposal of the Department of Health for this purpose. At the same time, special training centres for selected candidates were set up in Law Junction, Lennox Castle and Bangour Hospitals. At these institutions prospective nursing auxiliaries were given a three weeks' intensive course of training by experienced teachers before being posted for duty; and by the middle of 1942 some 650 nursing auxiliaries had been given their preliminary training under residential conditions in these centres.

During the following year, 900 women were trained in the special centres prior to their formal employment as nursing auxiliaries. Nevertheless, the apprehension of an acute shortage remained. Recruitment for all grades continued; but, except in the nursing auxiliary grade, resignations came to exceed enrolments; and this process continued, despite the fact that a new grade—that of supplementary nurses, who were trained in some special branch but lacked the general certificate—was established. At a census taken at the end of March 1943, 4,750 members of the Civil Nursing Reserve were found to be employed in hospitals, some 3,000 of this number belonging to the ranks of the auxiliaries. In March 1942, the number employed was 4,950, so that a wastage of 200 had occurred during the twelve months' period. The majority of the Civil Nursing Reserve members were occupied in the new and the extended hospitals; but, because of the general shrinkage in resources, it became increasingly necessary to give assistance from the Reserve to many other hospitals, including sanatoria and other institutions, which were not included in the Emergency Hospital Scheme. It should be added that certain members of the Reserve gave valuable assistance in the nursing of smallpox patients at Robroyston Hospital in 1942.

A factor of some possible importance had now to be recognised in connexion with the supply of nursing personnel for service not only in the emergency hospitals, but in institutional organisations as a whole. Under the provisions of the National Service Act women were already being registered up to an age limit of 45; but in April 1943, a special registration for nurses was instituted by the Ministry of Labour and National Service, and its upper age limit was fixed at 60 years. This in itself was an indication, and an admission, of the disquietude in regard to the situation which was being experienced by competent observers in possession of the facts. Simultaneously, the Ministry of Labour and National Service, under the guidance of its own nursing officers and in co-operation with the Department of Health, put into modified operation its powers of direction in respect of members of the nursing profession. It was, however, appreciated that the peculiarly personal work of the profession placed it in a category of its own and that overmuch activity in this connexion on the one hand, and injudicious use of emergency powers on the other, might well cause dissatisfaction and resentments which would, in the long run, conceivably aggravate an already difficult position—particularly since the Armed Forces were still insistent in their demands. Thus, at the end of March 1944, a further shrinkage had occurred in the civilian resources. At this time some 4,850 members of the Civil Nursing Reserve were employed in hospitals, and of this total 3,300 belonged to the grade of nursing auxiliary. The number of general trained nurses had fallen by over 100, this decline being more or less equivalent to enlistments in the Army Nursing Service. About this time a measure of relief was obtained at Killearn, Law Junction and Ballochmyle Hospitals by the seconding (with the approval of the Ministry of Labour and National Service) of nurses in the fourth year of their general training from the Glasgow Royal and Western Infirmaries.

By choice, therefore, methods of persuasion rather than of compulsion were adopted, and various appeals were made in the interests of recruitment. Nevertheless, numbers continued to fall. Thus, at the end of April 1945, the total number of Civil Nursing Reserve members employed was in the region of 4,250, of whom 2,900 were nursing auxiliaries. This represented a decrease of 650 over a period of 13 months, substantially due to a continued drift of trained nurses to the military services, and to the calling-up of nursing auxiliary Red Cross members for service with the Forces, and in India. At this time about 150 members of the Reserve were employed in hospitals not included in the Emergency Hospital Scheme, principally in sanatoria and institutions for the care of the chronic sick. With the end of the war in Germany, much of the incentive to continued effort disappeared; and, in view of the fear which had to be entertained that a sudden diminution in the number of effective members might occur, the Secretary of State, in May 1945, sent a personal message to all members expressing the hope that they would continue to serve as long as they were required. This appeal had some good results, but the wastage continued in such volume as to make the operation of the emergency hospitals increasingly difficult.

So far, the Civil Nursing Reserve alone has been considered in this brief survey. The nursing services of the country in general now call for notice; and the following details present in summary form the main points of interest during the war years:

(i) *General Nursing Council.* The numbers of newly qualified nurses admitted to the Register of the General Nursing Council for Scotland in the years 1940 to 1944 inclusive were:

1940	1,136
1941	1,172
1942	1,245
1943	1,320
1944	1,242

In 1940, an amendment to the Council's Rules was approved, enabling candidates, as an alternative to entering a recognised training school, to take the first part of the preliminary examination after a course of instruction in approved secondary schools, continuation classes or central institutions. The number of new entrants to the Register during 1943 was more than 250 over the average number registered in the five years before the war. This was a gratifying and important circumstance; but unhappily the following year saw a decrease in the numbers, which, although not significant in itself, indicated a continued fall which, because of a serious diminution in the number of applicants for training, was bound to manifest itself and cause concern in the near future. Additional evidences of nursing shortage in all classes of hospital service became ever more apparent throughout the year 1944. Not only in the Civil Nursing Reserve, but throughout all institutions, the total numbers employed diminished markedly, hospitals for tuberculosis, the chronic sick and the mentally deranged being specially affected. Consequently, the Ministry of Labour and National Service were obliged to direct that newly qualified general trained nurses were liable for twelve months' service in such hospitals unless they adopted midwifery or district-nurse training, or were employed in hospitals in which a particularly acute staff shortage existed.

The fact that the demand for student nurses by many of the training hospitals was not being met in any adequate way provided grounds for an increasing anxiety. With a view to stimulating recruitment, the Ministry of Labour and National Service, in consultation with the Scottish Education Department and the Department of Health, instituted a series of meetings in schools for the senior girl pupils. The Scottish Education Department also urged local authorities to establish pre-nursing courses within the school curriculum and to take steps, first, to encourage pupils to look upon nursing as a possible profession, and secondly, to prevent girls who were inclined towards nursing from being discouraged because of the probable interval between leaving school and entering a training hospital.

(ii) *District Nursing Service.* In 1940, arrangements were made by the Department of Health, with the assistance of the Queen's Institute of District Nursing, for the services of district nurses to be made available for the home nursing of transferred war workers in their billets. The inclusion of such workers in the list of those eligible for treatment in Emergency Scheme Hospitals naturally limited the calls made upon the district nurse, but nevertheless, she gave much valuable assistance. In 1941, at the request of the Department of Agriculture, there was an extension of the arrangements to cover the members of the Women's Land Army.

(iii) *Conditions in the Nursing Service.* In 1941, a committee was appointed under the chairmanship of Professor T. M. Taylor to consider existing conditions of service and to draw up scales of salaries and emoluments for State Registered Nurses employed in Scotland in hospitals and in the public health services, including the district nursing services, and for student nurses in hospitals approved as training centres by the General Nursing Council for Scotland. The committee consisted of two equal panels, representing respectively the employing authorities and the nurses themselves. The remit of the committee was later extended to include the salaries and emoluments of midwives, health and tuberculosis visitors and school nurses. The committee was further instructed that the term 'emoluments' might be interpreted to include conditions of service such as hours of work, length of holidays and interchangeability of pensions. It was understood that a grant would be paid to hospital authorities to cover part of the cost of any increased expenditure which might result from the recommendations of the committee.

In February 1943, an Interim Report was submitted by the committee, and this was followed in April of the same year by a Second Report.[1] These documents covered matters relating to nurses in general hospitals, in fever and sick children's hospitals, and in sanatoria; to midwives; to public health nurses and to district nurses. At this time problems relating to assistant nurses and nurses in public assistance institutions had still to be considered; and a special subcommittee associated with the Taylor Committee was appointed to deliberate upon the pay and conditions of service of nurses in mental hospitals and institutions. A second sub-committee undertook the duty of devising ways of securing uniformity of superannuation and interchangeability of pension rights for nurses and midwives.

The recommendations of the Taylor Committee, reinforced by a Third Report issued in February 1944,[2] provided for a substantial improvement in the pay and conditions of nurses generally, and the hope was warmly expressed that the important steps which had been taken would provide encouragement to women to adopt nursing as their career. On behalf of the Government, the Secretary of State, in 1943, offered to local authorities and voluntary hospitals a grant of 50 per cent. of the cost of increasing the salaries of nurses to the levels recommended by the committee. It was a necessary qualification for payment of the grant that employing authorities should adopt the committee's recommendations as a whole; and it specifically indicated that no grant would be paid in respect of expenditure which was in excess of the scales recommended.

Coincidently with the work of the Taylor Committee, the Department of Health considered possible ways and means of augmenting the supply of trained nurses for present and post-war needs. Methods of increasing the training facilities for nurses were, for example, suggested to hospital authorities. These included closer association between hospitals for training purposes, the seconding of student nurses from general hospitals to tuberculosis and fever hospitals for part of their training and, as a war-time measure, a reduction in the period of training. Again, the Department offered to set aside wards in the emergency hospitals to which student nurses might be seconded for part of their training and thereby enable the parent schools to increase their intake of students. It is regrettable to record that only a strictly limited advantage was taken of these suggestions, though it is fair to assume that the diminution in the number of applicants for training was an influential factor in the apparent failure to respond.

(iv) *Orthopaedic Nursing*. The development of orthopaedic treatment naturally increased the need for nurses specially trained for this particular work. Such training had been provided at three orthopaedic centres in Scotland, the courses having been arranged by the Department of Health in co-operation with the Scottish Orthopaedic Council and the hospital authorities.

(v) *Nurses (Scotland) Act*, 1943, *and Nurses Act*, 1945. The 1943 Act provided for the establishment of a Roll of Assistant Nurses and laid upon the General Nursing Council the duty of making regulations governing their training. The recognition of the grade assistant nurse was a new principle adopted in order to control this grade and incidentally to increase nursing strength. It also contained provisions regarding the licensing and conduct of agencies for the supply of nurses (excluding District Nursing Associations). The procedure under which such agencies must be licensed by local authorities was brought into force by Order of the Secretary of State on June 15, 1945;[3] and under the same Order the provisions regarding the conduct of the agencies came into force on October 15, 1945. Regulations made by the Secretary of State under the 1943 Act prohibiting the use of the title 'nurse' by other than registered nurses, enrolled assistant nurses and certain special classes mentioned in the Regulations, also came into operation on October 15, 1945.

TECHNICAL

Only a word need be said on this point, which, important as it is, does not call for any particular expansion here. When, however, it is remembered that pharmacists, technicians of various kinds, occupational therapists, qualified maintenance staffs and so on had to be recruited both for the wholly new and the extended hospitals, the size of the problem presented in this relation will be apparent—the more so when the demands of the Armed Forces and of war industry on the dwindling resources are kept in mind. Nevertheless, the difficulties encountered did not prove to be insurmountable, although the burdens assumed by many individuals were, when viewed against peace-time practice, disproportionately heavy. Responsibilities were, however, accepted and discharged as contributions to the common war effort. Most valuable advice and assistance were given by the universities and technical colleges, as well as by the voluntary and local authority hospitals; and, by the mid-term of 1941, what was to all intents and purposes a new series of services had been established—in certain districts, such as those in the neighbourhood of Ballochmyle and Stracathro hospitals, for the first time in their medical history.

DOMESTIC

Despite the most formidable shortage of domestic staff which demanded close and continuous consultation between the Ministry of Labour and National Service and the Department of Health, the policy of the latter in connexion with the domestic staffing of hospitals was one of progressive evolution and essential advance. It is true that, because of the requirements—and, indeed, the allurements material and otherwise, which tended to obscure the disadvantages—of the war factories, the number of women able and willing to carry on domestic work (by direction or otherwise) was relatively small; and, almost without exception, all institutions suffered in greater or less degree from the prevailing shortage. The latter, of course, had its reactions upon nursing because shortage of domestics imposed domestic functions upon ward nursing staffs. Notwithstanding this disadvantage, and within certain limitations, the policy of the Department of Health was based throughout upon the desirability of improving the lot of the domestic workers in general—including, of course, those who were employed in hospitals. The instrument which was particularly used for this object was the Report of the committee set up under the chairmanship of Sir Hector Hetherington to make recommendations on the subject;[4] and the net result of the Department's endeavours was much to the advantage of the workers. Advances were also made in 1944 by the appointment of catering officers to the base hospitals administered by the Department. It was thus possible to keep the standard of feeding for staff and patients under constant expert review. During the same year, and before the appointment, which followed later, of a senior dietitian to the Headquarters of the Department of Health, the Edinburgh Royal Infirmary generously lent the services of its sister dietitian for the purpose of making detailed dietetic surveys at the base hospitals. Her report indicated that the general standard maintained for both patients and staff was good; and dietitians were thereafter appointed to the base hospitals as they became available.

WELFARE

During the years 1943 and 1944 the desirability of supervising as closely as possible the welfare of patients in the base hospitals was increasingly recognised. From that time onwards, accordingly, welfare activities for staff and patients have been developed by the departmental hospital administration. Welfare officers were appointed to the base hospitals to deal with the more personal interests and problems of the patients; and the comprehensive monthly reports of these officers indicated the wide field of service which was open to them. The confidential nature of their work naturally prohibited the leakage of details of their activities, but the cordial relations which were established between patients and staff and themselves was in itself a sufficient indication of the acceptability of their work.

In order to promote harmonious working within the individual hospitals, welfare committees, representative of all sections of the hospital population and aided financially by State grants, were established in 1943 in all the Departmental base hospitals and nearly sixty of the auxiliary hospitals. Regular meetings were held by these committees for the purpose of discussing intra-hospital welfare activities, and valuable contributions were made by them to the common good. At the larger hospitals and at many of the auxiliaries grounds for recreational purposes were laid out.

THE ANCILLARY HOSPITAL SERVICES

Under the aegis of the Emergency Hospital Service in Scotland, the authorities contrived, even under the stress of war-time conditions, to establish satisfactory facilities for many ancillary services, of which those relating to transport of patients, bacteriology, radiology, physiotherapy, rehabilitation and the like were notably efficient and comprehensive. In the voluntary hospitals and some few local authority institutions resources already existed, and the strengthening of these within the limitations imposed by physical considerations provided the nucleus around which the ancillary services—with the exception of the transport services, which developed independently—were built up. The problem of providing resources for the whole of the widespread service were, however, considerable. They involved questions of accommodation, equipment and personnel; but these questions were resolutely dealt with, so that by the middle of 1941 appropriate functional arrangements covering the whole country had already been made. A short account of the other main developments, The Emergency Laboratory Services,

The Blood Transfusion Service and The Rehabilitation Service is given below.

THE EMERGENCY PATHOLOGICAL LABORATORY SERVICES

E.M.S. Clinical Laboratories. As the scope of the Emergency Medical Service came into focus, it became clear that the existing laboratory facilities in Scotland would be unable to cope with any substantial volume of work for the casualty services. Early in 1939 it was thought that the larger civilian hospitals might undertake routine work in pathology and biochemistry while the Emergency Bacteriological Service would be responsible for bacteriology. On closer examination of the problem, however, these initial proposals could not stand. Most of the key laboratories were located in vulnerable areas. The available staff and accommodation, already overtaxed, would be overwhelmed if burdened with even a moderate scale of additional duties. Everything led to the conclusion that the Emergency Medical Services would need to supplement the existing facilities by establishing a clinical laboratory service.

The provision of accommodation presented the least difficulty. In the hutted base hospitals, then being erected or about to be built, space for a laboratory was earmarked in the central administrative building immediately next to the admission block. This allowed for a commodious well-lit work room with a preparation room adjoining at the far end. In the base hospitals at Gleneagles and Larbert, suitable rooms were fitted out for laboratory purposes and, in due course, existing laboratory accommodation at Hairmyres and Stonehouse was modified and considerably extended to permit an increase in the scope and volume of work. The problems of finding staff and of supplying equipment were not so easily solved.

By the spring of 1940 the teaching hospitals were already depleted of junior staff. The seniors who remained found their commitments steadily increasing, but when their help and interest were sought for the new venture in the E.M.S., they willingly pledged their support and promised their co-operation. As a result, each E.M.S. hospital laboratory was linked with a central laboratory to which could be referred work which called for special experience, skill and apparatus. Owing to its peculiar geographical situation, Raigmore Base Hospital (opened in 1941) was associated with the Inverness Royal Northern Infirmary with the pathologist Dr. H. J. K. Kirkpatrick as Director of both laboratories. The other base hospitals were attached to the teaching departments of the four universities, the professors of bacteriology acting as Directors of the E.M.S. laboratories within their regions. The laboratory of the Royal College of Physicians served Inglis Street Hospital (Dunfermline). Professor T. J. Mackie, of Edinburgh University, acted as Consultant Adviser to the Department of Health for Scotland and worked in close co-operation with the Chief Medical Officer and his staff.

None of the central laboratories could second any staff, professional or technical, for duty at the E.M.S. hospitals. It was therefore arranged that one experienced resident physician on the E.M.S. staff should supervise each laboratory. This physician had the privilege of close consultation with the central laboratory where he could obtain advice and guidance from his Regional Director on matters of local interest within his own hospital. Under his Director this laboratory physician was responsible for the technical efficiency of his unit, for the interpretation of results and for the issue of reports to his clinical colleagues.

The dearth of experienced pathologists made it inevitable that all pathological histology during the war years had to be carried out within the departments of pathology in the central laboratories, and postmortem examinations were made by pathologists who came as required from the teaching centres. There was a notable exception to this rule. With the establishment in April 1942, of a neurosurgical unit at Killearn special provision was made for neuropathology. For routine clinical bacteriology, the services were obtained of women graduates in science either with honours in bacteriology or with bacteriology and biochemistry as degree subjects. These women were more than ordinary technicians and their grading and salary gave them a special status as professional technical officers to whom were entrusted most of the day-to-day bacteriological techniques. In the departmental hutted hospitals the biochemical member of the laboratory team was a pharmaceutical chemist (Ph.C.) who usually was also chief pharmacist to the hospital. These pharmaceutical chemists, carefully chosen for their experience in laboratory methods, proved invaluable, their technical accuracy being of a high order. From time to time informal refresher courses were available at the central laboratories for the non-medical bacteriologists and biochemists.

Because of staffing and equipment difficulties, the E.M.S. service was launched with laboratories equipped to carry out a standard minimum of work limited to a range which could conveniently be carried out with due regard to efficiency and economy. The simpler investigations, commonly called 'side-room' work, were done by the resident clinical staff who usually had bench space within the laboratory allotted to them. Professor T. J. Mackie prepared a practical manual which was issued by the Department in September 1940. This useful publication, intended solely as a technical 'companion', served as a guide to reliable routine procedures and indicated the kind of material which should be sent to the central laboratories for specialist investigation. In a covering letter the Chief Medical Officer made it clear that the division of technical work between central laboratory and hospital was not a deterrent to research. Anyone anxious to follow up a clinical problem by further study in the laboratory should seek the advice of his regional director to arrange for special study in either the hospital or the central laboratory as time and circumstances might permit. On the other hand, research work involving any considerable amount of reference to the central laboratory should not be undertaken at the E.M.S. hospital.

As each hospital came into commission, every effort was made to furnish equipment sufficient to enable a start to be made in the clinical laboratory. By the end of 1940 much of the basic equipment ordered earlier in the year had come to hand. Within another year each laboratory had been furnished to a common standard, with maintenance supplies available from the central stores administered by the Supplies Division of the Department of Health for Scotland. In the interests of a speedy service and economy of materials, full use was made of standard containers (*vide* Mackie & McCartney, *Practical Bacteriology*, Chapter IV, *et seq.*) and the supply of media, stains, etc., from the central laboratories. A steady flow of specimens, by post, by motor transport and by air, soon developed from casualty and convalescent hospitals and from field service units to the E.M.S. laboratories and from base hospitals to central laboratories. Work done by the central laboratories was paid for according to tariff charges agreed upon between the Department of Health and the central laboratories. The Supplies Division of the Department of Health planned many months ahead in successive stages for the ordering and delivery of apparatus and supplies in anticipation of the extension and development of work within the E.M.S. laboratories. As time went on every encouragement was given to each laboratory to develop along certain individual lines while maintaining a reasonable modicum of standardisation. In consultation with the Directors, laboratory medical officers and senior clinicians, apparatus was chosen of a kind which could be serviced under the difficulties of war conditions. For example, because of the lack of high pressure steam and coal gas supplies, it was necessary to instal Calor gas equipment and to use electrically heated autoclaves, hot-air ovens, etc. A reserve of essential spares was held by the department for maintenance purposes together with an adequate stock of glassware and sundries sufficient to meet unforeseen contingencies. The Department hospital laboratories acted as depots for the national reserves of sera, antitoxins, vaccine lymph, insulin and penicillin. They housed the blood and plasma bank for each hospital and, in collaboration with the clinical staff, the laboratory physician supervised the technical details of penicillin therapy.

During 1940-1, the use made of the clinical laboratories was limited by the restricted scale of available apparatus, but as supplies came to hand and as the laboratory staff gained experience and confidence, the volume of work steadily increased, to reach a maximum after D-day when convoys of wounded arrived. In 1942, a monthly return was instituted, using a tabulation compiled by Professor Mackie, which gave a useful picture of the range and amount of work within each laboratory and proved valuable in adjusting the flow of supplies and staffing arrangements. At the end of 1943, returns were made quarterly instead of monthly. The following table shows data for the E.M.S. clinical laboratories during the period 1944-6 together with an analysis of the output of one typical laboratory, to show the distribution of work in various sub-divisions :

E.M.S. Clinical Laboratories

Hospital	Total examinations carried out in base hospital laboratory			Total examinations referred to central laboratory		
	1944	1945	1946	1944	1945	1946
Ballochmyle	8,955	14,387	10,907	2,323	2,140	857
Bangour	24,185	20,933	21,341	681	570	698
Bridge of Earn	11,054	9,942	8,685	467	430	398
Hairmyres	15,544	24,553	24,451	566	508	525
Killearn	5,458	5,189	4,746	41	11	9
Larbert	20,064	3,004	2,259	947	431	197
Law	14,843	14,982	13,109	117	183	357
Peel	4,652	3,522	1,463†	505	803	125†
Raigmore	19,073	17,591	15,211	737	668	455
Stonehouse	2,396*	3,076	4,382	903*	553	366†
Stracathro	8,273	6,878	5,253*	295	222	184*

* Nine months only. † Half year only.

Raigmore Hospital

	Bacteriological examinations	Biochemical examinations	Haematological examinations	Microscopic examinations	Examinations referred to central laboratory
1944	7,486	6,673	3,297	1,617	737
1945	6,271	5,940	3,583	1,997	668
1946	5,509	4,142	3,843	1,717	455

From the end of 1945 onwards, as Service admissions to E.M.S. hospitals began to decline, the change from war to peace was reflected in the increase in the numbers of civilian patients admitted. The wartime tempo of the clinical laboratory service underwent a corresponding change, accelerated by the Departmental policy of preparing the hutted base hospitals for the forthcoming National Health Service. The limitations imposed by need for economy in the use of equipment were relaxed to permit of an upgrading both in kind and in quantity of apparatus. Advantage was taken of American and British surplus stocks of Service equipment to replace and replenish apparatus which already had been found scarcely adequate for the amount of work undertaken. At the same time, considerable changes in staff following demobilisation resulted in appointments more permanent than were possible under war conditions. With reduction in the load of work there followed an extension of the scope which the laboratories could undertake, a development which anticipated some of the recommendations of the Scottish Medical Advisory Committee in their Report (1947) for an integrated laboratory service for the country as a whole.[5] When the Departmental hospitals were handed over to Regional Hospital Boards, the clinical laboratories, which in 1940 had begun as the least mature service within the E.M.S. hospital scheme, passed on as departments of full stature to future fields of usefulness.

The Emergency Bacteriological Service. In 1938 the question of an emergency public health bacteriological service for Scotland was referred to the Scientific Advisory Committee of the Department of Health for Scotland. A special sub-committee was appointed consisting of the professors of bacteriology and representatives of public health bacteriology, the Services, and the Medical Research Council. This sub-committee prepared an operational scheme which led to the establishment of the Emergency Bacteriological Service, an organisation designed to serve both the civil and military authorities for epidemiological purposes in the event of war and to be available for scientific investigation if the enemy attempted to develop bacteriological warfare.

The arrangements made the existing resources throughout the whole country into an organised service, with supplementary additional laboratories at strategic points available for routine field work and, if occasion arose, for dispersal of the main centres situated in the vulnerable areas. In each Civil Defence Region there was designated a principal or central laboratory with area or district laboratories working in close association. The central laboratories were located in the bacteriology departments of the four universities; for the Highland district, the laboratory at the Inverness Royal Northern Infirmary was linked administratively with the Department of Bacteriology, Edinburgh University. In the West of Scotland two new laboratories were set up, one at Paisley and the other in temporary premises at Dumbarton. (The Paisley laboratory was not disbanded at the end of the war but was continued over into peace-time use.) The three fighting services all made use of the Emergency Bacteriological Service, and the Army laboratory unit, under Scottish Command, was housed within the Department of Bacteriology at Edinburgh University to ensure an organised link with the E.B.S.

In addition to the static centres, three mobile laboratory units were built up in readiness for any emergency arising in the rural areas or in the event of a catastrophe which might overwhelm the major centres. The mobile units were placed in Glasgow for the Western area, at Gleneagles for the Eastern area, and at Peel Base Hospital for the South-eastern area. At the end of the war, two of these units were dismantled to make equipment available for various laboratories and one was kept for future use in the event of a peace-time emergency.

THE BLOOD TRANSFUSION SERVICE

When, early in 1939, the Department of Health for Scotland asked its Scientific Advisory Committee to investigate existing facilities for blood transfusion and to advise on blood storage requirements in a national emergency, there was little which could be called a service in existence. In Edinburgh alone there was a small organised service with a panel of about 600 donors contributing some 400 pints of blood annually. In other parts of Scotland individual hospitals had small donor panels to meet their own requirements. As the clouds of war grew on the horizon, the Department encouraged the setting up of voluntary committees in the large cities to recruit panels of volunteer donors and to establish blood banks. By February 1940, single blood banks had been established in Aberdeen, Dundee and Edinburgh. Inverness was about to complete its arrangements and in Glasgow there were five blood banks each in a major hospital and co-ordinated by the local committee. All these local services were small in themselves and were without central guidance or co-ordination. On February 6, 1940, the Department set up a National Blood Transfusion Council under the chairmanship of the Earl of Rosebery to run the work as a voluntary organisation, to raise funds, recruit donors and to direct the local services with the assistance of a technical committee. The Government agreed to make a grant of up to 50 per cent. of the expenditure involved subject to a maximum of £5,000 annually. This council formally became the 'Scottish National Blood Transfusion Association' on March 5, 1940, having as its object 'the continuation, development, expansion, co-ordination and/or amalgamation of Blood Transfusion Services throughout Scotland, and, in general, the advancement of medical science in Scotland, with particular reference to the study of blood or other transfusion'. The policy of the Association, which remained unchanged throughout the war, was to assist in maintaining and co-ordinating existing services as a National service and to establish and maintain new services. The actual running of existing services was to be left to the local committees. The need for a large hinterland from which donors could be recruited and the obvious technical advantage of having a measure of Regional control soon produced the pattern which lasted throughout the war. The local committees in the main cities became, in fact, Regional committees and five Regional services came into being, viz.: Northern, centred on Inverness; Northeastern, centred on Aberdeen; Eastern, centred on Dundee; Southeastern, centred on Edinburgh; and Western, centred on Glasgow. These, and two smaller services in the Orkneys and Shetlands were run by local committees but were guided to a central policy by the Association with its headquarters in Edinburgh. From April 1, 1941, the Government grant was increased to 75 per cent. of the Association's expenditure up to a maximum of £7,500 annually, a figure which was maintained throughout the war years.

In keeping with its policy to develop new services to meet civilian needs, the Association decided in the latter half of 1941 to set up two depots for processing plasma, one in Edinburgh and the other in

Glasgow. It was decided that these depots should operate under central control and not under the Regional services. Both were in operation for processing liquid plasma early in 1942 and plans had been made to instal plant for drying plasma in Edinburgh. The drying plant, with a capacity of two hundred bottles per week, began to function in February 1943, and was formally opened by the Secretary of State for Scotland on March 26, 1943. From the time that the central depots began to function an adequate reserve of plasma for civilian needs was rapidly built up. Up to this date, assistance had been given to the Armed Forces stationed in Scotland in meeting their local needs, both for blood products and transfusion equipment, but from the time of the introduction of the drying plant, further assistance became possible both to the Services abroad and to the Merchant Navy. By the end of 1943, the reserves of dried plasma had exceeded 2,000 bottles and thereafter greatly increased assistance to the Services became possible. Detailed figures of the collection and issue of blood and blood products in the later years are included below.

The supply of blood was, of course, dependent on the goodwill of the volunteer blood donors, whose number steadily increased throughout the war years from a few hundreds in September 1939, until by June 30, 1945, the panel stood at 96,058. Donors were encouraged to offer their blood by continuous publicity and propaganda, and by the invaluable work and assistance given by other voluntary bodies, notably the British Red Cross Society (Scottish Branch) and the Women's Voluntary Services. The efforts of all concerned were co-ordinated by Regional organisers through whose untiring work the flow of blood kept pace with the demand. This demand reached new heights with the establishment of the Central Plasma Depots and it became necessary to introduce mobile teams which could visit small towns and villages all over the country to collect blood. Mobile withdrawal teams also visited Service camps and large industrial establishments to hold bleeding sessions. Two full-time teams were working at the end of 1941 and two more from early in 1943. These teams were based on the central depots but in the Regions many part-time teams were operating, and, by visiting suitable centres in their Regions, were able to tap hitherto untouched sources.

From the beginning of the war, the Department of Health had assisted the Association to obtain equipment it needed but in the main the Association obtained its own requirements locally. By early 1944, the Department had begun to supply routine equipment from its centrally purchased stores on repayment by the Association. This proved so satisfactory that the scope of central purchase was extended very considerably by the end of the war.

Close liaison was maintained with the National Blood Transfusion Service in England so that there would be no delay in imparting or receiving knowledge about the latest technical developments. Two members of the Association's Technical Committee were also members of the Medical Research Council's Blood Transfusion Committee. In both these ways every advance in technical knowledge was made rapidly available to the Scottish service and, after due trial, adopted.

The Blood Transfusion Service not only provided blood and blood products but prepared and assembled the equipment necessary for administration of blood and for the taking of blood from donors. Apart from a very few whole-time personnel, the great majority of the workers were part-time and gave their services entirely voluntarily to assist this important part of the war effort.

Detailed records of figures were not maintained centrally until 1943, but it was not until this year that the Service was really fully developed. It is known, however, that the number of bottles of blood withdrawn from donors in Scotland from September 3, 1939, to June 30, 1945, was 148,547. The figures given below illustrate how much the service expanded from very small beginnings :

Blood Withdrawals

	Bottles
1939 (from September 3 to December 31)	626
1940 (from January 1 to December 31)	5,580
1941 (,, ,, ,, ,,)	12,736
1942 (,, ,, ,, ,,)	22,779
1943 (,, ,, ,, ,,)	30,637
1944 (,, ,, ,, ,,)	53,379
1945 (from January 1 to June 30)	22,810
Total (September 3, 1939 to June 30, 1945)	148,547

Adequate records were kept in the later years of the war and these are included in the table below.

Blood Transfusion Service

	April 1, 1943 to March 31, 1944	April 1, 1944 to March 31, 1945	April 1, 1945 to June 30, 1945
Donor panel	57,184 (at March 31)	92,518 (at March 31)	96,058 (at June 30)
Donor attendances	37,973	56,919	12,049
Blood withdrawn (bottles)	34,885	53,598	11,496
Whole blood issued			
(a) for Civil use	11,081	11,079	3,648
(b) to Services	700	647	200
(c) Totals	11,781	11,726	3,848
Liquid plasma prepared	10,962	17,242	3,088
Liquid plasma issued			
(a) for Civil use	5,316	5,464	1,517
(b) to Services	407	163	18
(c) Totals	5,723	5,627	1,535
Dried plasma prepared	3,667	10,500	1,066
Dried plasma issued			
(a) for Civil use	64	510	158
(b) to Services	837	9,616	1,100
(c) Totals	901	10,126	1,258

Infusion fluid Service. The Department of Health for Scotland set up a service for the supply of fluids other than blood and plasma for intravenous use. The intention was to supplement existing sources of supply of infusion fluids and the service was wholly maintained by the Department under the Emergency Hospital Scheme. Any hospital coming within the Emergency Hospital Scheme was supplied free of charge. The scheme operated parallel with the Blood Transfusion Service but was independent of it.

The service operated from the following centres all of which received assistance in equipment and supply of material:

Aberdeen	(a) Royal Infirmary to serve North and North-eastern Regions (except Royal Northern Infirmary, Inverness).
	(b) City Hospital to serve Aberdeen Municipal Hospitals.
Dundee	School of Pharmacy, Technical College to serve Eastern Region.
Edinburgh	Department of Surgery, Edinburgh University to serve South-eastern Region.
Inverness	Royal Northern Infirmary to serve chiefly R.N.I.
Glasgow	School of Pharmacy, Royal Technical College to serve Western Region.

Each centre had a Director-in-Charge who was responsible for developing his own technique in preparing the fluids but, as a check, a Pyrogen Testing Service was provided at the Pharmacology Department of Edinburgh University where pyrogen tests were made on rabbits from any samples sent in by the Directors. All the Directors served in an honorary capacity. In 1943, bottles and the administration sets were changed so that identical equipment was used by both the Infusion Fluid and Blood Transfusion Services.

The output of the Infusion Fluid Service is summarised in the following table:

Year	Output in pints
1940 (from June 7)	2,354 (Edinburgh only)
1941	12,905 (All Regions)
1942	17,249 ,,
1943	21,698 ,,
1944	27,612 ,,
1945	35,279 ,,

REHABILITATION

In the planning of the Emergency Hospital Service the need for rehabilitation services was recognised, and, in designing the seven new hospitals and the larger annexes at existing hospitals, suitable buildings were included and equipment ordered. Certain of the base hospitals already had some provision: e.g. Bangour Hospital had a well designed department, including a hydro-therapy section, which had been used, and extensively developed, in the War of 1914–18: Princess Margaret Rose Hospital at Edinburgh, designed for orthopaedic work, had an existing physical medicine department, including a therapy pool: and Hairmyres Hospital in Lanarkshire had had a vocational training department whose functions included occupational therapy.

There were also physiotherapeutic out-patient facilities at all the main city general hospitals associated with the scheme, and at the orthopaedic and rheumatic clinic, Dundee, the Edinburgh orthopaedic clinic, and the Glasgow orthopaedic and rheumatic clinic.

One hospital—the Astley Ainslie Institution, Edinburgh—had for years been engaged on the work of general rehabilitation and was the only Scottish school for the training of occupational therapists. Since, however, the existing departments of the city hospitals already had heavy commitments, and their expansion was not, in most cases, physically possible: and since it was soon clear that it was the new and expanded country hospitals which would have to deal with the bulk of the work for Service and civilian long-term cases, the decision to provide rehabilitation facilities at the country base hospitals in the first place was natural and inevitable.

Provision of rehabilitation facilities began and progressed quickly. Much of the early Emergency Hospital Service had to be organised on the assumption of repeated and heavy air raids, frequent intakes of casualties employing all available beds, and followed perforce by redistribution of patients to home or billets for after-care. This never happened and the conception of a hospital service so heavily engaged in urgent life-saving work to the absorption of all its energies and all its staff gave place to the more acceptable and familiar view of hospital function—the fullest restoration of fitness and re-integration of the patient into the pattern of social, industrial and Service life.

The development of this function proceeded on several lines. As the base hospitals, under departmental or other management, came into commission, they were provided with physiotherapy, and usually with occupational therapy departments as well, either in specially designed buildings or in wards which could be spared from clinical use, and suitably adapted and equipped. The swimming pools existing at Gleneagles and Turnberry Hotels found a new use as sections of the physical medicine departments: but such ready-made facilities were a rather unusual bonus.

Certain of the auxiliary hospitals were developed for rehabilitation work and in course of time ten of these could show active and well-organised departments. They were usually linked with other general and auxiliary hospitals in the local group, which facilitated transfer of patients, consultations with specialists, and interchange of medical auxiliary staff. The Service specialists in physical medicine took a particular interest in this development, and their advice and influence quickly made itself felt throughout this field of work and not only in respect of Service patients. Through them also links were established with the Service Convalescent Depots, with much mutual benefit.

The Department of Health had a memorandum prepared by one of its consultants on methods and organisation of rehabilitation departments, which was circulated to all hospitals. Transfer of suitable patients from smaller to larger hospitals for rehabilitation was recommended and encouraged.

Staffing of rehabilitation departments was a very difficult matter throughout the war. Physiotherapists, whole-time and part-time, were recruited from the three Scottish training schools at Edinburgh Royal Infirmary, Glasgow Royal and Glasgow Western Infirmary, and through the local organisation of the Massage Corps.

Rehabilitation orderlies were available from time to time from the Services, and towards the end of the war a limited number of specially trained Army physical training instructors were attached to a number of hospitals and proved to be of the greatest value. One side-effect of the staff shortages was the development and encouragement of group exercises, classes and active methods, whose supervision consumed less staff time than individual treatments.

Occupational therapists were even harder to obtain. There was a training school in Scotland at the Astley Ainslie Institution whose beginnings and growth were much influenced by Canadian teachers and methods: but its output was limited to about twelve graduates a year, and even before the war hospitals had difficulties with staff shortages. Arrangements were therefore made for a number of students, mostly selected from the ranks of the Civil Nursing Reserve, to have six months' intensive course and thereafter take their places in occupational therapy departments as assistants. Most of them qualified for the full certificate at a later date.

Educational services were begun in the first place for Service patients and with the aid of the Army Education Corps. Local Education Authorities assisted in finding teachers for hospitals with numbers of child patients and were subsequently partners in the arrangements for the education of adult long-term patients. One quite remarkable feature of this field of work was the way in which hospitals enjoyed the help of volunteers who, though not always living in the neighbourhood, came regularly to teach and advise patients on the study of a surprising variety of subjects.

Welfare Officers were appointed to all the main emergency base hospitals and their associated auxiliary hospitals. They were either qualified hospital almoners or had general training in social work in various fields. They established contacts with Service Authorities, Government Departments, local authorities and voluntary agencies in many matters connected with welfare and after-care of patients. They also organised recreational and social activities in hospital and were valuable and versatile members of the team.

The problems of post-hospital rehabilitation and resettlement were quickly recognised. A series of follow-up surveys of men invalided from the Services was begun in 1941 and the results were discussed in *Industrial Health and Efficiency—Scottish Experiments in Social Medicine*, published by the Stationery Office for the Department in 1946.[6] The difficulties of resettlement were described and examples given. In a preliminary survey of 300 cases, it was found that, left to themselves, these men fared badly. The preliminary survey was followed by further investigation, to see what could be done to help them, and this was based on the records of 1,000 consecutive men and women invalided out of the Services in 1942. The report concluded:

'The difficulties described by the men themselves show how closely related are their social, medical and occupational aspects. Any attempts to meet these difficulties must take cognisance of these related considerations, and it is believed that an intensification of effort along the lines of the 1942 survey could reduce still further economic wastage and demoralisation.'

The Interim Scheme of the Ministry of Labour for vocational training was linked with the hospitals in 1941 and was steadily developed in the following years. The object was to ensure that any patient with residual disability should be put in touch with the Disablement Resettlement Officers of the Ministry as early as possible for advice and help on training and employment. The interim arrangements were eventually absorbed in the provisions of the Disabled Persons (Employment) Act, 1944.

Gleneagles Fitness Centre. Though, since 1935, the clinics of the Lanarkshire Orthopaedic Association had provided out-patient treatment for injured miners, there was not, until 1943, any residential rehabilitation or fitness centre for civilians in Scotland. The Miners' Rehabilitation Centre at Berry Hill in Nottingham had already shown what could be done: the publication of the White Paper on Coal[7] in 1942 awoke new interest, and the Department, which had organised Gleneagles Hotel as a war hospital, agreed to provide accommodation there for the rehabilitation of Scottish miners—an offer accepted by the Miners' Welfare Commission.

Adequate residential quarters, space for gymnasium and occupational therapy were available in the building, which also had a swimming pool and ample grounds for out-door activities. Staff was obtained and equipment provided: a planned day was organised, with selected and graduated activities for different injuries and different degrees of physical fitness. Recreation and social life were provided for and a canteen and library set up.

A consultative committee representing the two sides of the industry and the interested Departments was established.

In 1944 it was decided that patients other than miners might, in suitable circumstances, be admitted.

In 1946, with the return of Gleneagles to use as a hotel, the centre was moved to Bridge of Earn Hospital, at which it continued into the National Health Service. Much of its work was frankly experimental and much was learned.

Medical Advisory Committee Report. In 1944 the Secretary of State asked the Medical Advisory Committee to 'consider the types of condition for which rehabilitation facilities should be provided in a comprehensive medical service in Scotland and the nature and extent of the further facilities required'.

A sub-committee, with five specialists as co-opted members, was appointed and reported in 1947.[8] This report, which was published in the Stationery Office series, set out a description and definition of rehabilitation: the methods employed: the present practice: the conditions in which it is of value.

Other chapters considered rehabilitation in relation to industry and the nature and the extent of further facilities required. An appendix set out the organisation and aims of the Gleneagles Fitness Centre and made suggestions about the place and value of rehabilitation and the principles which should be observed in its application.

Following the publication of the Report, one of the specialist members of the sub-committee carried out a series of visits to all the principal hospitals and held discussions with representatives of hospital managements, local authorities and voluntary associations about the development of rehabilitation measures.

The experience of the war years in this field, though coloured by the particular circumstances under which it was gained, was full of significance for the future. The main lesson which emerged was that rehabilitation was not the sum of a particular set of techniques, nor something to be done in a special department of a hospital to which patients would graduate at one stage of their recovery and which in due course they would pass through and leave behind, but a continuous process, the fruit of an attitude of mind, which keeps firmly in view the maximum possible restoration of health, the education of the patient to live with any inevitable residual disability after its greatest possible amelioration, and the eventual reintegration in social, family and industrial life as an independent, confident and satisfied man or woman.

THE TRANSPORT SERVICES

Civilian Casualty Trains. The development of the emergency transport service involved the co-operation of the two railroad companies operating in Scotland—the London Midland and Scottish and the

London and North Eastern—the operators of the public road transport services and, above all, of the ambulance authorities. Five civilian casualty trains were provided for use in Scotland, and these, manned by doctors and nurses under the direction of the Emergency Medical Services, were situated variously and at different times at Glasgow, Edinburgh, Perth, Ayr, Law Junction, Inverness and elsewhere. In the actual event, they saw no service in Scotland except that which was associated with the evacuation of the London hospitals in 1944; but they were, nevertheless, maintained in readiness by the Department of Health and the railway authorities, and were exercised to keep them continuously ready for immediate operation. Each train consisted of some six coaches fitted for stretcher patients, four day coaches for ambulant casualties, and quarters for the train staff and for cooking.

The Inter-hospital Transport Ambulances. The bus companies lent their assistance by maintaining a fleet of twenty-eight to thirty-two seater buses for the transport of ambulant patients; and, in addition, they converted, on the instructions of the Department of Health, some sixty vehicles for stretcher use. The capacity of each was from eight to ten stretcher patients; and these bus ambulances were distributed at strategic points throughout the country—mostly in the Western District (the most vulnerable) and at such centres as the outskirts of Glasgow, Motherwell, Stranraer, Stirling and the like. While the ordinary buses were considerably employed in the inter-hospital movement of numbers of ambulant patients, the vehicles fitted for stretcher use were unsatisfactory from the point of view of the patient, and few calls were made upon them.

The mainstay of the hospital ambulance service was, as was to be expected, the extended facilities which were developed by the existing ambulance authorities in Scotland—namely, the St. Andrew's Ambulance Association and the Scottish Branch of the British Red Cross Society. These two bodies, like their counterparts in England, instituted a joint service and by a judicious distribution of resources, efficiently covered the whole country. In 1940, a welcome reinforcement came to the authorities in the form of the American Ambulance—Great Britain, which was brought into being through the generosity of the American community in England and Scotland. The quota of American vehicles provided in Scotland consisted of twenty large (4-stretcher) ambulances, twelve small (2-stretcher) utility ambulances, and twelve "sitting" cars, each of the latter being capable of transporting five ambulant patients in addition to the driver.

No limitation of duties was prescribed for the ambulance service, and they were consequently available for duties of all kinds—the collection of air raid casualties in co-operation with the A.R.P. ambulance service; the collection of casualties at railheads and seaboard destinations; and, above all, inter-hospital transport. A summary of the work done appears below.

St. Andrew's Ambulance Association. The maximum number of ambulances employed by the St. Andrew's Ambulance Association in each of the five Scottish Districts was as follows:

District	Ambulances
South-eastern	15
Eastern	70
Western	130
North-eastern	10
Northern	5
Total	230

The number of patients transported may be divided into the following categories:

Air Raid Casualties. During the air raiding in Scotland of 1940–1, particularly in Glasgow and the surrounding area, the entire service of the Association was placed at the disposal of the Government and the local authorities. The services were brought into operation while air raiding was actually in progress, and casualties were removed with expedition and efficiency. The conditions of these times, however, made it impossible to maintain accurate records of the casualties dealt with. In the course of, and following air raiding, when such hospitals as the Royal Hospital for Sick Children, Redlands Hospital, Drumchapel Home, Smithston Hospital in Greenock, and the like, had to be partly or wholly evacuated, the St. Andrew's Ambulance Association transported upwards of 700 patients to other hospitals.

Ordinary Inter-hospital Transfers. In the course of these operations, the Association dealt with no fewer than 179,480 patients.

From Hospital Trains. From the hospital trains which arrived at Scottish railheads between June 4, 1944, and September 12, 1945, the Association found transport for 9,919 patients and casualties.

To and from Docks and Harbours. 1,645 individuals were carried; and, in addition, 9,744 members of the U.S. Forces were moved from and to ambulance trains, airports, and docks.

Year by year between 1940 and 1945, the number of miles run by vehicles of the St. Andrew's Ambulance fleet amounted to:

Year	Miles
1940–1941	420,020
1942	510,000
1943	405,391
1944	553,202
1945	272,507

British Red Cross Society. In the month of December of each of the years in question, the number of ambulance vehicles operated by the Scottish Branch of the British Red Cross Society was as follows. The pattern of distribution was, in the case of the Red Cross vehicles, so

THE ANCILLARY SERVICES

subject to change that it is impossible to indicate figures for the respective Civil Defence Districts. The expansion of the service is, however, significantly indicated by the numbers given:

Year	Ambulances
1939	33
1940	153
1941	274
1942	298
1943	337
1944	389
1945	380

The comprehensive Red Cross transport figures given below include every patient carried and every mile run in the respective years, and the patients included British, Americans, Poles, French, Norwegians, Belgians, Dutch, Indians, etc.:

Year	No. of patients carried	Mileage
1939–1940	24,639	332,910
1941	155,012	1,531,418
1942	164,018	1,210,385
1943	229,258	1,789,833
1944	243,756	1,953,807
1945	224,825	1,535,653
Totals	1,041,508	8,354,006

In comparing these figures with those of the St. Andrew's Ambulance Association, it is to be borne in mind that the Red Cross Society had many direct military duties to perform, and also that the St. Andrew's Ambulance organisation had to carry its full quota of ordinary civilian work simultaneously with its specific war-time duties.

Other work done by the Red Cross Society during the period under review involved the use of the undernoted special resources:

Mobile dental units : patients treated	45,593
Mobile chiropody units : patients treated	155,301
Ambulance tender on Clyde : patients carried	5,046

American Ambulance, Great Britain. The total number of patients carried, mostly in inter-hospital transport operations, was approximately 360,000 between 1941 and 1945.

CIVIL DEFENCE CASUALTY SERVICES

FIRST-AID POST ORGANISATION

The Department of Health for Scotland was responsible for certain measures for Civil Defence which formed an important part of the Emergency Medical Service. The first-aid posts and associated mechanisms stood, as it were, in the field and exercised, at least in theory, a function comparable with that of the advanced dressing stations and casualty clearing stations in the military sphere, while the main fabric of the Emergency Hospital Scheme—although, under the expected conditions of warfare it might be in the front line also—stood behind them.

The first-aid post and ambulance services, forming collectively a part of the C.D. Casualty Service, thus constituted an important forward unit within the organisation for passive civil defence established and operated by scheme-making authorities in accordance with the terms of the Air Raid Precautions Act of 1937. Since the Casualty Service was essentially a medical service, the responsibility for its organisation, maintenance and operation was transferred, in October 1938, specifically to the health departments of the various local authorities, under the general guidance and supervision of the Department of Health for Scotland. The direction of the Department was both central and peripheral, and operational control in the different areas was one of the functions of the Hospital Officers who were appointed from 1938 onwards to the respective civil defence districts. The component parts were the scheme-making authorities of the five districts within the zone of the Scottish Region.

These five Districts, with their estimated populations and the names of the Counties and Burghs, which were given the powers of scheme-making authorities under the Act, have been recorded in Chapter 1, page 7, and therefore need not be repeated here.

This sub-division of the Scottish Region into five Districts or sub-regions, each with a Hospital Officer and his staff, representing the central authorities, had no parallel in England, in which the Emergency Medical Services had no intermediate executive representation between the Regional Hospital Officers and the local authorities in the Provincial Regions. In England it was found necessary to supply each Regional Hospital Officer with a staff consisting of a varying number of Assistant Hospital Officers, almost entirely employed with the Civil Defence Casualty Services; these were not required in Scotland.

In Scotland also the employment of a special staff of Group Officers such as was found necessary in the London Sector system and in some other areas was not found necessary as these functions were carried out by the District Hospital Officers.

The hospital offices were located at the headquarters of the District Commissioners for Civil Defence. Here also were situated the district offices of the Ministry of Home Security. This arrangement made possible the intimate co-operation and co-ordination which were necessary for the efficient operation of the medical services with the general A.R.P. services which were designed to function through local authorities under the direction of the Regional and District Commissioners. It is appropriate to repeat again the relative importance of the five Scottish Districts in respect of population; the figures are also a reliable index of vulnerability. The figures given are those for 1939, and the striking predominance of the Western District is at once apparent:

Civil defence district	Population
1. Northern	226,500
2. North-eastern	455,400
3. Eastern	684,500
4. South-eastern	802,900
5. Western	2,841,100

Geographical and social considerations, particularly those associated with density of population and industrial vulnerability, called for different applications of A.R.P. practice to different areas of the country. On the medical side, for example, fixed first-aid posts in remote country areas with sparse and scattered population would have been totally out of place; and in like manner unprotected meagrely equipped first-aid points would have been incompatible with the needs of congested localities. The scheme for the establishment and staffing of the first-aid post services of the various local authorities came to be divided into four sections, namely: fixed first-aid posts, mobile first-aid posts, public gas cleansing centres and first-aid points. By the spring of 1941, when the organisation attained its maximum development, there were in Scotland 271 fixed posts, 82 mobile posts, 145 public gas cleansing centres and 652 points.

Fixed First-Aid Posts. The main function of fixed posts was to afford early diagnosis and treatment of air raid casualties, and to relieve pressure at the emergency hospitals. Special facilities were provided in these posts for the cleansing and reclothing of unwounded or slightly injured persons who had been contaminated by or exposed to gas. The staff at each post consisted of at least one doctor, one trained nurse, and auxiliary personnel numbering 40 to 60 according to the density of the population and the vulnerability of the area. Although, as a matter of policy, as little use as possible was made of school premises for first-aid posts, it was found in several districts—especially in congested areas such as Glasgow, Paisley and Motherwell—that school buildings were, in fact, the only available accommodation. In such instances agreements were made with the Scottish Education Department and the local authorities to use such institutions as were necessary, appropriate adaptations and structural protection being supplied. According to the strict theory of first-aid post operation, all casualties were expected to pass through the post before those in need of hospital treatment were passed on to the Emergency Hospital Service. It was anticipated that congestion and confusion at the hospitals might thereby be minimised, and also that trained A.R.P. personnel would in the main be responsible for the completion of the important Ministry of Pensions documents for the Civilian Personal Injuries Scheme which were essential to claims for 'attributability'. In practice, however, quite properly, the seriously wounded were in most cases taken direct to hospital, to which also numerous slightly injured persons, impelled by peace-time habits, made their own way. Nevertheless, the first-aid post system worked on the whole successfully and with precision, and the scheme of co-ordination between first-aid posts and hospitals, prepared in complete detail by the Hospital Officers, was of the utmost value in aiding the orderly movement of casualties.

Mobile Posts. These consisted of specially adapted vehicles carrying in portable cases the equipment of fixed posts. Their function was to meet the requirements of towns and large villages in rural areas where fixed posts had not been established and to deal with 'substantial' local incidents in cities and large burghs. They also supplemented where necessary the resources of the fixed posts; and their ordinary personnel consisted normally of one doctor, one trained nurse and eighteen trained auxiliaries.

Public Cleansing Centres. The majority of the fixed first-aid posts (in the ratio of 6 to 1) were equipped from the outset of the war for cleansing people contaminated by gas. At the beginning of 1941, when fears of gas attack from the air became more urgent, the Department of Health took steps to augment the anti-gas facilities at the cleansing sections of first-aid posts. Additional sprays and equipment were installed in many of the posts, and separate centres were established in populous areas. Mobile gas-cleansing units were also organised, twenty-two of these being set up in the more densely populated areas. In only a few of the fixed posts could gas-contaminated stretcher patients be dealt with, but adequate provision for the cleansing and after-treatment of such persons was provided at the emergency hospitals, in many of which special construction had to be undertaken.

First-Aid Points. These were organised to serve the needs of small towns and villages in rural areas and were ordinarily located at the house of a doctor or district nurse, or in a village hall. They were equipped with simple first-aid outfits, splints and drugs; and they were operated by a small number of local part-time volunteers.

THE CIVIL DEFENCE AMBULANCE SERVICE

The C.D. Ambulance Services were built up under local authority control throughout the years 1939 and 1940. The service consisted of 'stand-by' ambulances—that is, vehicles purchased and converted by local authorities for whole-time duty, and 'on-call' ambulances—that is, vehicles which by arrangement might be called upon for use as ambulances when required. In addition, each local authority had available cars for sitting casualties. Some of these were maintained on whole-time and some on part-time duty.

The following table is a summary of the A.R.P. position in Scotland between the time of the completion of the organisation in March 1941, and the end of 1944. The disbandment of the Service followed rapidly upon the end of the German war, all scheme-making local authorities being instructed at the beginning of May 1945, to disband their first-aid post and ambulance services within two months.

Year	Fixed first-aid posts*	Mobile first-aid posts	Public gas-cleansing centres‡	Personnel attached to F.A.Ps. and cleansing centres	First-aid points	Ambulance service			
						Whole-time	On call	Sitting cars	Ambulance personnel
1941	271	82	145	22,454	652	972	970	1,852	7,941
1942	274	84	160†	21,025	700	1,014	926	1,798	7,125
1943	274	83	157†	25,881	682	929	832	1,496	6,172
1944	271	82	158†	34,466	676	957	772	1,365	6,182

* Mostly equipped for gas-cleansing.
† Including 22 mobile centres.
‡ Excluding cleansing centres for stretcher patients at E.M.S. hospitals.

THE WORK OF THE ORGANISATION

The fortunes of war decreed that the first-aid post organisation in Scotland was, in the main, but lightly tried by the hazards incidental to hostile air activity. With the exception of Aberdeen, Fraserburgh and Peterhead, where sporadic raiding and damage to first-aid posts occurred throughout the greater part of the struggle, only the communities in the Western District—including the City of Glasgow and the northern fringe of Lanarkshire, which were subjected to heavy attacks in 1940 and 1941 saw the operation of their Civil Defence mechanisms under serious conditions of stress. The most perilous situation of the whole war was that which faced the Clydebank authorities on the nights of March 13–14, and 14–15, 1941, when the whole of the first-aid post resources of the Burgh were substantially destroyed. This occasion was marked by the heroic work of the local C.D. organisation, efficiently and wholeheartedly assisted by mobile columns from the City of Glasgow (which was itself heavily involved on the same occasions) and the Counties of Dunbarton and Lanark. A similar situation confronted the Burgh of Greenock on the nights of May 6–7 and 7–8 of the same year; and in the earlier course of the former raid—on the night of May 6—the most devastating of all individual incidents occurred in the Burgh of Paisley where a first-aid post, fully manned and in action, was hit by a parachute mine. Although this particular post was of *ad hoc* reinforced concrete construction of approved design and standards it was completely demolished and reduced to dust. Every individual who was within its walls was killed, the death roll being ninety-nine.

Of all the Civil Defence organisations in Scotland, only sixteen came into active operation under stress of enemy activity. Only those of the City of Glasgow and the Burghs of Aberdeen, Greenock, Paisley, Clydebank and Dumbarton were called to strenuous endeavours. Over the whole country the number of casualties dealt with by the first-aid post and allied services in the field was 3,303. The number of Civil Defence personnel killed by enemy action was 56, and the number of wounded 91. First-aid posts were, however, put to many ancillary uses which were of value not only to the war effort but to the community as a whole. These included the use of cleansing stations for disinfesting persons suffering from scabies and pediculosis; for the mass vaccination which was called for after the arrival in the Clyde Anchorages of certain ships with smallpox aboard; for immunisation against diphtheria; and for the distribution of vitamin products.

A critical analysis of the work of the Civil Defence Organisation cannot be included in this history, but a few general observations may be made. In the first place, as might have been anticipated, the strength of the organisation lay primarily in the spirit of its personnel. Their morale remained high throughout the years of effort and even relative inaction failed to impair the conscientious acceptance and discharge of their duty by the vast majority of those concerned. Nevertheless, certain weaknesses in the general conception of the C.D. Scheme must be admitted, and these are to be ascribed primarily to unfamiliarity with a situation the possibilities of which could not, in the absence of experience, be intelligently predetermined. In a word, the fixed first-aid posts were vulnerable and static, and they were also unfamiliar and untried additions to the life of the ordinary citizen. Because of the first consideration they failed in some measure to fulfil the expectations which had been centred upon them; and by reason of the second they tended to evade the notice of many people who preferred to put their trust in the institutions which were already known, namely, the pre-existing hospitals. It was no uncommon experience, for example, during the series of air raids over the Clyde Basin, to find that wounded persons unable to find transport, dragged themselves past a series of first-aid posts and finally arrived at the door of a general hospital. Too little emphasis had been placed on mobility, which should have been the watchword of the Civil Defence plan so far as first-aid medical services were concerned. Mobility was, of course, not lacking; but it was insufficiently emphasised.

MORTUARIES

The expectation of fatal casualties in large numbers made it necessary for the Department of Health to give adequate consideration to the special duties which would fall upon local authorities in connexion with the collection and disposal of the bodies of people who might be killed in this country in consequence of war operations. The problem was a pressing one from both the humanitarian and public health points of view. While, in the majority of cases, it might be expected that conditions would be such that the relatives or friends of the victims would themselves be able to make the necessary funeral arrangements, it might often happen that, by reason of extreme mutilation or massive incidence of death, no straightforward procedure would be possible. Local authorities were therefore urged to make preparations to ensure that adequate mortuary services would be available should occasion for their use arise. They were accordingly asked to review (a) existing mortuary accommodation and suitable buildings which might be used to supplement it; (b) existing and potential burial grounds; (c) transport services; and (d) the availability and recruitment of staff capable of carrying out the necessary duties.

Following this survey, and according to the needs of individual areas, new mortuaries, with necessary equipment, were established, or, alternatively, suitable buildings were reserved for the purpose. Precise instructions were also issued on the procedure to be followed for the identification of bodies, registration of deaths and the keeping of records. By the end of 1941, some 500 buildings adequate for the purpose had been selected; and in addition five mortuaries had been constructed *ad hoc* in areas where existing properties could not be found. Of the selected buildings, 158 which were located in the more vulnerable areas had been adapted and equipped so that they could be brought into use as might be required. A number of local authorities had entered into mutual-aid pacts with neighbouring authorities.

AMENITY IN AIR RAID SHELTERS

A note on this subject may properly be included here. Until the end of 1940, questions relating to air raid shelters provided by public funds were dealt with by the respective local authorities under the direction of the Ministry of Home Security. In January 1941, however, many questions having been raised as to shelter accommodation in relation to the public health, the Department of Health became responsible for directing the modification of shelters in order to ensure a maximum of physical comfort. Intensive surveys were made by the Department's medical and technical staffs, and throughout the course of 1941, work in connexion with the following improvements was progressively initiated.

Drying was effected so far as possible by waterproofing wall surfaces and roofs, and installing heating stoves where necessary.

Ventilation was improved by the provision of additional small openings and, if need be, structural alterations at the doors.

Sanitation. Where possible, water-borne sanitation was provided in public shelters; and the dry sanitary appliances in such shelters as were so equipped were augmented.

Drinking water from the mains was led into many shelters. Where this was impracticable, containers for drinking water were provided.

Seating was provided in shelters exceeding a twenty-four person capacity—full seating being attempted in public and the larger communal shelters (if bunking allowed) and half seating in the smaller communal shelters.

Bunking was supplied in the first place in the smaller communal shelters; and the bunks were prepared, and put into temporary storage, to be immediately installed should the necessity arise.

Lighting was given special consideration because of its importance in relation to injury and general morale, as well as to conduct within the shelters. Where the cost was not prohibitive, wiring from the electric mains was installed. In other cases, battery lighting or oil lanterns were provided.

The scheme of improvements having been initiated, responsibility for its maintenance and development devolved upon the Medical Officers of Health, who were actively assisted by medical officers of the Department of Health. Progress was necessarily somewhat slow because of the shortage of labour and materials; but by June 30, 1942, it was possible to summarise results as follows:

Good progress had been made in all districts in eliminating dampness in all classes of shelter. Ventilation had been materially improved; roofs and walls had been waterproofed; and floors had been drained. Coal-burning stoves had been widely installed. Bunks for some 120,000 people had been distributed; and electric lighting had been installed in the great majority of basement shelters and also a substantial proportion of communal surface and domestic shelters.

CHAPTER 4
THE CLYDE ANCHORAGES

To deal with the increased volume of shipping expected to make use of the Clyde Estuary, the need was realised for a comprehensive and co-ordinated scheme to provide adequate Civil Defence and Public Health services.

The measures planned to deal with the maintenance of the Public Health by means of Port Sanitation and to prevent the importation of infectious disease will be dealt with in the Civilian Health and Medical Services Volumes; but the Hospital, Civil Defence and Ambulance Services specially organised to deal with marine and air raid casualties are appropriately included in this Volume.

These come under the following headings:

    A. Air Raid Precautions
    B. Marine Casualties
        (*a*) Landing and disposal of war injuries
        (*b*) Refugees and Repatriates
        (*c*) Welfare of Merchant Seamen.

A. AIR RAID PRECAUTIONS

Under the Civil Defence Act, the War Establishment for A.R.P. purposes of the local authorities had been fixed before the outbreak of war, and pre-war planning in this connexion resulted in the formulation of A.R.P. schemes in conformity with the standard pattern in the various scheme-making areas. The Act also provided for the setting up of appropriate safeguards and facilities at docks and harbours, and planning to this end was more or less straightforward.

The system of A.R.P. control which was established covered that area of the Clyde Estuary which lay within the protective boom, together with the adjoining sea lochs. All the government departments with interests in the anchorages were represented in its formation. The scheme consisted of the A.R.P. Services (Afloat) and the A.R.P. Services (Ashore), and the Port Boarding Medical Officer acted as Civil Co-ordinating Officer. The A.R.P. personnel consisted of male and female volunteers, who were trained by the Co-ordinating Officer and his staff. On the occurrence of an 'alert' they reported to their respective action stations and remained in readiness to undertake such rescue and first-aid work as might be required. Appropriate sea transport was provided both by the civilian and the naval authorities. Landing places, carefully chosen by reason of their strategic relations with ambulance, first-aid post and hospital facilities, were organised on both sides of the estuary;

and when these final dispositions were completed a defensive arm of considerable efficiency had been fabricated.

B. MARINE CASUALTIES

The problem of the treatment—and of responsibility for the treatment—of marine casualties and other survivors arose immediately after the outbreak of war. The German submarine campaign was launched simultaneously with the British Declaration of War; and at 9 o'clock on the evening of September 3, 1939, the Donaldson Atlantic liner 'Athenia' bound from Glasgow to Montreal, was torpedoed without warning and sunk 200 miles west of the Hebrides. Of the 1,400 passengers on board, well over 1,000 were saved. Seriously injured casualties were brought to the Clyde, twelve of these being accommodated in Greenock Royal Infirmary and twenty in the Western Infirmary, Glasgow.

(a) *The landing and disposal of war injuries.* It was, of course, clear from the beginning of the emergency that casualties resulting from enemy action at sea and landed at British ports must be regarded as the responsibility, for medical purposes, of the Government. Thus the category of 'Marine War Injury (Civilian)' appeared as No. 5 in the classified list of types of patient for whom, in Scotland, the Department of Health was required to make provision in the Emergency Hospital Scheme. In co-operation with the local authorities, therefore, of all possible landing places (of which, by reason of its geographical position, the Clyde Estuary was by far the most important) the Hospital Officers of the respective districts took appropriate action and made provision for the hospital care of survivors where such was necessary. Additional arrangements were made for those who were in need of first-aid care only. It speedily became apparent, however, that a narrow definition of the term 'Marine War Injury' would not meet the needs of the prevailing conditions; for it was difficult—and indeed impossible—always to differentiate between the injury due strictly to enemy action and that produced by the ordinary hazards of war-time travel at sea. The category was therefore widened to include sickness and injury to seamen attributable to any cause which was operative at sea.

So far as the actual care of seaborne casualties was concerned, seaboard medical officers of health were requested to establish, in consultation with the Hospital Officers, a continuously operating mechanism for the admission to hospitals of casualties coming ashore in their districts. In the interests of simplicity, it was suggested that all arrangements made should correspond as closely as possible with those which were then being devised in connexion with the Casualty Co-ordination Scheme, under which first-aid posts in each scheme-making area were affiliated with specific hospitals. The local arrangements which were made included the medical inspection at the ports of injured persons and of those who were sick through exposure or exhaustion; the availability of immediate first-aid treatment; and the marshalling of transport of the sick and wounded to hospital. As regards the last point, instructions were issued by the Department of Health that transport was to be held in readiness or in reserve at all times. In addition to the resources of the British Red Cross Society and the St. Andrew's Ambulance Association—both of which rendered notable service—the vehicles of the American Ambulance (Great Britain) were active; and the use of civil defence ambulances was authorised for the conveyance of sea-borne casualties.

The work of medical inspection at the landing points was carried out either by medical members of local authority staffs or by private practitioners willing to serve in this capacity and specially appointed for the work; and a scale of fees, payable in the last event by the Treasury and appropriate in amount to the service given, was formulated. In the Clyde Anchorages, medical attendance upon the landing of marine casualties and survivors was provided by a general practitioner panel until October 1941, the doctors concerned acting in part on behalf of the Government and in part—where ordinary sickness among ships' crews was dealt with—on behalf of the Shipping Federation. In spite of the complexity and often the urgency of the work involved, of frequently bad weather conditions in the Firth, calls being received at all times of the day and night, and the shortage of sea transport within the anchorages at this time, the practitioner panel achieved a remarkable record of admirable service during the first two years of the war. This arrangement was not, however, entirely satisfactory, and certain difficulties and undesirable elements in the situation led, towards the end of the year 1941, to the responsibility for all injuries and illness on incoming ships being placed upon the staff of the Port Health Office, under the general supervision of the Port Boarding Medical Officer. In view of the increased obligations of the Port Health Office, and its assumption of certain duties previously paid for by the Shipping Federation, additional medical and lay members were appointed to the staff, and the financial responsibility for these was accepted by the Shipping Federation. One single authority, with close liaison with all other departments which were interested, was thus established for the medical supervision of the anchorages, and from this time onwards the smoothest possible course of operation was pursued. The volume of the work undertaken between the end of 1941 and the end of 1944 is indicated by the following figures, which relate to the number of patients dealt with in the anchorages by the staff of the Port Health Office:

British	4,867
United States	3,259
Others	1,570
Total	9,696

The table below contains the number of admissions to hospital, during the war, of merchant seamen and civilians injured by enemy action at sea, and of merchant seamen injured in the course of their duty:

District	September 1939 to August 1940	September 1940 to August 1941	September 1941 to August 1942	September 1942 to August 1943	September 1943 to August 1944	September 1944 to August 1945
Western	1,048	657	608	678	414	210
South-eastern	110	52	30	56	57	49
Eastern	125	122	79	68	62	53
North-eastern	129	157	83	82	77	101
Northern	80	120	37	42	28	30
Totals	1,492	1,108	837	926	638	443

The periods of maximum activity at the anchorages were in the weeks preceding the invasion, first, of North Africa and, secondly, of Northern Europe. The general resources of the Clyde Estuary were then operated at maximum pressure, and the medical service shared fully in the activity as a whole. After the European 'D' Day, however, the volume of shipping fell off sharply, and there was a corresponding decline in the calls made upon the Port Health Office. In June 1945 consequently, the Shipping Federation gave notice that it proposed to discontinue the arrangements which had operated with such signal success throughout the war and to resume the earlier method of working through a practitioner panel. By the end of the year the process of involution was complete, and the various local authorities round the Clyde Anchorages had reverted, so far as their maritime activities were concerned, to their pre-war practices.

(b) *Refugees and Repatriates.* Early in 1940, when the situation in Western Europe made it probable that there would be a German invasion of the Low Countries, the Government took serious thought as to how provision might be made for the reception and disposal of Dutch and Belgian refugees. It was believed that many nationals of these countries would be driven to seek refuge on the British shores; in the long run, a vast cosmopolitan host had to be accommodated in England, Wales and Scotland, and the majority of those who travelled in organised parties arrived in the first place in the Clyde Estuary, from which they were later distributed widely throughout the country. By the end of 1941, the numbers and nationalities of war refugees in Great Britain had attained almost their maximum. Included in the totals were British refugees, from the Channel Islands, and from most of the European countries, as well as Belgians, Dutch, French, Norwegian, Danish, Polish, Austrian, and even Germans. It was at this period also, when the situation in the Mediterranean was most menacing, that evacuees in large numbers—men, women and children—began to arrive from Gibraltar and Malta. The mechanism of reception and disposal of the foreign refugees from Europe was as follows:

Before landing, each alien was subjected to the medical examination demanded by the Aliens Order. The procedure in cases of illness is mentioned below. Where sickness had not to be taken into account, the refugees then passed into the custody of the appropriate local authorities, who were influentially assisted by various Government agencies and by voluntary organisations such as the Women's Voluntary Services. Short-term accommodation was provided near the landing points; but, since these were the loci of successive disembarkations, parties were transferred at the earliest possible moment to inland centres from which a further redistribution was effected. Because of the need to conserve such accommodation as was available in the reception areas for the purposes of the official Evacuation Scheme, the refugees were for the most part housed in the sending and the neutral areas—at first in communal quarters and later, as opportunity arose, in private billets. Contacts maintained with the Ministry of Labour and National Service provided work for many; and the rapid extension of the war led to the absorption of all suitable males of military age into the fighting services of the nations whose Governments and military establishments had been set up for the time being in this country. The large residue who could not be cared for otherwise—women, children and older males—were housed in specially constructed hostels (such as those at Bridge of Weir and Neilston) the management of which was delegated to the Scottish Special Housing Association; and the many personal and international problems which were encountered were met and in the main brought to satisfactory solution by the tactful and sympathetic action of those who were concerned.

It was, of course, recognised that the health problems incidental to the arrival, possibly the precipitate arrival, of large numbers of refugees might well be serious. The conditions of their departure from home, and those under which they travelled to this country made it imperative to adopt special regulations to prevent the spread of infectious diseases, not only among the refugees themselves, but among the population exposed to the hazards of any unwelcome importation. Whenever it was possible, therefore, arrangements were made at the points of departure of organised refugee contingents to include a qualified medical practitioner in the complement of at least some of the ships. In such cases, a preliminary classification of patients was carried out before the arrival of the convoy. On the approach of refugee vessels to the anchorages the Port Medical Officer was given such notice as was practicable in order that he might arrange the boarding operations. The medical officers who actually conducted the latter carried out their inspection and completed the classification, in consultation with the ships' medical officers if such were available. Classification labels were provided for the following groups, namely, 'maternity', 'medical', 'surgical', 'infection', and 'cleansing'; and on disembarkation the several categories of patient were directed to special temporary shelters, arranged for in advance, which permitted the segregated housing of each individual type. An additional block of accommodation was set aside for refugees who, through lack of time or other circumstances, could not be adequately inspected on board ship.

In addition to these elementary procedures, it was understood that special measures would be needed for the infectious, for those women in an advanced stage of pregnancy and for individuals of both sexes who were suffering from wounds or serious illness. To meet such needs in a preliminary way, it was arranged that both the premises and the personnel of first-aid post organisation might be employed by the Port Medical Officer if it seemed desirable, while at the same time arrangements were to be put in train for the transport of patients to appropriate hospitals. The infectious diseases hospitals and the maternity hospitals of the local authorities were called upon to play their parts; and cleansing stations were established on the spot for the disinfestation both of patients and clothing. So far as ordinary sickness was concerned, the hospitals of the Emergency Hospital Scheme were freely opened to the refugees. While patients actually suffering from infectious disease at the time of landing were easily dealt with by admission to isolation hospitals, the problem of contacts and of persons in the phase of incubation was more difficult. It was clearly impossible to deal effectively with them at the point of landing, whose resources were apt to be severely strained; and where it was known, therefore, that certain refugees were contacts, notification of the fact was forwarded immediately to the medical officer of health of the area to which these refugees were sent. Apart from such specific notice, a general policy was adopted which required that all refugees were to be regarded as possible contacts and kept under medical observation for the first three weeks after their arrival. The additional medical and nursing staffs which were on occasion required during this period of special risk were obtained by the medical officers of health through the Local Medical War Committee and the Local War Committee for Nursing.

It may properly be said that one of the most remarkable features of the chain of circumstances connected with the reception and maintenance of large numbers of refugees in Scotland was the complete absence of any noteworthy medical complications. The possibilities of the situation were inassessable but undeniably menacing; yet in the actual event no serious embarrassment occurred. It would be neither satisfactory nor just to attribute this wholly to good fortune. Since potentialities of an explosive nature were ever present, particularly during the process of invasion, it is more likely that credit of a positive kind must be given; first, to those who recognised the dangers and took pains to make plans to counter them; and secondly—and this is of greater moment— to those who, charged with the obligation to execute these plans, fulfilled their appointed tasks with precision, understanding and mindfulness for responsibilities laid upon them.

(c) *The Welfare of Merchant Seamen.* During the course of the war, much was accomplished by the co-ordinated effort of Government and voluntary agencies in the promotion of a welfare for members of the Merchant Navy. This included the provision of adequate hostel and lodging accommodation for seamen, both British and foreign, and the development of recreational and educational facilities. Measures were also taken to promote regulations dealing with the safety of seamen in and around dock and harbour areas. For present purposes, however, the welfare activity of particular interest concerned an examination of the health facilities available for the medical treatment of seamen, and the steps which were devised to extend them. The general arrangements prevailing in the Clyde Anchorages have already been described; but, important and successful as these arrangements were, they covered only part of the problem and operated only in a restricted area. They served, in fact, to throw into some relief the fact that conditions elsewhere, and particularly in the ports themselves, left something to be desired; for outside the anchorages the precision with which the health services for seamen operated was by no means so exact as might have been desired. An important memorandum on the subject was prepared and circulated in February 1943, by the Medical Officer of Health for the City of Glasgow.[9] After detailing the facilities actually available in respect of merchant seamen, this document indicated the steps which had been taken to co-ordinate the work of the various departments and agencies concerned—departments and agencies which, in ordinary times, fulfilled their obligations and pursued their particular functions with little or no relationship one to another, and which, it was suggested, failed, even collectively, to provide a complete or even an adequate health service. The medical officer of health pointed out that the war-time medical arrangements had 'been carried out by virtue of the emergency powers vested in the Department of Health for Scotland, powers which will lapse on the termination of the war.' There followed a plea for the establishment, at least at the major ports, of a comprehensive and permanent medical service for merchant seamen, designed to cover the uncertain movements and the peculiarities of duty which are the lot of members of the Merchant Navy, and to provide both general practitioner and specialist connexions. So far as the Port of Glasgow itself was concerned, the plea was advanced that a special seamen's clinic should be established at the Southern General Hospital, and that consideration might be given to the desirability of setting up at Stobhill Hospital a special unit for the treatment of tropical diseases.

It may be said at once that neither of the two latter propositions was agreed to, although both were the subjects of active investigation and sympathetic deliberation. The resources of the Southern General Hospital—which, by reason of its geographical situation, was by far the most suitable for out-patient purposes, were already fully employed, and any additional responsibilities would, under the prevailing circumstances, have over-taxed it; and, while it was interesting to speculate whether a tropical disease unit could be profitably employed, it appeared to be doubtful whether the flow of patients would justify its existence. So far as the memorandum as a whole was concerned, it was seen that the ideas which it advocated involved the principle of sectionalising the community for medical purposes; and while it might be argued that seamen did indeed present a peculiar problem it did not appear to be a problem of such consequence as would justify the formulation of a special medical code. On the face of it, and despite certain arguments to the contrary, there seemed to be no good reason to suppose that the nationally operative arrangements of the National Health Insurance Scheme were in any significant measure ineffective in relation to British seamen in their home port, or, indeed, in any port in Great Britain, and it was proper to assume that the position would become even more satisfactory under the terms of the comprehensive medical service scheme which was even then under discussion. So far as alien seamen were concerned, medical arrangements were in the hands of the owners of the ships in which they sailed; but it was considered that it should not be difficult, from the administrative point of view, to include such sailors in a comprehensive medical service—by some arrangement with the owners, if on a British ship, or with the responsible shipping authority if on a vessel of foreign registration or nationality.

Nevertheless, so cogent in its details was the case presented by the memorandum that questions in regard to it were asked in the House of Commons on April 8, 1943.[10] In reply to these, the Minister of Health indicated that he was familiar with the contents of the memorandum, and on his own behalf and on that of the Secretary of State for Scotland he undertook to keep the document in mind during the discussions on the wider subject of the National Health Service. There followed a series of frank and mutually helpful discussions on the subject between the Department of Health and representatives of the Public Health Committee of the Corporation of Glasgow, the result of which was the institution by the former, in the latter half of 1943, of a special inquiry into certain aspects of the problem. This inquiry was informal but was nevertheless catholic in scope and comprehensive in its activity. In accordance with the terms of the remit, the consideration of the investigating officers was specially directed towards the following points:

(i) *The general practitioner medical service available to merchant seamen.* On signing off the Articles of a particular ship, every seaman was required to report to one of the Merchant Navy Reserve Pools established by the Ministry of War Transport. The Pools were administered by the Shipping Federation and to each was attached one or more medical officers who were usually the ordinarily employed Federation doctors. These medical officers had the duty of examining all seamen who joined the Pools, as only those who were physically fit were registered as available for further employment. The Pool doctors, however, were not required to give treatment to such seamen as were found to be in need of care. They were usually referred to a National Health Insurance practitioner, to a special clinic or to the out-patient department of a hospital; but, since most of the medical officers attached to the Pools were also members of a National Health Insurance panel, it was, of course, open to them as such to undertake such treatment as might be required.

The focus of this part of the inquiry was naturally the Port of Glasgow in the Merchant Navy Reserve Pool of which the names of some 1,500 men remained steadily upon the register, the individuals, of course, continuously changing. It was found that during the period of six months which ended upon June 30, 1943, those who reported sick or unfit for sea and were examined by the Pool doctors numbered 3,411. It was, however, found to be impossible to obtain the numbers of those who were referred to other agencies for treatment. A weakness in the chain of evidence thus occurred, and the deficiency was by no means relieved by the fact that it was represented to the investigating officers that many seamen presumably entitled to medical benefit were not in possession of a medical card or other documents which would establish their title. The substance of the latter statement was seriously weakened by the fact that, as has been indicated, the Shipping Federation was unable to give any information as to how many men had been referred to National Health Insurance practitioners, to special clinics or to out-patient departments; and the validity of the allegation was still further reduced by the subsequent evidence of the Clerk of the Glasgow Burgh Insurance Committee, who was able to say specifically that during the period in question only fifteen seamen patients had been referred to his committee, and that all of these had actually received the treatment necessary before being so referred. Thus it was to be inferred that the references to the committee were made primarily, not with a view to the authorisation of necessary treatment, but for the purpose of establishing the committee's liability for the doctor's fees.

So far as another allegation was concerned—namely, that difficulty was frequently experienced by seamen in obtaining the services of a National Health Insurance Practitioner when these were urgently required— it could not be shown upon investigation that such difficulties as may have occurred were any greater in the case of seamen than with other classes of insured persons, all of whom were subject to the delays imposed by the reduction in the civilian ranks of the profession. By and large, no good evidence was adduced to show that either the seamen or the national interest had suffered through delay or difficulty in obtaining medical attention; and this was, in fact, the considered opinion of the investigating officers.

(ii) *The extent to which the facilities of the Emergency Medical Services were utilised for merchant seamen, and whether these facilities could be extended or improved in this relation.* It was found that such criticism as was levelled from time to time against the mechanism of the Emergency Medical Services was largely ill-informed and without foundation. Practitioners in many instances failed to keep themselves familiar with the developments in the Service; and almost invariably an educative approach to the critics was all that was required to open up new avenues of understanding and perspective. It is nevertheless true that on two particular points minor weaknesses were discovered. These related to the practice of certain of the established general hospitals included in the Emergency Hospital Scheme, which failed for a time, quite innocently, to realise the importance in the national interest (i) of effecting the prompt admission to hospital of merchant seamen who were in need of care for minor ailments but who, unlike the ordinary citizen, had no home in which the necessary treatment could be administered, and (ii) of keeping the Seamen's Welfare Officer promptly informed of all merchant seamen admissions. Simple representations by the Department of Health speedily removed these causes of complaint.

(iii) *The dispersal of patients to hospitals, and the problem of the maintenance of contact with them by the Seamen's Welfare Officers and the voluntary agencies concerned with their affairs.* It is true that, throughout a considerable part of the war, operational necessities made it inevitable that merchant seamen should be admitted to widely scattered units of the Emergency Hospital Service. The complexity of the work of the Seamen's Welfare Officers was thus increased but the Hospital Officers consistently strove to simplify it by concentrating merchant seamen so far as possible in particular institutions. There can be little doubt that some of the criticism directed against the hospital services was, in part at least, dictated by certain anxieties related to the desire for the establishment of a special seamen's hospital in Glasgow. Nor can it be doubted that, had the volume of patients been greater than it was, such a proposition would have been given the most serious consideration. But as the facts were, even the Seamen's Welfare Officers, notwithstanding that the admission of all merchant seamen would have been of material benefit to them, agreed that a special establishment could not be justified.

CHAPTER 5

THE EMERGENCY MEDICAL SERVICES IN ACTION

THE HOSPITALS

THE PRELIMINARY MOBILISATION—1939

THE initial period of the war, up to and including the month of April 1940, was a quiet one so far as the Scottish hospital services are concerned. Except in a minor way, air raiding had not occurred and operations on the Continent were characterised by a quiet which was as misleading as it was surprising. Further, the amount of illness among the Service and civilian populations at home was not great; and the war industrial effort, which was later to produce many invalids, had not yet been speeded up appreciably. In consequence, the drastic measures which had been taken in regard to hospital accommodation at the beginning of the war were found, in effect, to have been largely unnecessary. These consisted in the main of the mobilisation of medical resources both in respect of personnel and of accommodation. Beds were cleared in such numbers at the beginning of September 1939, by sending home all patients who had progressed beyond the need for active hospital care, and transferring certain chronically ill patients who could not be cared for otherwise to secondary institutions that, of the 21,000 Scottish beds suitable for the immediate care of casualties, an average of some 15,000 remained empty throughout the winter. This circumstance was attended both by advantages and disadvantages. The former were related to lessons in preparedness which the continuing state of emergency afforded, and to the opportunity provided by the respite for the elaboration and consolidation of plans for the efficient staffing of the casualty units. The period of quiet was also of value in permitting the uninterrupted building of the new hospitals and annexes, and the preparation of a fully considered scheme for the co-ordination of the first-aid post and Emergency Hospital organisations. Under the co-ordination arrangements, particular first-aid posts were associated with particular hospitals towards which, in theory, the main stream of expected casualties would flow. It was obviously essential that each Hospital Officer should be familiar at any given time with the actual bedstate of all emergency hospitals in his area; and to this end, and as a routine measure, all institutions were required to provide the necessary information every twenty-four hours. During periods of air raiding returns of this kind were required more frequently.

THE RESTRICTION OF ADMISSIONS—1939

The provision and maintenance of empty beds for casualty reception involved not only the evacuation of patients but also the restriction of admissions to hospital except of the severely ill. Before the questions of the disadvantages of the scheme, and of the measures taken to minimise its effects, are dealt with, it will be useful to indicate in tabular form the rough detail of the Scottish hospital resources at the time of the outbreak of war. The four groups into which the institutions were divided have been defined in Chapter 2; the table comprises the whole of the hospital resources and not those which remained after the initial discharge and transfer of patients.

Scottish Bedstate, September 1939

District	Groups				Totals
	I	II	III	IV	
Western	5,701	2,152	4,950	1,768	14,571
South-eastern	3,877	—	1,394	187	5,458
Eastern	1,017	28	906	115	2,066
North-eastern	66	1,347	289	174	1,876
Northern	—	—	421	113	534
Totals	10,661	3,527	7,960	2,357	24,505

In the various districts, the total set forth above included 1,174, 253, 168, 213 and 3 cots respectively, the number of adult beds being accordingly 22,794. A large general distribution of cots and relative equipment took place later, but for the most part these were not required.

THE EFFECTS OF RESTRICTIONS—1939

The precautionary evacuation of hospital beds and the associated restriction of admissions among the civilian population to those who were urgently ill had certain untoward effects which had, of course, been foreseen, but which nevertheless had to be accepted as inevitable in the state of emergency. The first of these was the hardship which attended the virtual closure of the general hospitals to patients suffering from disabilities which could not be classified as acute. Such patients had perforce to await treatment with such patience and fortitude as they could muster; but it became apparent at an early stage that it was not only the individual who was thus placed at a disadvantage, but that the national effort which was called for in the industrial field, and which demanded a maximum degree of physical fitness, was also likely to be affected in a way which was by no means inconsiderable. A second disadvantage was that the specialist and nursing staffs of the general hospitals had too little to do—a circumstance which, in addition, threw additional responsibilities upon the thinning ranks of the general practitioners, who were already beginning to experience repercussions from the progressive attenuation of their ranks. A third disadvantage, which, in view of the possibility that a long war was to be expected was of considerable importance, was the fact that the restriction of hospital admissions naturally led to a diminution in the amount of teaching material available in the medical schools.

THE RELAXATION OF RESTRICTIONS—1940

With these facts in mind, the Department of Health took steps in January 1940, to modify the position to some extent. It was generally appreciated that there could be no completely satisfactory solution to the problem, which, broadly stated, was to find a reasonable compromise between the need, on the one hand, to maintain adequate facilities for the treatment of large numbers of air raid casualties and, on the other, to reduce to a minimum the necessary interference with the standards of the peace-time health services. The means adopted to reach an optimum position was the 'quota' system which operated successfully in practice throughout the whole of the remainder of the war. Since the existing policy of restrictions created peculiar difficulties in those hospitals in Groups I and II which ordinarily taught and trained medical students and nurses, the quota system was in the first place operated particularly in relation to such institutions. It was therefore agreed that in these hospitals, and in a few others which presented special problems, there might be some relaxation of the general restrictions. The procedure adopted was to fix a definite quota of beds which had to be reserved continuously for the reception of casualties; and the expectation was that the balance of beds for ordinary use might go some way towards providing for the legitimate needs of the civilian sick and also for reasonably adequate facilities for teaching and training. Examples of the actual quotas which were adopted are as follows:

Hospital	Bed complement	Reserved quota
Royal Infirmary, Glasgow	1,000	460
Western Infirmary, Glasgow	675	260
Royal Infirmary, Edinburgh	1,575	700
Royal Infirmary, Dundee	536	225
Royal Infirmary, Aberdeen	600	260
Totals	4,386	1,905

The ratio of total bed complement to reserved quota in these main institutions was substantially similar to that which obtained throughout Scotland as a whole, in which an affected total bed complement of 7,229 was related to a fixed quota of 3,321 beds. The quota system was successful, and led to a material diminution in the anxiety which prevailed, both in the professional mind and among the population at large, as to the availability of hospital services.

THE EXPANSION BY NEW CONSTRUCTION—1940-41

The situation was, of course, progressively ameliorated by the rapid progress which was made throughout the year 1940 in the construction of the new hospitals and of the annexes at many of the existing institutions. As a result of this progress whereby, in the course of twelve months, some 13,000 additional beds were provided for casualty purposes, it became possible to extend the quota system to hospitals in general. Not only so, but, as will be seen later, it became possible to provide widespread medical and surgical facilities for the civilian population both in the new hospitals and in the annexes. Other important developments took place, such as the release of certain existing accommodation for the reception and treatment of tuberculous patients. The increase in tuberculosis during the early years of the war was disquieting alike to the public health authorities and to the general public, and in due course the resources of the Emergency Hospital Service were called upon to assist in the control of the disease. In 1938, there were in Scotland 4,685 beds in local authority institutions, and 623 in voluntary institutions for the treatment of tuberculosis—a total of 5,308. On December 31, 1943, however, (and the position at this time was maintained throughout the remainder of the war) there were 4,005 such beds in local authority institutions, 632 in voluntary institutions and 1,549 in Emergency Hospital accommodation: a total of 6,186. This figure becomes the more significant when it is pointed out that, in December 1943, 680 tuberculosis beds in local authority institutions were still being employed for purposes of the casualty scheme; but they were more than offset by the provision of the 1,549 beds in the wards of emergency hospitals throughout the country. These Emergency Hospital Service beds, diverted from their intended purpose, were administered either by local health authorities or, in the case of sanatorium units at Law Junction and Bridge of Earn Hospitals, directly by the Department of Health.

The extension of the quota system was, as has been suggested, progressive; and it was such that, by the end of the year 1945, only some 1,000 beds belonging to institutions which were in existence before the war officially remained within the Emergency Hospital Service. Throughout the period of active hostilities, of course, the quota system was operated upon the understanding that the arrangement was entirely provisional and that, should heavy raiding occur, it might become necessary for the Hospital Officers to adopt measures which would secure additional beds for the casualty scheme. No particular interference with the quota arrangements had, in fact, to be instituted; but, in order that the hospitals affected might be enabled to make the best possible use of the resources placed at their disposal, a more or less routine system of transfer of convalescent patients from these institutions to peripheral hospitals was operated on the authority of the Hospital Officers. The granting of this authority relieved the parent institutions from further financial responsibility for the patients in question, of whom many thousands were actually transferred. A careful check upon the resources represented by the quota beds was maintained by the Hospital Officers; and in cases in which there was a substantial encroachment—say 20 per cent.—upon the permitted figure steps were taken to remedy the position by transfer.

By the summer of 1941, the programme of new building and of the adaptation of auxiliary accommodation was virtually complete, and at that time the resources of the Scottish Emergency Hospital Scheme were as follows:

Scottish Bedstate, July 1941

District	Group I	Group II	Group III	Group IV	Totals
Western	6,507	2,413	13,159	3,106	25,185
South-eastern	4,316	—	4,370	802	9,488
Eastern	1,234	34	4,239	1,044	6,551
North-eastern	156	1,631	271	632	2,690
Northern	—	—	1,184	352	1,536
Totals	12,213	4,078	23,223	5,936	45,450

In the early stages of their existence, the new hospitals and annexes, in common with the existing hospitals which became units in the Emergency Hospital Scheme, had no casualties (in the strict sense of the word) to deal with. Patients admitted to them, for whom the Government was responsible, consisted in the main of service personnel who were sick or who had been injured, and members of the Civil Defence Services injured in the course of their duty. The relaxations represented by the quota regulations were therefore thoroughly justified. Their absence, indeed, could hardly have been supported by any argument which might have been advanced. Thus it was that, when the situation changed dramatically in the summer of 1940, the Department of Health was reluctant to countenance the radical evacuation of hospital beds which had taken place in September of the previous year. That evacuation was by no means a panic measure, but one dictated by ordinary prudence; but in the nature of things its effects upon the civilian population were necessarily severe. The new measures which were decided upon in the late spring of 1940 combined a genuine consideration for the general public with an appropriate regard for the possible needs of casualties. The instructions dealing with the clearance of beds were issued from St. Andrew's House on May 18, 1940, and embodied the following points :

THE AMENDED HOSPITAL CLEARANCE POLICY—1940

If and when the Government decided that circumstances made necessary the clearance of hospital beds, the hospital authorities were requested to take the prescribed action on receipt of a request from the Hospital Officers. The action in question consisted of the sending home of all patients for whom the continuance of in-patient treatment was no longer essential, except in the case of patients who had no homes to which they could be sent at short notice; and the notification to the Hospital Officers of the completion of the action and a statement of the total number of beds which then became available. Daily, and if necessary more frequent, returns were to be made to the Hospital Officers by the individual institutions of the numbers of beds which remained available. It will be remembered that during the hospital evacuation of 1939, large numbers of patients were transferred to institutions other than those in which they were actually undergoing treatment; but in 1940 it was decided that there should be no recurrence of such mass transfers except when the Hospital Officers believed it to be necessary or desirable. In coming to this decision the Department of Health had in mind not only the general disturbance caused by mass transfer of civilian patients, but also the fact—a minor point, in the circumstances, but a definite consideration nevertheless—that all patients transferred on the instructions or authority of the Hospital Officers automatically became the financial responsibility of the Government so far as hospital care and maintenance was concerned. In the aggregate, this was a matter of no small significance, for during the early currency of the war several thousands of people were so dealt with. No great number of transfers by Hospital Officers did in fact take place in 1940, and at the end of that year a scheme known as the waiting list scheme, dealt with below, was formulated as a means of ending the need for transfers by Hospital Officers.

THE VARIATION IN BEDSTATES

Scottish Bedstate, July 1943

District	Groups				Totals
	I	II	III	IV	
Western	6,023	2,457	10,694	2,272	21,446
South-eastern	4,288	263	2,803	862	8,216
Eastern	1,948	35	1,352	1,159	4,494
North-eastern	—	2,240	1,391	782	4,413
Northern	—	616	588	335	1,539
Totals	12,259	5,611	16,828	5,410	40,108

Despite the misfortune which overtook the allied expedition into Norway, and despite the events which led to the deliverance of Dunkirk, no appreciable strain was thrown upon the Scottish hospitals, nor was their position affected by the casualties which resulted from the Battle of Britain. A further period was thereby secured in which the hospital system could be consolidated. The beds were now available, and what remained to be done was to secure adequate equipment, to organise their staffs, to secure so far as possible the protection of the buildings and to maintain and improve the ancillary services. The tabular statement, see previous page, of the bed position in the Scottish casualty hospitals at three specific periods shows the gradual diminution of the number of E.M.S. beds from the peak reached in July 1941.

From these figures it is obvious that the recession of the Emergency Hospital Scheme was already under way, although the majority of beds which had been lost could have been pressed back into service had occasion so demanded. A minor reallocation of beds between the different groups had also taken place. The losses are to be accounted for by an extension of the quota system already referred to, and by the return of certain beds—and in some cases of whole institutions—for the re-assumption of their ordinary function: the care, for example, of tuberculosis, which had become a disquieting problem. The two additional tables which appear below illustrate the continuous process of involution which occurred, a process which reached its conclusion at the beginning of 1947, when only some 5,000 beds remained to represent the once imposing Emergency Medical Services in their prime. The residuum comprised the beds in the completely new hospitals, the administration of which was continued by the Department of Health in anticipation of the coming of the National Health Service, together with a few hundreds in certain of the hutted annexes, as at Bangour, Hairmyres and Stonehouse hospitals, and a scattering in the older institutions:

Scottish Bedstate, July 1945

District	Groups				Totals
	I	II	III	IV	
Western	5,321	2,735	9,264	1,498	18,818
South-eastern	3,879	129	2,540	471	7,019
Eastern	1,896	—	1,706	677	4,279
North-eastern	—	1,778	1,391	577	3,746
Northern	—	507	672	142	1,321
Totals	11,096	5,149	15,573	3,365	35,183

Scottish Bedstate, July 1946

District	Groups				Totals
	I	II	III	IV	
Western	3,619	1,496	6,634	230	11,979
South-eastern	2,334	—	1,627	109	4,070
Eastern	552	—	966	246	1,764
North-eastern	97	673	923	150	1,843
Northern	—	—	486	—	486
Totals	6,602	2,169	10,636	735	20,142

THE CATEGORIES OF E.M.S. PATIENTS

While the reception of patients in Emergency Hospital Scheme accommodation began immediately after the outbreak of war, it was not until 1941 that actual casualties (apart from accidental injuries and marine war casualties) began to be admitted in any numbers. Until the middle of 1940, the types of patient for whom the Government assumed responsibility were included in one or other of the following categories:

Categories 1 to 4	Civilian war injuries
Category 5	Marine war injuries
Categories 6 and 7	Civil Defence Volunteers
Category 8	Unaccompanied child evacuees
Category 9	Refugees accepted for financial help by the Assistance Board
Category 10	Ordinary civilian sick transferred on the authority of the Hospital Officer
Categories 11 to 16	Army, Navy and Air Force sick and wounded
Category 17	Service dependants
Category 18	Prisoners-of-War

It is an interesting fact that, even in the aggregate, the sick and injured included in all these categories were, contrary to cautious expectations, insufficient to fill more than a relatively small proportion of the beds which had been prepared for them. As the new building progressed, the number of unoccupied beds was, of course, continually on the increase; and it is not to be wondered at that a spirit of restiveness, fostered by the quietness of the enemy both on land and in the air, led to an increasingly insistent demand for renewed hospital facilities for those members of the ordinary population whose treatment was a matter of expediency rather than of necessity. Those in urgent need were, of course, always admitted without delay. In addition, the process of marking time was disheartening and in some ways debilitating so far as hospital staffs were concerned, for both doctors and nurses, keyed up, as it were, to the uses of the emergency, felt that their services were largely unnecessary in the civil hospitals.

Marine Casualties. The one patient category which was in any way active was No. 5—that which related to marine casualties—for the German submarine arm was by no means quiescent and from the very outset of the war its effects were apparent. Relatively, the number of casualties was extremely heavy, and this number is not adequately represented by the number of hospital admissions. Many seamen were killed outright during U-boat attacks; and many others, only slightly injured by wounding or exposure, chose to recuperate at home rather than as hospital patients. In comparison, too, with the number of men serving in the armed forces, the number attached to the Merchant Navy was small; and the following figures covering the first year of the war become more significant when these facts are borne in mind. During the twelve months from September 3, 1939, till August 31, 1940, injured merchant seamen and other marine survivors were admitted to Scottish emergency hospitals in the following numbers:

Western District	1,048
South-eastern District	110
Eastern District	125
North-eastern District	129
Northern District	80

What this total of 1,492 represented, not only in loss of man-power but in the destruction of munitions of war and the means of transporting them, may well be imagined. The procedure devised for the landing of marine casualties and their subsequent disposal is dealt with in the section on the Clyde Anchorages. (See Chapter 4.) There are, however, two other points which represent Emergency Hospital Scheme activities during the early days of the war.

Convoys. Into the Clyde Anchorages came the great military convoys first of the Commonwealth and later of the United States. Each troop concentration which arrived brought its own quota of invalids and these had, of course, to be the immediate concern of the emergency hospitals. The latter not only accommodated the ordinary sick and injured, but had on occasion to make provision for large numbers of patients with infectious disease. A notable example was the great Australian convoy which reached the Clyde on June 17, 1940. While this concentration was passing into the North-western approaches a signal was received that mumps, measles and chicken-pox had broken out, and that a good measure of ordinary sickness was also prevalent. Since it was clear that the resources of the infectious disease hospitals of the local authorities might be unequal to the strain imposed upon them, it was decided that E.M.S. accommodation should be provided for practically all the patients. They were accordingly distributed as follows:

Hairmyres Hospital	209 cases of general illness
Knightswood Hospital	93 cases of mumps
Robroyston Hospital	170 cases of mumps

Cases of measles and chicken-pox were found to be few in number—about 40 all told—and were given ordinary accommodation in I.D. hospitals.

The second point concerns the extraordinarily cosmopolitan patient population in certain of the Scottish hospitals at various phases of the war. A single example only need be given. In 1941, patients of seventeen nationalities were under treatment simultaneously at Hairmyres Hospital, their places of origin being as follows:

Great Britain; France; Belgium; Holland; Norway; Poland; Czechoslovakia; Canada and Newfoundland; Australia; New Zealand; United States of America; India; Malay States; China; tropical Africa; Malta; Cyprus.

Additional Categories. With the formation of the Home Guard in June 1940, two new E.M.S. categories were necessarily created, namely, No. 19 covering accidents to members of the Home Guard on duty, and No. 20 relating to Home Guard war injuries. At about the same time, the increase in the tempo of war industry under the stimulus imparted by Mr. Winston Churchill's administration narrowed the gap between expediency and necessity in relation to medical treatment. That is to say, certain medical and surgical conditions, subacute or chronic in their clinical connotations, while not to be regarded as emergencies from the medical point of view, might properly be so described when associated with the increasingly intensive industrial effort. It was therefore agreed that war workers who had been transferred to new duties away from their homes should be given not only free but, so far as possible, priority access to E.M.S. hospitals for necessary care and treatment. Local nursing associations were also requested to give to such workers such services as might be required in cases of minor illness. The war workers' category in the Emergency Scheme was No. 21. Category No. 22 was added immediately afterwards. It applied to internees, towards whom the ordinary humanitarian obligations of society were recognised.

WAITING LISTS

Throughout the whole of this period, which extended up to the end of 1940, the numbers of those awaiting treatment among the ordinary population had markedly increased. That is to say, the waiting lists had steadily lengthened, and the situation which resulted was one of much embarrassment to the voluntary hospitals at large. In some of them, such as the Edinburgh Royal Infirmary and the Glasgow Western Infirmary, the figure was not far short of the 2,000 mark; and, while much of the illness thus represented was unimportant, it was undeniable that much anxiety resulted from the situation. Towards the end of 1940, Treasury authority was requested by the Secretary of State for Scotland for a scheme which he had formulated for dealing with the situation; and this was granted. Early in 1941, therefore, a waiting-list scheme covering general medical and surgical patients was inaugurated. It was later extended to include patients suffering from diseases of the ear, nose and throat, the eyes and, to a limited degree, the skin; and its last development took place in the autumn of 1941, when its scope was still further widened to admit women suffering from gynaecological diseases. Through the waiting-list scheme, the voluntary hospitals, on agreeing to make the moderate contribution of 30s. for each patient cared for and treated, were authorised to submit to the Hospital Officers lists of patients in relatively urgent need of treatment. The Hospital Officers, in turn, allocated the patients to geographically convenient 'associated' hospitals on the periphery of the cities or in the country areas, and the necessary admissions, investigations and therapy were promptly carried out. These admissions took place under Scheme Categories Nos. 23 and 24; and at the same time a special emergency category (S.E.C.) was created under which the medical superintendents of associated E.M.S. hospitals were authorised to admit emergency cases—the results of accidents, acute abdominal disease and the like—which might occur in the vicinity of the institutions. The initiation of the scheme led to the virtual abolition of Category 10, under which congestion in the voluntary hospitals had previously been relieved by transfers authorised by the Hospital Officers and without cost to the parent institutions. Category 10 transfers did, in fact, continue from certain of the local authority hospitals which, by reason of their statutory obligations, could not participate in the waiting-list scheme; but after 1941, such movements of voluntary hospital patients took place only in exceptional circumstances, and only for operational reasons. Such circumstances arose in the spring of 1944 when, by reason of the coming offensive operations in Europe, beds had to be made available for the expected casualties.

As may be inferred from the figures given below, the waiting-list scheme was an unqualified success from the point of view of numbers treated; and it may also be assumed that complete success attended it in the clinical field. Apart from its strictly medical connotations, it acted as a general tonic to the sick—a powerful instrument for the maintenance of morale and the reduction of anxiety among the civilian population. These effects were noted not only among the invalids themselves, but just as markedly among the relatives of those who were referred for admission to the associated hospitals; and it is impossible to estimate the added potential of the nation which might be attributed to the operation of the scheme. Reference has already been made to the extension of the scheme to almost the whole of the special fields of medicine; and it had side effects in stimulating the efforts which were made to provide more widely for patients in certain categories—such as the obstetrical, mental and tuberculous—which could not be covered by any E.M.S. arrangements. Although a trifle slow in getting under way because of the unfamiliar features of the plan, the progressively increasing use of the waiting-list scheme resulted in no less than 32,826 patients being cared for under its auspices from the time of its inception until the end of the German war. The figures to which reference is made at the beginning of this paragraph, and now tabulated, speak for themselves :

Admissions from	January till June 1941	750
,,	,, January 1941 till June 1942	5,695
,,	,, January 1941 ,, June 1943	16,080
,,	,, January 1941 ,, June 1944	30,000
,,	,, January 1941 ,, June 1945	32,826

The slackening in the tide of admissions during the last period referred to was due to the virtual suspension of the waiting-list arrangements which was necessary throughout the phase of major offensive operations on the Continent. At the same time there occurred the bombardment of the London area with the V-weapons; so that, apart from the need to provide for Scottish hospital accommodation for casualties from the fighting fronts, the additional need arose to provide beds for between five and six thousand patients who had to be evacuated from institutions within the range of the V-weapon bombardment. When the restrictions upon its activity were removed, however, the waiting-list scheme progressed afresh; and at the end of 1945, and over the five Scottish Districts, almost 40,000 patients had been dealt with through its agency. Officially the Scheme came to an end in 1946; but since, after that time, the new emergency hospitals were made available for the free admission of members of the general population, its effects continued as before.

Many civilian patients suffering from fractures were, of course, dealt with through the agency of the waiting-list scheme and sent by the hospitals to associated institutions in which special orthopaedic facilities had been established. This mechanism was, however, found to be too cumbrous for the needs of fracture cases, and to involve delays which, in the national interest, could ill be afforded; and consequently (and partly also as a means of engendering a greater familiarity with the location and work of the orthopaedic units) a special category—No. 25—was created in 1941 for War Industry Fractures. Since the definition of 'War Industry' was wide, and almost indefinitely resilient, practically the whole adult population could be covered in this way. As a result, much additional work—carried out with advantage to patients and staff alike—passed into the special units concerned. In the same year it became necessary to provide yet another category—No. 26—for patients rendered homeless by enemy action; and further arrangements were also made for patients who were the responsibility of the Ministry of Pensions for pensions' purposes and of the Department of Health in respect of treatment.

AIR ATTACKS ON SCOTLAND

A narrative of the events associated with hostile air attack on Scotland belongs more to the formal history of the war than to a medical report, however catholic the scope of the latter may be. Nevertheless, since the operational functions of the casualty services, with their medical connotations, were heavily involved in many Scottish incidents, a brief survey of the main features of enemy action must be included here.

It must be admitted that Scotland escaped lightly from a threat which was grave indeed. The failure of the Luftwaffe to strike any immediate and paralysing blow was a factor which told materially against its future success; for the delay permitted the home population to obtain a breathing space in which it was possible, as it were, to build up some resistance, and to make at least partial adjustments in anticipation of the potential destruction to come. The preliminary lull further permitted the pressing forward of the work of the various agencies for passive civil defence, without the assistance of which the possibilities would have been extremely serious. An early incident, in which a lone German raider dropped high explosive bombs upon the Shetland Islands—the only casualty being variously reported as a rabbit or a sheep—diminished the legend, fostered by German propaganda, that the Luftwaffe was at once unerring and invincible; and it was not without its influence in imparting the reassuring thought that every bomb dropped was not necessarily to be responsible for human casualties. The total effect of the respite was that, when serious trouble did in fact develop, a satisfactory measure of war-time stamina had already been engendered.

The first air raid on the Scottish mainland occurred on October 16, 1939, when two cruisers—H.M.S. *'Edinburgh'* and H.M.S. *'Southampton'*—were bombed in the Firth of Forth. No doubt the Forth Bridge was a main objective on this occasion; but the bridge escaped damage while some injury was sustained by the cruisers, and bomb hits were received by the destroyer *'Mohawk'* which was near at hand. Upwards of thirty casualties occurred, many of them fatal; but to balance the account four of the twelve Heinkel III bombers involved in the attack were destroyed.

There was no further aerial attack over the land for some nine months; but within the first three months of the war, shipping in the Scottish waters of the North Sea had already begun to feel the weight of German terror tactics. Thus Aberdeen had had experience of German ruthlessness long before the first bombs fell on the city. By November 1939, enemy aircraft opened savage attacks with bombs and machine-guns on unarmed trawlers and drifters. A number of ships were sunk, and others crept into port with members of their crews dead and wounded. Losses were severe, and the E.M.S. hospitals of the North-eastern District were influen ial in the work of succour.

It was not until June 26, 1940, that the enemy began his air attacks proper on Scotland. On that date the alert was sounded for the first time over the greater part of the country, but the only incident occurred in Aberdeen, where damage and casualties were caused. This was the first of some 400 alerts in that city, the worst of which took place on July 12, 1940, and in April 1943. On the former occasion, people homeward bound for lunch saw three Spitfires pursuing a single German bomber which, in the course of its manoeuvring to escape, dropped its bombs at random. The boilerhouse of a shipbuilding yard was hit, and the casualties numbered 34 killed and 74 injured. This was the heaviest death roll of any raid on Britain up till that time.

The most severe attack upon Aberdeen, that of April 22, 1943, which occurred after six months' quiet, was also the last. Some ten enemy aircraft succeeded in eluding the defences in a lightning raid. Ninety-eight people were killed and 235 wounded, and thousands of houses were damaged. The Royal Mental Hospital and a school were damaged, and rescue reinforcements had to be brought in from as far afield as Dundee. Over all, 178 people were killed in Aberdeen, and 588 injured. Three hundred and thirty-three houses were completely destroyed and upwards of 13,000 damaged.

For over eighteen months during 1941 and 1942 the Buchan Coast, especially the towns of Peterhead and Fraserburgh, were repeatedly attacked, and the latter sustained a fatal casualty rate of 5 per 1,000 of its population—a ratio equivalent to that of London during the period of its greatest trials. Damage and casualties in Peterhead were also heavy.

Altogether, over 250 militant operations were conducted against Scotland by the Luftwaffe. In only one county—Sutherland—and in five of the twenty-four large burghs—Inverness, Kirkcaldy, Perth, Airdrie and Dumfries—were no bombs dropped. Many localities, of course, escaped lightly, but the fear of possibilities was always present. Apart from a few isolated incidents, few anxieties were experienced in the Eastern District. The South-eastern District, though more seriously involved, was relatively free from hostile action; and even in Edinburgh the total death roll throughout the war was only 21. The worst raiding in this neighbourhood took place on the nights of July 18 and 22, 1940, over Leith, where 8 people were killed outright and 38 injured. It should be recorded here that not all the air raid casualties were British or Allied for on July 22, 1940, a prisoner-of-war camp in Banffshire was severely damaged. The British sustained 19 casualties on this occasion, two of them being fatal, while of the German prisoners 6 were killed and 17 injured.

The most trying experiences of the war over Scotland occurred in the Western District. In this area there were in all upwards of 105 incidents, which ranged from Appin in the north to Tynwald, near Dumfries, in the south; and from the Island of Mull in the west to Grangemouth in the east. By far the greatest weight of attack was directed against Clydeside which, in relation to the remainder of the District, bore the brunt of battle in the ratio 35:1. The first bombs were dropped, unproductively from the enemy point of view, on the Island of Mull on July 11, 1940, and the last, which were incendiaries only, in the Glasgow neighbourhood in the spring of 1943. The number of bombs scattered within this area was approximately as follows:

High explosive	2,300
Parachute mines	183
Incendiaries	72,500
Oil bombs	30

The total casualties (excepting minor wounds which demanded no formal care) caused by this mass of warlike material are shown in the table below :

Year	Month	Killed	Wounded		Totals
			Seriously	Slightly	
1940	July	7	18	100	125
	August	—	—	2	2
	September	2	3	60	65
	October	7	6	13	26
	November	7	6	23	36
	December	—	—	20	20
1941	February	2	—	15	17
	March	1,056	1,602	1,725	4,383
	April	100	74	316	490
	May	405	254	552	1,211
	Totals	1,586	1,963	2,826	6,375

These figures are significant when compared with the total of the Scottish casualties as a whole, the brief detail of which is as follows:

Place	Killed	Wounded	Totals
Glasgow	776	1,906	2,682
Greenock	307	647	954
Clydebank	534	1,088	1,622
Dumbarton	18	76	94
Paisley	101	43	144
Edinburgh	21	215	236
Renfrew County	99	271	370
Stirling County	3	43	46
Other areas	438	1,438	1,876
Totals	2,297	5,727	8,024

The first raid on Glasgow occurred on July 19, 1940, when 3 people were killed and 18 injured by bombs dropped by a single raider. The main property damage was the destruction of a tenement building, and the loss of life might have been much heavier. The first serious incident took place on the night of September 18, of the same year, when several raiders were over the city. By remarkable good fortune, civilian casualties on this occasion numbered only 65, of which two alone were fatal, and this happy eventuality was due to the fact that the very centre of the city, including George Square, suffered the most extensive damage at a time when the night population was at its minimum. In addition to the civilian casualties, however, the Royal Navy was a sufferer. A direct hit by a penetrating bomb involved H.M. cruiser '*Sussex*', which was berthed at Yorkhill Quay. The vessel settled to the river bed and blazed furiously for several hours, during which there was continuous danger of the ammunition in the magazine blowing up. The immediate population, in grave jeopardy, were evacuated by the police, and the Hospital Officer on duty decided that it was necessary to order the evacuation of the nearby and vulnerably situated Royal Hospital for Sick Children on Yorkhill. This operational movement was carried out with the utmost speed and efficiency by the staff of the institution, with the assistance of ambulances from the British Red Cross Society, the St. Andrew's Ambulance Association and the American Ambulance—Great Britain. The transfer of some 300 patients and staff, who were taken across the city and accommodated in Mearnskirk Hospital, was accomplished within the space of three hours in the dead of night. The efforts of the fire fighters prevented the detonation of the magazine; but a change of wind in the early morning led to the smothering of the Sick Children's Hospital in smoke which would, of itself, have rendered the institution uninhabitable. By a curious chance, it became necessary during a subsequent raid to evacuate the Country Branch of the Sick Children's Hospital, at Drumchapel, because of bombing in the neighbourhood; and about the same time the evacuation of Redlands Hospital for Women to the County Hospital, Cleland, had to be undertaken.

The gravest incidents were those on Clydeside on March 13–14, and 14–15, 1941, and on May 5–6 and 6–7, 1941. The former raids are considered to have been among the heaviest experienced in any part of Great Britain. On the first two dates, the objective was the stretch of the River Clyde between Dalmuir and Glasgow, and the areas most seriously devastated were those of Clydebank and Glasgow itself. On each night, raiding was persistent for a period of approximately eleven hours, and the conflagrations which occurred could be seen from aeroplanes as far as 150 miles away. In Clydebank itself, with a war-time population of 55,000, no less than 53,000 were rendered homeless, and the destruction of domestic property was such that only twelve buildings in the whole burgh remained intact. This circumstance was in curious contrast to the minor damage sustained by the great industrial works—including the shipyard of John Brown & Company—in the immediate neighbourhood. In fact, the number of houses damaged in Clydeside in the course of the two nights was 46,000—most of tenement type—and of these 4,300 were completely demolished; but the damage to the fabric of the industrial machine was negligible. The position in Glasgow, though serious, was by no means comparable with that in Clydebank, where the relatively meagre A.R.P. resources were speedily obliterated by the mass of falling masonry. The first-aid posts were put out of action, and mobile assistance from neighbouring parts of the country bore a considerable part of the burden of rescue. The City of Glasgow, in spite of heavy involvement on its own account, was able to extend material help, which was also enthusiastically forthcoming from the County of Lanark. The Civil Defence Services in general acquitted themselves with true heroism; and it should be recorded that in self-sacrifice and devotion to duty the workers on Clydeside stood second to none among their fellows of the United Kingdom. With high explosive and incendiary bombs dropping and buildings collapsing on every side, men, women and children toiled on heedless of danger or personal anxiety, rescuing victims buried beneath the debris, succouring the wounded, comforting the maimed, and performing the last rites for the dying. Even those who knew that they had suffered multiple bereavement maintained their efforts for the common good; and ambulance drivers performed prodigies of work in manoeuvring their vehicles into apparently inaccessible situations. Under the direction of the Hospital Officer as was required, the admission of casualties to hospital was carried out smoothly, although simultaneous raiding over Glasgow demanded the widespread employment of outlying hospitals such as Killearn, Lennox Castle, Gartloch, Larbert and Law Junction. In all, some twenty-three hospitals admitted patients from Clydebank, and the peripheral spread of casualties on their own account was remarkable, certain wounded individuals, for example, travelling as far as Oban before seeking medical care. In order to assist in the work of the first-aid services, the Hospital Officer instructed Killearn Hospital to send a Mobile Surgical Unit to Hardgate Farm, near Duntocher. Within an hour of the receipt of the message the unit was in operation at its appointed place, and in the course of the first night's raiding it dealt appropriately with 70 patients, many forms of treatment, including blood transfusions, being carried out on the roadside. So far as could be ascertained, only one of these casualties subsequently died.

With such an immense proportion of the population rendered homeless, the immediate aftermath of the raiding at Clydebank was a formidable task which faced the social service units of the Defence Services. As was to be expected, a mass evacuation of the neighbourhood occurred and the Vale of Leven experienced particularly trying times. In the course of a few weeks, however, appropriate reallocations of the displaced population were completed. It is a remarkable fact that, except for a period of two or three days after the catastrophe, the essential war industries of the region were not seriously interrupted in their task. It is true that the work was encompassed only with difficulty and that it demanded the exercise of additional fortitude upon the part of those concerned with it. Most of the workers had of necessity to be billeted in quarters which were more or less remote from their place of occupation, and, although arrangements were made to pay travelling expenses, the time spent in travelling, and the associated discomforts and congestion, might well have had an adverse effect upon industrial output. In the actual event, however, the principal anxiety was for the health of the men and women employed, and no effort was spared to secure the least possible fatigue. A word of commendation is here due to the Scottish Special Housing Association which, almost at once, undertook the responsibility of providing as much hostel accommodation as possible for homeless workmen. Within five weeks, a hostel containing living quarters for 170 people was in operation, and although there was a temporary reluctance to make use of it, initial prejudices were quickly overcome. This enterprise may rightly claim to have made no mean contribution to the prosecution of the war.

The simultaneous raiding over Glasgow produced about the same number of casualties as that on Clydebank, but it was less spectacular in the larger city. The recorded casualties which occurred in the course of the two nights were as follows:

Location	Killed	Wounded	
		Severely	Slightly
Glasgow	522	850	1,289
Clydebank	534	752	436
Totals	1,056	1,602	1,725

Sharp and apparently co-ordinated raiding occurred on the night of April 7–8, 1941, over the Glasgow district on the one hand and over the Gretna district of Dumfries on the other. In Glasgow, 64 people were killed, and 71 severely and 301 slightly wounded; in Gretna the numbers were 28, 3 and 12 respectively. On the nights of May 6 and 7, the second of the great Clydeside raids took place, Greenock, Port Glasgow, Dumbarton and Paisley being the main objectives. As in Clydebank, residential property suffered most severely, although industrial works were more seriously affected than in the earlier raid. Here again the Civil Defence Services were grievously pounded from the air, and damage was sustained by Greenock Royal Infirmary—from which most of the patients had to be evacuated—Larkfield Hospital, where blast produced material damage to the operating theatre, and Smithston Hospital. Reinforcements of all kinds were, however, available, and the work of succour went on uninterruptedly. In Greenock itself, the casualties totalled 307 killed, 221 severely and 500 slightly wounded. Paisley, on the same nights, though suffering relatively little material damage, had a death roll of 101 killed, 33 wounded severely and 10 slightly. The disproportionate number of killed was due to the melancholy fact that one of the first-aid posts sustained a direct hit from a parachute mine and was instantly reduced to dust. This incident, already recorded in the section on the first-aid post services, resulted in the death of every occupant of the post, 99 people in all.

EVACUATION OF THE LONDON HOSPITALS TO SCOTLAND, AUGUST 1944

A further matter to which reference must be made is the evacuation of the London area hospitals, mentioned above, which was rendered necessary by the serious random effects of the employment of the V1 and V2 weapons by the enemy. This new and disturbing phase of aerial warfare was initiated in the early summer of 1944, immediately following the invasion of Northern Europe; and it was marked not only by widespread destruction of property in general, but also by a material degree of damage to institutions. An already serious hospital crisis, which involved the drafting of emergency surgical teams from Scotland to the South of England, was thereby aggravated, both through interference with actual buildings and through the increased number of civilian casualties who had to be cared for in addition to the injured from the fighting fronts. In July 1944, therefore, the Government decided upon a policy of urgency which involved the evacuation from hospitals in the Metropolitan district of casualties and other patients who could reasonably be transported to regions of greater presumptive safety: not only for the sake of the patients themselves and a proportion of their nursing staffs, but also to create accommodation which could be employed for the care of new victims of the attack. Scotland was naturally willing and prepared to accept a part of the hospital evacuees, which naturally had to bear a just relation to the resources available. On August 2, the Scottish quota was tentatively fixed at 8,490 persons—4,000 'acute' sick and 4,490 'chronic' sick, each category to be transported to their respective destinations in 19 casualty evacuation trains—38 trains in all. As in the case of the official Evacuation Scheme, the Northern District was excluded from the arrangement by reason of its remoteness and the relative scarcity of casualty beds. In the other four districts the Hospital Officers in person made immediate provisional arrangements with the institutions designated for the reception of the hospital evacuees, and so quickly were the plans put into operation that the first of the evacuees arrived in Scotland on August 4, when two casualty evacuation trains arrived at Glasgow and Edinburgh respectively with 227 and 225 'acute' patients. Because of the shortage of nursing staff, it was arranged with the Ministry of Health that, while acutely ill patients would be cared for by Scottish nurses, chronically ill patients should be accompanied by a reasonable proportion of nurses. On the face of it, this arrangement was an equitable one; but, because of the preliminary failure to define 'acute' and 'chronic', it was found that in the actual event the vast majority of the patients designated 'acute' were, in fact, chronically ill, or so aged and infirm that they properly belonged to the chronic category. An additional burden of serious proportions was thereby imposed upon the nursing staffs of the Scottish hospitals; but the response to the situation was admirable and no insurmountable difficulties were encountered. (See E.M.S., Volume I, Part I, Chapter 6.).

The actual number of London evacuee patients received in Scotland was somewhat less than had been expected, as will be seen from the following table:

'Acute' trains :	15	
'Chronic' trains :	12	
'Acute' patients :		2,976
'Chronic' patients :		2,440
	27	5,416

Nursing and other staff accompanying the 'chronic' patients included:

Nurses	428
Male nurses	53
Orderlies	14
Domestics	95

The case of Turnberry Hospital was interesting. It was staffed by a complete administrative, medical and nursing unit of the London County Council, and it operated most successfully under these auspices from September 4, 1944, till July 11, 1945, inclusive.

The whole movement was completed by August 25, 1944.

The evacuation of so many South of England patients to distant and completely new surroundings might well, in view of age, exhaustion and injury, have been attended by many hazards apart from the difficulties of transportation; but in all its aspects the experiment was eminently successful. It is true that some complaints were received, both directly, from patients themselves, and indirectly through agencies in the home area; but almost without exception those were due to causes which ceased to be operative or irksome after appropriate investigation and explanation. As in the general evacuation, which is dealt with elsewhere, a drift home, affecting especially such patients as had made satisfactory clinical progress in Scotland, took place; and the number of patients was thus gradually reduced. Further diminution took place by reason of the considerable mortality among the aged patients; so that when the time came for the formal return of the evacuees to England—a process which was spread over a considerable period (April 22, 1945, to October 16, 1945)—a total of only 2,031 had to be provided for. Transportation was effected by means of twelve casualty evacuation trains.

Two additional trains were used (on October 26, and 28, 1944) for the earlier return of 243 patients, mostly belonging to the Royal National Orthopaedic Hospital, Stanmore, where special arrangements had been made for their readmission.

The maximum activity of the Emergency Hospital Scheme in Scotland occurred during the year which began on July 1, 1944—a few weeks after 'D-day'—and ended on June 30, 1945. In this period, the total number of Scheme patients in hospital was consistently over 25 per cent. (and at the peak over 70 per cent.) greater than in any previous year. About two-thirds of this total related to patients in Service categories. In the course of the year some 22,000 Service admissions were effected, including 13,287 British and Allied and 3,267 wounded German prisoners-of-war from North-west Europe, and 5,090 British and Allied casualties from more distant theatres of war. The latter reached the Clyde by sea, while the European casualties arrived in Scotland by ambulance train, most of them direct from the fighting fronts via the South of England. The movements of these patients by road from the railheads to the reception hospitals was carried out under the immediate direction of the Hospital Officers by the British Red Cross Society (Scottish Branch), the St. Andrew's Ambulance Association and the American Ambulance—Great Britain, with an efficiency which was all the more notable because the same organisations were involved simultaneously in the movement of a corresponding number of U.S. Army casualties and of thousands of others arriving from oversea in the Clyde Anchorages.

HOSPITAL OCCUPANCY STATISTICS

E.M.S. PATIENTS ADMITTED DURING THE WAR

The tables below indicate the volume of patients which flowed through the Scottish Emergency Hospitals in the course of the war, and show the differentiation which occurred between Service and non-Service patients. The figures in all the tables given below cover the years between September, 1939, and August 31, 1945 :

TABLE I

Total Annual Admissions

Year ending	Service	Non-Service	Total
August 31—1940	21,057	854	21,911
1941	55,776	9,871	65,647
1942	70,506	18,236	88,742
1943	87,807	30,106	117,913
1944	90,265	33,841	124,106
1945	79,530	31,427	110,957
Totals	404,941	124,335	529,276

The ratio of Service to non-Service admissions is thus seen to have been approximately three to one, although the increasing proportion of non-Service patients from 1942 onwards is strikingly apparent. The meagreness of civilian admissions throughout the whole of the first year of war is a notable phenomenon—noteworthy in itself, for it emphatically suggests the necessity for the relaxation of the regulations which severely restricted civilian admissions in the early months of the struggle.

Table II indicates the part played by hospitals of different denominations—voluntary, local authority and the like. From this table it will be observed that the heaviest part of the first impact of the war was borne (as was to be expected) by the voluntary hospitals which, largely bereft of their ordinary peace-time activities, were immediately in a position to assume the strain. These hospitals continued throughout to play their own honourable part in meeting their obligations, although they were rapidly outstripped in actual volume of E.M.S. admissions by the local authority and—perhaps more notably—by the newly constructed Departmental hospitals:

TABLE II

Year ending August 31—	Voluntary	Local Authority	Departmental	Auxiliary
1940	8,124	7,541	2,389	3,857
1941	13,863	24,629	12,085	15,070
1942	15,802	28,810	22,872	21,258
1943	18,661	41,158	32,847	25,247
1944	20,092	46,578	31,300	26,136
1945	18,888	39,873	32,213	19,983
Totals	95,430	188,589	133,706	111,551

The following tables indicate the average stay in hospitals of the various denominations of the different categories of E.M.S. patients. The immediately arresting feature of these tables is the short duration of treatment of all classes of patient in the voluntary hospitals, the approximate overall ratio being of the order of:

20 (Vol.):   42 (L.A.):   42 (Dept.):   26 (Aux.).

Since, in general, no particular differentiation was made in the immediate destination of patients by the admission authorities, these figures would seem at first glance to suggest a superior functional ability of the voluntary hospital arrangements. There is, however, a fallacy which is not apparent in the figures themselves. This consists essentially in the fact that the voluntary hospitals, in which the need for bed clearance was particularly acute, tended progressively to transfer their potential long-term patients to the peripheral local authority and departmental hospitals which contained the appropriate special units; and the average duration of stay in the latter was consequently much higher:

Average Duration of Stay in Days

TABLE III

Voluntary Hospitals

Years	Service	Civilian	M.N.	M. of P.	Waiting List	S.M.S.	Miscellaneous
1939-40	17	Nil	Nil	Nil	15	Nil	18
1940- 1	17	10	18	8	19	Nil	17
1941- 2	16	20	13	16	18	Nil	16
1942- 3	16	12	15	32	19	Nil	17
1943- 4	17	17	15	38	19	15	18
1944- 5	24	57	19	33	23	15	37
1945- 6	29	55	16	35	41	15	21
1946- 7	81	Nil	Nil	102	Nil	Nil	175
1939-47	19	14	16	34	22	15	22

Table IV

Local Authority Hospitals

Years	Service	Civilian	M.N.	M. of P.	Waiting list	S.M.S.	Miscellaneous
1939–40	30	Nil	Nil	15	5	Nil	11
1940– 1	30	25	52	43	23	Nil	28
1941– 2	27	109	38	40	28	55	40
1942– 3	27	47	38	61	27	31	35
1943– 4	24	47	32	65	26	32	32
1944– 5	31	84	39	70	32	36	87
1945– 6	41	14	43	64	33	39	41
1946– 7	151	155	Nil	149	186	85	106
1939–47	29	42	37	66	29	35	53

Table V

Departmental Hospitals

Years	Service	Civilian	M.N.	M. of P.	Waiting List	S.M.S.	Miscellaneous
1939–40	20	Nil	Nil	25	18	Nil	27
1940– 1	25	34	45	40	25	Nil	28
1941– 2	26	74	61	39	29	36	28
1942– 3	23	59	37	62	33	33	30
1943– 4	20	38	39	59	37	34	27
1944– 5	25	73	35	72	36	35	58
1945– 6	31	45	44	65	36	39	63
1946– 7	113	Nil	Nil	128	197	118	141
1939–47	24	44	44	65	36	35	45

Table VI

Auxiliary Hospitals

Years	Service	Civilian	M.N.	M. of P.	Waiting List	S.M.S.	Miscellaneous
1939–40	18	Nil	Nil	Nil	15	Nil	22
1940– 1	23	22	21	Nil	21	Nil	35
1941– 2	21	58	12	23	18	15	31
1942– 3	21	19	18	24	17	17	32
1943– 4	20	45	27	27	18	18	34
1944– 5	26	75	29	38	16	23	71
1945– 6	31	107	37	42	26	23	55
1946– 7	Nil	Nil	Nil	Nil	Nil	Nil	Nil
1939–47	22	29	20	34	18	19	41

CONCLUSIONS

These foregoing chapters tell the story of how the hospital and medical services were transformed under the force of the circumstances of the war from a heterogeneous collection of independent units into a homogeneous organisation which undertook the task of underwriting all the medical risks associated with war as well as the normal risks of ordinary life. The flexibility of the arrangements is brought out at each stage of the nation's changing fortunes. Although it can be said that the service was never as a whole highly tried, there were occasions when sections of it bore a very heavy burden and there is no reason to believe that, in the face of severe and universal testing, it would not have emerged with credit.

The decision that the civilian hospitals were to provide also for the needs of the Services in this country was a momentous one and led step by step to a degree of co-operation and rationalisation which, prior to the war, would have appeared far beyond the range of possibility. There were, of course, many difficulties to overcome and in the natural course of events one might have expected some, if not complete, reversion to the *status quo ante bellum*. It is now clear, however, that the lessons and opportunities created by war are not to be lost, for in the National Health Service there lies the administrative structure, not only for holding the position, but for improving it in the years to come.

REFERENCES

[1] Cmd. 6425. Interim Report and Cmd. 6439. Second Report of the Scottish Nurses' Salaries Committee, Department of Health for Scotland, 1943. (H.M. Stationery Office.)
[2] Cmd. 6505. Third Report of the Scottish Nurses' Salaries Committee, Department of Health for Scotland, 1944. (H.M. Stationery Office.)
[3] Statutory Rules and Orders, 1945, No. 652/S.24, Nurses (Scotland) Act, 1943, (Commencement). (H.M. Stationery Office.)
[4] Cmd. 6472. Report of the Committee on Post-War Hospital Problems in Scotland, Department of Health for Scotland, 1943. (H.M. Stationery Office.)
[5] Laboratory Services—Report of the Medical Advisory Committee (Scotland), Department of Health for Scotland, 1947. (H.M. Stationery Office.)
[6] Health and Industrial Efficiency. Scottish Experiments in Social Medicine: Department of Health for Scotland, 1946. (H.M. Stationery Office.)
[7] Cmd. 6364. Coal (1942). (H.M. Stationery Office.)
[8] Rehabilitation: Report of the Medical Advisory Committee (Scotland): Department of Health for Scotland, 1947. (H.M. Stationery Office.)
[9] Report of the Medical Officer of Health, City of Glasgow (1943), p. 56.
[10] Official Reports, Fifth Series: Parliamentary Debates—Commons, Vol. 388, Col. 792.

APPENDIX

Numbers of Scottish Hospitals (exclusive of the Auxiliary Hospitals) included in the Emergency Hospital Scheme, and their E.M.S. bed complements

The four groups under which they were classified were as follows:

Group I. Casualty Clearing Hospitals; that is, hospitals in areas most vulnerable to presumptive attack, which could give immediate surgical treatment to casualties occurring in their immediate localities.

Group II. Hospitals similar to those in Group I, but situated in areas believed to be less vulnerable and consequently suitable for continued as well as immediate treatment.

Group III. Base Hospitals; that is, hospitals in areas believed to be relatively safe and suitable for the immediate treatment of patients in their own localities and for the continued treatment of casualties transferred from more dangerous areas.

Group IV. Hospitals which had no facilities for surgical treatment but which could receive patients who no longer required such facilities.

| District | Group I | | | | Group II | | | | Group III | | | | Group IV | | | | All Groups | | | |
	No. of hospitals	Normal	Added by Dept.	Total	No. of hospitals	Normal	Added by Dept.	Total	No. of hospitals	Normal	Added by Dept.	Total	No. of hospitals	Normal	Added by Dept.	Total	No. of hospitals	Normal	Added by Dept.	Total
Western	23	4,824	1,041	5,865	4	1,266	869	2,135	37	3,693	8,655	12,348	17	1,476	663	2,139	81	11,259	11,228	22,487
South-eastern	13	3,329	996	4,325	—	—	—	—	12	754	2,977	3,731	6	301	81	382	31	4,384	4,054	8,438
Eastern	8	1,256	209	1,465	1	—	6	6	11	549	2,477	3,026	5	103	145	248	25	1,908	2,837	4,745
North-eastern	2	64	138	202	13	1,344	428	1,772	6	218	1,449	1,667	5	85	16	101	26	1,711	2,031	3,742
Northern	—	—	—	—	—	—	—	—	9	451	830	1,281	2	27	2	29	11	478	832	1,310
All districts	46	9,473	2,384	11,857	18	2,610	1,303	3,913	75	5,665	16,388	22,053	35	1,992	907	2,899	174	19,740	20,982	40,722

PART II

The Emergency Medical Services in Northern Ireland

INTRODUCTION
by the
Chief Medical Officer, Ministry of Health and Local Government

PLANS for the establishment of Emergency Hospital and Civil Defence Services in Northern Ireland were necessarily drawn up in close collaboration with the Ministry of Health in England and Wales and were therefore similar in policy and principle.

Certain minor differences in organisation were however inevitable owing to the system of local government in Northern Ireland. The whole of the Emergency Medical Services were therefore at first controlled by the Ministry of Home Affairs, then by the Ministry of Public Security and finally in 1944 by the Ministry of Health and Local Government after its formation. The evolution and work of the Hospital Services followed the same main lines as in England and Wales, and the Civil Defence Services though organised on somewhat different lines were founded on the same main principles.

The account of the heavy air raids on Belfast will be found in Chapter 13 of Part III of this volume.

The contribution which follows was compiled by my colleagues of the Ministry of Health and Local Government, and in very large measure we are indebted to Mr. Ewart Taylor, of this Ministry, who was intimately concerned with the day-to-day routine of the Emergency Medical Services during the war, and whose first-hand knowledge has facilitated the preparation of the history of the Emergency Medical Services in Northern Ireland.

May 30, 1952. JAMES BOYD

CHAPTER 1
EARLY STEPS TO CREATE A CASUALTY SERVICE IN THE PRE-WAR PERIOD

IT became clear after the 'Munich' discussions in 1938 that those who did not prepare for the eventuality of war would indeed be foolhardy. The Government of Northern Ireland decided accordingly to take steps to ensure that hospitals in Northern Ireland would be able to cope with a war emergency and the Ministry of Home Affairs, which was the responsible Ministry in Northern Ireland, turned for advice to the Home Office in London.

Acting on advice from that department, the Ministry immediately got into touch with the Northern Ireland branch of the British Medical Association with a view to securing the advice and co-operation of the profession in regard to the medical aspect of Air Raid Precautions and Emergency Hospital Services generally. The Ministry had in mind particularly the possibility of the evacuation of hospitals in Great Britain and the consequent necessity for special arrangements for the care and treatment of patients, Service or otherwise, who might come to Northern Ireland.

NORTHERN IRELAND MEDICAL WAR COMMITTEE

An invitation was accordingly extended to the local branch of the British Medical Association to allow its Emergency Committee to act in an advisory capacity to the Minister of Home Affairs.

In particular it was suggested that the committee might prepare a register of medical practitioners, showing in what way their services might be utilised in war-time, and might also have a census of hospital accommodation prepared.

It was also felt that Service departments and civilian services would to some extent be in competition for medical staff and for hospital accommodation in an emergency, and it was suggested that the committee might advise the Ministry in regard to the allocation of both staff and accommodation.

Finally it was suggested that the Chief Medical Officer of the Ministry and another member of the staff of the Ministry should be attached to the committee.

The invitation was readily accepted by the local branch of the British Medical Association in October 1938, and the Ministry's representatives joined the committee as suggested.

PRELIMINARY ACTION

A memorandum was circulated by the committee to Belfast Hospital staffs on July 4, 1939, giving a brief outline of a suggested Emergency Hospital Scheme and this was discussed at a meeting of the committee and Belfast hospital staffs on July 31, 1939, when general agreement was reached.

One of the recommendations from this meeting was that a Hospital Officer should be appointed by the Ministry to co-ordinate the work of the hospitals in an emergency and to evolve an organisation which would be acceptable to the hospital authorities, the medical staffs and the Ministry.

The Ministry was aware of the importance of providing instruction on the subject of poison gas, and particularly in the treatment of gas casualties, and had already on its staff a qualified lecturer on the subject in the person of Surgeon Captain H. Babington, R.N. With the co-operation of the committee, courses of instruction by Surgeon Captain Babington were arranged for doctors, dental surgeons, medical students and nurses.

Having secured the co-operation of the medical profession, the Ministry turned its attention to the following measures which it regarded as of first priority:

1. The erection of protective works at hospitals.
2. The provision of additional beds together with the necessary bedding and other ancillary equipment to be set up in existing wards of hospitals.
3. The bringing into use of additional accommodation at hospitals, e.g. annexes, etc., where necessary, by arranging for works of adaptation to be undertaken, and ordering the necessary beds and bedding, etc., for the new wards.
4. The placing of orders for such additional surgical and general equipment as would be necessary to improve the facilities generally at hospitals throughout the province.
5. The acquisition of reserve supplies of drugs and dressings and other consumable medical stores, including antitoxic sera, to be held in central store for issue to hospitals if required in emergency. Included in the list of items under this heading were portable X-ray apparatus and emergency cooking units.

APPOINTMENT OF HOSPITAL OFFICER

In August 1939, the Ministry appointed to its staff Dr. F. M. B. Allen to act as part-time Hospital Officer. Dr. Allen had been acting and continued to act as Secretary of the Emergency Committee of the British Medical Association (Northern Ireland Branch) which now became the Northern Ireland Medical War Committee. In addition to his hospital duties Dr. Allen advised the Ministry in regard to the medical aspect of all casualty services, i.e. the staffing of first-aid posts, etc., and acted as liaison officer between the Emergency Hospital Services and the Civil Defence organisations which were provided by local authorities. He immediately carried out a detailed survey of the facilities at all the hospitals in the province, on the basis of which he advised the Ministry generally in regard to the matters listed above.

EMERGENCY HOSPITAL SCHEME

Dr. Allen then turned his attention to the preparation of an Emergency Hospital Scheme the main features of which were to be:

(*a*) The enrolment of all general hospitals in Northern Ireland.
(*b*) The classification of these hospitals for the purpose of dealing with casualties.

Instructions were prepared for issue to hospitals in due course setting out the duties of hospitals in regard to (i) admission, (ii) records, (iii) disposal of casualties and outlining the powers and duties of the Hospital Officer.

These instructions included a definition of 'casualty'. The Scheme was primarily set up to receive and treat air raid casualties but it was decided at an early stage in the war that the services of the hospitals should be made available to sick and wounded members of H.M. Forces and Forces of the Allies. This was a wise decision, for although the Forces established several hospitals in Northern Ireland it would have been difficult for them to meet their needs without the aid of the ordinary hospital system. At all times co-operation between the Forces and civilian units was aided by the work of the Hospital Officer who acted as the link between them.

Acting on the advice of the Hospital Officer, the Ministry also set itself to organise:

1. The Emergency Medical Service which was to provide the additional medical personnel required to strengthen the existing medical staff of hospitals in an emergency. Full details of the history and development of the Emergency Medical Service will be found in Chapter 5.
2. The Civil Nursing Reserve which was to provide the additional nursing staff for hospitals in an emergency. Full details of the history and development of this Reserve will also be found in Chapter 5.
3. The Emergency Blood Transfusion Service at Belfast and Londonderry. Sir Thomas Houston and Professor J. H. Biggart of Queen's University, Belfast, had on their own initiative already devised a scheme for the provision of the additional supplies of blood which they foresaw would be required by hospitals in

an emergency and arrangements were made with Dr. J. A. L. Johnston, of Londonderry, to set up a similar scheme in Londonderry. Professor Biggart undertook to provide blood for South Antrim, Down and Armagh, while Dr. Johnston was to supply North Antrim, Londonderry, Tyrone and Fermanagh. Detailed information in regard to this service will be found under this heading in Chapter 6.

Control Room for Hospital Officer. In order to prevent the risk of the Hospital Officers being unable to secure telephone communication with the more important hospitals in Belfast because of congestion on the normal telephone circuits, the Ministry arranged to instal at Government expense a private line from the Hospital Officer's private residence to the following hospitals:

>Royal Victoria Hospital.
>Mater Infirmorum Hospital.
>Ulster Hospital for Children and Women.
>Belfast Hospital for Sick Children.
>Belfast City Hospital.

Arrangements were also made to provide a substantial shelter in his garden for use as a control room, and telephone extensions were provided to the shelter. During the period of heavy air raids the arrangement worked very satisfactorily.

'Shadow' Scheme. A 'shadow' scheme was prepared to operate in the event of a heavy air attack in which one or more of the casualty receiving hospitals might be put out of action. A number of suitable buildings in Belfast, mostly schools, were earmarked by the Ministry as 'shadow' hospitals which would be brought into use in the event of the parent hospitals being badly damaged.

Reserve Stores. In June 1939, acting on the advice of the Emergency Committee of the British Medical Association, the Ministry recommended all hospital authorities to acquire and hold as large reserves of drugs, dressings and consumable medical stores as they could conveniently store and turn over.[1]

BUS AMBULANCES

Arrangements made by the Ministry, immediately prior to the outbreak of war, for dealing with heavy air attacks on Belfast included provision for the evacuation of civilian sick from hospitals in the city to hospitals in safer areas.

It would not have been feasible to use the normal ambulance service for this purpose, and the Civil Defence Ambulance Service (i.e. converted private car chassis with specially constructed light weight bodies) was of course not yet in existence.

Arrangements were accordingly made in May 1940, with the Northern Ireland Road Transport Board, for the conversion by the Board of 10 Dennis Lancet single-decker buses.

The scheme provided that:

(a) the buses would be garaged by the Board in a safe place;
(b) the Board would ensure that the vehicles were regularly maintained and would supply drivers as and when required;
(c) the vehicles would remain the property of the Board but all expense in connexion with the scheme (including the cost of depreciation of vehicles) would be borne by the Ministry.

The bus ambulances were first used in June 1940, for the original evacuation and transfer of the chronic sick from the Belfast City Hospital to the Auxiliary Hospital established at Ballymena in converted workhouse buildings.

They were also used in that year for the evacuation of children from the two children's hospitals in Belfast to the annexes provided by these hospital authorities with the Ministry's assistance outside Belfast.

During the earlier years of the war their use was limited to the occasional further transfer of chronic sick from the Belfast City Hospital to the Auxiliary Hospital in Ballymena.

In 1942, they again proved useful for the transfer of civilian sick from voluntary hospitals in Belfast to the Ministry's Emergency Hospital at Purdysburn Hospital, Belfast. Details of this arrangement will be found in Chapter 3.

The last occasion of their use during the war period was for the transfer of patients from the Ministry's Emergency Hospital at Purdysburn Hospital to the newly-acquired premises for the hospital at Musgrave Park, Belfast.

In April 1945, the Ministry decided that in the light of the improved war situation the bus ambulances could safely be reduced to two, and the other eight were accordingly returned to the Transport Board.

At the end of the war the remaining two ambulances were returned.

REFERENCE

[1] Min. of Home Affairs C.D. Circular No. 1, June 22, 1939.

CHAPTER 2

EXPANSION AND WORK OF HOSPITALS FROM SEPTEMBER 1939 TO APRIL 1941

WHEN war broke out in September 1939, the Ministry immediately issued a memorandum[1] in regard to the Emergency Hospital Scheme which had been prepared for the purpose.

This memorandum provided for the enrolment of all general hospitals in Northern Ireland and for their segregation into four groups. A list of the hospitals showing the various groups and the special function allocated to each is contained in Appendix I to this chapter.

The hospitals in Groups I and II were instructed to reserve a number of beds and a communication was sent to each such hospital. Hospitals in these groups were also instructed:

(a) to restrict admissions to urgent cases;
(b) to direct patients where possible to go to hospitals in Groups III and IV;
(c) to send home patients who could be sent home without danger.

Preliminary instructions were issued to enrolled auxiliary medical personnel, and hospitals were informed of the names of those available. They were also told how they could obtain, if necessary, a surgical mobile team consisting of a surgeon, his assistant and an anaesthetist, while it was pointed out that to meet an exceptional temporary demand the services of a recognised specialist would similarly be made available. Detailed information with regard to this auxiliary medical service, which formed part of the Emergency Medical Services, will be found in Chapter 5.

Hospitals were also informed of the arrangements for the formation of a civil nursing reserve, full details of which will be found in Chapter 5.

DUTIES OF HOSPITAL OFFICER

A brief outline was given to the hospitals of the duties of the Hospital Officer. This officer was to exercise general control over the flow and clearance of casualties and the transfer of patients. Hospital authorities were to render reports of the number of their patients to him daily or more frequently if the flow of casualties became severe. It was also his duty to arrange for such movements of personnel as the situation might from time to time require.

INSTRUCTIONS ON PROCEDURE FOR ADMISSION AND DISCHARGE OF CASUALTIES

The Ministry then issued a memorandum[2] to hospitals on the procedure on admission, transfer, discharge or death of casualties and of normal sick from H.M. Forces.

A casualty bureau was set up in the Ministry to collect information regarding the number of vacant beds and the number of air raid casualties in each hospital, and arrangements were made to forward information in regard to individual casualties regularly to the Casualty Record Section of the Ministry of Pensions.

Bed Returns. On September 4, 1939, all hospitals in Groups I and II were requested by circular[3] to inform the Hospital Officer daily of:

(a) the number of empty beds available;
(b) the number which could be provided in twenty-four hours by sending patients home.

It was soon evident that the expected attacks from the air were not likely to happen for some time at any rate and the emergency instructions in regard to the restriction of admissions were relaxed by a circular[4] issued on September 8, 1939. In this circular instructions were, nevertheless, given that patients suffering from less urgent conditions should be recommended to seek treatment in hospitals in Group III as an alternative to postponing treatment for some time.

Additional Beds. The supplies of additional beds which had been ordered did not come forward as quickly as expected and as a temporary expedient, therefore, and in order to reduce the number of ordinary beds necessarily always kept vacant in hospitals, the Ministry issued to hospitals in Groups I and II a certain number of mattresses with appropriate bedding. These mattresses were stored in the immediate vicinity of the wards so that patients occupying beds might temporarily be moved on to the mattresses on the floors of the wards should a number of casualties occur as a result of a sudden emergency.

Treatment of Shock. One of the first steps taken in Great Britain had been the issue of a memorandum containing detailed instructions to hospitals on the administration of oxygen as part of the treatment of shock, based on research into the efficiency of various methods of oxygen administration. Copies of this memorandum were issued by the Ministry to each member of the Emergency Medical Services and to hospitals in Groups I and II of the scheme under cover of a circular.[5]

Resuscitation. Experience in Great Britain had shown the need for the setting aside of one ward in each casualty receiving hospital for use as a resuscitation ward for shocked casualties. It had also been found desirable to define more clearly the duties of the medical staff which would be provided by the Emergency Medical Service to supplement the regular staff of such hospitals if an emergency arose, so as to provide that :

(a) One should act as a casualty officer and be responsible for the admission of all casualties to the Hospital.

(b) One should act as resuscitation officer and be responsible for the treatment of all shocked casualties. For this work a number of Restor Shock Cages was ordered for each casualty receiving hospital.

(c) One should act as gas officer and be responsible for the treatment of gassed casualties.

DOMICILIARY MEDICAL ATTENDANCE

With a view to easing the pressure on beds in hospitals and to restricting admissions to those patients who could not be dealt with adequately outside the hospital, the Ministry issued a circular[6] detailing arrangements whereby domiciliary medical attendance would be given to certain air raid casualties. The purpose of the Scheme was to provide that a patient would, in the first instance, attend at a hospital and would receive a certificate there which would enable him to receive free medical treatment at his own home. The decision in each case was left to the medical officer at the hospital who was in charge of the treatment of the patient.

NEW MINISTRY FOR CIVIL DEFENCE FUNCTIONS

With the fall of France in June 1940, and the development of the long range bombing aeroplane it became clear that no part of the country could be regarded as safe from attack. It was also evident that the organisation which would now be required for civil defence in Northern Ireland would require the exclusive attention of a Minister of the Crown and it was decided to form a new department to deal with all matters of public security, particularly civil defence. A Ministry of Public Security was accordingly set up in June 1940, with the Rt. Hon. J. C. MacDermott, K.C., M.P., as its first Minister.

The division in the Ministry of Home Affairs dealing with hospitals and casualty services, in the charge of Mr. A. A. Farrell, was transferred to the new Ministry and the Hospital Officer also became an officer of the new Ministry.

RESTRICTION OF ADMISSIONS

On July 23, 1940, restrictions on admissions of the civilian sick were again imposed by circular[7] and medical officers were instructed to select patients who could be discharged to their homes at short notice—twenty-four hours or less. Hospitals were told to be prepared to notify the Hospital Officer by telephone or otherwise of any material change in bedstate.

It was also decided to extend to all areas the scheme of protection which had at first applied only to hospitals in the Belfast area.

DECENTRALISATION OF HOSPITAL OFFICER CONTROL

At this stage it was felt that the organisation generally was centred too much in Belfast which would be an obvious target for bombers, and the Ministry decided to divide the province into four areas, to leave the Hospital Officer in charge of Belfast and the surrounding area, and to appoint an assistant part-time Hospital Officer for each of the other three areas.

The doctors appointed and the areas for which they became responsible were as follows:

1. *West Area:* Lieut. Colonel A. H. M. Eaton, F.R.C.S.Ed., R.A.M.C., Tyrone County Hospital, Omagh.

    The southern portion of County Londonderry, south of Maghera;
    The County of Tyrone (excluding the north and west extremities and the towns of Strabane and Castlederg); and
    The County of Fermanagh.

2. *North Area*: W. F. Evans, M.A., M.D., Lislea, Coleraine, Co. Londonderry.

    The northern portion of County Londonderry, north of Maghera;
    The north and west extremities of County Tyrone (including the towns of Strabane and Castlederg); and
    The portion of County Antrim north of Ballymena.

3. *South Area*: N. E. H. P. Williams, M.B., B.Ch., Sandrys Place, Newry.

    The County of Down (excluding the north-east portion, Newtownards and Ards Peninsula and Hillsborough); and
    The County of Armagh.

These officers were to assist the Hospital Officer in the discharge of his duties which included:

(*a*) the direction of the Emergency Medical Service in Northern Ireland, including the assignment of officers to special duty, etc.;

(*b*) direction and control of the admission of casualties and patients to hospitals and their transfer from one hospital to another;

(*c*) the supervision and control of provision available for casualties in hospitals;

(*d*) control of the assignment of Emergency Nursing staffs to hospitals within the Emergency Hospital Scheme;

(*e*) the supervision of local casualty services and their co-ordination with the Ministry's Emergency Hospital Scheme;

(*f*) the maintenance of liaison between the civil casualty services as a whole and the military medical services.

The Assistant Hospital Officers were to undertake these duties within the areas assigned to them and under the general direction of the Hospital Officer but would act on their own initiative in any sudden emergency or when, owing to the failure of communications, it became impossible for them to keep in touch with the Hospital Officer.

Each Assistant Hospital Officer undertook a further detailed survey of hospitals in his area in the light of the new conditions and advised the Hospital Officer in regard to the day by day problems arising in his area. Each also suggested improvements in the organisation in country areas generally and undertook responsibility for the supervision of the storage and general care of the E.M.S. equipment, much of which by this time had arrived and was stored in hospitals throughout the country.

GAS-CLEANSING UNITS AT HOSPITALS

The gas-cleansing units set up at first-aid posts were to provide for the cleansing of all gas-contaminated walking cases. Provision had also to be made for the cleansing before treatment of stretcher cases contaminated with gas. At each casualty receiving hospital, therefore, a gas cleansing unit was provided either by the adaptation of existing buildings or by the building of a special annexe for the purpose.

The arrangements were designed to provide that the gas-decontaminated casualty passed through the gas-cleansing unit on his way into the hospital. A standard layout was provided by the Ministry for these units and a copy of this layout is contained in Appendix II.

Instruction in the Treatment of Gas Casualties. In March 1941, the Ministry arranged with the assistance of the D.D.M.S. British Troops in Northern Ireland to train doctors, other hospital staffs and members of the local casualty services in the treatment of gas-contaminated casualties. Lectures were arranged[8] at Londonderry, Coleraine, Ballymena, Armagh, Omagh and Enniskillen.

Further courses were arranged in August 1941, and lectures given in Belfast by Dr. J. Nairn Hay and Professor Noah Morris. The Ministry's circular[9] indicated that courses would be open to all members of the Emergency Medical Service in charge of gas cleansing units at casualty receiving hospitals and to Sister Tutors from all hospitals undertaking the training of nurses.

Furthermore, in October 1942, arrangements were made[10] for doctors who missed the previous practical demonstrations to attend further demonstrations given in the Institute of Pathology, Belfast.

Post-mortem Examination. With a view to research into causes of fatality from poisoning by war gases, arrangements were made for post-mortem examinations on such cases.

Specimens for histological and microscopical examination were to be sent to Professor J. H. Biggart, M.D., D.Sc., at the Institute of

Pathology, Queen's University, Belfast. Detailed instructions[11] were issued with regard to the collection and transport of the material.

Fire Fighting Facilities. The Ministry sought the advice of the Belfast Fire Brigade on the fire-fighting facilities of hospitals, and the additional fire-fighting equipment which they recommended was supplied to hospitals by the Department.

Emergency Lighting. Experience in Great Britain had also by this time shown the need for emergency lighting equipment at all casualty receiving hospitals in vulnerable areas, and emergency generating sets were ordered and supplied to all such hospitals in Belfast.

HONORARY CONSULTANT ADVISERS

Arrangements were made in October 1940, to appoint honorary consultant advisers to the Ministry in the various medical and surgical specialities and particulars of the names and specialities of those who undertook these services at the request of the Minister were communicated to hospitals by circular.[12]

This arrangement was revised a month later and hospitals were informed by circular[13] that all the members of the Emergency Medical Services who were of recognised consultant status would be available for consultation if and when required by the Ministry.

MOBILE SURGICAL TEAMS

Opportunity was taken at the same time to remind hospitals of the arrangements for surgical mobile teams, consisting of a surgeon, his assistant and anaesthetist, who were available to give general reinforcement where required. There were five such teams and the surgeons in charge were:

C. J. S. Woodside, M.B., F.R.C.S.I.
G. D. F. McFadden, M.B., M.Ch., F.R.C.S.
C. A. Calvert, M.B., F.R.C.S.I.
M. Lavery, M.B., F.R.C.S.
R. J. W. Withers, M.D., M.Ch., F.R.C.S.Ed.

HOSPITAL ACCOMMODATION AVAILABLE IN MAY 1940

The survey of accommodation at hospitals, which was completed in May 1940, revealed that there were approximately 4,700 beds in general hospitals throughout Northern Ireland at the outbreak of war. After consultation with the medical officers at various hospitals, the Hospital Officer estimated that either by reducing the space per bed in existing wards or by using as wards rooms formerly devoted to other purposes, approximately a further 1,000 beds could be accommodated. The adaptation of some disused buildings, e.g. old workhouses, for use as hospitals was expedited and 400 additional beds which it was estimated could be accommodated in those buildings were ordered. The adaptations referred to were undertaken at Londonderry, Ballymena, Omagh, Limavady and Magherafelt. A list of the twenty-five hospitals which were earmarked for the reception of casualties, together with a list of the remaining thirty hospitals which were earmarked for the admission of evacuees or of patients evacuated from casualty receiving hospitals to make room for casualties, are set out in Appendix III.

AIR RAIDS ON BELFAST, APRIL AND MAY 1941

So far hospitals had had a mere trickle of casualties, mainly of members of H.M. Forces stationed in Northern Ireland or children who had been evacuated under the Ministry's scheme for the evacuation of schoolchildren.

The first real pressure on hospitals came in April 1941, when Belfast experienced its first air raids. Fortunately the raids were few in number and were confined to a period of four weeks commencing early in April. Belfast was naturally the main target, although some casualties occurred in Londonderry and the Bangor-Newtownards area.

Two of the air attacks, those on the nights of April 15 and 16 and May 4 and 5, 1941, caused heavy casualties and great damage to property in Belfast. The casualty receiving hospitals, particularly the Mater Infirmorum Hospital (which sustained damage), the Belfast City Hospital and the Royal Victoria Hospital, had to cope with very large numbers of injured.

Two hospitals were completely demolished, namely, the Ulster Hospital for Children and Women and the Belfast Hospital for Diseases of the Skin. Another hospital, the Benn Eye, Ear and Throat Hospital was damaged but was able to carry on its services. Fortunately the casualties amongst hospital staff and patients were very light, due largely no doubt to the very effective protective works which had been carried out at the hospitals.

The 'shadow' scheme referred to in Chapter 1 came into operation when the Ulster Hospital for Children and Women received a direct hit and steps were taken to fit up a 'shadow' hospital at Haypark School in Belfast. The necessary adaptation works were carried out and the hospital was soon functioning normally.

Some idea of the pressure on the hospitals during the year 1941 is given by a comparison of the figures for the years 1940 and 1941 of 'casualties' admitted:

Year	Number of casualties admitted
1940	260
1941	3,500

Of the total 3,500 casualties, 680 were injured in the air raids, the balance being made up of other classes coming within the category of 'casualty' e.g. transferred sick, etc.

As will be seen from later chapters Belfast had no further visits from enemy bombers and hospitals were not again called on to deal with large numbers of casualties. The organisation had, however, been tested and while it suffered severe strain during this period, the devoted and untiring work by hospital staffs overcame the difficulties and won the admiration of the public.

Full details of the air raids in Belfast will be found in Part III, Chapter 13.

REFERENCES

[1] Min. of Home Affairs Memorandum C.D.21, September 1, 1939.
[2] Min. of Home Affairs Memorandum C.D. 22, 3rd Edition, June 1, 1940.
[3] Min. of Home Affairs C.D. Circular No. 24, September 4, 1939.
[4] Min. of Home Affairs C.D. Circular No. 32, September 8, 1939.
[5] Min. of Home Affairs Circular C.S. 120, enclosure (E.M.S. Gen./312), February 17, 1940.
[6] Min. of Home Affairs C.S. Circular and Memorandum 121, February 19, 1940.
[7] Min. of Public Security Circular H.1, July 23, 1940.
[8] Min. of Public Security Circular H.100, March 24, 1941.
[9] Min. of Home Affairs M.34, August 13, 1941.
[10] Min. of Home Affairs Circular H.O. 23, October 1, 1942.
[11] Min. of Public Security Circular H.94, February 1941.
[12] Min. of Public Security Circular H.41, October 24, 1940.
[13] Min. of Public Security Circular H.55, November 26, 1940.

APPENDIX I

Group I

Class A. Hospitals in Belfast which were expected to receive most of the general casualties:

> Mater Infirmorum Hospital
> Royal Victoria Hospital
> Belfast Union Infirmary

Class A1. Hospitals in Belfast which were expected to amend their special functions to receive a limited number of general casualties and to which casualties of a special nature could be sent:

> U.V.F. Hospital, Craigavon
> Ulster Hospital for Women and Children
> Samaritan Hospital
> Royal Maternity Hospital
> Belfast Hospital for Sick Children
> Belfast Ophthalmic Hospital
> Benn Hospital
> Claremont Street Hospital for Nervous Diseases.

APPENDIX I *(continued)*

Group II

Class B. Hospitals outside Belfast which lay in areas in which casualties were also expected to occur, and which were expected to receive such casualties and also casualties occurring in outlying parts of Belfast:

> Ards District Hospital
> Lisburn and Hillsborough District Hospital
> Antrim County Infirmary
> Bangor Cottage Hospital
> Larne District Hospital
> Smiley Cottage Hospital
> Massereene Hospital

Group III

Class C. Hospitals situated outside the area in which casualties were expected to occur and which would therefore receive only unexpected casualties occurring in their neighbourhood, but which were expected to maintain medical services for ordinary patients who might otherwise go to hospitals in Groups I or II, and to receive such patients and convalescent casualties from hospitals in Groups I and II:

> All hospitals in Northern Ireland except those specifically named in other classes and the Fever and Mental Hospitals and Sanatoria.

Group IV

Class D. Hospitals in Belfast with specially limited equipment or accommodation upon which no demand was expected unless in case of exceptional need:

> Throne Convalescent Hospital
> Rescue and Maternity Home, Malone Place
> Thorndale House
> Forster Green Hospital

EXPANSION AND WORK OF HOSPITALS 139

APPENDIX II

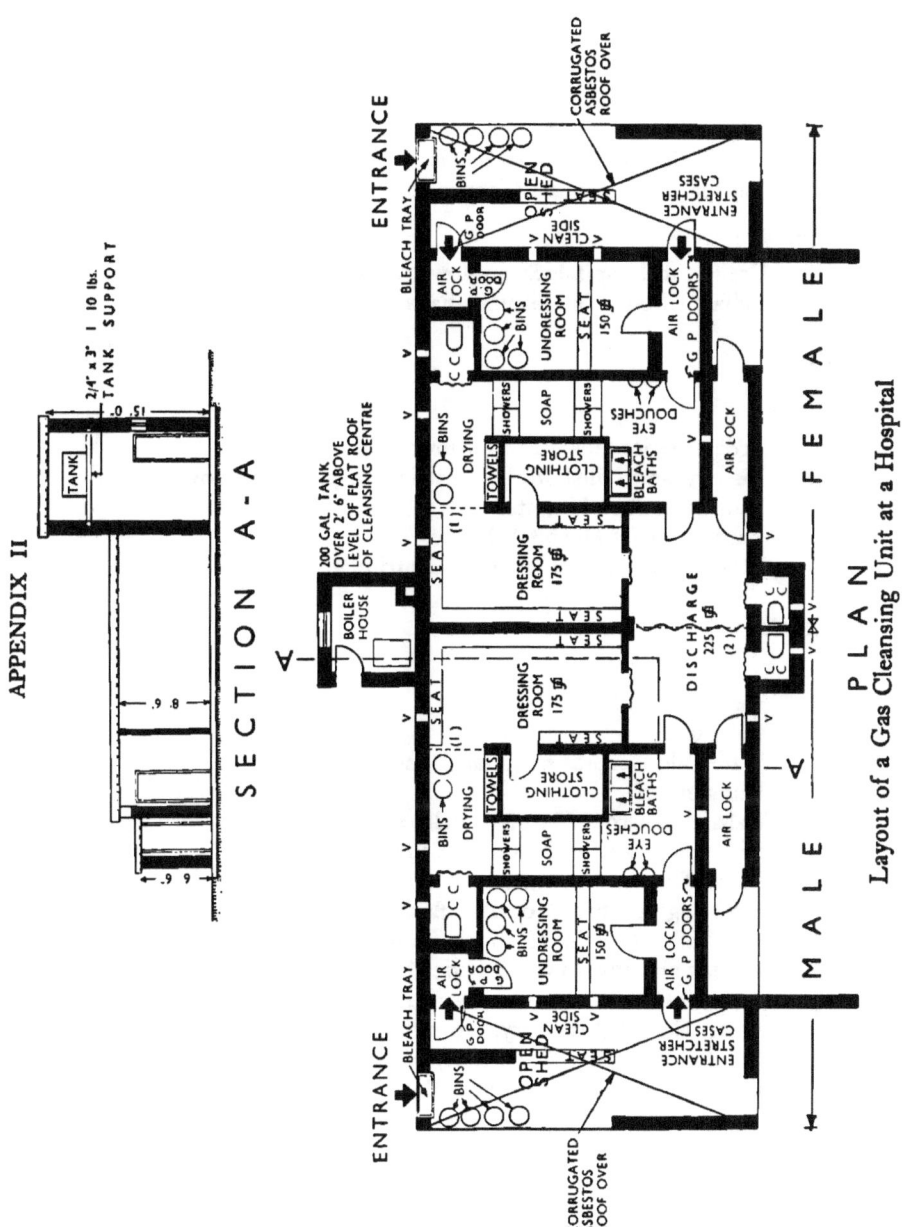

Layout of a Gas Cleansing Unit at a Hospital

APPENDIX III(1)

LIST OF CASUALTY RECEIVING HOSPITALS IN EMERGENCY HOSPITAL SCHEME

Group I

  Class A:

    Mater Infirmorum Hospital, Crumlin Road, Belfast.
    Royal Victoria Hospital, Belfast.
    Belfast City Hospital, Lisburn Road, Belfast.

  Class A1 :

    Craigavon Hospital, Strandtown, Belfast.
    Belfast Children's Hospital, Falls Road, Belfast.

Group II

  Class B:

    Ards District Hospital, Newtownards.
    Lisburn and Hillsborough District Hospital, Lisburn.
    Bangor Cottage Hospital.
    Larne District Hospital, Larne.
    Massereene District Hospital, Antrim.

Group III

  Class C:

    Newry
    Coleraine
    Waterside General Hospital, Londonderry.
    Dungannon
    Dalriada District Hospital, Ballycastle.
    Ballymena District Hospital, Ballymena.
    Route District Hospital, Ballymoney.
    Banbridge District Hospital, Banbridge.
    Roe Valley District Hospital, Limavady.
    Lurgan and Portadown District Hospital, Lurgan.
    Armagh County Infirmary, Armagh.
    Down County Infirmary, Downpatrick.
    Londonderry City and County Hospital, Londonderry.
    Fermanagh County Hospital, Enniskillen.
    Tyrone County Hospital, Omagh.

APPENDIX III(2)

LIST OF HOSPITALS SELECTED FOR THE ADMISSION OF EVACUEES OR PATIENTS EVACUATED FROM CASUALTY RECEIVING HOSPITALS TO MAKE ROOM FOR CASUALTIES

1. Belfast Emergency Hospital.
2. Ulster Hospital for Children and Women, Belfast.
3. Samaritan Hospital, Belfast.
4. Royal Maternity Hospital, Belfast.
5. Belfast Ophthalmic Hospital.
6. Benn Hospital, Belfast.
7. Nervous Diseases Hospital, Belfast.
8. Antrim County Infirmary.
9. Smiley Cottage Hospital, Larne.
10. Armagh Union Infirmary.
11. Downpatrick Infirmary.
12. Enniskillen Infirmary.
13. Magherafelt Infirmary.
14. Omagh Infirmary.
15. Castlederg Infirmary.
16. Clogher Infirmary.
17. Mourne District Hospital, Kilkeel.
18. Strabane District Hospital.
19. Londonderry and North West Eye, Ear and Throat Hospital, Londonderry.
20. Mary Ranken Maternity Home, Coleraine.
21. Ballymena Cottage Hospital.
22. Cushendall Cottage Hospital.
23. Portrush Cottage Hospital.
24. Robinson Cottage Hospital, Ballymoney.
25. Newry General Hospital.
26. Cowan Heron Cottage Hospital, Dromore.
27. Coleraine Cottage Hospital.
28. Thorndale House, Belfast.
29. Rescue and Maternity Home, Belfast.
30. Throne Convalescent Hospital, Belfast.

CHAPTER 3
WORK OF THE HOSPITALS FROM APRIL 1941 TO THE END OF THE WAR

HEADQUARTERS ADMINISTRATION

FOLLOWING the raids in April and May, 1941, a reorganisation of administrative work took place at Ministry of Public Security Headquarters, which involved the transfer of the administration of the Emergency Hospital Scheme to the Public Health Division of the Ministry of Home Affairs. That division already had a statutory responsibility for the supervision of the normal work of the local authority hospitals, all of which had been enrolled in the scheme, so that the new arrangement had much to commend it. Casualty Services remained a Ministry of Public Security responsibility.

LESSONS LEARNT FROM THE AIR RAIDS

Experience in the raids had revealed some defects in the organisation at the hospital end and the attention of the Hospital Officer was immediately given to them. As a first step he secured reports of difficulties encountered together with recommendations from all medical officers in charge of casualty receiving hospitals and in addition he secured confidential reports from hospitals in Great Britain showing how similar problems had been solved there. A circular[1] issued by the Hospital Officer on September 6, 1941, dealt with the following matters:

Resuscitation. The first matter requiring attention was the arrangements for the resuscitation of shocked casualties. Cases of shock which required resuscitation had been very numerous and, as the most valuable treatment was warmth, hospitals were advised to have the windows of resuscitation wards completely bricked up. It had proved impossible in some instances to provide adequate warmth where windows were blown in (or out). They were also advised to have emergency lighting in resuscitation wards.

Some hospitals had not set aside a special ward for use as a resuscitation ward and they were now asked to do so.

Classification of Casualties. Classification of casualties was considered to require attention and hospitals were advised to allocate an experienced member of the staff to this work. Classification on the following lines was suggested:

(*a*) minor injuries requiring little more than dressings;
(*b*) stretcher cases suffering from shock of varying degree;

(c) stretcher cases requiring immediate operation;
(d) stretcher cases who were moribund and dying;
(e) cases requiring operation, but not immediately.

Minor Injuries. Attention was drawn to the necessity for ensuring that patients with minor injuries were directed to a dressing room and not allowed home until they had been examined thoroughly in a good light. Cases had occurred where injuries originally suspected of being slight proved to be of a more serious nature and necessitated re-admission to hospital.

Casualty Team. It was found to be advisable to have a team of members of the staff readily available at the hospitals for casualties even though casualties might not arrive immediately. In the larger hospitals it was considered to be a reassurance to resident medical and nursing staffs to know that they were reinforced by at least a surgeon and a physician on the premises. In the case of smaller hospitals and those which had no resident staff, hospitals were asked to arrange that members of the auxiliary medical staff would attend at the hospital on the sounding of the alert. Experience had shown that members of staff had been prevented from reaching hospital later because roads had been damaged early in a raid.

Alternative Means of Communication. All reports and experience had emphasised the importance of the establishment of an alternative means of communication to the telephone, and authorities of casualty receiving hospitals which had not already done so, were reminded of the necessity to make provision for messengers to be allocated to the hospital and to be supplied with cycles or motor-cycles. Hospitals in provincial areas were advised in the event of a telephone breakdown to appeal to the police or nearest military authority.

Appointment of Regional Resuscitation Officers. The Ministry felt that the whole matter of resuscitation of shocked casualties and arrangements for the administration of blood transfusions was one which required expert attention and in the latter half of 1941 appointed Professor J. H. Biggart, Professor of Pathology, Queen's University, Belfast, and Dr. J. A. L. Johnston, Pathologist, Londonderry, to act as part-time Regional Resuscitation Officers and be responsible to the Hospital Officer for the necessary arrangements. Hospitals were informed of the arrangements by circular[2] and invited to consult these officers in regard to resuscitation problems.

The Ministry's Hospital Officer, Dr. Allen, resigned from this post on April 15, 1942, and he was succeeded by W. A. Brown, M.D., D.P.H., who was seconded from the Ministry's Medical Inspectorate.

One of Dr. Brown's first duties was to consider the first reports of the newly appointed Regional Resuscitation Officers and on their recommendation he arranged for:

(a) the issue of additional equipment to hospitals for the purpose of administering oxygen;

(b) the issue to each of eight selected hospitals of an 'Arcus' Set for oxygen therapy, capable of supplying oxygen to ten beds at a time. These sets were placed at selected hospitals but they were to be available for the use of any casualty receiving hospital on application to the Hospital Officer;

(c) the establishment of reserve stocks of oxygen cylinders at provincial agents of the British Oxygen Co. Ltd., to which hospitals were permitted to have access in an emergency. Hospitals were advised that for normal requirements they should hold adequate stocks of cylinders at their hospital;

(d) the issue of a circular[3] to hospitals to the effect that central blood banks and special reserves were now adequate to meet all demands and that application should be made to one or other of the Regional Resuscitation Officers as follows:
Professor J. H. Biggart—Counties of Down, Antrim and Armagh.
Dr. J. A. L. Johnston—Counties of Londonderry, Tyrone and Fermanagh.

(e) the issue of a circular[4] to casualty receiving hospitals, pressing those that had not already done so, to appoint a Resuscitation Officer who should be a doctor other than the medical officer or surgeon in charge of the hospital. The circular also dealt with arrangements for a course of instruction for Resuscitation Officers who would afterwards be expected to undertake the training of a Resuscitation and Blood Transfusion Team at their own hospital.

With a view to familiarising the staff of these Resuscitation and Blood Transfusion Teams with the use of the equipment which had been supplied, the circular suggested that the E.M.S. resuscitation and blood transfusion equipment be used for the treatment of the hospital's ordinary civilian patients.

Special Centre for Neurosis. Hospitals were advised by circular[5] of the existence of a special centre for the treatment of war neurosis at the Nervous Diseases Hospital, Claremont Street, Belfast, and it was pointed out that patients suffering from war neurosis could be transferred to this hospital on application to the Hospital Officer or the Assistant Hospital Officer.

MOBILE X-RAY VANS

The Joint War Organisation of the British Red Cross and St. John came forward, at this stage, with a very generous offer of two mobile X-ray vans for use in the event of a breakdown of the X-ray facilities at any hospital, and the Government very gladly accepted their offer. The vans were garaged at the Fever Hospital on the outskirts of Belfast for safety and arrangements were made for Mr. R. M. Leman, the Chief Radiographer of the Royal Victoria Hospital, to exercise a general oversight to ensure that they were kept in good working order and available for immediate use if required.

ERECTION OF HOSPITAL HUTMENTS

In August 1941, it was decided that in order to enable hospitals to cope with expected future demands the available hospital accommodation would require to be greatly increased. Arrangements were accordingly made for release by the War Office of pre-fabricated hospital hutments to accommodate 2,500 patients. These hutments were purchased and erected at various hospitals throughout the province. They were used mainly to supplement accommodation at general hospitals, both casualty receiving and other hospitals, but some were erected at sanatoria and at infectious diseases hospitals. Some hutments were also secured for the accommodation of nursing staff and full details of the hutments, and the hospitals at which they were erected, are contained in the Appendix to this Chapter.

ESTABLISHMENT OF BELFAST EMERGENCY HOSPITAL

While it was felt that hospitals outside Belfast were well equipped to deal with any emergency and would have adequate accommodation, particularly with their new hutments, it was considered that provision should be made against the possibility of damage by enemy action to one of the larger Belfast hospitals which had been earmarked for the reception and treatment of air raid casualties. With the co-operation and assistance therefore of the authorities of the Belfast Mental Hospital the Ministry arranged in November 1941, for the transfer of approximately 500 mental patients from Belfast Mental Hospital and adapted the vacated premises for use as an emergency hospital. After considerable adaptation the Belfast Emergency Hospital containing 400 beds within approximately five miles of Belfast was opened and made available for casualties.

The Resident Medical Superintendent of the Mental Hospital acted as the Medical Superintendent and a whole-time E.M.S. surgeon was appointed and attached to his staff. In addition a resident surgical officer and a house surgeon were appointed while the hospital was entirely staffed on the nursing side by trained and other members of the Civil Nursing Reserve.

Treatment of Civilian Sick at the Emergency Hospital. In order to avoid the anomaly of having a fully-equipped hospital complete with staff without patients and at the same time considerable waiting lists at certain voluntary hospitals in Belfast, arrangements were made with these hospitals whereby the Emergency Hospital undertook the treatment of as many as possible of the patients on their waiting lists. The main consideration behind this decision was that a large proportion of those on waiting lists were employed in essential war industries of shipbuilding, aircraft production, engineering, etc., and it was felt that in the national interest every effort should be made to make them fit for work as soon as possible.

Special Centres for Orthopaedic Surgery and Peripheral Nerve Injuries. Opportunity was taken at this time to develop an orthopaedic centre at the Belfast Emergency Hospital to which orthopaedic 'casualty' patients could be sent for special treatment. R. J. W. Withers, M.D., M.Ch., F.R.C.S. Ed., an orthopaedic consultant, was appointed to attend the hospital on so many sessions per week.

The whole-time E.M.S. surgeon of the Hospital, E. J. Crawford, F.R.C.S., undertook a special course in the treatment of peripheral nerve injuries and a special centre for this purpose was also established at the Emergency Hospital.

Fracture Clinic. Arrangements were made to refer casualty patients from other hospitals through the Hospital Officer to the Fracture Clinic, which was established by the authorities of the Royal Victoria Hospital, Belfast.

CIVIL DEFENCE EXERCISES

In May 1942, arrangements were made in consultation with the Civil Defence Services to stage a large-scale exercise of all civil defence and allied services. It was planned to make the exercise as realistic as possible and the various services were to act as though they were working under actual air raid conditions.

Hospitals co-operated to the full in this exercise which took place between the hours of 10 p.m. and 4 a.m. and they went through the whole routine of receiving casualties, classification of casualties, allocation to wards, treatment of 'injuries' and completion of all the necessary forms.

DEATH OF CHIEF MEDICAL OFFICER

In September 1942, the Ministry suffered a severe loss by the death of Dr. J. McCloy, its Chief Medical Officer, who had, because of the war situation, continued to serve beyond his normal retiring age. It is fitting that record should here be made of the valuable part which he played in the planning of the Emergency Hospital Scheme, the Civil Nursing Reserve and other services designed to meet war-time needs. The heavy pressure of work and anxiety connected therewith undoubtedly accelerated the onset of the illness responsible for his death.

He was succeeded by Dr. J. Boyd who had been Chief Medical Officer of the Ministry of Labour for Northern Ireland and who now acted as Chief Medical Officer of both Ministries.

VOLUNTEER CAR POOL

In December 1942, the Volunteer Car Pool was established. Under this scheme private car owners made their cars and themselves available for essential hospital journeys.

The Ministry's circular[6] authorised hospitals to use the pool:

(a) for the conveyance of patients to or from hospital or any place which had to be visited for purposes of treatment;
(b) for the conveyance of urgent medical supplies;
(c) for the conveyance of nursing or other medical staff attending sick persons.

FURTHER DECENTRALISATION OF HOSPITAL OFFICER CONTROL

In March 1943, the Ministry decided on the advice of the Hospital Officer to decentralise the control of air raid casualties in raids taking place outside Belfast. It was considered that the arrangements then operating whereby control was exercised by the Hospital Officer or an Assistant Hospital Officer situated perhaps some considerable distance from the scene of the air raid was impracticable. It was decided therefore to place the control in the hands of the medical officers of casualty receiving hospitals outside Belfast and Londonderry.

Full instructions[7] detailing action to be taken to implement this decision and action which would be required from the hospital medical and other staff, before, during and after an air raid were issued to the medical officer in charge of each of these hospitals.

PRIORITY IN HOSPITAL TREATMENT FOR KEY WORKERS

In consultation with the Ministry of Commerce the Ministry made arrangements with hospitals enrolled in the Emergency Hospital Scheme to grant priority of treatment to key workers employed in war factories. The purpose of this scheme was to ensure that workers employed in these factories were returned to their essential work at the earliest possible date.

CREATION OF MINISTRY OF HEALTH AND LOCAL GOVERNMENT

In December 1942, the Northern Ireland House of Commons decided to appoint a Select Committee on Health Services. This committee presented an Interim Report on July 6, 1943, dealing with the particularly pressing problem of the salaries and conditions of hospital nurses which it was felt demanded immediate attention.

The committee's recommendations were adopted by the government and new salaries and conditions of service were commended by the Minister of Home Affairs to, and adopted by, all hospitals in the province.

The Final Report[8] of the committee was presented to the House of Commons on January 18, 1944, and covered the whole range of the Health Services in Northern Ireland.

One of the most important recommendations was that a Ministry of Health should be set up at once which would be the central controlling authority for all health services in Northern Ireland.

This recommendation was accepted by the government and a new Ministry with the title 'Ministry of Health and Local Government' came into being on June 1, 1944. The Rt. Hon. W. Grant, M.P., was its first Minister.

The functions of the entire Public Health Division of the Ministry of Home Affairs, including the functions relating to the Emergency Hospital Scheme, were transferred to the new Ministry.

APPOINTMENT OF ASSISTANT HOSPITAL OFFICER

With the improvement in the war position throughout 1943 the duty of providing accommodation for air raid casualties gradually diminished in importance. Emphasis instead was laid upon the duty of making the maximum possible provision for accommodation in civilian hospitals for casualties amongst H.M. Forces which might arise from the projected invasion of the Continent of Europe.

Arrangements to this end were made in close consultation with the Deputy Director of Medical Services for Northern Ireland and involved many visits by the Hospital Officer to hospitals in country areas, for the purpose of dealing with problems arising out of the commissioning of hospital hutments, which had been erected in the grounds of hospitals but which had so far not been brought into use.

This presented a new problem for the Hospital Officer. Hospitals in the scheme were now taking a steady stream of Service casualties from overseas and, since all arrangements for the selection of a suitable hospital for particular casualties and for their transfer, if required, to special centres, etc., were arranged through him, he found that his enforced absences from Belfast prevented him from being able to cope with the day-to-day work arising from the operation of the scheme.

Furthermore, the possibility of air raids on Belfast had still to be reckoned with, since in that event his presence would be required in Belfast at the Control Room.

In the circumstances it was decided that an Assistant Hospital Officer would be required at Headquarters, and Dr. J. D. Mc-Clelland was appointed and took up duty in this post on November 1, 1944.

The new arrangement provided for the dropping of the three part-time Assistant Hospital Officer posts in provincial areas.

CONSULTANT ADVISERS IN MEDICINE AND SURGERY

The Ministry continued to keep the standard of facilities provided at hospitals throughout the scheme under continuous review and in November 1944, informed[9] hospitals that it had been decided to appoint as consultant advisers to the Ministry the Professors of Medicine and Surgery at Queen's University, Belfast, Professor W. W. D. Thomson and Professor P. T. Crymble respectively. These officers undertook the particular duty of advising the Hospital Officer on the treatment of a particular 'casualty' patient in any of the hospitals in the Emergency Hospital Scheme, but in addition they undertook the general duty of surveying the facilities for their speciality at each of the hospitals of the province. Their reports were forwarded to the Hospital Officer and recommendations based on their reports were issued to the hospitals in order to secure a general improvement in the standard of service.

TRANSFER OF EMERGENCY HOSPITAL TO MUSGRAVE PARK, BELFAST

In April 1945, arrangements were made by the Ministry to take over ex-military hospital buildings at Musgrave Park, Belfast, and the complete staff of the Belfast Emergency Hospital, together with the hospital equipment belonging to the Ministry, were transferred to these premises.

The purpose of the scheme was, on the one hand, to enable the evacuated mental patients to be returned to Belfast and on the other hand to enable the Government to secure much needed additional accommodation at Musgrave Park for the treatment of tuberculosis.

The premises at Musgrave Park were sufficiently large to provide that, after reserving the number of beds estimated to be required for Emergency Hospital Scheme purposes, there remained space for an additional 300 patients in an entirely separate section of the hospital. This section in due course became the tuberculosis wing of the hospital. Tuberculosis Committees were informed by circular[10] of the arrangements which had been made and were offered facilities for the treatment of their patients.

CONCLUSION

An attempt has been made in this and the previous two chapters to give a concise account of the organisation of the hospital services of Northern Ireland to meet the war emergency. Some idea of the extent to which hospitals in Northern Ireland were used for this purpose is given by the following statistics relating to 'casualties' treated in hospital during the war. Figures for each year were not available :

*'Casualties' treated in Northern Ireland Hospitals
during the period
September 3, 1939, to March 31, 1946*

Classification	Number
Navy	831
Army	4,989
Air Force	1,704
Total for services	7,524
Air raid	680
Others (*i.e.* evacuees, transferred sick, etc.)	14,721
Total	22,925

The task which fell to various Ministries of the Government of Northern Ireland which were involved in the administration of hospital services at one period or other of the war, was greatly simplified by the fact that a similar organisation, though on a necessarily much more elaborate scale, had been set up in advance in England and Wales.

For this reason an attempt has been made to avoid a mere repetition of what has been written in Part I of Volume I about the work of the Hospital Services in England and Wales and to direct attention rather to the points of difference between the arrangements in Northern Ireland and those made for England and Wales.

In general it can be said that the machinery created in Northern Ireland proved adequate to the demands made upon it. That this was so, was due in large measure to the willing co-operation and the initiative and resource of all those concerned with the actual provision of the Service.

It is but fitting, therefore, that tribute should be paid in conclusion to the devoted service which was given during those years by staffs of all grades, whether in hospitals or at Ministry Headquarters.

REFERENCES

[1] Min. of Home Affairs Circular H.O. 7, September 6, 1941.
[2] Min. of Home Affairs Circular H.O. 15, January 9, 1942.
[3] Min. of Home Affairs Circular H.O. 14, December 24, 1941.
[4] Min. of Home Affairs Circular H.O. 16, June 11, 1942.
[5] Min. of Public Security Circular, H. 111, April 10, 1941.
[6] Min. of Public Security Circular M. 125, December 22, 1942.
[7] Min. of Public Security Circular H.O. 46, March 15, 1943.
[8] Report of Select Committee on Health Circular H.C. 601, January 18, 1944.
[9] Min. of Health and Local Government Circular H.O. 122, November 8, 1944.
[10] Min. of Health and Local Government Circular M. 217, August 30, 1945.

APPENDIX

Hospital Hutments

Name of hospital	Casualty		Infectious diseases		Nurses	
	Number of hutments	Number of beds	Number of hutments	Number of beds	Number of hutments	Number of nurses accommodated
Ards District	2	100	2	50	–	–
Armagh County (Mental)	4	200	–	–	1	80
Armagh Union	3	100	–	–	–	–
Banbridge District	–	–	1	25	1	10
Coleraine Union	1	50	1	25	–	–
Dalriada District	–	–	1	25	–	–
Down County	1	25	–	–	1	6
Downpatrick Union	–	–	1	25	–	–
Dungannon Union	2	75	1	25	–	–
Dungannon Sanatorium	1	50	–	–	–	–
Enniskillen Union	2	50	1	25	–	–
Larne District	2	100	–	–	–	–
Lisburn and Hillsborough District	2	50	1	25		
Londonderry City and County	1	25	–	–	–	–
Lurgan and Portadown District	1	50	1	25	–	–
Magherafelt District	–	–	1	25	–	–
Mary Ranken Maternity	1	25	–	25	–	–
Massereene District	1	50	1	25	–	–
Mourne District	1	50	–	25	–	–
Newry Union	1	25	–	–	–	–
Omagh Union	–	–	1	25	–	–
Roe Valley District	3	150	1	25	–	–
Route District	1	50	1	25	–	–
Strabane District	2	100	–	–	–	–
Tyrone County	2	50	–	–	–	–
Tyrone County (Mental)	6	300	–	–	2	60
Ulster Hospital for Children and Women (Haypark)	1	50	–	–	1	12
Waveney District (Ballymena)	1	50	1	25	–	–
Whiteabbey Sanatorium	2	100	–	–	2	32

CHAPTER 4
CIVIL DEFENCE AND AMBULANCE SERVICES

EARLY ACTION

FOLLOWING the establishment at the Home Office in London in May 1935, of an Air Raid Precautions Department under Wing-Commander Hodsoll (afterwards Sir John Hodsoll), Assistant Under Secretary, the Secretary to the Ministry of Home Affairs, Northern Ireland, Major G. A. Harris, D.S.O., communicated with that Department to ascertain to what extent action in regard to air raid precautions should be taken in Northern Ireland.

The matter was discussed by correspondence and in May of the following year Wing Commander Hodsoll paid a visit to Northern Ireland when he discussed air raid precautions at length with the Prime Minister, (Lord Craigavon) and the Minister of Home Affairs (Sir Dawson Bates). He also addressed a representative meeting including delegates from the British Red Cross Society and the St. John Ambulance Brigade. The emphasis at these discussions and at the meeting was upon gas precautions, though the matter of training of first aid personnel was also discussed at length.

AIR RAID PRECAUTIONS ADVISORY COMMITTEE

At the end of the meeting Sir Dawson Bates announced that the Government of Northern Ireland had decided to appoint an Advisory Committee to investigate the matter generally and to advise the Government. Its terms of reference were 'to advise and assist the Government in the consideration and preparation of schemes for protecting the civil population and for the maintenance of an essential service in Northern Ireland in the event of attacks from the air in time of war and for this purpose to co-operate with similar committees in Great Britain'.

The committee held its first meeting on September 14, 1936, under the chairmanship of Lieut. Colonel A. R. G. Gordon, M.P., and local authorities, public utilities and the Joint Committee of the British Red Cross Society and the Order of St. John were represented.

Dr. C. S. Thomson, the Medical Superintendent Officer of Health, represented the Belfast Corporation.

The committee decided at their second meeting on September 28, 1936, to appoint two sub-committees, one for engineering and essential services and one for medical services. To the latter sub-committee Dr. C. S. Thomson, Dr. John Mackintosh, Mr. A. W. Mann, representing the British Red Cross Society and Order of St.

CIVIL DEFENCE AND AMBULANCE SERVICES

John, and Mr. J. Smith, Chief Officer of the Belfast Fire Brigade were appointed.

The committee and their sub-committees met on numerous occasions and heard expert evidence from officers of the Home Office in London and from those who were in a position to give advice as to the requirements in Northern Ireland. The committee's report[1] was presented to the Minister of Home Affairs on December 14, 1936. In the appendix to the report the committee outlined a sample air raid precautions scheme and the report recommended that local authorities should proceed immediately to frame schemes on these lines.

Several local authorities took steps immediately following the publication of this report to organise air raid precautions, to enrol volunteers and to lay the foundations of the services which would be required in the event of war.

The Ulster Joint Committee of the British Red Cross Society and the Order of St. John had already been active in arranging suitable courses of instruction in air raid precautions as far back as 1936 and the work was continued throughout the years 1937 and 1938. These courses were held at many centres in Northern Ireland and were instrumental, not only in awakening interest in the new problems of civil defence, but also in providing the trained personnel who formed the nucleus of the large Civil Defence Services which were later found to be necessary.

AIR RAID PRECAUTIONS ACT (N.I.) 1938

It soon became evident, however, that legislation was required to place the work on a satisfactory basis and a measure on similar lines to the Air Raid Precautions Act, 1937, for Great Britain was introduced in the Northern Ireland House of Commons on June 14, 1938.

This Act, which received Royal Assent on November 24, 1938, placed the duty of preparing air raid precaution schemes upon local authorities. In the period immediately following its passing there was a substantial increase in the study of civil defence methods throughout the country.

The Ministry of Home Affairs provided general guidance for local authorities in the preparation of their schemes and in turn were guided in the matter by the Home Office in London. Valuable advice and assistance were also given to the Ministry by the Northern Ireland Medical War Committee in determining the most suitable organisation of the Casualty Service (see Chapter 2).

Each local authority was advised by the Ministry of the probable requirements in its area and furnished with a copy of a model scheme to suit the needs of a typical area similar to that under the authority's control. The local authorities concerned were the two county boroughs —Belfast and Londonderry—a few boroughs, urban district councils and rural district councils. Unlike the Act in operation in Great Britain, the Northern Ireland measure did not make county councils scheme-making authorities. They had little connexion with the general organisation or operation of air raid precautions.

The Home Office Air Raid Precautions Department and the research workers acting in co-operation with that Department did valuable work in this period immediately preceding the war and the results of their labours and investigations were made available to the Government of Northern Ireland.

NEW DIVISION AT THE MINISTRY

A new division was set up in the Ministry of Home Affairs to deal with the administration of the Emergency Hospital and Casualty Services (see Chapter 2). Its duty in relation to casualty services was to guide and assist local authorities in carrying out the obligations laid upon them in regard to 'casualty' matters by the Air Raid Precautions (Schemes) Regulations (Northern Ireland), 1938. The more important duties were:

(1) Arrangements for dealing with casualties, including the organisation of first-aid parties, first-aid posts and ambulance services.
(2) Arrangements for decontamination of highways, streets, public places and buildings affected by poison gas and anything therein requiring decontamination.
(3) The recruiting and training of the personnel required for the Scheme.

The complete division was transferred to the newly-formed Ministry of Public Security in June 1940 (see Chapter 2) and the administration of the casualty services remained the responsibility of that Ministry up to June 1944, when the Ministry was wound up, and its responsibilities transferred to the Ministry of Home Affairs.

In general the pattern of the service followed closely on that of the Casualty Service in Great Britain, but certain differences are mentioned in the brief account of the organisation which is given below.

FIRST-AID PARTIES

The function of a first-aid party was to provide first aid at an incident and the action was limited to essential first aid which would remove immediate danger to life and guard against the deterioration of the patient's condition during his journey to hospital or first-aid post. In air raid conditions elaborate first aid was impossible and the standard training provided by the British Red Cross Society and St. John Ambulance Brigade was modified so as to provide for the quickest possible removal to hospital or first-aid post. For example, the cleansing of wounds at incidents was usually impracticable and rarely desirable.

Simple immobilisation of limbs by properly tied bandages was frequently preferable to the affixing of splints. In nearly all cases first-aid treatment for wound shock was given.

The first-aid party consisted of five men, including a driver for the motor car in which the party travelled from its headquarters to an air raid incident. The equipment required by the party was carried in the car or in a trailer attached to it.

Those comprising the first-aid party required extensive training in first aid. Generally the task of giving the necessary instruction fell on the medical officers attached to the Civil Defence Services and one of these officers, frequently the medical officer of health, was responsible for the general organisation of the complete casualty service.

At all times there was close co-operation between the rescue and first-aid party services and, at an early stage in the war, it was arranged that rescue parties should have training in first aid and first-aid parties should be trained in the less difficult branches of rescue work. When this was done the parties were better equipped to help each other and to avoid delay in clearing incidents.

The organisation of both Services in Northern Ireland had been on similar lines to those adopted in Great Britain, and they continued to be operated similarly in both countries up to 1943. During that year the authorities in Great Britain, influenced largely by the man-power situation, decided to amalgamate the first-aid party and rescue services. The Ministry of Public Security for Northern Ireland, which was the Ministry then responsible for Civil Defence Services, decided, however, after careful consideration, that the Services in Northern Ireland, where the man-power position was not so acute, should remain separate units.

The number of first-aid parties operating in Northern Ireland had by March 31, 1944, reached a total of 384.

FIRST-AID POSTS

It was obvious from the beginning of the organisation of Civil Defence Services that it was desirable that the limited accommodation and staff available at hospitals should be reserved for dealing with injured persons who could be given satisfactory treatment only at hospitals and that essential hospital work should not be hampered through the admission of persons suffering from minor wounds.

It was accordingly decided to establish a number of fixed first-aid posts on similar lines to Regimental Aid Posts of the Royal Army Medical Corps. The intention was that such posts would also provide early treatment for more serious casualties if the hospital serving the area was damaged or if it was a considerable distance from the air raid incident. The posts also proved helpful in classifying and treating casualties so as to ensure that the slightly injured were sent to their homes or rest centres after treatment and to prepare casualties, who required institutional treatment, for removal to hospital with the least possible discomfort.

The layout of first-aid posts followed generally the layout of similar posts established elsewhere throughout Great Britain and provided for the customary three rooms, namely, a reception room, a treatment room and a rest room. In general the units were located in church halls, schools and private houses, though in a few cases buildings were specially erected.

A gas cleansing station was erected at each first-aid post for dealing with persons (other than stretcher cases) who might be contaminated with persistent gas. Stretcher cases were dealt with at casualty receiving hospital gas cleansing stations. (See Chapter 3.)

The staff of the first-aid posts also was generally on the lines of that in Great Britain and provided for a doctor in charge of the medical treatment given at the post. Where possible the staff under his control included a trained nurse, together with a number of female assistants and a number of male volunteers to act as stretcher bearers and general assistants. In order to relieve pressure on the doctor in the treatment room, arrangements were made for the trained nurse who took charge of the reception room to deal with minor injuries (small cuts, etc.).

The final establishment of fixed first-aid posts was 45, of which 15 were authorised in the County Borough of Belfast and five in the County Borough of Londonderry. A few of the larger towns had two posts while other towns had one each.

MOBILE AID POSTS

The purpose of mobile aid posts was to set up a first-aid post at a suitable building near an air raid incident at which there had been numerous casualties. In each area a survey of premises had been made in advance and suitable accommodation had been provisionally selected for the purpose. If premises were not available the unit could, of course, operate in the open.

The post consisted of a van, fitted with removable cupboards and containers in which was stored all the necessary equipment of a first-aid post.

Each post had a medical officer-in-charge, together with a deputy medical officer where it was possible to obtain the services of a second doctor, and usually the staff consisted of a medical officer, a trained nurse and four nursing assistants, a clerk, a male assistant and the driver of the vehicle; plus 100 per cent. reserve.

The equipment carried by a mobile aid van was similar to that held at fixed first-aid posts. Originally the mobile first-aid service was provided with vehicles of the single-decker omnibus type and in a few areas these continued to be used throughout the war. This type of vehicle provided ample room for both staff and equipment but it often proved difficult to operate in narrow streets and it was found necessary at a later date to replace the omnibuses by vans which were easier to drive and could enter areas into which it would have been impossible to bring an omnibus.

The number of mobile aid posts authorised for Northern Ireland was 24, including 10 in the County Borough of Belfast.

MOBILE MEDICAL UNITS

Experience both in England and in Northern Ireland suggested that in vulnerable areas there was need for mobile first-aid units lighter than the mobile aid post but with similar duties. In Belfast and Londonderry, therefore, light units known as mobile medical units were established. Each unit consisted of two vehicles of the private car type, and was designed to provide a trained team, under medical guidance, to deal with casualties (especially trapped casualties) at an incident which did not require a large mobile aid post. The staff attached to these units varied and usually included a trained nurse, a nursing assistant and two male first-aiders.

Belfast had five such units, while Londonderry had four.

FIRST-AID POINTS

When the initial organisation of first-aid posts, fixed and mobile, had been settled it was thought advisable to make further provision for dealing with minor casualties in both the larger centres of population and in rural areas. This was done by the establishment of 'first-aid points' which were units similar to, but having less equipment and a smaller staff than, fixed first-aid posts. Extensive accommodation was not essential and many of the points carried on their work in single rooms.

Each point had a medical officer-in-charge and the authorised staff included six nursing assistants and two male first-aiders, plus an equal number in reserve.

The number of points authorised in Northern Ireland was 159 of which eleven were in Belfast.

AMBULANCES

Before the war, arrangements for ambulance services in Northern Ireland were briefly as follows:

In the County Boroughs of Belfast and Londonderry the County Borough Council in each case maintained and provided an ambulance service, which was run in connexion with the Fire Brigade.

Outside Belfast and Londonderry ambulances were maintained and a service was provided by Poor Law Authorities. There were in general two ambulances available for each Poor Law Union area.

It was obvious when Civil Defence Services were being organised that these ambulance services would be quite unable to cope with the task of providing a casualty ambulance service and it was decided to organise and operate an ambulance service as an adjunct to the first-aid party services referred to above.

It would have been very expensive to obtain entirely new and specially built vehicles and the alternative adopted by most local authorities was to build a light ambulance body on the chassis of a second-hand motor car, preferably with an engine of 14 h.p. or more.

The number of emergency ambulances provided in Northern Ireland varied between 350 and 400. Of this number Belfast had approximately 100 and the City of Londonderry approximately 20.

An emergency ambulance usually provided accommodation for four patients, and in addition to the driver an ambulance attendant travelled on the vehicle.

At least one ambulance was despatched with a first-aid party to each incident. The ambulance was brought to a convenient place near the incident by the party which gave the ambulance attendant information about casualties, both orally and by means of labels attached to the casualties.

In addition to the ambulances a service of 'casualty cars' was provided for 'sitting' cases. It was usual to send one car to each incident to which a first-aid party was despatched.

In the County Boroughs of Belfast and Londonderry the Civil Defence Authorities took over control of the City Ambulance Service which was previously operated by the Local Authority's Fire Brigade Service. The Civil Defence Authority in each case then accepted responsibility for the normal ambulance services in addition to the emergency services, and dealt with the victims of street accidents and accidents at industrial premises, etc.

Ambulances for inter-hospital transfers were provided by the Ministry of Home Affairs by arrangement with the Northern Ireland Transport Board and consisted of converted omnibuses. Full details of the arrangements which were made are contained in Chapter 1.

CO-OPERATION WITH ULSTER HOME GUARD

Each battalion of the Ulster Home Guard had a part-time medical officer and a number of trained stretcher bearers, but the force did not organise a complete medical service to meet the needs which were likely to arise if the enemy succeeded in reaching the shores of Northern Ireland. It relied largely on the assistance which could be made available by the medical services of the Armed Forces and the help which the Civil Defence Services were ready to provide.

The aid given by the Civil Defence Casualty Services provided for the establishment of more than 200 Civil Defence auxiliary first-aid points, situated near key points likely to be objectives of attack by the enemy if he succeeded in landing troops in Northern Ireland. In addition, all other Civil Defence Services, both fixed and mobile, were available to aid the Home Guard in that contingency, and many combined training courses and exercises were held to test the efficiency of the plans for co-operation in action.

The basic plan for dealing with casualties provided that after first aid had been given to a Home Guard casualty, he would be removed behind the lines by stretcher bearers to the nearest medical unit of H.M. Forces, or to a Civil Defence auxiliary first-aid point if there was one within a short distance of the scene of action. If there was no such unit near the place of injury, the casualty was to be taken to a pre-selected casualty clearing station. The further stages in the operational plan provided for the removal of the casualty to hospital or to a first-aid post by either a military or Civil Defence Ambulance unit. Adequate arrangements for the conveyance of messages to Civil Defence Headquarters were an essential feature of the scheme.

The course of the war changed and the Ulster Home Guard were never required to go into action as a fighting force, but during the air raids on Northern Ireland in 1941, certain units gave valuable help to the Civil Defence Authorities and proved the efficiency of this trained and disciplined organisation.

MEDICAL ASPECT OF REST CENTRE ARRANGEMENTS

In pursuance of the general policy to provide rest centres for persons whose homes were seriously damaged or destroyed by enemy action, arrangements were made whereby those requiring medical attention could be dealt with at the rest centre. Certain doctors undertook to visit these centres and supplies of bandages and simple drugs were held. The arrangements provided for one doctor and at least one nurse at each first line rest centre. Their responsibility was to examine all homeless persons who were to be billeted or evacuated. This was done to try to prevent the billeting of persons who might be suffering from illness or might require cleansing treatment. Where necessary, persons could be sent to hospital. Adequate medical supplies for the treatment of the less serious cases of infestation were placed in each first line rest centre. Three large disinfestation centres were established on the outskirts of Belfast to which the more severe cases of infestation could be sent for treatment. These centres also disinfested clothing. In addition there were in Belfast two special medical rest centres—one for the accommodation of eighteen aged and infirm persons not fit to be billeted but not so infirm as to warrant their admission to an institution, and one to accommodate thirty mothers and young babies or expectant mothers. Each of these had a doctor as superintendent and was staffed by volunteers attached to the W.V.S., the St. John Ambulance Brigade and the British Red Cross Society.

MORTUARY SERVICE

The principal task of the Casualty Services was to aid the injured, but each Civil Defence Authority had to make provision for the reverent treatment and burial of the dead. This task was entrusted to a special unit, known as the Mortuary Service, but this unit had, of course, to seek the help and co-operation of all Civil Defence Services.

The Mortuary Service usually operated under the control and direction of the medical officer of health. The plan under which it operated provided that bodies would be suitably labelled at the incident and, unless they were immediately claimed by relatives, would be subsequently conveyed to a properly-equipped mortuary where they would be dressed and prepared for burial.

In this matter, as in nearly all Civil Defence plans, the needs of the several areas in Northern Ireland differed widely. In Belfast a large Mortuary Service was essential; in rural areas and small towns, simple arrangements were considered to be sufficient.

The arrangements in Belfast in the earlier stages of the war provided for a number of small mortuaries. The assistance of certain undertakers in establishing the scheme was obtained, and volunteers were enrolled to undertake duty at a mortuary when required. Coffins and equipment were stored, graves were prepared in the principal cemetery in Belfast and a Mortuary Service Superintendent was appointed.

The heavy raid on the City on the night of April 15, 1941, made necessary an immediate change in the pre-arranged plan for action. There were hundreds of fatal casualties and it was found essential to open a large central mortuary in premises which had previously been used as a market and to convey to those premises the bodies which had been brought in the first instance to the small mortuaries specified in the original scheme.

The task with which the Belfast Mortuary Service was faced on April 16, 1941, was one which tested to the utmost the courage and administrative ability of all connected with that Service. A further severe test was experienced on May 5, 1941, when the Service had to deal with nearly 200 fatal casualties (see Part III, Chapter 13).

The lessons learned in April and May 1941, led to some reorganisation of the Mortuary Service in both Belfast and other areas in Northern Ireland. The Ministry of Public Security prepared a comprehensive code of instructions covering every aspect of the duties entrusted to the Service and steps were taken to improve certain arrangements which had been found to be inadequate to deal with exceptionally heavy raids.

Suitable premises were provided in all vulnerable areas and arrangements were made that they should be used for certain other Civil

Defence purposes during 'lull periods'. The new arrangements in Belfast provided for two large mortuaries (each capable of accommodating several hundred bodies) and the earmarking of other premises which could be used in an emergency.

After May 1941, Northern Ireland was free from attack by the enemy, but it was essential to maintain the Mortuary Service as a stand-by. Volunteers were recruited, instruction in procedure was given and exercises were held to test the working of the arrangements.

GAS CLEANSING ARRANGEMENTS

The arrangements made by the Casualty Services in Northern Ireland for dealing with gas contaminated persons (whether casualties in the ordinary sense or not) followed closely the lines of the arrangements made in Great Britain. They included the establishment of cleansing sections for persons and clothing at each first-aid post, and the training of personnel in the procedure to be adopted in handling gas contaminated casualties.

The only experience of particular interest from the medical point of view in connexion with the treatment of gas casualties arose from an accident which occurred in a training exercise in Belfast in January 1944, when nine boys received mustard gas burns and were admitted to hospital for treatment. None of the boys received any first-aid treatment whatsoever and no other treatment for at least twelve hours and in some cases eighteen hours after contamination.

The report of the medical officer in charge of the patients provided interesting material in that he was enabled to arrive at the following conclusions in regard to the treatment of mustard gas burns:

(1) Itch does not develop for some days and then is very severe. Various dressings were tried and of these calamine cream or oily lotion is most suitable. It does not prevent the burns from becoming septic; and it was concluded that all burnt areas should be covered by a dressing as soon as possible.

(2) Amyl salicylate causes pain and is only of use after a blister has been opened, to dry it up. It can only be used for a few days. For prevention of sepsis, vaseline gauze and sulphathiazole or sulphapyridine powder was useful, but the vaseline tends to keep the ulcer moist. Perhaps an oily calamine lotion with sulphonamide powder in it would be best. In the terminal stages sulphonamide powder alone is effective.

(3) One patient had received liquid in one eye in addition to burns elsewhere and though very ill at first he ultimately did well.

The accident was caused by the liberation of about 2 or 3 lb. of liquid mustard gas in a non-frequented area and it resulted in the equivalent of the occupation of a hospital bed for about 170 days. In addition, those not requiring in-patient treatment were prevented from carrying out their usual activities for a week to ten days. From this one can easily imagine the result of a mass attack by enemy planes each carrying some twenty or more mustard gas bombs of about 100 lb. each.

Photographs were taken of the burns at various stages in treatment and some coloured cine-pictures were obtained. These were retained and used for training purposes.

LESSONS LEARNT FROM THE WORKING OF THE ORGANISATION

Except in the description of the Mortuary Service no mention has been made above of the lessons learnt from the way in which the casualty organisation worked under air raid conditions. The explanation lies in the fact that apart from a few bombs in the Londonderry and in the Bangor-Newtownards area, Belfast alone in Northern Ireland suffered substantial air attacks. Apart from the normal exercises, therefore, the organisation outside Belfast was really not tested at any time. A full account of the work of the Casualty Services in Belfast and comments on the experience gained in raids will be found in Chapter 13 of Part III of this volume.

In general, it can be said that no part of the Civil Defence Services had a more loyal, conscientious or devoted band of workers than the Casualty Services and no history would be complete that did not record this fact. It is worthy of note that the names of four of its Belfast personnel appeared in His Majesty's Honours Lists.

REFERENCE

[1] Report of the Advisory Committee for Air Raid Precautions (Northern Ireland) December 14, 1936—Cmd. Paper (N.I.) No. 178.

CHAPTER 5

MEDICAL AND NURSING PERSONNEL

WHEN war broke out in September 1939, the Ministry, in its first memorandum[1] to hospitals dealt *inter alia* with the matter of medical staff. In the first place hospitals were invited to report to the Hospital Officer any difficulties which might arise out of obligations entered into by their medical staff for service with the Forces of the Crown. The Ministry promised that the Hospital Officer would take steps through the N.I. Medical War Committee of the British Medical Association to provide replacements. This committee, which came into being in November 1937, as an Emergency Committee of that Association, had agreed at the request of the Minister to act as a Medical Advisory Committee to the Ministry, and a full account of its activities under the heading 'Northern Ireland Medical War Committee' will be found later in this chapter.

It was pointed out that where extra demands of a semi-permanent nature fell upon the hospital as a result of the emergency, the Ministry's intention was to arrange, through the Emergency Committee, for the allocation of auxiliary medical staff to the hospital. Where, on the other hand, the extra demand was of a purely temporary or of a specialist nature, arrangements could be made for a mobile team consisting of a surgeon, his assistant and an anaesthetist to attend the hospital to deal with any urgent situation.

CIVILIAN HOSPITAL MEDICAL SERVICE

The memorandum also outlined briefly the Ministry's intention to recruit a civilian hospital medical service from among members of existing medical staffs who were not under engagement for active service with the Armed Forces. Members of this service were to be expected to sign an agreement to undertake routine or special duties entailed in the treatment of casualties in any hospital in Northern Ireland subject to the understanding that consideration would always be given to their personal desires and convenience so far as they could be reconciled with the needs of the situation. The service was to be open to all active and consulting members of the staff of the hospitals whether voluntary or rate-aided.

The memorandum also indicated that it was not proposed to follow the practice in England of employing doctors full-time on casualty work. It was considered that this system would not suit requirements in Northern Ireland. As an alternative the Ministry undertook to provide remuneration on a capitation basis which would be paid to the combined hospital medical staff, and which would be allocated by them at their discretion among the several members concerned.

The mobile teams were to be remunerated on a sessional basis, on the same lines as in Great Britain.

In October 1939, the Ministry issued its memorandum[2] detailing the terms and conditions of service of the new organisation which was given the title Emergency Medical Service.

The memorandum provided that the instructions of the Ministry in regard to duties were to be communicated to members of the Service by certain officers authorised by law (the Minister, Parliamentary Secretary, Permanent Secretary or an Assistant Secretary, or by the Chief Medical Officer or the Hospital Officer of the Ministry).

The Emergency Medical Service, like other Civil Defence Services, experienced a quiet period during the first nine months of the war. In June 1940, however, Northern Ireland came well within the range of the heavy enemy bomber and the requirements of the Service were re-examined. It was obvious that a certain amount of decentralisation of Hospital Officer control was necessary, and in October of that year three part-time Assistant Hospital Officers were appointed to assist the Hospital Officer in the discharge of his duties. They also were given the responsibility for the direction of the Emergency Medical Service, including the assignment of officers, directions as to special duty, etc., etc. Details of the areas which they served will be found in Chapter 2.

Consultants and Specialists. The Ministry also told hospitals that a panel of honorary consultant specialists had been appointed whose services would be available to all hospitals in the Emergency Hospital Scheme and their names and specialities were given in an appendix to the Ministry's circular.[3]

This arrangement was revised a month later by a circular[4] which provided that all members of the Emergency Medical Service who were of recognised consultant status or had specialist training and experience in particular branches of medicine or surgery, would be available for consultation or to exercise their speciality in any civil or military hospital where such assistance was required.

All applications for the services of consultants and specialists were to be made through the Hospital Officer or Assistant Hospital Officer.

Allocation of Additional Honorary Medical Staff to Hospitals. In March 1944, the Hospital Officer issued a circular[5] to hospitals pointing out that in an emergency certain hospitals could not, with their normal medical staff, cope with all the duties which it was planned to give to them, and that better staffed hospitals also would, no doubt, wish to have reinforcements available in the event of additional work falling upon them. He explained that it was, therefore, proposed to enrol in the Emergency Medical Services general practitioners living reasonably near to the hospital who were not normally on the hospital staff, and he invited hospitals to submit names of those whom they wished to have enrolled.

The questionnaire which was issued with the circular was so worded as to suggest to casualty receiving hospitals that in submitting names they should bear in mind the need to allocate a medical officer in an emergency to take charge of each of the following groups of duties:

(a) reception and classification of casualties;
(b) the treatment of casualties suffering from shock and requiring resuscitation;
(c) the treatment of gas contaminated casualties;
(d) the administration of anaesthetics.

The Ministry's suggestions were adopted and each casualty receiving hospital in the province appointed medical officers for these special duties. In a few instances the medical officers were already on the staff of the hospital in a part-time capacity, but most of them were general practitioners from the neighbourhood of the hospital.

COURSES OF INSTRUCTION FOR GAS OFFICERS AND RESUSCITATION OFFICERS

It was obviously desirable that doctors allocated to the special duty of taking charge of a gas cleansing unit should receive special instruction in the treatment of gas casualties, in particular in the duties of a gas officer of a hospital. A course was accordingly arranged by the Ministry for gas officers and was held in August 1941, at the Institute of Pathology, Grosvenor Road, Belfast. It included Lectures by Dr. J. Nairn Hay and Professor Noah Morris and practical demonstrations were given. This course was repeated on October 11 and 18, 1942, for gas officers who had not been appointed until after August 1941, or who had been unable to attend the first course.

Similar considerations applied to the resuscitation arrangements. It was considered desirable to provide training for doctors who undertook the duty of resuscitation officer at a hospital and courses on this subject were held on October 27, 1942, and November 3, 1942, at the Institute of Pathology, Grosvenor Road, Belfast.

All courses were well attended and were generally considered to be well worth while.

APPOINTMENT OF ADDITIONAL WHOLE-TIME MEDICAL OFFICERS AT HOSPITALS

It was clear to the Ministry that even with excellent arrangements for the attendance of honorary medical staff in an emergency, each casualty receiving hospital required at least one resident medical officer who would be available for duty immediately to deal with a sudden influx of casualties.

Several of the casualty receiving hospitals in the country had no such officer and were unwilling, either for financial reasons or lack of suitable accommodation for such an officer, to make an appointment.

The Ministry decided therefore to give financial help in the form of a grant towards the salary of the person appointed.

Where a house officer was appointed the Ministry's grant was at the rate of £120 per annum. Where on the other hand the officer appointed had the grade of resident surgical officer, carrying a salary of £350 or thereabouts, the grant was at the rate of £200 per annum.

Furthermore, where adaptation was necessary to provide suitable accommodation for the new officer the Ministry paid its customary grant towards the cost of the work (i.e. 100 per cent. in the case of voluntary hospitals and 70 per cent. in the case of local authority hospitals).

Under the above arrangements four officers of the grade of resident surgical officer and six house officers were appointed at hospitals throughout the province.

NORTHERN IRELAND MEDICAL WAR COMMITTEE

In the autumn of 1936 the Northern Ireland Branch of the British Medical Association, having noted developments in Great Britain, and in particular the setting up of an Air Raid Precaution Department at the Home Office in London, decided to invite Major H. S. Blackmore, L.R.C.P., Chief Medical Officer to that Department, to address the local branch on the medical aspects of air raid precautions with special reference to gas precautions.

Major Blackmore accepted the invitation and visited Belfast on February 5, 1937, when he addressed the local branch and outlined briefly the air raid precaution arrangements which had been made in Great Britain. He also dealt at some length with the probable nature of gas attacks and methods of combating them.

Emergency Committee of the British Medical Association. At the annual meeting of the branch which followed this address it was decided to follow the lead of the parent body in London and appoint an emergency committee which could be quickly summoned and could take all necessary action on behalf of the local branch in the event of the outbreak of war.

Committee's Activities Prior to the Outbreak of War. The first meeting was held on November 4, 1937, when Dr. R. M. Beath was elected to be chairman and Dr. F. M. B. Allen to be secretary of the committee. As a first step the committee decided to invite individual medical practitioners to state their intentions in a war emergency, and to prepare a register containing this information.

The second meeting which was held on October 10, 1938, was attended by Mr. R. P. Pim, Assistant Secretary of the Ministry of Home Affairs for Northern Ireland, and the Chief Medical Officer of that Ministry (Dr. J. McCloy). Mr. Pim told the committee that the Minister of Home Affairs invited them to act as a medical advisory committee to his Department, and for that purpose to allow additional persons to be added to the committee. The invitation was willingly accepted, and the committee decided to investigate immediately the following matters on which it was clear that their advice would in due course be sought :

(a) the number of hospital beds available in the Province;
(b) a plan for the evacuation of hospital patients from Belfast;
(c) the medical care of civilian air raid casualties;
(d) a plan for dealing with the allocation of medical personnel to meet the demands of the various war-time services.

At their next meeting on February 6, 1939, the committee decided also to prepare a register of nurses and special department staff on the lines of that prepared for doctors.

In April 1939, the committee decided to suggest to the Minister of Home Affairs that he should advise all hospital authorities under his control to order at least two months' reserve supply of medical supplies. He was also advised to arrange for the placing of an order for 3,000 beds together with the necessary bedding.

The committee meeting on May 15, 1939, was attended by officials of the Civil Defence Division of the Ministry of Home Affairs and discussions took place on the medical staffing of first-aid posts, the provision of additional medical staff for hospitals, the training of more nurses and the medical aspect of Civil Defence problems generally.

At their next meeting on June 28, 1939, the committee had before them a memorandum on an emergency scheme for hospital services which had been prepared by their honorary secretary in consultation with the Chief Medical Officer of the Ministry. It was decided to circulate the memorandum amongst the members of the honorary staff of Belfast hospitals and invite their comments.

Outbreak of War. The next meeting was not held until after war had broken out, and took place on September 29, 1939. The title adopted by the committee was now 'The Northern Ireland Medical War Committee', and its functions included advising the Government generally on all medical problems arising out of the emergency and carrying out for Northern Ireland on behalf of the Central Medical War Committee the functions of the latter in advising the Government on the allocation of available medical personnel amongst the different war-time services. Its main function was, of course, to deal with the steady stream of individual applications from doctors for permission to offer their services in one or other of the branches of the Armed Forces. No recruitment of

Northern Ireland medical personnel to the Forces was done without reference to the committee, whose recommendations in each case were forwarded to the appropriate Service Departments through the Central Medical War Committee in London.

From its inception the committee, as occasion demanded, added to its numbers by co-opting representatives of other bodies or associations interested in or connected with medical matters. The honorary secretary to the Northern Ireland Committee (Dr. Allen) had for some time been a member of the Central committee in London and he acted as liaison officer between the two committees.

Supply of Doctors to H.M. Forces. One of the main difficulties facing the Northern Ireland Committee was the fact that conscription did not apply to Northern Ireland. In general an attempt was made to follow the lead of the committee in London in matters of policy, within the limits imposed by the absence of conscription.

Every effort was made to increase the supply of doctors to the Forces. In May 1940, for example, the committee pressed the Central committee to relax so far as Northern Ireland was concerned the rule providing that applicants for commissions in the R.A.M.C. should have had at least six months' service in a hospital. It was pointed out that the number of newly-qualified practitioners coming forward from Queen's University, Belfast, was more than adequate to meet requirements of hospitals in Northern Ireland for housemen and as locum tenens. It was felt that if a newly-qualified doctor from Northern Ireland volunteered for service this condition might be waived; but the suggestion proved unacceptable to the Central committee.

The committee also passed the following resolution in May 1940 —'This committee suggests that in view of the present situation and the urgent demands of the R.A.M.C. no appointment to the University should be made of male medical graduates under 35 years of age who are physically fit and who have not signified to this committee their intention of giving immediate service, exceptional cases to be the subject of consultation between the Faculty of Medicine and the committee'. A copy of this Resolution was forwarded to the Dean of the Faculty of Medicine of Queen's University, Belfast. The University signified its willingness to restrict its appointments accordingly and throughout the period of the emergency consulted the committee before departing in any case from the general rule.

With a view to ensuring that potential recruits for the Forces obtained preference in securing hospital experience many voluntary hospitals of their own free will undertook not to appoint to house officer posts, doctors who were not prepared to sign an undertaking to join the Forces on completion of six months' service. The committee strongly supported this action and pressed the local authority hospitals to do likewise. The Rate Aided Hospital Association readily agreed to co-operate but the scheme had little meaning outside Belfast where the local authority hospitals had so much difficulty in filling their house officer posts that the question of a choice seldom arose.

Conscription. The committee was also mindful of the need in the absence of conscription for protection of the interests of doctors who had joined the Forces, and in March 1941, they passed the following resolutions which were forwarded to the Ministry of Home Affairs for Northern Ireland:

(1) All public medical appointments should be of a temporary nature for the period of the war and twelve months thereafter.
(2) The work of this committee in obtaining doctors for the medical branches of the armed forces would be greatly facilitated if hospital authorities would, in filling resident medical appointments, neither grant any extension of the six months nor appoint doctors who have already had six months' hospital experience elsewhere, without consulting this committee.

No complete guarantee could, of course, be given to doctors that their interests would not be adversely affected by joining the Forces. While therefore, there was little if any actual 'piracy' of the practices of those who joined the Forces, by May 1941, there was a strong feeling in the profession that conscription was the only solution. If conscription could not be applied generally to Northern Ireland, it was felt that it could at least be applied to the medical profession in Northern Ireland. The committee fully endorsed the profession's viewpoint and decided to forward to the Central Medical War Committee a resolution on the subject of conscription which it had received from the local branch of the British Medical Association and which read as follows:

The Northern Ireland Branch of the British Medical Association is of the opinion that conscription should be applied forthwith to the medical profession in Northern Ireland on the same basis as in Great Britain.

It was hardly to be expected, however, that the British Government would entertain the idea of applying conscription to a particular profession and the suggestion was not adopted.

The committee also kept in close touch with the Ministry of Labour in regard to admissions of doctors to panel practice during the war period.

Release of Medical Personnel. In the later period of the war much of the committee's time was devoted to dealing with requests from various bodies for the release of medical personnel from service with the Armed Forces for urgent and vital civilian duties. Where the request was considered reasonable the committee made representations to the Department concerned through the appropriate channels.

Prime Minister's Message. On V.E. Day, 1945, the Prime Minister of Northern Ireland (Sir Basil Brooke) addressed the following letter to the chairman of the committee (Mr. S. T. Irwin)—

Dear Mr. Irwin,

I feel that this is a fitting opportunity for me to express my appreciation and that of the Government, of the services you and your colleagues have rendered to the community during the war in dealing with medical questions.

Your co-operation in this sphere has been most valuable to the Ministry of Labour and other Departments of the Government.

The victory over the European enemy has not been achieved in this total war without the effort and co-operation of all members of the community and I should like to extend to you the cordial thanks of the Government for your essential and valuable contributions.

Yours sincerely,
Basil Brooke

MEDICAL PERSONNEL (PRIORITY) COMMITTEE FOR NORTHERN IRELAND

By the end of 1941, the shortage of medical personnel was acute. The Minister of Health in Great Britain, where the position was even more acute, had in June 1941, appointed a Medical Personnel (Priority) Committee to report on the position generally with a view to securing economy in the employment of medical personnel in H.M. Forces, the Civil Defence Services, and all other medical services including general practice and to ensure that the allocation of personnel amongst these services was fair and equitable. (See Volume I, Chapter 14.)

The Minister of Home Affairs accordingly decided to appoint a similar committee for Northern Ireland and on January 12, 1942, he appointed a Medical Personnel (Priority) Committee for Northern Ireland with Mr. David (afterwards Sir David) Lindsay Keir, M.A., Vice Chancellor of Queen's University, Belfast, as its chairman.

The terms of reference of the committee were 'to consider the most economical allocation of the available medical man-power in Northern Ireland and to promote measures for securing the maximum co-operation to meet civil and service needs in the area, and the elimination of overlapping'.

First Interim Report. The committee held its first meeting on January 13, 1942, and after three further meetings presented its first interim report on June 12, 1942.

In the first place it was pointed out that a survey had been made of the present medical man-power of Northern Ireland in relation to its population, of the number of hospital beds available for various types of case, the demands made on the medical services of the Province as a result of the war-time redistribution of the population, and the number of doctors in Northern Ireland who had volunteered for service with H.M. Forces.

The committee went on to point out that figures supplied by the Central Medical War Committee (Appendix I) showed that of the total number of doctors whose names appeared in the Northern Ireland section of the National Register of Doctors, 20·6 per cent. were then serving with H. M. Forces. It was, at the same time, pointed out that this figure was largely due to the good response which had been made by recent graduates; and that, of the men who had qualified since 1938, 60 per cent. had joined the Forces, the highest percentage in any one year being 72 per cent. and, if women graduates were included, the respective figures were 53 per cent. and 66 per cent. The proportion of medical practitioners per head of the population had also remained favourable in most areas. Tables were appended to the report showing the total number of doctors in Northern Ireland classified according to the type of practice in which they were engaged (Appendix I) and the ratio of population (in thousands) to doctors in active practice in the chief towns and districts (Appendix II).

The committee expressed the opinion that, in view of the demands which were being made by the Forces, it was important that this standard of recruiting should be maintained. At the same time they felt that the civilian health services in Northern Ireland should not be allowed to suffer and they therefore had to consider very seriously the situation which, as a result of recent changes in the medical curriculum at Queen's University, would arise in 1943 if no special steps were taken in anticipation.

They recommended therefore:

(i) That, in view of the demands which were being made upon medical man-power as a result of the war and of the relatively small number of students who under the present arrangements might be expected to graduate in June 1943, the Faculty of Medicine of Queen's University should be asked to consider shortening the present medical course by six months.

(ii) That the Ministry of Home Affairs, in making appointments in the Emergency Medical Service or sanctioning appointments in hospitals where the Ministry's approval is required, should apply the principles adopted and recommended by the Medical War Committee, namely, that appointments to junior resident posts in hospitals should, unless the post had been specifically designated a B post (for definition—see (iii) hereunder), be for a period of six months only and conditional upon a promise by the person appointed to volunteer at the termination of the appointment for service with the Armed Forces. This rule should apply to both men and women except where there are special circumstances, for instance, physical disability, which debar the individual from military service.

(iii) That, in view of the reduced numbers of students who were likely to graduate after June 1942, and in order to safeguard those hospitals whose needs are most pressing, junior resident posts at hospitals should be designated either as A appointments, i.e. held by a newly qualified practitioner for a period of six months only, or B appointments, i.e. held by a doctor with previous experience for any period of longer than six months. Normally the B posts at each hospital would be filled by prolonging the tenure of office of one of the existing A appointments.

(iv) That, in order to protect the practices of doctors who have joined H.M. Forces, and to encourage others to join the Ministry of Labour should be asked to consider the possibility of withdrawing for the duration of the war the present general right of entry into National Health Insurance practice, particularly in the case of doctors who had qualified since 1937.

Action taken on the Interim Report. With regard to the recommendation at (i) above, Queen's University immediately agreed to shorten the medical course by six months, thereby accelerating the supply of medical men to the Forces. The University also with the same general object in view discontinued all courses of post-graduate study for the duration of the war. The teachers engaged in instruction for these courses agreed instead to help in giving instruction to newly qualified doctors who were spending their six months in hospital before proceeding on service. The University was naturally reluctant to take this step in view of its position as a centre of higher medical studies, but the decision was unanimously reached in order to promote the national war effort.

With regard to (iv) the Ministry of Labour agreed to withdraw for the duration of the war in the case of doctors who qualified since 1937 the existing general right of entry into National Health Insurance practice.

With regard to recommendations (ii) and (iii) the Ministry of Home Affairs, while in sympathy with the intention of the committee, was doubtful of its powers to impose the conditions suggested in recommendation (ii) upon persons accepting appointments under local authorities. After it had obtained legal advice on the matter, the Ministry decided that in the absence of conscription in Northern Ireland it could not impose these conditions and its action was accordingly limited to the issue of a circular[6] asking for the co-operation of local authorities in the matter. A schedule detailing the A and B posts recommended for local authority hospitals by the Medical Personnel (Priority) Committee was enclosed with the circular.

A similar circular[7] was forwarded to voluntary hospitals enclosing a schedule of the A and B posts which the committee had recommended for voluntary hospitals, and asking that voluntary hospital authorities would have regard to these recommendations when appointments were being made.

Second Interim Report. The committee then turned their attention to the allocation of medical man-power between civil and Service needs with a view to determining to what additional extent the Services might draw upon existing medical man-power without detriment to the civil needs of Northern Ireland.

Five further meetings were held and on May 26, 1943, the committee presented their second interim report.

It was pointed out in the report that the committee had had before them a comparative statement showing the ratio of general practitioners to the civil population in (*a*) England and Wales, (*b*) Scotland, (*c*) Northern Ireland (Appendix II), and that they had attempted to arrive at an assessment in terms of man-power of the differences affecting practices in Northern Ireland as compared with other areas. The statistics available showed that the birth rate, infant mortality, and, for persons insured under the National Health Insurance Act, morbidity, were higher in Northern Ireland than in England and Wales or Scotland. As regards density of population, Northern Ireland occupied an intermediate position between England and Wales on the one hand and Scotland on the other. That was so also as regards frequency of prescribing under the National Health Insurance Act. The committee was also of opinion:

(*a*) that although statistics were not available there was reason to believe that relief was afforded to the general practitioner in Great Britain to a greater extent than in Northern Ireland because of the better midwifery service there and the more general adoption of adequate maternity and child welfare schemes; and

(*b*) that doctors in Great Britain tended to employ non-professional assistants such as dispensers and receptionists more than doctors in Northern Ireland.

Furthermore, they drew attention to the fact that one-third of the general practitioners in Northern Ireland had to fulfil obligations, imposed by the existence of the dispensary system, which had no counterpart in Great Britain.

Their conclusion, therefore, was that, leaving out of account the sparsely populated areas of Scotland, there was probably more work for a doctor per thousand of the population in Northern Ireland than in Great Britain.

The committee also submitted a table showing under seven main headings the number of doctors in Scotland and Northern Ireland. (Appendix III to this chapter.) They drew attention to the fact that the number of doctors of all classes in Scotland excluding those in the Services, those who were also dentists, and those retired from practice, was about five times the corresponding number in Northern Ireland, while the civil population of Scotland was then approximately 3·75 times that of Northern Ireland.

An examination of the numbers under the various headings showed that in proportion to population Northern Ireland had about the same number of general practitioners but considerably fewer doctors classified as consultants and specialists or holding hospital appointments or employed in the Public Health, Teaching and Research Services, and that the difference was most marked in hospital appointments. The conclusion which the committee reached therefore was that the general practitioner in Northern Ireland was being called on to do work which was done in Scotland by the hospitals or specialists or by the Public Health Services.

The report added that with the object of bringing the problem down to the individual practice the committee had examined the lists of insurance practitioners under the National Health Insurance Scheme, particularly those with less than 500 persons on their panel and had made such allowances as it could on the information available in respect of the private practice, dispensary, civil defence, or other duties of the doctors on the list.

The committee had also under consideration the possibility of making available a number of civilian practitioners, particularly consultants and specialists, for work in military hospitals in Northern Ireland in the event of it becoming necessary to withdraw existing Army medical personnel for service elsewhere. They reported that they had given this matter careful study but had reached the conclusion that, having regard to the fact that consultants and specialists were then fully employed and had commitments as members of the Emergency Medical Service in addition to their obligations to the civilian population, it did not appear to be practicable to provide from their ranks staff for the military hospitals.

At the same time the Minister was assured that consultants and specialists generally had undertaken to act in military establishments or to accept Service sick and wounded in civil hospitals in the event of their services not being required to the same extent for the Emergency Medical Service and normal hospital routine. The Service authorities had also been assured of their full co-operation in emergency and a liaison with the Deputy Director of Medical Services had been established to ensure the utmost assistance.

The tentative conclusion reached by the committee was that, if conscription were to be applied to the medical profession in Northern Ireland, it was unlikely that any further contribution would be possible from amongst the consultants and specialists, doctors holding hospital appointments or those engaged in the Public Health, Teaching or Research Services. A substantial contribution could, on the other hand, be called for from amongst general practitioners. In the opinion of the committee it would have been possible to maintain an efficient medical service for the civilian population under war conditions and at the same time to release for service in H.M. Forces at least fifty doctors engaging in practice as principals and also a small number of assistants. This took no account of the further release which would follow the application of conscription to the civil population as a whole.

In the ordinary course the younger doctors would be the first to be called up under conscription. In Northern Ireland a number of young men had entered practice in recent years and had shown no desire to respond to the appeals which had been made from time to time for volunteers for the Services. Some of them had small and apparently unremunerative practices. The steps which had been taken to close the panel and to restrict petrol prevented any growth in their numbers, but they presented a serious obstacle to the medical profession in Northern Ireland playing its full part in the war effort.

The calculations of the committee assumed a redistribution of the practices of the fifty or more doctors who joined the Forces so that those remaining in civil life would be fully occupied. The practical difficulty in the way of achieving this on a voluntary basis lay in the fact that the men who would probably respond would have to leave their practices to those, who, if conscription were applied, would be the first to go. It would have been impossible to defend a position under which young men would be provided with a practice and living, which they could not otherwise acquire, at the expense of patriotic and public-spirited older men.

Action on Second Interim Report. When the committee forwarded its report to the Minister it asked that the findings of the committee contained in this and its previous report should be brought to the notice of the medical profession as it was felt that they were not generally aware of the facts. To that end they recommended that copies of the reports be forwarded to the various medical journals with a request for publication of the committee's findings.

They also asked that steps should be taken to apprise the Service Departments of the committee's findings as to the availability of medical man-power in Northern Ireland.

Finally, they asked that copies of the report be forwarded to the Central Medical War Committee and the Northern Ireland Medical War Committee.

Action was taken by the Ministry on the lines suggested by the committee and the Ministry wrote to the medical journals drawing attention to the percentage of Northern Ireland doctors serving in H.M. Forces, and commented that the figures, though relating to a system of purely voluntary enlistment, were nevertheless reasonably close to those for the rest of the United Kingdom and added that it should also be borne in mind that a substantial number of Northern

Ireland medical men were recruited into the Forces elsewhere than in Northern Ireland.

Further Activities of the Committee. The committee held only one further meeting, which was called for the purpose of reconsidering their recommendations with regard to the number of A and B appointments at hospitals in the Province. Revised recommendations were forwarded to the Ministry and were communicated to voluntary hospitals[8] and to local authority hospitals[9] by circular.

The chairman of the committee continued to keep in touch with the activities of the corresponding committee for Great Britain with a view to calling further meetings of the Northern Ireland Committee should this be considered desirable but no occasion arose for further meetings.

Prime Minister's Message. On V.E. Day, 1945, the Prime Minister of Northern Ireland (Sir Basil Brooke) addressed a letter in the following terms to the chairman.

> My dear Vice Chancellor,
> May I take this opportunity to thank you and the members of your committee both personally and on behalf of the Government, for the valuable services which you have rendered during the war just now so successfully concluded so far as the European enemy is concerned.
> The problems arising in a total war demand for their solution the co-operation of all members of the community and I want you to know that the work of your committee has been keenly appreciated.
>
> Yours sincerely,
> Basil Brooke

CIVIL NURSING RESERVE

In June 1939, the Ministry of Home Affairs, having regard to the possible urgent need for additional nursing personnel, decided to constitute in Northern Ireland a Civil Nursing Reserve on the same lines as in Great Britain.

A circular[10] conveying this information was issued to all local authorities on June 28, 1939. It outlined the arrangements to be made for the training in nursing of any trained or partly trained persons who offered nursing services.

The Civil Defence Division of the Ministry undertook the administration of the Reserve and invited application for enrolment of nurses in the following categories:

1. *Trained Nurses* who were required to be either State Registered or to hold a Certificate of General Training given by a recognised training school before June 30, 1925.
2. *Assistant Nurses* who were required to be partially trained and have at least 2 years' experience in hospital work.

3. *Nursing Auxiliaries* who were required to have Certificates in First Aid and Home Nursing and to have had fifty hours' practical experience in hospital.

There was a good response to the call for volunteers and many trained and assistant nurses were enrolled straight away. There was also a good response from nursing auxiliaries. As a result of good work done in pre-war years by the St. John Ambulance Brigade and the British Red Cross Society many volunteers came forward who had already obtained their certificates. The Ministry arranged for them to obtain fifty hours practical hospital experience and, subject to a satisfactory report from the matron, they were enrolled as nursing auxiliaries.

Applicants who had not the necessary certificates were referred to their local authorities for training. Each of these authorities had a working arrangement with the Joint Committee of the St. John Ambulance Brigade and the British Red Cross Society whereby the committee provided the training and the local authority met the expense. Those who were successful in obtaining certificates were then referred to hospital for training and, subject to a satisfactory report from the matron they also were enrolled as nursing auxiliaries.

Applicants for enrolment could offer their services for hospital duties or first-aid duties or district nursing duties. If they had other obligations, e.g. home obligations, they were free to offer part-time service only. The arrangements provided for payment for full-time service at the same rates as those paid to members of the Reserve in Great Britain but part-time service was not paid for.

Each hospital in the Ministry's Emergency Hospital Scheme was allotted a quota of Reserve nurses and auxiliaries who had offered to serve in hospital. Each nurse or auxiliary so allotted was called in for periods of refresher training by the matron of the hospital to which she was allotted.

Members who offered to serve at first-aid posts were allocated by their appropriate local authority to first-aid posts situated within their area. These members were expected to attend the periodical practices which were carried out under the supervision of the medical officer or the senior nurse in charge of the first-aid post.

In the earlier stages of the war the Reserve was only called upon for whole-time nurses at first-aid posts in Belfast. It was not until the air raids in Belfast in 1941 that any real call was made upon the Reserve. Following these raids a number of Belfast hospitals engaged full-time nurses from the various categories of the Reserve, and country hospitals dealing with large numbers of evacuees also called up a number of the personnel allotted to them.

By the end of 1942, during which year the Ministry opened its Emergency Hospital at Purdysburn, Belfast, and established its

Emergency Evacuation Camps throughout the province, a considerable number of Reserve nurses were employed on full-time duty.

Appointment of Nursing Officer. In January 1942, the Ministry considered it essential to strengthen the Civil Nursing Organisation by the appointment of a Nursing Officer for Northern Ireland with functions corresponding to those of the Regional Nursing Officer in Great Britain (see Volume I, Chapter 15). Miss Florence E. Harrison, M.B.E., the Ministry's Inspector of boarded-out children, a State Registered Nurse, was temporarily seconded to this special work which she undertook in addition to her duties as the Ministry's Inspector. Miss Harrison assisted hospitals on the spot with their nursing problems, encouraged the recruitment of nurses to the Reserve and assisted generally in the promotion of training of nursing auxiliaries. She was responsible for the initiation of the schemes, referred to hereunder, for the employment of a mobile team of nurses with a guaranteed twelve months' employment and the institution of the six weeks' intensive course of training for nursing auxiliaries.

Mobile Unit. Experience at the time of the raids had shown that the arrangements for the calling up of nurses for service in hospitals in an emergency was not entirely satisfactory and did not work out as planned. It was found that the immediate nursing assistance which was so essential in such conditions was not always forthcoming and the Ministry decided, therefore, to establish a mobile team of trained nurses from the Reserve. The arrangement provided for a guarantee of twelve months' employment to be given to each of these nurses on the understanding that they would agree to work in any hospital in Northern Ireland coming within the Ministry's Emergency Hospital Scheme or in any of the Ministry's Evacuation Camps. By arrangement with the hospitals concerned the nurses were dispersed to various hospitals throughout the province and were regarded as supernumerary to the hospitals' nursing establishment.

The Ministry, which bore the full cost of the salaries of these nurses, was satisfied with the working of this scheme and while there were happily no further raids on Belfast the arrangement came to be regarded by the Ministry as an essential feature of any scheme for the provision of additional nursing services in a war emergency.

Intensive Course of Training for Nursing Auxiliaries. In 1943 the Ministry began to experience a shortage of nursing auxiliaries for the replacement of wastage in this grade of staff at the Emergency Hospital and in the evacuation camps. There was still a small number of nursing auxiliaries being trained by local authorities in this period but the numbers coming forward were so small as to make the courses infrequent and therefore slow and recruits were not coming forward in anything like sufficient numbers.

In September 1943, therefore, the Ministry decided that the only solution was to institute a special intensive course of training for applicants who expressed a desire to be considered for immediate employment.

Arrangements were made for such applicants to receive six weeks' intensive training at the Ministry's Emergency Hospital. During this period they were provided with free board, lodging and uniform and with 10s. per week pocket money. When trained, subject, of course, to satisfactory service, they were guaranteed full-time employment at ordinary civil nursing reserve rates.

It was made clear to local authorities in the Ministry's circular[11] to them on the subject that the arrangement was in addition to and not in substitution for the normal training arrangements for which local authorities were responsible.

Experience of the working of this course showed that it was an ideal method of recruiting those desirous of immediate employment and excellent results were obtained.

Statistics. The number of persons enrolled in the various categories of the Reserve during the period of the war were as follows:

1. Trained nurses	.	867
2. Assistant nurses	.	436
3. Nursing auxiliaries	.	3,222

Of the above the following numbers were employed on whole-time duties for various periods during the emergency:

Trained nurses	.	118
Assistant nurses	.	34
Nursing auxiliaries	.	310

The story thus far has inevitably been one of the Nursing Reserve which came into being to supplement the normal peace-time nursing services of the community. It is but right, however, to acknowledge that the greater part of the magnificent work done by all nursing staffs of hospitals throughout the war fell upon their permanent staffs. This is particularly true of the period of the heavy raids.

A tribute must also be paid to all nurses either permanent or temporary in other spheres including those in the Public Health Service and in district nursing for the valuable contribution they made during the war years.

REFERENCES

[1] Min. of Home Affairs C.D. Memorandum No. 21, September 1, 1939.
[2] Min. of Home Affairs C.D. Memorandum No. 63, October 1939.
[3] Min. of Public Security Circular No. H.41, October 24, 1940.
[4] Min. of Public Security Circular No. H.55, November 26, 1940.
[5] Min. of Public Security Circular No. H.O.1, March 25, 1941.
[6] Min. of Home Affairs Circular No. P.H.359, November 23, 1942.
[7] Min. of Home Affairs Circular No. M.124, November 30, 1942.
[8] Min. of Home Affairs Circular No. M.182, December 8, 1943.
[9] Min. of Home Affairs Circular No. P.H.389, December 10, 1943.
[10] Min. of Home Affairs Circular C.D. No. 2, June 28, 1939.
[11] Min. of Home Affairs Circular No. M.164, September 7, 1943.

APPENDIX I

CLASSIFICATION OF NATIONAL REGISTER OF MEDICAL PROFESSION IN NORTHERN IRELAND

(Figures furnished by Central Medical War Committee, January 1942)

Classification	Men				Women				Services	Totals
	Up to 41 years of age	41–50 years of age inclusive	51–69 years of age inclusive	70 years of age and over	Up to 31 years of age	31–40 years of age inclusive	41–50 years of age inclusive	Over 50 years of age		
1. Consultant or Specialist	14	23	26	7	—	2	5	2	13	92
2. General Practitioner	175	137	115	37	8	25	27	4	78	606
3. W.T. Voluntary Hospital	21	—	—	—	7	1	1	—	65	95
4. W.T.L.A. General Hospital	11	3	—	—	—	1	—	—	21	36
5. W.T.L.A. Specialist Hospital	12	5	3	—	1	—	1	1	5	27
6. W.T. Public Health Service	4	6	8	1	1	5	2	—	7	35
7. W.T. Government Service	2	6	10	—	—	—	1	—	—	19
8. W.T. Teacher	5	1	4	—	1	—	1	—	2	14
9. W.T. Research	3	—	1	—	1	—	—	—	1	5
10. W.T. non-Government Post	—	—	2	—	—	—	—	—	2	2
11. Dentist	3	1	29	49	—	4	11	14	5	7
12. Retired	1	1	29	49	—	4	11	14	5	114
13. Unclassified	66	5	2	4	27	8	6	—	52	170
Totals	317	187	200	98	46	46	55	21	252	1,222

Percentage in Services 20·62

APPENDIX II

STATISTICS SHOWING RATIO OF PRACTITIONERS TO POPULATION IN SCOTLAND, WALES AND NORTHERN IRELAND PRE-WAR AND AT APRIL 1942

		Population	Medical personnel		Population	
			Total	G.P.	Per doctor	Per G.P.
Scotland	Pre-war	4,993,126	5,501	2,444	908	2,043
	April 1942	4,779,758	4,222	1,985	1,132	2,408
Wales	Pre-war	2,420,586	1,830	1,065	1,322	2,273
	April 1942	2,471,564	1,510	932	1,637	2,652
Northern Ireland	Pre-war	1,279,745	1,222	606	1,047	2,112
	April 1942	1,275,832	955	565	1,336	2,258

APPENDIX III

STATEMENT PREPARED BY THE NORTHERN IRELAND MEDICAL WAR COMMITTEE IN MARCH 1943

	Northern Ireland		Scotland	
	Number of doctors (excluding doctors in Services)	Percentage of total	Number of doctors (excluding doctors in Services)	Percentage of total
		per cent.		per cent.
1. Consultants and specialists	79	8·27	440	9·35
2. General practitioners	565	59·16	1,985	42·19
3. Hospital appointments	67	7·02	651	13·84
4. Public Health, Teaching and Research Services	64	6·70	441	9·37
5. Dentists	5	·52	76	1·62
6. Retired	101	10·58	694	14·75
7. *Unclassified	74	7·75	417	8·87

* 'Unclassified' included newly qualified doctors not then in any particular post of whom a number were awaiting appointments in the Services, and a small number of doctors, particulars of whose activities were not known to the Northern Ireland Medical War Committee.

CHAPTER 6
THE LABORATORY SERVICES
PATHOLOGICAL SERVICES AT HOSPITALS AND PUBLIC HEALTH LABORATORY SERVICES

BEFORE the outbreak of war Pathological Services in Northern Ireland hospitals were inadequately developed. The Institute of Pathology of Queen's University, Belfast, which adjoined the Royal Victoria Hospital, provided a service for several hospitals in Belfast, but as a teaching unit was, of course, not an appropriate centre for the examination of routine samples. Professor J. H. Biggart, the holder of the Chair of Pathology, and Dr. N. C. Graham, the University's Lecturer in Bacteriology, had their headquarters at the Institute, and were always willing to receive and examine samples of special interest and to deal with cases where diagnosis was difficult.

By arrangement with the authorities of the University, a complete floor of the Institute of Pathology was used as a laboratory by the Royal Victoria Hospital. The hospital employed a senior pathologist, together with junior staff, and Professor Biggart acted as Honorary Consulting Pathologist.

The Belfast City Hospital had a small laboratory, which was controlled and supervised by one of the visiting part-time medical officers. A senior technician and two junior technicians were employed, and Professor Biggart acted as Honorary Consulting Pathologist.

The Mater Infirmorum Hospital had a small laboratory under a whole-time pathologist with Professor Biggart as Honorary Consulting Pathologist.

The Municipal Fever Hospital at Purdysburn, Belfast, had a small laboratory which was a branch of the Municipal Public Health Laboratory, the main portion of which was housed in certain rooms set aside for the purpose in Queen's University, Belfast. The work of the laboratory at Purdysburn was supervised by a whole-time bacteriologist who had charge of the complete Belfast Municipal Laboratory Service.

A few other hospitals had some laboratory equipment and undertook the routine examination of certain specimens, but none of them had a pathologist on their staff and the range of their services was extremely limited.

It was the practice, therefore, of all hospitals to consult one or other of the following in regard to major laboratory problems:

Professor J. H. Biggart, Institute of Pathology, Belfast.
Professor W. J. Wilson, Queen's University, Belfast.
Dr. J. A. L. Johnston, Londonderry.

The first named in general was consulted in regard to specimens of special interest from a teaching point of view.

Professor W. J. Wilson, on the other hand, who held the Chair of Public Health at Queen's University, Belfast, had been permitted by the Senate of the University to carry on a private practice as bacteriologist and clinical pathologist, and had been allowed to use the University Laboratory as the centre of his private practice. The County Councils of Antrim, Armagh and Down entered into contracts with him under which he supplied a Bacteriological Service for a fixed salary per annum, together with fees for certain special examinations. In addition, hospitals in these counties sent him clinical specimens for a pathological report.

Dr. J. A. L. Johnston, who practised as a physician and consulting clinical pathologist in Londonderry, held a similar appointment as bacteriologist to several Local Authorities in the North-west area of the Province. For the purposes of this appointment he had established a private laboratory, and hospitals in the North-west area, i.e. the counties of Fermanagh, Londonderry and Tyrone, also sent clinical specimens to him for pathological reports.

It will be observed that both in Belfast and in Londonderry public health and clinical work were done in the one laboratory. When war broke out, therefore, and consideration was given as to what action the Government should take in regard to laboratory services, the provision of public health and clinical laboratory facilities was treated by the Department as one problem.

In the latter half of 1941 Dr. J. McCloy, the Chief Medical Officer of the Ministry of Home Affairs, invited Professor Biggart to convene a meeting of all laboratory workers of standing in the province and to submit their considered recommendations in regard to laboratory services generally.

Professor Biggart convened several meetings of laboratory workers including Professor W. J. Wilson of Belfast and Dr. J. A. L. Johnston of Londonderry and on December 30, 1941, they forwarded a report to the Minister of Home Affairs which contained the following recommendations:

1. That an Emergency Public Health Laboratory Service be instituted in Northern Ireland, which shall be responsible for such bacteriological work as is required for the diagnosis, prevention and control of human infectious disease, excluding venereal diseases. The service will not include the examination of milk samples for the purposes of the Milk (Special Designations) Order, the chemical examination of foods, or the routine chemical examinations of water samples.

2. That the present existing laboratories be included in this Emergency Service, as much of their present work as pointed out above is the direct result of the war emergency.

3. That the present existing laboratories be strengthened in technical personnel, the new personnel to be a charge on the scheme.

4. That the cost of materials necessary to meet the additional work accruing as the result of the present state of emergency in the existing laboratories, be defrayed.

5. That inside this Emergency Public Health Laboratory Service a consultant service should be developed. This consultant service is to be available to those engaged in routine work in the Emergency Public Health Service.

6. That the medical and technical personnel of the Emergency Public Health Service including the consultant service should be reserved by the Government, and that certificates to that effect should be issued. It may here be pointed out that even with reservation of all available bacteriologists Northern Ireland relative to England or Scotland will still be very much under-staffed on a basis of population.

7. That arrangements should be made whereby alternative laboratory accommodation should be immediately available in the event of the destruction of any of the laboratories included in this service. Where necessary this should be done by the Government, or by the Local Public Health Boards at the Government's instigation. We regard the principle of continuity of the Public Health Service as a *sine quâ non* of any such service in this state of emergency.

8. That the Government provide as soon as possible a stock of laboratory apparatus so that in the event of destruction of a constituent laboratory by enemy action this continuity of service shall be assured.

9. That in order that the most recent information relative to infectious disease in the province should be available to the members of the service the heads of laboratories should notify Professor Biggart of their diagnosis of infectious disease, who will then be responsible for the notification of all the laboratories. It is felt that cases of such disease diagnosed in military hospitals should also be notified.

The final paragraph of the report stressed the desirability of creating a modern public health laboratory system on the advent of peace.

The committee's recommendations were accepted and the Ministry undertook:

(*a*) to establish an Emergency Public Health Laboratory Service;
(*b*) to provide and equip the emergency laboratory at Whiteabbey Sanatorium which would come into use in the event of damage to or destruction of the laboratories in Belfast or in the event of an outbreak of infectious disease;
(*c*) to provide a reserve stock of laboratory equipment;
(*d*) to purchase the necessary materials;
(*e*) to pay the cost of overhead expenses and technical staff required for the preliminary work;
(*f*) to enrol certain existing bacteriologists and to pay annual honoraria to them for their services.

The authorities of Queen's University, Belfast, undertook responsibility for the due functioning of the Service in an emergency and appointed Professor W. J. Wilson to direct it.

The improved premises and laboratory equipment at the Whiteabbey Sanatorium were placed by the Government at the disposal of that hospital and were used as a tuberculosis laboratory during the latter years of the war.

In accordance with the arrangements under (c) above the Ministry purchased three sets of side-room laboratory equipment, and stored them at hospitals on the outskirts of Belfast for use if required in an emergency. These sets were brought into use during the war at certain hospitals which desired to develop a laboratory service for minor routine examinations. One set was issued to the Belfast City Hospital and helped to supplement their existing facilities. One went to the Tyrone County Hospital which had previously had no laboratory facilities of any kind, and with the assistance of Dr. J. A. L. Johnston of Londonderry a limited service was provided at the hospital during the latter part of the war. The remaining set was stored at the Ministry's Emergency Hospital at Purdysburn, Belfast. When this hospital was transferred to Musgrave Park, Belfast, in April 1945, suitable premises were made available for laboratory purposes. Additional equipment was purchased and a full-time laboratory medical officer and two technicians were appointed. In due course this laboratory was competent to undertake all the normal laboratory work of the hospital and only exceptionally the hospital had to use the laboratory facilities of the Royal Victoria Hospital which the authorities of that hospital made available.

The authorities of the Ards District Hospital also decided during the war to provide a laboratory service. Equipment was purchased and a part-time pathologist was appointed to take charge of the work.

In March 1944, the surveyors appointed by the Nuffield Provincial Hospital Trust to survey Hospital Services in Northern Ireland presented their report[1] to the Northern Ireland Regional Hospital Council. The report recommended:

(a) a considerable increase of laboratory staff, medical and technical, both in Belfast and in the provinces, to meet the needs of the hospital service;

(b) that whatever system was inaugurated should link up the provincial hospitals with laboratory work in Belfast, and that the Professors of Pathology, Bacteriology, Hygiene and Bio-Chemistry should be available for expert advice in their respective subjects; and

(c) the establishment by the Regional Council before the end of the war of a small Committee of Inquiry to examine laboratory needs and to recommend a method of meeting them.

Before the war ended the Ministry had many consultations with interested parties and had reached the conclusion that a reorganisation of both public health and clinical laboratory services was urgent and essential. It was decided that, pending the establishment of a comprehensive Health Service for Northern Ireland which would be bound to make provision for a greatly improved laboratory service, the Ministry ought to make some temporary arrangements to cover the interim period. Plans to give effect to this decision were under consideration when the war came to an end and formed the basis of interim arrangements which came into operation in due course.

BLOOD TRANSFUSION

The blood transfusion arrangements in Northern Ireland before 1939 were confined to Belfast where a Blood Transfusion Service under the leadership of Sir Thomas Houston operated throughout the period between the two great wars. It was, of course, an entirely voluntary organisation and largely depended on the prompt response of enrolled donors when a demand for blood was necessary. The Service did not maintain a large 'blood bank' and the preparation of plasma and other blood products had not been introduced before 1939.

When the danger of war became serious there were consultations between the Belfast Blood Transfusion Service and the Ministry of Home Affairs and the following statement was issued by Sir Thomas Houston in August 1939:

'It has been realised that if a war emergency should arise and if Northern Ireland becomes the target of enemy bombers, thousands of blood transfusions would be required and that the present arrangements for this life-saving treatment would prove totally inadequate.

'The Ministry of Home Affairs for Northern Ireland and the Blood Transfusion Committee are convinced of the urgency of this matter. A joint meeting of the representatives of the Ministry of Home Affairs and the Transfusion Committee have discussed this problem and are making arrangements for such an emergency.

'The plan agreed upon is as follows:

'(1) An urgent appeal should at once be made for volunteers. Such volunteers should only be required to give their blood for transfusion purposes in the event of a war emergency.

'(2) The blood of such volunteers should be tested, as soon as possible, at two centres—the Mater Infirmorum Hospital and the Royal Victoria Hospital—and the blood type of each volunteer should be determined.

'(3) From these volunteers the universal donor types should be selected. When an emergency arises, relays of such universal donors should be requisitioned, their blood taken and stored for use when required.

'This plan in the case of an emergency means a great saving of time both to the donor and to the expert who is responsible for the blood transfusion. A similar scheme adopted in the recent Spanish war proved of great value and thousands of lives were saved by blood transfusion.

'Although it is impossible to say in the event of war whether Northern Ireland would be frequently bombed or not, the scheme suggested by the committee means that Northern Ireland, without much inconvenience to the volunteers, will be prepared for such an emergency, provided, of course, that the response to the appeal is adequate. The blood testing is a very simple procedure, absolutely painless, and requires only a few minutes.'

The expanded war-time service outlined above came into operation and as a result of more than a year's work about 4,000 donors were enrolled. Professor J. H. Biggart (Professor of Pathology) became Director of the Service and was aided by his colleagues in the Institute of Pathology and by other interested persons. In Londonderry, Dr. J. A. L. Johnston undertook to act as honorary director of a transfusion service for the North-west area (Derry, Tyrone and Fermanagh) and under his leadership the initial emergency arrangements made progress.

In May 1940, the Ministry of Home Affairs in its circular[2] to local authorities, hospital authorities and doctors generally on the organisation and co-ordination of emergency casualty services referred amongst other things to the arrangements which had been made in Belfast and Londonderry, and said that blood transfusion apparatus would be supplied as part of the hospital equipment which the Ministry was supplying to hospitals for emergency purposes. Hospitals were, however, to make their own arrangements for giving transfusions.

A further circular[3] on the subject was issued on June 4, 1940, detailing arrangements for the messenger and supply service which had been organised for the distribution of stored blood to casualty receiving hospitals. It drew attention at the same time to the need for arrangements to replenish the store of blood in the Central Blood Bank, and advised local hospitals to secure the names of local donors. When these had been obtained, they were to send the list of names to Professor J. H. Biggart, who was in charge of the services in Belfast. Professor Biggart would in due course make arrangements with the medical officer of each hospital for the donors to be tested by a team from the Institute of Pathology and for the collection of blood when necessary from those who were found to be suitable.

At the inception of these emergency arrangements the Government agreed to make a grant of £50 to aid the work, but it was soon obvious that this sum was inadequate and in October 1940, it was arranged that the Government should, in lieu of the £50 grant, pay a sum of £150 per annum to the Institute of Pathology and a sum of £50 per annum to

Dr. J. A. L. Johnston, with effect from September 1, 1939. In addition the Government agreed to pay for certain equipment. Subject to these grants, the emergency services continued to be voluntary.

Shortly before the first air raid on Northern Ireland, it was realised that further developments of the Blood Transfusion Service were necessary and appropriate action was taken.

In May 1941, it was agreed that Professor Biggart (with Dr. N. C. Graham, as Deputy) and Dr. Johnston should become salaried blood transfusion officers of a reorganised Emergency Transfusion Service financed by the Government as part of the general emergency arrangements, that the cost of professional assistance and the running expenses of necessary laboratory work should be met and that certain equipment should be provided at hospitals and in reserve centres. The duties of the two transfusion officers were defined as the administration of the Service in their respective areas, the recruitment and bleeding of donors, the processing of blood into citrated plasma, the maintenance of adequate reserves of plasma in Belfast and Londonderry and its distribution to hospitals and the supply to hospitals of the necessary prepared apparatus for giving blood transfusions.

The reorganised Service then came into operation and superseded the previous voluntary arrangements. The result was that hospitals generally soon relied entirely on the emergency service to meet their blood transfusion requirements. By this time (late in 1941) the Belfast area donor panel contained about 10,000 names and about 3,000 donors had been recruited in the North-west area.

In August 1942, the following information was conveyed by circular[4] to hospital authorities in Northern Ireland by the Ministry of Home Affairs:

EMERGENCY HOSPITALS BLOOD TRANSFUSION SERVICE

By means of a new filtration process, it is now possible to obtain supplies of filtered plasma which will keep almost indefinitely without refrigeration. It will, therefore, now be possible to place stocks of filtered plasma at all hospitals coming within the Emergency Hospital Scheme, and arrangements are being made for this to be done.

This Ministry understands that as a result of the absorption of existing blood transfusion services into the E.M.S. Blood Transfusion Service, hospitals generally are experiencing difficulties in obtaining supplies of blood for the treatment of civilian patients, and proposes accordingly to make these reserves available to hospitals for the treatment of civilian patients. A small charge will be made to cover the cost of processing, administration, and other expenses involved. This charge has been fixed provisionally at 10/- per bottle of blood or £2 2s. per bottle of blood plasma supplied. It is hardly necessary to point out that this figure is not intended to cover the cost of the provision of blood, which, as hospitals will be aware, is supplied by volunteer donors.

Hospitals requiring supplies of fresh blood should communicate with their Regional Resuscitation Officer who will arrange for supplies to be sent to them.

Hospitals which require plasma and already hold E.M.S. stocks are authorised to draw therefrom such amounts as they require.

In 1944 the number of transfusions given was over six times the number given before the inception of the reorganised Emergency Service.

In January 1945, a despatch rider service (provided by the National Fire Service) was instituted for the delivery of whole blood from the blood banks in Belfast and Londonderry to hospitals in Northern Ireland. This information was conveyed to hospitals by circular.[5]

In the year ended March 31, 1945, 805 bottles of blood and 483 bottles of plasma were issued to hospitals, nursing homes or general practitioners.

The Surveyors of the Nuffield Provincial Hospitals Trust in their Report on the Hospital Services of Northern Ireland (published early in 1945) stated:

> Blood transfusion is a method of treatment which has grown in importance greatly in the last ten years. Before the war, it was used but rarely in Northern Ireland, but under the Emergency Medical Service there has been a wide development which should not be allowed to lapse when the war ends. The value of the service has become obvious, not only in cases of war injury, but in many types of civil damage and disease. We need only mention here such conditions as internal haemorrhage, as from gastric or duodenal ulcer, post-partum haemorrhage, and the severe anaemias. For some conditions, filtered blood (liquid plasma) is preferable—notably extensive burns and surgical shock—and as plasma will keep under suitable conditions for six months as against a week for whole blood, and as it does not need typing, it is a valuable adjunct to a transfusion service.
>
> There should be no insuperable difficulty in maintaining a transfusion service in Ulster, but it needs direction and apparatus. The ideal form of storing plasma involves drying under special conditions; for this purpose the apparatus is costly (about £10,000 at the moment) and the cost of maintenance is so high that dried plasma costs three times as much to provide as does liquid plasma. The great advantage of the dried form is that it keeps indefinitely, and can be made available for use in a very few minutes.

The report also contained detailed recommendations as to how the service should be administered.

The Health Advisory Council which had been appointed by the Minister of Health and Local Government considered the matter in the early part of 1945 in connexion with their study of the particular problem of maternity services required for the province. They recommended *inter alia* that a permanent civilian Blood Transfusion Service should be developed out of the Emergency Scheme built up during the war.

The recommendations of the Surveyors of the Nuffield Provincial Hospitals Trust and those of the Health Advisory Council were carefully considered by the Ministry of Health and Local Government and when the war finished, plans were already well advanced for the institution of a peace-time service on the lines recommended by them.

PENICILLIN

In the early part of 1944 the Ministry of Health in London arranged for a limited quantity of penicillin to be made available for the treatment of civilians. Because of the great scarcity of supplies it was necessary to institute a system of rationing so that the drug would be used only for the treatment of conditions for which it was known to be suitable. The arrangements therefore provided for the allocation of so many units to each area throughout the United Kingdom, and Northern Ireland obtained an issue of twenty million Oxford units.

The allocation of the supply within each area to individual patients was to be done through the University Medical School and as far as Northern Ireland was concerned was undertaken by the Faculty of Medicine at Queen's University, Belfast.

The medical faculty appointed a Penicillin Committee to deal with individual applications but was not able to provide the necessary secretarial staff to deal with them. The Ministry of Health and Local Government arranged accordingly with the University that the staff of the Ministry which dealt with the Emergency Hospital Scheme should undertake the duty of collecting information on particular cases for submission to the Penicillin Committee. Hospitals and general practitioners were to be informed of the arrangements which had been made and asked to send their applications to the Hospital Officer of the Ministry (Dr. W. A. Brown) who would arrange a twenty-four hour telephone service. On September 8, 1944, the Hospital Officer issued a circular[6] to all hospitals and to all general practitioners outlining the way in which the scheme would work.

A further circular[7] on the subject was issued on October 3, 1944, modifying the original scheme in the light of experience. This circular specified a limited number of hospitals at which penicillin would be made available, and detailed the conditions which such hospitals would be required to fulfil before they could be approved for the purpose. It also outlined the method of application for supplies and detailed the particular infections for which supplies of penicillin would normally be made available. The decision on each application was, however, still to be taken by the Penicillin Committee.

The circular emphasised that application would have to be made personally by the hospital physician or surgeon in charge of the patient, and indicated that it would be necessary to confirm any telephone messages on the subject by the completion of a form to be despatched direct to the Penicillin Committee.

The scheme also provided for filling in a form on the completion of the treatment of each patient and for the return of any unused penicillin.

Since the drug would be available only in approved hospitals, medical practitioners were asked to take steps to secure the admission of patients requiring penicillin to one of these hospitals.

In many cases it was essential for supplies of the drug to be made available at short notice, for the purpose of urgent treatment, and under arrangements made with the National Fire Service, despatch riders of that Service undertook to convey supplies of the drug by motor cycle to where they were required.

The scheme worked quite satisfactorily and continued to operate in this way up to the end of the war.

REFERENCES

[1] The Survey of the Hospital Services of Northern Ireland (published by the Northern Ireland Regional Hospitals Council).
[2] Min. of Home Affairs Circular No. C.D. 175, May 20, 1940.
[3] Min. of Home Affairs Circular No. C.D. 197, June 4, 1940.
[4] Min. of Home Affairs Circular No. M.105, August 5, 1942.
[5] Min. of Health and Local Government Circular No. H.O. 141, January 25, 1945.
[6] Min. of Health and Local Government Circular No. H.O. 112, September 8, 1944.
[7] Min. of Health and Local Government Circular No. 115, October 15, 1944.

PART III

The Air Raids on Industrial Centres 1940-2

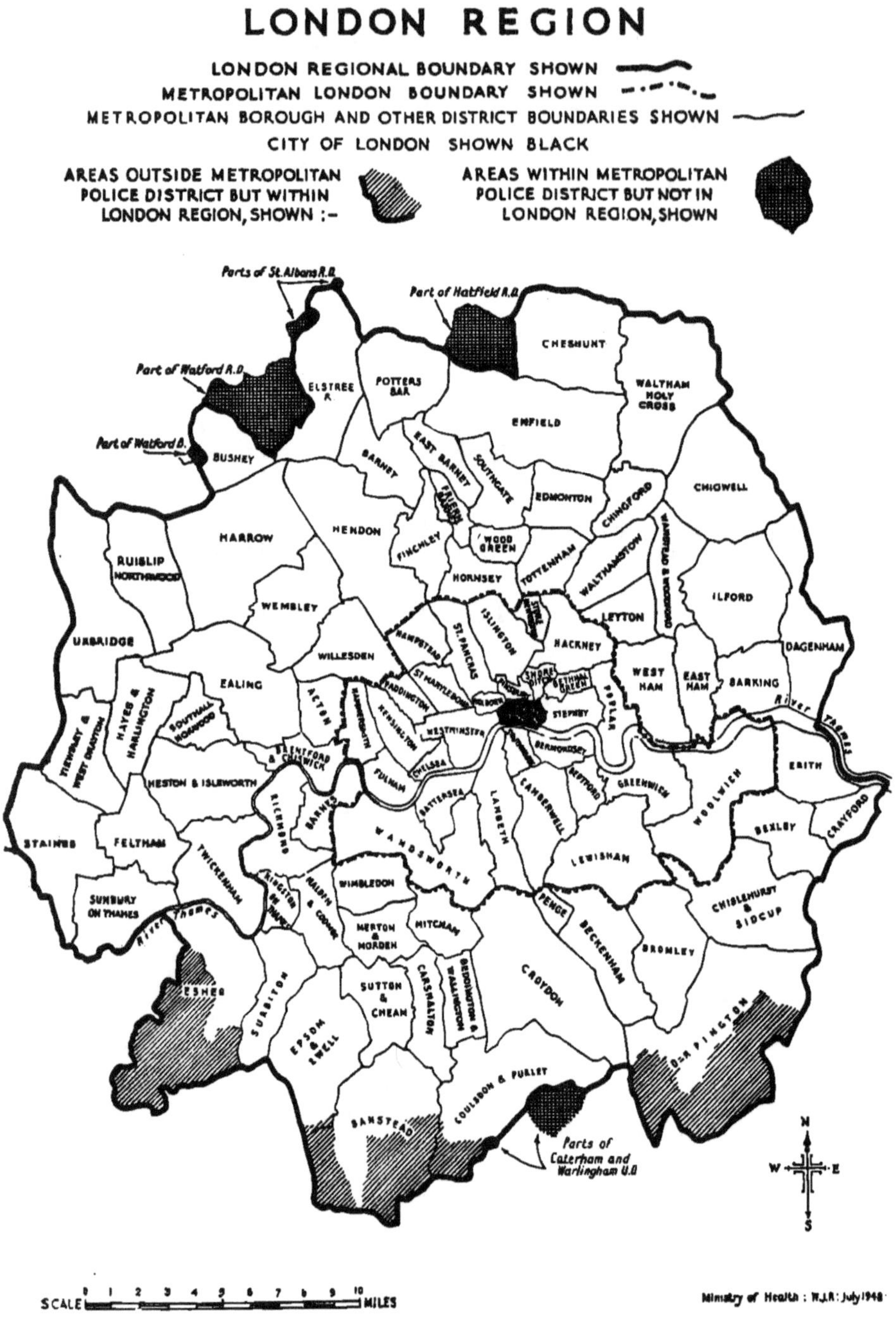
LONDON REGION
LONDON REGIONAL BOUNDARY SHOWN
METROPOLITAN LONDON BOUNDARY SHOWN
METROPOLITAN BOROUGH AND OTHER DISTRICT BOUNDARIES SHOWN
CITY OF LONDON SHOWN BLACK
AREAS OUTSIDE METROPOLITAN POLICE DISTRICT BUT WITHIN LONDON REGION, SHOWN :-
AREAS WITHIN METROPOLITAN POLICE DISTRICT BUT NOT IN LONDON REGION, SHOWN
Parts of St. Albans R.D.
Part of Hatfield R.D.
Part of Watford R.D.
Part of Watford B.
CHESHUNT
WALTHAM HOLY CROSS
ELSTREE R.
POTTERS BAR
ENFIELD
BUSHEY
BARNET
EAST BARNET
SOUTHGATE
EDMONTON
CHINGFORD
CHIGWELL
HARROW
HENDON
FINCHLEY
WOOD GREEN
TOTTENHAM
WALTHAMSTOW
ILFORD
RUISLIP NORTHWOOD
WEMBLEY
HORNSEY
LEYTON
UXBRIDGE
WILLESDEN
HAMPSTEAD
ST. PANCRAS
ISLINGTON
HACKNEY
DAGENHAM
EALING
WEST HAM
EAST HAM
BARKING
ACTON
PADDINGTON
ST. MARYLEBONE
HOLBORN
SHOREDITCH
BETHNAL GREEN
STEPNEY
POPLAR
River Thames
HAYES & HARLINGTON
SOUTHALL NORWOOD
KENSINGTON
HAMMERSMITH
WESTMINSTER
BERMONDSEY
YIEWSLEY & WEST DRAYTON
BRENTFORD & CHISWICK
FULHAM
CHELSEA
HESTON & ISLEWORTH
BATTERSEA
LAMBETH
CAMBERWELL
DEPTFORD
GREENWICH
WOOLWICH
ERITH
RICHMOND
BARNES
STAINES
FELTHAM
WANDSWORTH
LEWISHAM
BEXLEY
CRAYFORD
TWICKENHAM
SUNBURY ON THAMES
KINGSTON ON THAMES
MALDEN & COOMBE
WIMBLEDON
PENGE
BECKENHAM
CHISLEHURST & SIDCUP
MERTON & MORDEN
MITCHAM
BROMLEY
ESHER
SURBITON
SUTTON & CHEAM
CARSHALTON
BEDDINGTON & WALLINGTON
CROYDON
ORPINGTON
EPSOM & EWELL
COULSDON & PURLEY
BANSTEAD
Parts of Caterham and Warlingham U.D.
N
W
E
S
SCALE
0 1 2 3 4 5 6 7 8 9 10
MILES
Ministry of Health : W.J.R.: July 1948

CHAPTER 1

LONDON 1940-1

Compiled from contributions received from the Chief Medical Officer, London County Council, the Medical Officer of Health, City of London and the Medical Officers of Health of the Metropolitan and extra-Metropolitan Boroughs and other Local Authorities within the London Region, and from the Sector Hospital Officers of the London Sectors.

AREA AND POPULATION

BEFORE taking up the story of the heavy enemy attacks on London from September 1940 to May 1941, a brief reference must be made to the area and population of the battle zone and the distribution of the population within that zone, as the comparative casualty returns have all been based on these figures.

Area. The area covered by the Metropolitan Police District has been arbitrarily chosen as the area of operations, although many urban and rural localities outside its boundaries, especially to the east and southeast, were subjected to intermittent and ill-directed, but, nevertheless, heavy attacks. The statistics issued from time to time by the Ministry of Home Security about the weight of attack on London and the resulting casualties all referred to this area.

The London Region (Region 5) for civil defence purposes did not exactly coincide with the Metropolitan Police District, for the boundaries of the latter in some places passed through areas controlled by the peripheral local authorities, whereas the London Region, for obvious administrative reasons, either included or excluded the whole of the local authorities concerned. These small divergencies were as follows:

The Metropolitan Police District included small parts of Watford, urban and rural, St. Albans, Hatfield, Warlingham and Caterham, which were outside the London Region, but excluded parts of Esher, Epsom and Ewell, Banstead, Coulsdon and Purley and Orpington, which were included in the London Region. As both groups were wholly rural in character, the casualty returns were probably little affected by this arrangement of boundaries. (See Map.)

As regards the hospitals, this area included all the casualty clearing hospitals and some of the advanced base hospitals, the base hospitals being situated further afield.

The area of the Metropolitan Police District was 691·84 sq. miles or 442,777·6 acres. The inner zone consisted of the City of London (675 acres) and the 28 metropolitan boroughs in the administrative County of London, comprising 116·95 sq. miles or 74,848 acres or more than one-sixth of the total area. The metropolitan boroughs varied very much in size, the two largest being Wandsworth (9,107 acres) and Woolwich

(8,282 acres) and the smallest Holborn (406 acres) and Finsbury (587 acres).

In the outer zone there were 66 extra-metropolitan local authorities consisting of county boroughs, boroughs, urban district councils and rural district councils. The largest of these wholly within the Metropolitan Police District were the county borough of Croydon (12,672 acres) and the urban district of Harrow (12,558 acres) and the smallest, the urban districts of Penge (770 acres) and Friern Barnet (1,341 acres).

Population. The pre-war population of the Metropolitan Police District or Greater London was 8,575,700, of which 4,062,800 resided in the 28 metropolitan boroughs. The population of the City of London varied between about 10,000 persons at night and 500,000 in the daytime. By June 1940, through evacuation, recruitment for the Services and transfer of labour, the populations of Greater London and the County of London, including the City, were estimated to have fallen to 7,591,600 and 3,213,700 respectively (the City to 6,120). During the heavy enemy attacks these populations continued to fall by the evacuations, so that by the end of June 1941, the population of Greater London was estimated at 6,194,000 and that of the administrative County and City 2,259,800. The number of persons at risk, therefore, was greatly reduced at the end of the raids, especially in the inner zone, the whole population being less by about 2·4 millions, of which 1·8 millions came from the inner zone areas.

Of the metropolitan boroughs, Wandsworth was the largest in area and also in population, the pre-war estimate of which was 340,000. The next highest populations were those of Islington (292,000) and Lambeth (273,000). By September 1940, the numbers for the three boroughs had fallen to 278,000, 221,000 and 214,000 respectively. Holborn (34,000), Stoke Newington (51,000) and Chelsea (56,000) had the lowest populations, which by September 1940, had fallen to 26,000, 41,000 and 38,000 respectively.

In the whole of the outer zone the population decreased by about 600,000, as compared with a fall of 1,800,000 in the much smaller inner zone. In the outer zone, the largest populations were those of West Ham County Borough (254,900), Croydon County Borough (243,400) and Willesden Borough (203,734) and the smallest populations were in Waltham Holy Cross Urban District (7,164), Barnet Rural District (10,300) and Potters Bar Urban District (15,000).

Density of the Population. The density of the population in the inner zone as a whole in September 1940, was about 40 persons per acre. The most densely populated of the boroughs by September 1940, were Southwark (88 persons per acre), Bethnal Green (86 per acre) and Shoreditch (82 per acre), while in Woolwich, Greenwich and Wandsworth the density was 15, 19 and 31 persons per acre respectively. In the City of London the density at night time was under 9 per acre, but about 747 in the daytime. Of course, the population of the whole inner zone was much higher by day than by night, while that of the outer zone was correspondingly lower. In the outer zone the density of the population was under 12 persons per acre for the whole area.

In the areas of the 66 local authorities of the outer zone the population was densest in West Ham County Borough (54 per acre), Tottenham Borough (49 per acre) and Leyton Borough (45 per acre) and was most sparsely distributed in Waltham Holy Cross Urban District (0·7 per acre), Barnet Rural District (1·2 per acre) and Cheshunt (2·0 per acre).

The population figures given above, other than the pre-war figures, can only be considered approximate; they are based on the ration books issued by the Ministry of Food within the London area.

THE ORGANISATION OF THE EMERGENCY MEDICAL SERVICES
HOSPITALS

As mentioned in Volume I, Chapter 1, in September 1938, when the outbreak of war seemed imminent, the London County Council were asked to recommend one of their medical staff as Hospital Officer for the London Region and Dr. J. Nairn Dobbie was seconded for this duty and appointed to fulfil the same functions on behalf of the Ministry as those of the Hospital Officers already appointed to the provincial Regions. These functions had previously been carried out by the Ministry of Health without any specific appointment having been made. In June 1939, Wing Commander A. J. Brown, Medical Branch, R.A.F. (ret.), was appointed as an extra Hospital Officer for the London Region.

At the outbreak of the war a staff of Assistant Hospital Officers was attached to the London Region as in the case of the provincial Regions.

The Sector Organisation. As stated in Volume I, Chapter 2, this special scheme was devised for the hospital treatment of air raid casualties in the London Region. The London Region was divided into ten Sectors, each based on one or more of the large teaching hospitals at the apices of the Sectors in the Central Metropolitan area. These, together with other suitably situated voluntary or local authority hospitals, provided the primary casualty clearing hospitals. In the extra-metropolitan area certain hospitals were fully equipped and staffed as advanced base hospitals and others as local casualty clearing hospitals; the base and special hospitals were established for the most part in the adjacent provincial Regions into which the wide ends of the Sectors extended.

Ten Sector Group Officers recommended by the representative committee of the medical schools referred to in Volume I, Chapter 2, and ten Deputy Group Officers recommended by the London County Council to represent the interests of the local authority hospitals were approved by the Ministry of Health and appointed.

After these appointments were made, the Hospital Officer, London Region, was no longer concerned with the working of the hospitals except in a few minor matters, but the title, which thus became a misnomer, was not altered until a later period (see Volume I, Chapter 5). The hospitals were administered as in normal times by the owning authority, subject only to the reorganisation and supervision necessary to ensure that the requirements of the Ministry of Health for the efficient treatment of casualties were carried out. These functions were exercised on behalf of the Ministry by the Sector Group Officers, whose work was controlled and co-ordinated by Mr. C. Frankau, C.B.E., D.S.O., F.R.C.S. (afterwards Sir Claude Frankau), Director, Emergency Medical Services, London and Home Counties, on behalf of the Director-General, Emergency Medical Services.

Under the Sector scheme the established hospitals carried on their normal activities, but certain hospitals were selected to fulfil specific functions in the Emergency Hospital Scheme. Those designated as casualty clearing hospitals were required to maintain a specific number of beds unoccupied and available for casualties. This number on the average was about two-thirds of the total bed accommodation. These beds were kept empty by transferring casualties to the outer zone hospitals as soon as conditions permitted, but the Group Officers could also transfer to the outer zone as many ordinary civilian patients as they considered necessary, should a large number of beds be required. These civilian patients, as well as casualties, were sent to beds in the large hospitals equipped as base hospitals outside the London area or to others equipped as hospitals for the treatment of special diseases; thus the estimated requirements for casualties were duly maintained.

The Group Officers also arranged for the distribution of medical staff and equipment between the inner and outer zone hospitals in order that every hospital could adequately fulfil the functions allotted them in the scheme.

Besides keeping the casualty beds empty, certain hospitals were not allowed to use beds in top floor wards and in other unsuitable wards because of their vulnerability. These beds were described as 'frozen' beds.

It is obvious that, in order to bring the Sector organisation into being, an enormous amount of work was thrown on the Sector Group Officers and their staffs.

A graphic picture of the nature of the task which had to be undertaken is provided in an extract from a report by Dr. W. J. Pearson, Group Officer, Sector IV:

'On the sunny afternoon of August 28, 1939, two doctors, two hospital matrons and four laymen, with a number of lady clerks and typists left their modern hospitals and offices in London and met at an old house in Stanmore, Middlesex. There were no furniture, typewriters, or telephones. Lumps of the ceiling mingled with the dust on the floor. There was no gas or electric light and the natural light of the sun had difficulty in getting through the dirt on the windows; even the fireplaces were broken. The front garden had once been beautiful, but was a mass of weeds. The house appeared to have been unoccupied for years. It was now to become a hive of industry—the headquarters of Sector IV of the Emergency Hospital Services for London.

'The new staff looked at one another and at the dirty old building. They had been summoned by telegram; they came; they saw; they wondered. This team of pioneers, however, was soon active. A month after their arrival the building really looked a hive of industry, with telephones, typewriters, despatch riders, office furniture, files, etc., and bright fires burning in the grates. Much had been accomplished in a short space of time.

'Air raid casualties are not, however, treated at Sector headquarters and the real problem before the pioneers was to provide hospital beds for their share of the air raid casualties of the magnitude of 30,000 a day, which they had been informed was the estimate of the destructive power of Goering's gang. How they rushed round—always with that Damocles' sword of 30,000 casualties *a day* hanging over their heads.

'With the outbreak of the war on Sunday, September 3, 1939, the beds in the hospitals in Central London had been considerably reduced and a large staff and a great deal of equipment had been sent to hospitals and buildings which were to become hospitals, on the outskirts of the county and as far out in this Sector as Berkhamsted in Hertfordshire. Some of the first problems as regards accommodation were (*a*) to convert that delightful mansion, the Bonar Law College at Ashridge into a general hospital capable of doing surgical work; (*b*) to adapt for general hospital purposes an old Poor Law school at Leavesden, taken over by the London County Council in 1930 and used since then as a mental hospital; (*c*) to upgrade for general hospital purposes a Poor Law establishment at Hemel Hempstead, which had probably been used only for chronic sick and infirm types; (*d*) to adapt fever hospitals, like the North-western, Hampstead and Hendon Infectious Diseases Hospitals, so that they could deal with acute surgical cases.

'Looking back one is amazed at the keenness and the industry of the authorities of these establishments. Beautiful saloons at Ashridge with painted ceilings and oak panelled walls became hospital wards. Plumbing work was quickly undertaken in the large garage where it was at first thought that we might have to accommodate patients, if the casualties occurred as early and became as heavy as was contemplated. The canteen was rapidly converted into an operating theatre.

'At Leavesden all kinds of jobs were speedily undertaken by the staff and a good general hospital was soon in being. Looking now at the nurses' dining room one would not imagine that it had been an old swimming bath and that under the floor boards was the old swimming pool.

'The use of the Poor Law Institution at Hemel Hempstead involved the provision of more baths, bed-pan sluices, etc., and an operating theatre, but again this and many other improvements and adaptations were undertaken by the Institution authorities and general hospital cases were very soon being treated there.

'As, however, the accommodation became available for air raid casualties, it was found that there were no air raid casualties to treat! There were, however, the civilian sick still in need of treatment and arrangements were soon made for ordinary hospital patients admitted to hospitals in Central London to be evacuated to the new and upgraded hospitals on the periphery for treatment by up-to-date London hospital staffs.

'In addition to an ordinary general hospital service, special units—orthopaedic, neurosurgical, etc.—had been established at selected hospitals in the Sector and these special units became available, not only for hospitals in Sector IV, but also for certain other emergency hospitals. It also soon became apparent that accommodation in the emergency hospitals would be required for military casualties from overseas as well as from troops under training in England; arrangements were accordingly made at Ashridge, Hemel Hempstead, Leavesden and the country branch of the Royal National Orthopaedic Hospital, Great Portland Street, at Stanmore, Middlesex for the accommodation of these casualties. The first military convoy of 190 patients arrived at Leavesden on December 12, 1939.

'Two other problems confronting us throughout the period under review were staff and equipment. With the outbreak of the war there were many better remunerated services of national importance open to nursing and domestic staffs. These, together with the recruitment for the Services, made the staffing of the emergency hospitals a difficult problem.

'As regards equipment there is no doubt that the loss of many European sources of instruments, etc. presented the Ministry of Health with a very formidable problem in providing the hospital equipment needed for the very large increase in the number of hospital beds and it is appreciated that Dr. J. G. Johnstone, who was in charge of the supplies of hospital equipment at the Ministry accomplished an enormous amount of work in the face of very great difficulties. (See Vol. I, Chapter 9—Medical Supplies.)'

Anyone who has had any experience of the work entailed in adapting a large country house for use as a hospital and fully equipping it, will realise the enormous amount of labour thrown on many organisations; and when it is considered that this work was going on at hundreds of hospitals in outer London and in the rest of England and Wales, the results achieved in such a short time are worthy of the highest praise to all concerned. It should be realised that not only the Ministry of Health, but the medical departments of the combatant Services also were demanding the material for enormous expansion and were therefore competing for labour, technical experts and supplies. With the establishment of the Ministry of Supply, however, quotas were allotted as supplies became available.

In the other Sectors, the work of bringing emergency hospitals into being proceeded as rapidly and efficiently as in Sector IV, so that by the summer of 1940, although full expansion had not been attained, it could be said that the hospitals were ready to meet the strain which it was expected might be thrown upon them at any moment.

Medical Personnel. The staffing of these outer hospitals of the Sectors, even at this early stage of the war, presented considerable difficulties.

The skilled nucleus provided by transferring a large proportion of the staffs of the inner zone hospitals to the emergency hospitals, was supplemented by the recruitment of newly qualified medical officers as house physicians and house surgeons; but it must be realised that the staff was not on the peace-time scale and, in fact, as the war went on, the difficulties of adequately staffing the emergency hospitals increased. (See Vol. I, Chapter 14.)

Nursing Personnel. At the outbreak of the war, with the closing down of a large number of beds in the inner zone hospitals, nursing staffs could be transferred to the peripheral hospitals.

At first, with no casualties occurring, the nurses became bored and dissatisfied, and this frame of mind was aggravated by the poor conditions in their billets and other trials. Consequently, many nurses resigned from these hospitals to join the Services and to work in the Provinces; some even accepted posts abroad. This depletion of the originally transferred nursing staffs was followed by the gradual recall of transferred nurses to their London hospitals to staff wards and departments which were gradually reopened to meet the reflux of the civilian sick into the hospitals. While the number of nurses in peripheral hospitals diminished, the work steadily increased as the arrangements for the evacuation of civilian sick from the inner zone hospitals came fully into operation, and large numbers of troops were admitted, first from the surrounding areas and eventually in large numbers from France. The result was that both inner and outer zone hospitals were 65 per cent. full and the whole area had a hospital population of about 30 per cent. more than in peace-time.

In the early months of the war, the deficiency in nurses could always be made up by calling upon the fully trained Civil Nursing Reserve allotted to the Sectors, together with a large number from the Auxiliary Nursing Services; but it was found by experience that a considerable proportion of these nurses returned to their peace-time duties, and others would not work in the peripheral hospitals. The result was that by the time the heavy attacks on London began no hospital had a fully adequate nursing staff. (See Volume I, Chapter 15.)

Ancillary Services. The development of the ancillary services, such as the pathological laboratory service, blood transfusion service, etc., is given fully in the special chapters on the subject. (See Volume I, Part II.)

The Group Officers. The names of the Sector Group Officers during the period of the heavy raids is given below:

Sector   I. Russell John Howard, Esq., O.B.E., M.S., F.R.C.S., London Hospital.

Sector   II. Arthur Griffiths Maitland-Jones, Esq., O.B.E., M.C., M.D., F.R.C.P., London Hospital.

Sector III. Sir William Girling Ball, F.R.C.S., St. Bartholomew's Hospital.
Sector IV. Wilfred John Pearson, Esq., D.S.O., M.C., D.M., F.R.C.P., University College Hospital.
Sector V. Harold Esmond Arnison Boldero, Esq., D.M., F.R.C.P., Middlesex Hospital (afterwards Sir Harold Boldero).
Sector VI. Sir Charles McMoran Wilson, M.C., M.D., F.R.C.P. (afterwards Lord Moran), St. Mary's Hospital.
Sector VII. Anthony Feiling, Esq., M.D., F.R.C.P., St. George's Hospital.
Sector VIII. Professor Owen Lambert Vaughan S. de Wesselow, D.M., F.R.C.P., St. Thomas's Hospital.
Sector IX. John Bowman Hunter, Esq., C.B.E., M.C., M.Ch., F.R.C.S., King's College Hospital.
Sector X. Professor Thomas Baillie Johnston, C.B.E., M.D., Guy's Hospital.

Table I contains the number of casualty hospitals in each Sector, their total accommodation, frozen beds and average number of beds estimated to be available in the inner and outer zones respectively at the beginning of September 1940. The table does not include suspended hospitals:

TABLE I

Hospitals

Sector number	Inner zone				Outer zone		
	Number of active hospitals	Total number of active beds	Number of frozen beds in active hospitals	Number of casualty beds including reserves	Number of active hospitals	Total number of active beds	Number of casualty beds including reserves
I } II }	16	7,070	2,328	3,110	40	8,159	6,642
					17	6,518	4,050
III	10	2,452	1,170	1,526	12	4,690	3,931
IV	11	2,214	730	1,283	14	4,616	3,642
V	1	322	302	200	11	3,611	2,670
VI	4	1,997	856	950	16	6,595	3,741
VII	12	4,382	1,113	2,819	16	3,413	2,022
VIII	9	2,732	1,220	1,450	31	6,219	4,735
IX	4	1,631	426	855	34	11,811	9,268
X	13	3,888	1,882	2,270	25	11,489	10,172
Totals	80	26,688	10,027	14,463	216	67,121	50,873

CIVIL DEFENCE CASUALTY SERVICES

The history of the evolution of the Civil Defence Casualty Services in London is fully dealt with in Volume I, Chapter 7. The organisation in being by the autumn of 1940 is summarised below.

First-aid Posts. The first-aid posts, fixed and mobile and the first-aid points, as in the provincial Regions, were under the direct control of the local authorities and the supervisory control of the Hospital Officer of the Region and his staff.

Of the 1,911 fixed first-aid posts and 988 mobile first-aid posts in England and Wales in the summer of 1940, 392 fixed first-aid posts and 187 mobile units were in the London Region. There was therefore an average of four fixed first-aid posts and two mobile first-aid posts to each local authority. The average area served by each first-aid post was about 1,236 acres or 2 sq. miles; in the more congested areas there was one post to 500 acres or less—in Hammersmith for example there was one post to each 78 acres and one to 108 acres in Bethnal Green, but in some of the local authorities of the outer zone, the number of posts varied between 1 to 4 sq. miles and 1 to 20 sq. miles. Each post served an average population of 16,629. In 10 local authorities there was one post to less than 10,000 of the population and in 34 local authorities there was one post between 20,000 to 55,000 people.

The 95 local authorities concerned, 29 central and 66 peripheral, were formed into nine groups for mutual aid purposes in civil defence.

Personnel. The personnel attached to the first-aid posts consisted of one medical officer in charge of each post together with a rota of general practitioners who had volunteered for any duties in connexion with the posts which might be required of them. The rest of the personnel consisted of 579 trained nurses, 8,971 whole-time auxiliary nurses and 10,780 part-time volunteers.

Ambulance Services. In September 1938, when Dr. Nairn Dobbie was appointed Hospital Officer for the Region, the London County Council seconded Captain A. E. Reed, their officer in charge of the London Ambulance Service, as Chief Ambulance Officer for the London Region and under his supervision the emergency ambulance services were developed.

In November 1940, Captain Reed was succeeded by Mr. A. G. Naldrett, also seconded by the London County Council for this duty. Mr. Naldrett further developed and organised the ambulance services in the Region and remained in charge until the termination of hostilities. The Chief Ambulance Officer was responsible to the Hospital Officer for the operation of the inter-hospital transport and in supervisory control of the Civil Defence Ambulance Service.

Civil Defence Ambulance Service. To provide for the transportation of air raid casualties from streets and houses to hospitals and first-aid posts, the Government required scheme-making authorities (in the County of London, the London County Council), as an integral part of their casualty organisation, to establish and organise local ambulance services for the conveyance of casualties.

The London County Council was responsible for the organisation and administration of the Civil Defence Ambulance Service in the Administrative County of London but this service for the removal of casualties from incidents to hospitals or first-aid posts was directed by the Controller of the appropriate metropolitan borough.

For mutual support between local authorities the Region was divided into nine operational groups (subsequently reduced to eight). The London County Council area comprised Groups 1–5; Middlesex (with portions of Hertford) Group 6; and parts of Essex, Kent and Surrey within the London Region area formed respectively Groups 7, 8 and 9. At each Group Centre there was a Group Ambulance Officer, with assistants, acting under the direction of the Chief Ambulance Officer.

Although the primary purpose of the Ambulance Service was to convey air raid casualties from incidents to hospitals and first-aid posts there were many other uses to which the service was put such as the conveyance of:

(a) homeless from bombed houses;
(b) patients to and from hospitals and institutions;
(c) military sick between Army Units and static military and other hospitals;
(d) physically defective children to and from school;
(e) accident and emergency cases when the peace-time ambulances were fully occupied;
(f) medical officers and consultants on emergency work;
(g) midwives.

In the spring of 1940 the establishment of the Ambulance Service in the Region was:

Ambulances	2,264
Cars	1,516
Personnel	18,022

This establishment was just about half that recruited in December 1938, and it remained at these figures until 1942 when considerable reductions in personnel and vehicles were possible. Further reductions in the establishments in conjunction with other Civil Defence Services were also made in 1943 and 1944.

Inter-hospital Ambulance Transport. The inter-hospital transport was provided chiefly for transferring casualties and civilian sick from the inner zone hospitals to the outer zone and special hospitals and to form the connecting link between ambulance trains and hospitals. The service consisted mainly of Green Line Coaches of the London Passenger Transport Board converted to carry 8–10 stretcher cases according to the type of coach; in some coaches there was also room for a number of sitting cases.

In addition to the coaches a number of small ambulances and motor cars provided by the American Ambulance (Great Britain) was available and the service could be augmented if necessary by the use of vehicles of the Civil Defence Ambulance Service. Details of the administration and work of the Inter-Hospital Transport will be found in Volume I, Chapter 8.

CASUALTY RECORDING ORGANISATION

As mentioned in Volume I, Chapter 2, casualty bureaux were set up at the headquarters of each Sector on the lines of those established by the scheme-making authorities in the provincial Regions. The functions of these Sector casualty bureaux necessarily differed somewhat from those of the Regions. The latter, in addition to recording and disposing of E.M.S. forms 105 (notification in respect of all civilian casualties and Service and police cases—sick or casualties—admitted to hospital) in accordance with the instructions laid down in Memorandum 3 of the Ministry of Health, were also the agency for dealing with all inquiries regarding casualties by relatives and friends and they prepared for general information lists for posting in various places throughout the area of the scheme-making authority concerned.

In the Sectors these functions could not be adequately carried out. It was therefore considered essential to consult the Commissioner of the Metropolitan Police with a view to ascertaining whether the police would be prepared to carry out these functions in war-time as regards war casualties as they did in peace-time as regards ordinary casualties, missing persons, etc. Several conferences therefore took place between representatives of the Ministry of Health and the Metropolitan Police; and it was eventually agreed that the police would carry on these functions in the manner described in Volume I, Chapter 3 and, as therein mentioned, after a conference held in April 1940, the Commissioner of Police also undertook to compile complete casualty lists and supply statistics to the various authorities concerned.

For this purpose the Commissioner of Police, Sir Philip Game, issued Supplementary Police Order No. 52 on April 20, 1940, which was subsequently amended by Supplementary Police Orders No. 60 on May 28, 1940, and No. 111 on October 12, 1940, giving complete details of how the collection and notification of casualties was to be carried out. The salient features of the organisation were as follows:

Duties of the Station Police.

    (*a*) to collect particulars of casualties from hospitals and mortuaries as soon as practicable after air raids;

    (*b*) to notify relatives of casualties where the addresses were local;

    (*c*) to forward lists to Scotland Yard;

    (*d*) to receive by teleprinter collated lists prepared by Scotland Yard;

(e) to inform persons concerned at addresses in each station area if not already done under (b) above;

(f) to answer inquiries from the information contained in the lists.

Central Casualty Bureau, New Scotland Yard. The Police Orders mentioned above resulted in the establishment of the Central Casualty Bureau, the chief duties of which were:

(a) to receive particulars of casualties from the ten Sector Casualty Bureaux and from the mortuaries in the London Region through the local authorities and to compile casualty lists based on the information received;

(b) to issue copies of the casualty lists to all Police Stations in the Metropolitan and City Police Districts;

(c) to maintain a card index of all casualties;

(d) to answer inquiries which could not be dealt with at local stations;

(e) to circulate photographs of unidentified bodies submitted by the local authorities;

(f) to prepare periodic statistics of casualties.

The police action above was in addition to and not in lieu of the duties already laid upon the hospitals and local authorities, i.e. the notification of casualties to the Sector casualty bureaux and the duties laid upon the bureaux to inform the next of kin by post, etc.

The police at stations collected particulars of casualties personally at the hospitals and mortuaries in the areas attacked. Hospitals prepared lists in duplicate of casualties admitted, so that a copy was available to the police, separate records being kept for identified and unidentified casualties. The superintendents of mortuaries similarly prepared duplicate copies of lists of bodies received, identified and unidentified.

It was realised that after a raid involving many casualties a large number of people would be gravely concerned to know that relatives and friends were safe. They would not be content to wait for notification by post, but would turn at once to the police for information. The police were thus able to deal with these inquiries from information gathered at the earliest moment and render every possible help, as well as to notify the next of kin of all casualties with addresses in their areas. In some cases it was necessary to make further inquiries because persons to be notified were temporarily absent from home or had to move to other addresses.

If the lists showed that the addresses of next of kin of casualties were outside the Metropolitan Police District, notification was sent to the police station concerned direct from Scotland Yard. After the preliminary notifications of casualties had been completed, lists collected by the police were checked with the lists submitted by the casualty bureaux and any discrepancies found investigated and adjusted; the result provided a permanent record of identified casualties. The action taken as regards the unidentified casualties depended largely on the information available and on the general conditions. When it seemed likely to help, particulars were circulated by teleprinter or in printed form and photographs.

Most inquiries for missing persons thought to have been involved in air raids were dealt with satisfactorily at local police stations, but a large number of inquiries by letter received in the Central Casualty Bureau from all parts of the country and even from overseas had to be dealt with, many of them relating to persons who had been missing from their homes for considerable periods. In these cases liaison was maintained between the Central Casualty Bureau and the ordinary 'Missing Persons Branch' of New Scotland Yard.

If persons were missing and their bodies could not be found or identified in the normal way, the presumption of death, when there was no reasonable doubt, was established under the Defence Regulations. Under these Regulations the Registrar of Deaths was notified of such cases and passed the information on to the Coroner who held a private inquiry without a jury and, if satisfied, issued a certificate to the Registrar, who registered the death in the ordinary way. The number of deaths thus presumed in London for the whole war period was 575, of which 462 occurred during the period September 1940, to May 1941. Arrangements were made with the Registrar General for the particulars of deaths registered under the Regulation to be sent periodically to the Central Casualty Bureau in order to make the record as complete as possible.

As regards Service casualties the police action was restricted to informing the man's relatives or unit in accordance with the procedure in force all over the country; Service casualties were excluded entirely from the records of the Central Casualty Bureau.

The lists and statistics referred to above were restricted as regards injured persons to those who were officially received into the hospitals. The names of casualties who received first-aid treatment were recorded by the local authorities concerned and not by the police organisation.

There is little doubt that handing over these duties to the Metropolitan Police resulted in the earliest possible notification of casualties to relatives and friends. No other organisation could possibly have carried out these duties so efficiently and completely.

THE SCHEME IN BEING

This then was the medical organisation brought into being to serve the London Area and by the summer of 1940 it was functioning smoothly and efficiently. The hospitals had had several months of experience in dealing with Service sick and casualties in addition to the normal civilian sick and of close liaison with the medical services of the combatant Services to ensure the most efficient treatment of Service sick and casualties. They had also gained experience in the admission and distribution of large numbers of patients in a short space of time. The casualty bureaux had gained valuable experience in dealing with bedstate returns and in recording military, police and civil defence sick and casualties. The inter-hospital transport had also been regularly in action moving 'transferred sick' from the inner to the outer zone hospitals daily and dealing with convoys from ambulance trains. The Civil Defence Services alone had had no experience of actual casualties, but had had many opportunities of carrying out combined training exercises which, from the way they carried out their duties under the strain of heavy enemy attacks, proved to have been of the greatest value.

THE PERIOD OF INTENSIVE RAIDING

Preparations for the Attack. The fall of France and the evacuation of the British Expeditionary Force from the Channel Ports provided the Sector hospitals with their first war casualties (Volume I, Chapter 4) and with opportunity to show that a scheme designed to deal with air raid casualties, passing from the centre outwards could be adapted for the overseas casualties which were primarily dealt with in the peripheral instead of in the central hospitals.

Having dealt with these casualties, London had to prepare to deal with the expected invasion of this country by sea and a very probable heavy attack from the air, or with both at the same time.

The Coastal Belt Scheme (Volume I, Chapter 4) provided for the primary reception of casualties in Sector I and their evacuation to the north, through Region 4, and into and through the outer zones of Sectors II, III and IV, while the inner zone hospitals were kept clear. This scheme entailed a complete modification of the previous plan for evacuating air raid casualties from East London to the peripheral hospitals in Essex, while similar modifications and plans had to be made for the disposal of invasion casualties in Kent and Sussex.

At the same time London had to amplify and accelerate the extensive preparations already made for air raids by endeavouring to increase the numbers evacuated, especially of mothers and children, large numbers of whom had returned to their homes during the months following the primary evacuations.

On June 11 the arrangements for transferring all sick children in the inner zone hospitals were carried out and 561 children were sent to hospitals in reception areas. Plans had been made to evacuate 1,206, but 561 only were found fit to be moved on that date. Others were transferred later from time to time, when fit to be moved, together with civilian sick.

By this time the Battle of Britain had begun and it continued with increasing violence from June to September 1940. London, however, remained free from attack until the end of July.

The Progress of the Attack. Table II below gives the actual number of attacks monthly during the whole period:

TABLE II

Period	By day	By night	Totals
September 3, 1939 to August 31, 1940	8	15	23
September 1940	23	28	51
October 1940	29	31	60
November 1940	15	27	42
December 1940	8	17	25
January 1941	8	12	20
February 1941	3	14	17
March 1941	1	14	15
April 1941	—	5	5
May 1941	—	3	3
Totals	95	166	261

Initial Raids. The first bomb fell at Mill Hill near the northern boundary of the London Region on June 18, but caused no casualties and there also were incidents on July 3, 16 and 17 without casualties. The first casualties occurred in the outer zone in Loughton and Dagenham, Essex, on the night of July 26–27, 1940, when 2 persons were killed and 5 injured. Only one casualty was reported between this date and August 15, when a sharp attack was made on Croydon at 7 o'clock in the evening which resulted in 63 persons being killed and 45 admitted to hospital. On the following day during another attack on Malden at 5.30 p.m., 78 persons were killed and 108 admitted to hospital. These were short concentrated attacks by a small number of planes and were followed by short attacks by single planes almost daily until September 7, and from which small numbers of casualties occurred.

The Heavy Raids. On the night of September 7–8 an exceedingly heavy, widespread and prolonged attack was experienced, which resulted in 430 fatal casualties and 1,605 admissions to hospital. From that date onwards heavy attacks of varying intensity and duration continued, resulting in a considerable number of casualties daily, except from November 26, until December 7.

During December 1940, bombs were dropped in some parts of the London area on 21 days; in January 1941 on 17 days; in February on 13 days; in March on 7 days; in April on 5 days and in May on 3 days.

The attack on the night of September 7–8 caused the highest number of casualties in 1940, but heavy casualties also occurred on September 9–10 and 19; October 16–17; November 16 and 30 and December 9, 28 and 30.

P

TABLE III
Casualties

Date	Killed					Injured, Detained in hospital				Slightly injured
	Men	Women	Children	Unclassified	Totals	Men	Women	Children	Totals	Totals
September 1939 to June 1940	—	—	—	—	—	—	—	—	—	—
July 1940	1	1	—	—	2	—	4	—	6	3
August 1940	140	63	17	6	226	196	162	35	393	996
September 1940	2,241	2,541	757	7	5,546	3,375	3,179	613	7,167	13,200
October 1940	2,137	2,344	451	2	4,934	3,052	2,768	523	6,343	11,058
November 1940	914	871	194	—	1,979	1,304	1,175	245	2,724	5,026
December 1940	461	367	81	—	909	987	656	102	1,745	3,473
January 1941	403	248	49	—	700	567	350	77	994	2,062
February 1941	144	119	32	—	295	200	192	50	442	794
March 1941	643	461	124	—	1,228	895	642	129	1,666	2,435
April 1941	1,230	1,144	295	—	2,669	1,498	1,253	165	2,916	5,257
May 1941	752	606	132	—	1,490	857	564	83	1,504	2,367
June 1941	—	—	—	—	—	7	4	—	11	96
July 1941	48	39	18	—	105	45	51	12	108	195
August 1941 to May 1942	Nil	Nil	Nil	Nil	Nil	Nil	Nil	Nil	Nil	30
June 1942	5	3	11	—	19	10	16	9	35	54
Totals	9,119	8,807	2,161	15	20,102	12,993	11,016	2,045	26,054	47,046

Note. It should be noted that the deaths recorded as having occurred during the previous twenty-four hours can only be approximate figures, as after heavy raids many fatal casualties were not discovered for some days and a number of others had to be eventually recorded as missing, presumed dead. There were also many hundreds of fragments of human remains from which it was not possible to make any identification.

In 1941 the intensity of the attack greatly diminished, but there were occasional heavy raids. On March 20, 751 persons were killed and 1,110 seriously injured.

In April the heaviest raid of all occurred on the night of 16–17, when 1,179 persons were killed and 2,233 seriously injured and detained in hospital. This was followed by another heavy attack on the 20th, from which 1,208 fatal casualties resulted, with 1,061 seriously injured. After a lull the last heavy raid took place on the night of May 10–11, when 1,452 persons were killed and 1,792 seriously injured. There were no more heavy raids after this until 1944 and with the exception of a minor raid on the night of July 27–28, 1941, there were no raids at all until June 1942.

The Total Casualties. Table III opposite gives the total casualties killed, injured and detained in hospital, and those injured and treated at first-aid posts during the whole period.

The figures for the injured, admitted and detained in hospital are almost certainly accurate, as these were all verified personally by the Metropolitan Police and checked against the final hospital returns. The figures for slightly injured and treated at first-aid posts can only be considered approximate, as in a number of cases the first-aid posts were demolished or damaged and records destroyed. There were also a number of slightly injured persons who never reported at first-aid posts, but were treated by their own doctors or at chemists' shops and the majority of these cases were never reported at all. A certain number of

TABLE IV

Disposal of the Patients Treated at First-Aid Posts

Month	Sent home	Sent to hospital	Totals
1940:			
September	11,303	2,416	13,719
October	9,469	2,100	11,569
November	4,325	1,000	5,325
December	2,972	822	3,794
1941:			
January	1,834	647	2,481
February	655	222	877
March	2,992	789	3,781
April	4,327	1,370	5,697
May	2,848	747	3,595
Totals	40,725	10,113	50,838

Note. The figure 40,725, the number of people treated at first-aid posts and sent home, is less than the figure for slightly injured in Table III; the difference presumably represents the number of slightly injured treated at out-patient departments of hospitals of which no accurate number can be given because of loss of records, etc. In addition, as stated elsewhere, numbers of slightly injured attended neither hospitals nor first-aid posts, so that there is no record of these numbers.

TABLE V

Number of Bombs dropped and Casualties caused in the 29 Areas of the Inner Zone of London up to the End of the Period of Intensive Raids (May 31, 1941)

Metropolitan Borough	Estimated population Middle 1938 (in thousands)	Estimated population September 1940 (in thousands)	Acreage	Estimated population per acre September 1940	Bombs all calibres	Bombs per sq. mile	Casualties Killed	Casualties Admitted to hospital	Casualties Treated at first-aid posts	Casualties Totals	Casualties per 1,000 of estimated population	Casualties per bomb
Battersea	142	108	2,163	50	502	148·5	240	234	746	1,220	11·3	2·4
Bermondsey	97	71	1,503	47	875	372·6	617	942	1,230	2,789	39·3	3·2
Bethnal Green	93	65	760	86	287	241·7	270	448	1,007	1,725	26·5	6·0
Camberwell	222	173	4,480	39	1,228	175·4	585	1,624	740	2,949	17·0	2·4
Chelsea	56	38	660	58	256	248·2	376	572	499	1,447	38·1	5·7
City of London	11	6	675	9	413	391·6	204	362	790	1,356	*226·0	2·0
Deptford	96	76	1,564	49	740	302·2	275	645	880	1,800	23·7	2·4
Finsbury	57	39	587	66	225	245·3	295	432	858	1,585	*40·6	7·0
Fulham	138	106	1,706	62	424	159·1	235	351	613	1,199	11·3	2·8
Greenwich	96	75	3,858	19	924	153·3	239	475	918	1,632	21·8	1·7
Hackney	205	172	3,287	52	634	123·4	511	975	1,088	2,574	15·0	4·1
Hammersmith	125	99	2,287	43	314	95·1	248	530	364	1,142	11·5	3·7
Hampstead	91	73	2,265	32	347	98·0	141	161	259	561	7·7	1·6
Holborn	34	26	406	64	360	567·5	277	485	309	1,071	*41·2	3·0
Islington	292	221	3,092	71	569	117·8	554	1,162	1,322	3,038	13·7	5·33
Kensington	174	125	2,290	55	553	154·6	241	535	590	1,366	10·9	2·5
Lambeth	273	214	4,083	52	1,449	227·1	1,301	1,713	2,383	5,397	25·2	3·7
Lewisham	229	195	7,015	28	1,369	124·9	586	656	1,527	2,769	14·2	2·0
Paddington	137	96	1,357	71	288	135·8	266	445	906	1,617	16·8	5·6
Poplar	134	95	2,331	41	757	207·8	631	894	2,266	3,791	39·9	5·0
St. Marylebone	91	62	1,473	42	409	177·7	356	691	534	1,581	25·5	3·9
St. Pancras	179	132	2,694	49	651	154·6	724	799	1,829	3,352	25·4	5·1
Shoreditch	80	54	658	82	293	285·0	416	577	1,328	2,321	43·0	7·9
Southwark	145	100	1,132	88	605	342·0	695	1,250	1,339	3,284	32·8	5·4
Stepney	201	131	1,766	74	1,219	441·8	616	884	1,689	3,189	24·3	2·6
Stoke Newington	51	41	864	47	214	158·5	224	146	272	642	15·7	3·0
Wandsworth	340	278	9,107	31	1,363	95·1	683	710	2,286	3,679	13·2	2·7
City of Westminster	124	84	2,503	33	1,287	329·1	800	1,878	1,886	4,564	*54·3	3·5
Woolwich	151	124	8,282	15	1,487	114·9	351	1,251	1,248	2,850	23·0	1·9

* *Note.* The casualties per thousand based on the estimated night population of the City of London and the 28 Metropolitan Boroughs show some obvious discrepancies. For example, the casualty rate of 226 per thousand for the City of London is certainly much higher than the actual. Dr. Charles White, Medical Officer of Health of the City estimated that in addition to the resident population an average of about 20,000 persons from outside the City were sheltering nightly in the tube stations and basements and there were at least a thousand persons on A.R.P. duties of various kinds, public and private, at night. Also, up to midnight, there was always a number of people passing through the City in buses, or walking between the terminal stations. He considered, therefore, that the average nightly population at risk might be taken as about 28,000, which would give a casualty rate per those treated at first-aid posts requiring subsequent admission to hospital was recorded twice and unless the Ministry of Pensions Form 44 had been filled in and sent with the patient to the admitting hospital (which in many cases could not be done), the correct figures could not be recorded.

Distribution of the Attacks. Table V opposite gives the number of bombs dropped in the City and Administrative County of London during the period of attack, together with the density of the population in each area, the total casualties and the casualties per thousand of the population.

As regards the resident population, the records kept at the office of the City of London Police show that during the period in question the number of casualties actually resident in the City of London was as follows:

    Killed 41
    Injured and admitted to hospital . 70

From the records maintained by the Medical Officer of Health, i.e. Forms M.P.C.44, 75 persons giving City addresses were treated at the first-aid posts, but of these only 65 seem to have been actual residents, the others being fire-watchers. Of these, 15 were sent on to hospital and are therefore included in the 70 casualties above-mentioned. This leaves 50 as the actual number of persons treated at the first-aid posts. The total of casualties among residents was therefore 161, so that the casualty rate per thousand of the resident population was 26·3.

These considerations with respect to the City of London applied also to a lesser extent to certain other of the more central Metropolitan Boroughs, such as Holborn and Finsbury, but probably not to any great extent to the rest of the Metropolitan Boroughs.

In the City of Westminster the casualty rate of 54·3 per thousand of the population is also obviously too high, and is probably due to the fact that large numbers of non-residents were to be found in this area at places of amusement, restaurants, etc., at any rate up to midnight.

From the table opposite it will be seen that the greatest number of bombs, 1,487, fell in Woolwich, followed by 1,449 in Lambeth, 1,369 in Lewisham, 1,363 in Wandsworth, 1,287 in Westminster, 1,228 in Camberwell and 1,219 in Stepney, whilst the smallest number fell in Stoke Newington 214 and Finsbury 225, the boroughs with the greatest acreage as a rule receiving the largest number of bombs.

Apart from the exceptions mentioned above, the casualties per thousand of the population vary more or less directly with its density, so it would appear that Bermondsey with a population of 47 per acre suffered the greatest number of casualties among the resident population in the inner zone.

Table VI shows the number of bombs dropped in the 66 areas of the outer zone, together with casualties, etc.:

TABLE VI

District	Estimated population as at December 31, 1939 (in thousands)	Acreage	Estimated population per acre December 1939	Bombs all calibres	Bombs per sq. mile	Killed	Casualties Admitted to hospital	Casualties Treated at first-aid posts	Total No. of casualties	Casualties per 1,000 of population	Casualties per bomb
Acton B.	69	2,317	30	330	91·1	90	130	274	494	7·2	1·5
Banstead U.D.	30	12,821	2	462	23·1	7	23	34	64	2·1	0·13
Barking B.	85	4,174	20	505	77·4	129	261	654	1,044	12·3	2·1
Barnes B.	42	2,650	16	224	54·1	56	94	169	319	7·6	1·4
Barnet U.D.	25	4,290	6	128	19·1	111	68	103	282	11·3	2·2
Barnet R.D.	10	8,339	1	233	17·9	—	—	12	12	1·2	0·1
Beckenham B.	72	5,935	12	757	81·6	185	120	396	701	9·7	0·9
Beddington and Wallington B.	35	3,048	11	214	44·9	32	30	77	139	3·9	0·6
Bexley B.	80	4,869	16	605	80·0	89	318	538	945	11·8	1·6
Brentford and Chiswick B.	62	2,449	25	298	77·9	45	72	192	309	5·0	1·03
Bromley B.	60	6,519	9	759	74·5	166	224	316	706	11·8	0·9
Bushey U.D.	15	3,865	4	98	16·2	2	—	11	13	0·9	0·1
Carshalton U.D.	61	3,346	18	202	38·6	29	63	212	304	5·0	1·5
Cheshunt U.D.	18	8,479	2	230	17·4	3	9	49	61	3·4	0·3
Chigwell U.D.	27	8,972	3	653	46·6	70	68	86	224	8·3	0·3
Chingford B.	43	2,868	15	186	41·5	67	63	145	275	6·4	1·5
Chislehurst and Sidcup U.D.	70	8,957	8	836	59·7	94	154	285	533	7·6	0·6
Coulsdon and Purley U.D.	62	11,142	6	677	38·9	37	83	162	282	4·5	0·4
Crayford U.D.	26	2,700	10	390	92·4	32	51	69	152	5·8	0·4
Croydon C.B.	243	12,672	19	1,193	60·3	434	584	1,486	2,504	10·3	2·1
Dagenham B	107	6,728	16	485	46·2	129	259	334	722	6·7	1·5
Ealing B.	160	8,739	18	622	45·6	190	269	442	901	5·6	1·4
East Barnet U.D.	31	2,644	12	99	24·0	10	47	84	141	4·5	1·4
East Ham C.B.	131	3,326	39	778	149·7	364	401	675	1,440	11·0	1·9
Edmonton B.	108	3,896	28	237	38·9	90	187	285	562	5·2	2·4
Enfield U.D.	102	12,400	8	383	19·8	60	79	228	367	3·6	1·0
Epsom and Ewell B.	60	8,427	7	427	32·4	19	51	144	214	3·6	0·5
Erith B.	40	3,859	10	429	71·2	61	154	282	497	12·4	1·2
Esher U.D.	43	14,847	3	461	19·8	13	37	50	100	2·3	0·2
Feltham U.D.	45	4,935	9	228	29·6	6	22	77	105	2·3	0·5

Finchley B.	67	3,477	19	229	42·2	69	82	166	317	4·7	1·4
Friern Barnet U.D.	28	1,341	21	106	50·6	48	12	13	73	2·6	0·7
Hayes and Harlington U.D.	46	5,161	9	188	23·3	17	98	130	245	5·3	1·3
Harrow U.D.	184	12,558	15	418	21·3	102	115	203	420	2·3	1·0
Hendon B.	162	10,370	16	499	30·8	194	333	627	1,154	7·1	2·3
Heston and Isleworth B.	105	7,261	14	346	30·5	144	136	164	444	4·2	1·3
Hornsey B.	95	2,872	33	319	71·1	112	196	301	609	6·4	1·9
Ilford B.	170	8,435	20	769	58·3	213	750	855	1,818	10·7	2·4
Kingston B.	39	1,390	28	83	38·2	52	42	148	242	6·2	2·9
Leyton B.	117	2,594	45	441	108·8	170	287	480	937	8·0	2·1
Malden and Coombe B.	42	3,162	13	470	95·1	59	102	98	259	6·2	0·6
Merton and Morden U.D.	75	3,237	23	402	79·5	104	52	208	364	4·9	0·9
Mitcham B.	70	2,939	24	306	66·6	87	153	186	426	6·0	1·4
Orpington U.D.	52	20,842	2	1,278	39·2	51	60	172	283	5·4	0·2
Penge U.D.	28	770	36	145	120·5	38	50	209	297	10·6	2·0
Potters Bar U.D.	15	6,250	2	182	18·6	5	8	13	26	1·7	0·1
Richmond B.	39	4,243	9	355	53·5	84	160	114	358	9·2	1·0
Ruislip-Northwood U.D.	50	6,584	8	256	24·9	22	39	71	132	2·6	0·5
Southall B.	54	2,604	2	126	31·0	19	64	82	165	3·1	1·3
Southgate B.	65	3,764	17	218	37·1	91	201	202	494	7·6	2·3
Staines U.D.	32	8,247	4	117	9·1	14	45	174	233	7·3	2·0
Sunbury U.D.	22	5,689	4	176	19·9	19	10	48	77	3·5	0·4
Surbiton B.	51	4,709	11	251	34·1	29	42	69	140	2·7	0·6
Sutton and Cheam B.	87	4,338	20	305	45·0	80	177	80	337	3·9	1·1
Tottenham B.	149	3,014	49	302	64·1	194	501	505	1,200	8·1	4·0
Twickenham B.	90	7,078	13	495	44·8	100	153	169	422	4·7	0·9
Uxbridge U.D.	50	10,238	5	197	12·3	9	27	64	100	2·0	0·5
Walthamstow B.	133	4,343	31	482	71·0	125	194	865	1,184	8·9	2·5
Waltham Holy Cross U.D.	7	10,959	1	372	21·7	—	11	34	45	6·4	0·1
Wanstead and Woodford B.	56	3,824	15	312	52·2	124	143	225	492	8·8	1·6
Wembley B.	119	6,300	19	499	50·7	96	160	195	451	3·8	0·9
West Ham C.B.	255	4,706	54	1,525	207·4	823	1,094	2,836	4,753	18·6	3·1
Willesden B.	204	4,632	44	602	83·2	250	459	566	1,275	6·2	2·1
Wimbledon B.	60	3,211	19	276	55·0	104	112	218	434	7·2	1·6
Wood Green B.	54	1,607	34	192	76·5	52	76	172	300	5·6	1·6
Yiewsley and West Drayton U.D.	18	5,277	3	103	12·4	1	3	20	24	1·3	0·2

Note. As in Table III the total casualty figures in Tables V and VI contain a certain number of cases which were recorded both as treated at first-aid posts and subsequently admitted to hospital.

Table VI shows that some of these areas experienced even heavier attacks than any of the metropolitan boroughs, 1,525 bombs having fallen in West Ham, 1,278 in Orpington and 1,193 in Croydon, but Orpington and West Ham were much larger areas than any of the metropolitan boroughs. West Ham with an acreage of 4,706 appears to have experienced a heavier attack than any other area in the whole Region. The casualties caused in West Ham (4,753), because the density of population was higher than that of any of the other extra-metropolitan areas, viz. 54 per acre, shows a high figure per thousand of the population, viz. 18·6.

An examination of these tables shows that the eastern and southeastern areas as a rule experienced the heaviest attacks, the enemy's approach to London usually being up the river from the Thames Estuary and up the main line of the Southern Railway from the southeast coast. The areas which experienced the lightest weight of attack were naturally those to the west and north-west.

The Weight of the Attack. It is estimated that the number of bombs that fell in Greater London during the whole period of the raids of all sizes including mines, but excluding incendiary bombs, was 46,518. Of these about 20,000 are estimated to have fallen in the City of London and the 28 metropolitan boroughs and about 26,000 in the outer zone of Greater London.

Until the end of 1940, no special arrangements had been made for making a census of the number of bombs which fell, nor of the estimated weight or type of these bombs, but from January 1, 1941, the bomb census organisation was operating in the whole area and according to returns received 8,559 bombs fell during the five months ending May 31, 1941, of which 4,704 fell in the inner zone and 3,855 in the outer zone. The estimated weight of these bombs in metric tons was 1,742, of which 963 fell in the inner zone and 779 in the outer zone. Therefore, the bombs dropped averaged about 5 to the metric ton. If this proportion be applied to the bombs that fell in 1940, then the calculated total weight of bombs for the whole period would be about 9,300 metric tons. Table VII gives the distribution of the attacks throughout the whole period.

The Weight of Attack in Relation to Casualties. Dr. A. Bradford Hill of the Research and Experiments Department of the Ministry of Home Security compared the casualties reported by the medical officers of health of the local authorities in the London area with the number and weight of bombs which fell in each area. It was realised, as is mentioned above, that the casualty figures were subject to errors of varying degree.

There were certainly errors in counting and in estimating the bombs that fell especially in the earlier months; and large numbers of bombs fell in the river and could not be taken into consideration.

TABLE VII

	Period 1 June 18 to October 7, 1940	Period 2 October 8 to November 4, 1940	Period 3 November 5 to November 30, 1940	December 1940	January 1941	February 1941	March 1941	April 1941	May 1941	Totals June 1940, to May 1941
Number of bombs: inner zone	7,845	4,320	2,336	837	404	134	1,049	1,375	1,742	20,042
Number of bombs: outer zone	9,461	7,028	5,344	788	839	339	978	1,342	357	26,476
Totals	17,306	11,348	7,680	1,625	1,243	473	2,027	2,717	2,099	46,518
*Weight in Metric tons: inner zone	1,570	864	467	167	62	14	160	370	357	4,031
*Weight in Metric tons: outer zone	1,892	1,405	1,070	157	99	45	172	399	64	5,303
Totals	3,462	2,269	1,537	324	161	59	332	769	421	9,334

Calculated: It is probably an over-estimate, as in the opinion of many observers most of the bombs dropped in the later periods were heavier than those during the earlier attacks.

From this table it will be seen that by far the heaviest attacks were experienced during the first month of heavy raiding, and that the attacks continued on a fairly heavy scale until the end of November 1940. There was then a comparative lull during December 1940 and January, February and March 1941, followed by heavier but fewer raids in April and May.

In addition to these defects the bomb figures could not be obtained from all the 95 local authorities in the London Region for the whole nine months period. For the first three months, September to November 1940, returns were received from all the 28 metropolitan boroughs and 27 of the 66 local authorities in the outer zone but not from the City of London. In the second three months, December 1940, to February 1941, returns came from the City of London, the 28 metropolitan boroughs and 63 of the local authorities in the outer zone. In the last three months, March to May 1941, returns were available from all 95 local authorities. But, in spite of these defects, there were sufficient data to give a broad picture of what had happened to reveal the different experiences of various areas, and to permit of reasonably accurate estimates and conclusions of some statistical value.

Dr. Bradford Hill divided the London Region into seven groups moving roughly from the centre (with such areas as the Boroughs of Bermondsey, Southwark and Westminster) to the periphery (including such areas as Chigwell Urban District and Epsom and Ewell Municipal Boroughs). Groups A, B, C and D, included the metropolitan boroughs and E, F and G the county boroughs, boroughs and urban districts outside the County of London.

The table below gives the estimated casualty rates per bomb and mine dropped in the different groups of areas and the estimated density of the population per acre of each of these groups:

TABLE VIII

Group	Killed	Total casualties	Persons per acre*
A and B (centre)	0·94	4·39	45·5
C	0·72	3·75	41·4
D	0·53	2·53	26·4
E	0·36	1·92	17·9
F	0·35	1·80	13·9
G (periphery)	0·09	0·48	3·7

*Using the arithmetical mean of the populations at September 30, 1940, December 31, 1940 and March 31, 1941.

Note. It will be seen from this table that the casualty-causing effect of the bombs, as would be expected, gradually decreased in direct proportion to the density.

Dr. Bradford Hill also estimated the casualty rates per thousand of the population in each of these groups. These will be found in the table opposite:

TABLE IX

Group	September–November 1940		December 1940–February 1941		March–May 1941		September 1940–May 1941*	
	Killed	Total casualties	Killed	Total casualties	Killed	Total casualties	Killed	Total casualties
A	3·62	18·44	1·04	5·94	3·74	12·34	8·40	36·72
B	2·90	14·97	0·33	2·14	1·89	8·09	5·12	25·20
C	2·16	11·67	0·43	2·70	1·28	5·54	3·87	19·91
D	1·78	8·32	0·27	1·82	0·76	3·45	2·81	13·59
E	1·36	7·32	0·16	1·01	0·56	2·72	2·08	11·05
F	0·67	3·41	0·14	0·88	0·25	1·19	1·06	5·48
G	0·62	3·20	0·03	0·40	0·17	0·75	0·82	4·35

*Simple addition of the three quarterly rates, ignoring changes in population. Allowing for these changes would increase the rates slightly.

This table shows the same diminution in the casualty-causing power of the attack.

The weight of bombs in relation to casualties is given in the following table:

TABLE X

Persons per acre at March 31, 1941	No. of areas	Estimated metric tons of H.E. and mines	Average bomb weight Kg.	Casualties per metric ton		Casualties per bomb and mine	
				Killed	Totals	Killed	Totals
0–4	13	100	157	0·75	2·88	0·14	0·54
5–9	12	155	162	1·49	6·80	0·26	1·20
10–14	17	279	200	2·48	13·96	0·54	3·02
15–19	14	164	148	2·92	14·08	0·57	2·75
20–24	8	162	200	4·03	20·18	1·01	5·06
25–29	9	266	169	4·52	16·28	0·89	3·20
30–39	10	190	184	4·73	20·16	0·99	4·22
40–49	5	190	189	5·21	22·77	1·05	4·58
50–69	7	141	194	5·23	18·45	1·38	5·26
Totals	95	1,647	178	3·73	16·30	0·76	3·33

Note: This table deals only with the period January to May 1941, after the bomb census came into operation. It shows that the casualties per ton over the whole period averaged about five times the casualties per bomb.

Other investigations were made by Dr. Hill in various places to try to find the casualty-causing power of each type of bomb. It was found that the larger the bomb dropped in built-up areas the greater the number of casualties, but if the ton weight of bombs were taken the actual size of the bomb made very little difference; for example, the numbers killed by ten 50-kg. bombs did not greatly exceed those killed by one 500-kg. bomb, the deaths per ton being 3·6 and 3·0 respectively, while bombs of all sizes caused 3·7 deaths per ton.

It was further found that in three inner divisions of London and four large provincial towns, an average of 60 per cent. of all bombs fell in the open, an average of 30 per cent. on buildings, about 6 per cent. on railway bridges, docks, etc., about 1 per cent. on shelters and approximately 3 per cent. elsewhere.

As to the actual cause of death or injury, in the more densely populated areas, the greater percentage of casualties was due to falling buildings and flying debris.

Tables VIII to X are extracted from an appreciation of statistical data relating to air raid casualties, collected and analysed for the Research and Experiments Department of the Ministry of Home Security by Dr. Bradford Hill.

THE WORK OF THE HOSPITALS

This story of the Sector hospitals in action is not intended to be a chronological account of the work done; it is meant to be an appreciation of how the organisation functioned under heavy attacks, illustrated by examples covering every field of its activities, together with the impressions of those chiefly concerned with the direction and execution of the plans prepared for the treatment and disposal of casualties. It is based on special reports prepared by the Sector Group Officers for this purpose, together with reports from some of the larger hospitals concerned and other sources.

Owing to the geographical distribution of the enemy attacks, Sectors I, II, VIII, IX and X, situated in the Eastern and South-eastern areas, had the greatest amount of work thrown upon them, but as, with the exception of Sector I, all had their apices in the central area, nearly all the Sectors had to deal with considerable numbers of casualties (see Sector Map, Volume I, Chapter 2).

The Sectors have been dealt with separately, as it was found that this method presents a better picture than would result from an endeavour to deal with the Region as a whole, for the area of operations was too widespread and the period too prolonged for an adequate description of the chief events without some sub-division.

SECTOR I

This Sector, which contained 40 active hospitals in the E.M.S., was based on the London Hospital in Sector II and, unlike the other Sectors, had no hospitals in the metropolitan boroughs. It was all contained in the County of Essex and provided about 6,500 beds for casualties. It had some large hospitals in the crowded extra-metropolitan boroughs of the London area, such as Whipps Cross Emergency Hospital, Leytonstone, with 1,000 casualty beds; Goodmayes Emergency Hospital, Ilford, with 430 beds, and the Claybury Emergency Hospital, Ilford, with 570 beds. These hospitals and some others were meant originally to serve as advanced base hospitals for casualties occurring in the East End of London, but when in the autumn of 1940 the invasion of East Anglia became possible or even probable, the evacuation of civilian patients and air raid casualties from the inner zone hospitals to this area became undesirable. The line of evacuation was, therefore, changed, all the hospitals in the inner zone of Sector II being cleared in a northwards direction to their own base hospitals, while the advanced base hospitals of Sector I were usually cleared to base hospitals in Sectors III and IV. This line of evacuation was adopted as Sector II was generally affected at the same time as Sector I. There was no difficulty, apart from communications, in using this altered line of evacuation, as the Group Officers of these Sectors afforded every co-operation.

These large hospitals in Sector I were very useful as direct casualty receiving hospitals, for large numbers of casualties occurred in the crowded areas of Leyton, Ilford and Barking. The chief base hospitals in Essex were those in the Brentwood area affiliated to and staffed by the London Hospital, such as Highwood, Harolds Wood, Warley Wood and the London Hospital Annexe, with a total of over 1,000 beds provided chiefly by hutted additions to the existing hospitals. There were also large base hospitals with hutted additions at St. Margaret's Emergency Hospital, Epping; Black Notley Emergency Hospital, Braintree, etc. These hospitals also were only used for local casualties and for patients evacuated from the Coastal Belt of the County of Essex, such as the hospitals in Tilbury, Grays, Southend, Clacton and Harwich.

In order to regularise this changed situation, from July 1, 1941, all the hospitals in Sector I outside the London Region, except the four above-mentioned hospitals near Brentwood affiliated to the London Hospital, were transferred to Region 4, while those inside the London Region were transferred to Sector II.

During the heavy attacks on London and the Thames Estuary, this Sector had frequently to deal with small numbers of casualties from incidents in Essex, but it was unusual for an excessive strain to be put on a single hospital. For example, during the latter half of September, when the total casualties in six twenty-four hour periods varied between 55 and 86, only 8 to 12 hospitals were involved and the largest number received in a single hospital was 27. In one or two instances, major local disasters, which might have been expected to put a great strain on the adjacent hospitals, did not do so because of the large proportion of dead amongst the casualties. In the spring of 1941, when there were few day-to-day casualties and only two heavy raids, the distribution changed somewhat, but not sufficiently to throw an undue strain on any hospital. For example, on March 25, 367 casualties were admitted to 14 hospitals in the Sector, and the largest number for any one was 76.

On April 25, 394 casualties were distributed among 17 hospitals, the largest number admitted to any one being 70. In practice it was found possible to send quite a large number of the less seriously injured back to their homes without admission to hospital.

Damage to Hospitals. Most hospitals in the Sector received some damage and nearly all the inner hospitals were out of action on one or more occasions, but the Sector I hospitals were more fortunate in escaping major disasters. The most serious was at Queen Mary's Hospital, Stratford, where on September 7, 1940, a bomb struck a ward block and killed six patients and two nurses. The hospital reopened for receiving casualties on September 18 and the beds were increased to 100 by October. The East Ham Memorial Hospital was hit on October 9, and the kitchen and boiler house were destroyed without injury to patients or staff. The hospital was able to reopen wards to receive casualties early in December.

At Whipps Cross Hospital, wards containing 300 beds, almost full at the time, were rendered untenable by blast damage on December 8, but there were no serious casualties.

Other hospitals were temporarily put out of action from time to time by damage to public services, to their own services, or by unexploded bombs, but were able again to receive casualties within a few days. In all there were thirty-nine incidents, causing damage in nineteen hospitals.

No mobile surgical or resuscitation team in Sector I was ever in action in the London area, and on only one occasion was a surgical team called to a local hospital in Essex.

Telephone communications to inner London frequently broke down, but were remarkably quickly restored.

All demands for inter-hospital transport were promptly met by Group VII of the Ambulance Service, whose staff were extremely co-operative. The only recurrent difficulty was that the inner hospitals sometimes found it difficult to clear patients from the previous night's bombing early in the day, because loading was slow through lack of stretcher bearers.

SECTOR II

This Sector, containing sixteen inner zone hospitals providing 3,110 casualty beds and seventeen outer zone hospitals providing 3,570 casualty beds, was also based on the London Hospital, the total capacity of which had been reduced, in accordance with the policy of the Ministry, to 490 beds. The average number of beds occupied by patients was about 330, leaving 160 available for casualties.

The other large casualty receiving hospitals in this area were the L.C.C. hospitals at Bethnal Green, Hackney, Mile End and St. Andrew's, Bow, in each of which about 300 casualty beds were usually available, with a total reserve of about 700 beds. There were also a number of other local authority hospitals in the inner zone such as St. George's-in-the-East, Wapping; St. Leonard's, Shoreditch; St.

Peter's, Stepney and the Eastern Hospital, Homerton, but they could only provide a small proportion of casualty beds.

The chief advanced base hospitals were the Northern Hospital, Winchmore Hill and the North Middlesex Hospital, Edmonton, which had usually about 1,000 beds immediately available for casualties, with a further number of approximately 1,000 beds in reserve. The chief base hospitals were Haymeads, Bishops Stortford, with about 800 casualty beds, Chalkdell House, 400 beds and Chase Farm Emergency Hospital, Enfield, 800 beds; in the last of these were situated the special centres for head injuries and orthopædic surgery.

The Sector had extensive experience of evacuating large numbers of patients as well as small convoys. During the whole period of enemy attack, 4,135 patients were transferred from the inner to the outer zone hospitals, the peak period being between September 8 and 14, when 1,265 patients were transferred. All transfers were carried out promptly and efficiently.

The inner hospitals, both voluntary and municipal, helped their neighbours when blitzed, not only in dealing with patients but in giving hospitality to the staffs. There were sufficient beds in the outer zone hospitals not only to deal with all casualties but also to accommodate, for rest periods, nursing staff badly shaken as the result of bombing of their hospitals.

The work of the Ambulance Department was excellent, especially that of Group III.

Surgical teams had to be called on few occasions, for during the busiest periods it was possible to maintain an even distribution of cases to the outer hospitals in the Sector.

Despatch riders were of great service when telephonic communications had broken down.

Inter-Sector transfer between Sectors II and III was frequently used, and the aid received from Sector III was most useful in levelling out the distribution of cases.

Damage to Hospitals. In the inner zone, eleven hospitals were hit by a total of twenty-seven bombs, St. Peter's, Whitechapel, being hit four times. Plate I gives a typical example of the damage incurred—a wrecked wing of Mile End Hospital. In eleven of these incidents patients had to be evacuated. From only two hospitals was evacuation unnecessary, the London Hospital which was hit eight times and the Bethnal Green Hospital which was hit twice. If minor damage is included there were eighty incidents at twenty-five hospitals in the Sector.

A particularly striking feature of the period of raids was the speed with which each badly damaged hospital was able to get a temporary medical service back into action.

Four of the inner hospitals were unable to admit any patients for some time, but all maintained their out-patient clinics.

The only criticism was of delays in loading and unloading ambulances; partly due to the shortage of stretcher bearers and partly to the masses of debris in and around some of the inner hospitals immediately after they had been bombed.

The following is a Report contributed by Mr. George E. Neligan, M.C., F.R.C.S., Senior Surgeon at the London Hospital:

The London Hospital suffered from its geographical position. It is situated just outside the eastern boundaries of the City, and an equally short distance to the south is the river with its docks and warehouses, so that the bombing of either of these objectives put the hospital in the front line. Even when bombs were not dropping in the neighbourhood, planes frequently came up the Thames and then turned inland across the hospital on their way to other places.

Though the hospital was hit eight times by high explosive bombs and had showers of incendiaries causing two serious fires, damage was not so great as might have been expected. In fact, except for the loss of many windows and plaster from ceilings, the main part of the hospital was not seriously damaged.

The nightly alerts and the planes soon became part of one's life, and when the sirens sounded those on duty automatically reached for their tin hats and went to their allotted posts.

It is almost impossible to find words to express one's appreciation of the behaviour of the whole staff, whether they were sisters, nurses, students or the medical and lay staffs. It was a team that never faltered. The only noticeable differences from peace-time were the tin hats, worn usually at a jaunty angle, and the noise of the bombs or guns outside shaking the building. The old scrubbers, many of whom were over seventy years old, had for many years daily appeared at 6 a.m. and cleaned the same bit of hospital floor. No matter how severe the raid or whether transport had been knocked out and they had to walk from their homes, some of which had been ruined by bombs, these old ladies would turn up to time, pail in hand, and would settle down to their task, periodically stopping to argue with their scrubber friends as to which had had the biggest bomb near them during the night. They set a fine example and had lost none of their cockney humour.

Each of the staff had his own sphere of action. The House Governor looked after the running of the lay side of the hospital, the feeding arrangements and the porters, and organised emergency details such as clearing patients from dangerous wards in the neighbourhood of unexploded bombs, keeping in touch with Sector headquarters or maintaining liaison with neighbouring L.C.C. hospitals which had been badly blitzed and making mutual arrangements when necessary for the accommodation of patients. He was a tower of strength and encouragement. The Surveyor organised the protection of the hospital. If the windows got blown out and the blackout torn down, a telephone message to his control post brought a repair squad in a few minutes to repair the damage so that work in the wards could go on. He had a control post in the basement of one of the Homes and it was connected by telephone with every part of the hospital, including the roof. Long before the era of Government fire watchers, the hospital had its own. He also organised and trained the hospital's own fire brigade. There was a motor pumping engine, always manned, in a shelter in the garden ready to go anywhere at a moment's notice. They did splendid work and put out several minor fires that would otherwise have spread. There were two serious fires, one in the roof on one of the Nurses' Homes and one in the carpenter's shop, both from incendiaries. The hospital brigade not being sufficient, the N.F.S. Brigade was called in to extinguish the flames. My own work was to supervise the admission and treatment of casualties, the sorting of the cases, as during the last war in a C.C.S., being very important. All stretcher cases and severe walking wounded were admitted to the receiving room. The first thing to find out was their general condition. If they were obviously suffering from haemorrhage, a green label was pinned on to them, a clerk having written their names and injuries. They were then taken straight to the resuscitation ward. In practically no cases were dressings or splints removed from patients in the receiving room, only the external appearances of the dressings being observed.

Here I should like to pay tribute to the first-aid work of the stretcher parties and ambulance personnel. Considering the extremely difficult conditions they worked under, often in complete darkness and under fire, it was splendid the way the patients were dressed and the right diagnosis written on their tickets. It was good to see that very few tourniquets had been applied.

The resuscitation ward had been specially fitted up with oxygen tubes to each bed, and electric heaters—and, in case the electricity failed, with plenty of hot water bottles. Every bed had a blood pressure apparatus. Across the corridor was a small operating theatre where instruments could be sterilised and transfusions performed. In the corridor were refrigerators where the blood bank was kept. The ward was situated in a quiet side corridor of the hospital. It was in charge of a physician, helped by a medical First Assistant and four students. Charts were kept of all the patients, showing their pulse and respiration rate and, most important of all, their blood pressure. We soon learnt that though the pulse rate might drop, the only sure indication of improvement in the patient was a rise in blood pressure, and that it was useless to operate on any case when it was under 100. The patient's wounds were examined as soon as he was in bed and notes made of the type and extent. In the early days there was a tendency to start transfusions with blood or plasma too soon. Except, therefore, in cases where shock was obviously due to severe haemorrhage, the cases were given morphia and warmed up for half an hour and only then, if their condition showed no signs of improvement, were more active measures adopted. When a case was fit for operation, a note was sent to the theatre stating the patient's name and injuries. After operation, if it was considered that cases needed further resuscitation they were sent back to the same ward.

Cases in the receiving room not badly shocked and who needed operation were given a red label with their name, injuries and ward on it. They were then sent straight to a surgical ward where they were undressed, got ready for the theatre and given A.T.S. and morphia if in pain. A duplicate red label was sent to the theatre where they were sorted and as far as possible arranged in order of urgency. When ready for the next case, a trolley was sent for the patient and the red label from the theatre handed to the ward sister, so that it was known which case would be next and necessary premedication given. Cases not needing operation on admission, such as chest or head injuries or simple fractures, were given a blue label and sent to the surgical wards for appropriate treatment.

If fit enough, the head cases were transferred next day to the head unit at Chase Farm, Enfield, as these travel better before than shortly after operation. If the chest cases had sucking wounds, these were sutured in the wards and if fit to travel, were evacuated to a chest centre, otherwise they were dealt with in hospital by a chest surgeon. Simple fractures, if not too swollen, were put up in plaster next day, or if very swollen, put in splints and evacuated to the orthopaedic centre at Chase Farm.

Whenever possible, patients with lower limb fractures were evacuated. When put up in extension frames they are difficult to move from the ward in case of fire or direct hit. Every bed was fitted with a rope underneath the mattress so that in cases of emergency it could be twisted over the bed and the mattress and patient lifted to the floor and run out of the ward or downstairs in a few minutes. Practices were periodically held to teach the necessary technique. As the operating theatres are on the top floor, with large glass windows and roofs, two emergency theatres were established on the ground floor. In each theatre there were two lots of instruments and two operating tables divided by screens, so that when necessary the two table technique could be employed, thus saving time between the cases, as at times there had been long waits owing to a shortage of porters and the stream of admissions. There were two teams on duty each night and day, the team consisting of a surgeon, anaesthetist, theatre sister or nurse and a student assistant. Thus the whole twenty-four hours were covered. As the surgeons usually had to go and attend to out-patients after their night's operating, they only got a chance to sleep in the afternoon.

All patients with open wounds had a course of sulphonamide treatment. It was interesting to see how their spirits rose once the course was finished. In every case of penetrating wounds or fractures, an X-ray was taken in the wards with a portable apparatus. This worked very well except when the electric light failed, which it frequently did. On a few occasions the Red Cross sent an X-ray van to assist.

Before the war a small electric light engine had been installed in the basement and was sufficient to give light in the theatres and receiving room and four wards, so that when the main current failed the emergency light appeared a few seconds after turning on the switch. Later, a plant was installed sufficient to light the whole hospital and keep the refrigerators going. The gas failed on occasions and once the hospital was several nights without it, all the cooking having to be done by steam. Fortunately there was never a shortage of water, the storage tanks on the roofs being sufficient, even when the water mains were burst. Another annoying failure were the hydraulic lifts. In nearly every raid the water was cut off and the lifts put out of use, which meant that cases had to be man-handled if they overflowed to the wards in the basement or the first floor.

The day after each raid, a list of those fit for evacuation was made and the cases transferred in Green Line ambulances to the Sector hospitals in the country in order to make room for more casualties next night. The highest number of casualties admitted to hospital on any one night was 110, and it was possible to evacuate 50 the next day, though they were not all admissions of the previous night.

The first-aid post was fortunately under the control of the hospital and was situated in the basement of the out-patient department. Here attention was given to minor injuries, and the cases seen in the out-patient department next morning for further treatment or discharge. The largest number of cases seen in the F.A.P. on one night was 100.

The total number of air raid casualties attending this hospital was 1,330, a surprisingly small number when one considers that before the war started it was officially estimated there would be probably 320,000 casualties in the first fortnight in the London area. 697 were attended to at the first-aid post, 534 were admitted to the wards and 99 were brought in dead. Of the latter it was interesting to note the number who were brought in dead without any external sign of injury. Of those admitted to the wards, 56 died without operation, 203 did not need operation and 275 were operated on, 28 dying after operation. A large number of patients admitted were firemen, injured while trying to grapple with the many fires. Similar pluck was shown by the girls and men of the L.A.A.S., whose only anxiety seemed to be to unload their patients and get back through the blitz to the incident for more cases.

SECTOR III

There were 10 inner zone and 12 outer zone hospitals containing about 5,500 casualty beds in this Sector; of these beds about 1,500 were in the inner zone.

The chief casualty receiving hospitals were St. Bartholomew's in the City of London, the Royal Free, and the Royal Northern among the voluntary hospitals; the St. Mary's Hospital, Highgate and the Archway Hospital, Islington, administered by the L.C.C. There were two large advanced base hospitals, Wellhouse Emergency Hospital, Barnet, with 600 beds for casualties, and Friern Hospital, Barnet, with 750 beds.

The largest base hospitals were Mill Hill Emergency Hospital in Mill Hill School, which had been taken over by the Ministry and which provided 550 beds; Hill End Hospital, St. Albans, with 1,100 beds and the Three Counties Hospital, Arlesey, Bedfordshire, with 1,000 beds.

Mill Hill Hospital housed the headquarters of the Sector, and the hospital provided a neurosis centre for civilian and Service patients under Dr. W. S. Maclay and an 'effort syndrome' centre for the whole country. Hill End contained a large orthopaedic department and special departments for head, chest, maxillo-facial surgery and a centre for the special treatment of burns. The Three Counties Hospital, Arlesey, was also available when required as a base hospital for Region 4 and for Sectors IV and V.

St. Bartholomew's Hospital. As the inner zone included the City of London, which seemed likely to be a special target, preparations were made in anticipation of the reception of a large number of casualties in St. Bartholomew's Hospital, the only hospital in the City and the key hospital of the Sector. The top floors were emptied and more than half the beds were closed, only sufficient being retained to accommodate casualties and deal with acute civilian illness. A considerable organisation was carefully planned for the reception of casualties by opening up in a protected site in a basement, a large out-patient department as an admission and sorting room, with facilities for minor operations, emergency operations, resuscitation wards, blood transfusions, etc. This area acquired the title of the 'Casualty Clearing Station'. In another basement, a duplicate set of operating theatres was set up for use in the event of the originals being put out of action. Arrangements were made by which some of the honorary staff lived in the hospital, the remainder being posted to the hospitals in the outer zone. One experienced medical officer was put in control of the whole of the reception unit. His duties included sorting cases, making preliminary returns, etc., thus relieving the Medical Superintendent of the hospital, who had other urgent matters to attend to. In-patient admissions were limited to 15 patients per operating table; further cases requiring admission were directed to the nearest hospital with beds available.

These arrangements formed a pattern for the other hospitals in the inner zone of the Sector, of which the Royal Free Hospital was the most important. They were not really tested until the latter part of 1940. From then until May 1941, there were several occasions in which more than 50 air raid casualties arrived in a short space of time. The sorting arrangements carried out before casualties reached the hospital worked very well, so that the hospital received almost entirely stretcher cases. It was rare for a walking patient, or one who should have been walking, to arrive in the hospital. The heaviest nights for the reception of air raid casualties were October 9, 16, 26, December 27 and 29, 1940; and January 11, March 8, April 17 and May 11, 1941. Air raid casualties were received almost daily during this period, but on the dates mentioned 50 or more stretcher cases came to the hospital. The greatest number was on January 11, when 154 stretcher cases, mostly severely wounded, were brought to the hospital within the space of two hours; this occasion fully tested the hospital's arrangements. On that night the unloading of ambulances and delivery of the patients into the reception room never became overwhelming. The system of issuing fresh stretchers and clean blankets to each ambulance as soon as it was unloaded, so that it could move off, prevented congestion. There were never more than four ambulances unloading at once. The sorting of the patients in the reception room and their transport to the selected wards or to other parts of the hospital worked as well as had been expected and there were never at any one time more than 20 cases waiting for removal to the wards, resuscitation rooms, mortuaries or operating theatres of the hospital. From this point onwards, things became a little more difficult, as it proved that there were not sufficient surgical teams to deal with the type of injuries the patients had received that night and a call had to be sent for an additional team. This team was supplied.

Another occasion when the arrangements of the hospital were thoroughly tested was the night of December 29, 1940. Fifty-four air raid casualties had been received in the hospital two nights previously and there were also about 100 civilian sick in the wards, and on that night about 50 air raid casualties had been admitted by midnight. At 1.15 a.m. the Assistant Commissioner of Police informed the Medical Officer in Charge that there was only one route from the hospital still open, and this was threatened by fire. It was therefore thought advisable to reduce the number of patients in the hospital while the opportunity still existed. Sector headquarters provided transport immediately on request, and 102 patients were removed from the wards and put into Green Line ambulances in the space of two hours fifteen minutes. This work was done by porters and the resident students. In the absence of electricity to work the lifts of the hospital and in the absence of electric lighting, each patient had to be manhandled down the stairs from the wards. The normal rate of loading patients into Green Line ambulances at this hospital in daylight and with the lifts working was 60 per hour. That the students and porters got 102 patients into the Green Line ambulances, without electricity and without lighting, in the space of two hours fifteen minutes, was considered a reasonably satisfactory achievement.

Hill End Emergency Hospital, St. Albans. An appropriate alternative name which was often heard for this hospital was 'Bart's in the country', and the following short note on its work during the raids is of considerable interest:

The patients admitted to the hospital came from five sources:

1. Civilian sick from the admission list of St. Bartholomew's Hospital.
2. Civilian sick transferred from other Hospitals in the Sector.
3. Air raid casualties transferred from London Casualty Hospitals.
4. Service casualties and service sick transferred from Military and E.M.S. establishments, and
5. Direct admissions of air raid casualties from near-by incidents and Service patients injured in road accidents.

General Surgical Unit. Groups 1 and 2 contained patients similar to those treated at St. Bartholomew's in peace-time. The admission of patients in Groups 3, 4 and 5 was determined by the conditions of war; these groups constituted 50 per cent. of the admissions to the male wards and 25 per cent. of those on the female side. They made up 40 per cent. of the general surgical patients, but, since many of them were transferred after their initial treatment elsewhere, only 15 per cent. of our total operations were performed on patients from these three groups. Group 5 was the smallest. Only thrice during this period were groups of between 10 and 20 fresh air raid casualties received, and on these occasions the service rendered by the physicians in the resuscitation ward was of the utmost value. A serious difficulty at this time was the disposal of aged and infirm patients, especially those whose homes had been demolished, and beds were frequently 'blocked' till arrangements could be made for accommodation elsewhere. Though there is little to remark about operative procedures during the period under review, radical reforms in the routine of war dressings were introduced in order to combat cross infection. Much of the bacteriological research which paved the way for these improvements in dressing technique, which have since been widely adopted, was carried out at this hospital during the winter of 1940. (See Medical Research Volume.)

Plastic and Jaw Unit—under the direction of Mr. Rainsford Mowlem, F.R.C.S. From September 1940, to May 1941, 703 patients were admitted to the unit. Of these, 280 were air raid or Service casualties. The number of operations performed in this time was 560, of which 267 were on Service or air raid injuries. It appears, therefore, that the normal working of the unit was not affected by the additional burden imposed upon it and in fact the operative figures for this period show merely the normal rise, which has since been continued. The only outstanding point is the extremely heavy nursing burden imposed by the number of burns among the air raid casualties, but this had been expected and presented no very great difficulties.

Orthopaedic Unit—in charge: Mr. S. L. Higgs, F.R.C.S. During this period a total of 730 patients were admitted. This number was made up as follows: civilian sick, 245; air raid casualties, 185; Service cases, 300. A great majority of the fractures admitted to the hospital were treated in this unit.

Neurosurgical Unit—in charge: Professor (afterwards Sir) J. Paterson Ross, M.S., F.R.C.S., with Mr. J. E. A. O'Connell, F.R.C.S., as deputy. Cases admitted during the period were: civilian sick, 245; air raid casualties, 105; Service cases, 77; Total, 297. The majority of the Service cases and air raid casualties were treated for either head, spinal or peripheral nerve injuries. The civilian sick were the usual types of neurosurgical patients—brain tumours, spinal tumours, trigeminal neuralgia, etc.

Chest Unit—in charge: Mr. J. E. H. Roberts, O.B.E., F.R.C.S., with Mr. O. S. Tubbs, F.R.C.S., as deputy. The following cases were admitted: civilian cases, 174; air raid casualties, 77; Service cases, 56; total, 307. Most of the air raid casualties were received as early transfers from the London hospitals.

Damage to Hospitals. Damage to hospitals in the Sector was enormous. Direct hits were responsible for putting some hospitals wholly out of action, necessitating the total evacuation of all patients. In other cases only parts of the hospitals were put out of action. Damage by blast affected practically every hospital, some suffering on several occasions. Unexploded bombs from time to time caused the loss of essential services, temporary evacuations, partial or total, being necessary.

In all, twenty-three hospitals were damaged, either by direct hits or blast, on fifty-three occasions. St. Bartholomew's received direct hits by H.E. bombs on September 11 and 23, 1940, and on May 10, 1941, and on more than one occasion was almost completely surrounded by fires. The damage to the hospital and the medical school was considerable. On the first occasion a large amount of damage was done to the nurses' home, but no casualties resulted. On September 23 a considerable portion of the clinical medical school was demolished. On May 10 a H.E. bomb hit the west wing of the hospital and did some damage. In addition, the new medical college in Charterhouse Square received much damage in October, December and May, the chemistry and physiology departments were wrecked and the pathology block badly damaged. On several other occasions parts of the services of the hospital were put out of action. Fortunately no casualties were caused in the hospital at any time. Patients had to be evacuated one night in January, when the hospital was in imminent danger from fire.

In September the City of London Maternity Hospital, the Royal Chest Hospital and the Hornsey Central Hospital had to be completely evacuated, as had St. Matthew's Hospital and the Royal Free Hospital in October. In St. Matthew's three wards were demolished, 80 patients completely disappeared, and were presumed killed. In addition, 3 nurses were killed and 1 seriously injured and 45 patients injured. On November 16 a land mine destroyed two of the villas at the Friern Hospital and seriously damaged three others; 21 people were killed and 44 injured, some seriously. On the same night, Mill Hill Hospital was set on fire by incendiaries and 230 patients had to be transferred to other hospitals.

Commentary. Sir Girling Ball, the Sector Group Officer, said that considering that the hospitals were never designed to cope with the conditions of modern aerial warfare, the measures taken to deal with damage were extraordinarily effective; and it was surprising how quickly the damaged buildings were put into working order by the local authorities.

Communication by telephone was difficult on a few occasions, showing the advantages of despatch riders who knew the position of the various hospitals and the routes to them.

There was no difficulty on any occasion with the transfer of patients and 7,411 were transferred from the inner to the outer zone hospitals during the nine months. The close association between the inner and the outer zone hospitals proved to be a good arrangement as each came to know the others' methods.

SECTOR IV

There were twenty-five Emergency Service Hospitals in this Sector, twelve of which were in the inner zone and provided about 1,300 casualty beds; the remainder provided approximately 3,700 beds in the advanced base, base hospitals and local casualty receiving hospitals in the outer zone.

The key hospitals in the central area were Charing Cross, with 100 casualty beds, University College with 160 and St. Pancras with 136. Advanced base hospitals had been organised near the periphery of the London Region, such as Redhill County Hospital, Edgware, with 370 casualty beds, the Royal National Orthopædic Hospital, Stanmore, with 720 casualty beds and hospitals in Hendon and Watford. There were three large base hospitals outside the London Region, the Leavesden Emergency Hospital with 800 beds, Ashridge Emergency Hospital in the Bonar Law College, Ashridge, with 588 beds and Hempstead House, a converted Public Assistance Institution in Hemel Hempstead, with 400 beds.

The Headquarters of the Sector were at Stanmore. As an example of the kind of work done in the Sector hospitals before they had to deal with large numbers of casualties, the following figures show the numbers of patients dealt with in this Sector from the beginning of the war until September 1940:

In-Patients
Civilian Sick	37,755
Civilian Casualties	72
Service Sick (direct admissions)	2,547
Service Sick (overseas)	2,383
Total	42,757

Out-Patients
Civilian Sick	251,516
Civilian Casualties	505
Service Sick	1,750
Total	253,771

The maximum bed occupancy at any time was 4,460, and 5,960 patients had been transferred from the inner zone to the outer zone hospitals in order to keep casualty beds in the central area constantly clear to receive casualties.

From the beginning of September 1940, to the end of August 1941, the Sector dealt with the following patients:

In-Patients
Civilian Sick	38,008
Civilian Casualties	3,467
Service Casualties and Sick	3,616
Total	45,091

Out-Patients
Civilian Sick	151,801
Civilian Casualties	2,072
Service Casualties and Sick	2,911
Total	156,784

LONDON

PLATE I. A typical example of damage to a hospital. Wrecked wing of Mile End Hospital.

Plate II. Wreckage of St. Pancras Hospital.

In the inner zone Charing Cross Hospital dealt with 299 civilian casualties, University College with 199 and St. Pancras with 44. The Hampstead General Hospital also dealt with 230 from that area. In the outer zones, the majority of the casualties were dealt with at Redhill, 321; Royal National Orthopaedic, Stanmore, 360; Leavesden, 341; Hempstead House, 172 and Ashridge, 160. The resources of the Sector were never strained, as the maximum number of beds occupied in the inner zone was 1,480 out of 2,214 available on January 22, 1941 and 2,575 out of 4,616 available on October 23, 1940 in the outer zone, leaving 734 and 2,041 beds still available for further casualties.

The numbers of patients transferred from the inner to the outer zone were 9,375 civilian sick and 689 air raid casualties. To these figures should be added 876 air raid casualties and ordinary sick received from other Sectors.

Damaged Hospitals. As in the other Sectors, many of the hospitals in this Sector were damaged, St. Pancras Hospital (Plate II) on no less than ten occasions, which necessitated large numbers of the patients being transferred on four occasions. Charing Cross Hospital was damaged four times and University College Hospital five times, but not seriously enough for evacuations to be made. The total number of incidents causing damage was 65 in 22 hospitals.

The following account of the work of the Charing Cross Hospital was supplied by the Medical Superintendent, Mr. L. Graham Brown, M.C., M.D., F.R.C.S.:

> Charing Cross Hospital is situated on a small island site in the neighbourhood of Trafalgar Square and before the war it provided three hundred beds, filled by cases from all parts of London and the surrounding country. The local cases were drawn from Covent Garden Market, theatreland and the crowded streets. It was only natural that when war broke out, we should think our civilian work at an end, and that we could expect nothing but air raid casualties. In September 1939, many civilian cases were evacuated to the country, the upper floors were closed, and the old Westminster Eye Hospital (then an extension of the general hospital) was declared unsafe for use.
>
> Instead of air raid casualties, out-patients and ordinary casualties flowed in as before. Cramped even in times of peace, it was impossible to set apart separate out-patient rooms, theatres and wards for these cases. Each room had to serve a dual purpose and be ready for instant conversion from normal to air raid conditions. In August 1940, the out-patient department was functioning as in peace-time, and there were about 80 civilian cases in the wards, leaving 120 beds for emergencies. In this month we took over our first real war job. By arrangement with the Westminster City Council, we supplied a doctor and a trained nurse for the mobile unit stationed on the other side of the Strand at the Adelphi Depot. We also arranged to supply a medical officer and sister for the first-aid post at this depot.

When the air raids began in September 1940, the number of civilian cases in the wards was again reduced by evacuation to the country. The hospital switched over to its new duties, and we found that many preconceived plans had to be modified; nevertheless, neither casualty nor civilian emergency case was turned away. It soon became obvious that we all had to be versatile and prepared to tackle any job, or else the hospital would have required a much larger staff. In this connexion, the medical students excelled themselves and proved their adaptability by acting as stretcher bearers, medical orderlies, fire-fighters and clerks, as the occasion demanded.

When the sirens sounded each evening, two sisters and two doctors left the hospital to take up their duties at the Adelphi Depot. In old mackintoshes and rubber boots, tin-hatted and festooned with respirator and haversack, they did not look like the trim figures of their former selves, but in the few hours before they returned they had often done more than some of us had in weeks of peace-time. Few of us have administered morphia, hanging head down from a rope in a tunnel through fallen masonry and debris. Taking this work in turn was a great advantage to all of us, for when sitting together over our meals we could discuss the course of treatment of any casualty, not from the time he entered the hospital, but from the time he was first seen at the site of the bombing incident.

Besides these informal discussions, the medical staff themselves held a meeting soon after the conclusion of any big incident, and discussed ways and means of improving the organisation for the reception and treatment of casualties. Thus we soon had running an efficient system whereby treatment of casualties and the usual routine hospital work blended smoothly. The routine was made as simple but as elastic as possible. All cases were brought through into the out-patient hall, and from there, the ambulance attendants were issued with fresh stretchers and blankets. The case was rapidly examined—a case sheet affixed with name, provisional diagnosis and immediate treatment on it; while this was being done by a doctor, two students administered morphia and anti-tetanic serum as necessary. The case was then removed to a special resuscitation ward, the out-patient treatment rooms or the ordinary wards. The majority of cases went to the resuscitation ward. Here they were stripped, resuscitation was carried out and they were examined by a surgeon. Cases for operation then went to the theatres. They were returned to the resuscitation ward from the theatres as this enabled the blood transfusion officer to watch both acute and post-operative transfusions. The cases were then transferred to the general wards or the base hospitals in the next few days.

Air raids brought other problems besides the treatment of casualties. The nearby deep tube stations and large air raid shelters attracted many persons who were not local residents. In fact, many were living in these shelters after losing their homes in the East End. Amongst these people colds, sore throats, bronchitis and other minor illnesses were just as common as amongst other communities, but no longer could they be treated by a bottle of medicine and a day in bed. The hospital stepped in to their assistance, admitting to the wards for a few days any such cases as could not be handled in the shelter aid posts. A further arrangement was made with the Westminster City Council whereby three sisters took over the supervision of the health of about 32 shelters. The larger shelters were visited every night and others two or three times a week. Red Cross and St. John Ambulance personnel were on duty at these shelters, and, if faced with any difficult problem, they would call the sisters to their aid. These calls, in addition to their routine rounds, occupied them throughout the night from 8 p.m. to 6 a.m. or later. In these hours they came to know much concerning the intimate side of this strange night life of London, and by their knowledge, enabled us to solve many an individual's problem. The work of these nurses cannot be too highly praised. Walking from shelter to shelter, in the darkness of a London blackout, often during the height of an air raid and at great personal risk to themselves, they proved themselves indeed worthy successors of Florence Nightingale.

This new life soon became as much routine as any other, and it was difficult to realise that anything special was happening. Certain incidents, however, do stand out, as, for instance, an early raid, when we had to accommodate many patients from St. Peter's Hospital at 6 a.m., and evacuate our own medical block at the same time, on account of a delayed action bomb. Then there was the night when an incendiary bomb caught in the roof of the medical block and set it alight. We tried to telephone the Fire Brigade, but the line was dead. We heard later that the Fire Station had received a direct hit. The casualties from that Fire Station were actually being brought in while their comrades from another station were arriving to deal with our fire.

On another occasion, four medical students passed four hours axing, pumping and carrying water to control and eventually extinguish a fire in the medical school roof. They thought that others would be too busy to be worried by such a trifling incident. It was unfortunate that their good work was later on spoilt by a direct hit with high explosive. Even this disaster had its amusing side. The caretaker, firewatching on the roof, fell with the debris, extricated himself from the ruins, made a hasty survey, and then came over to make his report, 'The ferret is quite safe, Sir'.

The night of the Café de Paris incident on March 8, 1941, pushed us to our utmost, but, even then, no one was turned away, and every case needing operation had been to the theatre within twelve hours. Nevertheless, we were grateful for the altered arrangements which prevented such a strain being subsequently thrown on one hospital. The casualties which occurred as the result of this incident were 34 killed, 65 admitted to hospital and 30 treated as out-patients.

Only on one occasion did we have to close our doors, and then only for a few hours of darkness. A nearby land-mine put out all the electric light and blasted out the windows. The emergency lighting could not be used until daylight, because the black-out had been destroyed at the same time as the windows. Only three ambulance loads of casualties had to be re-directed. Temporary repairs, performed by the engineers' staff, enabled us to carry on as usual the same evening.

Like everyone else we had our bomb stories. There was the occasion when a paving stone was flung through a window on the fourth floor into the Skin Department's X-ray room, and damaged nothing but the window it came through. The X-ray tube fortunately had been removed to a place of safety downstairs. Another lucky escape was when the blast brought down the ceiling in the hall, just a second after two doctors had passed through.

Both hospital and school rapidly recovered from these damaging incidents, and both benefited from the careful plans which had been made for evacuation. Patients, personnel and equipment, were transferred outside London, when and as the necessity arose. We have much to be grateful for in the smooth working of these plans, and for the fact that the hospital received no great material damage.

Dr. Pearson, the Sector Group Officer, expressed the opinion that the casualty arrangements worked in a very satisfactory manner, and that medical and surgical services were given with complete efficiency. Reception and resuscitation facilities were good and the value of a system of distributing casualties in reasonable numbers to several hospitals was fully realised when large numbers had to be admitted as the result of the incidents at Hendon and the Café de Paris.

The special Head Centre at Leavesden under Mr. McKissock did exceedingly valuable work and ensured that head cases were treated at the shortest possible notice. About 250 cases of cranio-cerebral injuries were treated in this hospital, with a mortality rate of about 6 per cent. and operation mortality rate of about 16 per cent.

SECTOR V

This was a small Sector containing only twelve hospitals, of which one, providing accommodation for about 200 casualties, was in the inner zone and eleven with 2,657 casualty beds in the outer zone. The inner zone hospital was the Middlesex. In this hospital, of the total bed accommodation of 624, 302 beds in the upper floors were 'frozen', leaving 322 in use for all purposes.

The Mount Vernon Hospital, Northwood, provided an advanced base hospital of about 1,000 beds, and an *ad hoc* hutted hospital at Stoke Mandeville of 936 beds, administered by the Ministry of Pensions, was the only large base hospital.

Since the area served at its apex was small and the area it covered was not heavily attacked, the hospitals of this Sector were never put to any undue strain. The total casualties admitted during the raids were 450 to the inner zone hospital and 869 to those of the outer zone, a total of 1,319. These casualties never arrived in unwieldy numbers at any hospital in the Sector, but the Middlesex Hospital was occasionally fully taxed.

The scheme for evacuating hospitals was fully tested when the Central Middlesex County Hospital, Willesden, after having been hit more than once, was so badly damaged on October 5, 1940, that 400 patients had to be immediately evacuated to other hospitals. This transfer was carried out expeditiously and without incident.

PLATE III. A damaged ward. The Middlesex Hospital.

Ministry of Health

PLATE IV. Casualties being rescued in Bromley.

PLATE V. A typical rescue scene, Bromley.

Damaged Hospitals. The Middlesex Hospital itself was damaged on several occasions, but was never put completely out of action. In September 1940, it was slightly damaged by a direct hit near the out-patients' annexe and by blast from a bomb that hit the B.B.C. offices several hundred yards away. In January 1941, two bombs hit the hospital causing several casualties, of which one was fatal. In February a bomb hit the coal stores of the laundry, killing one of the staff and injuring many others. In April 1941, a large bomb hit the east wing, a new steel and concrete building, and penetrated three floors before exploding. As these floors contained only reserve casualty beds and stores, there was no loss of life. On the same night a shower of incendiary bombs was scattered over the roofs of most of the buildings and, the water supply having been put out of action, several fires were caused, the largest being in the out-patients' annexe and the north wing. The latter was also struck at the head of the stair-well with the result that three flights of stone stairs went crashing into the basement. There was no explosion, and it was thought that there might be an unexploded bomb, but when investigation became possible it was found that a winch and castings weighing several hundredweights had been blown out of the lift shaft of a block of flats 200 yards away. In these raids and in lesser ones, the sub-basement of the hospital was used as a small concentrated hospital unit, containing wards, nurses' quarters, staff rooms, operating theatres, a telephone exchange, etc. In addition to the sub-basement, the lower floor of the main new building, an exceptionally strong steel and concrete structure, was used as wards. This had three floors above and was considered to be reasonably safe. The correctness of the assumption was proved when the east wing was hit in April, as mentioned above.

Plate III illustrates the damage caused to a ward of this hospital.

The demands on the hospital were only occasionally very heavy, such as after the incident at the Café de Paris in Coventry Street in March 1941, when considerable numbers of seriously wounded patients were admitted, as Charing Cross Hospital was unable to deal with all the casualties.

The Central Middlesex County Hospital. This hospital was extensively damaged between September 28 and October 6, 1940. Six H.E.s and many incendiaries fell in the hospital grounds on September 28, causing extensive but not irreparable damage from blast and fires, to kitchens and other services, necessitating a partial and temporary evacuation of the hospital. On October 4, a large bomb fell between two blocks of wards and caused considerable damage to doors and windows by blast. On October 5, a large bomb fell in front of the children's ward which took fire. It also put a main kitchen out of action, so that the whole hospital had to be temporarily evacuated. Subsequently slighter damage was caused by oil bombs, anti-personnel bombs, etc.

The total number of bombs which fell in the hospital premises was 33 and the number of incendiaries about 150. But there were no casualties, except from slight shock and superficial bruises, among the hospital staff or patients.

The only other active hospital to be damaged was the Willesden Municipal Hospital.

Inter-hospital Transport. After nights on which more than normal numbers of casualties were admitted as well as civilian sick, as many patients as possible were evacuated to the outer zone hospitals as a routine measure in Green Line ambulances of the inter-hospital transport. Thus an adequate number of beds was always made available for fresh casualties and the turnover of patients could be considerably increased to the benefit of all concerned and with little disturbance and discomfort to the patients.

Commentary. The only criticism made by Dr. Boldero, the Sector Group Officer, on the working of the Sector Scheme was the failure of the authorities to arrange for the removal of the chronic sick from the central areas. This measure was carried out in October 1940, as the result of the insistent demands of the local authorities. (See Volume I, Chapter 4.) Even after this evacuation from the central areas, a number of first-class beds in the Stoke Mandeville base hospital continued to be unavailable for casualties because of their prolonged occupation by some of the chronic sick. He considered that separate accommodation suitable for this class of patient should have been provided. Dr. Boldero was not alone in this criticism, which was voiced by other Sector Group Officers and by the Hospital Officers of Regions in which considerable numbers of chronic sick from London and the Coastal Belt had been accommodated. It may be said, however, that the Ministry fully agreed with these opinions but, because large numbers of public assistance institutions all over the country had been requisitioned for up-grading, suitable accommodation was simply not available, and the demands of other Government Departments, especially the Fighting Services, made it difficult to obtain other buildings for conversion for this purpose.

SECTOR VI

The apex of the Sector was in the Borough of Paddington and it extended through North Kensington and Hammersmith into Buckinghamshire as far as Amersham and High Wycombe, but it also included as a base hospital, the Park Prewett Emergency Hospital, near Basingstoke.

Hospital Accommodation. The key hospital was St. Mary's Hospital, Paddington, and the Sector Group Officer was Sir Charles Wilson, M.C., F.R.C.P. (afterwards Lord Moran), Physician to St. Mary's Hospital and Dean of the Medical School. In the inner zone the other casualty receiving hospitals were the three London County Council hospitals—Hammersmith, where an independent school of the University of London, the British Postgraduate Medical School, was associated with the municipal hospital, Paddington Hospital and St. Charles Hospital, Kensington. These four hospitals provided on the average about 1,000 beds for casualties out of a total of about 2,000.

There were 19 hospitals in the outer zone with a total accommodation of about 6,500 beds, of which 3,700 were available for casualties. The chief of these was the Park Prewett Emergency Hospital, previously a mental hospital, the whole of which was taken over as a base hospital, thus providing 1,513 beds for casualties. It housed a maxillo-facial centre under Sir Harold Gillies, and a special centre for the treatment of burns, an orthopaedic centre and casualty beds for ordinary cases.

Other large base hospitals were the Amersham Emergency Hospital, with 202 E.M.S. beds, Hillingdon County Hospital, Uxbridge, with 328 casualty beds and Harefield County Hospital, Uxbridge, with 464 casualty beds.

This provision of base hospital beds was found to be ample for this sector.

Casualties: From September 1, 1940 to May 31, 1941, 1,380 air raid casualties were admitted to the Sector hospitals; of these 533 occurred in October, which was the peak period.

Transferred Sick: During the same period 2,786 cases of all kinds were transferred from the inner to the outer zone hospitals or to other Regions.

Damage to Hospitals. The Sector was fortunate in that, although several mines and bombs landed in hospital territory, comparatively little damage was done and all patients and personnel escaped injury. Minor damage was caused to ten hospitals as the result of seventeen incidents. At Hillingdon one ward block had to be pulled down, reducing the number of beds available. One medical officer at Clayponds Hospital won the George Medal for bravery for carrying an unexploded bomb from the precincts of the hospital.

Distribution of the Patients. Every hospital in the Sector received its share of casualties and dealt with them most efficiently and expeditiously. The evacuations from the inner zone hospitals took place at regular intervals, but also on other occasions when such additional action seemed necessary to maintain an adequate number of beds unoccupied. The receiving hospitals in the outer zone were chiefly Park Prewett, Harefield and Amersham. These transfers were at all times dealt with promptly by the ambulance services.

Special mention might be made of the splendid service rendered by the local authority hospitals. Additional strain was thrown upon them because voluntary hospitals were not permitted to encroach upon their casualty bed reserve to any appreciable extent, with the result that the municipal hospitals had to cope with additional civilian sick as well as with air raid casualties, for they had to continue to admit many cases under the London County Council regulations. Although short of staff and with their bed capacity strained to the utmost they maintained the highest efficiency.

The work of the nursing staff in all the general hospitals was magnificent. Many of these were only young girls undergoing their training but they carried on and protected and comforted their patients in the most exacting and hazardous circumstances.

St. Mary's Hospital. The account of the working of the Key Hospital is based on notes supplied by Mr. R. M. Handfield-Jones, M.S., F.R.C.S., Surgeon on the honorary staff of the hospital, and by Mr. V. Zachary Cope, M.S., F.R.C.S., who succeeded Lord Moran as Sector Group Officer in the summer of 1941:

St. Mary's is situated in a densely populated area on which many incendiaries and high explosive bombs fell and it is remarkable that the hospital Medical School and Nurses' Home escaped serious damage. The hospital is five or six storeys high and only the ground floors, first floors and basements were used for casualty work.

Organisation. At the time of the Munich crisis five members of the honorary staff were appointed to prepare plans for adapting St. Mary's to meet the threat of aerial bombardment. All had served for long periods in the last war and their joint experience covered every aspect of the collection, evacuation and treatment of wounded men. Their recommendations were accepted without amendment and stood the test of all the calls made upon the hospital during the bombing of London.

Subsequent changes of central policy crystallised in the Sector system of evacuation and altered the status of the hospital, but apart from easing greatly some of our problems imposed no change upon our arrangements.

The rapid handling of a sudden influx of recently wounded demands:

(1) free ingress and egress,
(2) a reception room manned by teams trained to work quickly and with precision,
(3) a system of classification and distribution of different categories of wounds, and
(4) a pre-operative and resuscitation unit adjacent to the theatre.

By taking two large wards on the ground floor immediately opposite to the main entrance a compact self-contained war unit was created. No comment is needed on the organisation of the six-table theatre, pre-operative and resuscitation rooms, but the reception room presents certain features which may be of interest.

The reception room contained six registration tables each with a pair of trestles in front for a stretcher. Slung on a metal rod between the trestles was an inverted 'Restor radiant-heat cradle' whereby every patient obtained warmth from the moment of arrival all through the process of registration and identification of his or her injuries. The registration was done by an almoner; clinical examination by a receiving room officer who dictated to a senior student. The destination of each patient was entered on the record card and, so that the stretcher bearers should make no mistake, a coloured star was stuck to each card. These colours corresponded to those of large direction arrows in corridors, stairways and ward entrances. It was therefore the simple rule of 'follow the colour'.

While in the reception room each patient received the regular injection of sera and if needed, morphia, all details being entered on the record card.

The System in Action. In spite of the proximity to Paddington Station and the considerable damage to the Borough of Paddington, the casualties reaching St. Mary's fell far below expectations. On the first night of the bombardment of London, September 7, 1940, a number of slight casualties and three serious were admitted and during the rest of the month there was a steady trickle of small numbers. The week-end of October 13, 14, 15 and 16 stretched the physical endurance of the staff to near the limit, as each day and night produced considerable numbers of very seriously wounded people. On the 14th two bombs hit the Metropolitan Station just after a main line train had arrived and the tube platforms were crowded. During the months of November and December the bombing reached a high peak of severity but the district served by St. Mary's seemed to have providential protection and there were comparatively few severe casualties. In the two great final raids on April 17 and May 10, 1941, numbers of seriously wounded were dealt with by teams of surgeons; on May 10 especially, the work was heavy and extra members of the staff had to be called in.

On several occasions the hospital was deluged with incendiaries, but the magnificent efforts of the student fire-fighters prevented any serious damage to the hospital, medical school or nurses' home.

St. Mary's Hospital can claim no outstanding experience over and above that shared by many others, but it remains a great surprise that the hospital escaped direct hits when its proximity to Paddington Station is considered. A great volume of work fell on young people—nurses, doctors, students and almoners—to none of whom had war's noise, mess, blood and fear ever come before. To one who served in France throughout 1914–18, their steadfastness, cheerfulness and gallantry was an inspiring and memorable experience. In those days the War Staff all lived in the hospital, and there developed a camaraderie and team spirit which made the busiest nights go smoothly and efficiently.

Park Prewett Hospital, Basingstoke. The organisation, work and experiences of various hospitals during the period of the heavy raids have already been sufficiently described to illustrate the dangers and difficulties which all hospitals had to be prepared to meet and overcome. The same spirit of service inspired the work of the base hospitals as that which found more dramatic expression in the target areas. The outer zone hospitals, whose geographical position ensured their relative safety, naturally had a less colourful history than those in the inner zone which took the first shock of the air attacks. But in war the base hospital is no less essential than the first-aid post, the dressing station, the clearing hospital and the field hospital. It is at the home base that the chain of treatment is reviewed and extended and the patient is given the benefits of the fuller resources and facilities provided to hasten his complete recovery or, where that is not possible, to mitigate his disability.

Park Prewett, largest of the Sector's outer hospitals, besides acting as a base hospital for air raid casualties and urgent cases of civilian sick from London and the suburbs, also shared in the work of caring for the wounded after Dunkirk as a receiving hospital for Service casualties. The following table—supplied by Dr. Reginald Miller, Medical Director—shows that Service cases formed over 75 per cent. of total admissions during one period of the heavy raids with which this chapter deals. This high proportion of Service cases reflects the situation of the hospital. Cases were transferred from Southampton and Portsmouth as well as from London, and there were also many direct admissions of cases of all sorts from Service camps in the neighbourhood of Basingstoke. The number of admissions of air raid casualties which had received only first-aid treatment was, however, very small. These came from raids at Basingstoke, Odiham, and very rarely, from Southampton.

During the year from the start of the Dunkirk Evacuation in June 1940, to May 31, 1941 the monthly admissions to Park Prewett were as follows:

		Service	Civilian		Total
1940	June	767	35	=	802
	July	352	31	=	383
	August	587	31	=	618
	September	894	168	=	1,062
	October	396	216	=	612
	November	301	343	=	644
	December	238	312	=	550
1941	January	623	203	=	826
	February	525	194	=	719
	March	571	184	=	755
	April	835	281	=	1,116
	May	604	155	=	759
	Total	6,693	2,153		8,846
		75·7 per cent.	24·3 per cent.		100 per cent.

The 6,693 Service cases were made up as follows: British Army, 4,943; Royal Navy, 1,250; Royal Air Force, 332; Canadian, 96; Australian, 8; Free French, Polish and Dutch, 64.

Subsequent developments included the provision of various additional special units, and from D-day, Park Prewett acted as a transit hospital. Its administrative arrangements as such are described in Volume I, Chapter 6.

SECTOR VII

The number of active hospitals in this Sector was 28, of which 12 were in the inner zone; the number of beds immediately available for casualties was usually slightly over 4,000 with a reserve of about 600.

The chief casualty receiving hospitals in the central area were: St. George's with 167 casualty beds, including reserve; the Westminster Hospital with 211; the West London Hospital with about 120 and the L.C.C. Hospital at Fulham with about 200 beds; St. Mary Abbot's 190; St. Stephen's, Chelsea, 200; St. Luke's Chelsea, 200 beds, and the Western Hospital, Fulham, 150 beds.

The chief hospitals scheduled as advanced base hospitals were: Staines County Hospital with 380 casualty beds and reserve beds; West Middlesex Hospital, Isleworth, 200 beds; Windsor County Emergency Hospital, 230 beds and the Slough Emergency Hospital, 120 beds; while the Park Prewett Hospital, Basingstoke, administered by Sector VI, was the chief base hospital. In practice these advanced base hospitals functioned as base hospitals and Park Prewett was not called upon to receive casualties from Sector VII. The number of casualties admitted to the hospitals of this Sector during the raids was 2,488 and at no time was any shortage of beds experienced.

Damaged Hospitals. Damage to hospitals was caused on 33 occasions to 14 hospitals. The Fulham Hospital was damaged four times, and twice temporary evacuations were necessary. St. Mary Abbot's, Kensington, was also damaged four times, and the number of beds was permanently reduced. St. Luke's Hospital, Chelsea, was badly damaged on May 10, 1940, and all the patients had to be evacuated and the hospital closed. St. Stephen's Hospital was severely damaged on two occasions, resulting in the permanent loss of two ward blocks. In other hospitals evacuations also became necessary, chiefly through damage to the essential services, especially water and gas. Only once was a large-scale evacuation necessary during the hours of darkness. This happened when a large unexploded bomb was found to have fallen near St. George's Hospital. In the early hours of the following morning, all the patients and staff, medical, nursing and domestic, were removed either to other hospitals near London or to accommodation provided in a nursing home. Except for this one instance it was found feasible for the hospital staffs to look after the patients until daylight. The emergency lighting which had been installed in the Emergency Medical Service hospitals was found to be a great boon on many occasions when the lighting service failed.

St. George's and the Westminster Hospital on other occasions received direct hits, but there was no evacuation of patients.

On the whole, it was remarkable how few serious casualties occurred among the staff and patients in hospitals which received direct hits from high explosive bombs.

Dr. Feiling, the Sector Group Officer, considered that the arrangements made in the Emergency Hospital Scheme proved satisfactory in practice; a far greater strain was placed on hospital staffs by air raid damage to hospital premises and their essential services than was ever produced by the admissions, treatment and subsequent evacuations of the casualties.

In the early raids there was a tendency to send all casualties from a large incident to one hospital, the result being that this particular hospital got overwhelmed with urgent work, while perhaps other hospitals at a short distance from the incident received few or no casualties. Steps were taken as soon as possible to avoid this uneven distribution of casualties.

Dr. Feiling found that the arrangements made for resuscitation in the casualty receiving hospitals were of the greatest value and that without them many lives would have been lost.

He considered, as the result of experience, that full X-ray facilities were required at all times and that the services of an ophthalmic surgeon were constantly necessary. Until experience had been acquired after the admission of large numbers of casualties, it had not been realised how extensive a clerical staff of some kind was needed to deal quickly with the forms required by the Police and the Emergency Medical Service authorities about the identification of casualties and the nature of their injuries.

As in other Sectors, a shortage of stretcher bearers at some hospitals gave rise to considerable difficulties. It was suggested that this shortage, owing to the man-power difficulty, might be met by arrangements with the military authorities by which members of the Home Guard could receive training in loading and unloading and be available on a rota system to supply reliefs of stretcher bearers to hospitals requiring them.

Dr. Feiling paid a high tribute to the efficiency, patience, skill and care of the Ambulance Officers and their staffs.

The following account of the work of St. George's Hospital was contributed by Lieut. General Sir George Cory, deputy treasurer of the hospital and Mr. A. H. M. Siddons, M.Ch., F.R.C.S., assistant surgeon:

> St. George's, in common with other teaching hospitals in London, came into the Ministry of Health Emergency Scheme as a key hospital in one of the Sectors, and on the outbreak of war was prepared to receive and treat air raid casualties and to evacuate as regularly and quickly as the state of these patients allowed. The arrangements to carry out these duties were made in great detail during the period of tension before the war actually started, and on the whole stood the test of experience and were little altered as time went on.
>
> From the point of view of the victims' reaction, the main difference, perhaps, between the reception and recording of air raid casualties and industrial or traffic accidents, was the worry over the family and house property, the consciousness that the danger was still present, and the darkness. The worry of 'what had happened to the others' must be dealt with at once. For this the record staff at St. George's Hospital found the co-operation of the 'B' Division Police most efficient and sympathetic, as also

was the courageous energy of the voluntary car drivers (subscribers to the hospital) who went out amidst the raids, burning buildings and glass-strewn roads to find and fetch relatives. On the other hand, there was an astonishing acquiescence on the part of the casualty, as compared with the sense of resentment felt, for instance, by the victim of a motor accident.

During the nine months from August 1940 to May 1941, St. George's admitted 396 air raid casualties, many more receiving out-patient treatment.

The staff soon found that in one night they could deal satisfactorily with 35 to 40 casualties, completing all the necessary emergency surgery within ten hours of the injuries. When about 35 patients had been admitted, further ambulances were diverted to neighbouring hospitals. Only on the night of December 21–22, 1940, did they have their hands full, when a total of 69 casualties was admitted. The emergency operating was completed by mid-day, eighteen hours after the onset of the raid.

Casualties were sorted in the large board room (in which John Hunter had died 150 years ago). They were examined there very briefly and those requiring resuscitation were sent to that department, the remainder being distributed to the wards. It was found that as only 10 per cent. of the casualties required transfusions, the fourteen-bedded resuscitation ward was never overcrowded. This ward, which was on the ground floor, had in peace-time been the maternity ward. The adjoining labour ward was equipped and used as an operating theatre, and this, together with one other operating theatre with two tables, was found to be sufficient.

The evacuation of patients the day after a raid required careful organisation. By 9 a.m. a list of those suitable for evacuation was prepared. These were divided into two main classes—those requiring transfer to special centres, such as neurological, orthopaedic and chest centres, and those for transfer to general hospitals outside the centre of London. The latter included a number of sick other than air raid casualties, for the hospital continued its routine work and many patients were found to be willing to come into hospital in spite of the danger of air raids.

Before the cases were transferred in the early afternoon, the secretarial staff found time to make out adequate clinical notes, and copies of these kept in the hospital provided records of all but 14 of the 396 casualties admitted.

Arrangements had been made to segregate hysterical patients as these were expected in considerable numbers. In fact, they did not arrive; there were only two or three patients that were difficult to manage and noisy, and after being quietened with morphia one of these was found to have a penetrating wound of the skull.

Of the total 382 casualties, eight died in hospital and it is believed that not more than two or three died of their injuries after transfer to other hospitals.

The events of two particular nights stand out in the memory of the hospital staff. On December 21–22, 1940, several adjacent buildings had been hit and most of the hospital windows had been broken and the blackout blown down and it was suggested that casualties should be diverted to neighbouring hospitals, but it was found that they too were working to capacity. The hospital, therefore, continued to treat the casualties.

The other night, December 11–12, was the only occasion on which the hospital received a direct hit—though the hospital was hit several times with incendiaries—and fortunately the one 1,000-lb. bomb did not explode.

There was no difficulty in getting patients moved on their beds to parts of the hospital out of range of the bomb, and after this such casualties as had been admitted were treated. A captain of the Royal Engineers inspected the scene and reported that it was a delayed action bomb and obtained permission to render it safe. He was aided by a small party of volunteers from the A.R.P. organisation and from the hospital staff. It was, however, found impossible to render it safe in the time allotted and the 122 in-patients and entire hospital staff were evacuated in the early hours of the morning. This was organised by the A.R.P. authorities under whose direction it proceeded without incident. Seven days later the Royal Engineers had removed the bomb and St. George's was open once again and ready for the next raid.

SECTOR VIII

The Headquarters of this Sector was housed in the Surrey County Council Hall, Kingston, and was based on St. Thomas's Hospital, with its accommodation for 330 patients (reduced from 440). The other principal hospitals in the central area were the Lambeth Hospital (L.C.C.) with 120 casualty beds, St. James's Hospital, Balham (L.C.C.) with 20 casualty beds, but with a large reserve of 354 beds, and the Grove Hospital, Tooting, with 59 casualty beds and a reserve of 60 beds.

The Kingston County Hospital with 85 casualty beds and 109 reserve beds; St. Helier's, Carshalton, with 30 casualty beds and 90 reserve beds and others were scheduled as advanced base hospitals. The main reception or base hospital was the large hutted hospital at Botley's Park, Chertsey, with 1,351 beds which housed special centres for orthopædic surgery and peripheral nerve injuries; others were Warren Road Hospital, Guildford, with 217 beds, Woking War Hospital with 243 beds, the Royal Surrey County Hospital, Guildford, with 151 beds and 92 in an annexe, and St. Thomas's Hospital, evacuated to Hydestile, Godalming.

Other hutted hospitals projected for this Sector had been handed over to the New Zealand and Australian Medical Corps and to the War Office and were not used by the Sector.

There was in addition Queen Mary's Hospital, Roehampton, which was administered by the Ministry of Pensions. At the time of the big air raids it functioned as an orthopaedic centre and a maxillo-facial centre, with 184 beds. It was afterwards much enlarged and became the limb fitting centre for the whole country. The account of its work will be found in the Ministry of Pensions section of this History.

The central areas of this Sector sustained some heavy attacks, but the casualties were fairly equally distributed in space and time; thus in the inner zone Lambeth Hospital received 685 casualties, St. James's 486, South Western 336, South London Women's 298, St. Thomas's 274, etc. Occasionally smaller hospitals in the outer zone were flooded with casualties from local incidents, a thing difficult to avoid in the middle of heavy attacks, but these hospitals were rapidly cleared on the following day.

The bed position was never strained but on May 14, 1941 there were only 300 beds returned as vacant in the inner zone and 1,068 in the outer zone. Professor de Wesselow, the Sector Group Officer, was of the opinion that the figure for the outer zone gave a false picture of the position, as many of the vacant beds were in the numerous small hospitals in the suburbs kept vacant for local incidents and he calculated that there were really only 450 beds available for transfers from the inner zone on that day.

As the Wilson Hospital, Mitcham, the Kingston County Hospital, the Nelson Hospital, Merton and the Royal Hospital, Richmond, admitted 173, 123, 210 and 112 casualties respectively during the raids, the necessity for keeping vacant beds in these smaller hospitals was fully proved.

The total number of air raid casualties admitted to hospital up to June 19, 1941, was 4,298; during the same period 4,701 sick civilians were transferred from inner to outer hospitals to free beds for air raid casualties.

Damage to Hospitals. In all, nineteen hospitals were damaged thirty-nine times, mostly in a minor degree. The only hospitals to be seriously damaged from the point of view of functional efficiency were St. Thomas's, Lambeth, and to a minor degree, the Battersea General Hospital. The usable beds in the two former hospitals at the end of the raids were reduced to 281 and 40 respectively. St. Thomas's was damaged on eight occasions and Lambeth on six. Evacuation of patients in considerable numbers was necessary on three occasions. On September 9, 1940, 192 patients were transferred from St. Thomas's; on September 15, 1940 and on January 11, 1941, 319 and 130 patients respectively were transferred from Lambeth.

Mobile Surgical Teams. Professor de Wesselow considered that these teams were less necessary in the Emergency Hospital Scheme than in the Army in the field. In his opinion the need for them could be avoided by close attention to the primary distribution of patients in the available hospitals.

Resuscitation. Professor de Wesselow was of opinion that at the beginning of the raids insufficient attention was paid to resuscitation and that it was often neglected in favour of immediate operative intervention, but this was soon remedied. He considered, however, that blood transfusion in some hospitals was carried to extremes, and that hospitals using smaller amounts of blood obtained results just as good as those using larger quantities.

He considered that the liaison with the Civil Defence Services was not fully effective in the inner zone, though in the outer zone it was excellent, largely because his headquarters were in the same building as Group 9, Civil Defence Headquarters.

He praised the work of the Ambulance Services in both zones and found the Despatch Rider Service adequate and satisfactory.

The following account of the work at St. Thomas's Hospital was contributed by Mr. A. P. B. Irwin, the House Governor:

During the months preceding the outbreak of war, the Governors took certain precautionary measures to reduce casualties in the event of the hospital being struck by missiles or blast. These measures included:

(a) The evacuation of the top floors of the hospital.
(b) The provision of additional fire-fighting appliances and the detailing of fire parties to certain key positions.
(c) The replacement of glass lantern lights by concrete roofs.
(d) The preparation of an emergency operating theatre in the basement.
(e) The removal of two-thirds of the ward windows; their replacement by shutters, and the protection of the remaining windows by adhesive strips.
(f) The building of sandbag revetments and blast walls.

A system had also been worked out, and practised, for the evacuation of patients from the wards in the event of the lifts becoming useless. For this purpose, volunteer squads of medical students were used and proved to be most efficient.

Under arrangements made with the Ministry of Health, the bed complement was reduced to 200 casualty beds and 130 beds for civilian sick.

During the second week in September the hospital was struck on three separate occasions by heavy bombs, all of which fell on the line of the main corridor and caused great destruction. The first bomb destroyed the nurses' home in Block I and the home for paying patients which fortunately had been closed, besides blasting all the wards in Block II and rendering them unusable. The patients in Block II were transferred by stretcher bearer squads to Block VII without incurring any casualties. As the lifts were out of action and the gas and water supplies had failed, it was decided to send to their homes all patients who were sufficiently fit to be discharged, and the next day the remaining patients were transferred to Sector hospitals in order to make possible intensive repairs with the object of reopening a total of 206 beds in two days' time.

The second bomb destroyed the night nurses' home and in consequence the housing problem for nurses and maids became acute. Eventually it was temporarily settled by placing mattresses for some of the maids under the beds in the nurses' dormitory.

The third bomb struck the centre of the hospital, severing all communications on the ground and basement levels, and destroying the medical out-patient department, the resident medical officers' house and the canteen, and wrecking the kitchen and administrative block, besides putting all the essential services of the hospital out of action. The destruction of the kitchen created a problem in the supply of meals for resident staff, and this might have proved insoluble if the Governors had not been able to take over, at the invitation of the Dean, the kitchen and dining room of the Medical Students' Club.

On two subsequent occasions the hospital suffered very heavy damage, and the total casualties to medical, nursing and lay staff amounted to 10 killed and 60 injured.

The only in-patient to become a casualty suffered minor injuries from flying glass.

During all these months the hospital received a steady flow of air raid casualties, which were dealt with at the first-aid post organised in conjunction with the hospital's casualty department. Two wards, improvised from out-patient departments, had been prepared for the reception of air raid casualties in the basement, and were in constant use, as was the underground theatre. These arrangements worked very smoothly, the wards being cleared on the following mornings by sending convoys to Sector hospitals, under arrangements made with the Group Officer.

The highest number of admissions of air raid casualties on any one day was 38, though of course a large number of walking cases were treated for minor injuries on most nights during the period of intensive bombing. The hospital could have undertaken the care of a much greater number and was easily able to deal with all the demands made upon it.

Meanwhile the hospital dealt with civilian emergencies and arranged for their evacuation to Sector hospitals by Green Line ambulances, as in the case of air-raid casualties.

Between September 1940, and May 1941, the numbers of patients evacuated were: Civilian Sick, 571; Air raid Casualties, 168.

The bed complement was severely affected by the destruction caused to so many parts of the hospital, and the fluctuations were as follows:

August 1939	440
September 1940	57
April 1941	15
May 1941	35

After that date the bed complement steadily increased and stood at 180 in February 1944, while out-patient attendances had become nearly normal again.

The Governors regret the loss of so many valuable members of the staff, and the appalling destruction caused to the buildings during the autumn and spring of 1940–41, but they can look back with much satisfaction to the remarkable fact that there was no loss of life amongst the in-patients of the hospital. They can also recall with pride the exemplary behaviour of all members of the staff, who carried out their duties courageously and efficiently under conditions of difficulty, discomfort and considerable danger.

St. Thomas's Hospital, Hydestile, Surrey. Mr. R. Pelham Borley, Clerk to the Governors, sent the following account of the country branch of the hospital:

Owing to the crippling damage inflicted on St. Thomas's by enemy action, the Governors were compelled to open a country branch in order to maintain full facilities for the treatment of patients, and the education of medical students, nurses and physiotherapists. This branch was opened in April 1941, at Hydestile, near Godalming, the site being provided by the L.C.C. and the buildings by the Ministry of Health, in a hutted hospital formerly used by the Australian Forces. Although the bed complement remained more or less the same as when it was taken over, the change from being purely a military hospital to a general teaching hospital involved extensive alterations and improvements.

Among these were the provision of an administrative block, lecture rooms, library, chapel, nurses' sick quarters, canteen, dining-rooms, diet kitchen, an enlarged main kitchen, pathological laboratory, casualty, massage, electro-therapy and lady almoner's departments; accommodation for lay, nursing and medical staffs, a linenry, and a hut for occupational therapy. The completion of these and other alterations practically doubled the size of the hospital.

It was obviously not practicable to open the hospital completely at first but gradually ward after ward was made ready until 334 beds were available, the full complement. 274 of these beds were allocated for civilian sick, and the remainder for casualties under the Emergency Medical Service Scheme.

The necessity for establishing a hospital in the country owing to the exigencies of war, proved to be a most interesting experiment, providing much useful data, and giving an insight into the possibilities and difficulties of maintaining a large (London) teaching hospital permanently outside of the Metropolis—a scheme which has had its advocates from time to time.

From this experience, the St. Thomas's Hospital authorities have concluded that the advantages were outweighed by the disadvantages. The opening of the branch at Hydestile inevitably meant much dislocation of the family life of many of the staff. It was impossible to find accommodation for wives and families unless houses were built specially for them and when, after much trouble, billets and quarters were ultimately found, much was left to be desired.

The same difficulties were met with in arranging accommodation for the nursing staff, and this obstacle was only overcome by finding quarters for them, spread over an area of ten square miles. This meant the provision of a private bus service, and as all the food had to be conveyed from London by lorry thrice weekly, the transport bill was naturally a very heavy one.

The actual administration of the country branch from the outset was directed from London in order to avoid unnecessary over-lapping but, with a branch situated over forty miles away, it was inevitable that there must be duplication of staff, which involved considerable difficulties and expense. Another important point was the arrangements for treating patients at both hospitals by a medical staff seriously reduced by the numbers who had gone into the Forces. Medical staff who were busy at Hydestile in the morning were often back at St. Thomas's, London, performing operations or taking clinics in the afternoon.

Two interesting features at Hydestile were a ward for children, named 'America Ward', which was largely made possible by the generous gifts called 'Bundles for Britain', and the provision of a Victor X-ray Therapy apparatus, which was presented by the American Red Cross.

With regard to the treatment of patients, it became increasingly evident that Londoners being transferred so far away from home, especially after the end of the war, were a source of anxiety, not only to themselves as patients, but also to their relatives, who found it difficult to continue their visits. Experience at Hydestile provided no evidence that the type of case normally treated in a teaching hospital, where the average length of stay is 17 days, benefited particularly by being in the country.

SECTOR IX

This Sector, whose headquarters were at Epsom, was based on King's College Hospital. It spread out through the eastern half of Surrey and to east and west of Sussex as far south as Horsham and Haywards Heath. The estimated population of the Sector was normally about a million, of which nearly half a million were in the metropolitan area and about a quarter of a million in the county borough of Croydon.

It had more hospital accommodation than any of the other Sectors, for it had 38 active hospitals, of which four only were in the inner zone, and over 10,000 casualty beds, of which about 9,000 were in the outer zone. King's College Hospital, Denmark Hill, had a normal bed accommodation of 452, but because of the policy of 'freezing' about one-third of the beds, only 220 beds were available for casualties.

Other large hospitals in the metropolitan area were two L.C.C. hospitals, i.e. St. Giles', Camberwell, and the Dulwich Hospital, with about 100 casualty beds immediately available and a reserve of about 360 beds; the South-eastern hospital in Lewisham could also usually provide 70 casualty beds. In the extra-metropolitan area were situated the Epsom County Hospital, with about 120 casualty beds and a reserve of 82; the Sutton Emergency Hospital, with 800 beds available for casualties, which also had an annexe for children in the Queen Elizabeth Hospital, Banstead, with about 200 available beds.

Croydon was served by the Croydon General Hospital with about 150 available beds and the May Day Hospital, Thornton Heath, with about 350 beds.

Outside the London area the chief hospitals were the Horton Emergency Hospital, Epsom, which had been taken over from the L.C.C., with about 2,000 active beds and a reserve of 300, and housed special centres for orthopaedic surgery and chest surgery; Hurstwood Park Hospital, Haywards Heath, with 220 beds and special head and spinal centres; Queen Victoria Hospital, East Grinstead, with its annexe, with 150 beds and special centres for maxillo-facial surgery and burns. There were in addition other large hospitals, such as Redhill County Hospital, Reigate, with about 270 available beds; Leatherhead Emergency Hospital, with 612 active beds and a reserve of 311; St. Lawrence's Hospital, Caterham and Cane Hill Hospital, Coulsdon (wings of mental hospitals) with 250 beds and 261 beds respectively; and Queen Mary's Hospital, Carshalton, with 76 active and 124 reserve beds.

The report of the Sector for the year ending April 30, 1941, shows that during this period, which included the reception of battle casualties from Dunkirk and air raid casualties chiefly from London, more than 25,000 patients were dealt with. Of these, 14,351 were from the combatant Services, 4,562 were air raid casualties and 6,753 were transferred civilian sick from the inner zone hospitals. Approximately two-thirds of the beds were constantly occupied and about half the patients were E.M.S.

The shortage of medical staff even at this period is shown by the fact that the whole medical staff consisted of only 150 whole-time medical officers and 77 part-time. The nursing staff was better as there were 3,500 whole-time nurses, of whom about 1,200 were fully trained.

The following appreciation of the work of the hospitals during the raids has been extracted from the report of Mr. J. B. Hunter, Sector Hospital Officer.

Reception of Casualties. It was soon found that the number of casualties received from any raid was such that they could easily be accommodated in nearby hospitals; on only one occasion did any hospital become unduly crowded. The arrangements by which each casualty receiving hospital stopped admissions when the number reached a figure based on the number of operating tables available, ensured that there was no overcrowding. It was usual for the casualties to arrive in driblets, the less seriously injured generally coming first. In order that the serious cases subsequently arriving should not have to wait, the general rule was not to operate during a raid unless the operation could not be safely postponed.

The importance of an experienced casualty receiving officer to sort out the cases into those requiring resuscitation and early surgery and those who could wait transfer to outer zone hospitals was soon realised. The important rôle that efficient resuscitation played in the management of air raid casualties was fully established, and an adequately equipped and staffed resuscitation suite was found just as important as an operating theatre.

Transfer of Casualties. It was rarely found necessary to transfer cases from the receiving hospitals during the progress of an air raid. To attempt to transfer blocks of patients in the black-out during a raid would have placed an unnecessary strain on the medical and nursing staffs, already fully engaged in dealing with the casualties. Even when hospitals were damaged it was found advisable, except on one occasion, to await daylight before starting evacuation.

The inter-hospital transport, despite the heavy demands made on it after a raid, was always immediately available, even when the patients and staff of a bombed hospital had to be moved.

Damaged Hospitals. St. Giles's Hospital received a direct hit from a heavy bomb, necessitating the evacuation of the whole hospital which contained over 500 patients, and it was two months before 100 beds could be brought back into commission. There was only one casualty.

At the St. Lawrence Hospital, Caterham, evacuation was also necessary when the main sewer of the hospital was broken. There were no casualties.

The Sutton Emergency Hospital received a direct hit on a crowded ward block, which is fully described below in a summary of the report on the work of this hospital submitted by Dr. Louis Minski, Medical Superintendent.

Altogether sixteen hospitals were damaged on thirty-two occasions, but apart from the above-mentioned, the damage was trivial.

The advantage of having underground reception and resuscitation rooms was appreciated at King's College Hospital, when over 180 cases were admitted and attended to without interruption, despite extensive damage to windows and black-out.

Mobile Surgical Teams. On ten occasions mobile surgical teams were made use of, to act as reliefs when the surgical staffs of hospitals had a number of heavy operations on hand.

Special Teams. Special mobile teams for cranio-cerebral, maxillo-facial and chest surgery from the special centres had been arranged for and equipment provided to enable these teams when necessary to visit hospitals in the Sector or even in other Sectors and Regions. As it was obviously better to move the patient to a special centre than for the centre to move to another hospital, especially during a raid, it was found convenient that the special surgeons should visit each hospital in advance of the team in order to decide whether it would be necessary for the team to come to the patient.

Medical Education. King's College Hospital Medical School was the only teaching hospital in the Sector and students were mostly taught at Leatherhead, Horton and King's College, but went to certain other hospitals for instruction in special subjects. In Mr. Hunter's opinion the students did not suffer from this arrangement, the examination results showed a smaller percentage of failures than in peace-time.

Mr. Hunter considered that on the whole the original conception of the E.M.S. Scheme was good and produced a complete hospital service for the fighting forces and for some of the sick and injured who would normally have been dealt with in the metropolitan hospitals. The equipment was found adequate for dealing with air raid casualties and for the special cases in the special centres, but showed numerous defects for normal hospital practice, which constituted about half the work of the hospital. He recorded his view that the co-operation and mutual goodwill which existed between the voluntary and municipal hospital authorities had been a vital factor in enabling the Sector to meet the varied demands made on it from time to time.

A wide choice of consultant assistance was always available in all the hospitals in the Sector.

The total number of casualties occurring during the raids was 4,716, the monthly admissions being:

1940		1941	
August	197	January	115
September	1,423	February	53
October	1,231	March	164
November	426	April	478
December	366	May	263

The largest number of patients admitted on any one day was after the raid on the night of April 16–17 when 355 casualties were admitted, the next highest figure being about 200 casualties admitted on May 11. The fluctuation in the monthly admission is a fair example of what occurred in the other Sectors because of the varying severity of the attacks.

The following short summaries of the work of two hospitals may be of interest as typical examples of the experiences of large Sector base hospitals during the raids:

Horton E.M.S. Hospital. By far the largest hospital in this Sector was Horton Mental Hospital on which the work of conversion into a general hospital, with full medical and surgical services, had been started in June 1939. Within eight hours of the 'clear hospitals' order of August 27 it had been emptied of some 2,200 patients who, with part of the staff, were transferred to other mental hospitals in the neighbourhood. The Medical Superintendent, W. D. Nicol, M.D., F.R.C.P., together with his deputy, the Matron and other administrative officers remained in charge of the hospital and of their appropriate departments. By September 3 there were 45 doctors and 643 nurses on duty and 2,000 beds were available for use.

The absence of casualties during the first few months of the war enabled the work of conversion to be continued. The hospital was separated into civilian and military divisions, and a separate building, with accommodation for 50, was reserved as an officers' hospital.

In addition to general medical and surgical work, special units were established to deal with injuries and diseases of the chest and with orthopaedic conditions. An ear, nose and throat centre to serve the Southeastern area of England and an extensive physiotherapy and rehabilitation centre were set up and later, a peripheral nerve injury unit was added. The small, self-contained malaria therapy unit, of 30 beds and laboratories, which had been established before the war under the auspices of the Ministry of Health and the London County Council, continued its work under Dr. Nicol.

During the first year of the war, Horton, which was capable of expansion to 2,300 beds, dealt mainly with civilian sick, who formed approximately 74 per cent. of the total number of patients under care on January 1, 1940.

At that date the hospital contained 1,159 civilian and 354 Service sick, plus only 57 other Service casualties and two civilian air raid casualties—a total of 1,572 patients. Thereafter the number of civilian sick fell and casualties increased, the average numbers on January 1 for the next five years being: civilian sick 617, Service sick and wounded and civilian air raid casualties 687.

Some idea of the work of the hospital may be gained from the following figures (to the nearest hundred in each case) for the period September 1939 to August 15, 1945:

Civilian sick and accident cases	26,100
Civilian air raid casualties	3,400
Service sick	15,900
Service battle casualties (including 5,400 in transit from Normandy) Service air raid casualties and accidents	15,500
Total	60,900

During this period approximately 36,500 operations were performed and over 78,000 X-ray examinations were made.

The heavy raids of 1940–41 and the flying bomb attacks of 1944 were reflected in the number of admissions of civilian air raid casualties shown in the following table:

Year	Number
1939 (from September 3)	2
1940	979
1941	698
1942	248
1943	393
1944	962
1945 (to August 15)	88
	3,370

Civilian air raid casualties formed less than 6 per cent of the total number of patients at Horton, where both civilian and Service sick and injured were admitted in large numbers and retained for treatment for all conditions except those for which special provision had been made elsewhere, e.g., cases of psycho-neurosis, mental disorders, fevers, maxillo-facial injuries, head injuries and children's diseases.

It may be recalled that Horton Hospital had previously been used as a war hospital from 1915 to 1919, and thus it again played an important part in the nation's hospital services under emergency conditions.

Sutton Emergency Hospital. This hospital was brought into being in under three months by adapting the L.C.C. Training Centre at Sutton, which when completed was fully equipped and staffed to accommodate 800 patients, 600 beds for general medicine and surgery, and 200 beds for a neurosis centre. It provided two operating suites with two operating tables in each, fully equipped X-ray and physiotherapy departments, a pathological laboratory, an electro-encephalographic department and a section for occupational therapy. It also had a fully equipped dental clinic.

Before the raids the staff had considerable experience in dealing with large numbers of admissions. The hospital opened from October 10, 1939, by admitting weekly batches of transferred civilian sick from the inner zone hospitals and treated numbers of Service sick from units in the vicinity. It also took in convoys from the base hospitals in France and on May 22, 1940, admitted 250 battle casualties from Dunkirk. In June three further convoys of seriously wounded patients from France were admitted. These convoys threw a far greater strain on the medical and nursing staff of the hospital than the London raids did at any time for the proportion of seriously injured requiring major operations was very high. After the receipt of the first of these convoys all four operating tables were in continuous use for three days. The first air raid casualties began to come in towards the end of August 1940, mostly from local incidents connected with the Battle of Britain, a considerable part of which was fought in the outer areas of this Sector. The hospital was slightly damaged at this time by a shower of incendiary bombs which were promptly dealt with by the staff; the damage was only minor and was mostly due to the water used to extinguish the bombs. On September 9, as a result of the heavy raid on the inner zone on the night of September 7–8, patients began to arrive from the central hospitals in a steady stream which continued throughout September, October and November, after which the admissions gradually diminished except for rises in the third week of April and the second week of May. The hospital was kept busy during the whole of this period because the admission of batches of transferred civilian sick continued as usual, as did the treatment of Service sick.

The total number of air raid casualties admitted during the raids was 607; the total number of patients dealt with up to the end of August 1941, was:

Civilian casualties	427
Service sick and casualties	1,349
Police casualties	6
Civil Defence casualties	46
Civilian Sick	1,562
Total	3,390

These patients were dealt with in the surgical and medical wards of the hospitals and did not include admissions to the neurosis centre. These were as follows:

Civilian casualties	41
Service sick and casualties	2,023
Civil Defence casualties	16
Civilian sick	726
Total	2,806

The figure for neurosis cases among civilian casualties is strikingly small and apart from the period following Dunkirk, when the men went through a time of severe stress coupled with exhaustion, lack of sleep and food, a feeling of inability to strike back and continuous retreat, very few of the Service cases admitted could be called war neurosis. Nearly all were found to be neurotic before they entered the Service and broke down because they were unsuited to Army conditions and/or from stresses having little or no relation to the war.

Damage to the Hospital. High explosive and incendiary bombs fell in the hospital premises on several occasions, but only once did serious harm. On October 7, 1940, a high explosive bomb struck a three-storey block housing medical and surgical patients and caused considerable damage; twenty patients and three members of the staff were killed and eleven patients and six members of the staff were injured. All the members of the staff behaved in an exemplary manner and it was largely due to their efforts that the casualty list was not greater. They crawled into the debris without hesitation in spite of escaping gas and in some cases with water running down their backs, and patients were passed out, or given morphia when they could not be moved. The local A.R.P. service were on the spot very quickly and rendered yeoman service. Everyone worked throughout the night without rest and about 200 patients fit to be moved were transferred to another hospital smoothly and quickly. By early morning everyone had been accounted for. For the next few days the admission of casualties was stopped to restore order and clear up the mess. It was found that 151 beds had been put out of action, but by making use of the concert and recreation halls as wards as a temporary expedient, the lost beds were quickly replaced.

On October 11, the neurosis block was put out of action by damage from the blast of a large bomb which fell just outside and 180 patients had to be transferred to other hospitals. In a few weeks the damage had been made good and the neurosis block was again opened.

On December 30, seventy-five patients from Guy's Hospital, which was evacuated as it was ringed by fire, were admitted and the first ambulance contained mothers and new-born babies. The hospital had no equipment for dealing with such cases, but cots were improvised and babies' bottles and other articles borrowed from a nearby children's hospital. In addition a large part of the X-ray and laboratory apparatus from Guy's Hospital also arrived for storage, and a number of Guy's nurses for whom accommodation was found. When Guy's was again functioning the equipment and staff were returned.

Dr. L. Minski, the Medical Superintendent, paid a tribute to the loyal co-operation of the Sector Authorities, the London County Council and all the members of the staff.

SECTOR X

This Sector was almost as large as Sector IX and also contained thirty-eight active hospitals, of which thirteen were in the inner zone. It provided about 10,000 casualty beds, of which about 2,250 were in the inner zone. The area it covered contained the highly congested metropolitan boroughs of Deptford and Bermondsey at its apex and also the large metropolitan boroughs of Greenwich, Woolwich and Lewisham. It then projected down the south of the Thames Estuary and the Southern Railway main line as far as the River Medway in the north and Tunbridge Wells in the south and contained practically all the largest hospitals in Kent. The whole Sector was probably the most vulnerable to air attack, since experience showed that the Thames Estuary and the Southern Railway main line to Folkestone and Dover were the chief routes of the enemy bombers in attacks on London. It was also the area in which they jettisoned large numbers of unused bombs when retreating.

The headquarters of this Sector were well situated in Orpington. Guy's Hospital was the key hospital. Its normal pre-war capacity of 691 beds had been largely reduced so that it only provided about 400 casualty beds including reserve beds. Other large inner zone hospitals were St. Olave's, Bermondsey, with 400 casualty beds; St. Alfege's, Greenwich, with 340 casualty beds, Lewisham Hospital with 150 casualty beds and St. Nicholas Hospital, Woolwich, with 150 casualty beds. Further out were the large Southern Hospital in Dartford with 1,254 casualty beds and a reserve of 250 beds and the Joyce Green Hospital, Dartford, with 1,340 beds. These were both L.C.C. hospitals.

The chief base hospitals were the Orpington Emergency Hospital with 800 casualty beds and a nearby county hospital at Farnborough with 200 beds, also Queen Mary's Hospital, Sidcup, with 300 beds. There were further the Kent County Hospital, Pembury, with 500 beds and the Kent and Sussex Hospital with 300 beds in the Tunbridge Wells area.

As in Sector I on the north of the Thames Estuary, it was not considered advisable to use many of these large hospitals, in an area vulnerable to invasion, for receiving air raid casualties from London. Nevertheless, 6,648 air raid casualties were dealt with in the Sector hospitals; 5,458 were admitted to the hospitals in the metropolitan area, 902 to the Kent hospitals outside this area and 288 from the extra sectorial portion of Region 12. In each case more than 50 per cent. of the admissions were during September and October 1940. These figures omit many patients with slight injury, who were discharged to their homes after treatment and rest for periods of two to six hours.

Casualties admitted to Guy's and St. Olave's, however, were not evacuated to the base hospitals of this Sector, but by arrangement were transferred to the base hospitals in Sector IX, and 543 patients were thus transferred. In addition, as many beds as possible in the outer portion of the Sector were kept vacant for possible battle casualties.

In May 1940, the Group Officer, Professor Johnston, issued a circular letter to all Sector hospitals on the importance of informing the Sector headquarters at once when air raid casualties were being admitted and of subsequently submitting progress reports, because in such a large and vulnerable Sector, it was essential that information at headquarters should be right up-to-date. When these reports were received it was a routine measure to ask whether help of any kind was required by way of mobile surgical teams, etc. In practice it was found that the larger hospitals proved reluctant to ask for outside help, and thus placed an unnecessarily heavy strain on the willing shoulders of their own staffs. At first there was a failure to appreciate that most of the patients were suffering from varying degrees of shock and there was therefore a tendency to rush them to the operating theatre. There was also a tendency to admit more patients than could be coped with before informing the Sector headquarters. Apparently the hospital staffs did not realise that this excessive zeal might be detrimental to the continued efficiency of their work, and also to the patients, for a tired operator cannot possibly produce his best. It was also quite unnecessary, because fresh reliefs were always available. The smaller hospitals frequently asked for help which was always forthcoming. But when these errors were corrected, the treatment given to air raid casualties could hardly have been improved upon.

Damage to Hospitals. The greatest difficulties experienced in Sector X arose from (1) direct hits on hospital buildings and services, (2) delayed action bombs within the curtilage of a hospital and (3) damage to telephone exchanges and lines. No fewer than 16 hospitals, many of them on several occasions, sustained serious damage from direct hits. In nearly every case water mains, gas mains or electric cables were also involved. On account of the size of most of the hospitals, it was the damage to services which determined whether or not the whole hospital had to be evacuated for the time being. When evacuation in part or in whole proved necessary, the arrangements worked without a hitch and the delays were minimal. Of the other hospitals six suffered extensive damage from blast.

Only eight Class IA hospitals, including four of the smallest, escaped with practically no damage. During the period there were no fewer than 85 instances in which hospitals sustained damage from enemy action, but fortunately the casualties among the personnel and patients were relatively light. They amounted to 42 killed, 17 seriously injured and a small number of minor injuries.

Distribution of the Casualties. In the metropolitan area sixteen hospitals dealt with more than 100 casualties each. Of them Guy's (923) and St. Olave's (767) were much the hardest worked, showing that the adjoining postal areas of S.E.1 and S.E.16 suffered more than other districts. The Greenwich district (St. Alfege's 443, Miller General 426, St. John's 60 and Dreadnought 28) came next, followed by Woolwich (Woolwich War Memorial 386, St. Nicholas 269 and the Brook Hospital 268), Lewisham and Hither Green (Lewisham Hospital 487 and Park

Hospital 106). The Sidcup, Bromley, Beckenham and Farnborough hospitals each dealt with 200–250 cases, Orpington with 128 and Erith with 129, all direct admissions. In addition, however, the County hospitals at Farnborough and Orpington, in their capacity as advanced base hospitals, received many hundreds of casualties transferred from the inner London hospitals.

On the nights of the heaviest raids it was not uncommon for as many as 13 or 14 hospitals to be admitting casualties on the same night. So long as telephone communications remained intact, there were few avoidable delays. On many occasions, however, telephone communications were interrupted and it was not easy to maintain contact with all the hospitals.

The Ambulance Controls and the Police were most helpful in passing on messages and the despatch riders proved invaluable.

Throughout the whole period the transport arrangements were most efficient. Delays were rare and the interval between the summoning and the arrival of ambulances at hospitals was minimal. After an incident casualties were transported to hospital much more quickly than had been expected, a fact which reflected the greatest credit on the organisation of the Civil Defence Ambulance arrangements.

General Comments. Region V Headquarters and Whitehall were most co-operative and were always willing to provide help when it was sought.

The evacuation of casualties from inner London to advanced base and base hospitals, which had the advantage of expert surgical advice, provided a means of assessing the immediate treatment given to the patients. Surgeons of experience and seniority were encouraged to visit the smaller hospitals when there was reason to believe that the methods of treatment were open to criticism. Tactfully carried out, these visits, far from causing any resentment, were welcomed by the staffs of the hospitals concerned. Later the appointment of Advisers to groups of hospitals with wider duties was sponsored by the Ministry.

The Casualty Bureau arrangements at Sector X Headquarters proved of great value. Bedstate figures were subject to sudden and substantial fluctuations but, thanks to the efficiency of the Casualty Bureau, it never happened that casualties were directed to a hospital which was unable to cope with them.

Two features stood out during the period. (1) The way in which the staffs of the hospitals, medical, nursing and lay, reacted to heavy bombing was beyond all praise. Everyone was always ready to lend a hand. Doctors and nurses took an active share with the porters in rescue work when this had to be done, or in clearing wards and evacuating the patients. There were many shining examples of courage and self-sacrifice, only a few of which received official recognition. They included the posthumous award of the George Cross to Porter A. E. Dolphin, South-eastern Hospital and the award of the George Medal to Dr. Laura Bateman, Brook Hospital, Shooter's Hill, S.E.18. (2) The other gratifying feature was the willingness displayed at all hospitals to work far beyond normal limits without complaint or request for relief.

The following account is based on and the quotations are taken from an article 'Guy's and the German War' by P. M. F. Bishop, M.D., Medical Officer-in-Charge (Emergency Medical Services), Guy's Hospital (*Guy's Hospital Gazette*, July 21, 1945).

Guy's Hospital. After the fall of France, when daylight raids on the South of England and enemy preparations for invasion indicated that the long expected aerial attack on London could not much longer be delayed, London hospitals re-awoke to the need for action and at Guy's, as elsewhere, practices and rehearsals, which had begun to pall and were maintained only with difficulty during the waiting period, were resumed with a renewed sense of urgency. Everything possible was done to perfect every detail of the casualty reception organisation. The toil and sweat were there, the blood and tears were to come. As air raid alerts became more frequent and armed reconnaissances began to disturb the peace of night there was a growing apprehension of imminent danger until, on September 7, the heavy night raids began with an attack on the London docks.

Warned to expect casualties to be brought up by the River Emergency Service, Guy's prepared to receive 200 and, after admitting 75 casualties from its own district, decided to evacuate 35 patients in order to make room for the dockland convoy. But it never arrived, for fires from the South bank had made the river impassable. Night after night the bombers returned and on twenty-five consecutive nights from September 7, Guy's admitted casualties. The hospital suffered serious damage. On the second night of the attacks three incendiaries which fell—one on the roof of the Eye Ward theatre, one in the Park and one on the roof of the Nurses' Home—were extinguished 'with ease and zest'. On September 10, another penetrated the roof of the Matron's House. On September 15 at 9.55 p.m., a stick of three 50-kg. high explosive bombs straddled the hospital.

> 'One penetrated the dome above the main staircase of Hunt's House and burst at the level of the third floor, causing considerable damage to the Clinical Wards and the Children's Ward. Both these wards and Mary Ward on the floor below had been emptied in the course of the previous week, during which night bombing had been intense. The main staircase was completely demolished and collapsed in a heap of rubble which reached from the ground floor to the first floor level and blocked the entrance to the building. Both lifts were destroyed. Mains from the water storage tanks in the tower were fractured and cascades of water poured down into the debris. The electric, gas and steam mains were cut, and gas and steam escaped into the building. Fire broke out in the debris of the Clinical

Research Laboratory on the third floor and was finally extinguished by the fire squad using hand buckets and tin helmets filled with water.'

From the first two floors sixty patients were carried down fire-escape staircases on the outside of the building and bedded down in the out-patient hall in twenty-three minutes. Though there were about 230 people in the building at the time it was struck, there was only one casualty, and that one was fortunately not fatal.

The second bomb penetrated the basement of Hunt's House and exploded in the coal cellar; the third fell in the Works Department Yard, fracturing gas and water mains. The basement of Tabard House, which was used as a sleeping shelter for the maids, was flooded and had to be evacuated. As on a number of subsequent occasions, essential services were menaced by flooding of the engine room. On the same night further damage was done to the hospital buildings and protective measures had to be taken because bombs—one thought to be un-exploded—had fallen nearby.

> 'The night had been crowded and exciting. Standing on the roof to watch the dawn and the fires, one's sensations were of relief and thankfulness that so little injury could accompany so much destruction, and of admiration for the resourcefulness, energy and bravery of nurses, students and works department staff.'

The raids continued for seven months, during which casualties, nearly a thousand of whom were admitted, were received in the hospital on seventy-one days. On ten nights the hospital was involved in incidents either on its own premises or so close as to require emergency steps. Water, gas and electricity all failed from time to time. For over a week the only drinking water was brought up from the country in milk cans, and a small dam set up in the park and filled with home-chlorinated water supplied all other needs. Paraffin stoves were brought into use for ward cooking. Since lack of sleep is the chief enemy of stamina and morale, as far as possible everyone slept in a basement and staff were encouraged to spend their off-duty periods outside London.

As a result of the loss of the staircase in Hunt's House, wards in the surgical block had to be re-occupied and the hall of the Massage Department was converted into a ward; eighteen beds were set up in the northern end of the out-patient hall, and this became the main Casualty Reception Ward. The limited accommodation made it imperative to evacuate as many casualties as possible to base hospitals by midday following a raid.

> 'On the night of December 29, the City of London was largely destroyed by fire. Guy's on the fringe of the fire was nearly surrounded by an inferno of blazing warehouses, the flames from which destroyed the College and the Deep Therapy Department. In contrast to these locked and unattended warehouses, Guy's remained largely undamaged, though thirty incendiaries

fell on the hospital itself and serious fires were started in Doyle's House, the Externs' Room and the Artificial Sunlight Department. Owing to the intensity of the surrounding conflagration the police eventually ordered the complete evacuation of the hospital. Only twenty people holding key positions remained behind.

'But in addition to this ordeal by fire, a stick of three 50-kg. high explosive bombs fell on the hospital at 7.30 p.m. One demolished part of the east wing of Guy's House and patients in Dorcas had a lucky escape. The second penetrated the subway beneath the Guy's shop and the bakery. Blast wrecked the Linen Stores, the basement of the Massage Department and a small mess-room in the subway, the occupants of which were trapped for a short time; four of them suffered minor injuries. The blast extended as far as a locker room under the Nurses' Home and blew up the floor of Martha Ward, turning a piano upside down; no patient was injured. The third bomb penetrated through the wall of the Dental Department in White Hart Yard, causing much damage to windows and to the basement of the Hostel from blast.

'In the New Year the intensity of the bombardment diminished to some extent, though on February 17 a bomb fell on a large public shelter in Stainer Street Archway under London Bridge Station. Eighty-one casualties were admitted and sixty people were killed; many were drowned in the shelter by flooding from a fractured water main. On March 8, two bombs fell in the hospital—one just in front of the Superintendent's House, and one in the western quadrangle of Guy's House. Both were thought to be unexploded and all the buildings in the front quadrangle and Guy's House were evacuated and cordoned off for over a week. The second bomb was, in fact, unexploded and was removed by a bomb disposal squad.

'On April 16 the hospital suffered its last and most tragic loss. At 2.20 a.m. a canister of incendiaries fell on the hospital. A fire started in the roof of the Nurses' Home and was troublesome to deal with. In the meantime an incendiary was smouldering in the roof of the Court Room. By the time it was discovered the fire had already taken such hold that it could not be controlled with stirrup-pumps and buckets. It was not until 5 a.m. that a fire-engine arrived (from West Ham); even then no water could be obtained from the hydrants, and it was 9 a.m. before the fire was eventually extinguished. Before the roof of the building collapsed everything movable was carried out of it by students and others.

'On the two final terror nights of April 20 and May 10 the hospital was lucky to escape damage. A 1,000-kg. bomb fell on the bombed out site immediately behind where the 'Ship and Shovel' had been, but fortunately the hospital received no more than a severe shaking.

'So ended the 'Blitz'. That it was a period of strain every citizen of London would agree, but perhaps it submitted certain classes of people working in hospitals to a rather considerable strain. All-night work was the rule rather than the exception, but yet the routine work of the hospital had to be dealt with during the day-time as well, and in exceptionally difficult circumstances, requiring good temper, initiative and a flair for improvisation. Those especially affected were the senior members of the nursing staff, the staff of the administrative offices, works department staff, kitchen staff and the students. No praise can be too high for the invaluable service these people rendered to the hospital at this time.'

CONCLUSIONS

There is little doubt that the Sector Scheme for the hospitals was in every way a success, with which in practice little fault could be found. It provided skilled treatment for all classes of casualties from the moment they were admitted from an incident or a first-aid post until they were finally discharged from hospital. They received the best treatment available in the country from specialists of the highest standing when such treatment was required.

The scheme eased in every way the day-to-day evacuation of casualties from the battle area to fully equipped and staffed hospitals in the comparative safety of the outer zone, and thus permitted a large number of beds to be available always for the casualties caused by the almost continuous raids. Ordinary civilian sick also received the benefits of this system and had only to put up with the minor inconvenience of spending most of their time in hospitals at greater distances from their homes than they were used to in peace-time. Even this inconvenience was to a great extent mitigated by the regulations made by the Ministry to facilitate frequent visiting by friends and relatives. So successful has the scheme been that many of those chiefly concerned with its organisation and working have thought that a scheme of this kind might be of benefit to the patients if applied to large urban areas as a routine procedure.

The opinion has also been expressed that it would have been better, if it had been possible to do so, to provide bomb-proof casualty clearing hospitals in the central area in order to permit of urgent operations being carried out in the safest conditions possible, in the interests of the patients and of the medical staff, and to clear these emergency casualty stations daily of all patients who could be moved without detriment. Some of the central hospitals did their best to meet these requirements by establishing emergency operating theatres and post-operation wards in the basements of their hospitals; some operations could not have been justifiably carried on had these emergency arrangements not been made.

As regards the civilian sick, the evacuation of all those daily requiring admission to hospital would have presented a major problem. It would have meant a considerable increase in the inter-hospital transport, which in accordance with the policy of the Ministry continued to evacuate an average of about 7,000 patients per month from the inner to the outer zone hospitals both during the period of active raids and periods during which there were no attacks.

THE WORK OF THE CIVIL DEFENCE SERVICES

The story of the work of the Casualty Services in the London area from the beginning of the war until the end of intensive raiding in May 1941 can best be told by the medical officers of health of the metropolitan and extra-metropolitan boroughs, upon whose shoulders much of the burden fell. A large number of excellent reports of their work during this period were furnished for the purposes of this History, and tribute is due to all those London medical officers of health who ungrudgingly gave their time to preparing suitable material, often in trying and arduous circumstances. A list of the contributing medical officers of health in the metropolitan and extra-metropolitan area will be found in Appendix I.

Had space permitted, many of the reports furnished could have profitably been published *in extenso*. In the circumstances it was felt that the best manner of presenting this material would be to give in greater detail the experiences of two extra-metropolitan boroughs in the line of the Luftwaffe's approach and that of a number of metropolitan boroughs in the inner area, some on the south bank of the river and some on the north, as examples of their experiences and the lessons learned.

The boroughs selected for this purpose are:

1. *In the Outer Area.* Bromley, Kent
   Croydon (County Borough)
2. *In the Inner Area.* The City of London
   Bermondsey
   St. Marylebone
   Hackney

BOROUGH OF BROMLEY

(*From the Report of Dr. K. E. Tapper, O.B.E., M.B., D.P.H., Medical Officer of Health*)

PREPARATIONS

Between the year 1936 and the falling of the first bomb in August 1940, the A.R.P. Services experienced a series of alternating periods of intense activity and of *laissez faire*. Looking back through records it appears that the Casualty Service Scheme originally submitted in 1936 had very little wrong with it and that the principles laid down stood the test of experience. The medical officer of health's objections to the standard text-books and his support of the principles of rendering first aid on the site—i.e. the minimum of splinting, the early treatment of surgical shock and the necessity for speed and priority of evacuation of patients to hospital and first-aid post—are duly recorded. In addition the records show a strong plea against over-training in anti-gas measures, at the expense of training in first aid, and a note appears in his report to the Emergency Committee to the effect that as wardens would be the first people on a site their training in gas at the expense of first aid was a matter of considerable concern. In this Borough alone, and before the outbreak of war, over two thousand persons passed through first-aid training lectures, and many of the oral and practical examinations passed into the early hours of many mornings.

Much of this preparatory work entailed anxiety, long hours and not a little impatience, since, as in most cases, the prime duties of a medical officer of health were being seriously interfered with.

EXPERIENCES OF THE RAIDS

Bromley, a dormitory town within ten miles of London and outside the balloon barrage, covered an area of 6,519 acres of which 595 were scheduled as open spaces. Its pre-war population was 61,000, living in some 16,000 houses, with a density of population of nine persons per acre. Taking these facts into consideration and allowing for the voluntary evacuation of some 8,000 persons from this neutral area, a high casualty figure was not to be expected, unless raiding were concentrated on the district. And indeed during the whole raiding period up to March 1943, although more than a thousand H.E. bombs fell within the area, the total casualty figure was only 706, i.e. less than one casualty per bomb. The casualty returns showed 166 killed, 224 seriously injured and 316 slightly injured. The damage to property was extensive, no less than 516 buildings being destroyed, 510 seriously damaged and 14,786 suffering minor damage. In addition fires caused by enemy action amounted to 531, 332 of which were dealt with by wardens.

As typical of minor bombing, the medical officer of health describes a twenty-four hour period in October 1940, commencing at 5 o'clock on the evening of the 17th and finishing at about the same time on the 18th:

'After a day of the usual Public Health duties, I returned home for a meal, knowing that within an hour or two I would be back in the Control Room for the usual evening siren. In fact, before I had finished eating I was disturbed by a 'purple' message from Control, the siren following about fifteen minutes later. After a hurried journey into the town, I reported to Control Room to await the first sign of attack. Except, however, for the droning overhead of planes on their way to London, we were not troubled until about 22.15 hours.

'Then the real business of the night began. An express message from the wardens informed us—"H.E. at Blenheim Road, direct hit on house—casualties trapped." Despatching a stretcher party and an ambulance to the site, I handed over Control Room duties to my assistant and proceeded to the incident, taking with me my Casualty Officer. After a hectic drive of about three miles, the darkness only broken by searchlights sweeping the sky and the flashes of the anti-aircraft barrage, we arrived at Blenheim Road within twelve minutes of the first intimation that a bomb had fallen. The rescue party, stretcher party and ambulance were already on the site, proceeding with what had now become their routine duty. Number twenty-two had been just an ordinary little suburban house—there are hundreds like it in any town in the country—now it was nothing but a heap of bricks and timber, the bomb having pitched just under the front footings of the house and blown it completely apart. There were three trapped casualties and all were found within a comparatively short time—all dead, husband, wife and son. Two or three additional minor casualties had meanwhile been transferred to the nearest first-aid post, after being treated by the stretcher party and temporarily taken in by neighbours.

'On the site I was informed by Control that further casualties had occurred at Oaklands Road, on the other side of the town, and we immediately made our way thither. This incident was very much the same as the last, except that here it had been a very large house and obviously a very large bomb. In this case a mansion had received a direct hit in the centre of the building, the bomb having gone right down to the basement and then exploded, thus shattering the house completely. The road was strewn with rubble and the picture the following morning was of nearby trees covered with all sorts of personal and private belongings which had been blasted to the four winds. It was known that there were three people in this house —a man, his wife and their maid. The search among the debris proceeded and after some time, the body of a woman was discovered—dead.

'By this time the Salvation Army canteen had arrived and tea was never more welcome, for the amount of dirt that one collects from the atmosphere and from the site not only proves the necessity for wearing old clothes when on duty, but it also gets well into one's throat, so that hot drinks are most refreshing, especially on such a bitterly cold, pitch black night. All the while searchlights criss-crossed the sky, enemy planes droned overhead and we could hear the whistling of bombs, which necessitated our grovelling on the ground. Pride is forgotten on these occasions.

'After further work on the site, keeping in touch with Control all the time, we found a second body, this time the dismembered corpse of a male, but it was not until two days later that parts of the third missing body were found embedded in the crater. Leaving a casualty service representative on the site with necessary instructions to report should the third victim be discovered, we returned to Control, with enemy activity still proceeding and shrapnel pinging off the roofs of the houses. It was then after midnight. We had more hot tea and a sandwich, and then commenced to fill in the necessary forms, so that the returns of casualties could be completed. Meanwhile, the usual preparations had been made, by the opening of Rest Centres, to receive any dehoused persons who would require shelter until the end of the raid.

'In the early hours of the morning, in fact at 02.15 hours, a message was received—"Parachute mine seen floating over the town". Glancing at the wind indicator, we raised a prayer that the wind was strong enough to blow the cursed thing out of our area. Alas! our hopes were short-lived.

Suddenly there was a violent explosion and earth tremors were felt throughout the building. This time there was no waiting for a message, clearly there was devastation somewhere fairly close at hand. Again the Casualty Officer came with me and we went searching. Not a soul was in the streets, but we proceeded in the direction in which we believed the mine had fallen. What varied opinions one receives on the direction of sound and how deceiving sounds can be!

'We saw a woman who had come out of a damaged house and we asked her where this thing had fallen, but all she could tell us was that her own ceilings were down as a result of the explosion. So deciding to use our own initiative, we continued on our way until we had traced the site by the smell of explosion and the rubble on the road. We contacted two stretcher bearers, who had arrived in search of the mine, closely followed by wardens and other A.R.P. personnel. This mine had burst at the bottom of a garden and the blast had torn several houses to pieces. Prospecting round the edges of the damage we heard a faint cry from the top of the wreckage and on investigation a young woman was found lying on what had once been the roof. She was seriously injured, but conscious, suffering from a compound fracture of tibia and fibula besides other injuries and very severely shocked. In transit to the ambulance, which had arrived through Control having been contacted from a private house within a hundred yards where the telephone was still working, this very brave young woman persisted in telling us that there were eight people in the house, some of whom had been bombed out of their home in London only the previous night. She told us in which rooms they were sleeping and where we were likely to find them. It was from this information that we were ultimately able to locate all the casualties.

'Another woman, who was crushed and seriously injured, died before we could completely release her. Deep in the wreckage, and only visible through a crack in what had once been the outside wall, was a man who was completely trapped—fixed by his legs—and only after hours of skilled work by the rescue personnel could he be extricated, morphia having been administered early in the proceedings. Parties continued with their work, which was expedited by the sounding of the 'All Clear' and the subsequent opportunity to make use of unshaded lights, until all eight casualties had been discovered—three were dead, three seriously injured and two only slightly injured. Eventually, we returned to Control Room for the necessary action in connexion with the disposal of the dead, the recording of casualties and the completion of returns, for the work of the Casualty Officer does not cease with the 'All clear'.

'When daylight came, it brought the discovery by the wardens of yet another mine, this time unexploded, which called for the evacuation of twelve hundred people. By the prompt action of police and wardens and the calling up of necessary transport, these twelve hundred persons were all evacuated in time to receive their breakfast from the Air Raid Relief Committee. The bomb disposal service of the Navy rendered the mine harmless later in the morning, and the majority of the evacuees were able to return home the same afternoon.

'In the meantime, after completing all casualty returns for the information of Police and Information Bureau and the various reports necessary for

London Region, and visiting all bombed sites and Rest Centres, I proceeded home for a bath and breakfast. At 11 o'clock I returned to the office to commence the day's routine work on Public Health, knowing that there would be many queries and inquiries to be cleared up before the decks could be cleared for action during the coming night and knowing that the staff of the Rest Centres and the Casualty Officer would still be working.'

As a contrast the heavy raid which occurred in Bromley on the night of April 16–17, 1941, is described as follows by the medical officer of health:

'Actions are not quite so clear cut in a heavy raid as compared with minor bombing, for here one may have, as did Bromley, to cope with 214 H.E. bombs within a few hours, with messages coming into Control at the rate of six a minute during the first hour and an average of two and a half messages a minute over the succeeding four hours, and with telephones in some cases out of action.

'It all started with a chandelier flare over the town, which lit up the streets on my way to Control, where I arrived as incendiaries fell all over the town. Almost at once came the first report of casualties at the Grand Theatre shelter, and I left Control to find half the town alight and the Municipal Offices on fire amid a gay confusion of hose pipes and fire engines and the strident shouting of urgent instructions. After inverting a couple of dustbins over incendiaries in the car park, I proceeded by car to the Grand Theatre shelter only to find minor walking casualties. But it was not long before the H.E.s began to fall, so that, having regard to the shattered glass from shop windows, flying splinters, bouncing shrapnel, one found it more pleasant to walk than to go by car on such a night. I dashed down a side street where two furnishing stores were well alight with a canopy of flames overhead, to reach a site of devastation caused by a mine. A stretcher party arrived "out of the blue" and an ambulance was standing by for casualties. A rapid survey showed that hours of rescue work were entailed; so I returned to Control to gather some information as to where the Services were most needed, on the way picking up my car which I had left parked in the main street. Control Room was flooded with paper, but the personnel were miraculously coping with the situation. Two nearby sites with casualties were next visited on foot, and two old people found sitting by a wooden table amid their ruined house, drinking a cup of tea. No rest centre for them, this was their home and they were sticking to it.

'A visit was then made to Church Road to find the Parish Church a mass of ruins, the tower only remaining, licked in flames. The nearby houses were wrecked from the blast and the Observer Corps were evacuating their headquarters at Church House, which was burning savagely, the fire completely out of control. Yet, amid all this inferno, there was only one casualty, a firewatcher within the church, and she unfortunately was killed by the explosion.

'Stumbling over a dead Home Guard in the street, placing him under cover of the sidewalk and passing private houses on fire and blazing furiously out of control, with bombs falling, the atmosphere laden with dust and smoke, ambulances, stretcher parties and fire parties nobly carrying on with their work, and miraculously without injury, I returned to Control

Room. Finding there a Regional Officer, I decided to take him with me, this time by car, to sites as yet unvisited. It was an exciting journey and we had narrow escapes from unlit bomb holes in the road, but ultimately we reached a stretcher party depot which had been in action for hours and although their own depot had suffered damage from a nearby mine, they had established on their own initiative a casualty clearing station for casualties from the mined area. The activity with the coming and going of ambulances and the departure and return of stretcher parties was war in reality. The hot and dirty personnel indicated by their persons more than by any words that they were coping with the situation, with high credit to themselves and to the service which they represented. The adjoining site was another one of devastation. Rescue parties and those manning the canteens were doing valiant work, but here again hours of labour lay ahead. A check up of the casualties was made and on we went to the next site and the next, to find them all covered by our own Casualty Services and Rescue Service, and so, after visiting the first-aid posts, which although functioning under strain, did their work well and without fuss, we arrived back in Control in the early dawn, to get the picture of the raid from that end. Here we found more work to do, for the post-raid problems are perhaps the most difficult of all—the collection and identification of dead and the opening of rest centres at dawn, the tracing of missing persons, the collection of statistical returns and finally re-visiting of sites where parties were still working.

'The reaction following the 'blitz' was one of pride in the fact that we had dealt with it without calling for mutual aid, and a consciousness of the fact that we could deal with anything that the enemy could give us. This was the 'blitz' on Bromley, which gave us a casualty list of 74 killed, 72 seriously injured and 128 lightly injured, while the damage to property amounted to 299 houses demolished, 256 seriously damaged and 7,105 with minor damage. Plates IV and V show typical rescue scenes in Bromley.'

COMMENTARY

The medical officer of health, as a result of his experience of raiding of the types detailed above, recorded what he considered to be certain fundamental principles for an efficient casualty service.

First: the decentralised distribution of combined depots of light rescue parties and ambulances if sites are to be covered quickly and adequately. Through the ordinary channels of message transmission a period of at least ten minutes must elapse between the falling of the bomb and the receipt of the message whereas by direct action this delay can be almost entirely eliminated. Control should, of course, continue to be informed of the movement of parties, in order that a comprehensive picture may be built up.

Second: first aid on the site must be efficient and yet limited, for speed and priority of evacuation of the patient to hospital or first-aid post are prime essentials. The application of first aid in the dark is difficult, the diagnosis in many cases impossible, and in these conditions it is a good axiom that the patient is always worse than you believe him to be. This is especially true of trapped casualties, as in the excitement of his release the patient masks his symptoms, with the result that in many cases crush syndrome, traumatic pneumonia and such like are not infrequently missed if the patient is not sent to hospital. The early administration of morphia by a doctor or person trained in its administration is of proved value. A doctor on the site is of a greater importance, in my opinion, than a doctor standing by at a first-aid post or in Control Room. Much of the first-aid work at the first-aid post can be carried out under the supervision of a trained nurse, a doctor only being called for as and when necessary.

Third : all depots should have an adequate messenger service.

Fourth : I would place among the first considerations of an adequate casualty service, a complete organisation for the identification and disposal of the dead, with a well situated mortuary, sufficiently large to retain bodies in an orderly manner up to seven or ten days. The mortuary should possess an adequate reception room for relatives who come to identify their dead immediately following the raid, and this waiting room should be brightly decorated and comfortable if one is to maintain the morale of the public and give them the sympathetic handling which they deserve.

Fifth : there must be complete liaison between first-aid parties, stretcher or light rescue parties, first-aid posts, rest centres, hospitals, wardens and police, and all personnel should be trained in all services, so as to allow for interchangeability and mobility in case of need.

Sixth : the work following a raid is frequently more difficult than the work during a raid—the functioning of rest centres, rehousing of the homeless, emergency feeding and tracing of missing persons are all activities in which a medical officer of health is called upon to take an active part if the casualty services are to be efficient and complete.

Seventh : a complete list of all persons passing through hospitals, first-aid posts, rest centres and the mortuary must be compiled as early as possible following the raid, for not infrequently missing persons, afterwards found to be in a rest centre, are being searched for among bombed property.

Finally : the service must conform to the pattern set for the whole country, but must be modified to cope with the local problems—the size of area, the population per acre, the types of buildings and the proximity of hospitals. These factors are important ones in each branch of the casualty service, and the time may come when whole-time personnel are placed on an Army basis, living in barracks and being detailed to action stations as a daily routine. Above all increased mobility is an essential.

COUNTY BOROUGH OF CROYDON

(Based on a Report from O. M. Holden, G.M., M.D., D.P.H., Medical Officer of Health)

AREA AND POPULATION

Croydon is a large county borough situated in the southern part of the London Region with an acreage of 12,672. To the north its boundaries touch the Metropolitan Boroughs of Wandsworth and Lambeth, and the southern part extends to the boundaries of Greater London. The estimated population in 1939 was 243,000.

CIVIL DEFENCE SERVICES

The Civil Defence Services were organised on lines similar to those common in most scheme-making authorities. There were eight *ad hoc* first-aid posts, three attached to hospitals, and three mobile units. The operational scheme conformed generally to that followed in other boroughs, but in Croydon as with other local authorities, there were variations from the usual procedure. One most important variation was the practice of sending out a reconnoitring party on the first sound of gunfire or of bombs exploding, instead of waiting until incidents were reported to the Control Office. In the early days, this consisted of a first-aid party accompanied by an ambulance and a sitting-case car. The plan proved of great value; these parties frequently arrived at incidents before the wardens and before any report of incidents had been received. The Control Centre was kept notified of the movements of the reconnoitring parties from time to time in order to prevent any unnecessary reduplication of services at incidents. The personnel of the first-aid parties fully appreciated this arrangement, and there is no doubt that lives were saved on several occasions by their early arrival. Croydon was the only authority in which this scheme was in force from the very beginning. In other places, it usually was adopted only after several raids had occurred.

THE HOSPITAL SERVICES

Apart from some small hospitals, most of which had been suspended or withdrawn from the E.M.S. scheme, there were two main casualty hospitals, viz. the City General (voluntary) with an expanded capacity of 250 beds of which it was estimated that 151 would be available for casualties, and the May Day Hospital (municipal) with 660 beds and 342 available for casualties. There was also a Class II hospital with 754 total beds, of which 342 were available for the treatment of minor casualties and convalescents. These hospitals came under the authority of the Sector Group Officer of Sector IX, Mr. John Hunter, M.C., F.R.C.S., for the admission, treatment and transfer of patients. The procedure regulating the admission of casualties to primary receiving hospitals and their subsequent transfer to large base hospitals and special hospitals was in conformity with that of the other London Sectors in the southern and south-eastern areas.

THE RAIDS

The first bomb was dropped in the borough at 0015 hours on June 19, 1940, when eight H.E.'s fell on a farm at Addington causing no casualties. The first raid causing casualties was a short sharp attack on the Croydon Airport and its vicinity which occurred at 1900 hours on

August 15 and which only lasted five minutes. The warning was late, the sirens only being sounded at 1914 hours and although only twenty H.E. bombs were dropped the casualties were high, 63 persons being killed, 45 seriously injured and 104 slightly injured. There was also much damage to property.

On August 18, there was a heavier raid at 1324 hours lasting twenty-one minutes, but on this occasion the sirens sounded at 1306 with the result that there were no fatal casualties, only 16 persons being seriously injured and 11 slightly injured. Minor raids of varying severity continued, mostly in daylight, on practically every day during the rest of the month of August, and during September, October and November, 1940, causing as a rule small numbers of casualties. The attacks in December were limited to six days, in January to four days, in February to three days, in March to four days, in April to two days and in May to one day. Only one of these caused more casualties than the original raid on August 15, a heavy and widespread attack on the night of April 16–17 lasted over six hours during which 86 H.E. bombs and three paramines were dropped and caused 85 fatal casualties, 83 serious and 187 slight injuries. During the nine months, it is estimated that 1,193 bombs of all calibres, excluding incendiaries, exploded in the borough causing the deaths of 434 persons. Some 953 casualties were taken to the hospitals in ambulances, of whom 584 were admitted and detained, while 1,486 were treated at the first-aid posts.

THE HOSPITALS

Casualties. At the May Day Hospital the total number of air raid casualties received was 507, of whom 347 were admitted direct to the wards. Sixty were found to be dead on arrival at the hospital, ten were admitted to the wards from the first-aid post attached to the hospital and 90 were sent home or to a rest centre after treatment at the post. At the Croydon General Hospital the total number of casualties received was 496, of whom 206 were admitted to the wards, 261 were sent home or to rest centres; 29 were found dead on arrival. The raids during which the highest number of casualties were admitted were on August 15, with 45, on October 28–29, 33, and on the night of April 16–17, 83. In addition to these two hospitals a small number of casualties were also admitted to the Norwood Cottage Hospital from time to time, as this hospital served the area of Upper Norwood on the Lambeth border.

Damage. The May Day Hospital was hit on several occasions by bombs and one ward block was put completely out of action. Fortunately, no patients were hurt, but one of the staff was killed and several injured. On another occasion, part of the maternity block was destroyed and two patients killed. The hospital services also suffered on one occasion, the electric, gas and water supplies being temporarily put out of action.

FIRST-AID POSTS

Casualties. Of the total number of 1,486 cases treated at first-aid posts, approximately 14 per cent. were sent to hospitals, 67 per cent. sent home and 18 per cent. sent to rest centres. Six casualties were found to be dead on arrival or died shortly afterwards.

Damage. The Ingram first-aid post received a direct hit from a small bomb which put four rooms out of action, but after the transfer of equipment to the other side of the building, work was resumed within two hours. This post was also set on fire on April 16, but little damage was done. The Kingsley first-aid post had a direct hit on October 12, which necessitated the post being transferred to an adjoining building. Three of the staff were seriously injured. Later in the month this post had to be evacuated to a stretcher party depot for three weeks, until a delayed action bomb which fell just outside the building had been disposed of. At the Portland first-aid post the roof was damaged on the night of October 19–20 and the windows blown in by blast; the telephones and water were cut off, but the post continued to function with lamps and torches. The Benson first-aid post received similar damage without injury being caused to any of the staff. First-aid party and ambulance depots, fortunately, escaped any major damage, except one, which was partly demolished by a direct hit and had to be removed to another building.

REST CENTRES

Admissions to rest centres, of which seven had been established, were 743 and another 120 were admitted to rest homes.

DAMAGE TO HOUSES

The number of houses totally destroyed was 353, so damaged as to be incapable of repair 831, severely damaged but capable of being made habitable 1,406 and slightly damaged 1,224. The number of persons who had to be rehoused as the result of the above damage was 2,021, and the total number of persons for whom billets were found in the borough, including the persons rendered homeless in other boroughs and people evacuated from the coast, was 5,542. These figures do not include a considerable number of people who found accommodation for themselves.

PUBLIC HEALTH CONSIDERATIONS

No serious post-raid problems arose in Croydon as the result of the raids. The chief problem was the temporary housing of the homeless. This was met by taking empty houses in the town and furnishing them. Damage to water supplies was localised and there was no cessation of supplies to any large area. As a precaution, the water was constantly chlorinated but the general distribution of material for chlorination, which had been stocked, was never found necessary. The air raids generally affected the public health services very little, so that the activities of the health departments were able to continue fully and normally. The raids put 100 beds in May Day Hospital out of action for about four months and the maternity block for a longer period, but the latter deficiency was met by using private maternity homes.

GENERAL COMMENTS

The casualty services gave an excellent account of themselves under the strain of the raids and as in other towns there were many instances of conspicuous devotion to duty even though the staff had been affected in their own families by their homes being destroyed. Dr. Holden, the Medical Officer of Health, received the George Medal for conspicuous bravery and devotion to duty.

The first-aid services answered every call made upon them, and the casualties never suffered from lack of prompt attention in the posts, in the ambulances or in the hospitals.

CITY OF LONDON

(*From the Report of C. F. White, O.B.E., M.D., D.P.H., Medical Officer of Health*)

PRELIMINARY CONSIDERATIONS

The problem to be dealt with in considering the organisation of the Civil Defence Services in the City of London, differed somewhat from that presented in other areas. In the latter the provision of first-aid posts, first-aid parties and ambulances usually varied directly with the estimated resident populations of those areas. In the City of London, however, with a very small night population and an estimated day population 100 times greater, different standards had to be applied, especially since heavy day raids were expected and not the night raids over a prolonged period which actually occurred.

First-aid Posts and Depots. In consequence it was decided that, if possible, first-aid posts should be underground or at least on the ground floor of modern steel framed buildings in order to ensure the greatest possible protection from direct hits. Arrangements were therefore made to establish first-aid posts on the ground floor of Unilever House, Blackfriars; in the basements of the Central Criminal Court, The Old Bailey; the Chartered Insurance Institute, Aldermanbury; Bishopsgate Institute, and St. Helen's Court. The owners of these premises generously gave the use of the necessary accommodation rent free, subject only to reimbursement for heating, lighting, etc., and to reinstatement after the war. Similar arrangements were made for combined depots for first-aid parties and rescue parties.

The staff of the first-aid posts and depots was recruited on the lines laid down originally by the Home Office and amended later by the Ministry of Health.

A sanitary inspector was appointed at each of the first-aid posts and depots to act as liaison officer. All did splendid work in organising the posts and particularly the depots in the early and more difficult stages. In addition, arrangements were made with St. Bartholomew's Hospital for nine clinical students, six for day and three for night duty, to be sent to each first-aid post at the outbreak of war. The first-aid auxiliaries, who by the time heavy raiding started were well trained, had had no real experience in dealing with casualties; and it was felt that the medical students could be depended upon not to quail before the sights and sounds which it was expected would be seen and heard in a first-aid post when raids began. Actually, as the medical school closed down until the beginning of 1940, the students were paid as whole-time A.R.P. personnel and lived in the first-aid posts. Later, when the school opened again the students became part-timers and were not paid, but were billeted at the hospital at the expense of the Corporation and reported to their first-aid posts on every alert. The students were selected by the Warden of Studies and held their appointments for three months only, so that their studies were not unduly interrupted. This scheme, though quite unofficial, was continued until the end of March 1942, and worked very well and economically.

Mobile First-aid Posts. Two large Bedford vans were earmarked as mobile first-aid posts and were duly delivered with drivers at the outbreak of war. The equipment was supplied by the Ministry of Health, and the staff, a doctor, a trained nurse and four medical students were supplied from St. Bartholomew's and auxiliary first-aiders were supplied from the first-aid post at the Criminal Court. As the expected air raids did not come, these two units were demobilised, but at the beginning of 1940, when the reduction in the number of A.R.P. personnel and of fixed first-aid posts took place, one of the mobile units was recommissioned and stationed at the first-aid post at Unilever House, with a part-time medical officer, a trained nurse and the authorised number of auxiliary first-aiders. The staff lived at the first-aid post and worked there unless the mobile unit was called out.

First-aid Parties. In the City there was great difficulty in getting recruits to enrol for stretcher bearer duties. At the outbreak of war, however, about 180 men had volunteered and had been trained and when they were called up at the end of August 1939, the response was excellent, though the numbers were only about half of the authorised strength.

Staff cars. Before the outbreak of the war, the City Corporation made arrangements with the London General Cab Company to supply forty taxis with drivers immediately, for duty with the stretcher parties. All of these reported promptly on or before September 3, 1939 and continued in service until early in 1940, when the local authorities were instructed to purchase cars at not more than £30 each.

Ambulances. The ambulances and cars were the responsibility of the L.C.C., but the three ambulance stations were established in the City.

Private A.R.P. Arrangements. In the City many big business houses had developed excellent A.R.P. schemes of their own. The smaller concerns did very little in this way.

ORGANISATION AT THE COMMENCEMENT OF THE RAIDS

Before heavy raiding started, the City of London had at its disposal an organisation partly in accordance with the standards laid down and partly unofficial. The medical officer of health's views, however, on the recruitment and training of A.R.P. personnel—views which subsequently obtained the support of the Borough Medical Officers of Health's Committee of the Metropolitan Branch of the Society of Medical Officers of Health, but which before the war had not been accepted by a number of the councils of the metropolitan boroughs—did not meet with the agreement of the central authorities. These views and his subsequent comments were as follows:

'Under modern conditions, war may be expected to come with appalling suddenness, and consequently the minimum forces for passive defence should be constantly maintained, trained and equipped, so that they may be mobilised at a few hours' notice. The essential requirements have been recognised by the fighting forces of all countries since the dawn of history. These comprise discipline, training, physical fitness, delegation of command through officers and non-commissioned officers, and provision of appropriate weapons and equipment, including uniform and the distinguishing badges of rank.

'In place of such a force, what was actually available was a civilian force consisting mostly of volunteers with inadequate training, and with little or no discipline. These volunteers could please themselves whether they continued in the service or not; they were not subject to any examination as to their physical fitness, nor were they required to undergo physical training. There was no proper delegation of command, because there were no officers, and they had no uniforms and no badges of rank. They were a collection of civilians, some of whom had volunteered because they desired to serve their country and some who had joined the A.R.P. services as a means of earning a living, or in some cases to avoid being called up for the Fighting Services.

'The long period of freedom from air raids gave the opportunity for some of these difficulties to be remedied, and in action the A.R.P. personnel displayed courage and devotion to duty beyond all criticism, though this does not mean that the work was always performed with the highest efficiency.

'Once it was deemed necessary after the outbreak of the war to employ whole-time paid personnel in the A.R.P. Services, this staff should have been organised on a military basis on Territorial Army lines, with officers, non-commissioned officers and other ranks, all in uniform and with a definite obligation in regard to training as was done when the National Fire Service was formed. The main objection to this scheme seems to have been that it would have meant the loss of the enormous amount of voluntary service which was being given throughout the country, particularly in residential areas, but there appears to have been no reason why part-time voluntary service could not be linked with a Civil Defence Territorial Army, just as it was with a whole-time Civil Defence Service. Under such conditions, part-time voluntary service would have been more popular and more efficient, particularly if uniforms had been issued to the part-timers. On mobilisation, such a Civil Defence Territorial Army would have been immediately available and highly efficient and local authority officials would have had far fewer difficulties in the administration of the Civil Defence Services.

'The policy of the central authorities seemed to consist of a timid effort to suggest to the general public that air raids were a possibility in the future and gas was chosen as the bogey with which they were to be mildly startled. The necessary precautions were, apart from the central issue of gas masks, to be undertaken by and at the expense of, such individuals and such local authorities as chose to take the dangers seriously, but nobody must be really frightened, nobody must be forced to do anything and no heavy expenditure must be incurred for which the central Government might have to take the responsibility. The result was a great waste of money, enormous waste of effort, much discontent and less efficiency.

'After the experience of heavy raids, the central authorities realised that many of the proposals originally made and detailed above were soundly based, and ranks and uniforms were introduced, but the organisation continued to be an entirely civilian one and continued to be less efficient than it would have been if it had been organised, trained and disciplined on the lines of the Fighting Forces from the very beginning.'

DESCRIPTION OF THE HEAVY RAIDS

Bombs were dropped in the City during 57 of the raids on the London area. The first bombs to fall in the City were on August 25, 1940 and none fell after the night of May 10–11, 1941 until January 1943, with the exception of a few which fell on four or five occasions, which caused, with one exception, little damage and few casualties.

Only once did bombs fall during the daytime, on January 30, 1941, when a few explosive incendiary bombs fell, and caused four casualties which were treated at a first-aid post; one patient was sent to hospital. Altogether 1,247 incidents were reported to the City Control Room; these related to the fall of 348 H.E. bombs; 772 incendiary bombs; 19 oil bombs, 10 parachute mines; 12 A.A. shells; 83 unexploded bombs and three unexploded parachute mines. The estimated weight of H.E. bombs (including parachute mines and unexploded bombs) was 100 tons. The actual number of incendiaries which fell in the City must, of course, have been much greater, probably several thousands, and no doubt many non-reported H.E. bombs may have fallen into the large areas on fire.

The three greatest raids were on the nights of December 29–30, 1940, when a large part of the City, including the Guildhall, was destroyed by fire; the night of January 11–12, 1941; and the night of the heaviest raid, May 10–11, 1941.

That on the night of December 29 will always be remembered as the night of the Great Fire. A large part of the City was destroyed. Fortunately only a small number of H.E. bombs was dropped. Probably owing to a sudden change in the weather, the enemy did not follow up with H.E.s as was expected. The casualties were not heavy, six persons being killed, 44 injured and taken to hospital and 87 treated in first-aid posts.

On the night of January 11, 1941, the City suffered its heaviest casualties; 111 persons were killed, three of whom remained unidentified; 136 were admitted to hospital, 125 treated by the mobile unit (four of whom were sent to hospital) and 172 were treated in first-aid posts and at the medical aid posts in the Tube Station at Liverpool Street. At this time the medical aid post at the Bank Station had not been put into commission. One of the nurses from Liverpool Street, however, walked along the railway to the Bank, with dressings, and helped to deal with casualties on the platform. Eight casualties were dealt with at the medical aid post at Liverpool Street on that night. The casualties on this night were caused almost entirely by three bombs which fell, one on the crossing at the Bank of England, piercing the roadway and exploding in the Underground booking hall, one in Bishopsgate near Liverpool Street Station and the third at the junction of Cheapside and St. Martins-le-Grand. On May 10–11, 32 were killed (one of whom remained unidentified), 40 injured and admitted to hospital and 203 treated at first-aid posts.

Other serious raids from the casualty point of view occurred on the night of October 9–10, 1940, when a bomb hit a private shelter in Dean Lane, Fetter Lane, killing 20 persons, and on the night of March 8–9, 1941 when Cloak Lane Police Station received a direct hit, three police officers being killed and thirteen injured.

THE WORKING OF THE CASUALTIES SERVICES UNDER THE STRAIN OF AIR RAIDS

First-aid Parties. The casualty services in the city were never fully extended, as heavy raids took place only at night when the population was small and mainly in good shelters. Though there were occasions when all the stretcher parties were out because of the number of incidents, it was never necessary to call for assistance from other areas in the Group, because the individual incidents were usually small so far as casualties were concerned. On the other hand, on a number of occasions parties from the City were sent to help in neighbouring boroughs. Before the heavy raids, a great many exercises were held to develop a scheme to ensure that there would be no delay in the Control Room, however many incidents were reported. If a warden knew that a building hit by a H.E. bomb was occupied he sent an express message immediately and completed his report later when he had reconnoitred the scene. On receipt of this message, an express party, consisting of a stretcher party, a rescue party, an ambulance and a sitting-case car, was immediately despatched from the nearest depot to the incident. It frequently happened that the persons in the bombed building emerged unharmed, so that the number of incidents at which casualties occurred was no indication of the number of times on which stretcher parties were called out. Never did any stretcher party hesitate to answer a call immediately during a raid and only once was there any complaint of delay in attending to casualties, and that was at the Bank Tube station incident, when it was not at first realised that there had been casualties on one of the platforms below, which could only be reached from the Lombard Street entrance. There were several occasions on which from one to three persons were known to be trapped, and it was impossible to reach them because of the intensity of the fire. So great was the heat that in several instances nothing recognisable as human remains was found subsequently, in spite of the most careful excavation.

Ambulances. The ambulance services worked promptly and efficiently and exhibited the utmost bravery and resource in fulfilling their difficult and dangerous duties.

First-aid Posts. The fixed first-aid posts also were never fully extended; in fact, owing to the extent and duration of the fires in the city they were often busier attending to firemen suffering from minor injuries, particularly to the eyes, than attending to actual injuries from bombs.

Mortuaries. The mortuary accommodation was always greatly in excess of requirements and, except on one occasion, the staff of the City mortuary and disinfecting station were able to deal with the fatal casualties without outside assistance. At the time of the Bank tube station incident, stretcher parties were asked to volunteer for mortuary duties, and under the supervision of the medical officer of health, members of his clerical staff and the mortuary superintendent, they did the necessary work satisfactorily. Only four bodies received at the mortuary were unidentified, though in a number of cases it was several days before identification was established, and then rather from articles of clothing than from any recognisable features. The City was fortunate in having to deal with a remarkably patient population who accepted the fact that the bodies of their missing relatives could not be ready for identification the morning after the raid, and were prepared to give the mortuary staff reasonable time to deal with the situation. In most cases the relatives made private arrangements for the burial of their dead, but in 25 cases it was necessary for the corporation to bury persons killed in air raids, provision having been made for the transport to, and interment at, the corporation's cemetery at Ilford, of considerable numbers of dead.

COMMENTARY

Generally, therefore, it may be said that the Civil Defence Casualty Services dealt satisfactorily with the effects of the particular type of raids which developed. Whether they would have been equally successful had the raids been of the type which they were designed to meet is a matter for conjecture. Of the courage and willingness of the personnel during the raiding period there was no doubt, but their readiness to accept disciplinary control and constant training in every aspect of their work has not been so evident. But that was not their fault, it was the result of the disinclination of the central authority to introduce any vestige of militarism into the Service.

DAMAGE TO FIRST-AID POSTS, DEPOTS AND CENTRAL CONTROL

First-aid Posts. Two of the first-aid posts were put out of action. On the night of December 29, 1940, the Chartered Insurance Institute was surrounded by burning buildings and the staff were evacuated. The upper part of the building caught fire and also the main entrance doors. The post in the basement was unharmed, but the premises were without water and lighting for some weeks. A temporary post was established in Basinghall Street where the staff carried on for several weeks until the Chartered Insurance Institute could be reopened—even then the water had to be obtained from the tanks on the roof, which were replenished by the National Fire Service.

The post at the Central Criminal Court was put out of action on the night of May 10 when high explosive bombs hit the building. The post in the basement was practically undamaged, apart from a quantity of debris from the building above. The staff were evacuated to Unilever House but were able to return the next morning.

Combined First-aid and Rescue Party Depots. Two depots were put out of action. One at St. Martins-le-Grand received a direct hit from a land mine which exploded on the roof, destroying the upper floors. There were about eighty of the first-aid and rescue personnel in the basement and fortunately all escaped without injury through an emergency exit in the pavement and were able to continue to use the depot, although for some days it was partially flooded by rising water which had to be pumped out. The depot at Swan Street School, Minories, was damaged by fire and the personnel was evacuated to Ibex House. Later when the school was practically ready for re-occupation it was totally destroyed.

Ambulance Stations. Each of the three ambulance stations was damaged or destroyed in raids: No. 73 once, No. 74 once and No. 76 three times. No. 76 unit was afterwards stationed at the Old Bailey until they were disbanded in February 1942.

Central Control. On the night of December 29, 1940, the central control room was surrounded by fire and had to be evacuated. The 'all clear' had just been given when it was decided to evacuate. The premises were later extensively damaged by fire, although the control room itself stood; in fact, some of the telephones—those which were on the Avenue Exchange—were still working for some days. All records and equipment were removed. 'Control' continued to operate from a reserve control room at Lloyds in Leadenhall Street, until a new one was constructed in Moorgate.

Administrative Offices. The offices of the Medical Officer of Health were destroyed by fire on the night of May 10–11, 1941. Fortunately, most of the records were in the strong room in the basement, and in spite of the fact that the door to the strong room was wedged open to comply with 'fire escape' requirements and that the building had to remain burning some hours owing to lack of water, only a small part of the records was destroyed.

CASUALTIES

Hospitals. There were no casualties amongst the patients or staff of St. Bartholomew's Hospital, the only hospital in the City. One hundred and two patients had to be evacuated to Friern Hospital on the night of December 29, on account of fire risk and 152 were evacuated to Sector hospitals on May 11, because of temporary lack of utility services.

First-aid Posts. There were no casualties among the personnel of the first-aid posts. The following table shows the number of casualties among members of the Civil Defence Services.

	Killed	Injured taken to hospital	Treated at F.A.Ps.
Rescue and First-aid	2	1	91
Ambulance Services	Nil	1	1
Wardens	3	3	15
Police	8	56	10
Fire Service	20	?	214
Totals	33	61*	331

* Excluding Fire Service.

From this table, it is seen that the number of firemen treated at first-aid posts was 214, just over one-quarter of the total, and that there were 91 members of the first-aid rescue service treated. Most of these injuries were not caused directly by bombs, but were received during fire-fighting and rescue and demolition work, after raids. No record is available of the number of firemen injured in the City and taken to hospital, because the fire service areas differ from the A.R.P. areas and no separate record was kept for the City.

Casualties among the personnel of the three ambulance units stationed in the City were fortunately very small, but in addition to those shown in the above table there were seven slightly injured, one suffered from shell-shock and was discharged and sixteen suffered from carbon monoxide poisoning. These were treated by members of their own units.

Other Casualties. It is difficult to give accurate figures of the killed and wounded in an area such as the City of London, where there was a very small resident population and the majority of casualties occurred amongst persons residing outside the area. The number of killed is substantially correct, although there may have been a few bodies removed from within the boundaries of the City into other areas. Also some persons, injured within the City, may have been taken to hospitals outside, where they died. The number of dead, 204, includes those taken to the City mortuary or St. Bartholomew's Hospital, from incidents in the City.

The number of persons removed to St. Bartholomew's Hospital, who were known to have been injured within the City was 362. No record is available of any who may have been sent to other hospitals outside the City.

The number of casualties treated in first-aid posts was 765, including 131 treated by the mobile first-aid unit at incidents. In addition eight were treated at the medical-aid post at Liverpool Street Station and 17 at a first-aid post at the G.P.O., making a total of 790. Of these 456 were civilians, three members of H.M. Forces and the remaining members of the Civil Defence Services (including police and firemen).

Casualties per Ton Weight of Bombs. The estimated weight of H.E. bombs of 100 tons, gives a figure of 2·04 killed per ton and 3·62 seriously injured per ton.

Mutual Assistance. Although on a few occasions all the stretcher parties in the City were out at incidents and none was left in the depots, some had always returned before it became necessary to call for outside assistance. On the other hand, City parties were often called to help in neighbouring boroughs.

LESSONS OF THE RAIDS

As has already been observed, the City was not a typical area and conclusions drawn from the heavy raiding may not be applicable to areas where there was a large resident population housed in less substantial buildings.

Casualties were much fewer in number than was expected. This was largely due to the fact that raiding was at night when most of the population were in shelters or at least dispersed in their own houses or in other buildings. In the City the way in which modern steel and concrete buildings resisted high explosive and incendiary bombs, in comparison with the destruction wrought upon the older buildings was very evident. Fortunately, there was no experience, as in Germany, of the results of 'crash' raids with perhaps 1,000 tons of bombs of weights up to 8,000 pounds all dropped on one target within an hour. Again, as bombing took place when there were few people in the open, casualties were for the most part killed or seriously injured. There were few of the comparatively minor cases for which first-aid posts were established, and it certainly appears that these were too numerous and too elaborately staffed and equipped. For the same reason the heavy mobile first-aid post had not many calls. It was, however, important to get a doctor and a trained nurse as quickly as possible to every large incident and there was, therefore, no doubt as to the value of the light mobile unit.

It soon became evident that first aid at the incident should be simple and confined to the arrest of severe haemorrhage, the immobilisation of fractures and the minimising of shock. The important thing was to get the seriously wounded to hospital with the minimum of delay. The standard of the St. John Ambulance Brigade and British Red Cross Society training was excellent for the accidents of peace-time, but needed modification in its application to air raid conditions, when the work had to be done with very little light and the casualties were numerous, mostly serious and covered in dust. It was difficult to teach stretcher bearers to appreciate what cases should be dealt with immediately and what should wait until the urgent cases had been dispatched to hospital. The details which gain points in a St. John Ambulance competition were frequently impracticable or a waste of valuable time when the effects of an air raid had to be dealt with. Even if the casualties at an incident were few, incidents followed in rapid succession and it was important for the stretcher bearers to complete their work and to report that they were back in their depots and ready for the next call. The peace-time training of the St. John Ambulance Brigade is apt to be fussy and the first-aider does not appreciate that in doing something to the patient he is not necessarily doing something for the patient. The virtues of 'masterly inactivity' on occasion are not recognised.

The developments of the war made the demand for man-power and materials insistent. The result was that establishments were drastically reduced and the stretcher bearers and the heavy rescue personnel each had to learn something of the other's job. This was ideal, but better results would have been obtained if some incentive to attain and maintain proficiency in various types of Civil Defence duties had been held out to the men. Small additions of pay should have been given in respect of each additional qualification and the continuance of such proficiency pay made dependent on the maintenance of efficiency. Here again, as the medical officer of health for the City has pointed out, organisation on a military basis would have been helpful. Moreover, under such an arrangement, it would have been easy, as the age of call-up for military service advanced, to draft Civil Defence personnel into the Fighting Forces and to draft into the Civil Defence men from the Forces who, though physically unfit for the prolonged strain of active service, were yet capable of comparatively short periods of strenuous exertion, generally with opportunities for rest and recuperation in between.

Experience of voluntary service has shown that while it was offered freely, even insistently, at times of acute crisis, it was very apt to lose interest and enthusiasm in periods of lull, and there was no feeling of confidence that in the event of a sudden call it would still be available and efficient. It was afterwards found necessary to issue 'freezing orders' in relation to part-time Civil Defence personnel, but it would have been better if volunteers had been attached to a military organisation and had been made more clearly to recognise that, having undertaken obligations, they should hold themselves always in readiness to fulfil them.

METROPOLITAN BOROUGH OF BERMONDSEY

(From the Report of D. M. Connan, M.D., D.P.H., Medical Officer of Health)

SPECIAL FEATURES

Bermondsey, one of the smaller metropolitan boroughs, was distinguished by two features, one political and one physical, both of which had an influence upon the war-time medical service. As regards the political feature, at the outbreak of war, and for some time before, the Council, except for five or six members, was so strongly pacifist as to hamper seriously all efforts towards civil defence.

So far as the physical features are concerned, of an eight mile perimeter, nearly half was river frontage lined by wharves and warehouses; indeed, the eastern portion of the borough was surrounded on three sides by the river, in the loop of which lay the Surrey Commercial Dock. Between the Surrey Dock and the river ran Rotherhithe Street, at one time the longest street in London. In peace-time this part of the borough had a population of about three thousand and as access to this area at both ends was by bridges, the whole area had to be treated as an island and required a separate and self-contained medical service.

HOSPITALS AND FIRST-AID POSTS

Guy's Hospital was situated at the north-western end of the borough, St. Olave's (L.C.C.) Hospital in the Rotherhithe or eastern district, and the small hospital of the Bermondsey Medical Mission was centrally placed. In addition to the medical staffs of these hospitals, there were twenty-seven doctors practising in the area, the population of which consisted almost wholly of manual workers and, before evacuation, numbered about 100,000. Six first-aid posts were provided in accessible positions, so that every part of the borough was within a mile of at least one post. This number was afterwards reduced to three posts in active commission and two reserve posts, a number which fully met the needs of the area when bombing began. Of these three active first-aid posts, one was situated in the central baths, a modern building with little possibility of protection; a second in St. Olave's Hospital, and the third in an elementary school in the dock area. In addition to first-aid posts, there were three stretcher party depots, the post in the dock area being a combined first-aid and stretcher party post. Each first-aid post was placed under the control of a responsible member of the permanent staff of the Public Health Department, generally a sanitary inspector. These officers were on duty for twenty-four hours every third day and they had the task of welding a rather motley staff into a team. They controlled the entire operation of the post, and all instructions and requests to and from the Medical Officer of Health were made through them. Each post had one trained nurse, usually a member of the staff of the Public Health Department, and one or more general practitioners always available for the treatment of casualties, besides a staff of first-aid assistants.

This arrangement of the first-aid posts was conspicuously successful, both in quiet times and during the raiding period. The efficiency of the stretcher parties never reached the same standard, and, although they worked quite well at incidents, a lack of discipline and therefore of order was noticeable in their work. A much smaller number of men disciplined and trained would have been far more effective. The most satisfactory of the first-aid posts was that at the central baths where there was plenty of room for sorting and resting patients, and this plenitude of space contributed both to the orderly working of the post and very much to the comfort of the patients and of their accompanying relations. As all the casualties were extremely dirty, the lavish supply of hot water available at this post was also a very great advantage.

THE RAIDS

The bombing began with a light rain of incendiaries on August 29, 1940, and this was followed by heavy raids which occurred almost nightly in September and October, but fell off in November and subsequently followed at the rate of three or four a month until May 1941. Several of these raids were really heavy, but two stand out as memorable occasions in Bermondsey. These were the raids of September 7, 8 and 9, 1940, and that of May 10, 1941. Altogether, in September, heavy bombs fell on twenty-one occasions, but no subsequent week equalled the first week and although there were many further serious incidents and trying nights, no time was so terrifying. This effect of terror was partly mingled with awe, for the burning of the timber yards in Surrey Docks on the night of September 7, was a magnificent sight unlikely ever to be forgotten, and for Bermondsey unrivalled, even by the burning of the City of London.

On that night the combined first-aid and stretcher party post in the dock area was burnt out and the whole of the dock area had to be evacuated. Some two or three hundred of these folk were put up in a rest centre, but unfortunately this also was hit later in the night and thirty-four were killed. About 140 heavy bombs fell in the borough during this week-end and although casualties were light, this was a sudden and severe introduction to that which we had all anticipated with fear for so long. The first-aid post was re-established temporarily in the Cambridge University Mission premises in Jamaica Road, and these premises were badly damaged by blast in January 1941. The post was again re-established in Amos Estate and escaped further damage. The first-aid post at St. Olave's Hospital was struck and partially demolished towards the end of September, but none of the staff was hurt and sufficient of the premises remained to allow the post to continue in service until a new one could be fitted out at the Rotherhithe Town Hall. In these same weeks of September, the Bermondsey Town Hall was hit and wrecked, and the stretcher party post in Rotherhithe New Road was so badly damaged that it had to be evacuated; in addition, two ambulances and several stretcher party cars were destroyed. The first-aid post at the central baths was slightly damaged on May 10, 1941, and the mobile unit stationed at this post was damaged. Each of the three hospitals received some damage, but none of them was put out of action. Damage to St. Olave's has already been mentioned; the Medical Mission Hospital was damaged slightly by fire and by flying debris, and part of Guy's Hospital was destroyed by fire. The control centre was in the basement of the Municipal Offices, adjacent to the Bermondsey Town Hall, but although the Town Hall and the adjacent depot were hit by several bombs, the control centre escaped. The raid on May 10, 1941, was a very heavy one and it was in this raid that the mayor was killed. One member of the stretcher party staff and one of the Public Health Department were killed in the September raid in which the Town Hall was wrecked; and a woman doctor and two nursing assistants were killed when a heavy bomb fell directly into the medical aid post of a shelter on February 17, 1941.

The ambulance service was operated by the London County Council and the arrival and despatch were prompt and always adequate to the need.

Two mortuaries were provided, one in each end of the borough, giving a total accommodation for 300 bodies, but the greatest number of bodies in either of the mortuaries at any one time never exceeded one-quarter of this figure. A senior clerk in the Public Health Department was appointed Mortuary Superintendent and the mortuary assistants were all volunteers. The work of these men was more trying and unpleasant than that of any other service, and it was performed with exemplary care. All bodies, limbs, and parts, were washed and shrouded, and an immense amount of trouble was taken to secure identification, though in many instances this proved to be quite impossible.

During the heavy raids, 617 people were killed, 922 admitted to hospital and 1,230 treated at first-aid posts. A few very slight casualties went to their own doctors, and a few were treated in the medical aid posts of some of the shelters; these are not included in the numbers given above.

COMMENTARY

Relations with other boroughs were excellent and free and friendly exchange of ideas was constant. The borough was called upon to assist a neighbouring authority with mortuary accommodation and received help from the stretcher parties of a neighbour. On the whole, however, it was remarkable that so little outside help had to be called for, and the defence system was not at any time fully extended in this area. There was a striking disparity between the number of casualties and the corresponding damage to property. Over two thousand properties were completely demolished, and in addition a further 15,000 properties suffered damage more or less severe. As contrasted with less than 700 killed, this figure seemed disproportionate. More effective dispersal of the population would undoubtedly have reduced the number of casualties, since it was noticeable that a large proportion of the killed were in large shelters which were hit. No acute problems followed the raids. When raiding was severe there was an exodus from the borough, and the population dropped to about half that of peace-time. Although there was very extensive damage of property, overcrowding did not become an immediate problem, though it was thought certain to become acute the moment hostilities ceased. This is a small borough with a well-staffed Public Health Department, and the relations between that staff and the general public have for long been almost intimate. The Medical Officer of Health was convinced that this relationship was of great value in times of stress and that both sanitary inspectors and health visitors exerted a powerful steadying influence on the population in general. A similar remark applied to the relation between the medical staff of the Public Health Department and the general practitioners of the borough. This relation, for many years friendly, became intimate during the war, no doubt to the lasting benefit of the doctors and public.

METROPOLITAN BOROUGH OF ST. MARYLEBONE

(*From the Report of H. A. Bulman, M.R.C.S., D.P.H., Medical Officer of Health*)

THE OUTBREAK OF WAR

On August 31, 1939, the order was given for mobilisation. All volunteers whose names appeared on the then current register were asked to report immediately at the post or depot to which they had been allocated. Of roughly 2,000 who had at one time or another enrolled and trained, 230 men and 700 women now remained nominally active. Of these, however, only some 150 men and 400 women actually reported to take an active part in the functioning of the services. Much shadow but little substance. But those who did report were to be the mainstay of the organisation.

The new recruits came from every walk of life, salesmen, labourers, actresses, writers, people on leave from overseas who had been caught up in the tide of events, folk who had rarely been further afield than Edgware Road or Oxford Street. Some did not stay long, but for the most part they quickly trained and became efficient and many were later to do great work amidst the blasting and burning which was to come.

FIRST-AID POSTS

By September 3, 1939, six fixed first-aid posts, two mobile first-aid units and three first-aid party depots were manned, and the doctors who had been appointed under the Ministry of Health Circular No. 1789 took charge. A proportion of auxiliary nurses also worked at these posts.

To facilitate administration, it was considered advisable to have a member of the staff of the Public Health Department attached to each post. Health visitors were therefore appointed to act as liaison officers between the doctors in charge and the Medical Officer of Health. It was their duty to take care of the domestic and clerical work at the posts and to be primarily responsible for the maintenance of equipment.

The full-time war establishment at each consisted of twenty-four women and six men, supervised by a trained nurse. In addition, part-time unpaid volunteers gave great assistance. Some three hundred continued to perform regular hours of duty. Especially was this the case at first-aid posts Nos. 2 and 5 where, after the authorised paid establishment for the borough had been reduced, the posts were run almost exclusively by unpaid workers.

MOBILE FIRST-AID UNITS

At each establishment there was close co-operation between the doctors in charge of the individual units, but the teams kept to their own units and maintained a friendly rivalry, which also existed between the two stations.

STRETCHER PARTIES

When war came, the first-aid parties, by then known as stretcher parties, were established at their three depots. At these depots were also stationed the London County Council's personnel of the rescue service.

The Divisional Superintendent of the local St. John Ambulance Brigade acted as officer-in-charge of stretcher parties at all three depots and was directly responsible to the Medical Officer of Health for their discipline and efficiency. Upon mobilisation, the men were put into squads of five, including a car driver. One man in each squad was appointed leader. They worked in shifts of twenty-four hours, there being a company officer-in-charge of each shift of ten squads and a supervisor in charge of both shifts at each depot.

As with the first-aid posts, from time to time during the first year the establishment was reviewed and modified in the light of experience. In January 1940, the number of full-time personnel was reduced from 300 to 240 and soon after to 210. Unlike the first-aid posts, the stretcher parties relied almost entirely upon a full-time paid personnel but, from the start, a few part-time volunteers did regular turns of duty at the depots.

MORTUARIES

In September 1940, the staff was as follows: 1 male mortuary keeper (permanent staff), 1 mortuary superintendent (temporary), 3 mortuary assistants, 8 van drivers.

The van drivers were stationed at a first-aid post and the other staff at mortuary premises. A sanitary inspector was made responsible for each mortuary and the clerical staff of the Public Health Department were relied upon to do what was necessary in the way of clerical work. It was arranged also that bodies from hospitals in the borough should be transferred to one of the Council's mortuaries.

VEHICLES

Before September 1939, some of the larger firms in the borough had been consulted on transport and a number of their delivery vans and other vehicles earmarked for emergency use. But these sources were insufficient and it was not possible to obtain enough cars of the right type, or indeed sufficient vehicles at all, without interfering unduly with business. To provide transport for the stretcher parties, therefore, during the first few days of the war, thirty-three saloon cars, mostly 16 h.p., were hired from a large firm of motor dealers, under the provisions of A.R.P. Circulars Nos. 193 and 199 of 1939. At the same time a number of private cars were loaned or given to the Council by residents. These were mostly used for general purposes.

In accordance with Home Security Circular No. 338, within a few weeks of its issue on December 14, 1939, all the hired cars had been returned and had been replaced by vehicles of more or less the same type, purchased at an average cost of £30 each. From then the transport arrangements were conducted according to the directions issued from time to time by the Ministry of Home Security. Some of the vehicles which had proved uneconomical in use were replaced in the course of time. After the London County Council car pool came into operation, all redundant vehicles were gradually returned.

THE PERIOD OF HEAVY RAIDING

The Test. The first bombs fell on the night of September 7–8, 1940, and for nearly four months few nights were to pass without an attack. Towards the end of November, incidents became fewer and the attacks gradually waned. There were casualties, including some deaths, in December, particularly on the night of the 8–9th, but little more extensive damage until the nights of April 16–17 and May 10–11, 1941.

When the first casualties occurred, the people whose task it was to deal with them were, in general, well trained and used to team work. But apart from doctors and trained nurses, their knowledge was mainly theoretical. A few who had served in the St. John Ambulance Brigade and British Red Cross Society in peace-time had some acquaintance with practical casualty work. Others had spent a limited number of hours in hospital under a special training scheme, but by and large they lacked real experience. One wondered how they would react to actual operations. When the test finally came, almost without exception they stood up to it magnificently. The words of one medical officer when speaking of first-aid post personnel are equally well applicable to those in the other branches of the casualty service. 'They behaved', he said, 'in the best professional tradition, combined perhaps with a little extra kindness and tenderness.'

FIRST-AID POSTS

In practice, the injured were normally brought to a first-aid post or hospital, as the case might be, by members of one of the services. There was no evidence of lightly wounded persons rushing the hospitals. Conduct was always orderly and there was no panic.

The largest number of patients dealt with on any one occasion occurred on December 8–9, 1940, when 71 casualties were recorded at First-aid Post No. 2. Just after midnight a land mine fell on a large block of flats quite near to the post, which itself had doors, windows and skylight blown in. Although this caused considerable damage at the post, fortunately none of the staff was hurt. In spite of difficulties, particularly with lighting while some of the blackout was being restored, they were quickly tending the casualties, all of whom arrived within three-quarters of an hour. The injuries were mainly cuts, abrasions and shock, but there were fifteen head and scalp wounds and one fractured ankle.

Eighteen were sent on to hospital. All were evacuated from the post within nine hours and though resources were extended, the medical officer in charge has recorded that 'the co-ordinated work of the shift as a team was beyond praise'. Of this and other occasions he says 'there was never any hurry, flurry or fuss, everything being done promptly, quickly and with that useful self-confidence bred of sound knowledge'.

At all first-aid posts it was the practice of the medical officer in charge to decide priority of treatment and destination on discharge. Usually treatment was carried out under his immediate direction or under that of another doctor, and procedure followed as in exercises.

The great majority of casualties were brought to the posts during the hours of darkness, but First-aid Post No. 5 was most fully extended when during the afternoon of October 11, 1940, a bomb on a disposal squad lorry exploded almost outside the premises. Seventeen casualties, including one dead and seven seriously injured, were brought to the post. Only a skeleton staff was on duty at the time. Staff from the adjoining hospital gave assistance. One auxiliary nurse was herself slightly injured outside the post, as she was going off duty, but returned to work among the casualties. She was specially commended for her action. Superficial damage to the premises did not interfere with the functioning of the first-aid post.

In other respects the work of this post is typical. Of the 118 cases recorded, 68 were males and 50 females, the ages varying between $2\frac{1}{2}$ and 83 years. Fifty-four were injured in the open, the high proportion being partly accounted for by the bomb explosion mentioned above. Seventeen cases were sent on to hospitals, the remainder being discharged to their homes or elsewhere after receiving treatment. Cuts and abrasions accounted for 79 cases, fractures of the long bones, four, and of the skull, one, and ribs, two. There were five burns, three wounds of leg or thigh, two penetrating with injury to tibia, four puncture wounds from explosive incendiaries. There were two maternity cases. The remainder were suffering mainly from shock, but it is recorded that in all cases, except those with the severest injuries, shock was slight and perhaps the word 'shaken' would better describe the condition. No tourniquets were used. Morphia was administered in five cases, and of a large proportion injected with anti-tetanus serum only three reported moderate reactions. Only a very small proportion of those treated returned for further attention.

First-aid Post No. 1, at the Middlesex Hospital Annexe, suffered more serious damage than any of the other posts. On September 13, 1940, windows were broken by a nearby bomb and the premises had to be temporarily vacated because a delayed action bomb had fallen in Foley Street. However, this delayed action bomb eventually caused no additional damage to the premises and the post was reoccupied after a lapse of about twelve hours. A fortnight later a small high explosive bomb fell in the forecourt to the building, demolishing the men's undressing shed of the gas cleansing section, but otherwise causing only superficial damage. Finally, on April 16–17, 1941, a large part of the premises was badly damaged by fire and the post had to be abandoned. Although the first-aid treatment rooms were beyond reasonable repair, the gas cleansing section remained serviceable. The first-aid work was transferred to the casualty department of the hospital in the main building, and only the gas cleansing arrangements retained in the annexe.

MOBILE FIRST-AID UNITS

The mobile first-aid units treated casualties at major incidents on four occasions. The first incident in the borough which resulted in casualties gave the units an early opportunity of action. This was on September 9, 1940, when a high explosive bomb demolished Madame Tussaud's Cinema and caused a large number of injuries from flying glass and falling debris amongst the inmates of the St. Marylebone Institution opposite. A unit from Berkeley Court was sent and set up in the Institution premises. Thirty-one casualties were attended, some being sent on to hospital. They were all old men who had been in bed when the bomb fell and the work done was particularly valuable as it saved them the journey to a first-aid post, which, in their shocked condition, was best avoided. A second unit from Health Centre No. 2 was set up in the entrance of Madame Tussaud's building, but dealt with only three patients.

After this start, there were few incidents of a type where the units could be profitably employed. No part of the borough was more than about half a mile from a fixed first-aid post and, although the units were again in action on September 25 and October 16, it was soon realised that the retention of all five was not justified. Consequently, by degrees all but one were disbanded, the staff being largely absorbed on shelter or other work.

STRETCHER PARTIES

Although for nearly a year the stretcher parties had been stationed at the same depots as the rescue parties, in September 1940, the two services had little in common. The stretcher parties, under the Borough Council, were trained as first-aiders, the London County Council rescue parties were skilled in the technique of dealing with dangerous buildings and extricating those who might be trapped. The theory was that stretcher bearers should be sent to incidents to give immediate first aid to the injured, the rescue parties being called upon only where there were complications from the presence of debris, dangerous wreckage or the like. Their work was therefore complementary but directed in detail by different officers and more or less clearly defined in scope. After the first few raids, it was found that in practice it nearly always happened that some amount of rescue work had to be done before the stretcher parties could function as first-aiders. This had been foreseen, and locally an attempt had already been made to teach them some of the elements of rescue work. But there was then no official recognition of this type of instruction for first-aid personnel. Moreover what was done was inadequate to give them the necessary skill and confidence to deal with any but the most straightforward rescues.

SPECIFIC INCIDENTS

The incidents described below are of general interest, but exceptional only in that the 'Tussaud's' incident was the first in the borough involving casualties and that the Marble Arch tube incident was the first where there were many dead and where the unseasoned services were subjected to a particularly gruesome ordeal. In considering the earlier incidents, it should be realised that during training it had been impossible to reproduce immediate post-raid conditions. The confusion, the mess, the great piles of debris which blocked and isolated one road from another—these were impossible to simulate. When, therefore, they became reality, it is not surprising that, quite apart from first-aid considerations, experience was necessary before better methods of reporting and incident control could be instituted.

The occasion when Tussaud's Cinema was demolished and a large number of the inmates of the St. Marylebone Institution opposite were injured by flying glass has been mentioned in connexion with the mobile first-aid units. The bomb, a high explosive of large calibre, fell about 4 o'clock on the morning of September 9, 1940. Blast damage extended more than 100 yards along Marylebone Road, both east and west from the cinema, and also over a large area north and south, particularly in Baker Street. Flats, etc. at the south-east corner of Chiltern Court had been wrecked, and brick and plaster Georgian-type houses nearby in Cornwall Terrace had collapsed. Minor damage had been caused at Berkeley Court and Baker Street Station. It was to the station that the first party was ordered to proceed. The message was received at 0410 hours and the leader of the party which immediately left Depot 1, reported later that when they reached the station much debris was encountered, but no warden or other persons able to give any reliable information as to what had occurred could be contacted. It was still blackout and in the darkness the situation was confused. One casualty was found in the middle of the roadway, and the leader conducted his own investigations in the absence of any specific directions. In Baker Street Station the party found a few other casualties, but no sign of the primary damage. In the meantime, on a report of what presumably was another incident, another party was sent to Cornwall Terrace. Again they failed to contact anyone in authority. They searched as best they could, and reached the south-east corner of Chiltern Court where the

Fire Service was dealing with a fire in one of the flats. They also found a heavy rescue party removing debris from the passageways of Chiltern Court. On reports of casualties in the St. Marylebone Institution and at Madame Tussaud's, two mobile units had been despatched to the site with two stretcher parties to assist them. About 0500 hours, two more parties who had been sent to Berkeley Court upon a report of damage there also made their way to the main incident. Thus there were no less than six parties in attendance, each unaware of the presence of the others. Much time was wasted by parties searching ground already covered by others. This first operation of the stretcher parties illustrated the need for co-ordination on the site. It was also an example of one large high explosive bomb giving the impression of several different incidents and was typical of some of the earlier operations.

Very different in character was the occurrence at Marble Arch Underground Station on the evening of September 17, 1940. Here a small bomb exploded in a confined space, having penetrated the roadway into the subway leading from Hyde Park to the booking hall. Over one hundred people were sheltering there at the time and there were many killed and injured. The casualties were mainly caused by blast, the effect of which was very great, travelling in the narrow tunnel as if down a gun barrel. To add to the difficulties, the lighting had failed, and working with the inadequate A.R.P. torches the men had to distinguish between blood-stained debris and mutilated bodies, some without head or limbs. Six parties from St. Marylebone were employed, and so gruesome was this terrible work that many of the men became temporarily ill and had to be relieved. The men from Westminster who attended the disaster, as well as burly policemen, were similarly affected. Apart from this aspect, the incident presented the difficulty of not knowing how many people were to be accounted for, and again there was not yet efficient co-ordination of services on the spot. Time was lost by the parties in searching for somebody who could say what was required of them.

MORTUARIES

The first two deaths from war operations in the borough occurred on September 9, 1940. From September 17 to 30, 1940, 129 bodies were admitted to the mortuary, Paddington Street. On September 18, 1940, 43 bodies were received and on September 25, 31 bodies. During this critical period the mortuary staff stood the strain of the work very well indeed. In addition to the unpleasantness of their duties, there were frequent raids during the day, but the men carried on steadily.

After September 1940, there was a considerable reduction in the number of fatalities. There were, however, large numbers killed on April 16–17, and May 11, 1941, and, resulting from the raid on the latter date, 53 bodies, the highest number ever received in a day, were brought to the mortuary at the Mansergh Woodall Club. The following is a statement of the number of bodies received each month in the raiding period:

1940—	September	132 bodies
	October	54 ,,
	November	12 ,,
	December	29 ,,
1941—	January	2 ,,
	February	1 body
	March	—
	April	43 bodies
	May	66 ,,
		339 bodies

Identification of the dead proved to be the chief difficulty of the mortuary service. Transport of the dead was effected rapidly and at no time did this part of the service break down, in spite of the fact that the work often had to be carried on during night bombing. Most of the bodies were so mutilated that identification was often difficult. Many were not recovered from the debris until some weeks had elapsed, but identification was established in all cases, except ten from Marble Arch Subway on September 18, 1940; some mutilated remains from Marylebone Road on September 24, 1940; and one from Jackson's Garage, Rathbone Street, in which instance the charred remains were not recovered until February 25, 1941 when the debris was being cleared—five months after the incident.

THE LESSONS LEARNED

First-aid Posts. First-aid posts were originally established at hospital premises so as to act as buffers between hospital and public. Experience during the heaviest raids indicated that there need have been no fear that the lightly wounded would interfere unduly with the functioning of the hospitals. In fact, the maintenance by the Borough Council of separate first-aid posts, in view of the relatively small numbers of casualties encountered, was not justified where alternative arrangements could be made for the hospitals to treat walking wounded. Such an arrangement is more economical of man-power, accommodation and money. It avoids also to some extent duplication of equipment and facilitates administration.

Mobile First-aid Units. The reduction in the number of mobile first-aid units from five to one was made because their retention was not justified in a borough no part of which was much more than about half a mile from a first-aid post. Where first-aid posts and hospitals were fewer and further apart, there was little doubt as to the great value of these units as first-aid posts. Especially was this the case in rural districts. But in St. Marylebone the principal value of the units was found to be in their potentialities for the treatment of shock and in the aid which could be given by the doctor and trained nurse to trapped casualties. There were also beneficial psychological results arising from the presence of women nurses at some types of incident.

To secure these advantages, however, a heavy unit, which was cumbersome and expensive, was seldom necessary in a metropolitan district. The necessary staff and equipment could quite well be carried in a medium-sized saloon car. This fact was recognised by the Ministry of Health, who directed that with each heavy unit there should be a satellite car to transport the doctor and a nurse to incidents at which the attendance of the full team was unnecessary. They also introduced the 'light first-aid unit' which was in effect the same as the 'satellite car', except that it operated independently of a heavy unit.

Stretcher Parties. As a result of experience, many changes were effected in this branch of the service. There had been a continuous wastage of trained personnel mainly due to the younger men being called up for service with the Forces, so that the average age became considerably higher than formerly.

Largely as a result of operational experience, the type of instruction given was greatly modified. Before the period of heavy bombing, practical rescue training had no place in the official curriculum for stretcher parties. The unofficial instruction which had been given in the subject dealt chiefly with such processes as the removal of casualties from difficult situations as, for example, from upper rooms of wrecked houses *via* the windows. As we have seen, it proved to be totally inadequate when they came to deal with actual war incidents. Time and again they were despatched to the site of bombing only to find that the casualties were trapped. Before they could be reached, operations involving a knowledge of building construction or technical rescue methods and the use of special equipment were necessary. This not only caused delay while rescue parties were summoned, but only too often when these parties arrived, the stretcher bearers were not sufficiently skilled to assist them materially. Hours were sometimes wasted standing by, while rescues were being effected.

The first few raids made the position clear and, locally, steps were taken to train the stretcher parties more adequately so that they might be competent to undertake rescue work of the simpler kind themselves and give useful assistance to the rescue service instead of standing idly by. The officer in charge of the rescue service readily co-operated in arranging this training. It was in progress when the Ministry of Home Security, having seen the same need, directed that similar instruction should be given officially. The result could be seen in the handling of the later incidents, where the stretcher parties were often able to give real assistance to the rescue personnel and, moreover, on several occasions successfully tackled, unaided, rescues which would have been beyond their powers without the special training.

On March 1, 1942, in accordance with L. R. Circular No. 579, the stretcher parties did, in fact, become light rescue parties and from that date were so designated. Their equipment now included tools and other necessities for essential rescue operations, carried either in a van or in a trailer towed behind the party car.

GENERAL CONCLUSIONS

Some of the lessons taught by experience have been outlined and developments and modifications sketched. The whole system was necessarily not static, but required constant adjustment to meet changing conditions. Nevertheless, certain principles persisted, more particularly the need for securing effectiveness, elasticity, economy of man-power and money, and ease of administration. The additional suggestions made are either fundamental in character or involve a degree of speculation, but it is with these principles in mind that they are put forward:

First-aid Posts and Mobile Units. Their functions are a logical extension of the work of hospitals, by whom they should be absorbed wherever possible.

Rescue Service. At the time the light rescue service was so named, the former rescue parties—or rescue, shoring and demolition parties to give them their full title—became the heavy rescue service. The general trend of policy was in accord with local experience of operational requirements, but it is considered that the development was not sufficiently fundamental. The outstanding lesson taught by the functioning of the stretcher and rescue parties was the need for their fusion. The closer co-operation and mutual assistance between the two is a very definite advance, but the next logical step forward is a combined service under the jurisdiction and control of one authority, or even as part of a national service on the lines of the National Fire Service.

To secure the optimum of efficiency and economy of man-power, parties consisting of nine men seem to be indicated. These might well consist of a leader who is primarily a skilled rescue technician, an assistant leader who is essentially an experienced first-aider, a driver, one building-trade craftsman, and five other men all trained in first-aid and rescue work. Vans as at present employed by the heavy rescue service would be used for transport.

Not only would this composite party be fitted to tackle nearly any type of rescue and first-aid work, but distinct advantages would come from the abolition of dual control. Although the relationship which exists between the Borough Council and London County Council officers concerned with the two services as they exist is good, there is necessarily a certain amount of duplication in administration. Moreover, arising from the fact that the two sets of men working closely together are each under a different authority, anomalies sometimes become apparent which would be better avoided. Both at the depots from day to day and on operations, therefore, single control would result in greater efficiency and economy in man-power, equipment, etc.

Dealing with the work of the light rescue parties in more detail, experience has shown that a good leader is the keystone of efficiency. On reaching the site of an incident, he should quickly obtain from the incident officer all essential relevant information and then make his own reconnaissance. Many lives have been saved by 'looking round the corner' in this way. At the same time, the leader should direct his men and dispose them as the situation warrants. Having assessed the position as accurately as possible, the leader should deal with the tasks involved in order of their urgency. He should himself undertake the more difficult or delicate work and be assisted by the others rather than allow them to act on their own initiative. When he does not need the immediate help of all the rest of the team, he should detail his No. 2 man and any others he can spare to do some particular job and never let them remain idle. The parties should always return to their base immediately their work is done.

As to actual first aid, it has been found that what is required is the minimum of treatment with the maximum of care. This rule cannot be too strongly stressed. In other words, all that circumstances permit must be done to combat shock and the patient should be removed to first-aid post or hospital with the least possible delay.

The standard first-aid training has always been that laid down in the St. John Ambulance Brigade and British Red Cross Society handbooks. This provides an excellent groundwork but contains much that is impracticable for the work of the parties under operational conditions. For example, the handbooks use triangular bandages, but the standard bandage supplied to the light rescue service is the mines dressing. Again, in this essentially peace-time training, too much elaborate splinting is encouraged. The stress is on treatment rather than on the observation and recognition of signs and symptoms. Locally efforts have been made to correct these tendencies, but it is recommended that the course should be revised for war purposes. It is also suggested that each scheme-making authority should have a central training establishment for all services under their control.

METROPOLITAN BOROUGH OF HACKNEY

(*From the Report of G. H. Dart, M.D., D.P.H., Medical Officer of Health*)

THE FIRST-AID POSTS

The opening phases of the raids on London found Hackney with five fully equipped and staffed first-aid posts trained and ready to tackle a job of unknown dimensions. The staff had been told to expect casualties in their hundreds, but nobody suggested that raids might last from dusk to dawn, and after.

With one exception, all the first-aid posts were situated at ground level. The exception was in the form of a Nissen Hut constructed partly below ground level. Of the four remaining, one was a small two-storey private hospital, and three were converted church halls.

To say that the first-aiders worked under dangerous conditions would be a truism that was never voiced by any of them. Once heavy raiding started, there was simply no time to think about the dangerous aspect of the job to be done. They got on with it, finished it, went home to sleep, and came back the next night to do it all over again.

The personnel were, for the most part, young girls who, before the war, had absolutely no experience of casualty work; to make up for this drawback the staff from each post were in the habit of attending the out-patient and casualty departments of the local general hospitals for some time before raiding began; the object, of course, was to get them used to the atmosphere, and to the appearance of wounds.

In addition to the first-aid posts there were two heavy mobile units based at one of the posts. Apart from the professional nurses in charge, the auxiliary nurses were recruited and trained in the same way as their colleagues in the fixed posts. They volunteered quite freely—many gave up well-paid positions to do so; they took their first-aid training, passed their examinations, attended demonstrations and exercises every day, and got on with the job of making themselves capable of doing what they had volunteered to do. In passing, it should be added that the attraction of a uniform was non-existent—there was no uniform provided in the first place—just a metal badge followed later on by the issue of an arm-band.

During the Battle of London, there was always the possibility of the enemy using gas, and apart from the first-aiders being responsible for treatment of casualties due to high explosive bombs, they were trained and ready to cope with poison gas casualties in a special section of the post set aside for that particular purpose. To ensure that both anti-gas and first-aid treatment could be given at the same time, the staff were put on a rota which meant their returning sometimes to their posts, even though they had just completed a heavy night's work. They were, in fact, 'on call' when they were off-duty. If they were at home when the 'alert' was sounded, they had to run the gauntlet. To make these journeys less hazardous, staff were allocated to posts near their homes; in fact, with a few exceptions, personnel were grouped within a circle, in the centre of which was the first-aid post. There were five of these groups covering the whole of the borough, and in addition to these posts there were five reserve first-aid posts. They were not staffed, but were maintained and equipped for emergencies.

The First-aid Posts in Action. Saturday, September 7, 1940 saw three of the five posts go into action. An onlooker would have seen only cool, calm efficiency—the personnel had been waiting and training for this moment. When it came—very suddenly—they rose to the occasion like veterans and did a perfect job. When it was over they barely had time to talk about it, when the early evening brought a repetition in the shape of an even heavier raid. Periods of interval were, for the most part, taken up with sleep.

One post had two delayed action bombs dropped close by, forcing evacuation into a reserve first-aid post where the staff continued casualty treatment. Shortly afterwards a delayed action bomb was dropped within fifty yards of this reserve post. Again the staff had to be evacuated. There was a very heavy raid in progress at the time, but the whole of the staff were moved by lorry and were dealing with casualties in the space of half an hour. In those days there was no knowledge as to when these bombs would explode, and in this particular case the bomb had dropped in a church, the vicar of which had offered his services to the reserve post, and did in fact, help the staff to get away. He happened to be in the church when the bomb exploded. He was killed.

An unusual case was brought into a post one night. The casualty, a man, was brought in with the back of his head laid open from ear to ear, but although the wound exposed his skull, he was quite conscious and able to describe what had happened. It appears he was in bed upstairs when the raid started, and within a few minutes of taking shelter in his 'Anderson' in the garden, was blown through the back wall of his bedroom with the shelter wrapped around him.

Another unusual type came into another post—a woman, who upon being questioned could do no more than make unintelligible sounds. Upon examination, it was found that two of her top teeth had been forced right through and below her lower lip literally 'buttoning up' her mouth. Once her mouth was freed she had little to say that bears repeating!

A warden hurried into a post one night and handed the officer-in-charge a small child of about nine months or so. He only had time to say that he had found the child wrapped in a blanket lying on the pavement near an 'incident'. The police and report centre were notified and a description of the child passed on. Later the child's mother went to the post and found him happy and contented, and strangely enough quite unhurt. Apparently the child was blown out of her arms, and could not be found when she recovered her senses.

Some casualties who walked into first-aid posts for light treatment were completely unaware of more serious wounds. For instance, a man with a slight wound in his arm walked a distance of roughly half a mile to the post. He had also been severely wounded in the buttock. The flesh had literally been gouged out about two inches across and two inches deep. When he was questioned he said he knew nothing about it. With him on this particular night there came a young lad with practically the whole of one ear blown off. He too, had walked the same distance, but in his case he was so badly shocked that he was unable to speak for about an hour.

Around October 1940, the weight of raiding increased, and although the first-aid posts catered for 'walking wounded', they often had to accept serious stretcher cases. This, it seems, was because of 'incidents' close to the posts, and where there seemed to be a likelihood of the cases proving fatal without immediate surgical assistance.

All this brought first-aiders into close touch with treatment that was well outside the scope of first aid. Even so, first-aid training in the form of revision went on every day, and in one post the medical officer was in the habit of collecting the staff on duty and giving short lectures in the middle of an air raid to fill in the time between casualty treatment.

Casualties were most grateful to the post nurses, and often showed their appreciation later by gifts of chocolates and cigarettes. Incidentally it was found that a cigarette did more for men than for women; for the latter the equivalent was a cup of tea.

Up to January 1943, Hackney first-aid posts treated casualties running into four figures. The heaviest month was October 1940. The post situated in the centre of the borough did most work, although one post on the edge of the borough was 'rushed' with fifty-five casualties; all of whom practically walked in one behind the other. This was common when dealing with the result of a 'parachute mine'.

First-aid posts, for the most part, have always been something in the nature of a 'silent' service. The general public has never really appreciated what the girls went through. They were never seen during the daytime, in fact, the only way in which one could appreciate them was to receive treatment at their hands. They started in with no experience of bombing to help them, and when it came they uncomplainingly treated their casualties through the whole period without the slightest show of fear. If anyone had walked into a first-aid post in the middle of a heavy raid, he would have marvelled at what he saw. It may be asked whether the nurses took shelter seeing that they were at ground level? They did not. So long as there were casualties to be treated, the shelters were empty, and when casualty work was done they had to be forced to go to shelter; they preferred to wait in their sections for what might come in.

THE STRETCHER PARTIES
(AFTERWARDS LIGHT RESCUE PARTIES)

An attempt to describe in detail the work of the first-aid parties in this borough would require more space in any work than can be allocated to it. The following summary, though it will serve some purpose in giving figures and totals of such things as the number of casualties attended, the number of incidents at which services were given, etc., cannot present a satisfactory picture of the true services rendered to the public.

Apart from the actual rendering of first aid to air raid victims, a greater work was done in keeping up the morale of the public, by the inspiring example which was set by the personnel whilst working under fire. Victims and their relatives were undoubtedly heartened by the knowledge that fully trained men were available to render first-class aid, despite the risk to their own lives from still falling bombs.

The training of the personnel for this work was a long, arduous and tedious business often provoking complaints from the men themselves, but that it was satisfactory was borne out by the results. How they would react when the bombs began to fall was always an unknown quantity, but when the test came the response from the men far exceeded all expectations. In fact, from reports received, the greatest crime that any of the depot officers could commit was to despatch a party to an incident out of turn, unless it was before its turn became due. Not a single case of refusal to leave for an incident has been recorded. When the bombs and parachute mines were falling any fear felt by the men was rarely shown, but everywhere very strong language was used because they were unable to hit back. The least used parts of the depot during an alert were the shelters provided for the men's safety. This was not bravado on the part of men, but they preferred to amuse themselves by playing billiards, snooker or darts whilst awaiting their call for despatch to an incident. During the comparative quiet of the daylight hours, the men would pay particular attention to their equipment and still more attention to the squad cars. Should a defect in the latter be found, the officers-in-charge were asked hourly whether the defect had received attention.

Although the personnel could not rightly be held responsible for a breakdown on their way to an incident, they seemed to assume that responsibility and looked upon it as a serious let-down for their particular depot. Not infrequently, men who had worked most of the previous night dealing with air raid casualties could be seen, although off duty, helping their fresher mates on new incidents.

One leader of a stretcher party, a member of the St. John Ambulance Brigade, when off duty would follow on his cycle the sound and direction of falling bombs for the purpose of using his skill as a first-aider. On another occasion a stretcher party officer had to despatch a squad to his own home which had been damaged by a bomb. Despite his anxiety and concern for his family's welfare, he refused to leave his post until long after the raiders' passed signal had been given and he had satisfied himself that another responsible officer was in charge. Other similar cases are on record.

It was ever apparent that the risk to their own lives from falling bombs was not so upsetting to the men as the injury and loss of life among the child population of the borough, which frequently brought oaths of condemnation from the men against the parents for not having taken advantage of the Government evacuation scheme. Throughout the whole period, the stretcher party staff were, without exception, fully alive to and proud of their job i.e., the preservation of life. Complaints from the men were very few, and they asked nothing more upon return from incidents than to know that cups of tea were available. Often, on arriving at an incident, a squad could not find the incident officer or warden. Realising that they were probably busily engaged elsewhere, the leader immediately took charge of the incident, dealt with casualties, and if ambulances were not available, despatched hospital cases in a heavy rescue party lorry.

Incidents such as the following are examples of the kind of work which was done:

Having crawled through a very narrow opening into a trench shelter which had received a direct hit, a stretcher party officer supported for three hours a badly injured woman, whilst on either side of him were the woman's two children, dead. Whilst encouraging and supporting the injured woman, he was called upon to answer her questions concerning her children's welfare and to administer the morphia handed down by a doctor. Immediately after the woman's release, this officer continued to work and did so for a further five hours.

Among the many acts of bravery on record is one which was particularly outstanding. The leader of a heavy rescue party squad had decided to withdraw his men from a collapsed building, because of the grave risk from falling debris. It was the leader's intention to return in daylight. However, an officer in charge of the stretcher parties at work on the incident refused to leave this particular site and at great personal risk, not only from falling bombs but also from being buried by 40 or 50 tons of debris, burrowed into the debris sufficiently to enable him to grasp a trapped woman's hand and so comfort her and to render such first aid as was possible. Three people were finally extricated alive and the part contributed to this by the leader was undoubtedly immeasurable.

PORT OF LONDON AUTHORITY

(*From the Report of F. Harris White, M.R.C.S., D.P.H., Medical Officer P.L.A.*)

The history of the Battle of London would not be complete without a short account of the work of the Port of London Authority over the activities of which the boroughs have no jurisdiction.

AREA AND POPULATION

The Port of London Authority were responsible for the Civil Defence Services in an area of about 2,300 acres exclusive of land required for development. This area naturally had a floating population, but the normal average was about 60,000. It was directly administered by the Port of London Authority and was covered by buildings of various types

—storage warehouses, transit sheds, factories, mills, etc., and by the docks, but did not include the numerous wharves, factories, etc. lining both banks of the river for many miles of its length. These came under the various local authorities. whose boundaries touched the river. The Port of London Authority, however, were responsible for all vessels in the stream.

There were five distinct systems of docks, viz:

(1) The London and St. Katherine Docks
(2) The Surrey Commercial Docks
(3) The East & West India and Millwall Docks
(4) The Royal Victoria, Albert, and King George V Docks
(5) The Tilbury Docks.

Each of these systems was physically separated from the others by distances varying between one and fifteen miles.

PRE-WAR ARRANGEMENTS

It is obvious that a separate and self-contained civil defence organisation in each of these dock systems was necessary, which was capable of functioning alone, but which in emergencies could obtain support from the others or from the neighbouring local authorities.

The pre-war arrangements and equipment were those required by the Factory Acts, viz., first-aid boxes distributed over the dock area and an ambulance room with an ambulance for each system.

From 1936 onwards, the Port of London Authority organised and expanded the first-aid services to meet war conditions. Courses of lectures were conducted on first-aid and anti-gas measures and first-aid stations were provided. By the outbreak of the war, eleven such stations conforming to the standard laid down by the Ministry of Health were equipped and a civil defence depot was set up in each of the dock systems. For the transport of casualties 29 ambulances were provided and a certain number of taxis were chartered. As regards personnel, 400 men were trained during this period. They were chiefly volunteers from the staffs of the Port of London Authority and their tenants. As the Port of London Authority had only one medical officer, medical practitioners from the residential areas near the docks were allocated to attend the first-aid stations as required.

OUTBREAK OF THE WAR

From the outbreak of the war, whole-time medical officers were appointed to each of the first-aid posts, but as time went on it became evident that many of the precautions taken were not necessary; the full-time medical officers were gradually absorbed into other activities and medical practitioners were paid retaining fees to continue the training of the personnel and to attend first-aid posts during enemy attacks. The posts were staffed by trained first-aid men and women at night only.

RIVER AMBULANCE SERVICE

In addition to the arrangements on land, the Port of London Authority formed a River Ambulance Service to deal with casualties occurring on ships in the stream and in parts of the area not readily accessible from land. Fourteen ships of the pleasure steamer type were suitably adapted as ambulance vessels; each had accommodation for sixteen patients in the saloons (Plate VI), and the decks could accommodate additional cases on stretchers as well as walking and sitting cases. About seventy motor boats were brought into the Service to act as tenders to the ambulance craft and a small number of speed boats were employed for communication work. The personnel was recruited from among the local yachtsmen and river clubs. Each of the ambulance steamers carried one doctor, two trained nurses, ten auxiliary nurses and two orderlies. (Plates VII, VIII and IX illustrate the River Ambulance Service in action.)

THE RAIDS

The raids began with the heavy attack on the night of September 7–8, 1940, and from that date onwards the dock areas experienced several heavy attacks, but owing to the nature of the area and type of attack delivered, the casualties were surprisingly low. During the whole period between September 1, 1940, to May 31, 1941, the casualties treated in the Port of London Authority first-aid posts were as follows:

India Docks	49
Tilbury Docks	7
London Docks	75
Head Office	22
Surrey Docks	29
Royal Docks	17
Total	199

Of the above number, 85 cases were conveyed by Port of London Authority ambulances to hospital. The River Ambulance Service only had to deal with a very small number of cases, probably about 20 in all, but the exact numbers are not available as the records were lost owing to enemy action. These casualties were mostly on ships coming into the Port of London.

On several occasions parties consisting of a medical officer and nurses were landed to give assistance to casualties in the various boroughs alongside the river.

Experience showed that the River Ambulance Service was very little used, and the ambulance steamers and the motor tenders were gradually demobilised and taken over by the naval authorities for other purposes.

The greatest destruction was caused by the huge fires at the Surrey Docks on the night of September 7–8, when there were many casualties among the fire services and the first-aid post in the docks was totally destroyed.

The largest number of casualties caused by one bomb was when one of small calibre fell on the concrete road immediately outside the Superintendent's Office on the evening of November 15, when eight members of the staff were killed, ten seriously injured and a considerable number slightly injured.

COMMENTARY

Considering the extensive area concerned, the number of casualties caused during the whole period was exceedingly small, which must chiefly be attributed to the fact that the great majority of the bombs fell in the river or the docks, thus causing little damage. Casualties were few even when ships in the river received direct hits, such as H.M.S. *Helvellyn* on March 19, when there were only six. When the *Clan Forbes* was hit in the Tilbury Docks on August 16, 1940, a small number of casualties occurred among the crew and workmen, chiefly from ammunition in the ship exploding. The largest number of casualties in a ship was caused by a bomb which penetrated the firemen's quarters of the s.s. *Ben Nevis* lying at the North Quay of the West India Dock, six Chinese seamen being killed and nine being treated at the first-aid post; other casualties were removed by police ambulances direct to the Poplar Hospital.

Plates X to XVII may serve further to illustrate certain aspects of the work of the Civil Defence Services in the Metropolitan area during the heavy raids. They are included as pictorial examples of the devotion to duty and heroism displayed by the members of these Services to which an endeavour has been made to pay an adequate tribute in the preceding pages.

GENERAL REVIEW

As previously mentioned, this story of the great raids on the London Area is an endeavour to give a representative picture. Many of the experiences during the raids and the lessons learned are common to all the London Boroughs. There were, however, considerable differences and variations. There were differences in the manner in which some boroughs reacted to the early call for preparedness—some were quicker off the mark than others. Borough councils were not all of the same mind. There were also differences in the interpretation of experiences and in the views of what might have been done better, now that events are seen retrospectively.

Some of the impressions of the medical officers of health of the metropolitan boroughs and extra-metropolitan areas are summarised below:

LESSONS OF THE RAIDS

Many of the medical officers of health commented on the lessons they learned from their experience during the raids and many of the suggestions made by them were subsequently given effect to by the Ministry of

Health in the complete reorganisation of the Civil Defence Services carried out in 1942. This subject has been fully dealt with in the chapter on the evolution of the Civil Defence Services. (Volume I, Chapter 7.)

FIRST-AID POSTS

Fixed Posts. The type of raiding which the R.A.F. considered within the powers of the Luftwaffe (see Volume I, Chapter 2) and the estimated number of casualties as the result of such attacks, necessarily formed the basis of the Ministry of Health's plans for the provision of first-aid posts, but this type of attack was never delivered and the casualties per ton of bombs dropped only amounted to a small fraction of the estimate. It was soon evident that the number of first-aid posts was much in excess of requirements although considerable numbers were wholly or temporarily put out of action. Naturally some posts which happened to be near major incidents had to work under heavy strain for short periods, but most of them usually had to deal only with a small number of casualties at considerable intervals.

During the month of September 1940, when the heaviest raiding occurred, the total number of casualties treated at first-aid posts was 13,719 and as the number of fixed posts was 392, the average number dealt with at each post was 35 in the whole month, only slightly more than one per post per day. After the raids the Ministry of Health reconsidered the position in the light of experience; and felt that the number of posts and the size of their staffs could be considerably reduced by abolishing some and putting others on care and maintenance. Most medical officers of health emphasised in their reports the desirability of making these reductions.

Mobile Posts. In the opinion of most of the medical officers of health, the mobile posts, of which there were 187 in the whole of London, were of little use and were practically never used for the purpose for which they were intended, i.e., to open out in a convenient building near a large incident at which many casualties had occurred, or to replace a post which had been put out of action. It was generally almost impossible to find a suitable building conveniently situated adjacent to an incident, in which to open a post, especially in the blackout. It was found to be better practice in the interests of the casualties to render immediate first aid at the incidents and send the casualties either direct to hospital or to a fixed post. In Paddington mobile units were much more used than in the other boroughs.

Treatment. Many of the medical officers of health found the equipment of the first-aid posts much too lavish, especially the multiplicity of surgical instruments, splints and similar appliances; for example, Thomas splints were scarcely, if ever, used, nor were the great majority of the instruments, as the numbers of seriously injured admitted to first-aid posts requiring immediate surgical treatment only averaged about 2 per cent., but 25 per cent. of all cases received at first-aid posts were subsequently sent to hospital. The seriously injured who did not require immediate surgical treatment were given the minimum amount of first-aid necessary, the object being to get them into hospital at the earliest possible moment; other cases were sent for special examination, but the treatment required in most cases was for shock. Dr. J. MacMillan, Medical Officer of Health, Woolwich, expressed these views in graphic terms in his report as follows:

'Before actual experience of the types of casualties which would have to be dealt with at first-aid posts as the result of an air raid, expectations ranged from the slightest of injuries to men with "several leg fractures" or worse. In theory a regular procedure for treatment had been laid down. Casualties of all types were to be admitted to a reception room where they would be classified, diagnosed and a certain amount of clerical work completed and treatment ordered. From there they would walk or be carried to the treatment room and receive attention for their injuries. They would then proceed to the recovery room for tea, coffee, cigarettes and the completion of the clerical work and also for a time to recover somewhat from their experiences.

'Exceptions to the above would be urgent hospital cases, which, after receiving essential treatment in the recovery room, would go straight into an ambulance.

'Experience provided a totally different picture. The majority of the casualties were slight, but a proportion of these had to be sent to hospital for X-ray examination or as out-patients; the immediate urgent hospital case was very infrequent. Most of the slightly injured arrived covered in dust, dirt and debris, with glass splinters in their hair, etc., and with their throats full of grit. They emerged from a blackness in which a terrible upheaval had taken place. Possibly they had lost everything, the home of years; little things that mattered and gathered with care—the dog, the canary, etc. Perhaps their own household had not been traced, no one knew as yet whether they were dead, injured, or safe. All the air raid casualty could appreciate was that the thing that couldn't happen had happened to him and that in a brief space of time life had stopped being a thing of security and had become a thing of dirt, grime, pain and confusion. They arrived among unknown people calling, shouting, directing and removing them from one place to another where more unknown people wished to help. This then was the "patient" whom we were prepared to classify, whose arm or leg we would bandage and who would ultimately get a rest and a cup of tea. From the very first day, therefore, our preconceived system of treatment was turned completely upside down.

'The treatment of minor injuries was the last consideration; treatment of shock and an effort to achieve sympathy with, and restore confidence to, the patient was the first. Consequently a visitor to a first-aid post would find dirt begrimed men and women in any room, sitting or lying, wrapped in blankets and with hot water bottles and anything else we could provide, drinking tea, smoking, talking, until a certain degree of steadiness returned and it was felt that they could be worried to the extent of being washed and receiving treatment for their injuries. All that happened to them during the "recovery" period was that a casualty card was tied on; ultimately the treatment written on it if possible and an effort made to obtain their name and address, which together with "home", "hospital" or "rest centre" was added. Finally, after a clean up and treatment of injuries the casualty did arrive in the recovery room where more tea was provided and more sympathetic conversation took place and the individual was given some idea of what would happen to him next. Volunteers from the first-aid staff took messages to relatives, etc. Finally, the casualty left or was removed to whatever appeared to be the best place for him, and the night's work was over.

'Thus we learned that first aid meant primarily treatment for shock, both mental and physical; secondly treatment for injuries; and the next most important work was a social service bureau, where information about the varying types of assistance and how and where to get it, was given.'

Dr. MacMillan's views were shared by several other medical officers of health, whose admirable reports revealed much similarity of experience and opinion, both in doing and reviewing the work of the Civil Defence Services during this period.

PERSONNEL

No one could read these records unmoved by the heroic courage displayed by unassuming men and women who, unaccustomed to the sights and sounds of battle and claiming for themselves no exceptional devotion or patriotic virtue, refused no call and shrank from no danger in rescuing and tending the victims of air attack. To this courage and devotion general tribute was paid.

No less commendable were the passive endurance and high morale of the casualties themselves, and the absence of panic among the general population, factors which, as emphasised by Dr. Thompson (Lambeth), contributed in no small measure to the efficient working of the civil defence machine.

But, while there was no difference of opinion as to the keenness and steadfastness of civil defence workers in action, various suggestions were made regarding their recruitment and training.

In the first place, in many boroughs—e.g. Bethnal Green (Dr. Borland), Lewisham (Dr. Miller), Southwark (Dr. Stott), Lambeth (Dr. Thompson)—great difficulty was experienced in obtaining suitable recruits as volunteers for the first-aid parties, and even when whole-time paid staff was sanctioned the difficulty still continued. Volunteers of the quality of the St. John Ambulance Brigade member who 'when off duty would follow on his cycle the sound and direction of falling bombs for the purpose of using his skill as a first-aider' (Dr. Dart's report) were the elite of the service; but one medical officer, who had recourse to obtaining recruits from the Labour Exchanges, remarked that about

75 per cent. of those sent to him were "known to the Police"! Nevertheless, such men, who were not lacking in physical courage, were among the keenest workers when the testing time came.

It is not surprising, however, that complaints were made of apathy and indifference to discipline during the period of training. That this was a substantial problem was evident in the reports of Dr. White (City of London), Dr. Allan Young (Poplar), Dr. Symes (Chelsea), Dr. Freeman (Islington) and Dr. Caley (Wandsworth). In Kensington, and to less extent elsewhere, boredom and apathy during quiet periods were combated by employing the staffs to the fullest extent possible in the ordinary public health, clerical and other activities of the borough.

One medical officer of health considered that much time had been wasted in giving a rigid and elaborate training to first-aid personnel, with not enough emphasis on simple treatment, especially for shock (Dr. Oates, Paddington). Another (Dr. Borland, Bethnal Green) considered that too much stress had been laid on anti-gas training and too little on first aid.

Radical changes in organisation to meet these difficulties were advocated by Dr. White and Dr. Caley. To the former (see his report) a military organisation appealed as being the best solution. Dr. Caley considered that the Civil Defence Services suffered in efficiency because they were set up as a separate organisation under an entirely new administration which had to be created for the purpose. He thought that greater efficiency and economy of man-power would have resulted if these services, except for the staffs of the first-aid posts, had been placed under the Metropolitan Police, which is a disciplined force with an efficient administration. He pointed out that in peace-time the Metropolitan Police were in the habit of dealing with considerable numbers of casualties from traffic, fire and other causes. Large numbers were trained first-aiders and were fully acquainted with the hospital organisation of the London Region and the type of casualties with which they could adequately deal. They summoned ambulances and disposed of casualties with the greatest possible efficiency and expedition. They also were accustomed to deal with the disposal of fatal casualties and unidentified bodies. Dr. Caley therefore thought that this organisation formed an efficient framework, which could have been expanded to meet the additional requirements resulting from heavy raids more rapidly and efficiently than any other. Their value as a casualty recording organisation was recognised and used by the Ministry, but not their experience in dealing with casualties.

FIRST-AID POSTS

The treatment of the lightly injured was found to be better in the out-patient departments of hospitals and at first-aid posts attached to hospitals than at separate and independent first-aid posts. This, of course, was what might be expected, the staff of a hospital having had much more experience in what was required than that of a first-aid post. Attention was drawn in the report of Dr. Barnes (Camberwell) to this point, on which there was general agreement, and the Ministry subsequently adopted the policy of staffing and administering the posts from hospitals as far as was found possible.

Dr. Struthers (Holborn) thought it important that the medical officer in charge should see all cases and select those for immediate treatment, allowing other casualties to wait their turn. Another medical officer strongly deprecated patients being worried with questions for record purposes when they were not in a fit condition to give coherent answers.

Opposing views were expressed regarding the size and number of first-aid posts. Westminster (Dr. Shinnie) favoured a few large well protected posts, with plenty of room to deal with the various types of casualties, but in Kensington the Medical Officer of Health (Dr. Fenton) preferred a large number of small first-aid posts, his point being that the casualties would receive attention quicker, and that this system avoided the confusion sometimes caused by dealing with large numbers. Dr. Oldershaw, Hampstead, supported this view. It should be borne in mind, however, that the object might be defeated by a large influx of patients to the first-aid post nearest to an incident at which many casualties had occurred, and by the difficulties of distributing casualties to a large number of small posts by first-aid parties who would have no knowledge of the numbers being attended to already at each post.

Many other boroughs like Bermondsey considered it essential to supplement the establishment laid down by the Ministry of Health for first-aid posts, by using permanent members of the Public Health Department, such as sanitary inspectors, trained nurses, health visitors and other trained lay staff to organise, control and administer the first-aid posts. Others drew attention to the inadequate sleeping accommodation for the staff on duty at first-aid posts and first-aid party depots, and for feeding those on duty for long periods during raids. The authorities apparently had not expected all-night raids for many consecutive nights. In most boroughs these needs were gradually met by extra provision for night staffs and mobile canteens to supply food.

The general consensus of opinion was that every part of first-aid posts should be protected as strongly as possible against the effects of bombing and many medical officers of health would have gone much further than the Ministry, whose policy was only to provide protection against blast and over-head protection of one room for personnel. Many first-aid posts in schools, public baths and halls proved to be very vulnerable to heavy attack.

Homeless Persons. Many of the medical officers of health drew attention to the inadequate provision made to deal with the post-raid problems of housing persons rendered homeless by the destruction of their houses, and contrasted these with the lavish arrangements made for treating casualties.

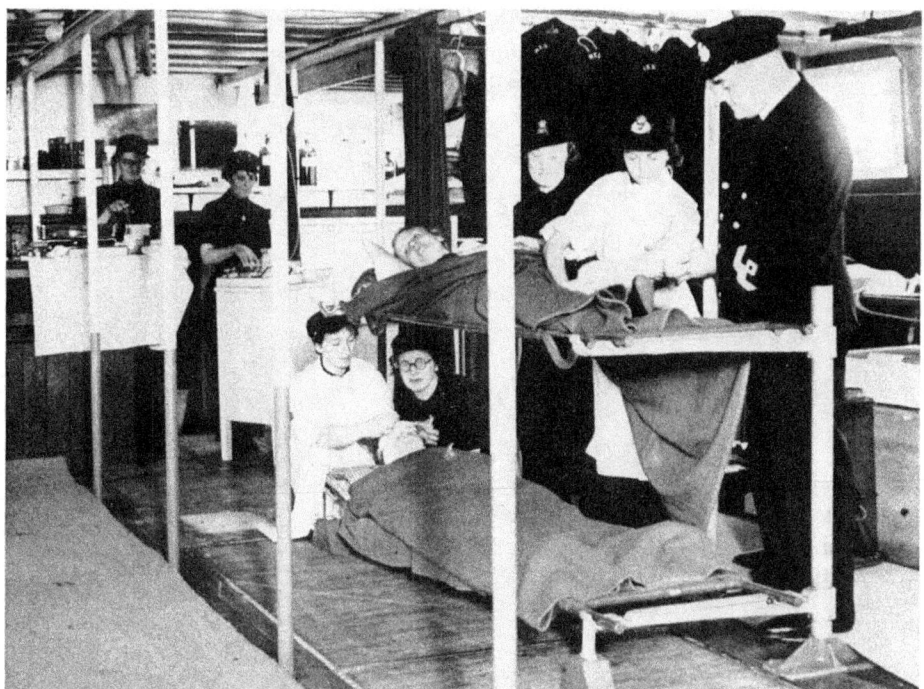

PLATE VI. River Ambulance Service. Accommodation in saloon.

PLATE VII. River Ambulance Service. Stretcher parties at work.

LONDON

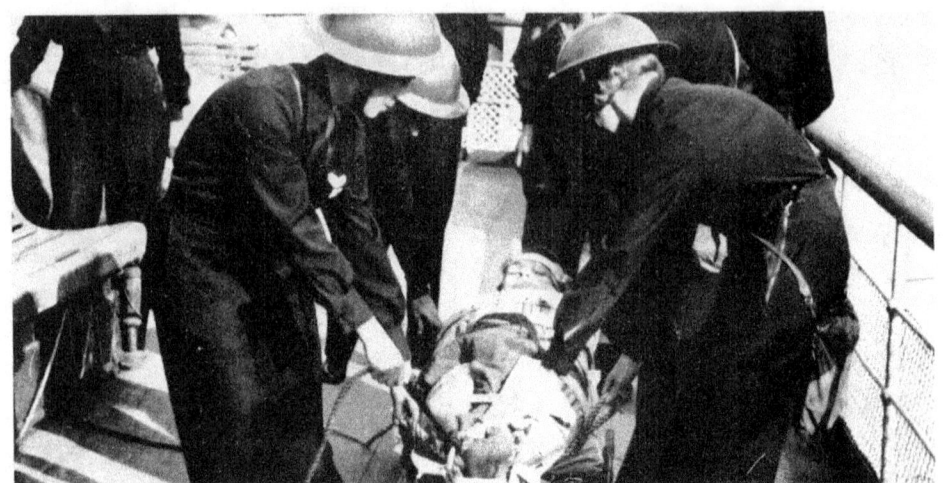

PLATE VIII.
River Ambulance
Service. Stretcher
parties at work.

PLATE IX.
River Ambulance
Service. Stretcher
parties at work.

PLATE X. Rescue scene: Releasing woman trapped for several hours.

PLATE XI. Rescue scene: Trapped child being saved by rescue workers.

Graphic Photo Union

PLATE XII. The Medical Services in Action: Doctor waiting for victims being released from debris.

Associated Press

PLATE XIII. The Medical Services in action: A Specialist preparing instruments for an operation on trapped victim.

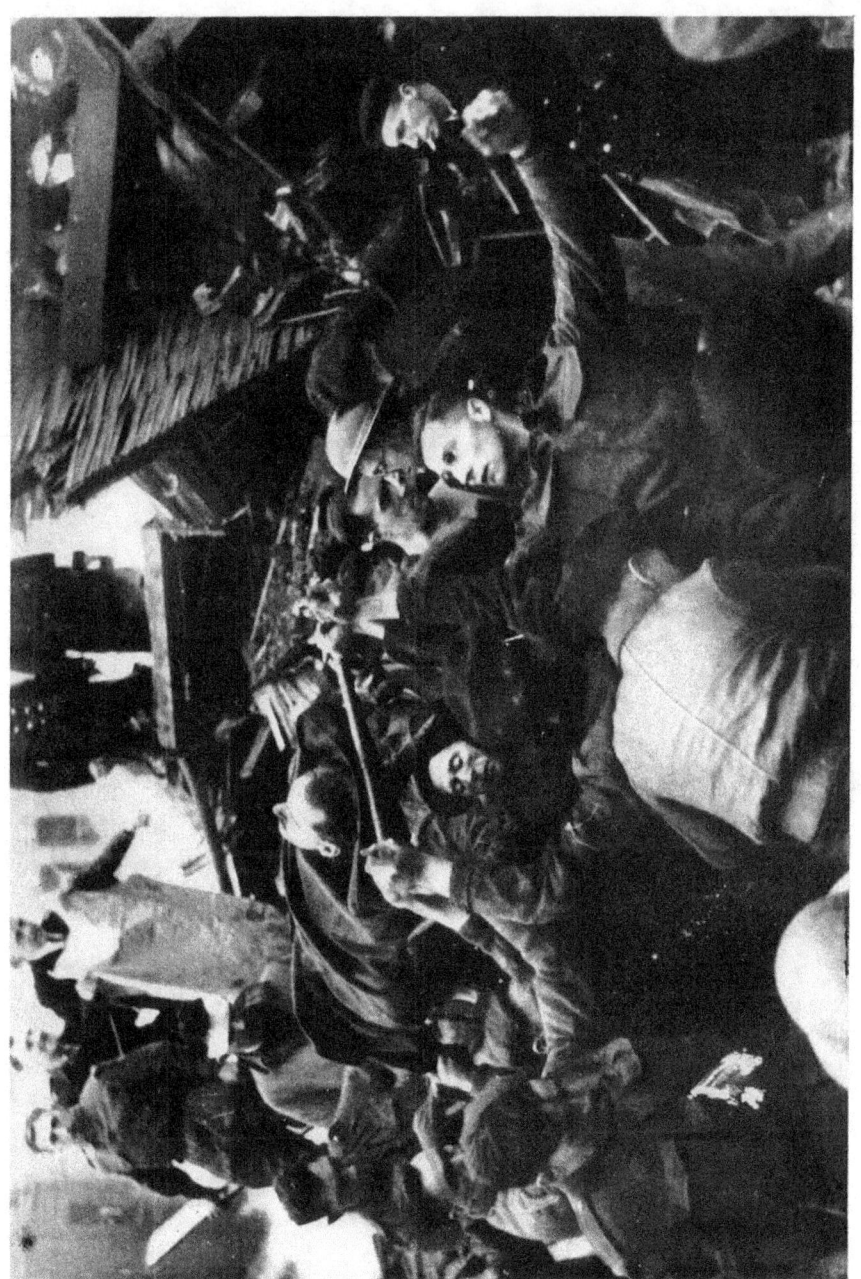

PLATE XIV. Rescue scene: Victim being carried away after operation.

General Press Photos

PLATE XV. The Medical Services in action: Women patients evacuated from a bombed hospital to a school.

PLATE XVI. The Medical Services in action: Clothing for casualties being got ready by nurses, Guy's Hospital.

PLATE XVII. Anglo-American Ambulance Corps in action.

MERSEYSIDE

Liverpool *Daily Post & Echo*

PLATE XVIII. The wrecked Mill Road Hospital.

Daily Herald

PLATE XIX. The wrecked operating theatre, Mill Road Hospital, May 3–4, 1941.

The result of this lack of foresight was that temporary rest centres for feeding, clothing and accommodating the homeless had to be improvised and an organisation brought into being for passing them on to billets and other accommodation both inside and outside the area. It can be well understood that with continual raids, a great strain was thrown on the borough councils to meet these urgent requirements and great credit is due to the local authorities for the steps they took to deal with these problems, and by the end of September 1940, little complaint could be made of the arrangements made in the whole of the London area.

CONCLUSIONS

In conclusion it may be said that the general consensus of opinion was, that on the whole, the plans made by the Government, as amended in the light of experience during the period between the declaration of war and the beginning of the heavy raids, were soundly based. As indicated, certain deviations from these plans in order to fit them to local conditions, were found necessary by the local authorities and these, in such areas, added to the efficiency of the services.

In such a vast and thickly populated area as Greater London it was only to be expected that many errors and omissions in the organisation would be found; and it was the experience gained during the heavy attacks that led to the reorganisation of the Civil Defence Services.

There is still, however, a great deal to be said for the views expressed by Dr. White, Medical Officer of Health of the City of London and Dr. Caley, Medical Officer of Health of Wandsworth, that either a military organisation or a civil one based on the Metropolitan Police Service would have still further improved the efficiency of the Civil Defence Services. An organisation of this kind would undoubtedly have led to a more rapid evolution of efficiency from the beginning, to a saving in man-power and possibly to an increased saving of life.

Similarly, the general opinion that the first-aid posts would have functioned more efficiently if they had been organised originally not only as ancillary services to the hospitals, but staffed and administered by them, is based on sound grounds. Such an organisation would undoubtedly have been more efficient at the outbreak of the heavy raids, by being better trained through their close association in dealing with patients in hospital and with out-patients, and would probably have provided better treatment for casualties, and also have reduced the death rate.

As regards the Ambulance Service, although some Medical Officers of Health and Sector Group Officers had had an uneasy feeling that their control in the inner zone by the L.C.C. as a separate authority might lead to lack of cohesion and delay, it is satisfactory to record that no Sector Group Officer or Medical Officer of Health had anything but praise for the efficiency of this Service.

The above account of the Battle of London, giving a summary of the medical preparations made to meet the attack, and the work of the three services into which the organisation was divided—viz. the Hospital Service, the Civil Defence Service and the Ambulance Service—administered by separate authorities, would not be complete without some appreciation of how this division of authority functioned under the stress of heavy attacks.

Among the Group Officers, Professor de Wesselow, Sector Group Officer of Sector VIII has recorded his opinion that the liaison with the Civil Defence Service was not fully effective in the inner zone, but that in the outer zone it was perfect, because his headquarters were in the same building as the headquarters of the Civil Defence Service for his area.

As already stated the division into three authorities only existed in the inner zone, i.e. the City of London and the 28 metropolitan boroughs. In these there were three distinct and separate authorities; one for the hospital service (the Sector Group Officers), one for the ambulance service and one for the casualty services, i.e. medical officers of health under their respective borough councils. In the outer zone there were only two authorities, the hospital service and the borough councils; in other words, the organisation was similar to that in the large provincial cities. In spite of this division of authority, very little criticism on the working of the organisation as a whole, or of lack of liaison between these three services, has been expressed by any of those chiefly concerned with the running of the organisation. The ambulance service in particular has been given universal praise.

One criticism, however, has been voiced by some of the medical officers of health of the inner zone as follows:

When cases were sent in ambulances direct from incidents to hospitals the first-aid parties did not know to which hospital the cases were being taken, only the ambulance driver knew this and sometimes ambulance drivers continued to take cases to hospitals which already had more patients than they could adequately deal with, so that the ambulances had then to convey the casualties to the next hospital on the list. This system in some cases must have been detrimental to the patients. Similarly, casualties sent from first-aid posts to hospitals had sometimes to go to a second hospital before being admitted. In the outer zone the necessity for making this extra journey should never have arisen as in this area the hospitals were in close touch with the control centres. When any hospital had admitted all the casualties it could efficiently deal with, the control centre was informed and the information was distributed to the incidents and first-aid posts, giving the names of the hospitals to which the casualties should be taken. It should have been possible to introduce similar arrangements in the boroughs in the inner zone. Elimination of any unnecessary journeys for an ambulance could not fail to have been of great advantage, especially in view of the fact that blocked roads, blackout and other obstructions, made the difficulties of rapid admission to hospital very great.

APPENDIX

LIST OF CONTRIBUTING MEDICAL OFFICERS OF HEALTH IN THE LONDON REGION

Sir William Allen Daley, M.D., F.R.C.P., D.P.H., London County Council.
Dr. C. F. White, O.B.E., M.D., City of London.
Dr. G. Macdonald, D.P.H., Battersea Metropolitan Borough.
Dr. D. M. Connan, M.D., D.P.H., Bermondsey Metropolitan Borough.
Dr. V. Borland, D.P.H., Bethnal Green Metropolitan Borough.
Dr. H. W. Barnes, D.P.H., Camberwell Metropolitan Borough.
Dr. W. H. L. McCarthy, D.P.H., Chelsea Metropolitan Borough.
Dr. F. L. Keith, M.D., D.P.H., Deptford Metropolitan Borough.
Dr. A. B. Stewart, M.D., (Acting Medical Officer of Health), Finsbury Metropolitan Borough.
Dr. J. A. Scott, O.B.E., D.P.H., Fulham Metropolitan Borough.
Dr. C. Porter, M.D., (Acting Medical Officer of Health), Greenwich Metropolitan Borough.
Dr. G. H. Dart, M.D., D.P.H., Hackney Metropolitan Borough.
Dr. W. H. Brodie, (Acting Medical Officer of Health), Hammersmith Metropolitan Borough.
Dr. H. L. Oldershaw, M.D., D.P.H., Hampstead Metropolitan Borough.
Dr. J. A. Struthers, M.D., D.P.H., Holborn Metropolitan Borough.
Dr. V. Freeman, D.P.H., Islington Metropolitan Borough.
Dr. J. Fenton, C.B.E., M.D., D.P.H., Kensington Metropolitan Borough.
Dr. A. G. G. Thompson, M.D., D.P.H., Lambeth Metropolitan Borough.
Dr. J. W. Miller, D.P.H., Lewisham Metropolitan Borough.
Dr. G. E. Oates, M.D., D.P.H., Paddington Metropolitan Borough.
Dr. W. Allan Young, M.D., D.P.H., Poplar Metropolitan Borough.
Dr. H. A. Bulman, D.P.H., St. Marylebone Metropolitan Borough.
Dr. W. Stott, D.P.H., Southwark Metropolitan Borough.
Dr. F. R. O'Shiel, D.P.H., Stepney Metropolitan Borough.
Dr. S. King, M.D., D.P.H., Stoke Newington Metropolitan Borough.
Dr. F. G. Caley, D.P.H., Wandsworth Metropolitan Borough.
Dr. A. J. Shinnie, M.D., D.P.H., City of Westminster.
Dr. J. MacMillan, D.P.H., Woolwich Metropolitan Borough.
Dr. G. E. B. Payne, M.D., D.P.H., Acton Borough.
Dr. E. J. MacIntyre, M.D., D.P.H., Banstead Urban District.
Dr. C. Leonard Williams, Barking Borough.
Dr. W. F. Twining McMath, M.D., D.P.H., Barnes Borough.
Dr. A. L. Hyatt, Barnet Urban District.
Dr. T. Philips Cole, D.P.H., Beckenham Borough.
Dr. Chas. A. Bentley, C.I.E., D.P.H., Beddington and Wallington Borough.
Dr. G. F. Bramley, M.D., D.P.H., Bexley Borough.

Dr. R. C. Leaning, D.P.H., Brentford and Chiswick Borough.
Dr. K. E. Tapper, O.B.E., D.P.H., Bromley Borough.
Dr. F. Lawrence Smith, D.P.H., Carshalton Urban District.
Dr. Brian Russell, M.D., Cheshunt Urban District.
Dr. L. S. Fry, M.D., D.P.H., Chigwell Urban District, Waltham Holy Cross Urban District.
Dr. W. D. Hyde, D.P.H., Chingford Borough.
Dr. P. N. Cave, M.D., D.P.H., West Kent United Districts.
Dr. F. R. Edbrooke, D.P.H., Coulsdon and Purley Urban District.
Dr. C. M. Ockwell, M.D., F.R.C.S., Crayford Urban District.
Dr. O. M. Holden, G.M., M.D., D.P.H., Croydon County Borough.
Dr. C. Herington, D.P.H., Dagenham Borough.
Dr. T. Orr, M.D., D.Sc., Ealing Borough.
Dr. C. M. Scott, East Barnet Urban District.
Dr. D. Regan, D.P.H., Edmonton Borough.
Dr. D. H. Geffen, M.D., D.P.H., Enfield Urban District.
Dr. Horace A. Nathan, (Acting Medical Officer of Health), Epsom and Ewell Borough.
Dr. R. Leader, Erith Borough.
Dr. J. Fanning, M.D., Esher Urban District, Malden and Coombe Borough.
Dr. A. A. Turner, M.C., M.D., D.P.H., Finchley Borough.
Dr. J. W. Poole, M.O. for A.R.P., Friern Barnet Urban District.
Dr. J. Stanley Lloyd, M.D., F.R.C.S., Hayes and Harlington Urban District.
Dr. Caryl Thomas, M.D., D.P.H., Harrow Urban District.
Dr. A. Fairgrieve Adamson, M.D., D.P.H., Hendon Borough.
Dr. A. Anderson, M.D., D.P.H., Heston and Isleworth Borough.
Dr. G. F. Rigden, Hornsey Borough.
Dr. A. H. G. Burton, M.D., D.P.H., Ilford Borough.
Dr. J. W. Starkey, D.P.H., Kingston Borough.
Dr. A. Wallace Johns, D.P.H., Merton and Morden Urban District.
Dr. A. Ashworth, M.D., D.P.H., Mitcham Borough.
Dr. B. E. Hawkins, Penge Urban District.
Dr. W. E. Hayes, (A.R.P. Medical Officer), Potters Bar Urban District.
Dr. E. Pereira, D.P.H., Richmond Borough.
Dr. L. D. Bailey, C.B., N.C., Ruislip-Northwood Urban District.
Dr. E. Grundy, M.D., D.P.H., Southall Borough.
Dr. A. C. Mann, M.C., Staines Urban District.
Dr. Alex Urquhart, M.D., D.P.H., Sunbury Urban District.
Dr. E. J. MacIntyre, M.D., D.P.H., Sutton and Cheam Borough.
Dr. G. H. Hogben, D.P.H., Tottenham Borough.
Dr. J. Maddison, M.D., D.P.H., Twickenham Borough.
Dr. W. Townsend Dobson, Uxbridge Urban District.
Dr. R. F. Vere Hodge, M.D., Wanstead and Woodford Borough.
Dr. A. G. Morison, M.D., D.P.H., Wembley Borough.
Dr. G. F. Buchan, M.D., F.R.C.P., D.P.H., Willesden Borough.
Dr. H. Ellis, Wimbledon Borough.
Dr. M. Manson, G.M., M.C., M.D., D.P.H., Wood Green Borough. (Also Acting Medical Officer of Health, Southgate Borough.)
Dr. P. Bobbett, D.P.H., Yiewsley and West Drayton Urban District.

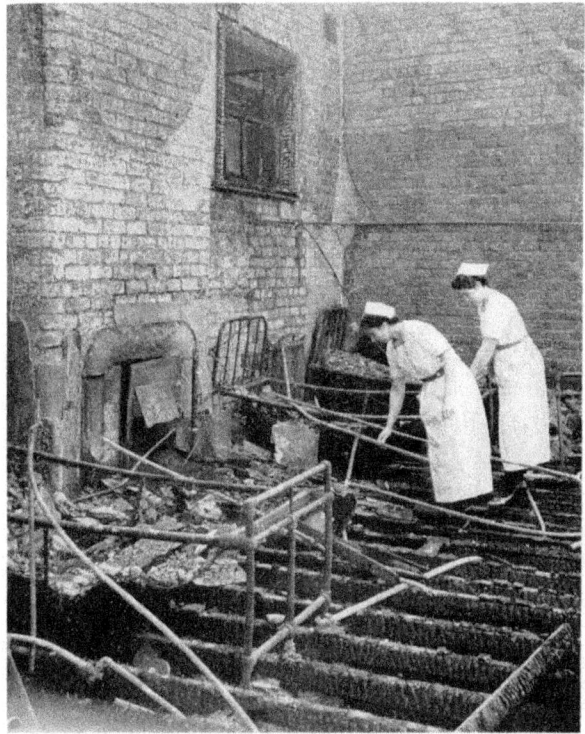

Topical Press Agency

PLATE XX. Burnt out ward in the Maternity Hospital, Liverpool.

Liverpool *Daily Post & Echo*

PLATE XXI. The home of Professor McMurray, Professor of Orthopaedic Surgery, Liverpool University, May 4, 1941.

William Cull

PLATE XXII. A wrecked block, Birkenhead Municipal Hospital.

Wallasey Borough Police

PLATE XXIII. A damaged First-Aid Post, Wallasey.

CHAPTER 2
MERSEYSIDE
August 1940 to May 1941

Based on Contributions received from
K. W. Monsarrat, T.D., M.B., F.R.C.S. Ed., *Group Officer*; W. M. Frazer, O.B.E., M.D., *Medical Officer of Health, Liverpool*; D. Morley Mathieson, M.D., *Medical Officer of Health, Birkenhead*; R. B. Berry, M.D., *Medical Officer of Health, Wallasey*; *and* F. T. H. Wood, O.B.E., M.D., *Medical Officer of Health, Bootle*

AREA AND POPULATION

Area. For the purposes of the Emergency Hospital Scheme the inner zone of the Merseyside area consisted of four county boroughs, Bootle and the City of Liverpool on the north-east or Lancashire bank of the Mersey and Wallasey and Birkenhead on the south-west or Cheshire bank. The total area of the four county boroughs was 44,041 acres, the area of Liverpool being 27,321, Birkenhead 8,598, Wallasey 5,908 and Bootle 2,414, exclusive of the bed of the river. The built-up areas of the two boroughs on each bank of the river were practically continuous, the chief line of docks being those of Bootle and Liverpool with shipbuilding or ship-repairing yards higher up on both sides of the river.

Population. The dock area and its environments were very thickly populated, the population consisting mostly of dock labourers and the employees of large industrial concerns. The estimated population in December 1939, was in Liverpool 856,072, Birkenhead 145,500, Wallasey 98,900 and Bootle 74,080, a total for the whole area of 1,174,642 as compared with an estimated population of 1,152,722 in December 1938. The population per acre of the four county boroughs was: Liverpool 31, Bootle 31, Birkenhead 17 and Wallasey 16. In the beginning of September 1939 large numbers of children were evacuated, some with their mothers, under the Ministry of Health Evacuation Scheme and there was also a fairly considerable amount of voluntary evacuation. There was, however, a considerable influx of population after the outbreak of war, consisting chiefly of additional dock labourers, munition workers and employees of the shipbuilding yards, which, together with the natural increase of population, appears to have more than balanced the evacuation.

The population decreased rapidly during the winter of 1939–40, and the following spring, through recruitment to the Services and to further movements of labour. The following table gives the Registrar General's estimates of the population of the four county boroughs from June 30, 1940, before the period of enemy attacks began, to June 30, 1941, when the attacks had definitely ceased:

	June 30, 1940	September 30, 1940	December 31, 1940	March 31, 1941	June 30, 1941
Liverpool	763,100	753,700	732,600	718,740	679,720
Birkenhead	135,800	134,900	130,900	125,800	117,100
Wallasey	91,230	91,300	89,230	80,390	67,250
Bootle	68,490	67,760	66,100	61,130	50,470

These estimates were based chiefly on food ration books and are probably fairly accurate. It will be noted that there was a progressively rapid decrease in the population during the period of enemy attack which was most marked in the quarter ending June 30, 1941, there having been very considerable evacuation of homeless people during the month of May. Proportionately, Bootle and Wallasey were most affected. As the result the population per acre on December 31, 1940, had come down to 27 in Liverpool, 15 in Birkenhead and Wallasey and 27 in Bootle, and by June 30, 1941, to 25 in Liverpool, 12 in Birkenhead, 11 in Wallasey and 21 in Bootle.

MEDICAL ORGANISATION

Group Officer. The hospitals of the four county boroughs and certain advanced base and base hospitals outside the area, extending as far north as Southport and as far south-west as Chester, comprised the Merseyside group of hospitals of which the Group Officer was Mr. K. W. Monsarrat, F.R.C.S. Ed., and responsible to Dr. W. H. C. Patrick, Regional Hospital Officer, North West Region (Region 10), for the staffing and equipping of the hospitals in the group. His chief function was to maintain the highest standard of treatment of casualties and make available to them whatever special treatment they needed. The Group Officer exercised the powers of the Regional Hospital Officer as regards the movement of inter-hospital ambulances within his group to permit of the transfer of patients from the inner zone hospitals to the outer zone or base hospitals, in accordance with the requirements for keeping an adequate number of beds empty for casualties in the inner zone hospitals; these, to use the military phraseology, acting during operations as casualty clearing hospitals. He was also entrusted with the duty of distributing to the appropriate hospitals within his group, or under the instructions of the Regional Hospital Officer to hospitals outside his group, patients arriving in his area in hospital ships or by ambulance trains.

Inter-hospital Transport. For these duties the Group Officer had at his disposal twenty ambulances (ten-stretcher) consisting of converted single-decker coaches garaged in Liverpool and ten garaged in Chester for the transport of stretcher cases, and as many 32-seater single-decker coaches for sitting cases as he might require, there being a large number of these vehicles available in Liverpool, Chester and Southport. He had at his disposal one ambulance (four-stretcher) one sitting case car and four first-aid cars garaged in Liverpool from the Regional fleet of the American Ambulance (Great Britain), whose regional headquarters were in Manchester, and, also, a call on ambulances and sitting case cars belonging to the four local authorities, when the numbers to be transported were small.

Staff. To assist the Group Officer, an Assistant Hospital Officer, Dr. Broomhead, was deputed from the staff of the Regional Hospital Officer; and Miss M. E. Jones, O.B.E., R.R.C., Matron of the Liverpool Royal Infirmary was appointed Sector Matron for the group of hospitals, her duties being to assist the Group Officer in the staffing of the hospitals with nurses and nursing auxiliaries.

Civil Defence Services. The Group Officer was not concerned with the Civil Defence Services, which were the responsibility of the four county boroughs in their own areas, working through their emergency committees. These were organised in accordance with the policy laid down by the Ministries of Health and Home Security. The medical officers of health were responsible for organising the first-aid posts, local ambulances and sitting case cars for the removal of casualties from incidents to first-aid posts and hospitals, and for recruiting and training the first-aid and ambulance staffs. Local emergency committees were responsible to the Ministry of Health for the working of this part of the Civil Defence Services, and to the Ministry of Home Security for the other parts, such as first-aid parties, rescue parties, decontamination services, etc., the medical officers of health being responsible for the first-aid training and operational control of the first-aid parties.

Operational Control. During enemy attacks, the operational control from incidents to first-aid posts and hospitals was vested in the Controllers of Civil Defence Services in the four areas, the medical officers of health acting as their advisers regarding the first-aid posts and ambulances. In practice, in the control rooms of the local authorities, the movement of patients to first-aid posts or hospitals was carried out under the instructions of the medical officers of health. In Merseyside, where in the inner zone four local authorities were included in a group in which the hospitals were supervised by a Group Officer, the medical officers of health worked in close liaison with him in planning the direction of patients to hospitals, in order to regulate the flow of casualties in accordance with their needs and the varying accommodation available in the hospitals. Similarly, in the outer zone close liaison was maintained between the Group Officers and the medical officers of health of the Counties of Lancashire and Cheshire and the County Boroughs of Southport and Chester, where the base hospitals were situated.

Hospitals. At the beginning of the war, a large number of hospitals, about 50 in all, were included in the Merseyside group of hospitals; during the winter of 1939–40 a certain number of these were either suspended or withdrawn from the Emergency Hospital Scheme, owing to their being found unsuitable for the treatment of casualties or too small to serve any useful purpose, except in a grave emergency. By August 1940, therefore, the hospital situation was as follows:

Inner Zone (Liverpool, Bootle and Birkenhead)
1. Number of hospitals 19
2. Total number of beds 12,055
3. Number of casualty beds . . . 3,242
4. Number of vacant beds on August 10, 1940 . 3,761

Outer Zone (Southport, Ormskirk, Rainhill, Whiston, Chester, Upton, Clatterbridge, Wallasey)
1. Number of hospitals 10
2. Total number of beds 5,499
3. Total number of casualty beds . . . 4,072
4. Number of vacant beds on August 10, 1940 . 2,916

The number of vacant beds in the inner zone hospitals was greater than that allotted for casualties, owing to the intake of civilian patients being at that time less than the normal; in the outer zone a number of casualty beds were already occupied by Service cases.

Although the Wallasey hospitals were at this time included in the outer zone hospitals, it was found, owing to the severity of enemy attacks on Wallasey, that these hospitals had to be used entirely as clearing hospitals. In these there was a total of 428 beds, of which 116 were estimated to be available for casualties. At the beginning of the war the Royal Southern Hospital, the David Lewis Northern Hospital in Liverpool and the Bootle Hospital, which adjoined the docks, were removed to situations farther from the docks, as their original locations were considered too vulnerable. The Royal Southern Hospital was removed to the City of Liverpool's Isolation Hospital at Fazakerley about three miles from the river bank, the Northern Hospital to Childwall about the same distance from the dock area and the Bootle Hospital to the Bootle Isolation Hospital about two miles from the docks. As a result of these transfers the bed capacity of the receiving hospitals had to be increased.

In the Merseyside Group the outer zone hospitals were independently staffed, but each was linked to one or more inner zone hospitals, which supplied the senior members of the nursing staffs. These hospitals, however, were not affiliated to the outer hospitals in the sense of transferring any of their equipment or of their medical staff there, nor was any control exercised by the central over the outer hospitals, as was done in the inner and outer zone hospitals in the London Sectors. The London system was not possible in Merseyside, as none of the inner zone hospitals was even partially evacuated, and their staffs, therefore, were fully occupied on the ordinary civilian work, as well as providing a primary casualty service. Proposals to allocate certain members of the consultant staffs to permanent residence in the outer zone hospitals were considered, but discarded as involving a waste of personnel. The alternative chosen was to call upon consultant surgeons for temporary additional duty in the outer hospitals, to maintain in each of these at least one resident surgical officer of experience, and to use all the experienced local surgeons available. This system was found to work well, even under the heavy strain of enemy attack. Each outer hospital had its own establishment of resident medical officers, but when the admission of casualties was high, additional residents were lent from the staffs of the inner hospitals.

Recommendations for all whole-time resident medical officers employed in the Emergency Service hospitals in the group were made by the Group Officer. By arrangement with the University of Liverpool, the medical officers of health and the medical boards of hospitals, appointments to junior resident posts in the voluntary and municipal hospitals were unified throughout the group, the Group Office functioning as the clearing house by general consent. The appointment of senior medical students as resident medical officers for resuscitation duties was organised through the office of the Assistant Registrar of the University, the Dean of Faculty of Medicine and the Group Adviser on Resuscitation. For a hospital group centred on a medical school this general pooling of medical personnel for resident service was most advantageous to the hospitals. Special mobile surgical teams were also arranged to relieve any pressure which might occur in the outer zone hospitals.

First-aid Posts. In the inner zone area there were thirty-four first-aid posts either in connexion with hospitals or in suitable buildings adapted for the purpose, and these were fully equipped and staffed in accordance with the plans laid down by the Ministry of Health. There were also a few mobile units to serve as a reserve. The personnel of the first-aid posts was mostly women, the majority being part-time volunteers.

Ambulances. There were 240 ambulances (four-stretcher) and 200 sitting case cars in the four county boroughs, staffed by over a thousand drivers and attendants. These were nearly all women and the majority were employed whole-time. In all the boroughs the ambulances were mostly cars with suitable chassis on which ambulance bodies had been constructed in accordance with the Ministry's specification. In Wallasey, however, trailers had been tried and found unsuitable. It was found that turning in narrow streets was sometimes difficult or even impossible and that the fumes of the exhaust from the cars gained access to the trailers to the detriment of the patients carried. Converted vans had also been tried, but they were not a success.

First-aid Parties. Over a thousand men made up the staff of these parties, nearly all employed whole-time. This number was sufficient to provide a hundred parties in Liverpool and proportionately smaller numbers in the smaller boroughs. Rescue squads, decontamination squads, etc., in accordance with plans laid down by the Ministry of Home Security, had also been recruited and trained.

Mortuaries. In view of the large numbers of killed which it was expected would have to be dealt with the local authorities had very largely increased their normal mortuary accommodation: in Liverpool 1,400 places in mortuaries had been provided; in Birkenhead 350 places; 300 in Wallasey and 300 in Bootle.

THE ATTACK ON MERSEYSIDE

Scale of Attacks and Casualties. The enemy attacks opened in August 1940, with raids on Birkenhead on the 9th, Wallasey on the 10th, Liverpool on the 17th, and Bootle on the 29th, when a few H.E. bombs accompanied by incendiaries caused a small number of casualties and fires. These were apparently in the nature of reconnaisance raids. The first raids on a fairly extensive scale occurred on the four nights August 28 to September 1 when about 200 H.E. bombs were dropped. These caused 175 casualties in Liverpool of which 31 were killed and 77 admitted to hospital. There was only a small number of casualties in the other parts of the area.

Raids of varying intensity continued frequently during the autumn, there being 334 alerts up to the end of the year; bombs were dropped on about 25 nights during this period. Liverpool was the chief target during September, October and November 1940, the heavier raids being on September 17–18 and 18–19 when 87 people were killed and 252 injured and on the night of November 28–29 when 270 were killed and 322 injured. The first heavy and sustained attack on the whole area occurred on the three consecutive nights of December 20–21, 21–22 and 22–23 when 309 H.E. bombs and paramines fell in Liverpool, 198 in Wallasey, 65 in Bootle and 60 in Birkenhead, a total of 632 in addition to large numbers of incendiary bombs. According to the returns submitted by the medical officers of health, 618 persons were killed, 705 admitted to hospitals and 535 treated at first-aid posts during this period, so that 0·97 persons per bomb were killed and 1·1 admitted to hospital. Several hospitals were damaged in this raid.

Dr. A. Bradford Hill of the Research and Experiments Branch of the Ministry of Home Security made an analysis of the effects of this attack, based on data supplied by the bomb census officers. It related to 576 H.E. bombs and 35 paramines, which were definitely identified, and excluded unexploded bombs. The bombs dropped were of various sizes, from three of 1,000 kg., down to 351 of 50 kg., and the total weight of bombs was estimated at 84·3 metric tons. Only 33·3 per cent. of the bombs caused casualties. Dr. Hill found it difficult accurately to estimate the casualties per bomb on the returns of the three nights, the data being incomplete, but the returns of killed on the second night, on which 396 bombs and 21 paramines fell, were considered sufficiently accurate to warrant a statistical analysis. The result of this showed that 0·49 persons per bomb and 0·58 per mine were killed. In Dr. Hill's opinion the record of numbers killed was possibly deficient but not unreasonably so, but the figures for the injured, giving an injured rate of only 0·14 per bomb, were obviously of no value. The number killed per metric ton was found to work out at 3·5. This figure was approximately the same as the figure found in an analysis made in Birmingham of five nights of raiding when 169·35 metric tons were estimated to have fallen, the number killed per metric ton being 3·8. Taking the analysis of the two raids together, Dr. Hill estimated that the killing power per ton of bombs of the categories 500 kg., 250 kg., and 50 kg., were about equal.* These figures although not claiming to be strictly accurate were of interest; as in conjunction with others from other areas they formed the basis on which calculations regarding hospital and mortuary accommodation, civil defence provisions in the way of first-aid posts, ambulances, etc., and personnel could be made.

In proportion to its population, Wallasey was more heavily attacked than the other areas; 180 H.E. bombs were dropped and caused casualties amounting to 119 killed, 176 admitted to hospital and 312 treated at first-aid posts.

There were no more heavy raids on the area during the rest of this year; in fact raiding continued on a much less extensive scale during the whole of January and February 1941, there being only two small raids in January and one in February.

The next extensive raids occurred on the nights of March 12-13 and 13-14, the main targets being Birkenhead and Wallasey. 300 H.E. bombs and 50 mines fell in Birkenhead causing many casualties of which 277 were killed, 286 seriously injured and many slightly injured. In Wallasey 195 H.E. bombs and 11 mines fell, 174 persons being killed, 239 seriously injured and over 300 slightly injured; in Liverpool 90 H.E. bombs and 7 mines fell causing the death of 85 persons, 115 seriously injured and about the same number slightly injured. In Bootle only three H.E. bombs were dropped and caused no casualties. In this raid a great deal of damage was done to public services in Birkenhead and Wallasey and the Birkenhead Municipal Hospital was damaged for the second time.

After this raid a comparative lull occurred until May 1, when the Merseyside area experienced a more severe series of attacks which continued up to May 8, the heaviest being on May 2 and 3; it was described in the German communique as 'the heaviest raid yet delivered on any English town'. During this period 583 H.E. bombs, 69 mines and 21 oil bombs fell in Liverpool; 191 H.E. bombs in Bootle and 64 H.E. bombs in Wallasey. Birkenhead escaped comparatively lightly. During the week, 1,454 persons were killed in Liverpool, 1,065 seriously injured and 599 slightly injured. In Bootle, 257 killed, 295 seriously injured and 481 slightly injured. In Wallasey, however, only 3 persons were killed, 8

---

* Ministry of Home Security, Research and Experiments Department, Bomb Census Data Statistical Report No. 3 (Secret) of March 7, 1941.

seriously injured and 33 slightly injured. The attack was therefore nearly wholly confined to the north-east bank of the river.

After these heavy raids the enemy attacks gradually died away; there were only four more raids in the area during the year 1941, these being by single planes which dropped very few bombs and caused only a few casualties.

During the whole period from August 1940, to May 1941, the number of alerts was 485 and bombs were dropped on about 50 nights.

Total Weight of Enemy Attacks and Casualties caused

	Liverpool	Birkenhead	Wallasey	Bootle	Totals
Total number of bombs dropped	2,484	800	657	313	4,254
Proportion to population	1–295	1–163	1–136	1–212	1–248
Total casualties:					
Killed	2,711	464	320	425	3,920
Admitted to hospital	2,548	697	488	441	4,174
Treated at First-aid posts	1,600	751	721	983	4,055

Numbers Killed and Injured per Bomb

	Liverpool	Birkenhead	Wallasey	Bootle
Killed	1·1	0·58	0·48	1·35
Admitted to hospital	1·03	0·87	0·74	1·4

COMMENTS ON THE CASUALTY RETURNS

Comparison with the scale of Operations. In the opinion of Dr. W. M. Frazer, Medical Officer of Health, Liverpool, casualties there were by no means high in proportion to weight of attack, in spite of the fact that the chief target was the thickly populated area near the docks, where houses in some parts averaged 48 to the acre. He attributed this to the adequate provision of shelters which undoubtedly saved many lives, and explained the low proportion of slightly injured among the casualties as due to the fact that the raids took place at night when people were mostly indoors, either in shelters or at home. Among civil defence workers on duty, which entailed their being out of doors, the numbers killed were 206, seriously injured 155, and slightly injured 547, a totally different proportion.

In Birkenhead, Wallasey and Bootle, the casualty returns differ from those of Liverpool in that the admissions to hospital were in each case greater than the killed, and the slightly injured were still more numerous, especially in Bootle. In fact, the figures from the latter three areas approximate to those for most other towns and urban districts in the country, as regards the proportion of killed, seriously and slightly injured.

The casualties per bomb were highest in Bootle, a thickly populated area, and lowest in Wallasey, which was much less congested.

Proportion of Casualties to Damaged Houses. Damage to buildings, sufficient to cause injury to persons inside, usually involved serious injury owing to the fall of debris and flying glass, splinters of wood, stone or bricks. A large proportion of the injuries were crush injuries or due to missiles of various kinds and were, therefore, serious. The damage to buildings was very severe in Liverpool, where 2,804 houses were completely destroyed, 2,615 damaged beyond repair, 18,758 seriously damaged but found capable of repair, and 99,687 received damage necessitating some degree of repair, but were still habitable. The total number of houses damaged was therefore 123,864, and if the total number of houses destroyed or damaged is compared with the total number of casualties killed or injured, it appears that only one person was killed or injured for every eighteen houses destroyed or damaged. The ratio of casualties to damaged houses was found to be higher in Birkenhead, Wallasey and Bootle. In Bootle, a thickly populated dockside area, the damage to property was especially severe. During the heavy raids in the first week of May 1941, 3,500 of Bootle's 17,000 houses were rendered uninhabitable and 11,500 were less seriously damaged.

Proportion of Casualties to the Population. A more accurate picture of the incidence of casualties is provided by the numbers of killed and injured per thousand of the population of each of the four county boroughs:

	Estimated population December 1940	Total killed	Killed per 1,000 population	Total admitted to hospital	Admitted per 1,000 population
Liverpool	732,600	2,711	3·70	2,548	3·48
Birkenhead	130,900	464	3·54	697	5·32
Wallasey	89,230	320	3·59	488	5·47
Bootle	66,100	425	6·43	441	6·67
Totals	1,018,830	3,920	3·8	4,174	4·0

These figures are based on the estimated populations on December 31, 1940 and cannot be considered strictly accurate, but may be regarded as an approximate average for the whole period. On the whole, it may be assumed that the casualties per thousand of the population were somewhat higher than these figures tend to show, especially in Bootle, where the estimated population at the beginning of May, when the heaviest raids occurred, was under 60,000.

THE EMERGENCY ORGANISATION IN ACTION

Headquarters. The authorities were fortunate in only having to deal with minor raids in August–October 1940, and therefore had the benefit of practice under actual enemy attacks of gradually increasing severity. It was found from the very beginning that each section of the casualty services displayed a high sense of duty, volunteer part-time workers reporting with the utmost regularity, even after sleepless nights due to consecutive raids, and the whole-time personnel were almost continuously on duty. The liaison between the Group Officer and Medical Officers of Health was maintained without any friction; and local authority ambulances and sitting case cars, when required for short inter-hospital and other urgent journeys, were readily placed at the disposal of the Group Officer, 539 journeys being made by these cars from September 1940, to May 1941.

In the first week of May 1941, during the heavy raids, great assistance was also rendered by the Army authorities, the 159th Field Ambulance being placed at the disposal of the Group Officer and 317 patients were carried in their ambulances. The Field Ambulance also provided stretcher bearers and despatch riders during this period, both being found exceedingly useful. The stretcher bearers relieved the overworked hospital bearers to deal with the large numbers of admissions during this week, and the despatch riders ensured rapid communication between the Group Officer and the inner and outer zone hospitals, when telephone communication was interrupted.

At the local authority control centres, work went on smoothly during all the raids, but it was found difficult from the reports at some of the report and control centres to picture the exact dimensions of an incident both in casualties and in damage to buildings; the tendency, therefore, was to send more personnel than was found necessary to earlier 'incidents'. Sometimes during heavy raids this led to a lack of personnel at places where they were most wanted, and it often proved difficult to ensure the return of the surplus services to their depots.

Much extra work was thrown on the headquarters medical staff when heavy damage was done to hospitals by bombs, or when they had to be evacuated because of unexploded bombs; arrangements had to be made to provide fleets of ambulances and cars to evacuate the patients and medical and nursing staffs, and for their accommodation in other hospitals, etc., usually at night and often by messenger or despatch rider.

The telephone, lighting, gas, water and sewerage services were severely strained. When these services were thrown out of gear by bombing, the authorities in charge had to organise as rapid repair as possible, in order to minimise the difficulties thrown on all concerned and the effect the absence of these services might have on the health of the population. Certain areas were without normal water and gas supplies for several days and without telephones and lights for shorter periods. Arrangements had to be improvised to distribute chlorinated water in all sorts of suitable receptacles, and to chlorinate the main reservoirs to ensure potability of the water in those parts of its distribution system that were still partly in action. Emergency cooking and lighting for the hospitals and rest centres had to be provided. In the latter, after heavy raids thousands of cooked meals were supplied to homeless people, many of whom also required medical attention, for which a staff of doctors and nurses had to be detailed. In Bootle, extensive arrangements were required for these purposes.

Hospitals. The group system of hospitals under the Group Officer, Mr. K. W. Monsarrat, in spite of certain difficulties which arose because the voluntary hospitals had to surrender a certain amount of their independence, proved an unqualified success. The group of hospitals, spread over a wide area both urban and rural, provided extensive and varied accommodation, and functioned as a single unit during heavy raids which caused considerable numbers of casualties. Patients were taken into the casualty clearing hospitals in the inner zone, received expert attention and were transferred, as soon as their condition warranted it, to special hospitals for treatment, or to the outer zone base hospitals. Thus sufficient beds were always available for casualties in the target areas during subsequent raids. All the casualty clearing hospitals continued to fulfil their normal civilian duties in addition to dealing with casualties. All were provided with well-equipped resuscitation wards and an adequate number of operating theatres and sufficient X-ray facilities. The base hospitals were similarly equipped and in addition, certain of these hospitals were designated as special centres. The Alder Hey Hospital on the outskirts of Liverpool was the chief orthopaedic centre, the Broadgreen Emergency Hospital in the same area contained the chest and maxillo-facial centres, the Southport Emergency Hospital, the neurosis centre, etc. The chest centre for the group was later transferred from Broadgreen to the Clatterbridge Emergency Hospital, a base hospital four miles from Birkenhead.

In practice, the greater number of the casualties could be transferred to outer zone or special hospitals within forty-eight hours, most of them in under twenty-four hours. The early transfer of patients with serious head, chest and other injuries was not generally approved by the clinical staffs of primary receiving hospitals; and they were also slow to avail themselves of special surgical teams, even when the casualty admissions were exceptionally heavy. In this respect only was their procedure open to criticism.

During the periods of greatest strain such as the nights from December 20 to 23, March 12 to 14, and May 1 to 8, no sign of the organisations breaking down was apparent, even when the hospitals were so seriously damaged that it was necessary to transfer immediately all or a portion of the patients to other hospitals, in addition to dealing with a heavy inflow of casualties.

The total number of patients transferred from inner to outer hospitals in the whole Merseyside area during the period of heavy raids was 5,567, the largest numbers being 829 between March 11 and 15 from Birkenhead and Wallasey and 2,435 in the first week of May from Liverpool and Bootle. The total number of casualties admitted to the inner zone hospitals during this latter period was 2,178, so the evacuations were well ahead of the admissions.

The above figures do not include temporary transfers from one inner zone hospital to another for special treatment, or because parts of hospitals were temporarily out of action.

Of the casualty clearing hospitals the Group Officer named the Royal Infirmary, Liverpool, and the Walton and Broadgreen Emergency Hospitals as having rendered services of outstanding merit. The largest numbers of casualties in one night were received by the Alder Hey Hospital (315) and Walton Hospital (276).

Mr. Robert Kennon, F.R.C.S., Senior Surgeon, Royal Infirmary, Liverpool, commented on the work of the institution as a casualty receiving hospital:

> The attachment of a first-aid post to the hospital was found to be invaluable, as the cases could be dealt with by a staff accustomed to casualty work, the lightly wounded being dealt with by them and heavier cases or unexpectedly difficult ones passed on to more experienced hands. This arrangement proved its value more and more as the weight of the attacks developed and casualties increased. Minor injuries requiring such treatment had their wounds excised in an underground theatre and remained several hours in adjacent recovery rooms. The quiet orderliness of these rooms was most impressive and conducive to quick recovery of morale. The more seriously injured were dealt with by being passed through a joint receiving and resuscitation ward, from which those requiring operation were passed on to experienced surgeons.
>
> During the whole period of the heavy attacks, the routine evacuation of casualties and normal civilian patients fit to be moved, maintained an ample supply of beds in the casualty clearing hospitals of the inner zone, thus permitting the trained staffs to devote their undivided attention to the casualties being admitted, a factor which contributed greatly to the patients' benefit. This was not at first fully appreciated by doctors accustomed to see their patients through their illness, as in normal civilian hospital practice.
>
> There was, however, a great shortage of stretcher bearers. Hospital staff, medical students and some volunteers from the St. John Ambulance

and British Red Cross helped as far as possible, but the necessary movement of the patients took a considerable time. In one hospital, where the help of the trained staff of a Field Ambulance was obtained for the evacuation of the patients to other hospitals, the work was done with rapidity and precision, the time occupied being about one-third of that taken by the volunteers.

As the months passed, a quiet confidence in the medical organisation was established. It was felt that it would be able to stand up to any strain put upon it at any time.

The following is a rough analysis of the patients received at this central receiving hospital during the blitz period in May 1941:

Total number of cases 757; admitted to hospital 415.

Of these 14 were brought in dead and 29 died within 24 hours of admission.

Nature of the Injury

Shock, no obvious injury	89
Burns and scalds	20
Coal gas poisoning	2
Gas gangrene	5
Head and neck	270
Chest	17
Back	32
Pelvis and buttocks	7
Abdomen	12
Upper extremity	153
Lower extremity	150
Total	757

The comments of the Group Officer, Mr. K. W. Monsarrat, F.R.C.S. Ed., were:

The most important lesson on the organisation of an air raid hospital service to be drawn from Merseyside experiences is the inadvisability of using hospitals within the target area, except as receiving stations, and then only such accommodation as can be provided underground.

Those used for primary casualty reception within the target area on Merseyside were:

The Royal Infirmary	360 beds
The Stanley Hospital	120 ,,
Mill Road Infirmary	762 ,,
Bootle General Hospital	150 ,,
Wallasey Victoria Central Hospital	135 ,,
Birkenhead General Hospital	172 ,,
Birkenhead Municipal Hospital	560 ,,

It cannot be questioned that all these hospitals rendered valuable service to air raid casualties, in so far as conditions permitted, but even in the case of the more fortunate such as the Birkenhead Municipal Hospital and the Liverpool Royal Infirmary, which were never rendered wholly unusable, the work was carried on under highly unfavourable conditions. With regard to the other five hospitals, their vulnerability resulted in their being liabilities rather than assets.

The experience of Merseyside permits of certain definite conclusions as follows:

(*a*) The built-up area within three miles of the river on each side should be treated as a battle ground. Underground receiving stations should be provided within this area and no other accommodation there should be used for casualties.

(*b*) Night casualties admitted to these receiving stations should be evacuated at daylight to outlying hospitals. Day casualties should be evacuated direct to outlying hospitals.

(*c*) Resuscitation, warmth, fluids, first aid and splinting should be provided at the underground receiving station, but no other surgical treatment attempted.

(*d*) All hospitals within the target area should be evacuated, either to suitable buildings well outside the area or to hutted hospitals specially erected. Such accommodation might house the staff and equipment of two or more smaller or special hospitals.

These conclusions are based on the following observations:

1. Medical and surgical treatment cannot be appropriately provided either for ordinary civilians or for casualties in half protected buildings within a target area.

2. Only first aid and resuscitation are needed within the first few hours after injury in all but a small proportion of cases.

3. Within the target area patients should be retained for this first-aid treatment only in invulnerable accommodation where staff, patients and equipment are safe.

4. The maintenance in full working of the principal hospitals within the target area, as was approved on Merseyside, is incompatible with the provision of adequate medical staff in evacuation hospitals outside.

DAMAGED HOSPITALS

Liverpool. On the night of May 3, 1941, the Mill Road Hospital, 494 beds of which were available for casualties, was completely demolished by a land mine (Plates XVIII and XIX). All the surviving patients, who numbered about 400, had to be transferred to other hospitals; 83 persons in the hospital were killed and 27 injured, including 17 members of the staff killed and 22 injured. The Deputy Medical Superintendent, Dr. Gray, the Deputy Matron, Miss L. Handley, two resident medical officers, eleven nurses, a clerk and a porter were killed, and the Medical Superintendent, Dr. L. Findlay, the Matron, Miss G. Riding, fifteen nurses, the chaplain and four porters were wounded. In addition to the above, fourteen drivers in the Emergency Ambulance Depot at the hospital were killed and three injured. This mine, therefore, was responsible for the deaths of 97 persons.

On other occasions, 136 patients from the Fazakerley Sanatorium, 398 from the Royal Infirmary, 281 from the Southdown Road Hospital, and 37 from the Stanley Hospital had to be transferred owing to damage to the buildings or to unexploded bombs. Plate XX illustrates a burnt-out ward in a Liverpool maternity hospital. It may also be of interest to illustrate here (Plate XXI) the wreckage of the house of Professor T. P. McMurray, Professor of Orthopædic Surgery, Liverpool University, which was destroyed on May 4, 1941. This house has been called the home of orthopædic surgery in Liverpool, as it was occupied by Hugh Owen Thomas, the pioneer in this field, and by Sir Robert Jones the world-famous surgeon.

The following account by Mr. W. M. Beattie, F.R.C.S., R.S.O., Liverpool Royal Infirmary, is the story of an escape because the bomb was of relatively small weight and the building very strongly built:

> The raid of December 21, 1940, had been in progress for some hours and had caused a large influx of casualties. The organisation of the reception room, resuscitation ward and operating theatres for major and minor casualties was working well, having been well tested in the smaller raids of the previous three months.
> The work in the reception room had dwindled, but the resuscitation and operating teams were working at full pressure. A certain number of the staff also was detailed to attend to the medical and surgical in-patients who had been moved, wherever possible, to the more protected areas of the hospital at the beginning of the raid.
> We were operating upon a patient who had sustained a depressed fracture of the skull, when there was a loud crash, the doors of the theatre were blasted open and the room was filled with dust. A bomb had fallen into the main corridor which connected the reception and resuscitation rooms immediately outside the reception room and about twenty yards from the operating theatre. Fortunately, nobody was hurt, but two members of the medical staff and the night sister, who were standing only six feet from the point where the bomb fell, were undoubtedly saved from injury by a low thick dividing wall which resisted the blast.
> The absence of any excitement was most noticeable and in a few minutes the work continued. Members of the nursing staff did much to reassure the patients by their composure.
> It was clear on the next morning—a very cold December day—that evacuation of patients would be necessary, as many windows had been damaged by blast and problems of blackout and heating were temporarily insoluble. Some patients went home, others were evacuated in ambulances to outlying emergency hospitals and the remaining few were moved to the undamaged wards. By the evening the hospital was once again fully prepared to receive its quota of casualties.

Birkenhead. The Convalescent Home of the Children's Hospital of 30 occupied beds received a direct hit on September 7 and was so seriously damaged that all the children and staff had to be evacuated. The Birkenhead General Hospital was also partly out of action owing to blast damage in September and October. The Birkenhead Municipal

Hospital was damaged by blast in December, which entailed the evacuation of the maternity block. On March 12–13, six H.E. bombs fell in the grounds of this hospital, two of which hit the buildings; one ward was wrecked and the patients were transferred to another part of the hospital. The General Hospital was again damaged in March; 62 patients had to be evacuated and admissions had to be stopped. The Children's Hospital was severely damaged by blast, and was unable to admit any casualties at all.

The following are notes by Dr. R. A. Grant, Medical Superintendent of the Municipal Hospital, on conditions on the night of March 12–13:

> The other two hospitals being out of action, the Municipal Hospital had to bear the brunt of the raid. Some 380 casualties were admitted during the night. The resources of the hospital were put under a heavy strain, but it carried on in spite of the fact that it was being heavily bombed itself. Two patients were killed in one ward, which was wrecked, and two infirm patients sheltering in the basement of the institution attached to the hospital were also killed by a bomb which penetrated three floors before exploding.
>
> The entire casualty staff of the hospital were called into action to deal with the casualties and for the succeeding 24 hours the operating theatres were working continuously. Among those injured, compound fractures, dislocations and head injuries predominated. An analysis of the injuries among air raid casualties admitted to all the Birkenhead hospitals elucidated the fact that out of 697 casualties 186 were head injuries—26·6 per cent. of the total. There were also a few injuries to the chest and abdomen. A large number were only suffering from minor injuries and shock and could very well have been treated at the first-aid posts. In addition to the civilian casualties, a large number of Service casualties were admitted owing to a land mine having been dropped close to a school occupied by the military authorities. The majority of these cases were mortally injured and, indeed, many were dead on admission. The admission of casualties was greatly hampered by bomb damage which obstructed the ambulance traffic.
>
> After receiving urgent attention, the casualties were rapidly classified into those fit for immediate transfer and those unfit to be removed without further treatment. At dawn, the former were evacuated to the Clatterbridge County Hospital, four miles from Birkenhead, and others to the Upton Emergency Hospital, Chester: the more seriously injured, numbering 123, had to be retained. Some of these were subsequently transferred to the special centres dealing with head injuries, etc., but the majority were operated on and recovered in the Municipal Hospital. Although work was hampered to some extent by the blackout arrangements having been destroyed, fortunately no damage was done to the admission units or operating theatres and the utility services of the hospital were well maintained.

Dr. Grant commended the behaviour of all the hospital personnel, especially singling out the work of the stretcher bearers and the nursing and medical staff.

Plate XXII shows the ward wrecked by a high explosive bomb.

Wallasey. The Victoria Central Hospital of 135 beds had to be evacuated owing to damage on December 20, 69 patients being transferred to other hospitals and the remainder sent home. The boiler-house was completely out of action and no gas or electric light was available. In addition, 86 casualties had to be temporarily admitted, which increased the strain thrown on the staff, but the transfer of patients was carried out without a hitch. The hospital was out of action until January 13, 1941, during which period there was fortunately no heavy raid. Some damage was caused in later raids, but usually was not extensive enough to prevent the hospital carrying on. A complete evacuation was, however, made necessary after the first night of the heavy raids in March 1941, by the interruption of the gas, water and electric services, and the fact that practically all the windows were blown in. Again the staff had to deal with casualties after the damage had occurred, fifty being temporarily admitted during the night.

The Liverpool Open Air Hospital for children, Leasowe, an orthopaedic hospital for 200 children and 38 adult females, had 40 additional adult beds added for air raid casualties. It was also arranged for emergency beds to be available in the Railwaymen's Convalescent Home adjoining in case of need. This home was required in the heavy December raid to accommodate the staff and patients from a private nursing home who had to be evacuated because of an unexploded bomb, and, owing to the damage to the Victoria Central Hospital, 70 casualties had to be admitted during the night and teams of surgeons worked for twenty hours. Except for slight damage and a few fires caused by incendiary bombs this hospital suffered no damage.

The Wallasey Cottage Hospital of 45 beds was not supposed to be a first line casualty clearing hospital, but in the heavy March raids, owing to the Victoria Hospital being evacuated, 79 patients had to be temporarily admitted; this caused serious overcrowding as the patients had to be placed between the beds in the wards and in the offices and waiting rooms on stretchers. Surgeons operated by the light of emergency batteries and torches under blackout difficulties owing to the extensive destruction of glass windowpanes. In spite of the overcrowding, the work of treating the casualties was adequately carried out and the patients fit to be removed were transferred the following day.

The diphtheria ward of the Infectious Diseases Hospital was wrecked on the night of March 12–13 and two patients were killed. Other wards were damaged by debris and blast. This hospital and the adjacent Highfield Maternity Hospital had to be immediately evacuated because of an unexploded H.E. bomb and because a paramine had fallen in close proximity to the buildings. The evacuation was to the Egerton Grove School and, with voluntary help, it was functioning as an Infectious Diseases Hospital and a Maternity Hospital in a few hours. Great care was taken to separate the maternity cases completely from the infectious cases. Within three days, all the patients were transferred to suitable accommodation outside the town.

It is obvious that the hospital accommodation provided in Wallasey was quite insufficient. This was because it was not expected that Wallasey, which was not predominantly an industrial or shipping town, would be heavily attacked. Before the war, only a small part to the south of the borough was scheduled as an evacuation area, the rest of the borough was regarded as a neutral area.

Bootle. As recorded earlier, Bootle had the highest number of casualties in proportion to its population. It experienced eight fairly heavy raids, two in September and two in December 1940, and four in May 1941, the heaviest being on the night of May 7–8.

Bootle General Hospital had a normal capacity of 130 beds, which only permitted of 30 to 40 beds being available for casualties. As previously stated, this hospital had been moved from its vulnerable site near the docks to the Bootle Isolation Hospital farther away from the danger area. In view of its proximity to other hospitals in Liverpool, this accommodation was considered adequate, as arrangements had been made for the daily transfer of patients to certain Liverpool hospitals. But it was found quite inadequate to deal with the local casualties during the heavy raids. On the night of May 7–8, it was so extensively damaged by blast from land mines and bombs as to make it necessary to evacuate immediately the whole of the patients and staff during the hours of darkness. This was so well organised by the authorities that it was completed by 4 a.m.; the patients were evacuated to the Royal Southern and Walton Hospitals, the hospitals to which casualties were sent direct from the first-aid posts and 'incidents' during the heavy raid on the night of May 8–9.

In a report on the conditions at Bootle General Hospital on the night of May 7, 1941, Mr. James Moroney, F.R.C.S., acting R.S.O., who was transferred from Ormskirk Emergency Hospital to Bootle General Hospital on May 5, to relieve the R.S.O., Mr. R. A. C. Owen, recorded that in the first hour of the raid on May 7, 1941, 60 major casualties were brought to the hospital. At the end of this hour the hospital was damaged and the wards were in chaos. Some patients were in bed, some on stretchers under the beds. The thin fabric of the huts and glass was scattered over everything. As the blackout had been blown away, torches could not be used. Meanwhile, ambulances continued to arrive and no connexion with Control was possible as telephones were destroyed. The dead were laid on the lawns and the injured given what shelter the damaged hospital afforded. About 3 a.m., a fleet of ten-stretcher ambulances arrived and all the patients were evacuated by 5 a.m. Mr. Moroney commented on the 'impossibility' of giving proper service to casualties in a building of the Bootle type within the target area. It afforded no protection either for staff or patients and the only result of selecting it for the reception of casualties was to accumulate large numbers on one spot where the probability of further injury was high, where crowds of friends and relatives collected and where the staff were rendered helpless by damage. Mr. Moroney was of opinion that immediate transport to Ormskirk, ten miles away, was the proper solution of the Bootle problem.

Mr. A. L. Cooper, Superintendent of the Bootle General Hospital, gave his impressions of the occurrences on the night of May 7–8 as follows:

One of the many incidents of the May 1941 air raids on Merseyside was the damaging of the Bootle General Hospital and its subsequent evacuation at the height of a prolonged raid. It is said that troubles never come singly, and this proved true as far as the hospital was concerned on the night of May 7-8. Up to then we had escaped with only minor damage, but within one half hour we had scores of incendiary bombs, a direct hit on the first-aid post, a delayed action H.E., only twenty yards from where raid casualties were being received, and finally two landmines fell near the boundary wall and finished the job. A hasty tour of the hospital revealed that there were only three casualties from these incidents, but the wards were clearly unusable. A remarkable calmness prevailed among both patients and staff.

The system whereby patients were placed on one mattress underneath their beds, while a second mattress remained on the wire springs of the bed to afford protection undoubtedly saved many from injury. The staff were told to wrap patients in blankets and prepare for evacuation.

The next problem was to establish contact with Control centre for assistance. Electrical, gas and telephone services had long been interrupted, but with that hope which springs eternal in every breast a visit was made to the telephone room.

The light of the moon, its coldness now enriched with the glow of many fires, revealed the operator still sitting patiently in front of her 'dead' switchboard, windows gone and debris all around. Just at that moment providence intervened and an indicator dropped. A thoughtful operator at the exchange inquired if the hospital had any messages.

Contact was made with Control and transport requested for evacuation. Before the conversation could be completed the board again became 'dead'. For a second time fortune favoured us, as on leaving the telephone room, there unmistakably was a solitary bus coming along the road. This stopped in response to signals and once again the kindness and helpful spirit which seemed to prevail on these occasions was in evidence, as the driver immediately agreed to take a bus load of patients to the nearest hospitals. Sitting cases from the wards were transferred to the bus. Further transport soon began to arrive in response to the S.O.S. and before the raid was over, all patients had been evacuated and without a further single casualty. Within six weeks the damage to the hospital was repaired and once again we were ready for any eventuality.

The main impressions left were the magnificent behaviour of both patients and staff. The greatest ordeal was the waiting period for casualties to arrive, but once there was something to do, all feelings of fear disappeared and everyone worked regardless of personal danger. We found that the deadliest thing was not the bomb, but continued lack of sleep. Four and five nights and days of receiving, treating and transferring casualties, yes, but when it came to the sixth and seventh nights, we felt only a few more would bring work to a standstill.

There was a great deal of humour, too, even from the old lady of 70 years who, although a casualty, and in spite of being lucky to have just escaped with her life, insisted that her son went back to find her false teeth as she was 'ashamed to appear before company looking like an old hag'.

FIRST-AID POSTS

During the raids, eight first-aid posts in Liverpool were damaged; one at Mill Road Hospital was completely destroyed, while four others were put out of action for a few days. Strangely enough, none of the first-aid posts staff was killed or injured. In Birkenhead, only one out of eight first-aid posts was wholly put out of action, but a gas cleansing centre attached to a first-aid post and in a separate building was also completely destroyed. Seven members of the Civil Defence Service were seriously injured and eleven slightly injured. Of these only two were medical personnel. In Wallasey, two first-aid posts were badly damaged, one had a direct hit in May (Plate XXIII) and although there were 88 persons in the building there were only five casualties of which one was serious. In March the roof of another post had been blown off and most of the windows blown in, with the result that, owing to debris, plaster, glass and broken doors, the post was in an appalling state. In spite of this the staff reduced chaos to order in a very short time and attended to over 300 patients during the night. In Bootle, one of the three first-aid posts was completely destroyed on the night of May 3–4, but the casualties to the staff were only four.

Dr. Berry, Medical Officer of Health of Wallasey, expressed the opinion that separate accommodation for the treatment of the sexes in first-aid posts under raiding conditions was quite unnecessary and that a few portable screens in the treatment room would have been all that was required. This opinion has frequently been expressed by other medical officers of health. Dr. Berry further thought that many of the first-aid posts in adapted buildings proved most unsatisfactory and expensive, especially in view of the ultimate necessity for restoring these buildings to their original condition. It would probably have been cheaper and better to have built more properly designed first-aid posts which could have been used after the war as clinics, etc., by the local authorities, but owing to the demands of the combatant services, it would have been difficult at the time to provide the necessary labour and materials.

AMBULANCE SERVICES

Apart from the single incident in Liverpool at Mill Road Ambulance Depot when fourteen of the drivers and attendants were killed and three seriously injured, the casualties among the ambulance personnel were surprisingly low, only four more being killed and four seriously injured during the whole period, in spite of the fact that varying proportions of the ambulance drivers and attendants were on duty in their vehicles at all incidents occurring during the nine months of night raids and were driving through blocked streets, past falling buildings and fires to and from incidents for long hours. No praise is too great for the work of these drivers and attendants who were nearly all young women. Two ambulances, seven cars for sitting cases, and one mobile unit were completely destroyed by enemy action in Liverpool and 85 vehicles damaged to some degree at various times. Three of the large ten-stretcher ambulances were also destroyed. In Birkenhead three ambulances were seriously damaged and two cars for sitting cases totally destroyed. In Wallasey two vehicles were totally destroyed and seven damaged. In Bootle, the ambulance depots suffered damage by blast; and on the night of May 7–8, extra ambulances had to be requisitioned from the Regional pool, but on account of difficulties in communications, they did not arrive until the afternoon following.

FIRST-AID AT INCIDENTS

As the result of experience, it was found impracticable, and indeed undesirable, to undertake more than a minimum of first aid to casualties at sites of incidents. The observance of the minutiae of first-aid procedure was found to be less important than the expeditious removal of serious casualties to a hospital where efficient measures of resuscitation could at once be undertaken. This was especially true in the urban areas which had a large number of hospitals conveniently situated so that casualties had to be transported only short distances. Little splinting was therefore done—the Thomas splint was rarely used—and apart from the use of sandbags to immobilise limbs while patients were on stretchers and the supply of hot-water bottles and blankets, the primary objects of the first-aid parties were to get casualties into the ambulances as soon as possible and to assist in rescue work. The training of first-aid party leaders was found to be good in first aid, but deficient in rescue work. The modifications in training instituted at a later date, when the Civil Defence Services were reorganised, ensured the removal of these defects.

Mobile units were very seldom used for the purpose they were intended to serve. In Wallasey, all they did was to establish small fixed first-aid posts at their own depots. In the Merseyside area, except in Birkenhead, no organisation for obtaining the attendance of doctors at incidents was introduced as was done in many other places, though occasionally doctors in practice in the vicinity voluntarily attended incidents and rendered useful assistance, but the medical officers of health and their staffs personally attended major incidents when it was possible to do so.

In Birkenhead, 'incident doctors' had been brought into association with the work of the first-aid depots, and their services were found of great value by Dr. Morley Mathieson, the Medical Officer of Health. He particularly commended the work of Dr. Laing on the night of March 12–13, 1941, at a serious incident.

In Wallasey, Dr. Berry found it necessary to economise his first-aid party personnel during heavy raiding. Complete parties of five men were seldom sent to incidents. If the warden's report indicated few casualties, either one ambulance or a sitting case car, together with one or two first-aid party men who travelled in the same vehicle, were sent out.

MORTUARIES

As already stated, in Liverpool 1,400 places for bodies were at first provided, but they were increased to 2,100 after the first heavy raids and the extra provision was found very necessary for the large numbers of killed during the raids in the first week of May 1941. In Birkenhead, the 350 places first provided were afterwards increased to 650. In Wallasey and Bootle the 300 places provided were considered sufficient, but in the latter town a mortuary containing approximately 180 bodies was totally destroyed by fire on May 3 and alternative accommodation had quickly to be made in a school taken over for the purpose. In Bootle also, although an experienced undertaker had been engaged on whole-time duty to deal with the bodies and had the assistance of three members of the bath staff, sufficient labour for the duties entailed was never available. From the nature of the task, it was difficult or impossible to get temporary labour from the labour exchanges. Eventually, eight experienced undertakers were obtained on loan from the Manchester Corporation for a fortnight to deal with the situation caused by the heavy raids. No special difficulties appear to have been experienced in dealing with the bodies of the killed in other parts of the area.

EVACUATIONS

As was only to be expected, many people left the target areas during the period of heavy raiding. Large numbers of expectant mothers and children had been evacuated under the Ministry of Health scheme at the outbreak of the war, but most of them had returned before the heavy raiding began. During the raids the Ministry of Health again made extensive arrangements for the evacuation of children. For example, in Wallasey, 819 children were evacuated after the December raids and 2,671 in the March raids. Large numbers of homeless adults both in and outside the town had also to be billeted to clear the rest centres, in which 10,000 meals were served during the March raids. According to the Food Office returns, over 2,000 persons left the town in the autumn of 1940 and 20,000 in the spring of 1941. In Bootle, 2,715 children were evacuated during the May raids and over 7,000 by June

30, 1941, out of a total population of 11,000 children. Over 20,000 homeless people had to be evacuated, mostly to outside the town. In the rest centres 39,000 meals were served during the May raids. In addition to complete evacuations, about 2,000 travel vouchers were daily issued to workmen for a nightly exodus to the rural areas.

Dr. F. T. H. Wood, the Medical Officer of Health of Bootle, said that the evacuation, although it gave him a great deal of work, provided much greater problems of public health and sanitation to the medical officers of health of the rural areas to which people migrated or were evacuated. In these reception areas large numbers of special buildings had to be acquired to house thousands of people who had work of national importance in the inner zone area. In Birkenhead 3,000 people were evacuated during the raids and 17,000 homeless people were billeted elsewhere in the borough.

GENERAL COMMENTS

During the long period of enemy attacks of varying intensity, which extended to nearly nine months, it proved that the medical organisation brought into being to cope with heavy air raids was fully competent to deal with all the calls made upon it, even under the heaviest strain.

No one who has not experienced heavy night raiding over a long period can wholly realise the difficulties which had to be met and overcome. All the work of collecting the casualties at incidents, rendering essential first aid, transferring them to first-aid posts and hospitals and from first-aid posts to hospitals, had to be carried out in the dark, hour after hour. The first-aid services had to find their way to incidents, mostly by circuitous routes because roads were blocked by craters and debris, and they had to collect casualties, mostly from ruined buildings and buildings rendered dangerous of access by direct hits and blast. Tunnels through unstable materials had to be dug in order to release trapped casualties. Ambulances had to find their way through streets partly or wholly blocked; the personnel of first-aid posts had to deal with hundreds of casualties, often in partly wrecked buildings, with blackout rendered ineffective, by the light of torches and lanterns, and to make quick decisions as to priority of treatment or despatch to hospital of those who required more expert attention.

In the hospitals, physicians, surgeons and nurses had to deal with many serious cases as rapidly as possible, and operational treatment often continued all night and well into the following day, necessitating relief teams of surgeons, anaesthetists and nurses. Frequently, this skilled attention had to continue without adequate lighting and other conveniences. On the days after raids, patients had to be carefully examined and those fit for transfer evacuated to base hospitals, and this work threw great strain on the medical, nursing and lay staffs who, after a sleepless night, had to prepare to do it all over again the next night.

In many hospitals during heavy consecutive raids, sleep could only be snatched at very short intervals. When there were also direct hits or blast damage, order had to be produced out of a chaotic mass of debris and broken glass, patients removed to other parts of the hospital and there attended to, or evacuated to other hospitals in darkness, cold, rain or even snow, and all the while the drone of enemy planes, the crash of bombs and the rumble of falling buildings continued. This was front line work equivalent to that of the Fighting Services. As in all services, mistakes were made—occasionally one hospital was overcrowded while another was comparatively empty, first-aid posts were swamped with patients and arrivals at incidents were delayed. Most of these mistakes were, however, unavoidable owing to the breakdown of communications.

In addition to the above essential work, the homeless had to be fed and often clothed and found temporary homes, and the necessary services had to be restored as rapidly as possible.

The devotion to duty of all services deserved the greatest praise and the following cases of courage and endurance received recognition:

Liverpool. The Medical Superintendent of Mill Road Hospital was awarded the George Medal.
The Matron of the Mill Road Hospital: The Order of the British Empire.
One woman ambulance driver and one first-aid party leader: The British Empire Medal.

Birkenhead. Three George Medals and one British Empire Medal were awarded to men of the Civil Defence personnel for extreme bravery in rescue work.
Two women members received the British Empire Medal and four men and one woman commended for bravery.

Wallasey. The doctor in charge of the Church Street First-aid Post was made a Member of the Order of the British Empire for extreme courage and devotion to duty when the post was severely damaged in March. One nurse and three auxiliary nurses and one first-aid party member were commended for bravery.

Bootle. Commendations for bravery were received by one stretcher bearer and three first-aid party men.

These recognitions should be looked upon as a tribute to the whole of the Hospital and Civil Defence Services, whose high morale and courage under the most trying conditions and the heaviest strain were universal, and many deeds of courage deserving high commendation were passed unsung.

CHAPTER 3
THE MANCHESTER GROUP
August 1940 to June 1941

Based on Contributions received from
A. H. Burgess, M.Sc., F.R.C.S., *Group Officer*; C. Metcalfe Brown, M.D., *Medical Officer of Health, Manchester*; J. L. Burn, M.D., *Medical Officer of Health, Salford*; J. Yule, M.D., *Medical Officer of Health, Stockport*; and F. Hall, C.B.E., M.D., *County Medical Officer of Health, Lancashire*

AREA AND POPULATION

IN an area so thickly populated and so heavily industrialised as the environs of the Cities of Manchester and Salford, its division into an inner zone of casualty clearing hospitals and an outer zone of base hospitals presented a problem different from that of the Merseyside Group. In the latter the target area could be presumed to be the dock and shipbuilding areas on the banks of the Mersey, for there were few industrial concerns in the areas immediately surrounding the towns of the inner zone.

In the Manchester Group, only in the area to the south of these towns was there any obvious dividing line between urban and rural conditions. In the north, north-east and north-west it was difficult to find any rural area at all. For miles in these directions there were more or less continuous built-up areas connecting large industrial centres such as Bolton, Bury, Rochdale, Oldham and Ashton with each other, and with Manchester and Salford. These towns, and the areas between them, contained large numbers of cotton mills, factories and collieries. The most likely targets were the large industrial concerns in the Cities of Manchester and Salford, mostly near the docks on the Manchester Ship Canal, but some in Stockport and Stretford, which is geographically a part of Manchester. These were therefore chosen as the inner zone, and in this area were situated all the hospitals most suitably placed to be casualty receiving hospitals. The estimated population in this zone and the population per acre are given in the table below:

	Population December 1938	Population December 1939	Acreage December 1938	Population per acre December 1938
Manchester	751,371	747,318	27,256	24
Salford	201,800	199,400	5,202	39
Stockport	133,700	134,800	7,976	16
Stretford	67,608	68,958	3,530	19
Totals	1,154,479	1,150,476	43,964	26

It will be seen that there was little change in the population of the area during the year 1939. The evacuation of mothers and children under the Government scheme and a certain amount of voluntary evacuation could hardly be said to have been reflected to any extent in the slight differences in the population, as the figures were obscured by many other factors, but by June 1940, considerable decreases in the estimated population, based on food ration books were noticeable, especially in Manchester and Salford. These decreases were attributed to recruitment to the Armed Forces and transfer of labour from the cotton industry.

The table below shows the quarterly estimates of the population from June 1940, to June 1941:

	June 30, 1940	September 30, 1940	December 31, 1940	March 31, 1941	June 30, 1941	Population per acre June 30, 1941
Manchester	619,600	618,800	615,800	596,850	593,710	22
Salford	172,300	174,500	175,100	162,670	157,710	33
Stockport	131,800	132,300	132,500	131,800	131,100	16
Stretford	54,330	56,280	55,860	48,260	46,690	13
Totals	978,030	981,880	979,260	939,580	929,210	21

There was little change in the population until after the heavy enemy attacks on the area in December 1940, but from that time the populations of Manchester, Salford and Stretford decreased progressively by the evacuation of homeless people after much damage to houses, and by an increase in voluntary evacuation. It was noticeable that in Stockport, where the damage was slight, the population remained practically stationary. The decrease was more apparent in the densely populated City of Salford than in Manchester, the boundaries of which included a considerable area of parkland and semi-rural area in the County of Cheshire to the south.

EMERGENCY MEDICAL SERVICE ORGANISATION

HOSPITALS

Inner Zone. The casualty clearing hospitals of the inner zone consisted of ten in Manchester with 3,255 beds available for casualties, two in Salford with 955 casualty beds, two in Stockport with 525 casualty beds and one in Stretford with only thirteen casualty beds—a total of 4,748. This was the number of beds which could be made available by sending home all patients whose further treatment could be carried on in their own homes, plus the beds issued by the Ministry to increase the normal capacity of the hospitals by 'crowding'. In these hospitals 3,089 beds were vacant on August 10, 1940, before the raids began. There was also, of course, a large number of other hospitals in the area which had either been suspended or withdrawn from the hospital scheme, some of which could have provided extra beds in a grave emergency. The Stretford Memorial Hospital, with a total accommodation of 121 beds, had been suspended and was only kept in the scheme in order that very urgent cases occurring in the vicinity might receive immediate attention. It was nearly always full of local patients; therefore the operational plans provided that all casualties in Stretford requiring hospital treatment, except very urgent cases, should be taken straight from incidents to the large Withington Hospital, in Manchester, but close to the Stretford boundary.

Outer Zone. For the reasons given above, it was not found feasible, except to a limited degree in the south, to set up a ring of especially designated base hospitals outside the expected target area as was done in London and in the Liverpool area. In the north and east there were many well-equipped hospitals within ten to twelve miles of Manchester or Salford, but as they were situated in the crowded industrial county boroughs of this area they were allocated as casualty clearing hospitals for these potential targets. Large advance base hospitals on the outskirts of these towns were also available and were equipped for this purpose. These conditions prevailed in the County Boroughs of Bolton, Bury, Rochdale, Oldham, etc., and each constituted a smaller example of the Group System, with the medical officer of health acting in the same capacity and with the same functions as the Group Officers in the larger groups of hospitals in the Provinces.

In the south, three hospitals in Macclesfield (18 miles) with 801 casualty beds, one in Buxton (22 miles) with 300 casualty beds expansible to 450 in a grave emergency, one in Knutsford (16 miles) with 385 casualty beds, the Baguley Sanatorium (12 miles) with 281 casualty beds and a block of the Winwick Mental Hospital (24 miles) with 500 beds, were allotted to the outer zone of the Manchester Group. In the spring of 1940, however, the function of the Royal Devonshire Hospital, Buxton, was changed to that of a special hospital for the spa treatment of rheumatic Service cases and in the summer the Bucklow Hospital, Knutsford, was handed over to the War Office as a hospital for prisoners-of-war. The Winwick Hospital was chosen as a special orthopaedic centre, a head and spinal injuries centre, and a centre for the treatment of peripheral nerve injuries, while the Baguley Hospital was designated as a special chest injury centre, and a centre for plastic surgery and jaw injuries. Winwick was also allotted as a 'convoy' hospital.

These changes seriously depleted the number of beds available for ordinary casualties in the outer zone hospitals, and only 703 beds were available and vacant on August 10, 1940. It was therefore decided to provide 680 beds in huts at Baguley Sanatorium and to give up the existing casualty beds in the sanatorium as beds for civilian T.B. cases, for which there was an increasing demand. It was also arranged to take over more of the mental accommodation at Winwick to provide a total of 800 casualty beds at that hospital. But this new accommodation was not ready when the heavy raids on the Manchester Group began. The North-west Region was, however, well provided with large all-purpose base hospitals, such as Whittingham Emergency Hospital (35 miles) with 900 beds, Calderstones Emergency Hospital (28 miles) with 906 beds and other smaller base hospitals so that with the base hospitals above referred to near the large county boroughs, there was never any difficulty in providing beds for air raid casualties or convoys; especially as none of these large county boroughs outside the Merseyside and Manchester Groups was ever attacked except in occasional small sporadic raids.

Experience has shown that even if a concentrated attack on the whole industrial area of Lancashire on the scale of the London raids had been made, the provisions made for casualties in the Region would have been fully equal to the strain.

Group Officer. The Group Officer for the Manchester Group of hospitals was Professor Arthur H. Burgess, F.R.C.S., Emeritus Professor of Surgery, Manchester University. He was responsible for the proper distribution of all available equipment in the hospitals and for their adequate staffing with consultant and resident staffs of surgeons, physicians and house officers in accordance with their special functions. This duty included providing the whole professional staff for the Winwick, Baguley and Macclesfield Hospitals, which except in the Macclesfield General Infirmary, had previously no medical staff available for casualties.

When it was required, the Group Officer transferred medical personnel from the staffs of the inner zone hospitals to those of the outer zone, interviewed all candidates for house officers' posts and recommended them to the Hospital Officer for appointment. For dealing with nurses, the Group Officer had the services of Miss Duff-Grant, Matron of the Manchester Royal Infirmary, as Sector Matron, who regulated the distribution of nurses by detailing to the outer zone hospitals senior trained nurses from the inner zone hospitals and auxiliary nursing personnel from the Civil Nursing Reserve pools maintained by the medical officers of health of the inner zone towns or from the County or Regional pools.

The lay Sector Officer, Mr. Cotton, seconded from the staff of Dr. Veitch Clark, Medical Officer of Health of Manchester, was a tower of strength to the Group Officer, and his right hand man in ensuring that the hospitals of the group were provided with their requirements in lay staff, etc.

The medical and nursing staffs had been appointed to these outer zone hospitals during the winter of 1940–1, as they were used to receive convoys from the base hospitals in France; the staffs were, therefore, at the outbreak of enemy attacks well acquainted with their hospitals. They were not fully staffed but were reinforced as and when necessary.

Mobile Surgical Teams. The Group Officer had arranged for nineteen mobile surgical teams based on the inner zone hospitals, and maintained a duty rota, so that surgical teams were always ready on call to go to any hospital in the group or, if necessary, outside the group. The names of the members of each team who were on call for each night, together with the hospitals on which they were based, were posted on the notice-board in the Manchester Central Control, together with those next for duty, so that a mobile team was always available on short notice. During enemy attacks all the teams were available.

Operational Control. The Group Officer was in control of the admissions and discharges of patients to the inner and outer zone hospitals, and copies of the daily bedstates submitted to the office of the Regional Hospital Officer were sent to him to aid him in these duties. His office was in the medical department of the Town Hall in Manchester and near to the office of the Regional Hospital Officer, so that the two were constantly in close liaison, which greatly facilitated the control of the movement of patients and the provision of mobile surgical teams to hospitals requiring them.

Inter-hospital Transport. As Manchester was the headquarters of the North-west Region, there was nothing to be gained by deputing to the Group Officer the functions of the Hospital Officer in controlling the inter-hospital transport as was done in Liverpool. In the Manchester Group there were ten Manchester Corporation bus ambulances, ten Salford Corporation bus ambulances and six bus ambulances of the North-western Road Car Company, all carrying ten stretcher cases each, and their movements were controlled from the Regional Hospital Officer's office, through the transport officers. For the transport of sitting cases, thirty-two seater coaches were always available. The Regional Hospital Officer also controlled the fleet of Anglo-American (G.B.) ambulances, sitting case cars, etc., garaged in the building next to the Regional Office. This consisted of three four-stretcher ambulances, three smaller general purposes cars, four mobile first-aid posts 'A' which could be used as ambulances and sitting case cars, and four first-aid post 'B' units which were used for sitting cases or personnel.

Local Ambulance Transport. This transport was distributed in the four inner zone areas, see table following page.

Their movements were under the operational control of the civil defence controllers of the four areas, but medical officers of health indicated the hospitals to which casualties were to be sent. The number of beds available in each hospital during raids was sent by telephone or messenger at very frequent intervals in order that the flow of casualties might be adequately controlled in accordance with the capacity of the surgical staffs.

	Man-chester	Salford	Stock-port	Stret-ford	Totals
Ambulances					
Whole-time	106	33	17	13	169
Part-time	122	23	24	15	184
Sitting case cars					
Whole-time	37	19	—	15	71
Part-time	179	51	100	36	366
Personnel					
Male—Whole-time	200	75	29	7	311
Part-time	128	124	148	77	477
Female—Whole-time	329	75	27	12	443
Part-time	185	47	198	213	643

First-aid Posts. These were, as elsewhere, under the control of the medical officers of health of the local authorities concerned and were distributed in the area as follows:

	Man-chester	Salford	Stock-port	Stret-ford	Totals
First-aid posts	20	8	7	2	37
Mobile units	12	2	2	1	17

The first-aid post personnel recruited for duty at their posts before the beginning of the raids was as follows:

	Man-chester	Salford	Stock-port	Stret-ford	Totals
Male Whole time	156	31	16	7	210
Part-time	398	—	220	12	630
Female—Whole-time	375	143	56	24	598
Part-time	731	228	388	166	1,513

The Medical Officer of Health of Manchester had commented that some of the premises selected as first-aid posts or civil defence depots were found to be unsuitable, and steps had been taken to rectify defects as far as practicable. For example, four of the fixed first-aid posts were situated in public swimming baths in which adequate overhead and lateral protection was not possible and the danger from flying glass and debris was obvious. In three of these the first-aid posts had been transferred to the basements where full lateral and overhead protection could be provided before the heavy raiding started.

THE RAIDS

Scale of Attacks. The first raid to produce casualties in the area was a small one in Manchester on August 29, 1940, and from this date until

June 3, 1941, there were 261 alerts, but only 24 raids producing casualties in Manchester, 15 in Salford, 10 in Stretford and 10 in Stockport. All these raids were minor ones and caused comparatively few casualties, except for two very heavy raids on the nights of December 22–23 and 23–24, 1940, and a sharp attack on the night of June 2–3, 1941.

Weight of Attacks. The table below shows the number of bombs dropped in the area during the periods of the raids, together with the numbers dropped during the heavy raids from December 22 to 24:

Bombs dropped of all kinds except incendiary bombs	Manchester	Salford	Stockport	Stretford	Totals
Minor raids	295	227	59	117	698
December 22–24, 1940 . .	343	330	23	115	811
Totals	638	557	82	232	1,509

It will be seen that over 50 per cent. of the weight of the attacks occurred on the two nights in December.

No estimated weight of attack in metric tons for the whole period of the raids is available as the bomb census in this area was not started until January 1, 1941, and even then the whole area was not covered, the census only being taken in a circle within a radius of five miles of Manchester Cathedral.

Casualties. The table below gives the numbers of casualties:

	Manchester			Salford			Stretford			Stockport		
	Killed	Seriously injured	Slightly injured	Killed	Seriously injured	Slightly injured	Killed	Seriously injured	Slightly injured	Killed	Seriously injured	Slightly injured
Minor raids . .	207	146	628	66	94	288	42	48	104	9	4	23
December 22–24 .	369	453	728	213	177	648	110	87	184	4	2	18
Total . . .	576	599	1,356	279	271	936	152	135	288	13	6	41

On the night of June 2–3, 1941, that of the second heaviest raid, there were 48 persons killed and 183 injured in Manchester, 44 killed and 138 injured in Salford, 1 killed in Stockport, and 2 killed and 19 injured in Stretford.

Proportion of Casualties to Bombs Dropped. In Manchester and Salford 1,195 H.E. bombs and mines of various calibres were dropped during the raids, as the result of which 855 persons were killed and 870 admitted to hospitals, a proportion of 0·72 killed and 0·73 admitted to hospital per bomb—a ratio very similar to the casualty rates in other towns. Stockport has not been included in these figures since the weight of attack there was comparatively negligible. In Stretford the figures were: 232 bombs (not including incendiaries) dropped; 146 people killed outright or died from injuries (0·63 per bomb); 232 hospital cases (0·58 per bomb). (Of the total number of H.E. bombs dropped on Birmingham during the two heavy night raids of November 19–20 and 22–23, 1940, it was estimated that only about one in six (16·2 per cent. and 17·4 per cent. respectively) caused casualties—a ratio which was approximately doubled in the three attacks on Liverpool and the Merseyside area on the nights of December 20–21, 21–22 and 22–23, when casualties were attributed to one in three (33·3 per cent.) of bombs dropped.)*

Casualties per 1,000 of the Population. The casualty rates per thousand of the population in Manchester and Salford for the nine months' period were only about one per thousand killed and the same for admissions to hospital. If Stockport and Stretford were taken into account the rates would be still lower. These low rates show that the weight of the attack in the area was light compared with the Merseyside area where the figures were 3·8 and 4·0 per thousand.

Raids on December 22–23 and 23–24, 1940. The heavy raids in December, during which 696 persons were killed and 719 admitted to hospital, were chiefly concentrated on the most thickly populated areas, and were equal in severity to any attack on a similar area in the rest of the country. These raids caused nearly double the number of casualties which occurred in all the other raids during the nine months period; and also caused extensive damage to houses, including huge fires, some of which took days to extinguish. The first raid started on the 22nd at 6.38 p.m., and went on continuously, with the exception of an interval of less than half an hour about 10.30 p.m., until 7.06 a.m., wave after wave of bombers passing over the target area. It began with the dropping of large incendiary bombs and flares, followed by large and small H.E. bombs. The calibre of the bombs appeared to increase as the raid went on. On the 23rd, the raid started at 7.12 p.m., and appeared to be heavier than the first while it lasted, but it suddenly came to an end at 1.29 a.m., on the 24th. In this raid more large paramines and oil bombs were dropped than on the first night.

It was fairly obvious from the beginning that Manchester and Salford were the chosen targets. On many previous occasions when alerts were sounded enemy planes passed over the area from the south and south-west and dropped no flares and incendiaries and few, if any, bombs. It was usually found that these planes, after passing over the Manchester area by the old K.L.M. route over the Pennines, were on their way to attack the Merseyside area. But this time many flares and incendiaries were dropped at the beginning of the raid on the southern suburbs of

---

* Ministry of Home Security, Research and Experiments Department, Bomb Census Data, Statistical Reports Nos. 1 (January 29, 1941) and 3 (March 7, 1941).

Manchester, then over the centre of the city, and then even in larger numbers on Salford. Incendiaries started a large number of fires, especially in the centre of Manchester and the dock area of Salford. The planes then appeared to circle round and pass over the now brilliantly lit area and began to drop their bombs, the outer suburbs to the south and north escaping comparatively lightly. After the half-hour's lull between 10 and 11 p.m., heavier bombs and many paramines were dropped indiscriminately, some of the latter falling on the southern suburbs of Withington and Fallowfield, three or four miles south of the centre of Manchester. On the second night practically the same procedure appears to have been followed; but the attacks, though six hours shorter, were heavier while they lasted than those of the night before. On this occasion the track of the raiders seemed to be more to the west, with the result that the Borough of Stretford, which had escaped comparatively lightly on the first night, came in for a heavy attack which was continued into Manchester and Salford.

EMERGENCY SERVICES IN ACTION

First-aid Parties. In Manchester, first-aid parties were called out 211 times, but on 92 occasions no casualties were found.

In Salford first-aid parties were called to 157 incidents out of an estimated total of 330, caused by 301 H.E. bombs, of which 51 did not explode, and 29 mines, including 3 unexploded. The number of incendiary bombs was estimated to be well over 10,000.

In Stretford the estimated number of H.E. bombs, including nine land mines, was 115. The first-aid parties were called out on 117 occasions.

The Medical Officer of Health of Manchester commented very favourably on the work of the first-aid parties. He stated that on the 124 occasions out of 211 of which records were taken, the first-aid parties reached the incidents in under 15 minutes on 97 occasions, under 30 minutes on 21 occasions and only on six occasions in more than 30 minutes. After the raids, the quality of the first-aid given at incidents was checked by enquiries at the casualty clearing hospitals, and the medical officers in charge of the reception of casualties were specially complimentary on the quality of the work done.

In Salford the Medical Officer of Health recorded that, in spite of the weight of the attack and the special difficulties caused by disasters to the only two casualty clearing hospitals in the city, and the damage to first-aid posts and ambulance depots, every call was answered immediately and personnel or vehicles were never found deficient in numbers or efficiency. The casualties were removed in the shortest possible time and at only one incident was there any delay. The delay of two hours in this case was due to the fact that both the wardens in the area were killed and the telephone service, not only to the central control, but also to first-aid posts and first-aid party depots, was put out of action. For the rest of

350　THE EMERGENCY MEDICAL SERVICES

the raid the information was transmitted by a messenger service which functioned most efficiently, but, of course, more slowly.

In Stretford the services operated promptly and efficiently, in spite of temporary difficulties caused by failure of the telephone system. A messenger service was substituted and proved expeditious and reliable even under severe bombing. The morale of the workers was high and was a source of encouragement and confidence to injured persons and their relatives. Under the exacting conditions of the raids, municipal midwives upheld the highest traditions of their profession. The inspiration and confidence which these nurses brought to their patients and families under terrifying conditions merited unstinted praise.

Disposal of Casualties. In Manchester, according to the reports of the first-aid party leaders, 257 stretcher cases, 80 sitting cases and 135 walking cases, a total of 472, were dealt with at incidents, but at first-aid posts 841 cases were recorded as having been treated, so that many of the slightly injured casualties must have gone direct to the first-aid posts or to the out-patient department of hospitals, without treatment at incidents. The classification of the two nights' casualties in Manchester is given in the table below:

	Male	Female	Children	Totals
Dead { Hospitals	27	13	5	45
Dead { Mortuaries	137	129	58	324
Seriously injured	225	189	39	453
Slightly injured	498	180	50	728
Totals	887	511	152	1,550

In Salford no record of the numbers treated at incidents was kept but at the first-aid posts 468 cases were treated.

The casualties for the two nights in Salford are classified in the table below:

	Male	Female	Children	Sex unknown	Totals
Slightly wounded	466	145	37	—	648
Seriously wounded	105	63	9	—	177
Dead	84	76	34	3	197
Missing (believed killed)	10	4	2	—	16
Totals	665	288	82	3	1,038

The proportions of killed and slightly injured appear to conform to the average at other places, the killed and the seriously injured being more or less equal, and the slightly injured being about double the number seriously injured. The proportion of male to female casualties, however, is somewhat different from that found by the Research

Department of the Ministry of Home Security in other parts of the country, where it appeared that the numbers of male and female casualties during night bombing were approximately equal. In Salford, there was a marked excess of male casualties. The number of child casualties (about 10 per cent.) closely approximated to the proportion occurring in other places.

First-aid Posts. In Manchester, nineteen of the twenty fixed posts and all the twelve mobile units were in action on the first night of the attack, and on the following night sixteen fixed posts and eleven mobile units were used, one of the mobile units having been completely wrecked on the first night when three of them were standing by for further duty at their station, and it received a direct hit by an H.E. bomb. One medical officer and three of the staff were killed, eleven seriously injured and six slightly injured. The superstructure of the fixed first-aid post at Withington Baths was wrecked by a paramine, but luckily the first-aid post had already been transferred to the basement and escaped damage. In Salford eight first-aid posts were in action. Two were damaged by blast and one had its roof set on fire by incendiaries. All light was cut off in these posts, but the staff of all three carried on their work by the light of hurricane lamps and torches. Of the two mobile units only one was used.

Ambulance Services. The work of the ambulance services was beyond praise. They were on almost continuous duty for 48 hours taking casualties from incidents to first-aid posts and hospitals and aiding in the transfer of patients from bombed-out hospitals to others.

In Stretford, all calls were answered by the first-aid posts and ambulance depots during the height of the raids. No whole-time personnel were injured or killed, but some part-time volunteers were injured while coming on duty.

DAMAGE TO HOSPITALS

The damage to hospitals in Manchester and Salford was one of the chief features of these raids and this fact added considerably to the amount of work thrown on the whole organisation. The following hospitals received serious damage which entailed the loss of beds for the reception of casualties for considerable periods.

Manchester Royal Infirmary. The new nurses' home of this hospital had been completely put out of action by a direct hit in a previous raid. On the night of December 22–23 many windows were broken by blast, and admission had to be stopped for one hour while the blackout was temporarily repaired. The next night a delayed action bomb fell on the administrative block and exploded the following afternoon. It caused considerable damage, chiefly to the X-ray department, but there were no casualties among the staff or patients.

The Royal Eye Hospital, next to the Royal Infirmary, received a direct hit on the night of December 22–23 which demolished a part of the south wing, and put the heating, cooking and other services out of action. A mobile canteen was sent to the hospital, and next morning, the whole of the staff and patients were evacuated to the Withington Hospital where they remained for over three months, until the Eye Hospital was able to open again in April 1941. A doctor and nurse were killed but no patients were injured.

Manchester Victoria Jewish Hospital. This hospital received a direct hit on the night of December 22–23 and all services were put out of action. No patients were injured, as they had previously been removed to shelters, but five members of the staff were killed and three injured. A mobile canteen supplied the hospital during the night and with the arrival of daylight the patients and staff were all evacuated to the Crumpsall Hospital. The Jewish Hospital was able partly to resume its activities after a month and in two months was again working at full capacity. It was, however, again damaged by fire during the raid on June 2 and evacuated, but was able to resume work after a short time.

Withington Hospital. This hospital received a direct hit on December 22 by a small explosive bomb which did considerable damage to the top and middle floors of one pavilion. No patients were injured but two of the nursing staff were wounded, one seriously.

Hope Hospital, Salford. In Salford the worst catastrophe occurred. On December 22, a paramine struck the administrative block of the Hope Hospital, a large modern hospital of 1,200 beds belonging to the Salford Corporation, and reduced it to a heap of rubble. The rest of the hospital was so badly damaged by blast that of the 1,200 beds only 256 in a new block were capable of being used as a separate unit. All services were completely out of action. No patients were injured, but the Medical Superintendent, Dr. J. Dudgeon Giles, O.B.E., the Matron, Miss M. J. C. Ross, R.R.C., and four members of the staff who were in the basement shelter under the administrative block were buried under tons of debris and were all dead when the bodies were recovered after several days. The pre-arranged plans for the evacuation of patients were immediately put into action; local and inter-hospital transport were assembled and 673 patients were evacuated in a few hours, most of them to the large base hospitals at Winwick, near Warrington, Whittingham near Preston, Queen's Park near Blackburn and Townley's Hospital, Farnworth near Bolton. A few patients unfit to make the longer journey were admitted to the Crumpsall Hospital, Manchester.

The Salford Corporation, by strenuous efforts were able to reopen certain parts of the hospital for serious casualties and urgent cases. One ward was made the receiving ward for the admission and distribution of patients on December 27, 1940; on January 19, 1941, a second ward was ready to receive about 40 child patients; and on January 22, a further three wards were made ready for the admission of additional patients. Each of these wards had a bed accommodation of 38 patients. Other wards in the hospital were gradually brought into service after renovation and essential repairs had taken place.

The catastrophe entailed temporary arrangements for the reception of very urgent casualties in the Salford Royal Hospital and for all other casualties in the Crumpsall Hospital, Manchester, which was the nearest large hospital to the Salford boundary.

Salford Royal Hospital. Worse was to follow, for on the night of December 23–24, the only remaining casualty clearing hospital in the city, the Salford Royal Hospital, was put out of action by blast from a paramine that caused much damage to the fabric and services of the hospital, so that all the patients and staff had to be evacuated. This was done at daylight and arrangements were made to admit all Salford casualties to the Crumpsall Hospital, Manchester. It was fortunate that a large first-class hospital with a total accommodation for 1,500 patients was available at such a short distance. The Salford Royal Hospital was able to function again on the following evening, December 25, to the extent of 40 beds; 120 beds were available within seven days and 200 within ten days. The remainder were out of use for about six months until repairs to the roof over the two top floor wards were completed, but it received another direct hit on June 2, when thirteen nurses met their deaths by being buried under debris, but again by a strange freak of fortune, no patients were injured.

The Hope Hospital had further trouble after it had partially reopened; incendiary bombs caused damage to the roofs of several pavilions and the nurses' home in a later raid, so that 89 patients had to be evacuated to the Winwick Emergency Hospital. In addition to these casualty clearing hospitals, the Ladywell Infectious Diseases Hospital was damaged on two occasions, once during the December raids and afterwards in March, when a bomb demolished the operating theatre and damaged some of the wards. Ninety patients had to be evacuated as the result of the damage in December and 94 in March.

DAMAGE TO SERVICES

In addition to actual damage to the hospitals, temporary difficulties were caused in nearly all the hospitals by damage to the telephone and lighting services, water supply and sewerage. Repairs and temporary adjustments were usually quickly made, but in Salford the sewerage system was seriously damaged; the low level sewage disposal system was partly out of action until February and crude sewage had to be permitted to flow untreated into the Ship Canal. The sewers were broken at eighty-five different places; forty-six of these breaks occurred in the December raids. All precautions were taken to ensure the purity of the drinking water supply and there was no evidence of any ill effects on the health of the inhabitants.

WORK OF THE HOSPITALS

In spite of the very considerable damage to hospitals, the alternative accommodation for casualties was so plentiful that never did any of the patients suffer anything more than unavoidable inconvenience.

The flow of admissions to hospitals was controlled in accordance with pre-arranged plans. All hospitals were required to notify the control centres of the first admissions and thereafter to communicate the numbers admitted at regular intervals, which were as short as fifteen minutes when necessary, so that the medical officers of health on duty at the control centres could ensure that no hospital received more casualties than it could adequately deal with; quotas for each hospital had previously been agreed upon. In this way rapid surgical and medical treatment for all casualties could be ensured, mobile surgical teams could, when necessary, be provided as reliefs for hospitals, and arrangements could be prepared in advance to evacuate patients to base hospitals and provide bed accommodation for further casualties.

In Manchester it was noted that small hospitals tended to admit casualties in excess of the agreed number, so that the excess had to be transferred to other hospitals.

Admissions to Hospitals. The number of patients admitted and retained in the casualty clearing hospitals on the two days of the raids was 717.

Types of Injuries. In Manchester the following percentages of the various types of injury were admitted to hospital:

	per cent.
Fractures	12
Eye injuries	15
Head and facial	12
Lacerations	22
Abrasions	10
Shock accompanied by injury	15
Miscellaneous	14

Resuscitation Wards. All the casualty clearing hospitals had fully equipped resuscitation wards and at each hospital at least one blood transfusion team had been arranged. The Regional Blood Transfusion Services had not fully come into action at the time of these heavy raids, but the hospitals of Manchester and Salford were fortunate in already having a well organised blood transfusion scheme, which was brought into being in August 1939. The processing plant was under the direction of Dr. J. F. Wilkinson, of Manchester University, and was housed in the Manchester Royal Infirmary. Between September 1939, and May 1942, 21,500 bottles of blood were collected. Of these, 5,468 bottles were used in the Manchester and Salford hospitals, and during the raids in December 234 bottles of plasma were used in transfusions for casualties.

Stretcher Bearers. In addition to the porter staffs of the hospitals relief squads of stretcher bearers had been provided by arrangement with the

British Red Cross Society and St. John Ambulance Brigade. These reliefs were fully employed and proved exceedingly useful in the heavy work of receiving casualties during the raids, transferring patients from bombed hospitals, and the evacuation of patients to base hospitals—duties which necessitated continuous stretcher bearing from the evening of December 22 to the evening of December 24.

Transfers from Hospitals. As the result of the damage to hospitals and in order to clear beds by transfer of patients to outer zone hospitals, 941 patients were transferred to other hospitals during December 23, 24 and 25. On the morning of December 22, there were 2,284 vacant beds suitable for casualties in ten hospitals in Manchester. On the evening of December 25, the beds available were 1,402 in seven hospitals. In Salford on December 22, there were 303 vacant beds in two hospitals and on the 25th, no vacant beds.

No strain was therefore thrown on the bed accommodation, but although reliefs were arranged, the resident medical, surgical and nursing staffs of the hospitals necessarily got little rest for the whole period of 24 hours. During the whole period from August 1940, to June 1941, 7,640 patients were transferred from the inner zone hospitals to hospitals outside the area. These were mostly 'transferred' civilian sick and Service cases transferred to free beds in the inner zone hospitals.

MORTUARY SERVICES

In Manchester, five mortuaries had to be brought into use with fifteen vehicles which were adequate to cope with the 324 bodies brought into the city mortuaries. Bodies unclaimed for several days were preserved by carbon dioxide snow. Small parts were kept in formalin.

The City Director of the Pathological Services gave valuable assistance in training personnel and in identifying mangled bodies. An identification bureau had been organised, but the premises in which it was located were destroyed on the night of the 22nd: alternative premises were rapidly brought into use with the help of the Casualty Services and the Police.

In Salford the number of casualties dealt with in the Corporation's mortuaries during the period of the raid was 223.

CASUALTY BUREAUX

The casualty bureaux functioned most satisfactorily. Casualty lists were received from hospitals, first-aid posts and mortuaries and lists made were forwarded to the Chief Constable daily. It was thus possible, even after heavy raids, to publish the first lists of casualties within eight hours of the end of a raid.

Difficulties had to be met in dealing with hundreds of inquiries by letter, telegram and telephone, and large numbers of personal callers also had to be dealt with. Other difficulties, such as incomplete records, incorrect names and addresses and illegibility of the records resulted in some mistakes in the published lists, which sometimes caused grave and unnecessary anxiety to friends and relatives.

HOUSES DAMAGED BY ENEMY ACTION

In Manchester, over 50,000 houses were damaged, of which about 44,000 were only slightly damaged and could be repaired; 5,051 were so badly damaged that they had to be evacuated and accommodation had to be found for 2,806 families, comprising 10,800 persons. In Salford, out of the 53,000 houses in the city, 25,000 were damaged, of which 3,943 were found to be beyond repair; 26,700 persons had to be found temporary or permanent accommodation elsewhere in or outside the city.

In Stretford, 186 houses were totally demolished; 321 were damaged beyond repair and 14,604 were damaged but reparable. Accommodation had to be found for 2,541 families totalling 8,354 persons.

Persons rendered homeless were in the first place accommodated, fed and where necessary, issued with clothing at the rest centres, and adequate medical and nursing aid was provided.

STORES AND EQUIPMENT

In Manchester a large and complex system of storekeeping had been organised. Supplies were held in eleven stores in various parts of the city in order to minimise bombing risks. Nearly two million articles of all kinds were stocked in these stores, which were manned day and night so that the urgent requirements of the hospitals, first-aid posts, ambulances, etc., during raids could be met immediately.

GENERAL COMMENTS

The careful planning of the Emergency Medical Services in the Manchester Group by the Regional and local authorities resulted in the most harmonious and efficient working of the scheme. The plans for the collection of casualties at incidents, their first-aid treatment, despatch to first-aid posts or hospitals, their reception and treatment at these institutions and their subsequent dispersal to other hospitals, worked without a hitch. The liaison maintained at each stage was effective, the only delays being caused by the destruction of communications and the necessary substitution of messenger services. The liaison between the Manchester, Salford and Stretford controls was good, as was shown by the arrangements speedily put into effect for the transfer of patients from bombed out hospitals in Salford to Crumpsall Hospital, Manchester and thereafter for the direct transport of all the Salford casualties from incidents and first-aid posts to the same hospital. The transfer of Stretford cases to Withington Hospital direct presented no unforeseen difficulties. The supply of inter-hospital transport in the form of large ten-stretcher ambulances for the evacuation of hospitals and their staffs was also prompt and efficient. This was shown by the fact that all the necessary arrangements for the transfer of patients in the area and evacuation of patients to base hospitals after the heavy raid on December 22–23 were completed and the evacuation begun by 2 p.m. on the 23rd, and was continuing when the second raid started at 6.30 p.m. This raid ended at about 1 a.m. on the 24th and the supplementary arrangements for decanting patients were completed by 5.30 a.m. and the move timed to begin at 9.15 a.m. All the moves were finished by 12 noon on the 24th.

The work done by the Civil Defence Services at incidents, by the Ambulance Services, both inter-hospital and local, the first-aid posts, the hospitals and the controlling staffs was highly commended by the Regional Commissioner, Sir Harry Haig, who remarked that one service that could be said to have worked without a hitch was the Casualty Service.

CHAPTER 4
BIRMINGHAM
1940 to 1942

Contributed by
H. P. *Newsholme*, M.D., F.R.C.P., *Medical Officer of Health, Birmingham*

AFTER a brief outline of the composition of the Civil Defence Casualty Services, the treatment of casualties in the air raids is reviewed, and a short description given of the more important raids. The report concludes with one or two descriptions of actual experiences, contributed by members of the casualty services.

THE COMPOSITION OF THE CIVIL DEFENCE CASUALTY SERVICES

Control. There were nine control centres co-ordinated by central control. The medical officer of health or one of his assistant medical officers was always on duty at central control, and was assisted there by the air raid precautions officer in the control of the casualty services. The medical officer of health had no direct representative at any of the control centres, as distinct from central control.

Hospitals. Eight hospitals were originally scheduled to receive air raid casualties. One of these was afterwards militarised, but two emergency basement hospitals were added to the list, and proved their worth. One of these was sited in a large, modern department store in the centre of the city, and was near to the large voluntary hospital which acted as parent hospital for equipment and staffing purposes to both basement hospitals. The other was situated in the vaults of a large brewery about one mile from the city centre. Each was fully equipped to deal with 100 casualties, and operating theatres and X-ray facilities were provided. Casualties going to these two hospitals during a raid were moved out to base hospitals early the following day, and these patients generally did remarkably well. The basement hospital in the centre of the city was ready to receive casualties at the end of January 1941, and was able to give most valuable help during the heavy raids of April 1941, when approximately 100 casualties were received. The other basement hospital came into operation at a later date, and fully justified its existence by dealing with 80–90 cases during the explosive incendiary bomb raids of July 1942.

First-aid Posts. There were 32 first-aid posts, the majority in schools or baths and so sited that no casualty should have more than a mile to walk to get to one of them. They fulfilled their function, and in relieving the hospitals of a considerable number of casualties performed most useful work. Although they were planned to deal with minor casualties, more serious cases inevitably on occasion found their way to a first-aid post, i.e. cases from incidents close to the post, cases brought in by members of the public, or occasional cases in urgent need of medical attention rushed in by civil defence workers.

Mobile Units. There were twelve mobile units sited at six stations. Although the big incidents with large numbers of casualties for which these units were designed occurred infrequently in this city, nevertheless, mobile units were used extensively. It was often difficult to assess the gravity of an incident from the preliminary report message, and it was the practice to send out a mobile unit to any incident which appeared likely to have more than a dozen casualties. At first the whole unit was sent, but it was soon found that a light unit, consisting of a doctor and two first-aiders with equipment, was usually sufficient.

Incident Medical Officers. In the early raids there was some difficulty and uncertainty in getting a doctor to go to an incident, consequently, in conjunction with the general practitioners of the city, a system of incident medical officers based on first-aid posts was prepared; so that, if a doctor was wanted at an incident it was only necessary to contact the nearest first-aid post. This scheme was linked up with a general practitioner service for the public during air raid periods, under which a member of the public urgently needing a doctor for a case of illness or accident during an air raid applied to his nearest first-aid post.

First-aid Parties, Ambulances and Sitting Case Cars. These were sited at twenty-five depots scattered strategically about the city. The approximate numbers available at each raid were as follows:

First-aid parties	. 100 to 120
Ambulances .	. 190
Sitting case cars	. 90 to 100

These proved adequate to deal with all the casualties, although in two or three of the bigger raids they were stretched to their utmost capacity, and reserves were asked for from Region as a precautionary measure. These first-aiders, working at the site of the incident, and with all the handicaps which that involves, such as darkness, dirt and danger, deserved the highest praise for the way in which they successfully discriminated between hospital cases and first-aid post cases—a truly remarkable achievement. (Plate XXIV shows ambulance assistants helping in rescue.)

Medical Services in Shelters. Schemes were prepared on the lines suggested in the Horder report, and these provided medical-aid posts in seven of the most populated shelters, but those facilities were little used, for the shelter problem in this city was not in any way comparable with that in London.

Mortuaries. There were nine mortuaries, staffed voluntarily by members of the Birmingham Funeral Directors' Guild, who, throughout, co-operated whole-heartedly with the Public Health Department.

Casualty Bureau. This was established in the Public Health Department and was run in close co-operation with the Birmingham Hospitals Contributory Association. Details of the total number of casualties dealt with during the raids up to July 31, 1943, were as follows:

	Males	Females	Children	Total	
Killed	1,172	858	211	2,241 (25·1 per cent.)	
Admitted to hospital	1,945	846	218	3,009 (33·7 per cent.)	8,934
Treated at first-aid posts	2,557	925	202	3,684 (41·2 per cent.)	

Further information is given in the account of individual raids which follows:

AIR RAIDS ON THE CITY OF BIRMINGHAM

The heaviest raid so far as weight of bombs is concerned, occurred on the night of April 9–10, 1941. There was a much smaller raid on the following night, which for statistical purposes cannot be separated from the raid of the night before. The Research and Experimental Department of the Ministry of Home Security provided the information that on these two nights 896 H.E.s fell on the city, their total weight being about 110 tons. The casualties totalled 1,404 and comprised 403 fatal, 473 hospital cases and 528 first-aid post cases. Roughly this meant that for every ton of bombs dropped four people were killed and nine injured, four of them seriously.

The average population at risk during the raids is estimated to have been some 970,000.

For the convenience of description it is proposed to divide the raids as follows:

(a) August 1, 1940—September 30, 1940.
(b) October 1, 1940—July 31, 1941.
(c) July 1942.

(a) August 1 to September 30, 1940.

These raids were linked with the Battle of Britain.

On the night of August 9, 1940, the first bombs were dropped on the City of Birmingham, and this raid was followed by eleven further raids in August and seven in September. Although these early raids were light compared with the heavier raids which were to follow, they were of extreme value in giving experience to all branches of the Civil Defence Services. As a result the casualty services were fully and efficiently prepared for the later heavy raids.

PLATE XXVI. Mobile Canteen in operation.

BIRMINGHAM

Birmingham *Post & Mail*

PLATE XXIV. Ambulance attendants assisting in rescue.

Birmingham *Post & Mail*

PLATE XXV. Searching the debris for victims.

Casualties in the two months totalled 498, the details being as follows:

	Killed	Hospital cases	First-aid post cases
Males	57	77	163
Females	34	45	90
Children under 16	12	11	9
Totals	103	133	262

In one of these raids, an aircraft factory received a direct hit before the sirens sounded and there were about 150 casualties from this incident. In another raid three hospitals received damage, but all were able to carry on without serious handicap. Two first-aid posts also received minor damage in other raids during this period.

(b) *October 1, 1940 to July 31, 1941.*

The first fortnight of October was quiet, but from the middle of the month onwards and throughout November there was a visit almost every night from the enemy, culminating in the heavy raids of November 19–23, which followed quickly on the heels of the heavy Coventry raid.

The raids in October and those occurring before November 19 do not call for very much in the way of comment, and all branches of the casualty services worked smoothly. In one of these raids one of the casualty hospitals received a direct hit from a powerful bomb, but although the material damage was marked there were only a small number of casualties and the hospital continued to function satisfactorily. This hospital contained on this particular night, purely as a temporary measure, a considerable number of evacuees from London, but none of these received any major injury. In another raid one of the first-aid posts had an incendiary bomb on the roof which caused a fire. No sooner had this been extinguished with great promptitude by the staff, than the post received a direct hit from a H.E. which wrecked the post and caused casualties to the staff, three being fatal and four seriously injured. A mobile unit was summoned and did most valuable work. In a further raid, another first-aid post received a direct hit on the main entrance, but the post was able to continue in action and only five of the staff were injured.

Tuesday night, November 19–20. This was a heavy raid, nearly 1,000 incidents being reported. The services, although strained, were able to deal with all problems. The raid was perhaps remarkable for the very minor damage suffered by the casualty services, having regard to the number and weight of bombs dropped. A very serious incident occurred at a large factory, involving 54 fatal and 98 seriously injured casualties as well as many minor injuries.

Wednesday night, November 20–21. About 200 incidents were reported, the majority being due to incendiary bombs, of which a number were of the explosive type, causing casualties to those attempting to deal with them. This was shown by the casualty figures for this raid, which showed an undue proportion of injured to killed, i.e. killed 14, hospital cases 94, first-aid post cases 222.

Friday night, November 22–23. This raid opened with heavy bombing in the early evening of Friday, November 22, and continued with undiminished intensity for approximately eleven hours. It was the heaviest raid to date on the city, with 1,300 incidents. Although the centre of the city bore the brunt of the attack, few districts escaped.

The casualty services were taxed to their full capacity and additional ambulance units were asked for from Region, but were not actually needed. Practically every first-aid post dealt with casualties and several handled large numbers. Two of these asked for extra medical help. Several posts had near misses and suffered slight damage. The only post which suffered severely was one which had already suffered heavy damage in a previous raid, and was only functioning in a minor capacity. All the twelve mobile units were in action repeatedly, being sent out to no fewer than 33 incidents; they were able to give valuable help. Use was also made of several medical practitioners to go to incidents. In the course of the raid three hospitals were damaged, but all were able to continue to function satisfactorily. As the raid progressed, it became obvious that a good deal of damage had been done to water mains; but the seriousness of the position was not apparent until after the raid was over, when it was reported that unlucky hits had severely damaged two out of the three large mains carrying the supply to the city from the waterworks. This meant that roughly three quarters of the city was immediately deprived of a piped water supply, and this state of affairs persisted for several days. All precautions were taken, and as far as could be ascertained not a single case of enteric fever, or for that matter any other disease, arose as a direct result of this damage.

The total casualties during this week were:—killed, 796; hospital cases, 1,127; first-aid post cases, 1,202.

The number of fatal casualties threw a heavy strain on the mortuary arrangements, but all difficulties were satisfactorily overcome. Apart from one heavy raid in December, and twelve very minor raids, bombing practically ceased until April 1941.

Raid on the night of December 11–12, 1940. This raid was again most intense around the city centre; a comparatively large number of H.Es. were dropped together with a number of parachute land mines. Mobile units were used extensively and once again proved their value. One unit dealt with about 30 casualties in an area devastated by a land mine, while another unit was sent to an ambulance depot which had received a direct hit. A third unit had to be evacuated owing to an incendiary bomb on its depot. No single outstanding item of major damage was apparent, and the services worked well and were sufficient to cope with the raid. Five first-aid posts received minor damage and one of them had to be evacuated on account of the close proximity of a serious fire. Plate XXV shows a typical rescue scene.

The casualties were: killed, 263; hospital cases, 245; first-aid post cases, 298.

Night of April 9–10. This raid, during which 864 incidents were reported, was more concentrated than the previous heavy raids, only occupying about five hours, and the feature of the raid was the large number of H.Es. dropped. The greater part of the city was affected, but the bulk of the attack was on the city centre and the eastern suburbs.

The casualty services were fully used. At one time, twenty ambulances were received from Region, but they were not required as the existing services proved adequate to deal with the heaviest raid yet experienced. Extensive damage to the telephone system made it very difficult to keep in touch with all the services throughout the raid. The mobile units were used to capacity and attended sixteen incidents in all. One first-aid post received considerable damage, but was able to carry on; miraculously there were no casualties among the staff or patients. All but two of the first-aid posts were in action, and in all they dealt with 423 casualties.

The casualties were: killed, 290; hospital cases, 408; first-aid post cases, 423; total, 1,121.

Night of April 10–11. This raid, though not comparable in size with that of the previous night, was nevertheless significant. More than 162 incidents were reported, but there was nothing of outstanding importance. Total casualties: killed, 25; hospital cases, 43; first-aid post cases, 96.

After this raid, apart from four minor raids in May, June and July 1941, there were no further raids until July 1942.

Total casualties for the October 1940–July 1941, raid period were as follows:

	Killed	Hospital cases	First-aid post cases
Males	1,006	1,517	2,074
Females	764	714	756
Children under 16	193	207	183
Totals	1,963	2,438	3,013

(c) *July 1942—The Explosive Incendiary Bomb Raids.*

This small series of raids during the last week of July 1942, consisted in the main of a sharp incendiary attack followed two nights later by the first use of the explosive incendiary bomb on a large scale. A third raid occurred the succeeding evening but was of no special significance.

The first raid, on July 28, was mainly an incendiary attack and lasted about two hours, there being about 300 incidents. About two-thirds of the first-aid posts were in action, and mobile units were sent out to six incidents. Two incident medical officers were also sent out. One of the large voluntary hospitals in the centre of the city suffered damage from H.Es., one of which put the operating theatres out of action, and another the heating system, so that hot water was unobtainable. In addition, a delayed action bomb was suspected in the grounds of the hospital. As a result, the patients and staff were moved to such wards as were still available and relatively safe, and at dawn complete evacuation was started. Eighteen bus ambulances were used, first-aid parties acting as stretcher bearers. The evacuation was completed without incident. The delayed action bomb, after careful examination in daylight, was eventually reported to be a camouflet. One of the first-aid posts suffered serious damage from blast, but was able to continue in operation, and in addition three other posts suffered minor damage.

Casualties were: killed, 50; hospital cases, 114; first-aid post cases, 156; total, 320.

Two nights later, on July 30, a similar raid was staged, but with the difference that most of the incendiary bombs dropped—of which there was a very large number, over 500 incidents being reported—were of the explosive type. On this account casualties were relatively heavy, and most of them occurred at many incidents reported almost simultaneously from all over the city. This created a sudden demand for ambulances, and for a time this service was stretched to its full capacity. The large voluntary hospital, evacuated two nights previously of all but a very small number of patients too ill to move, was again hit, and a serious fire broke out in one of the wings. This was eventually got under control, and the ultimate damage was found to be lighter than had been expected.

This hospital was out of commission, as far as air raid casualties were concerned, and all but two of the remaining casualty hospitals eventually filled to their switching figure. This was the first time that an opportunity of trying out the switching scheme had presented itself, and although there were one or two hitches the scheme worked relatively smoothly. One hospital asked for additional surgical assistance, which was provided by a mobile surgical team. Three hospitals in addition to the one already mentioned suffered damage, but were able to continue to function. One first-aid post was also damaged slightly.

Casualties were: killed, 71; hospital cases, 264; first-aid post cases, 161; total, 496.

Some of the fatal casualties, many of the hospital cases, and most of the cases dealt with at first-aid posts were caused by incendiary bombs of the explosive type. The casualty services generally received a real test in this raid and came through with great credit.

There was a minor raid the next night, following which there was a long period of immunity, only broken on the night of April 23, 1943, by a single plane which dropped two H.Es., and caused a small number of casualties.

The total casualties for this period were as follows:

	Killed	Hospital cases	First-aid post cases
Males	108	352	320
Females	60	87	79
Children	6	—	10
Totals	174	439	409

PERSONAL EXPERIENCES RECORDED BY MEMBERS OF THE CASUALTY SERVICES

The following three accounts of personal experiences recorded by the members of the casualty services are included. They add the human touch to this report :

THE INCIDENT MEDICAL OFFICER

On the night of November 19, 1940, occurred the dreadful disaster in St. George's Street. A land mine was dropped here by an enemy raider. The resulting explosion was devastating. Most of St. George's Street was destroyed. We were told that a group of men saw a long dark shape, suspended from a parachute, descending during the height of the raid. They thought this was a German airman who had 'bailed out', and they ran to capture him. The land mine not only made awful havoc of St. George's Street, it blew down an adjacent part of Hospital Street.

An urgent telephone call came to the post. 'Was the M.O. on duty ?' 'Yes'. 'Would he go at once to Hospital Street and take some morphia'.

A few minutes later, the doctor, post officer and one of the staunchest of the volunteers were hurrying to Hospital Street. Pavements and roadway were strewn with broken glass, fragments of wood and all sorts of rubble. It was dark, but not too dark to see the outlines of such houses as were still standing. A fire was raging not far away, and throwing now a flickering light amid clouds of smoke, and now a lurid glare. Stumbling along, our three turned into Hospital Street. At first they went down the street towards the Brearley Street crossing, but, seeing no signs of a rescue party, they retraced their steps and reached the St. George's Street corner. Here was the trouble—no question about it. The fire in the background disclosed a scene of awful ruin. Over an enormous mound of broken bricks our trio clambered, to find themselves on the edge of what looked like a black pit. The sloping sides of the pit were composed of shifting, silting rubble covered with a thick layer of fine black dust. The bottom of this pit was about twelve feet down. At the bottom a man was trapped. He was partially embedded in the broken bricks, shattered woodwork and other wreckage of what had once been his home. He was lying prone, face downwards, his legs and outstretched arms deeply embedded. An electric torch in the hands of one of a group of five or six men shone down on him.

Slinging the first-aid bag over his shoulder, the M.O. lowered himself down. He had to move cautiously for fear of knocking pieces of brick and slates on to the trapped man's head. The back of a kitchen chair stuck out of the rubble at the bottom of the hole. The doctor braced one foot against this, and stretched his other foot to the opposite side of the declivity. He was now bestriding the embedded man. The poor trapped fellow could just raise his head about an inch. He was fully clothed and was wearing an overcoat. His face and head were smothered in the black dust and his features could hardly be discerned.

By the light of flash lamps the doctor examined the trapped man carefully and tried various expedients to release him. Then taking a pair of scissors from his pocket, the doctor cut away a portion of the man's overcoat and under-garments and injected a pain relieving dose of morphia with his hypodermic syringe. It was no easy matter to bend in that cramped attitude to give the hypodermic, fearful that an unwary movement might start the rubble sliding downwards to cover the victim's face. The morphia soon began to give relief. The sufferer began to talk and asked for a little water. The doctor gave him sips of water from an egg-cup. The space between the man's mouth and rubble was so restricted that only a small egg-cup could be used.

All this time a cold bleak wind was rising as the hour of dawn drew near. A towering gaunt piece of shattered wall rose overhead like a chimney stack, almost overhanging the black pit beneath. This ruin seemed to shake in the wind, and the watchers directed upon it the beams of their torches, as if dreading that it might collapse.

It was impossible to remove the man without first shifting many more of the bricks; so a wooden door was sawn in two halves, placed over the poor fellow at the bottom of the pit to protect him from falling pieces, and the rescue party went hard at it, removing obstructions as fast as possible. No one seemed to pause to consider what other dire destruction the enemy might be doing in the meantime. Another bomb might have descended at any moment, but all were too busy and pre-occupied to spare one glance at the lowering sky. By this time the morphia had acted fully—the injured man could tolerate the movement of the obstacles that prevented his release. Soon he was freed and hurried off to hospital.

THE MOBILE UNIT IN ACTION

On an evening in the middle of November 1940, a yellow warning was received at the unit at 6.40 p.m. followed by a purple five minutes later, and sirens began their wailing in a further few minutes. The staff manning the unit were quickly augmented by the arrival of volunteers and the medical officer. The ambulance engine was tested, hot water bottles refilled, gas clothing, steel helmets and gum boots put ready. By this time the droning of enemy aircraft and the noise of anti-aircraft fire was becoming intense and was quickly followed by explosions of bombs on all sides. The glow of fires began to make their appearance in many parts, which soon lit up the entire city.

Just before midnight a call by telephone was received to proceed to a serious incident in the centre of the city, and within a few minutes the unit, consisting of a pilot car, the ambulance and an escort car, set off. The personnel consisted of twelve including the medical officer, eight being women. Bombs were still falling, fires were still raging, and it was not long before detours had to be made where roads were blocked with debris, craters, hose pipes and fire engines. The crunching of glass over which the unit passed almost synchronised with the crackling of raging fires. On more than one occasion the pilot car just pulled up in time to prevent going headlong into a crater, which had as yet not been discovered or guarded by A.R.P. wardens. After doing two or three times the normal distance the unit arrived at the end of the street where lay the serious incident, a hundred or more yards away. The incident was one of a land-mine that had dropped in a back courtyard in which were several Anderson shelters, and many people were buried, both in these and in the wrecked houses.

As it was impossible to set up a proper station, each member was handed from the ambulance as much equipment in the form of blankets, hot water bottles, splints, dressings, drugs, instruments, etc., as he could carry, and proceeded with the utmost difficulty over piled up masonry to where we discerned the figures of police and a rescue squad, who were already at work with crowbars, picks and shovels. The groans of the trapped people made one curse with hatred the Nazis, as further bomb explosions could be heard round about. The groans, however, were a guide towards these unfortunate people. All the members of the unit set to work with their hands and with any tools available to assist the police and rescue squad in removing debris which was piled up on top of half a dozen Anderson shelters, which lay around the edge of an enormous crater, a youth from the neighbourhood giving a good idea as to their exact positions.

After the work had been going on for some time, a voice suddenly shouted 'Doctor wanted'. The medical officer proceeded to the spot and found that a limb had been uncovered, the remainder of the body being firmly wedged by the roof of the shelter which had been forced in by sheer weight of brickwork. It was obvious that others were underneath and some alive, but without doubt seriously injured, as groans and heavy breathing could be clearly heard coming from below. The medical officer examined the limb and announced that the victim was no doubt dead and was obviously obstructing the way to others. With great care the roof near which once was the entrance of the shelter was elevated by crowbars and eventually the body was pulled through a small tunnel; it was that of a young woman who had sustained severe general injuries as a result of crushing, and who also showed severe signs of the effect of the blast. The tunnel was widened to enable the medical officer to crawl into the wrecked shelter, and with his torch he found several people, old, young, and babies lying in various positions, some dead, others seriously injured. They were all wedged by debris, chairs, and corrugated iron. The medical officer asked for morphia to be passed down, and he gave each live casualty an appropriate dose.

While this was being done the tunnel into the wrecked shelter was being enlarged and volunteers were asked to come down into the shelter to help release the trapped people. As there was only room for one other person at a time the medical officer remained and directed the release of each victim in order to avoid further injury to the casualties. As each one was released ropes were attached under the shoulders and they were gently pulled out through the tunnel. The smell of coal gas grew rather pungent and it became necessary to come up for spells of fresh air. One by one each victim was released, brought to the surface, and laid on a stretcher, the medical officer giving instructions to the personnel in the dressing of wounds. Three little babies under one year old were found dead, being clasped firmly in their mothers' arms—they had obviously been suffocated as a result of the maternal protection. An old man of seventy-five was the last to be rescued. He was sitting at the far end of the shelter on an old wooden chair completely covered with debris up to his neck; he was perfectly conscious and chatted cheerfully throughout the proceedings and indicated the possible positions of the various people who were in the shelter. He was the least injured of any, and by the time he was rescued after many hours, the debris had been sufficiently cleared for him to walk out. His only thoughts were for his daughter and her child, both of whom unfortunately were dead.

The dressings of the wounds were inspected by the medical officer. Hot drinks, hot water bottles, and blankets were given to the patients, labels with doses of morphia given were attached to each one, and they were despatched by ambulance to hospital at the earliest moment.

Similar rescue work had to be undertaken with half a dozen other shelters and several houses, everyone working to the utmost capacity, and it was nearly daybreak when it was decided that everybody had been accounted for. One old lady in the region of eighty was found sitting in her chair in front of the kitchen fire, and had been killed by falling masonry. The conscious victims behaved in a heroic manner. They kept up their spirits and cracked jokes whilst they were being rescued. The rescuers, the personnel of the mobile unit, and others all worked heroically in the face of the danger of falling debris and the presence of coal gas.

When the last of the casualties had been despatched to hospital—there were between twenty and thirty in all—the unit, tired out, ankles sprained, and with clothing torn, proceeded back through the shattered and deserted streets to their headquarters, where they were greeted with those cups of tea which never tasted better, feeling at least they had done a good job of work.

THE FIRST-AID POST RECEIVES CASUALTIES

Here we are at the first-aid post in the midst of factories and slums. After weeks of lecturing and practices I began to feel more comfortable about the capabilities of my girls. My only worry was, how would they react to a raid—indeed, how would I myself react? Then came our first raid—my girls keen and excited; I, feeling sick and worried. Our first casualties arrived, some hurt in the black-out—all minor things, but still dressings to be done. Then the real thing: bombs falling all around us, fires everywhere, casualties being brought in, in a steady stream. How wonderfully those girls reacted!

But for their white faces I would have thought they didn't mind one jot. They worked quietly and, for novices, efficiently; all my fears for them vanished and I must confess I felt ashamed of myself, for right down in my heart I knew they would give a good account of themselves.

All that we had been told as to what would happen, and how we must act in theory, went 'phut'; in actual practice everything is totally different. We went through those grim nights never knowing which would be our last, for I think the Jerries had a particular liking for our area, or so it seemed to us!

Screaming and whistling bombs all round us, fires everywhere. Twice we were on fire ourselves, casualties lying about our floors. How wonderfully everyone worked, joking and smiling with an occasional 'Gosh, that was a near one', or 'I hope our Mam and Dad are alright'.

We worked sixteen, eighteen, twenty hours a day. The extraordinary pluck and fortitude of the casualties was more than wonderful; no hysteria or complaints, grateful for any little thing done, some brought in after the terrible ordeal of being buried for some time, others terribly wounded.

My reactions to the first sight of wounded little children was the most dreadful experience, horror, red-hot anger, then utter helplessness. One little girl stands out in my mind—about nine years old—a direct hit on their home, the whole family being buried, including this child, blood streaming from her mangled face and her poor little body a mass of bruises. As she was sitting on the stretcher making pathetic shuddering noises, I put my arms around her and said 'Don't be frightened darling, we'll soon have you clean and comfy again'. Her indignant and scornful answer was: 'Frightened, who's frightened? I'm not frightened of Hitler's bombs, my daddy is a soldier and wait till he hears what has been done to our home and then see what he does to Hitler'. That was the spirit of all our casualties : hot resentment and indignation.

On another occasion when, towards the end of a particularly gruesome night, all our windows, doors and blackout had been blasted out, and when, without gas or electricity, we were working with the aid of hurricane lamps, a man came in and placed a bundle in my arms with the remark 'A little child, I don't know how much of it is there'. I felt cold and sick wondering what further horror was to meet my eyes. My knees literally knocking, I sat down with the bundle on my knees and fearfully removed a corner of the blanket, and to my utter amazement I saw a pair of bright blue eyes and a little voice piped out 'Hello, I's full of bricks'. You can imagine the inexpressible relief of that moment.

Plate XXVI illustrates a mobile canteen unit in action after a raid. These units proved themselves to be of great value as auxiliaries to the first-aid services.

CHAPTER 5
COVENTRY
August 1940 to July 1941

Contributed by
Arthur Massey, C.B.E., M.D., Medical Officer of Health, Coventry

COVENTRY had a population of 220,000 in 1938 which was estimated to have increased to 233,000 by June 1940, and 238,000 by September of that year. After the first heavy raid in November, the population fell by about 38,000 owing to the evacuation of homeless people, and continued to decrease until in June 1941, it was about 188,000. It is evident, therefore, that no large scale evacuation took place on account of the raids.

In the city the cycle industry was born about half a century ago, and from this there sprang in natural order the motor-car, machine tool, electrical and aircraft industries for which the town is famous. When civil defence first began to receive serious attention before the war, the Ministry of Home Security placed Coventry high in the list of likely target areas. The justification for this was shown all too well by subsequent events.

THE SCHEME OF EMERGENCY MEDICAL SERVICES

It was a feature of the local scheme that first-aid posts, ambulance depots and first-aid party depots were in all cases housed together under one roof. The separation in the central administration of the first-aid party service (Ministry of Home Security) from the first-aid post and ambulance services (Ministry of Health) was thus countered.

In the initial scheme there were nine such combined posts and depots. Of these, numbers 1 and 2 were located in clinic buildings, number 3 was in a public baths and numbers 4 to 9 were in large elementary schools. (See Plate XXVII). School buildings were found to be by far the most suitable, and moreover they were readily available at first on account of the large-scale evacuation of school children. But when, because of long periods of respite from enemy raids, the children returned home in numbers, difficulties arose in regard to the continued occupation of these buildings by the E.M.S. It was, however, deemed impossible to relinquish them, although in four cases joint use by E.M.S. and Education Authority was finally arranged. The posts covered the city area in such a way as to comply with the requirement, as then laid down, that no injured person should have to go more than one mile to reach a post. Medical and nursing staffs, ambulance drivers and first-aid men were allotted to the various posts and depots reasonably near to their homes.

A feature of the local staffing arrangements was a scheme whereby the leading engineering firms were 'affiliated' to nearby posts for the purpose of supplying squads of part-time trained first-aid men to the posts from among their workers. This greatly stiffened the city's first-aid party service.

Thirty full-time E.M.S. first line ambulances were allotted in the scheme. The original vehicles were converted commercial vans, which were crude and most unsatisfactory. Happily, these were quickly superseded by converted car ambulances, which proved quite suitable, and were eminently better than the various forms of trailer ambulances by which at that time a few scheme-making authorities were attracted. In addition to the Ministry of Health allotment of ambulances, ten new ambulances were presented to the city E.M.S. by Sir Alfred Herbert, K.B.E., and proved of very great value throughout the war. Then again, a dozen ambulances owned by the Coventry Hospital Saturday Fund and manned by St. John Ambulance Brigade personnel were available during raids. These also gave great assistance on the frequent occasions they were called. There were six mobile first-aid units located at selected fixed posts. The mobile units consisted of medically-equipped vans in which flying squads of doctors and nurses went to air raid incidents.

There were two centrally situated casualty clearing hospitals in the city, namely, the Coventry and Warwickshire Hospital (voluntary, 425 beds) and the Gulson Road Municipal Hospital (350 beds). Under the Ministry of Health group scheme, these hospitals were linked up for 'decanting' purposes with outside hospitals in the surrounding reception areas. For the necessary inter-hospital transport eight converted bus ambulances were provided.

The available emergency mortuary accommodation originally made provision for 450 bodies. The local casualty bureau was organised as a part of the Public Health Department office.

Anti-gas Arrangements. At each first-aid post a fixed anti-gas cleansing unit was provided for the cleansing of injured contaminated persons. In 1941, six mobile cleansing units were supplied, consisting of boilers and showerbath apparatus mounted on motor lorries. The idea of mobile services was further developed in Coventry by the use of marquees in association with mobile cleansing units and mobile first-aid units working together. A marquee was carried on each vehicle. The whole combined unit under cover could be set up in twenty minutes. In the first marquee the showers were accommodated, divided into male and female sides by canvas screens. The second marquee was joined endwise to the first and in it was set out the medical and surgical equipment from the mobile first-aid van. Thus complete movable units were available for combined cleansing and first aid.

There were also provided certain showerbath units for the cleansing of uninjured contaminated persons. A feature of the Coventry scheme was the installation of these units near or in local laundries. The advantages of this were that hot water supplies were already at hand and skilled laundry workers were available as volunteers to staff the units. Tanks for the decontamination of gas-fouled clothing were also provided as a part of these units.

In the absence of enemy gas attacks, the cleansing arrangements were often employed usefully in the campaign against lousiness and scabies. After the big air attacks on the city when water supplies were cut off in many districts, the cleansing units still in commission were made available to the public as baths and were widely used.

THE AIR RAIDS

The table opposite sets out the sequence of enemy air attacks on the city and gives information as to the casualties and material damage sustained. It will be seen that there were several small raids before the first big attack. This was as well because the local civil defence services thereby became progressively experienced in their work, and when later the supreme demand came, they were equal to the task.

WEIGHT OF ATTACK AND CASUALTIES

Having regard to the number and weight of enemy attacks on Coventry, the casualties were not heavy. In all raids collectively, 1,248 persons were killed, 1,851 seriously injured and 1,189 slightly injured.

Estimates of weight of attack and of resultant casualty rates varied widely. Local estimates gave bomb weights of over 1,000 tons for all attacks, the estimated weight of H.E. for the three heavy attacks of November 14–15, 1940, April 8–9 and April 10–11, 1941, being 500, 210 and 153 tons respectively. Based on these figures, supplied by the Police and Observer Corps, the casualties per ton weight of bombs dropped were: for all raids killed 1·11, seriously injured 1·69 and slightly injured 1·08. In the individual large scale raids the figures were: November 14–15, 1940, 1·14, 1·73 and 0·79; April 8–9, 1941, 1·33, 2·71 and 0·70; April 10–11, 1941, 1·27, 0·86 and 0·95.

The Research and Experiments Department of the Ministry of Home Security, on the other hand, estimated that the total weight of bombs in all attacks was only 440–510 (metric) tons. ('The Effects of the G.A.F. Raids on Coventry, Based on the Results of a Social Survey'; Ministry of Home Security Report R.E.N. 441, Table I.) Taking the middle figure (475 tons) the casualty rates per ton for all raids were: killed 2·6, seriously injured 3·9, slightly injured 2·5. For the heavy raid of November 14–15, 1940, which occurred before the bomb census was extended to Coventry, the weight of attack estimated by the Department (200–250 metric tons) gave the following rates per metric ton: killed 2·5, seriously injured 3·8 and slightly injured 1·75. On November 19, 1940 the bomb census was started in Coventry, the census area being a circle of radius

Air Raids on the City of Coventry

No. of raid	Date of raid	Persons killed M.	Persons killed W.	Persons killed C.	Persons seriously injured M.	Persons seriously injured W.	Persons seriously injured C.	Persons slightly injured M.	Persons slightly injured W.	Persons slightly injured C.	Damage to houses Demolished or practically so	Damage to houses Substantially damaged
1	August 18, 1940	—	—	—	—	—	—	—	—	—	—	—
2	20	—	—	—	—	—	—	—	—	—	—	20
3	25	—	—	—	—	—	—	—	—	—	—	—
4	26	—	—	—	2	1	—	11	—	—	2	26
5	28	—	—	—	1	2	—	2	2	2	—	2
6	September 16	10	5	1	9	2	1	19	6	4	5	281
7	26	9	8	1	3	1	3	10	17	3	12	287
8	October 12	16	10	5	4	9	—	30	13	—	—	84
9	14	7	14	1	18	9	—	35	13	—	23	373
10	19	6	9	—	32	8	—	62	12	—	39	269
11	19	—	—	—	14	8	—	28	—	—	43	551
12	20	17	7	—	24	10	2	34	14	1	72	1,127
13	21	8	8	1	19	18	—	38	27	—	102	979
14	22	16	6	—	10	5	1	20	12	—	11	110
15	26	—	—	—	1	—	—	—	—	—	—	—
16	27	2	3	1	5	5	2	11	2	—	16	333
17	29	2	2	—	5	4	5	10	2	9	5	212
18	November 1	5	5	3	15	10	4	18	12	—	8	239
19	2	—	—	—	1	1	—	—	—	—	—	—
20	5	—	—	—	—	—	—	2	2	2	5	7
21	7	—	—	—	—	—	—	—	—	—	4	4
22	8	—	—	—	—	—	—	—	1	—	1	116
23	12	—	—	—	—	—	—	—	—	—	—	—
24	14	282	189	97	509	303	51	272	102	19	2,067	87
25	16	—	—	—	—	—	—	—	—	—	—	40,061
26	19	—	1	—	—	—	—	—	—	—	—	—
27	December 11	4	2	—	2	4	1	9	9	—	4	—
28	January 7, 1941	—	—	—	—	—	—	—	—	—	—	—
29	8	—	—	—	—	—	—	—	—	—	4	500
30	March 11	1	—	—	—	1	—	—	—	—	—	147
31	April 7	—	—	—	—	—	—	—	—	—	3	71
32	8	—	—	—	—	—	—	—	—	—	—	—
33	9	195	74	11	327	227	16	102	28	11	948	18,188
34	10	—	—	—	—	—	—	—	—	4	—	—
35	June 5	121	61	12	101	30	1	100	41	—	—	—
36	10	—	1	—	—	—	—	—	—	—	—	—
37	July 5	3	3	—	8	2	4	3	3	1	17	331
	Totals											

Killed 1,248
Seriously injured 1,851
Slightly injured 1,189

M = Men W = Women C = Children

three miles centred at the Cathedral, and roughly equivalent to the city boundary. On this basis, the Department reported that in the heavy raid of April 8–9, 1941, 683 bombs fell, weighing in the aggregate about 85 metric tons, giving casualty rates per ton: killed (280) 3·3, seriously injured (570) 6·7, slightly injured (141) 1·7.

These differences between the casualty rates calculated by the local Medical Officer of Health and those given by the Research and Experiments Department of the Ministry of Home Security emphasise the fact that all are based on bomb weights which could not be definitely ascertained. Estimates made before the bomb census could be hardly more than guess-work, both as to the number of bombs and especially as to their size. In the latter respect even the bomb census findings rest on no firm foundation, for while the fact that a bomb had fallen was obvious to persons in the vicinity of the explosion, it required previous experience and the application of a process of reasoning to determine its size and weight. There could be no certainty of finding sufficient fragments for identification of a bomb which had already been shattered or destroyed by its own explosion, and in the absence of such a means of identification the sizes of bombs were estimated on the evidence provided by the nature and extent of the damage caused. Obviously, weights of attack thus determined could only be approximate, but the method provided a useful means of comparison between the various raids to which it was applied.

Of the 568 fatal casualties in the November raid, 53 persons were killed while taking refuge in public air raid shelters. The corresponding figures for the two April raids were 474 and 40. The largest number killed at any one time in a shelter was 27.

THE GREAT RAID OF NOVEMBER 14–15, 1940

The attack began at 19.15 hours on November 14, and ended at 05.35 hours the next morning. There was a full moon. The first wave of enemy aircraft dropped a large number of flares and soon the whole city was almost 'as light as day'. Thereafter waves of bombers came over at half-hourly intervals for over ten hours; some thirty thousand incendiaries, twelve hundred high explosive bombs and fifty parachute-mines were dropped. The city centre was soon a mass of flames and big fires were widespread in other parts. The reinforced fire service was handicapped by an early shortage of water and the water supply in fact gave out completely during the night; the fires burnt themselves out in some cases over a period of days. The damage by fire and explosion was devastating. This raid was the first large scale attack on a provincial town. Coventry took the headlines of the world press and the word 'coventrate' was added boastfully by the Germans to their vocabulary.

Casualties. The casualties were not as numerous as the severity of the attack might have led an observer to suppose. The killed numbered 568,

863 persons were seriously injured (hospital cases) and 393 slightly injured (first-aid post cases). The population at risk had been much reduced by evacuation after previous raids. During and after the big raid, there was a large exodus of people from the city, but it never degenerated into a panic. The outgoing crowds were fed by mobile canteens and army field kitchens and were sheltered in accommodation quickly found or improvised in the rural areas around.

Damage to First-aid Posts, etc. Three of the nine first-aid post depots were destroyed. Fortunately, the personnel and vehicles were withdrawn from the demolished posts before the final destruction—in two cases on account of early unexploded bombs on the premises. The only casualties among E.M.S. personnel were one killed, three seriously injured and ten slightly injured. The central E.M.S. stores was hit with incendiaries and gutted by fire with a total loss of contents. Of the vehicles, 22 ambulances and two first-aid party cars were appreciably damaged.

Damage to Hospitals. Of the two local casualty clearing hospitals, one, the Coventry and Warwickshire Hospital, was extensively damaged, although some 200 beds were left intact. The other, the Gulson Road Municipal Hospital, was less seriously damaged. All patients from the two hospitals were successfully evacuated by bus ambulances to peripheral hospitals in neighbouring reception areas under the Ministry of Health Scheme.

Central Control. The Council House, which accommodated the municipal administration and which housed in its basement the civil defence central control, escaped major damage. This was miraculous, for around it on three sides was a sea of fire which gutted the adjacent Cathedral and many other important buildings nearby. The survival of the central administration contributed greatly to effective control during the raid and to the reconstruction of essential services afterwards.

Ambulance Work. The street collection of casualties was carried on by the ambulance and first-aid party services throughout the night—as far as possible in the intervals between the waves of the attack. At first, the stretcher cases were conveyed to the two hospitals near the city centre. The concentration of bombing on the central area and the damage to the central hospitals themselves, however, soon indicated the necessity of directing all casualties to outside hospitals or to first-aid posts at or near the city perimeter. All the injured were got away to external hospitals by noon on November 15.

Mortuary Services. The collection of the dead then began. It was necessary to use ambulances because the mortuary lorries were insufficient. The bulk of the bodies were brought in during the following forty-eight hours, but for some weeks afterwards occasional remains were unearthed in the course of debris clearance. The emergency mortuary sustained extensive damage to the roof and the mortuary office was totally destroyed. The water supplies were cut off. These conditions, together with the large number of bodies to be dealt with and the severe mutilation of many of them, caused difficulty and embarrassment. Staffing the mortuary also presented a problem because most of the volunteers previously enrolled did not report. The problem was met by obtaining the assistance of a number of first-aid party men who volunteered for these duties and of volunteer military personnel supplied by the Army Authorities. The necessary work at the mortuary was successfully accomplished despite all difficulties.

Interment of Air Raid Victims. Each body had a separate coffin. The bodies were reverently interred in large trench-graves at the London Road Cemetery, and two public funeral services were held, on November 19, 1940 and November 23, 1940 respectively. For various reasons, private funerals were prohibited. The general verdict was that the public funerals were most impressive and certainly those who attended will never forget the experience.

Assistance. At the height of the raid, the mutual assistance scheme was invoked by the Region and ambulance services were drafted to the city from neighbouring midland cities and towns, notably Birmingham. It was most difficult for the incoming services to contact the Coventry posts owing to smashed roads and like obstacles. But the services managed to gain an entrance and were of great assistance. The St. John Ambulance Brigade in Coventry gave valuable help in this and all other raids, notably in the unloading squads supplied to the hospitals and in ambulance work. The British Red Cross organisation also assisted greatly with ambulances and equipment, notably by the loan of mobile X-ray units. In the casualty bureau, certain of the local clergy gave useful service in helping to deal with the mass of relatives' inquiries.

E.M.S. Personnel. The E.M.S. personnel worked magnificently throughout and several members later received well-earned recognition.

Lessons of the Raid. Of the three first-aid posts destroyed in the November 1940, raid, two were not replaced while the third was re-established in a school building near the city boundary. Experience had shown that the majority of air raid casualties were outside the minor injury category for which the first-aid posts were originally intended. The policy therefore was to reduce the number of posts, to retain mainly the peripheral ones and to widen their functions.

Experience confirmed the view that treatment given by first-aid party men at incidents should be minimised, and that in fact their chief job was quick collection and loading of casualties and participation in rescue work.

Though the mobile first-aid units had been most useful in dealing with scattered incidents in small raids, they were not practical—for their original purpose of 'setting up' near incidents—under concentrated attack.

PLATE XXVII. A typical First-Aid Post in a school.

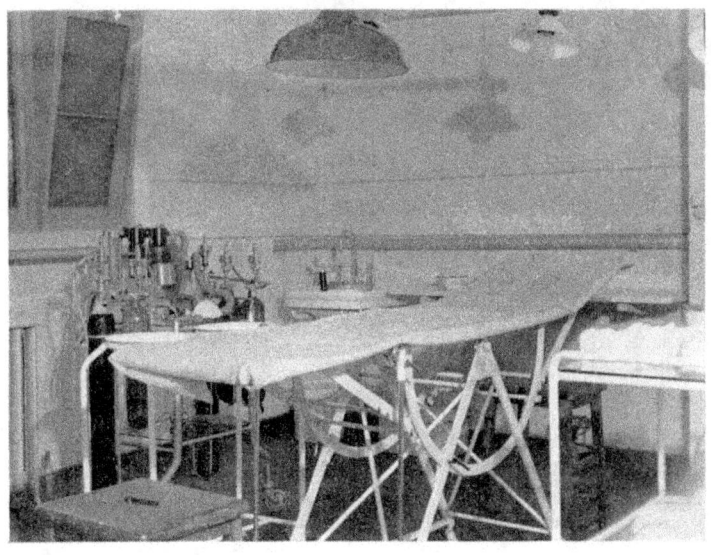

PLATE XXVIII. Operating theatre in upgraded perimeter First-Aid Post.

Coventry Evening Telegraph

PLATE XXIX. Coventry and Warwickshire Hospital, a wrecked wing, April 1941.

Coventry Evening Telegraph

PLATE XXX. Coventry and Warwickshire Hospital, scene following raid, April 1941.

Doctors at incidents were invaluable, not only for the immediate administration of morphia and like services, but also as custodians of morale. A local scheme had been formulated, whereby a rota of doctors willing to attend incidents was available at selected posts. This worked well in the big raid and there were notable instances of gallantry in this work.

Clearance of Casualties at the Perimeter. The major lesson taught by the November 1940, attack was the danger resulting from a central location of casualty clearing hospitals. The enemy technique was to 'plaster' the inner circle of the town and the supreme difficulties of clearing casualties at hospitals sited in the zone of maximum bombing were very soon apparent. During the raid, it became necessary to improvise a scheme of perimeter clearance by reversing the flow of ambulance traffic and directing it outwards to peripheral hospitals in the surrounding reception areas in Warwickshire. Many stretcher cases were also perforce delivered to the first-aid posts in the outer ring of the city and difficulties were encountered from the serious nature of the injuries with which the posts, with their necessarily limited equipment, were called upon to deal. The difficulties were somehow overcome, however, and the lesson was duly registered.

In consequence, a concrete scheme of casualty clearance at the perimeter was devised. This was described in the *British Medical Journal* of July 26, 1941 ('Clearance of Urban Air Raid Casualties at the Perimeter' by A. Massey, G. G. Alderson and C. F. Brockington). The following is an outline of the local scheme:

Five perimeter casualty clearing stations were established in selected existing first-aid posts located in large school buildings situated respectively in the northern, eastern, southern, south-western and western sectors of the city. The posts in question were 'upgraded' to meet the needs of their extended function. The upgrading included the provision of beds, operating rooms (see Plate XXVIII), resuscitation facilities and full surgical equipment. The medical and nursing staffs were strengthened as necessary. The clearing stations were linked up on a geographical basis with the outside base hospitals in the reception areas. Thus the northern station linked with Nuneaton, the eastern station with Rugby, the southern station with Warwick and Leamington, the south-western station with Stratford-on-Avon and the western station with Marston Green (Canadian War Hospital). Under the scheme, city ambulances were responsible for the conveyance of casualties from city incidents to the perimeter stations, while Warwickshire county ambulances (by arrangement between county and city) conveyed from perimeter stations to outside hospitals. The county ambulances reported automatically at the perimeter stations on intimation from city control to county control that the scheme was to operate.

The perimeter scheme, although not completed at the time, was sufficiently advanced to work successfully in the two big raids on

Coventry in April 1941. The scheme was later completed in all details. The value of the scheme will be appreciated when it is mentioned that in the April 1941, raids, now to be described, one of the city's two central hospitals was destroyed, while the other was again badly hit.

THE RAIDS OF APRIL 1941

The attacks took place on April 8–9 and April 10–11, 1941, in moonlight. The usual technique of preliminary flares was adopted. On these occasions a considerable weight of high explosives was dropped, but the weight of incendiaries was small compared with the November 1940, attack. The number of casualties in the two April raids together was about the same as that of the single big attack in the previous November.

A Hospital destroyed. The city's voluntary hospital, the Coventry and Warwickshire Hospital, was largely destroyed in the attack on April 8. The main blocks were struck time after time during the night with high explosive bombs and by early morning the hospital was a mass of wreckage (Plate XXIX). Some 200 beds were put out of commission in the one night; an equal number had been lost in former raids, notably in the previous November attack. The first bombs on the hospital on April 8 struck the out-patient department and damaged the reception hall. A few air raid casualties had already been brought in and operative work was in progress at the time. After the early direct hits on the out-patient building, admissions ceased, and by then in any case central control had brought the perimeter casualty clearing scheme into operation. But the hospital had already a considerable number of routine acute cases. While the bombs were striking the hospital buildings, the patients as far as possible were transferred on stretchers to the basement. Patients and staff braved the inferno until the 'all clear' was sounded at daybreak. At this stage the evacuation of patients from the basement of the hospital began (Plate XXX). The culminating disaster was the explosion of a delayed action bomb which had apparently buried itself in the ground on which at the time of the explosion doctors and nurses were at work arranging the evacuation of patients. Two doctors and seven nurses and a number of patients were killed in this incident. The task of evacuating the hospital was then carried on to completion; the patients were taken in bus ambulances to various outside hospitals in the group.

Casualties at the Hospital. The casualties at the hospital were as follows:—Killed: 21 patients, 2 doctors, 7 nurses and 2 male porters; injured: 14 nurses. Throughout the ordeal, the hospital staff worked splendidly and the behaviour of the patients was exemplary. There were many acts of gallantry, several of which later received recognition. A graphic account of the suffering of the hospital was contributed by the House Governor and Secretary, Mr. S. C. Hill, to the 1941 *Hospitals Year Book*.

The Municipal Hospital. The Gulson Road Municipal Hospital also received hits in both April raids. Although the picture was not nearly so dramatic as that at the Coventry and Warwickshire Hospital, there was, nevertheless, wonderful work performed there, and here again there were many acts of bravery. The Municipal Hospital, owing to its vulnerable central position next to a big engineering works, had for some time previously been run on the lines of a casualty clearing station, and there were very few patients in the hospital before the raids. Such few patients as there were, together with air raid casualties admitted, were safely evacuated to outer hospitals. There were no casualties among the Municipal Hospital staff. Among E.M.S. personnel (excluding hospital staffs) there were no fatalities and but two injured in the April raids. The first-aid posts escaped serious damage.

Public Funerals. The mortuary arrangements after the raids worked smoothly. Again it was necessary to prohibit private funerals. All the dead were buried on April 15, and a most dignified public funeral marked the occasion.

Although they had performed well in the November attack, the city's E.M.S. worked even better in the April 1941 raids. It was evident that the November experience had been assimilated to advantage. The perimeter clearing scheme operated with marked success.

DISTINGUISHED VISITORS

H.M. The King visited Coventry on November 16, 1940, immediately after the big raid and toured the stricken city on foot. His visit was a source of great inspiration and comfort to the citizens. The King again visited the city on February 25, 1942, this time accompanied by H.M. The Queen. Their Majesties made a special inspection of the bombed voluntary hospital.

On two occasions H.R.H. The Duchess of Gloucester visited the town and inspected St. John, British Red Cross and E.M.S. personnel, hospitals, first-aid posts and ambulance depots. This gave great pleasure and encouragement to the staffs concerned. Another fillip to civil defence morale was given by the visit in 1941 of the Prime Minister, The Rt. Hon. Winston Churchill.

Among the further welcome visitors were the Minister of Health, The Rt. Hon. Ernest Brown, who made a tour of hospitals, war-time day nurseries and air raid shelters, and Surgeon-General Thos. Parran of U.S.A., who came in early 1941 to inquire at first hand about post-raid epidemiological problems.

COMMENTARY

Before concluding this account of the E.M.S. in Coventry, mention must be made of the work of the Regional organisation and the Ministries concerned. Guidance and help on the spot were always forthcoming from these sources, alike in the initial organisation of services, in the heat of the air attacks and in post-raid reconstruction. The splendid work of the National Emergency Committee of the Coventry City Council is also recorded, for the chairman and members of this committee were a tower of strength to the officers charged with the direction of the E.M.S. The personnel of the city Public Health Department and of the E.M.S. were unremitting in their devotion to duty. They did a great job as 'mere civilians' without military glory.

POST-RAID PUBLIC HEALTH CONSIDERATIONS

The damage to property in the heavy raids was widespread and included extensive injury to sewerage, drainage and water communications.

The Typhoid Hazard. The consequent typhoid hazard occasioned much concern. Fractured or smashed sewers allowed sewage to flow into basements and bomb-craters. Wide damage to water pipes deprived many districts of water supplies. This at any rate limited the problem of escaping sewage by causing in the affected districts a suspension of the water carriage system. Water mains and sewers usually run in widely separate channels and thus damage to both in common craters was comparatively rare. Nevertheless, the general menace to the public water supply was considerable.

Chlorination of Water. In consequence of former raids, routine chlorination of the water supply was in operation before the first heavy attack; after it an increased dose was put in. The augmented dosage was continued for some weeks after each large-scale raid. A tribute is here due to the City Water Department for their care and vigilance.

Advice to Public. Intensive local propaganda was used on each necessary occasion to urge the boiling of drinking water and milk. Press, posters and Ministry of Information loud-speaker vans were freely used. The absence of gas supplies in many parts of the town did not make matters easier, but it is certain that the public did all they could to co-operate. Publicity was also invoked to impress upon makers and purveyors of foodstuffs the special need for cleanliness in spite of difficulties due to water shortage. Not the least important of the spheres of propaganda was that which gave advice to the general public, to protect themselves against typhoid fever by means of inoculation.

Sanitation Problem. All possible steps were taken by the Corporation Departments concerned to secure the early restoration of sewers and water pipes. Engineers and sanitary inspectors worked together in locating and assessing damage to sewers, and gangs directed by the City Engineer's Department did rapid 'first-aid' work. Sewage was pumped out of each crater and was taken away in tumbler carts. First aid then consisted in rodding the distal section of the broken sewer and making an open clay channel to permit a resumption of flow. The permanent making good of broken sewers followed on as soon as possible.

Restoration of Water Supply. In the districts temporarily cut off from the piped water supply, regular water-cart patrols were at first arranged. But surface water mains were quickly brought into use with stand pipes at appropriate points.

Anti-typhoid Inoculation. After the November 1940, attack, three typhoid immunisation clinics were opened—two at hospitals and one at a large central first-aid post. In addition one of the mobile first-aid units was used as a mobile immunisation clinic. These clinics were run by Public Health Department staff. The employees of large factories were inoculated at their places of work either by the works' medical officers or by private practitioners called in for the purpose. The factory managements feared at first that reactions after the inoculations might lead to serious loss of working time. Misgivings in this connexion proved to be unwarranted. About 18,000 persons were immunised during the four weeks following the November raid. This was not a big response for the large population at risk, but it is to be remembered that there were no precedents for mass anti-typhoid inoculation of civil populations and moreover the supreme stimulus which the occurrence of actual typhoid cases would have given was not present. No typhoid cases attributable to raid conditions did in fact occur.

The Rat Menace. Beneath many of the bombed sites, foodstuffs and bedding lay buried near to broken and unsealed drains. These conditions favoured rat infestation on a large scale and for a time there was a veritable menace. Concentrated measures of attack were brought to bear, however, and the position was relieved.

Housing. The table shows the enormous damage to houses which resulted from the local raids. A big programme of first-aid repair work soon restored a considerable percentage of the damaged houses to use. Nevertheless, the net loss of housing accommodation was serious and could not be set off by new building in war-time. This, together with the general return of population to the city, gave rise to much overcrowding. There was one bright feature of the bombing, namely, that many of the demolished houses were slum properties. Of the 2,213 unfit dwellings included before the war in a local slum clearance programme, which was to have taken place during the period 1940–4, 891 were demolished in air raids.

HOSPITAL POLICY AND CITY PLANNING

The events of the war, and in particular the effects of the heavy raids on the hospital services of Coventry, demanded a complete review of local hospital policy. As already described, the Coventry and Warwickshire Hospital lost all its in-patient accommodation as a result of enemy action in April 1941. The hospital authorities during the following year provided some replacement by re-establishing the hospital nucleus at their Convalescent Home just outside the city boundary and by the erection of certain emergency wards there. This action helped the immediate situation without prejudicing the future broad issues of hospital policy.

The Gulson Road Municipal Hospital was hit by enemy bombs on several occasions as previously mentioned, and could only be used as a clearing hospital. This was a consequence of its central site in the shadow of a large engineering works. Apart altogether from war considerations, evidence had long been accumulating to emphasise that in any case the Gulson Road site was quite unsuitable for a Municipal Hospital worthy of the city, the modern idea being all in favour of siting hospitals on the perimeter. In March 1942, the City Council decided on the policy of providing immediately after the war a large new general hospital on a perimeter site already acquired. Consultations later took place between municipal and voluntary hospital authorities both of whom were facing radical post-war hospital reconstruction. The outcome was the formation of a joint committee to consider how the city's general hospital services could be unified—potentially an epoch-making development.

The razing by enemy action of large central areas of Coventry has given wide opportunities of future redevelopment and ambitious plans to this end were adopted during the war by the City Council. Among the new buildings provided for in the scheme are the large general hospital foreshadowed above and a chain of district health centres from which it is hoped the new concept of medicine will radiate.

CHAPTER 6
SOUTHAMPTON
June 1940 to July 1941

Contributed by
H. C. Maurice Williams, O.B.E., M.R.C.S., L.R.C.P., D.P.H., *Medical Officer of Health, County Borough and Port of Southampton*

THE area of Southampton in December 1938, was 9,599 acres, excluding tidal waters. The estimated population in December 1938, was 180,100. By June 1940, the estimated population based on ration cards was 172,900. This gradually decreased during the succeeding quarters, until by the end of June 1941, the population was only 126,000. The whole of this reduction was due to evacuation. The use of the docks was given up and all engaged in loading and unloading ships, etc., were transferred to other ports. Many homeless people were billeted in rural areas.

THE CASUALTY SERVICE BEFORE THE WAR

As in other towns, the first steps to bring a local casualty service into being were considered in 1936, and, in Southampton, it was felt by all concerned that the necessary organisation should be in readiness in case of war, because this busy port was almost certain to be a special object of enemy attacks. But between 1936 and 1938 there was no clearly defined policy or plan. In his Annual Report in 1938, the Medical Officer of Health drew attention to this state of affairs and urged the formation of such a policy and plans, based on peace-time experiments, 'rather than mental vacillation'. Instead of relying on purely voluntary effort, he recommended a system in which personnel would be under contractual obligation and that officers of various grades exercising control over the rank and file should be appointed. He further recommended that a full-time assistant medical officer of health for the A.R.P. services should be appointed to train personnel in first aid and other duties and Surgeon Rear-Admiral R. W. G. Stewart, O.B.E., R.N. (ret.) was appointed, Southampton being the first County Borough Corporation to make such an appointment.

THE OUTBREAK OF WAR

And then the war came. War, with all its excitement, its tenseness and its grim forebodings. That calm Sunday morning in September 1939, when Mr. Chamberlain told the world that Britain had gone to war, found Southampton's youth population already depleted by many thousands, for the evacuation of school children had started a few days before. With banners announcing the names of their schools, the evacuees marched in long lines to the Central Station, where a mobile first-aid unit performed the first war task of the medical services. This unit had been detailed to deal with first-aid work that might be necessary, or to examine any children suspected to have infectious disease. Although evacuation was the responsibility of the Education Department, who had laid their plans well, the medical services were closely concerned with the transfer of thousands of children and expectant mothers to reception areas, and could sympathise with the evacuation authorities in the difficulties with which they had to contend. The schedule was often upset by the last minute withdrawal of children who had been registered for evacuation; and by the last minute and unexpected arrival at the station of hundreds of children who had not been registered. Altogether, about 14,000 children, including those from secondary schools, were evacuated to the outlying parts of Hampshire and, further afield, to Dorset and Somerset.

Because the expected raids did not come, it was not very long before many of the parents were bringing their children home again. Although in the first few weeks of the war the housewives who received the little refugees could scarcely do enough for them, the novelty of having guests frequently wore off, and there is no doubt that the combination of homesick letters, unsuitable billets and complete quiet on the home front, decided many parents to bring their children back. After a few months, the whole scheme was in danger of being completely upset, for evacuation began to be a 'shuttle' business. Nearly 50 per cent. of the evacuees were back in the town when the raids started, and further emergency evacuations took place.

Code messages which had been coming in throughout the week before September 3, 1939, emphasised the imminence of war, and decided the chief officers of the Corporation to make their departments their homes. Beds were installed, and for days and nights on end, many scarcely left the Civic Centre, in which Southampton's administrative departments are grouped.

One of the tasks of the Medical Officer of Health's Department was to clear the town's hospitals in readiness to receive expected air raid casualties. This evacuation was carried through in conjunction with the Group Officer, who, together with the Medical Officer of Health, was responsible to the Hospital Officer of the Region. When all this had been done, there remained in Southampton approximately 1,000 beds in Class I hospitals, and about 1,200 in Class II hospitals. The sand-bagging of wards, the construction of underground operating theatres, and the provision of shelters, were among the many emergency works which had to be put in hand.

By this time, thirteen first-aid depots, in conjunction with ambulance stations, had been established. There were also nine fixed first-aid posts, and nine mobile first-aid units. The fixed establishments, some of which were in the first instance attached to hospitals, were mainly staffed by part-time personnel. It was soon found that the establishment of these depots in hospitals was not a satisfactory arrangement, through the failure of some of the personnel to conform to normal hospital discipline. Eventually, alternative accommodation had to be found for these depots, first in schools, and when these were again required by the Education Department, in private houses requisitioned by the Corporation.

Quite prudently, the Government expected much heavier casualties than occurred, and the Ministry of Home Security fixed the full-time establishment for first-aid parties in Southampton at 600. This figure was never attained, the maximum reached being 265. As the war progressed, and the demands on man-power became more acute, this figure of 265 was reduced by about one-half.

On the evening of May 18, 1940, a strange-looking and pathetic 'armada' sailed up Southampton Water. It was made up of an extraordinary miscellany of craft ranging from fishing trawlers to 'hopper' barges, from a harbour master's launch to stoutly-built tugs. And the decks of every craft in the long lines that headed for Southampton Docks were crammed with the first of the refugees from Europe. Here was urgent and unexpected work for the medical services. Within a week, thousands of Belgians, Dutchmen and Frenchmen, and women and children had sought sanctuary. They all had to be medically examined as they came ashore. Cubicles were erected in the customs sheds on the quays, and through these they filed for examination. Some were verminous and had to be bathed; some were suffering from infectious diseases; many were ill through worry.

Right up to the end of July the refugees came—in their thousands at first, and later in a thinning stream. By September 4, 6,147 Belgian, Dutch and French refugees had landed. Of this total, 1,098 French subjects were sent back to France. In the middle of these landings, there also came 2,424 refugees from the Channel Islands, all of whom arrived between June 20 and 29. Public assistance institutions, a sportsdrome and other buildings in the town were used to give them shelter, until arrangements could be made for their permanent care. Most of the Channel Islanders were sent to Barnsley or Wakefield.

THE FIRST RAIDS

Those who had to administer the medical services encountered many difficulties during the early days of the war, when the lack of activity brought about a marked decline in enthusiasm and discipline of personnel. All this was immediately altered when the first bombs fell on Southampton, early on the morning of June 20, 1940. The casualty services, in common with all other branches of A.R.P., showed themselves ready and equal to their first test. The first bomb to fall on the town hit a garage and petrol filling station in the Millbrook area, and seemed to signal the end of waning enthusiasm and flagging interest in A.R.P. work, a branch of Civil Defence which, up to that hour, had been increasingly criticised as a waste of money and man-power. Naturally, there were many lessons to be learned from this first raid, chief among them, the necessity for the utmost care in reporting incidents to the report centres. There was, on this occasion, much exaggerating of casualties and damage; there was also overlapping. Many of the services sent out much more equipment than was required. The total casualties in this raid were six seriously injured, who were taken to hospital; and two slightly injured, who were treated in a first-aid post.

And then there was a lull until August 13, 1940, when the town had its first daylight raid. Twenty-three H.E. bombs were dropped, one of them demolishing a furniture depository at the lower end of the town, near the docks. A cold storage company's building was set on fire, and burned for ten days. This fire was a menace to public health, because of the noxious fumes from burning fat and the rapid breeding of flies which resulted. The Food Salvage Department, then in its infancy and untested, was not able to deal with the situation with the speed it demanded.

The first George Medal conferred upon a Southampton man was awarded to William Wyatt Fisher, a labourer employed in the docks, who was raised in a crane sling to the roof of the cold storage building where, amidst anti-aircraft shells which were being exploded by the heat, he rescued an A.A. gunner who was lying injured near his gun.

From the early autumn of 1940, heavy and frequent daylight and night attacks began to be made on the town, and during the night hours there was almost incessant gunfire, not only night after night, but also week after week. This accustomed the Civil Defence Services to the more persistent attacks which led up to their severest tests during the winter of 1940–1. It also focused attention on the immediate need for protecting the population from possible outbreaks of the typhoid group of fevers because of the danger of drinking water which might get contaminated by sewage, although the necessity for boiling water after a raid had long been emphasised in pamphlets and through the Press. Clinics were established, and free inoculation was offered to the public. Approximately 30,000 people availed themselves of this protection.

It was thought that with so many thousands of people spending many hours nightly in public and private shelters, the incidence of infectious disease would increase greatly, but this did not happen, except for a widespread outbreak of scabies. Both diphtheria and scarlet fever remained at pre-war level.

On September 9, 1940, because of the threat of invasion, instructions were received to 'clear hospitals' in coastal areas on the following day. Patients from Winchester, Romsey, Lymington, Milford-on-Sea, Lyndhurst and Cold East Hospitals were brought to Southampton, and, with patients from hospitals in the borough, were evacuated in two casualty evacuation trains and one hospital ambulance train. A total of 448 patients were evacuated, the movement being completed by 1551 hours on September 10. In spite of a few minor difficulties, the arrangements, on the whole, worked smoothly.

Not only had Southampton been well provided with Anderson and public shelters, but the public had, by spoken word and through the press, been made shelter-minded. This accounted largely for the fact that, as is shown later in this account of the many assaults on the town, casualties were much lower than might have been expected from the number of bombs dropped. A small section of shelter-users showed their appreciation of the protection offered in a strange way, by stealing electric lamps and fittings, by damaging the structures, and by fouling the shelters. But gradually there was a noticeable improvement in the conduct and habits of shelter-users. There is no doubt that the formation of shelter committees, the appointment of a shelter superintendent, and appeals to the people's sense of decency and civic pride all contributed to this improvement. Another factor which undoubtedly had a bearing on the total number of casualties in Southampton was the pre-war clearance of congested slum areas in the heart of the town and the transference of many thousands of workers to homes in the outlying districts.

The first objective raid on the town occurred on September 11, 1940. Up to this time, although the working class and residential areas had suffered extensively, establishments created for war industry had, in the main, escaped damage. A portion of an aircraft factory was demolished in daylight. The magnitude of the raid did not seem to be appreciated. The first call for aid did not come from the factory itself, but from a member of the general public who saw the bombs fall and who telephoned from a public call box, three-quarters of a mile away. Because casualties were underestimated, insufficient services were sent to the factory, although valuable aid was given by naval medical officers stationed at the airport adjoining the factory. Casualties had to be removed to hospital in any vehicles which happened to be passing or handy, ranging from lorries belonging to the factory to laundry vans and bakers' carts without any proper fitments. When the casualties reached hospital, the great majority were found to be severely shocked, and it appeared that the condition of many of them had been aggravated by the failure to await satisfactory transport. There was considerable difficulty in identifying the dead, because the majority of those killed were in dungarees and had left their identification cards in other parts of the factory. This emphasised the necessity for identity discs. In this raid there were 49 killed, 38 seriously injured, and 54 slightly injured.

It is both interesting and useful to compare the raid on this factory with what happened on September 24 and 26, 1940, when bombs were dropped on the Supermarine Works at Woolston. In the factory raid, there was little realisation of the extent of the damage or the number of casualties; improvisation was the only method of coping with the situation. On September 24 and 26, the situation was altogether different, for on these occasions all the medical services were mobilised and dispatched expeditiously. On September 24, bombs were dropped at 1330 hours before the receipt of the air raid warning 'red', and fell on the northern end of the Itchen Works, and on several trench shelters which were adjacent, but in which there were only a few workers since the 'red' warning had not been given at the time. The firm's first-aid post, situated in the Woolston block, about 600 yards from the actual damage, was untouched.

Two mobile first-aid posts were dispatched to the scene. One went to the Itchen Works, and, after the medical officer had carried out a survey of the casualties, was utilised as a 'classification point'. The other reported to the firm's first-aid post, and the staff, including the medical officer of the unit, co-operated with the firm's personnel. About 80 casualties were treated at this first-aid post. This raid followed almost exactly the pattern of an exercise which had been held at the Works some months previously, to obtain the co-operation of industrial firms; and one realised on this occasion the value of these exercises in accustoming personnel to co-operate with firms' first-aid personnel. Other parts of the town suffered damage on this day, and the total casualties were 42 killed, 65 seriously injured, and 98 slightly injured.

THE HEAVIER RAIDS

During the next attack, on September 26, also on the Supermarine Works, the Woolston Works, Itchen Works, and the block in which the first-aid post was situated were all very badly damaged. Emergency heating and lighting which had been provided by the firm were both put out of action. Oil fuel, the primary source of heating, flooded into the first-aid post, and added to difficulties by preventing the use of naked lights, such as hurricane lamps. Although a considerable area of Woolston adjacent to the factory was damaged, the original estimate of casualties, 250, proved to be an over-estimate, the total number being 147. For this reason, reinforcements were called in from other areas, and, although not needed in such large numbers, proved of considerable help in dealing with trapped casualties. Incidentally, throughout one's experiences of raids, there was almost invariably this inclination to overestimate both damage and casualties. Although, on this occasion, all the reinforcements could not be used, useful experience was gained in handling reinforcement problems, which proved of value when such help was really required two months later.

Another lesson learned from the happenings of September 26, was the great importance of all personnel and equipment proceeding direct to the incident to which they had been dispatched. It happened that on this occasion an attempt was made to divert first-aid parties to deal with a few casualties at Pear Tree Green, which was en route. The personnel had already been given strict instructions never to deviate from the route over which they had been sent, to ignore all attempts to divert them or their vehicles, and therefore proceed direct to the main incident.

It was on this day that the gas works were put out of action. For eight days there was no gas supply, and it was about one month before a complete supply was restored. A considerable amount of property in the vicinity of the gas works was destroyed, but casualties were surprisingly light, the totals for the day being 55 killed, 49 seriously injured, and 43 slightly injured. After these two big raids, there were small raids on September 29, and October 8, 1940.

It was a comparatively clear afternoon when, on November 6, at 1445 hours, raiders swept across the town and dropped twelve 500-lb. bombs on the centre of Southampton. One bomb hit the Art Gallery of the Civic Centre, penetrating the roof, and two floors, and exploding in the basement shelter. Seventeen children, who had been attending a class in the Art School, and who had been taken to the basement for safety, were killed. They were badly disfigured by burns from the explosion, and by falling debris. As it happened in the centre of the town, this incident attracted a big crowd of people who, to a certain extent, impeded the rescue operations. Mobile first-aid posts were soon in action, and on this occasion were found most useful. About 300 yards from the Civic Centre, in the commercial part of the town, solicitors' offices were demolished, and from the ruins of one of them a man of 68 was extricated alive after being buried for sixty-three hours. He lived only two-and-a-half hours after admission to hospital, but his survival for so long in the ruins was due to the fact that he was in a chair which had apparently fallen under a table as the result of the explosion, and to the fact that man, chair and table were all enveloped in the carpet of the room, which seemed to have diminished the shock.

Southampton had its first experience of parachute mines at 0500 hours on November 17, 1940, when they were dropped on several parts of the town, causing very considerable damage. Later in the day there was a raid with H.Es. The casualties from both these raids were: 55 killed, 57 seriously injured, and 65 slightly injured. At one of these incidents, where many houses were damaged, and where it was expected that there would be heavy casualties, the equipment from a mobile first-aid post was transferred to a veterinary surgeon's house, which was used as a temporary first-aid post. The casualties at this incident were: 14 dead, 5 seriously injured, and 2 slightly injured. Raids were increasing in frequency and intensity, and while there were no indications that the preparations made for them were inadequate, experience taught many ways and means of improving Civil Defence Services.

Before continuing the story of the actual raids, it may be instructive to summarise the arrangements at one of the hospitals—the Borough Hospital—as an illustration of the way in which Emergency Medical Services were organised. The first essential, it was found, was the provision of a suitable room for the reception of casualties, placed centrally and in such a position as to provide easy admission of the wounded from the ambulances. It was found important to have a highly experienced medical officer present in the reception hall to control the sorting of casualties, and so secure a minimum of interference with them. It was also of importance not to overload a particular ward with too many casualties at one time. In this hospital it was so arranged that there were four ground floor wards continuously in use for the reception of casualties: two male and two female. Arrangements were made for one of the resident medical officers to be on duty in each of the four wards, assisted by outside practitioners.

At least 50 per cent. of the casualties were found to be suffering from shock, and the main part of the ward doctor's work was to carry out a preliminary examination, apply resuscitation measures, and decide which casualties were in need of immediate operative treatment. The provision of heat cradles, saline, plasma and whole blood transfusions was an essential part of the emergency equipment. Those who had suffered from severe haemorrhage were given whole blood, but blood plasma was also found most effective for the treatment of shock. In patients who suffered from penetrating wounds of the chest, and where there was marked cyanosis and shock, oxygen was administered, usually by means of Tudor Edwards spectacles, as the B.L.B. oxygen mask often caused discomfort by compressing the nose. Great difficulty was found in getting volunteers to act as stretcher bearers, and ample stretcher trolleys were found to be essential in conveying patients between the reception hall and the ward, and between the ward and the operating theatre. Although there were three surgical teams allocated to the hospital, it was seldom, except in the very heavy raids, that the three teams were operating all at the same time.

Southampton had its first heavy night raid on November 23, 1940, when a warning at 1816 hours was followed almost immediately by many incendiary bombs in the east division of the town. First-aid posts and depots in this division were damaged. Early in the raid, Sydney House, a municipal clinic, was set on fire, and later demolished by H.Es. A mobile first-aid post stationed in the grounds was gutted by fire. For more than three hours bombs rained down incessantly on the east and central divisions, and in the former division, a passenger train received a direct hit. A mobile first-aid post was sent to the railway station nearest to the scene of the incident, and dealt with nine casualties, mostly foot and ankle injuries. When a report came that a cinema in the centre of the town had been damaged, another mobile first-aid post was sent to the incident, but it was found that the cinema had been emptied before it was struck. Resources were so taxed in this raid that reinforcements were sent for and a total of 20 first-aid parties, 22 ambulances, 6 sitting case cars, and 2 mobile first-aid posts arrived during the night from Winchester, Stockbridge, Bramdean, Bournemouth, Reading, Godalming and Guildford, in addition to those from adjoining parishes. Bournemouth sent mobile first-aid posts. The total casualties in this raid were 77 killed, 134 seriously injured, and 177 slightly injured. After the destruction of Sydney House, the tuberculosis, ante-natal, child welfare, and school clinics were all moved to a secondary school half a mile away, and continued to operate from there.

The following Saturday night, November 30, Southampton had one of the heaviest of all its raids, which lasted for eight hours. On this occasion, all services were hampered by the fact that the telephone exchange was out of action early in the raid. Certain direct lines belonging to the Police and Fire Brigade continued to operate for a considerable time, and two mobile first-aid posts were dispersed to suburban police stations, where the personnel could be contacted by telephone. Although the raid was distributed over the three divisions of the town, the heaviest attack was on the southern end of the central division, where a public shelter received a direct hit causing a large number of casualties. Early in the raid, the nurses' home at the Royal South Hants and Southampton Hospital was set on fire, and it was necessary to evacuate 78 patients from the hospital, while the raid was at its height. Eleven of the patients were removed to the Borough Hospital, and 67 to the Isolation Hospital, until arrangements could be made for their evacuation to base hospitals next morning.

It was also necessary to evacuate 50 patients when St. Mary's Public Assistance Institution was damaged. Some patients remained in the institution until it was finally evacuated next morning. Ringed by fires, Mount Pleasant first-aid post, the headquarters of the casualty services, had to be transferred. Casualties who had been taken to this post, but who were not in need of immediate hospital treatment, were taken with the staff to Itchen Secondary School. When this school was examined at daybreak, it was found that there was an unexploded bomb in the cleansing station, and seven more in the grounds. This, however, did not necessitate evacuation of the whole of the premises, as it was possible to use the eastern part of the school as a first-aid post.

At this time, first-aid party and ambulance service personnel were stationed at three depots, one in each division of the town, and there was a small subsidiary depot for part-time personnel in the east division. It became urgently necessary to evacuate personnel from the central division depot to the west division, and this transfer emphasised the importance of dispersal. As a result of this experience, three depots were afterwards established in each division, an arrangement very similar to that existing at the outbreak of war. Buildings gutted by fire during the night included the municipal clinic in East Park Terrace, and the municipal laboratory in the same road. The dental department, adjoining the clinic, was also damaged, but not sufficiently to prevent the maintenance of a skeleton service of all the clinics in this building, until alternative arrangements were made. A temporary municipal laboratory was set up at the Borough Hospital.

While rescue parties were still digging in the ruins, and many fires were still burning—the firemen were helpless because there was not enough water pressure to supply the hoses—and while everything was in a state of chaos, the raiders came back soon after dusk the next night. During this day, strenuous efforts were made to restore the essential medical services to meet a further attack. It was realised by this time that the German policy was to deliver on consecutive nights a series of concentrated attacks on particular towns. The first essential was to restore as quickly as possible the number of vacant beds in hospitals for the reception of other casualties. With this in mind, an early start was made in transferring 91 of the previous night's casualties that were fit to travel to base hospitals in the Region; 408 hospital patients were also removed out of the town to less vulnerable areas.

Telephones were constantly ringing with appeals for the evacuation of aged and infirm people whose homes had been destroyed or whose relatives had left. The department tried, as far as possible, to meet these requests by arranging with nursing homes and public assistance institutions outside the town to receive as many as possible. Mount Pleasant first-aid post had been evacuated on the previous night because of nearby fires. By daybreak, these fires were under control, and the staff returned to their headquarters in preparation for the next attack.

The central first-aid party depot and ambulance station, which had been transferred to the west division, was also able to return during the day. The casualty bureau was inundated with inquiries from relatives and friends seeking news. Five different casualty lists were published, identifying 12 dead and 90 of those in hospital seriously wounded. Reinforcements of medical personnel, who had arrived on the previous night, were housed in depots and first-aid posts.

Thus, Southampton awaited its next merciless attack, which started at 1808 hours and lasted until 0130 hours. It was the most difficult situation that the town's Civil Defence Force had had to face up to then. Even the Central Control had had to be moved to the edge of the town, where it was re-established at Bassett House, because some telephone communication was still possible in that area. Because of the almost complete breakdown of communications, which now could only be maintained rather unsatisfactorily by messenger services, instructions had been issued that each first-aid party and ambulance depot was to act independently, and deal with any calls which they might receive, at the same time maintaining what contact was possible with the corresponding report centre. In this way, a general, but rather vague picture of the situation was obtained throughout the raid.

As on the previous night, incidents were again scattered over the whole of the town. A large number of casualties occurred in the Portswood area, and a direct hit on a trench shelter in the centre of the town accounted for a further large number of dead. The Casualty Service buildings again suffered considerable damage. The first-aid party and ambulance depots at the Hampshire Girls' Orphanage, at Grosvenor Square Garage, and at Oatlands House, were all damaged, and an unexploded bomb near the Grosvenor Square depot necessitated its evacuation once again. On this occasion the depot was transferred to the Deanery School and University College first-aid posts. A public washhouse in Cook Street, which had been adapted for decontamination of protective clothing, was also damaged. Stoppage of a pump because of the failure of the electricity supply, resulted in the flooding of the underground first-aid post at Mount Pleasant School, which borders on a river, and by early morning the water had reached a depth of six inches. The control room of the medical services in this building was fortunately a few inches above water level. Movable equipment in the post was carried up to the ground floor of the building.

Medical services reinforcements, which had been drawn from a wide area, were divided between the west depot at Shirley, and the central depot at University College. Rescue work went on for days after these two shattering raids, and, until they were released on December 6, the reinforcements assisted as stretcher bearers in hospital, and helped at the mortuaries. After a few first-hour difficulties, the billeting arrangements made for the reinforcements worked smoothly, and, under extraordinarily difficult conditions, the canteen department provided ample and suitable food. As they had not expected a stay of more than a few hours in the town, most of the reinforcements were without a change of clothing, or shaving and washing requisites, and many had no money. But all these minor discomforts were overcome.

On this occasion the military authorities gave invaluable assistance. R.A.M.C. officers dealt with casualties at several incidents, and the military also provided despatch riders and sanitary inspectors. The work of the latter was of enormous help in supplementing the town's sanitary staff during this, its greatest testing time, when water mains and sewers had been damaged at many points. The sanitary inspectors assisted with the purification of the water, and water carts were used in certain districts of the town to provide fresh drinking water. The Red Cross organisation in the town also provided valuable assistance with rest centres and in other departments of the Emergency Service.

Because the Royal South Hants and Southampton Hospital had been damaged, the brunt of the work in this raid fell on the Borough Hospital.

During and after these two raids, a total of 256 casualties were admitted to this hospital, including 14 found to be dead on admission. A large-scale evacuation of hospitals had to be arranged, and between December 1 and 7, a total of 366 patients were removed from the Borough Hospital to hospitals outside the town. Sixty-seven patients who had been transferred from the Royal South Hants Hospital to the Isolation Hospital, were evacuated on December 1, and 17 infectious diseases cases were removed on December 3 to the Isolation Hospitals at Aldershot and Winchester. The huge number of homeless presented a most difficult problem. Some of the cases admitted to hospital were chronic sick who had been able to manage until their homes were damaged, or relatives were no longer available to nurse them. They were admitted to the Borough Hospital and later removed to a base hospital. During these two nights, two serious casualties occurred to first-aid party personnel. One man was seriously injured by an explosive incendiary bomb, and another received cuts from a plate-glass window. Both were eventually invalided out of the service. Conduct of the personnel, as a whole, was extraordinarily good, and special credit must be given to the women ambulance drivers, two of whom received the B.E.M. Casualties resulting from the raids on these two nights were: 137 killed, 242 seriously injured, and 149 slightly injured.

Raids between December 28, 1940, and March 26, 1941, resulted in 198 casualties of which 36 were killed, 68 seriously injured and 94 slightly injured.

Twelve parachute mines which were dropped in widely separated parts of the town on April 11, 1941, caused widespread damage. Mount Pleasant School was again damaged, but the first-aid post in the basement was able to function satisfactorily. Other first-aid depots which were damaged were those at Ludlow Road Schools and the Royal South Hants and Southampton Hospital. The total casualties in this raid were: 14 killed, 41 seriously injured, and 51 slightly injured.

On June 22, 1941, parachute mines were again dropped—18 on this occasion. Several fell in the Shirley area. The total casualties were: 12 killed, 35 seriously injured, and 42 slightly injured.

There was another heavy raid on July 8, 1941, when about 150 high explosive bombs were dropped, mainly in the central and west divisions, doing extensive damage. Casualties were: 38 killed, 30 seriously injured, and 65 slightly injured. This ended the period of heavy raiding and, apart from casual raiders, there were no further concerted attacks on the town; 2,400 bombs had been dropped, of which the estimated total weight was $410\frac{1}{2}$ tons. The casualties were 591 killed, 861 admitted to hospital and 939 treated at first-aid posts, a total of 2,391. The numbers killed and seriously injured per bomb were therefore 0·25 and 0·36 respectively and 1·4 and 2·1 per metric ton of bombs of all categories; comparatively speaking low figures. The proportion of seriously injured to killed was higher and the proportion of slightly injured lower than in other towns of this size. It is interesting to note that on April 11, 1941, and June 22, 1941, when the casualties were all caused by 30 paramines only, estimated to weigh one ton each, 26 persons were killed and 76 seriously injured, or 0·86 killed and 2·5 seriously injured per ton. This tends to bear out the findings of the Research and Experiments Department of the Ministry of Home Security that the casualties per ton weight of bombs dropped were much the same irrespective of the type and weight of bombs used.

CHAPTER 7
PORTSMOUTH
1940 to 1941

Contributed by
A. B. Williamson, O.B.E., T.D., M.D., M.A., B.Sc., *Medical Officer of Health, Portsmouth* and T. E. Roberts, M.B., B.S., M.R.C.S., *Acting Medical Officer of Health (September 1939 to October 1940)*

THE area of the City of Portsmouth was 9,223 acres and the estimated population at mid-1939 was 260,300. By the middle of 1940 this had decreased to 199,200 and in succeeding quarters enemy attacks resulted in further evacuation, so that at the end of September 1941, the population had declined to 136,500. The night population during the first half of 1941 was further considerably reduced, as many people left the city at night and returned to work in the daytime.

MEDICAL ORGANISATION

Preliminary Arrangements. Because of its association with the premier naval port of the Empire, Portsmouth took up passive air defence seriously from the beginning and was one of the first local authorities to prepare a scheme.

As early as March 1935, a plan for the treatment of casualties was presented to the Town Clerk by the Medical Officer of Health, and a foundation was laid for the casualty services, specific duties being allotted to all members of the Health Department. In January 1936, liaison was established with representatives of the Order of St. John and the British Red Cross Society; a committee called the First-aid and Medical Services Voluntary Committee was formed to assist the Medical Officer of Health in the recruitment and training of personnel and in the course of the next three years a large number of voluntary personnel was enrolled and trained. During 1938, a model first-aid post—gas-proof, blast-proof, and proof against the smaller bombs, with emergency lighting and filter plant and water supply—was erected at Milton Road in the grounds of St. Mary's Municipal Hospital. It was the first of its kind in the country and was the subject of special interest at the conference of the Royal Sanitary Institute in July of that year, when a large scale A.R.P. exercise was held and papers on A.R.P. subjects were read and discussed. Other existing buildings, such as halls and schools, were selected for first-aid posts and gas-cleansing centres, and at the time of the Munich crisis in September 1938, these were equipped and staffed at short notice.

The city area generally was divided into three parts, Southern, Northern and Cosham, in each of which a report and control centre was established, the A.R.P. Main Control being situated at the Guildhall. As far as possible combined first-aid party and ambulance depots were established in the same buildings or immediately adjoining first-aid posts, so that these sections of the casualty services might work in the closest co-operation, and districts were defined for which the various depots would be responsible in the event of a breakdown in communications.

Throughout the year 1939 preparations for an emergency proceeded systematically, so that when war broke out there were over 2,000 volunteers enrolled, the hospitals were prepared, the adaptation of the seven first-aid posts in schools was nearing completion, and equipment had been packed ready for immediate despatch to the various hospitals, posts and depots. There were, naturally, many things still to be done, and for a few weeks the strain on the department was tremendous. Unfortunately, some hundreds of those who had volunteered for service, many of whom had been trained, did not come forward, and it was, therefore, necessary to enrol numbers of absolutely untrained men and women. The position was considerably eased, however, by help given by Portsmouth Field Ambulance (Territorial) in manning the posts and depots with personnel of its stretcher bearer companies for a period of six weeks from the outbreak of war until the unit left for its concentration area. The work on the posts was completed within a very short time, and immediate steps were taken to train the new recruits.

Civil Defence Casualty Services. On the outbreak of war the Portsmouth Casualty Services consisted of:

(a) Ten combined first-aid party and ambulance depots with 84 first-aid parties and 60 on-call ambulances, each depot being in charge of a male superintendent.

(b) Ten first-aid posts, i.e. the model post at Milton Road, seven adapted schools, and two out-patients' departments of hospitals, together with four mobile first-aid units. Several medical officers were attached to each first-aid post, one of whom was appointed to be in charge and responsible for supervising and training the personnel. A trained nurse acted under his control, and in most instances a lay superintendent was appointed.

(c) Casualty clearing hospitals provided 973 Class I and 266 Class II beds at St. Mary's Hospital and Institution, Infectious Diseases Hospital, St. James' Hospital, Royal Hospital, Eye and Ear Hospital, and Queen Alexandra Hospital. These hospitals were linked with base hospitals in the county area.

(d) Decontamination laundry at the Infectious Diseases Hospital, if required.

(e) Twelve ambulance coaches for inter-hospital transport of casualties.
(f) Casualty bureau.
(g) Three emergency mortuaries.

Owing to the calls of industry and the armed forces, a large number of trained men was lost to the service in the earlier months of the war and the difficulty experienced in getting replacements was such that selected women were used in first-aid parties. The reservation of men in first-aid parties at 30 years of age was granted in July 1940, and prevented men in this service from leaving without permission.

In April 1940, a training school for the casualty services was opened, and by the end of the year between four and five hundred men and women had received preliminary or more advanced training. This school, one of the first of its kind, was visited by various officers of the Ministries of Health and Home Security who expressed high praise of the work being done there.

E.M.S. Hospitals. From the beginning of 1939 rapid progress was made in preparing Portsmouth's hospitals to play an effective part in the treatment and evacuation of war casualties. St. Mary's Hospital and the Infectious Diseases Hospital were classified as Grade 1A hospitals with the Royal Portsmouth and Queen Alexandra Hospitals, and the Portsmouth and Southern Counties Eye and Ear Hospital was graded as 1B, whilst Langstone Sanatorium, a section of St. James' Hospital, and of St. Mary's Institution, were classified as Grade II hospitals. (The Eye and Ear Hospital, Langstone Sanatorium and St. Mary's Institution were subsequently withdrawn.) Protection against blast, additional fire fighting measures, and at St. Mary's Hospital a cleansing station for gas cases were provided, and steps were taken to guard against possible failure of lighting or water supply. Semi-underground shelters for hospitals staffs were also provided, and in the case of St. Mary's Hospital an underground operating theatre was adapted and equipped.

The Ministry's scheme provided for the evacuation of casualties from Portsmouth hospitals to base hospitals in the Chichester Group. Thus, after the preliminary decanting of certain classes of patients at the beginning of the war, the local hospitals were able to reserve about 1,000 vacant beds for air raid casualties.

A local branch of the Ministry of Health's Civil Nursing Reserve was established in February 1939, and by September about 120 trained, 90 assistant nurses and over 400 nursing auxiliaries had been enrolled. Of this number 271 nursing auxiliaries were already in training.

A co-ordinated scheme for the typing, collection and storage of blood was prepared by the Medical Officer of Health in June 1939, and developed with much success by the deputy medical superintendent of St. Mary's Hospital.

AIR RAIDS

The Earlier Raids. The first raid on Portsmouth occurred on July 11, 1940, at 1800 hours, when about fifteen aircraft crossed the city from west to east dropping bombs of small calibre, (see Plate XXXI). One of these made a direct hit on Drayton Road first-aid post and depot, killing twelve of the staff and injuring a number of others. By the excellent work of the rest of the staff, assisted by those of other establishments, most of the equipment was salvaged and the post and depot were, within twenty-four hours, re-established in shadow premises ready for operation.

The next raid occurred about mid-day on August 12, when Green Row first-aid depot was destroyed by fire due to H.E. bombs, but, fortunately, on this occasion there were no casualties amongst the staff.

On August 24, 1940, at about 1600 hours, Portsmouth sustained a concentrated attack by a large force of aircraft. Nearly 70 H.E. bombs of various sizes including some of large calibre and three delayed action bombs which exploded some hours after being dropped, fell on the city in five minutes; 125 people were killed, and 107 seriously injured and admitted to hospital. There was a direct hit on the Princes Cinema in Lake Road, but at the time of the warning there were only a few people in it, most of whom took cover. Of those remaining eight were killed and twelve injured. Water, gas and electricity mains sustained extensive damage. Two days later another heavy daylight raid occurred, but most of the bombs fell into Langstone Harbour, and there were very few casualties. A direct hit was scored in Hilsea Gasworks and several high explosives fell on Eastney Sewage Works, damaging the outfall tanks.

During the remainder of the year twenty-five further raids occurred—the majority of those in the later months being during hours of darkness. The heaviest of these raids were on the evenings of December 5 and 23. In the former 44 people were killed and 76 seriously injured, the Carlton Cinema at Cosham receiving a direct hit. In the latter raid 18 people were killed, 59 seriously injured and nearly 500 admitted to rest centres because of extensive damage to property from severe blast over a radius of one mile. The reverberation was felt at Ryde, Isle of Wight.

In the last six months of 1940 there were 305 alerts and 29 raids. About 250 H.E. bombs were dropped, killing over 250 persons and seriously injuring about 380. Over 12,000 houses were damaged.

The Raids of January 1941. The next extensive raids occurred on January 10–11, 1941; the first lasting from 1800 hours to 2225 hours and the second attack from 2335 hours to 0230 hours. Flares fell soon after the first warning and then thousands of incendiary bombs and hundreds of H.Es. were dropped by successive waves of aircraft, mainly over the southern part of the city. The electricity power station received two direct hits by H.E. early in the raid, so that the current failed throughout the city and in surrounding districts. Thereafter all controls, posts and hospitals worked with emergency lighting. Many large fires developed which involved the three main shopping centres in Southsea and Landport. Gas and water mains were fractured in many places, severely handicapping the fire services.

At 1915 hours incendiary bombs were reported to have fallen on the Portsmouth and Southern Counties Eye and Ear Hospital and it was soon after hit by H.E. The hospital, including the nurses' home and the cleansing station of the first-aid post was extensively damaged. Fortunately, all the patients had been evacuated to the basement of the adjoining Royal Naval Club, whence they were transferred later that night to E.M.S. beds in the Infectious Diseases Hospital. The first-aid post accommodated within the hospital was transferred for a few days to the adjoining Cathedral crypt.

Incendiary bombs also fell on the Royal Portsmouth Hospital causing what promised to be a major fire. Moreover, adjoining business premises were already well alight and there was a serious shortage of water. It was, therefore, decided to evacuate the hospital and between 2220 hours and 0230 hours while the raids were still in progress, 70 sick and 33 air raid casualties were transferred by ambulance coach to Queen Alexandra Hospital, Cosham. Although five H.E. bombs fell within 100 yards of it, the first-aid post at the hospital continued to function until the next day, when the staff was distributed temporarily among other posts pending the reinstatement of the out-patient department. Three H.E. bombs fell in the grounds of St. Mary's Municipal Hospital causing damage to the nurses' home. One delayed action bomb lodged in the main corridor of the hospital near the kitchen and underground operating theatre and exploded at about 0600 hours next morning, and did considerable damage to the hospital services, but, fortunately, without serious injury to the staff. The west wall of St. George's Square first-aid post was blown in by a H.E. bomb falling nearby. Most of the personnel were in shelter and escaped serious harm and the post was transferred temporarily to an adjoining school. The Cottage Grove district was showered with incendiary bombs, some of which fell on the post and depot and on ambulances in the school yard. The resulting fires were put out by the staff, but as the safety of the building was seriously endangered by major fires in adjoining property, evacuation was ordered to premises nearby which had previously been earmarked as a shadow post. Incendiary bombs also fell on many other depots and posts but were quickly extinguished. An emergency mortuary at Swan Street was hit by H.Es. and incendiaries and destroyed.

The only individual incident producing a large number of casualties was one in Arundel Street, where a public air raid shelter was hit, but the extent of the raids was such that a shortage of services was expected, and reinforcements were accordingly called for, with the result that twelve first-aid parties and twenty-five ambulances from adjoining areas arrived before midnight. These reinforcements were deployed to depots as they arrived and the normal services were augmented by a large number of keen part-time personnel, so that at no time was there any shortage of first-aid parties or ambulances. Local collecting personnel had been trained to keep 'on the spot' first-aid to a minimum and to get casualties to fixed treatment points rapidly, paying due regard to anti-shock measures and smoothness of transport.

During the first alert, incendiary bombs fell on the Guildhall and were extinguished. Later, it was again set on fire and since water pressure was low because of the heavy demand being made by fires in the Commercial Road area, the fire could not be controlled, and at 0115 hours the Controller ordered evacuation of Main Control to Cosham. The Guildhall was completely gutted and Main Control continued to function at Cosham for several days, until an alternative control was set up in the Royal Beach Hotel, where the municipal offices were again partly established.

In these two raids of January 10–11, 1941, 202 persons were killed (or missing and ultimately presumed dead), 47 of these by a direct hit on a semi-underground shelter, and 212 were seriously injured. The following day most of those admitted to hospital were transferred in ambulance coaches to Chichester and Basingstoke. Some days later a mass burial of some of the dead took place at Kingston Cemetery. Hundreds of business and private premises, including churches, schools, hotels, cinemas, the Guildhall and three hospitals, were seriously damaged or destroyed by H.E. or fire which devastated the three main shopping centres in Southsea and Landport.

Over 3,000 persons were rendered homeless.

The Raids of March and April 1941. After a relatively quiet period of two months, a series of raids began on March 8, aimed at the destruction of certain battleships which were in the port. These culminated in a heavy raid on March 10–11, lasting from 2000 hours to 0300 hours, in which a large number of incendiaries and at least 250 H.E. bombs were dropped, mainly on the southern half of the city. A large number of fires were again caused and the railway line received a direct hit which stopped train services temporarily at Cosham and Havant. The electricity supply failed in some parts of the city early in the raid and gas and water mains were extensively damaged.

Shortly after midnight a H.E. fell in the road just outside Penhale Road first-aid post causing damage to the building and throwing an ambulance on to the roof of a house about 30 yards away. Fortunately, there were no serious casualties amongst the personnel, who were under cover at the time. Two other H.E. bombs caused much damage to the cinema and stores of the Queen Alexandra Hospital. Many windows in the main hospital building were blown in and two of the operating theatres were temporarily put out of action. A total of 117 persons were killed and over 180 seriously injured. On March 11, there were nine air raid warnings during the day.

In an attack on the night of April 8, 1941, 32 H.E. bombs and about 500 incendiary bombs were dropped. Casualties amounted to 20 killed and 30 seriously injured.

Six other less severe raids, involving 57 fatal and 71 serious casualties, followed at intervals and on the night of April 27, 1941, there was another fairly heavy attack, mainly by parachute mines. One of these made a direct hit on the Royal Hospital out-patient department and first-aid post which was completely demolished. Fortunately, most of the staff had taken shelter in the basement, but three nurses of the post, two hospital porters, two special constables acting as stretcher bearers, and one patient were killed (see Plate XXXII). A house surgeon was seriously injured and died in hospital the following day. Maddon's Hotel was destroyed by another parachute mine, with heavy casualties, and the adjoining Town Station and General Post Office were damaged by blast. A total of 117 persons were killed or missing and presumed dead, and nearly 150 seriously injured.

Subsequent night raids occurred at irregular intervals, the heaviest of these being (a) on May 3, 1941, when 41 H.E. bombs, six unexploded bombs and five delayed action bombs fell on the city, 19 persons being killed and 30 seriously injured; (b) on June 14, 1941, when 20 H.E. bombs and one unexploded bomb of 1,800 kg. fell on the northern part of the city. This bomb was ultimately discovered after much searching and removed by a local disposal company in 1946; (c) on August 15, 1943, when there were 62 incidents, 37 persons being killed and 36 seriously injured, and (d) on April 27, 1944, when over 20 persons were killed, most of them by a direct hit on an air raid shelter of some corporation flats in Crasswell Street.

Two flying bombs fell in the city, the first at Locksway Road on the night of June 25–26, 1944, resulting in 14 seriously injured, 19 not seriously injured, and the second at Newcomen and Winstanley Roads on the night of July 14–15, 1944, resulting in 15 dead, 35 seriously injured and 63 not seriously injured.

Up to the end of August 1944, there had been 1,581 alerts in Portsmouth, and during sixty-seven raids there were dropped 1,320 H.E. bombs and 38,000 incendiaries, excluding some hundreds of both types that fell in the sea, and 38 parachute mines. The total casualties in Portsmouth have been: killed 930 (males 456, females 349, children 125); seriously injured and admitted to hospital 1,216 (males 745, females 406, children 65), and not seriously injured and treated at first-aid posts 1,621 (males 965, females 536, children 120).

Control and Communications. Although there was no complete breakdown of telephone communication in any raid, interruption occurred in various districts on several occasions and the system of 'local control' whereby each combined depot had been made responsible for a particular district in its own vicinity, proved of great value. In the raid of January 10–11, 1941, when the fire could no longer be controlled, the Main A.R.P. Control situated in the Guildhall was transferred in the early hours of the morning to Cosham. The three local report and control centres continued to function, so that no disturbance of control resulted.

GENERAL COMMENTS

All the medical and first-aid services were found to be generally sufficient; only on two occasions, i.e. on January 10 and March 10, 1941, were ambulances and first-aid parties called in from outside as reinforcements by the Controller.

The policy of establishing a first-aid post either within or close to each of the four general hospitals was found to be well justified (*a*) by assuring closer co-operation between the post and the hospital and easier transfer of cases found on examination to require hospital treatment; (*b*) by relieving the hospital of the treatment of minor casualties who go there independently, and (*c*) by providing possible reserve hospital accommodation in the event of severe damage to the hospital. The original hopes entertained for the four heavy mobile first-aid units were not realised. The Portsmouth experience accords with that of other cities, namely, that the heavy mobile first-aid post is really not required within a built-up area. On the other hand, a light mobile first-aid unit, i.e. consisting of a car with medical officer and one or two nurses with a small amount of equipment including morphia, etc., proved most useful, and this was despatched to all incidents where casualties were trapped.

The administration of 3,000 units of anti-tetanic serum to all casualties with an open wound on admission to a hospital or first-aid post proved a wise precautionary measure, for no case of tetanus occurred in any of 2,836 injured treated.

In regard to treatment at the incident, the giving of sodium bicarbonate and other appropriate treatment for crush injuries, was tried on one occasion only, but this proved not to be a real test, so that no definite conclusion as to their efficacy could be reached.

The hospitals proved adequate to the calls made on their services in spite of the dislocations caused by destruction and damage. The evacuation of patients was efficiently and smoothly carried out. The practice of evacuating during heavy raids from hospitals in the centre of the city to the Queen Alexandra Hospital on the outskirts was well justified.

The personnel of the civil defence casualty and health services carried out their duties efficiently and enthusiastically at all times and with disregard of personal safety.

Below is a list of personnel who received well deserved recognition for their services to civil defence:

Kerr, Mr. Patrick	F.A.P. Service	G.M.
Lane, Mr. William	F.A.P. Service	G.M.
White, Mr. A. Samuel	Depot Supt.	G.M.
Wickens, Mr. Raymond	Depot Supt.	G.M.
Wilson, Mr. Leonard	F.A.P. Leader	G.M.
Keen, Miss E.	Matron, Royal Portsmouth Hospital	O.B.E.
Williamson, Dr. A. B.	Medical Officer of Health	O.B.E.
Gay, Miss M. L.	Matron, St. Mary's Municipal Hospital	O.B.E.
Davis, Miss K. L.	Sister i/c X-ray Dept., St. Mary's Hospital	M.B.E.
Mulvaney, Dr. Una	M.O. i/c F.A.P.	M.B.E.
Scarlett, Miss B. F.	Supt. F.A.P.	M.B.E.
Taylor, Dr. Churton	M.O. i/c F.A.P.	M.B.E.
Welldon, Miss V.	Lay Supt., F.A.P.	M.B.E.
Farr, Mrs. M.	District Midwife	B.E.M.
Phillimore, Miss A. M. D.	Mobile Asst. Nurse	B.E.M.
Walker, Miss Jessie	Ambulance Driver	B.E.M.
Lowlett, Mr. Charles	F.A.P. Service	Commendation
Williams, Mrs. M.	Section Leader Ambulance Service	Commendation

PORTSMOUTH

Portsmouth *Evening News
and Hampshire Telegraph*

PLATE XXXI. Scene following the first raid.

Portsmouth *Evening News
and Hampshire Telegraph*

PLATE XXXII. Salvaging after raid which damaged the Royal
Portsmouth Hospital.

PLYMOUTH

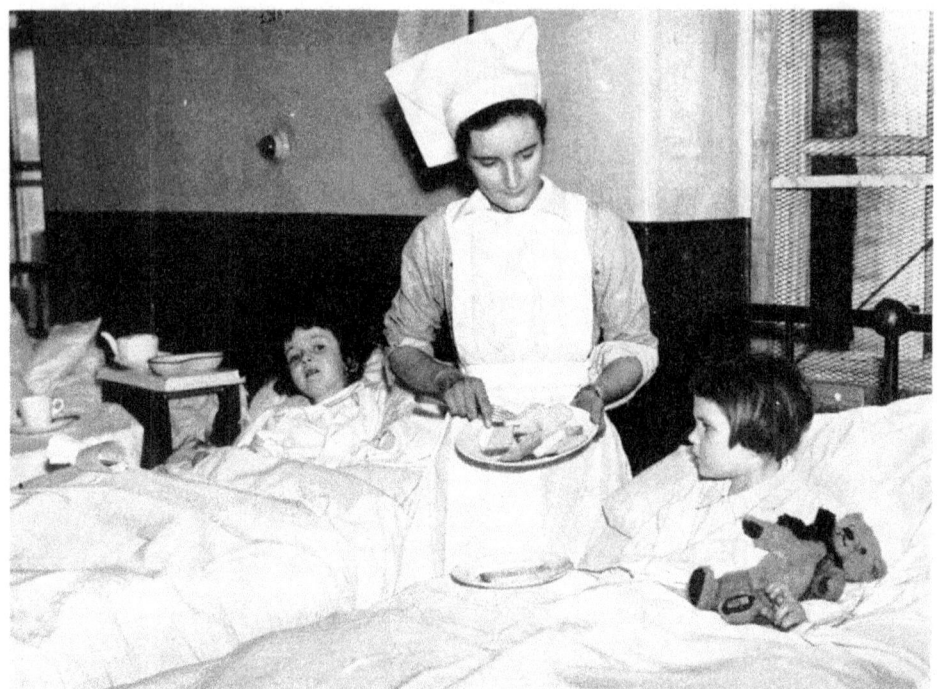

Western Morning News

PLATE XXXIII. City Hospital, children and nurse.

Western Morning News

PLATE XXXIV. City Hospital, bombed wing; 32 babies killed.

CHAPTER 8
PLYMOUTH
July 1940 to June 1941

Contributed by
T. Peirson, M.D., M.R.C.S., *Medical Officer of Health, Plymouth*

THE area of Plymouth in December 1939, was 9,515 acres, excluding tidal waters, and the estimated population was 221,229. By the end of the second quarter of 1940, the population, estimated chiefly on food ration books, had decreased to 200,500 and in the succeeding quarters the effects of the enemy attacks were responsible for its gradual reduction to 183,400 by the end of March 1941, when the heavy raids accelerated its decline to 135,870 by the end of June 1941. The night population in this last quarter was further considerably reduced as many people moved out of the town at night and returned to work in the daytime.

MEDICAL ORGANISATION

E.M.S. Hospitals. The Class 1A Hospitals of Plymouth included in the Emergency Hospital Scheme were the three branches of Prince of Wales Hospital (the main one at Greenbank and the others at Devonport and Lockyer Street), the City General Hospital and the Mount Gold Orthopaedic and Tuberculosis Hospital. The normal total bed complement of these hospitals was 1,245 but by 'crowding' and using other rooms this total was increased to 1,446. A fortunate feature was the dispersal of these beds amongst five different hospitals which made it unlikely that many first class beds would be lost in the same raid, although two principal hospitals, the City General and the Prince of Wales (Greenbank) were situated close together.

The figure of 1,446 beds mentioned above included, however, about 150 beds on the upper floors of very old blocks in the City General Hospital and these were later excluded as being quite unsuitable. Other Plymouth hospitals which were capable of receiving casualties if the need were urgent, were the Royal Eye Infirmary (90 beds) and the Pearn Convalescent Home (50 beds). The Public Assistance Institution, Ford House, was also included in the scheme, but it was never really suitable, and in any case it was completely demolished in an early raid before the heavy raids began.

There were two first-class Service hospitals in the city, each of about 600 beds, the R.N. Hospital and the Stoke Military Hospital. The latter was completely evacuated and dismantled in April 1941. Certain schools were also selected for use as reserve hospitals.

During the heavy raids of March and April 1941, as will be shown later, the first line hospitals, in spite of repeated damage to all of them, were never overwhelmed and always managed to deal with their casualties and evacuate those fit to be moved to distant hospitals the following day.

Civil Defence Casualty Services. Before the outbreak of war it had been considered desirable to link up as closely as possible all first-aid and ambulance services. Ten first-aid units were established in the city, use being made of existing buildings such as the church halls, clubs, etc., all of which required considerable internal alterations. An entirely new first-aid post was erected in the grounds of Swilly Isolation Hospital.

These first-aid units were for administration placed under the control of part-time unit commanders whose normal occupations were those of a dental surgeon, a sanitary inspector, a chief clerk, etc.; each unit commander had two whole-time assistant unit commanders.

Each first-aid unit consisted of a first-aid post (fixed or mobile), a first-aid party and an ambulance depot, and later a public gas cleansing station. The great advantage of this arrangement was the ease of interchangeability of personnel, all being trained in the various sections. There were usually four ambulances at each unit and twelve in reserve.

Two and sometimes three medical officers were attached to each first-aid post. The senior medical officer of each post was responsible for supervising and training the post personnel and the trained nurse of the post acted under his direct control. Calls for medical assistance were made to the nearest first-aid post when doctors were required at raid incidents or for cases of sickness in shelters and rest centres for the homeless.

The first-aid and ambulance service was for general purposes controlled by a staff officer under the Medical Officer of Health. He was a port health inspector in peace-time.

AIR RAIDS

The Earlier Raids. The earlier raids on Plymouth were carried out by occasional aircraft usually in the evening and early in the morning, and caused isolated incidents of damage and a few casualties. They were dealt with expeditiously by the civil defence services, which appeared almost to welcome some real activity after a long period of inaction. The first air raid damage occurred on July 6, 1940, when a few houses at Swilly were hit. On December 28, 1940 and again on January 13, 1941, severe damage was inflicted upon the gas and electricity undertakings and for many weeks large areas of the city were deprived of all gas and electricity. This was very trying for the inhabitants of those areas during the cold weather, and cooking meals was a difficult problem. Parts of the city were without gas for periods varying up to ten months. Up to March 15, 1941, the total civilian casualties were 127 killed, 180 seriously injured and 322 slightly injured.

The Later Raids. Intensive raids were carried out on the city on March 20 and 21 and again on April 21, 22, 23, 28 and 29. Very severe damage was done to property including public buildings and churches, but, considering the amount of material damage, the casualty lists were remarkably light. This must be largely attributed to the excellent shelter accommodation. The policy of dispersal into small private shelters proved to be sound and there were one or two tragic disasters when large public shelters received direct hits.

The March Raids. On the evening of March 20, 1941, advance warning of probable intensive raiding was received by the civil defence services. The raid commenced at 8.37 p.m., and the 'all clear' sounded at 12.51 a.m. Flares were dropped at the beginning and there was then a very heavy fall of incendiary bombs accompanied and followed by approximately 200 to 250 high explosive bombs. There were 25 large fires, 5 medium and 117 small fires and very many minor outbreaks. Most of the damage to property was due to fire. On the following night, March 21, the raid developed at 8.35 p.m. and continued to 12.13 a.m. It was again preceded by flares, a heavy fall of incendiaries, mixed with and followed by about 300 to 400 high explosives of varying calibre. On this occasion there were 14 very large conflagrations, 7 medium and 97 small fires. It was estimated that between 150 and 200 planes took part in each of these attacks.

These two attacks were concentrated upon the centre of the city, although a large number of bombs also fell in the Stonehouse district, in Devonport and in the outlying areas. The public buildings which were either destroyed or seriously damaged included the Guildhall, Municipal Offices, General Post Office and the County Court. The A.R.P. Report Control Centre in the Guildhall and the Public Health Central Offices were completely destroyed.

The Prince of Wales Hospital, Lockyer Street, received a direct hit and had to be completely evacuated, the male patients going to the R.N. Hospital and the females to the Prince of Wales Hospital, Greenbank. The City General Hospital was hit by four high explosive bombs which fell upon the children's wards and the new maternity block which had been opened only five weeks previously. Twenty-two children and six nurses lost their lives in the City General Hospital. Many outstanding examples of personal gallantry were performed at this hospital, and a resident medical officer, Dr. Alison McNairn, was awarded the George Medal for the part she played. (See Plates XXXIII and XXXIV.)

The Princess Square first-aid post was set on fire early in the second raid and although the staff managed to keep it under control for some time, it eventually had to be abandoned, as all the buildings in the immediate vicinity were on fire and there was a danger of the patients and staff there being cut off.

The Stonehouse first-aid post received a direct hit by a high explosive bomb which wrecked half of the post. One patient was killed, but, fortunately, the staff were unharmed and were able to carry on in the remaining half of the post.

The story was repeatedly heard that lack of water prevented many buildings being saved from fire. During these two raids it was estimated that 750 dwellings were destroyed or damaged beyond repair, 5,000 dwellings were seriously damaged but reparable and 13,500 dwellings suffered slight damage. The business and shopping centre of the city including the principal streets such as Bedford Street, George Street, Old Town Street, Westwill Street, and Princess Square was completely destroyed.

After each of these two raids, the hospitals had to begin evacuating their casualties while still dealing with a flow of cases. This was necessary to ensure that beds were available for the next raids. Evacuation was carried out by hospital train and ambulance buses to Exeter, Bodmin, Exminster and further afield. Stretcher bearers for loading were never available in sufficient number at the hospitals and first-aid party men were always used for this work.

Many other tasks were performed during the aftermath by the civil defence ambulances and first-aid party men. These included the transport of homeless persons, clothing them and salvaging their furniture from bombed houses and the collection of information regarding billets, for all records of available billets which had been prepared beforehand had been lost in the municipal offices.

The way in which the members of the civil defence casualty services carried out their duties was excellent. No instance came to notice of any reluctance to turn out again and again to bring in casualties. Forty-three ambulances (each carrying four stretchers) were on duty. It soon became obvious that the second line ambulances, which were trade vehicles which had to be called in and adapted with stretcher carrying fitments, were of little value since it took too long to make them available. Assistance, however, was obtained from the naval ambulances.

As a result of the two raids on March 20 and 21, 328 civilians were killed, 279 seriously injured and admitted to hospital and 438 were slightly injured.

Control and Communications. During the second raid, the A.R.P. Headquarters Control Room situated in the basement of the Guildhall was destroyed by fire and the staff were evacuated without casualty to the Devonport part of the city. The A.R.P. Control was established in the Devonport Report Centre which was under the Devonport Market in the centre of the shopping area. Although Devonport had suffered comparatively lightly in the first two heavy raids, it was generally expected that the enemy would devote his attention to the dockyard and the neighbourhood. This he did the following month, the control room being destroyed, and the controller and his staff, the medical officer of health and the city engineer again having to change their headquarters after salvaging what they could. This time they found refuge in an old private mansion, Pounds House, situated in the Central Park.

The destruction of the control centre on two occasions naturally caused a certain amount of dislocation, but a probable breakdown of communications had been provided for and in accordance with pre-arranged plans the officers in charge of the first-aid party and ambulance depots acted on their own initiative, despatching services to incidents upon information they received locally. During the height of the raids, parties and ambulances were moved from one incident to another without returning to their depot. A messenger service had not been developed, but heroic service was given by Cadets of the Naval Engineering College acting as despatch riders.

Another heavy raid upon the third successive night was expected and the usual hour of starting, namely, 8.30 p.m., found nearly all personnel again on duty and ready for the third dose. As the evening wore on and nothing happened, there were many feelings of relief.

Water Supply. During these two raids the damage to the water services was very extensive, and approximately 80 mains were burst. The ends of broken drains and water mains were frequently in the same bomb crater, and the absence of any untoward result from a polluted water supply was remarkable. Before restoring the supply in repaired water mains a heavy dose of chlorine was injected and the chlorination of the service reservoirs during all this time was kept well stepped up. Large areas of the city were without a main supply for nearly a fortnight and were served by mobile water tanks. At the end of a fortnight, however, the water supply in the city was practically normal. The public were urged to boil all water and milk for the time being and anti-typhoid inoculation was advised and offered free, but only about 200 people took advantage of this offer.

April Raids. There was a brief respite of a month after the March raids and during this period the city gradually resumed its normal life. There was, however, worse to come and in April the enemy again attacked with heavy raids on five out of nine consecutive nights. The first of these came on April 21 and it was repeated on April 22, 23, 28 and 29. The raids began each night between 9.30 and 10.0 p.m., and lasted approximately six hours on each of the first two nights and about four hours on the other three nights. The raids on April 21 and 22 were the most severe, about 300 high explosive bombs were dropped each night, and the number dropped during the subsequent attacks varied from 100 to 150. These were accompanied by a heavy fall of incendiary bombs; a feature of the raid on April 29 was the dropping of 17 paramines with devastating results.

Although the damage was widespread, the western or Devonport half of the city suffered most, particularly the areas adjacent to the Service establishments. The Devonport shopping centre, comprising Fore Street and the immediate vicinity, was destroyed and, in the east, Drake Circus and Old Town Street were further devastated. It is estimated that as a result of the five raids, 3,750 dwellings were demolished or damaged beyond repair and 44,000 dwellings were damaged but capable of being repaired; large numbers of people were of course rendered homeless.

Considering the extent of the material damage, the casualties were again, as in March, not heavy. A total of 590 civilians were killed, 430 were seriously injured and detained in hospital, and 583 slightly injured received treatment at first-aid posts.

During the night of April 21, the Prince of Wales Hospital (Devonport) was damaged, but although no further casualties could be received there, it was able to retain its patients that night. A mobile first-aid unit was sent to assist the hospital staff during the night as their heating and water supplies were interrupted, and the hospital was evacuated the following day.

On the night of April 22, the Ker Street first-aid post and depot were struck by a high explosive bomb, which carried away a corner of the building. The bomb landed on the pavement, failed to explode, and was removed by the bomb disposal squad within half an hour of its fall.

The Royal Eye Infirmary and the Three Towns Maternity Home had to be evacuated because of damage during the night of the 22nd and the patients were moved by ambulances to other hospitals in the city. At the City Isolation Hospital, Swilly, the central kitchen was demolished and one ward block set on fire. This necessitated evacuation of half the patients in the hospital. The smallpox hospital at Lee Mill about 12 miles from Plymouth was opened and about 40 patients were sent there, others going to the Truro Isolation Hospital. The following day a field kitchen was set up in the grounds of the City Isolation Hospital and the staff were able to carry on with the remainder of the patients there.

The Prince of Wales Hospital, Greenbank, received a direct hit which seriously damaged the private patients' wing. Three of the nursing staff were killed and several injured.

Each day after a raid, all the cases fit to be moved were evacuated, either by hospital train or ambulance buses to the Royal Devon and Exeter Hospital, Exeter City Hospital and the Exminster and Bodmin Emergency Hospitals. This was necessary in order to keep a sufficient number of beds available in case of a raid the following night. It imposed a heavy task on the hospital staff who had to begin evacuation while still dealing with the casualties.

Control and Communications. As previously mentioned, the control room and report centre which since the destruction of the Guildhall had been housed under Devonport Market, again had to be evacuated because of damage by fire on April 22 and it was installed in Pounds House, Central Park.

The breakdown of telephone communication was a severe handicap and the alternative system of messengers for reporting incidents to the report centre and sending instructions to first-aid party and ambulance depots was comparatively speaking, slow. Consequently, the officers in charge of these depots acted on their own initiative and out of a total of 225 incidents involving casualties on the three nights of April 21–23, 99 were attended by the casualty services without awaiting instructions from the report centre.

As a result of this experience a new system of alternative communications and 'local control' was evolved. In order to make the complete interruption of telephone communications between report centre and party depots less likely, both the ordinary post office exchange and direct lines were installed. The ten first-aid units were constituted 'Centres of Direct Local Action' which meant that when cut off from Central Control, they became autonomous units in their own areas which were defined; all reports from wardens and other services were sent direct to them and the commanders of these units were responsible for taking any necessary action in their own areas. To make these centres more self-contained, rescue parties were also posted to them when the telephones broke down.

It was necessary, however, that these centres of direct local action should be kept well informed of the incidents in their own area so that when they were cut off from the Central Control they could assume local command without any hiatus. To enable this to be done, each unit was as a routine sent details of the incidents in its area from the beginning of every raid and these were kept plotted on a map at the unit.

This scheme of direct local action was not looked upon with favour by the Regional Office of the Ministry of Home Security, and it was many months before approval was given to it.

Personnel and Vehicles. During these heavy raids of April 1941, there were available on an average each night thirty-five ambulances and the same number of first-aid parties. This was always an adequate number. It was usually found advisable to move ambulances and parties from quiet areas to units which were having a busy time. The morale of the personnel was excellent. This was evident from the following figures: For the first-aid posts, ambulance and first-aid party depots, the total number of whole-time personnel it was possible to maintain on duty during a normal night shift was 140, whereas during these raids in April when part-time volunteers and whole-timers off duty reported to the units for duty, the number rose to 516 one night and never fell below 358. This was at the end of a winter of particularly heavy action.

During the heavy raids of March and April, eight ambulances and three first-aid party cars were either destroyed or damaged beyond repair and thirteen ambulances and six cars were damaged but reparable. The St. Budeaux mobile first-aid unit was badly damaged, but most of its equipment was salvaged.

First-aid Posts. In the opinion of the Medical Officer of Health, the usefulness of fixed first-aid posts inside a town, as judged by the number of casualties dealt with by them, was very doubtful. He considered that they certainly should, as far as possible, be situated at or very close to a hospital. They were, however, always regarded as possible reserve hospitals, in the event of severe damage to the hospital accommodation. The two mobile first-aid units were complete 'white elephants.' The idea before the raids appeared good, but in practice it was always found that they took too long to set up and by the time they were ready for action the casualties had been adequately dealt with by other means. In rural districts, however, they would no doubt have some excellent uses.

What was found to be of great value was the dispatch to an incident of a party consisting of a medical officer and one or two nurses with a small amount of equipment including chloroform and morphia. This service was later officially recognised as a 'light mobile first-aid unit'.

Evacuation. It was not until the beginning of May 1941, that Plymouth officially became an evacuation area. The City Council had applied on two previous occasions for the city to be regarded as an evacuation area but it had always been scheduled as neutral. The general clearing up after these April raids, therefore, was made more complicated by organising the evacuation of children, expectant mothers and other evacuable classes. The task of the Health Department was not made any easier by the complete destruction of its central office and records. It had been decided earlier that in the event of this happening, the department would re-establish itself in the main tuberculosis dispensary at Beaumont House.

Scale of Attacks and Casualties. Between July 6, 1940, and June 29, 1941, bombs were dropped during 53 attacks, 6 of which caused no casualties.

The attacks on the nights of March 20–21 and 21–22, 1941, were the first heavy attacks. During these two nights 470 H.E. bombs and thousands of incendiaries fell on the city. The estimated weight of H.E. bombs was 104·88 metric tons.

The casualties were 328 killed, 279 admitted and detained in hospital and 438 treated at first-aid posts.

On the five nights of April 21–22, 22–23, 23–24, 28–29 and 29–30, 1941, it is estimated that 862 H.E. bombs and 18 paramines were dropped weighing 178·95 metric tons.

The casualties were 590 killed, 430 admitted and detained in hospital and 583 treated at first-aid posts.

In the two series of raids therefore about 3·2 persons were killed and 2·5 seriously injured per metric ton of bombs. It was estimated that 55 per cent. of the bombs were 50 kgs., 30 per cent. 250 kgs., 5 per cent. 500 kgs. and 10 per cent. 1,000 kgs. In the circumstances the casualties were not considered heavy when compared with the weight of attack on other towns. During the whole period of the raids the estimated number of bombs of all kinds, excluding incendiaries, which fell was 1,727 including 112 U.X.B., while the total casualties were 1,071 killed, 933 seriously injured and 1,449 slightly injured.

GENERAL COMMENTS

The system of devolution of control to ten first-aid units in the city, each unit consisting of a first-aid post, a first-aid party and an ambulance depot, was unusual, but certainly proved its usefulness in action, especially when the Central Control was disorganised and telephones completely put out of action for considerable periods, so that the slow system of messengers had to be used.

The number of ambulances was found insufficient, owing to the large number put out of action, but the mutual aid arrangements for the supply of ambulances and relief first-aid parties from other areas functioned well.

The supply of blankets at the rate of two per stretcher was found to be quite insufficient, especially as many were temporarily unavailable for various reasons.

The Medical Officer of Health considered that cocaine should be added to first-aid post equipment because of the large number of cases with grit in the eyes.

The personnel of the civil defence services were put to the greatest strain in the heavy raids, but stood up well to all the calls on their endurance until relieved by outside aid.

The hospitals proved adequate to the calls made on their services in spite of the dislocations caused by damage and consequent loss of beds.

The evacuation of patients was efficiently and smoothly carried out.

Awards for Gallantry. The following personnel of the civil defence casualty services received well deserved recognition for their work in connexion with casualties:

Fletcher, Percy	F. A. Party man	B.E.M.
Lloyd, Mrs.	Ambulance attendant	Commendation
McNairn, A., Miss	Doctor	G.M.
Clancy, V. A., Miss	Probationer nurse	B.E.M.
Edwards, G. J., Miss	Probationer nurse	Commendation
Giles, K. M., Miss	Probationer nurse	Commendation
Yearling, W. M., Miss	Sister	Commendation
Burn, G.	Ambulance driver	Commendation
Stanton, M., Miss	Ambulance attendant	Commendation
Fitzgerald, M., Mrs.	Ambulance driver	G.M.

CHAPTER 9
BRISTOL
June 1940 to April 1941

Based on material contributed by
R. H. Parry, M.D., F.R.C.P., *Medical Officer of Health, Bristol*

THE area of the City of Bristol was 24,383 acres and the population before the war was estimated to be 419,000. In June 1940, the estimated population was 412,500 from which time it slowly fell until it had reached 347,000 by the end of June 1941. There appeared to be very little evacuation of the city on account of raids, as the diminution could be wholly accounted for by recruitment to the Services.

HOSPITAL SERVICES

There were three casualty receiving hospitals in the city:

(1) The Southmead Municipal General Hospital with a normal capacity of 423 beds which had been extended, by crowding and using other accommodation, to 620. Of this total about 400 beds on the average were occupied by ordinary civilian sick, so that about 220 beds were usually available for casualties.

(2) The Bristol General Hospital (voluntary) with a normal capacity of 188 beds, of which 63 were in reserve. This hospital, however, had an annexe at Westbury-on-Trym, near Bristol, which could accommodate 110 patients; an average of 170 beds in the hospital and its annexe were occupied by civilian cases, leaving over 120 beds usually available for casualties.

(3) The Bristol Royal Infirmary (voluntary) with a normal capacity of 351 beds which had been expanded to 471. Of these about half were usually occupied by civilian sick.

The city, therefore, could provide nearly 600 first-class beds for the reception of casualties. A reserve of beds was provided by other hospitals such as Cossham Memorial Hospital (voluntary), with about 40 beds usually available, and a few smaller suspended hospitals. For minor cases a further number of beds was available in an emergency in certain Class II hospitals. The Ophthalmic Hospital was also used for the treatment of the large number of eye cases which occurred, especially for out-patient treatment.

CASUALTY SERVICES

First-aid Posts. There were eight fixed first-aid posts and ten mobile units and, in addition, fourteen first-aid points, which were subsequently increased in number to sixteen.

BRISTOL

Ambulance Services. A fleet of 75 ambulances was ready at the beginning of the raids, but owing to the demand on these services the number was increased to 115 early in the period, 57 cars for sitting cases on whole-time duty and 23 on part-time duty together with 45 trailers, were also available. For the first-aid parties 39 full-time and 110 part-time cars were in use.

Personnel. The table below gives the establishment employed in these civil defence services at the end of the series of raids:

Summary of Personnel Position, June 1941

	Full-time		Part-time		Totals	
	Men	Women	Men	Women	Men	Women
1. *First-aid Post Service*						
Fixed first-aid posts (8)						
Doctors	5	3	8	–	13	3
Trained nurses	–	9	–	5	–	14
Auxiliary staff	20	172	104	255	124	427
Mobile first-aid posts (10)						
Doctors	10	–	11	1	21	1
Trained nurses	–	10	–	–	–	10
Auxiliary staff	27	142	3	26	30	168
Separate gas cleansing stations (16)						
Auxiliary staff	4	–	–	–	4	–
Mobile gas cleansing unit						
Auxiliary staff	–	–	–	–	–	–
First-aid posts (14)						
Auxiliary staff	–	–	43	189	43	189
2. *Ambulance Service*						
Controlling officers	15	–	24	–	39	–
Drivers and attendants	55	177	115	430	170	607
3. *First-aid Party Service* (afterwards merged with Rescue Service)	240	–	354	–	594	–
Totals	376	513	662	906	1,038	1,419

THE RAIDS

The city was subjected to intermittent raiding between June 1940, and April 1941, after which no further attack was made until the end of August 1942, when one H.E. bomb fell in the centre of the city and caused 102 casualties, of which 46 were fatal; this high figure was due to the fact that the incident occurred at 9.30 a.m., when the streets were crowded.

During the period of heavy attacks, casualties resulted from 51 of the raids, amounting to 1,253 killed, 1,277 injured and admitted to hospital and 1,992 treated at first-aid posts.

The table opposite shows the numbers of bombs and casualties in the six extensive night raids and one day raid from which heavy casualties resulted.

There were, in addition, two heavy raids on the docks on the nights of April 3 and 4, 1941, during which it was estimated that 540 H.E. bombs and about 17,000 incendiaries were dropped, but the casualties only amounted to 25 killed and 77 injured, of which 43 were treated at the first-aid posts.

THE WORK OF THE HOSPITALS

The City Hospital at Southmead and the two voluntary hospitals, the Bristol General and the Bristol Royal Infirmary, were able at all times to meet the demand made upon them as primary casualty receiving hospitals. They dealt with all the casualties requiring admission to hospital, except a few which happened in the locality of Cossham Hospital, near the city boundary, to which these were admitted as a matter of convenience.

The admissions to the hospitals were regulated by the casualty bureau. This unusual arrangement was found to be of great benefit in preventing a hospital from receiving more patients than could be efficiently dealt with.

A team of specially recruited part-time messengers was found of great value in maintaining up-to-date information as to the position of each of the hospitals at frequent intervals. They also carried urgent messages and even supplies of serum on occasions.

All the hospitals were damaged to some extent, but no casualties occurred except on April 11, when three patients and two nurses received slight injuries from flying glass. In no case was the work of the casualty receiving hospitals interrupted, except that the first-aid post housed in the Bristol General Hospital was put out of commission for about a week by damage received on that date. Plate XXXV shows the damage to a ward in the Homœopathic Hospital.

Injuries, Causal Agents, etc. Speaking generally, the principal types of case treated were fractures of limbs, other fractures, burns, incised wounds, crush injuries and eye injuries caused mainly by falling masonry, flying debris and glass, bomb fragments, blast, coal gas and fire. Major haemorrhage was very rare; the tourniquet was only used once, on a wrist wound, and even then it is doubtful whether it was necessary.

There were a few instances of perforation of the abdomen and chest, and of cerebral compression.

Shock was notably absent in the majority of slightly injured; the degree of shock usually varied directly with the severity of the injury and the age of the patient.

A few cases of hysteria were encountered, chiefly due to bereavement and anxiety for others.

PLATE XXXV. A damaged ward of the Homœopathic Hospital.

BRISTOL

PLATE XXXVI. Incident in street. First-Aid Parties at work.

Bristol *Evening World*

County Borough of Bristol
Table of the Heavy Air Raids on the Borough

Date	Duration of attack	Locality attacked	Estimated number and type of bombs		Killed		Admitted to hospital		Treated at first-aid posts	
			I.B.	H.E.	Civilian	Service	Civilian	Service	Civilian	Service
1940:										
September 25	1129 to 1215	Filton	No record		105	11	130	24	163	8
November 24	1821 to 0008	City centre	5,000	1,000	196	4	150	13	495	31
December 2	1816 to 0015	City centre	7,000	700	153	3	142	7	107	14
December 6	1843 to 2328	City widespread	7,000	650	87	13	69	11	91	17
1941:										
January 3	1821 to 2058 / 2103 to 0621	City widespread	5,000	250	142	7	130	3	211	7
March 16	2026 to 0140	City widespread	6,000	790	256	1	144	5	235	7
April 11	2147 to 2353	City widespread	10,000	700	173	7	138	8	232	4

Bristol was fortunate in being the headquarters of the Army Blood Supply Depot under Colonel L. E. H. (afterwards Sir Lionel) Whitby, so that expert transfusion teams were readily available, in addition to the ordinary hospital arrangements.

It is noteworthy that on the occasion of the first heavy raid on November 24, 1940, about 60 per cent. of the total casualties were slight injuries, as compared with about 40 per cent. in all other raids. This extraordinarily high proportion was probably largely accounted for by foreign bodies in the eye, for which no less than 170 cases were treated at the Eye Hospital out-patients department alone, and to slight burns sustained mainly in putting out incendiary bombs.

The following figures regarding the raid on March 16, 1941, present a typical picture of the distribution of casualties among men, women and children and of the causal agents:

Casualty Figures for Raid on March 16, 1941

	Killed		Seriously injured	
	Number	Per cent.	Number	Per cent.
Men	117	51·1	110	63·2
Women	90	39·7	51	29·3
Children under 16	22	9·2	13	7·5
Totals	229	100·0	174	100·0

Approximately 76 per cent. of the deaths were caused by splinters, 16 per cent. by crushing or falling masonry, and 8 per cent. by blast. Of the seriously injured casualties approximately 52 per cent. were caused by crushing or falling masonry, 39 per cent. by splinters and 9 per cent. by blast. The reason for the high percentage of crush injuries is suggested in the following sample analysis, which includes the great majority (88·5 per cent.) of the total number of seriously injured casualties in this raid, although less than half (46·7 per cent.) of the fatal casualties. It will be seen that most of the casualties occurred in private houses and public shelters, including two church crypts which received direct hits:

Situation Analysis of Casualties (sample only) from a heavily bombed area of the City

	Killed		Seriously injured	
	Number	Per cent.	Number	Per cent.
Open streets	9	8·4	13	8·4
Private houses	18	16·8	65	42·2
Public shelters (including communal shelters)	14	13·1	74	48·1
*Church crypts	52	48·6	—	—
Private shelters	14	13·1	2	1·3
Totals	107	100·0	154	100·0

* The majority of public shelter casualties were due to hits on two large church crypts.

The sample refers to casualties concerning whom reasonably accurate information is known. In this sample there were 107 killed and 154 seriously injured.

From the figures as a whole, it appears that a considerable percentage of the casualties were caused by damage to houses; and Dr. Parry, the Medical Officer of Health, considers that a substantial proportion of these might have been prevented by the use of indoor shelters, sufficiently strong to bear the weight of fallen material.

THE CIVIL DEFENCE SERVICES

First-aid Posts. The eight first-aid posts had no difficulty in meeting all the calls made upon them. In addition to the first-aid post at the Bristol Central Hospital mentioned above, the post at the central clinic was put out of action for one day; others were damaged but able to carry on their work without interruption.

The ten heavy mobile units were not found to be of much value and at only two or three incidents during the whole period were they required to fill the rôle for which they were provided, there were very few incidents where large enough numbers were affected to justify setting up a post nearby. After the early raids, as an experiment, the medical officer-in-charge of one unit was given a roving commission. He travelled in his own car with one or two nurses in search of incidents, but kept in touch with the report centre for directions. This experiment was considered to have fully justified itself and, as in other towns, it was the precursor of the subsequently introduced light mobile units.

First-aid Points. These were manned by part-time volunteers and did valuable work, so much so that they were later increased in numbers.

First-aid Parties. The work of the parties, both full-time and part-time, was found to be speedy and efficient. They showed excellent judgment in classifying the injuries at incidents, with the result that very few cases sent to first-aid posts afterwards required transfer to hospital (see Plate XXXVI.)

Ambulance Services. The fleet of 115 ambulances and 57 sitting case cars was fully extended during the more severe raids and Regional reinforcements had to be called for on a few occasions. The high proportion of female drivers stood up to the strain magnificently, as did also the part-time personnel.

The trailers which had been allocated to the city were found to be of little use in the conditions under which the ambulances had to work, for in the blackout, with streets blocked by debris, access to casualties was too difficult. This condemnation of trailers for casualty work was almost universal.

Several ambulances were damaged but only six were put entirely out of action.

Among the civil defence personnel a total of 32 were killed and 63 injured. The wardens suffered most, 28 being killed, 26 of whom were part-time workers.

Mortuary Service. The original part-time service having proved inadequate in the early raids, a special staff of superintendents, clerks and attendants was recruited, which became highly efficient. In the 'Baedeker' raids it afforded much assistance to Bath, and also to Weston-super-Mare on the occasion of the heavy raids there.

DOCTORS' EXPERIENCES IN THE RAIDS

The following examples of experiences of medical men on duty during the Bristol raids, as related at a meeting of the Bristol division of the British Medical Association held on June 12, 1941* are of interest:

Dr. Golding. (Medical officer-in-charge of a mobile first-aid unit.) Until November, Dr. Golding's unit was practically immobile. At the first incident to which it was sent, no suitable building in which to set up a post could be found within a quarter of a mile. It was therefore partly opened out in a shelter where, under the most difficult conditions and with an audience consisting of people who had taken refuge in the shelter, it had to treat patients with injuries varying from a sprained ankle to a depressed fracture of the skull. During the whole period the unit could practically never be used in accordance with pre-arranged plans, but Dr. Golding attended incidents without the unit and found that his mere presence was a great relief to first-aid parties, wardens and others concerned.

The conditions of casualties coming for first aid made a lasting impression on his mind; they were indescribably dirty, with hair full of plaster and eyes full of grit. This impression has been recorded by many observers in other places, especially by Dr. McMillan, Medical Officer of Health of Woolwich (see Chapter 1). Dr. Golding found that the degree of shock did not depend on the severity of the wound. In his experience some casualties with a mere scratch were sometimes profoundly shocked, while he instanced a case of a man with a ruptured patella ligament and a forward dislocation of the knee joint, in whom practically no shock was evident. He recorded, as had others, that the tourniquet, thought to be so important in pre-war plans for first-aid, was never used.

Dr. A. M. Fraser (Assistant Medical Officer of Health, Bristol), related his experiences in connexion with the work of the control centre. The central control received reports from the divisional report centres of which there were six in Bristol. These reports all had to be pieced together to give a proper picture of the incident. Each division

---

* Bristol Medico-Chirurgical Journal, Vol. lviii, No. 219, pp. 57–73.

was independent, but only as regards its own resources, which included about twenty ambulances and two mobile first-aid units. When help was needed, aid was sent from other local divisions to the area most affected. This was found to be a better procedure than asking for outside help which would have to be met on arrival, organised and, being unacquainted with the locality, supplied with guides. The value of outside help was less during a raid than as a relief after a raid to give the local personnel the necessary rest. Regional reinforcements arriving in daylight after a night raid were distributed throughout the city to work as part of Bristol's own organisation if a repetition occurred on the following night. The central control had to maintain close and frequent touch with the hospitals and also with the Region in order that reliefs of medical and surgical reinforcements could be rapidly obtained if required and to ensure the speedy evacuation of patients after raids to clear beds. Early reports of damage to hospitals were especially essential.

It was found by experience that wardens could not be expected always to estimate accurately the number of casualties to be dealt with at incidents. Ambulances and first-aid parties were therefore sent to every incident from which damage by H.E. bombs was reported. This meant that about 30 per cent. of journeys were useless, but it was better to have an excess of ambulances than to have casualties waiting for varying periods before expert first aid could be given.

Dr. M. E. J. Packer (Medical officer-in-charge of a mobile unit), who considered that the mobile unit was on the whole a white elephant, adopted the plan of going in his own car, without his unit, to incidents and treating casualties, often going down tunnels dug by the rescue parties in order to attend those who were trapped. He emphasised the value of having a few nurses with him and leaving them at various places to look after casualties, thus freeing him to see as many casualties as possible in the shortest space of time. He saw some cases of severe haemorrhage and shock, which first-aid parties would have had to send to hospital and which probably would have died before arrival.

Dr. J. Morton Evans, Jun. emphasised the advantage of carrying a rubber-capped bottle containing a solution of morphia for administration at incidents, where conditions were unsuitable for the use of tablets or ampoules. Darkness, lack of sterile water and the indescribable dirt of the casualties made any form of asepsis hopeless.

Although in charge of a mobile unit, Dr. Evans never functioned as such, but worked as a medical officer in attendance with the first-aid parties. Among 250 cases treated at a first-aid post he found that about 10 per cent. required to be sent to hospital, half of them directly, as urgent cases, and half, after further investigation and preliminary treatment, on the following day.

Dr. R. J. Stephens also treated a large number of casualties at first-aid posts, the majority being eye cases and burns. He, too, used previously prepared morphia in liquid form at incidents.

Dr. W. H. Hayes deplored the fact that earlier arrangements had not been made for using general practitioners who were not members of the official organisations. There was no lack of willingness to serve at incidents, and he had gone to several to volunteer his help before joining the rota which was subsequently formed for the purpose.

Dr. H. D. Pyke emphasised the strain, especially on lay workers, of being in attendance at digging out operations, and mentioned the instance of a civil defence officer having broken down so badly as the result of his experiences that he had been unable to face the work again.

CHAPTER 10
SHEFFIELD
August 1940 to May 1941

Contributed by
John Rennie, M.D., D.P.H., Medical Officer of Health, Sheffield

THE area of Sheffield in December 1938, was 39,596 acres and the population was estimated to be 518,200. By June 1940, the estimated population had fallen to 493,900, the decrease being attributable to recruitment to the Armed Forces. By December 1940, the estimated population had slightly increased to 498,660, probably by the influx of labour to the munition factories being greater than the outflow due to recruitment. This was followed by a fall during the next six months to 480,200, so that the heavy raids in December 1940, did not result in an excessive evacuation of the city, which might have followed extensive raiding.

CIVIL DEFENCE CASUALTY SERVICES

First-aid Posts. By June 1940, twenty-six fixed first-aid posts and three mobile units had been established and a sufficient whole-time and part-time first-aid service had been trained and enrolled. The numbers reporting for duty at the beginning of the heavy raids were: whole-time males 49, females 170; part-time males 129, females 202, thus giving an average of six males to twelve females to each first-aid post. In Sheffield the provision of twenty-six fixed first-aid posts for a population of about half a million was above the average. In Manchester and Liverpool with populations of about 750,000 and 850,000 respectively, twenty first-aid posts only were provided, and were found to be quite sufficient, even during the prolonged raids which occurred in Liverpool. Of the first-aid posts four were attached to hospitals and twenty-two were situated to serve areas with no hospitals.

Ambulances. There were 86 four-stretcher whole-time ambulances and 16 whole-time and 135 part-time cars for sitting cases. The whole-time staff recruited to serve these ambulances and cars consisted of 72 males and 212 females; the part-time staff numbered 70 males and 67 females.

First-aid Parties. There were twenty-one first-aid party depots and 294 whole-time males and 488 part-time had been recruited and trained.

HOSPITALS

The city contained seven Class 1A casualty clearing hospitals, namely:
Voluntary: Royal Hospital; Royal Infirmary; Children's Hospital (suspended); Jessop Hospital for Women.

Municipal: City General Hospital; King Edward VII Hospital; Lodge Moor Hospital (suspended).

There were in addition annexes to the Royal Hospital and the Royal Infirmary and three Class II hospitals, one of which, the Edgar Allen Institute, was used for the out-patient treatment of casualties only. In addition to these active hospitals there were other small special hospitals which were not called upon to receive casualties unless in a grave emergency. At the beginning of the raids there were about 1,000 vacant beds for the reception of casualties.

THE RAIDS

The first bomb dropped on the city fell on August 18, 1940; neither this bomb nor two more dropped on the following night caused any casualties. The first casualties occurred on August 28, when twenty-four H.E. bombs were dropped, of which only twelve exploded. Four persons were killed, seventeen admitted to hospital and 61 treated at first-aid posts. There were four more raids from September to November; but very few bombs were dropped and only a few casualties resulted.

In December, the city was heavily attacked on the nights of 12–13 and 15–16. On these two nights approximately 540 H.E. bombs and 11 paramines fell on the city together with thousands of incendiary bombs. The estimated weight of heavy bombs of all calibre was 300 metric tons. On the first night the attack lasted for about nine hours; on the second night for about three hours, during which 100 H.E. bombs and five paramines were dropped. In these two raids 616 persons were killed, 488 admitted to hospital and 1,096 treated at first-aid posts. On the other fifteen occasions on which bombs were dropped only 36 persons were killed, 82 admitted to hospital and 167 treated at first-aid posts. Seventy-eight bombs were dropped in these smaller raids. The total weight of attack was 618 H.E. bombs and 11 paramines, of an estimated total weight of about 330 metric tons. The casualties were about one killed and ·9 seriously injured per bomb and about two killed and 1·7 seriously injured per metric ton. If these figures are correct the average killed and injured per bomb was higher than the average in other towns, but the rate killed and injured per metric ton was lower. It seems reasonable to assume, however, that the average weight of the bombs dropped was not more than half a ton, and that the estimate of 330 metric tons was therefore too high.

During these attacks four hospitals were hit by bombs and six patients were killed; 501 patients had to be transferred to other hospitals. Two first-aid posts were put out of action, one ambulance destroyed and twelve seriously damaged. Among the Civil Defence Services there were eighteen fatal casualties.

The table opposite contains details of the various attacks on the city.

No.	Date	No. of H.E. bombs	Duration of attack	Number and type of bombs	Killed	Admitted to hospital	Treated at first-aid posts
	1940:						
1	August 18		2355–0112	One H.E.	—	—	—
2	19		2310–0356	Two H.E.	—	—	—
3	28		0135–0310	24 H.E., including 12 unexploded	4	17	61
4	31		2205–0305	Three H.E.	—	3	20
5	September 11		0130–0056	Nine H.E.	1	2	1
6	26		2216–2315	Several, including four H.E.	3	11	11
7	October 14		2230–2326	Over 50 incendiaries, two H.E.	—	—	—
8	December 12–13	450	1900–0417	Thousands of incendiary bombs, approximately 450 H.E., including six parachute mines	616*	488	1,096
9	December 15–16	100	1910–2215	Incendiaries, 100 H.E. bombs, including five mines			
	1941:						
10	January 9		2330	One H.E.	—	—	1
11	February 16		—	10–15 incendiaries, four H.E.	—	1	2
12	March 14		2104	One H.E.	1	2	3
13	May 8		2127–2130	Two H.E., two land mines	14	29	26
14	October 13		0050–0300	Approximately 100, including 20 H.E.	2	11	25
15	20		2330	Three H.E.	9	5	17
16			2200	Incendiaries	2	—	—
17	1942: July 28		Early morning		—	1	—
				Total	652	570	1,263

Date	No. of H.E. bombs	Deaths	Seriously injured	Slightly injured	No. of patients killed	Patients transferred to other hospitals after raid	F.A.P.s put out of action	C.D. personnel killed or wounded	Houses evacuated	Persons found accommodation
1940: December 12–13, 15–16	450 100	616	488	1,096	6	Royal Hospital 91 Royal Infirmary 123 Jessop Hospital 32 Nether Edge Hospital 255 —— 501	1 1	14 wardens killed 5 Fire Service killed: 34 injured 4 Casualty Service killed	6,471	6,000

* Of these, 487 were deaths registered in the city; seven were deaths of Sheffield residents registered outside the city (Wharncliffe Emergency Hospital); eight were deaths registered on the certificate of the Coroner; 81 were presumed deaths registered on the authority of the Registrar-General; two were unclassified, and there were 31 deaths of men serving in His Majesty's Forces.

THE WORKING OF THE CIVIL DEFENCE SERVICES

There were 1,012 incidents reported during the two nights of heavy raiding and first-aid parties were called out to 263 incidents. Ambulances were sent out on 272, and cars for sitting cases on 99 occasions. 899 patients were carried to the hospitals and first-aid posts in these vehicles. 614 men, 390 women and 92 children, a total of 1,096 persons were treated at first-aid posts. Of these, 268 men, 124 women and 25 children were treated at the four first-aid posts in connexion with hospitals and retained there until they could be sent home. At first-aid posts not connected with hospitals, 346 men, 266 women and 67 children, a total of 679 persons were treated, of whom 541 were retained at the posts until fit to return home. Of the remainder, 133 persons were sent on to hospitals for admission and five died at the posts.

The figures given above include only those recorded at posts; but it is known that a considerable number of persons were treated in addition, of whom no record was kept through the difficulties caused by damage to posts and improvised lighting when the electric supply was cut off.

COMMENTS BY THE MEDICAL OFFICER OF HEALTH ON THE WORK OF THE CASUALTY SERVICES

General. During the first raid the weight of the attack fell mostly on the central, southern and western divisions of the city, while in the second the attack was heaviest on the eastern and northern divisions. Thus during the two raids the casualty services were all severely tested.

The turn-out of personnel both whole-time and part-time was exceedingly good and the staff of the casualty services were found to be fully competent in carrying out their duties. At no time were the resources of the first-aid parties or ambulances found inadequate.

The work of the three sections of the casualty services proceeded smoothly and efficiently and there was never any breakdown; the conduct of all concerned was beyond praise. Their complete absorption in their work and cool indifference to danger was something of which the city may justly be proud.

Interference with telephone communications occurred very early and was extensive, but these difficulties were overcome by the resource, initiative and bravery of all concerned. The early failure of telephone communications showed the lack of foresight displayed in Sheffield in not having organised a messenger service for the casualty services in addition to the official warden's messenger service.

The work of the controls was efficient, even when handicapped by the breakdown of the telephone and lighting services. Many first-aid parties and ambulances were called out to incidents by wardens direct from their depots when communications with the control centres had been cut.

The experience of these raids emphasised the desirability of having simple rescue equipment available at each party depot, as in a number of incidents first-aid parties could have rescued persons trapped in cellars much more speedily if they had been supplied with the necessary apparatus, such as pickaxes, crowbars, etc. After the raids this defect was rectified, and, since these experiences in Sheffield were similar to those in all parts of the country, the complete reorganisation of the Civil Defence Services was undertaken in order to meet these defects.

The First-aid Parties. The first-aid party leaders showed good judgment in their selection of cases for hospital treatment. This was proved by the fact that 87 per cent. of the cases treated at the first-aid posts did not subsequently require hospital treatment. Even in cases where the patients afterwards went to hospital, it was undoubtedly greatly to their advantage to have been given some preliminary resuscitation, warmth, rest and morphia.

The Ambulance Service. The work of the ambulance section was well carried out. The personnel, who were for the most part women, showed invariable coolness and heroism throughout these raids. The numbers of ambulances and sitting case cars were found to be sufficient and after the service had answered every call there were still vehicles ready to be sent out. The blanket and stretcher exchange system of the hospitals did not work well during the first raid, but was better in the second raid. During the course of the action on December 12-13 the ambulance headquarters became untenable and the Ambulance Officer transferred his headquarters and that of another ambulance depot, which was bombed out, to the Sheffield Royal Hospital, from which they operated for the remainder of the raid. A further move to the Sheffield Royal Infirmary was necessary on the following day because of a delayed action bomb near the Royal Hospital.

The First-aid Posts. The fixed first-aid posts proved their value in both raids and carried out their duties with marked success, often working under great difficulties owing to 'blast' damage to the posts. But the experience of these two raids showed conclusively the relative uselessness of mobile first-aid units in a city like Sheffield. While it might be useful to retain several mobile units in reserve to meet special contingencies, it was quite apparent that mobile units could not in any way replace fixed first-aid posts. In view of the experience during these two raids, it must be counted as extremely fortunate that the instructions which had been received to convert a number of fixed first-aid posts into mobile units had not been carried out. Homeless people thronged in large numbers to several of the first-aid posts, and in two instances it was several days before the rest centre organisation could relieve them of this burden. These extra duties were specially felt by the first-aid posts' staffs who had, by the end of the raid, already carried out a great deal of very hard and trying work. The burden was willingly borne, but it was found essential that these homeless people should be removed from the first-aid posts at the earliest possible moment in order that they could be prepared for further action.

It was found difficult during these raids to supply the casualty services personnel with a good meal, so essential to many of them after their prolonged exertions. Arrangements were subsequently made for mobile canteens to call at each post and depot and deliver hot meals to the staff as soon as possible after a raid. This provided a satisfactory solution to the difficulty.

The central casualty stores at Nether Edge hospital were hit on the night of December 12–13 and a fire was started among the stores. About 75 per cent. of the stores were saved and were moved to accommodation in Winter Street Hospital and Crimicar Lane Sanatorium.

THE WORK OF THE HOSPITALS

During the two heavy raids, 488 seriously injured casualties were admitted to the various hospitals, the three main receiving hospitals being the Royal Hospital and its annexe, the Royal Infirmary and the City General Hospital. Firvale House, a Class II hospital, admitted a certain number of patients who required hospital care on account of their age and infirmity. After the raids, arrangements were made to transfer both the ordinary civilian sick and air raid casualties from the Royal Hospital and Royal Infirmary to the Wharncliffe Emergency Hospital, a base hospital just outside the city boundary, thus reducing the number of patients in the centre of the city and making provision for further raids.

The number of casualties arriving at the hospitals was always well within the capacity of the medical and nursing staffs to deal with, such difficulties as there were being the result of damage to hospital buildings during the raids. In spite of this, patients were treated and made comfortable in the most expeditious manner. There was some delay in the almoner's and clerical departments in compiling accurate returns for publication by the Casualty Bureau. This was only to be expected as large numbers of admissions were made during a very short period. In all the hospitals the telephone communications were broken.

The Jessop Hospital for Women was put out of action very early in the first raid, from which time it was unable to receive patients, and had eventually to be completely evacuated. The Royal Hospital suffered extensive damage to its windows early in the raid and for a time casualties were received in the hospital basement. When this was no longer possible, a mobile surgical team was sent to the Fulwood Annexe on the outskirts of the city and ambulances were diverted from the Royal Hospital to the annexe direct. On the following day, access to the Royal Hospital was found to be difficult, because there were delayed action bombs close by and it was necessary to transfer a considerable number of the patients to the Wharncliffe Emergency Hospital. Many bombs fell near the Royal Infirmary, and after the first raid as many patients as could be moved were also evacuated to the Wharncliffe Emergency Hospital.

Nether Edge, a Class II hospital, was much damaged by fire and high explosive bombs. There was a direct hit on one ward in which six patients were killed. The medical and nursing staffs were engaged all through the night transferring patients to the less damaged wards and did magnificent work under the most trying circumstances. After the raid an attempt was made to carry on, but the absence of water, gas and electricity and the condition of the buildings made necessary a complete evacuation, which was carried out on December 15 and 16. The chronic sick patients were sent to Dean House Emergency Hospital, Huddersfield; the maternity patients either to their own homes or to the City General Hospital, and the tuberculous patients to the Winter Street Hospital. Only 80 patients who could not be moved, remained in this hospital. A certain amount of damage to windows, ceilings, etc., was suffered by the Children's Hospital, but the staff was able to function normally.

From the experience gained during the raids, it appeared necessary to augment the clerical staffs of all the hospitals in order to deal adequately with the recording and notification of casualties. It was important for friends and relations of casualties to receive the earliest possible information, so that their anxieties might be relieved.

The value of adhesive linen mesh on the glass of windows, etc., as a protective measure was found to be most satisfactory. In the Nether Edge Hospital most of the windows were blown in by blast, but none of the patients or staff was injured by flying glass.

Dr. A. G. Yates, the Group Officer, has given the following account of the work of the hospitals during the two heavy raids:

THE ROYAL INFIRMARY

Night of December 12–13, 1940. As soon as the 'Alert' sounded all staff reported to their various duty points. Stretcher bearer volunteers (of whom approximately 25 reported) were joined for the time being with the porter staff and posted to the casualty department, and as look-outs on the top floors of the different buildings. The latter proved a wise and timely measure, for at an early stage of the raid incendiary bombs (50–60 in number) fell in the infirmary grounds and on different blocks—notably the nurses' home, Victoria block, old building, Norfolk block and laundry. These fire bombs were quickly attacked and only in the nurses' home, Victoria block and laundry did the building take fire. These fires were promptly controlled or extinguished before they assumed serious proportions. Stirrup pumps or sand were used to deal with these incendiary bombs, and proved successful.

When the fire fighting had been completed, look-outs were again posted on the top floors, and porters and stretcher bearers were sent to assist and hasten the work of transferring patients to accommodation which had been prepared under ground level. All possible basement accommodation was used, and, although conditions were not ideal, the patients seemed comfortable and calm. The casualty department, which by this time was dealing with air raid casualties, was also transferred as far as possible to the greater safety of the basement of the dispensary and to rooms adjoining. The stairway down to this basement proved rather difficult to negotiate but alterations which were carried out after the raid improved the position here. The infirmary buildings suffered no direct hit from high explosive bombs, the main damage being caused by blast; fortunately, there was little flying glass, probably because most windows had been covered with protective substance of one kind or another. Members of the works department were promptly called in by telephoning to an address near their homes (which was on record) and before dawn wards which were required to accommodate casualties and other in-patients had been made habitable. The stock of materials which had been accumulated against this need proved invaluable. In common with other establishments the hospital was, after the raid, without gas or water—electricity only being maintained. As regards the lack of gas, which affected cooking arrangements in particular, prompt measures were taken to install oil-fires and coke-fired cooking stoves and these gave good service. Water supplies were resumed in all buildings except the nurses' home, within 24 hours, and in the home a mobile tank was obtained without delay and supplies obtained therefrom until an emergency pipe-line had been carried through from the adjoining Prince George block. Although electricity supplies were not affected on this occasion it was thought advisable to obtain supplies of various equipment to provide emergency lighting in case of need in the future.

Night of December 15–16, 1940. On this occasion the action taken was on the same lines as on the previous raid, but, fortunately, the main attack was centred to the east of the infirmary area and did not appear to be so severe. All staffs, however, were mobilised for action and met the demands made upon them, and patients were again brought safely underground.

Casualties treated were:

December 12–13, 189 casualties of whom 37 were admitted, and 4 died after admission.

December 15–16, 64 casualties of whom 22 were admitted, and 8 died after admission.

A warm tribute was paid to all sections of the infirmary staff (and volunteers attached thereto), who with courage and determination carried out their duties with little thought for their personal safety.

THE ROYAL HOSPITAL

For more than nine hours on December 12–13, 1940, and for three and a half hours on December 15 the city was continuously bombed, but neither the hospital, the annexe, nor the two nurses' homes were directly hit. Damage from blast was sustained by the hospital, the sisters' wing of the home and at Crookes. The hospital windows generally were shattered, but the central block and connecting bridge received less damage than elsewhere. All wards were previously closed except the Keeling and Arthur Jackson, and the nurses' dining room in the basement was made into a ward. There was an adequate staff on duty, and the only two incendiary bombs which fell (one on the roof of the pay bed wards outside the theatre, the other in the courtyard) were quickly dealt with. Two men on roof and courtyard patrolled throughout the raids.

Casualties commenced to arrive about 8 p.m., and under the direction of Dr. Imrie were at once treated. The number increased until the hospital was full, after which ambulances were directed to Fulwood, which also became a casualty station. One of the surgeons, Mr. Hynes, took a batch of nurses and a houseman up to the Annexe at Fulwood at 1 a.m., to deal with the cases that were being transferred there. The number of cases treated altogether was 328, of which 37 were admitted to the hospital and 89 to the annexe.

CITY GENERAL HOSPITAL

During the two major attacks on December 12 and 15, 1940, 116 cases required admission to hospital, i.e. 60 and 56 respectively.

There was a high proportion of serious cases and 57 patients required immediate operation. Twelve patients died; nine in the first 24 hours, two within 48 hours and one on the 9th day after injury.

The operating theatres were ready during the raids, but on each occasion the 'all clear' had sounded before the patients had sufficiently recovered after admission for operative work to begin. Elaborate methods of resuscitation were not used, as all the patients recovered with simple warmth by blankets, hot bottles, warm drinks, rest and sedatives. Only six cases received transfusion.

JESSOP HOSPITAL FOR WOMEN

This hospital was put out of action early in the raid of December 12–13 and the old block was rendered unsafe, but no patient was injured. Seventy-six patients were removed to the ground floor when the raid started, and after the building was damaged, were transferred to the basement of the new unfinished wing. Only two casualties were received. All the patients were evacuated the next morning.

NETHER EDGE HOSPITAL (MUNICIPAL)

This hospital was very seriously damaged, and six patients were killed in the raid of December 12–13. No casualties were admitted. Most of the patients were evacuated to Huddersfield on Sunday, December 15.

DAMAGE TO WATER SUPPLIES AND SEWERAGE

The damage to the water mains meant that about 300,000 people, including some residing in areas outside the city, were temporarily deprived of piped water supply; 170 mobile tanks, 32 stationary tanks, and, where possible, street standpipes were brought into action and people were advised to boil for at least fifteen minutes all water which was to be used for drinking purposes or preparing food. Most of the mains were repaired and supply restored by the end of the month. All fractured mains were chlorinated before being again brought into use. Serious damage to the sewerage system, which had contaminated the pipe water supply, made this essential. No epidemic of any kind due to water-borne diseases supervened.

The absence of water supply temporarily put out of action the water closets in several parts of the city, and hundreds of chemical closets were supplied. These had to be emptied and disinfected three times daily, and thus threw a good deal of additional work on to an already attenuated conservancy staff. The rest centres and public air raid shelters had already been supplied with chemical closets; these were much used and in spite of repeated emptying some grossly insanitary conditions supervened in certain parts of the city. An additional strain on the cleansing department was caused by the need to collect refuse from every house daily because the power house at the refuse disposal works had been put out of action.

REST CENTRES

Fifty-four rest centres had been provided of which twelve were 'first line', i.e. fully equipped and staffed day and night. Of these twelve, four were damaged and of the others only ten were usable because of damage to the buildings in which they were situated. Homeless people had therefore to be housed temporarily in all sorts of premises such as schools, church halls, cinemas, etc. The highest number of persons housed in these temporary premises at one time was about 23,000. By 6 a.m. on December 14, 60,000 hot meals had been served from mobile canteens, many having been sent by other towns to supplement the city's own resources.

CHAPTER 11

HULL

June 1940 to August 1941

Contributed by
Nicolas Gebbie, M.D., D.P.M., D.P.H., Medical Officer of Health, City of Kingston upon Hull, Medical Officer of Health, Hull and Goole Port Health Authority

INTRODUCTION

IT was obvious that Hull was likely to be very open to air attack should war break out between Britain and Germany. The city's geographical situation, its importance as Britain's third port and its experiences of Zeppelin raids during the War of 1914–18 left no doubt of this in the minds of the civil and military authorities. At the time of the Munich conversations, a policy of appeasement found favour here as elsewhere, but certain Corporation officials, notably the City Engineer and Medical Officer of Health, had already begun to review the local position and to plan certain measures for the safety and welfare of the population. Hospital provision, clinical services and the availability of medical, surgical and nursing staffs were reviewed by the Medical Officer of Health and discussions were opened with the officers of the Hull Corps of the St. John Ambulance Brigade.

Locally, the activities of the British Red Cross Society had been in abeyance in the interval between the War of 1914–18 and this conflict, but the St. John Ambulance Brigade had continued to function and it was expected that the officers and members of the brigade, men and women, would provide the nucleus of the casualty services in the event of air raids. All ranks in the brigade were eager and willing to volunteer for service in dealing with casualties, but when the war did eventually break out, the St. John Ambulance Brigade members were unable adequately to staff the first-aid depots and first-aid posts then established. Unfortunately there were many other urgent calls for their services, e.g. many of the men were employed by the railway company and immediately found themselves required to work long periods of overtime. The staffing of the casualty services thus created a very difficult problem.

On the outbreak of the war and for some time before, a severe strain had been placed upon the officers and staffs of local authorities and especially upon the staffs of the public health departments. In addition to the normal work of the Public Health Department, the administrative officers and the senior members of the clerical staff, handicapped by shortage of clerical assistance as the result of recruitment to the Services, had to organise and administer an entirely new service for dealing with air raid casualties. It was indeed a miracle that, with no previous experience to guide them, they were able in so short a time to forge an instrument which was to prove equal to all demands made upon it and to maintain its efficiency, not only during heavy raids, but also through long periods of inactivity and boredom.

THE CASUALTY SERVICES

The dual control of first-aid posts by the Ministry of Health and of first-aid depots by the Ministry of Home Security, presented a major problem to the staff of the Public Health Department. There were, in peace-time, no stretcher bearers to provide a nucleus for the Casualty Service, whereas the gangs of workmen in the City Engineer's Department were readily available for the new Rescue Service.

The keynote of the city's policy in regard to air raid precautions was dispersal. Shelter provision by the City Engineer for the members of the public at home, at school, at work or in the streets, was designed to prevent large numbers of people being in any building during raids and no shelter with accommodation for more than fifty persons was kept in use.

A similar policy was adopted by the Medical Officer of Health as regards the personnel of the casualty services in order to secure as wide dispersal as possible of the trained staff and of the cars and ambulances. For this purpose, thirty-three premises for use as first-aid depots and thirteen for use as first-aid posts were selected. However, on the outbreak of the war, there was a shortage of male staff, and only twenty-one first-aid depots were manned, the remaining twelve sets of premises being held in reserve. A recruiting campaign for volunteers, paid and unpaid, was embarked upon and meetings were held, which were addressed by the Medical Officer of Health, the Deputy Medical Officer of Health and by a member of the City Council, who had interested himself in the organisation of the casualty services. Courses of instruction of the volunteers in first aid (St. John Ambulance Association Course) and in anti-gas measures were held and many of these trainees obtained the certificate in first aid of the St. John Ambulance Association. During the period from December 1938, to June 1941, 2,817 persons were trained in first aid and of these 2,456 were successful in obtaining certificates. In widely dispersed depots such as have been described, discipline was necessarily less rigid than would have been possible had the personnel of the casualty service been concentrated in a few large depots, but this difficulty was more than compensated for by the additional safety secured.

Throughout the whole period it was difficult to secure enough part-time unpaid volunteers for the casualty and ambulance services and their attendance at practices and exercises was unreliable. However, the organisation was tested at a limited number of exercises and the services had not long to wait till the city had experience of the real thing, the best test of all. Fortunately the early raids on the city were light. Experience during these raids made the members of the casualty services alert and keen and they gave an excellent account of themselves, and there is no doubt that an efficient casualty and ambulance service, coupled with a good casualty information bureau, played a most important part in maintaining public morale at a high level.

THE RAIDS

The City of Hull, occupying 14,433 acres, had a pre-war population of 320,000 which dropped to an average of about 260,000 during the raids. As already mentioned, it was considered by the authorities to be highly vulnerable. An intense blackout was enforced and barrage balloons appeared in the sky. After the raids started in June 1940, alerts were numerous, and varied in duration from a few minutes to over eight hours. In the early days, daylight alerts sent the people off to shelters, but very soon no one took the slightest notice of the sirens during the hours of daylight. During the darkness, however, practically everyone not on civil defence or other duty sought the protection of house or shelter as soon as possible after the air raid warning had sounded. There were eighty-two raids during which bombs were dropped within the city boundaries. The routine of most of the raids followed closely that which was generally experienced elsewhere, viz. flares, followed by incendiaries and/or H.Es. with or without parachute mines, and in the later raids, anti-personnel bombs.

The first occasion on which bombs were dropped on the city was on June 22, 1940, so that the city was one of the first places in the country to have to meet an enemy attack.

Raiding on the city can be divided roughly into the following periods:

(i) Minor raids—from June 1940 to May 1941.
(ii) Heavy raids—from May 1941 to August 1941.
(iii) Subsequent minor raids.

THE NATURE OF THE RESULTING CASUALTIES

(1) *Unwounded Victims of Air Raids.* This category includes not only those who were within range of blast and flying debris and escaped injury, but also those who suffered from shock or who were rendered homeless.

The range of blast effect on human beings is a wide one—from slight momentary deafness to death. There were found at every incident some people stunned by their experiences. There they sat, head in hand, staring blankly into space, dazed, irresponsive to stimuli, unable to help themselves. They had to be taken to a reception centre, not sent unaccompanied or they would wander about. The different reactions of adults and children were most marked. At the reception centre, after a hot meal, the children dropped off to sleep, but the adults chattered in groups for hours. This observation was confirmed by the reception centre staffs and members of the W.V.S. who had a very wide experience amongst all classes of the community.

The beneficent effects of hot drinks at the site of the incident and at reception centres cannot be overstated. Mobile canteens and their efficient use did much to maintain morale, to lessen shock and to comfort the homeless. Raid and post-raid welfare was found to be of great importance. At one time there were over sixty reception centres with sick bays (one or two beds) at each, and two medical rest centres, and up to the end of June 1943, 103,000 homeless people had been dealt with, i.e. officially recorded as homeless. In fact, approximately half the city's population were at some time rendered homeless and many made private arrangements, e.g. through the good neighbour scheme, etc. The maintenance, control and hygiene of shelters and the care and welfare of the people using them became of such importance as to necessitate the setting up of a Shelter Welfare Department.

Frequent and prolonged alerts caused so much loss of sleep that some people, especially the workpeople, found themselves unable to carry on. They trekked out of the city to get a night's rest. Some of them started off on foot early in the afternoon, but there was no congestion so police control of road traffic was not required. The trekkers went to all sorts of accommodation, much of it very unsatisfactory—barns, pigsties, stables, hedgebottoms, etc, etc.

The Emergency Committee set itself to solve the problem, which was not a serious one till July 1941, and arranged for the use of school shelters in the playing fields of schools on the periphery of the city, to which buses were run from collecting points in the blitzed areas. They also arranged for blankets and for entertainments in the form of concerts, lectures, cinemas, dances, classes for the children, gardening, etc. Medical-aid posts were set up, with a rota of general medical practitioners to attend them. Thus the 'trekker' problem was solved.

(2) *Wounded*. The most marked feature of the wounded of all types was their dirty appearance. Skin and clothing were alike affected. Particles of dust, soot, plaster and often glass were driven into the skin, and the clothing, if it had not been partly or completely removed by blast, was very dirty. The patient might be almost unrecognisable and skin-pencil marks on the forehead were generally useless. Tag labels were used on every case and fastened to the patient.

The nature of the casualties differed from expectations, speaking generally, in that the slightly wounded were less numerous than was anticipated.

The first-aid posts fulfilled their function of minimising the rush of the slightly wounded to hospitals and the numbers never put an excessive strain on the organisation. The number of killed was proportionately higher than estimated. Killed and hospital admissions were about equal. Shrapnel wounds and cases of what was known in the last war as 'shell shock' were not common. The use by the enemy of H.E. and the fact that the people sought shelter from A.A. shrapnel accounted for the paucity of shrapnel wounds. The high death-rate in those subjected to near misses by bombs with powerful H.E. may explain the absence of 'shell shock' cases. Haemorrhage too was less serious than was expected. In fact, occasions for the use of tourniquets were very rare. At one hospital, which bore the heat and burden of heavy attacks on several nights, only three cases had tourniquets applied before admission, and of these only one was really necessary. Crush injuries with serious sequelae were very rare. Among the seriously wounded, it was found that few required immediate operation and experienced medical superintendents maintained that one of their chief functions during and immediately after raids was to restrain the excessive enthusiasm of the resuscitation and surgical teams. Of 956 cases admitted to hospital, 54 died after admission.

(3) *The Killed*. The dead were reverently dealt with at the incidents and full particulars entered on the labels so that identification later was simplified and the casualty bulletin could be published without delay. The dead were removed to the mortuaries as soon as possible.

The numbers of casualties from June 1940, to August 31, 1941, were:

	Men	Women	Children	Totals	Deaths in Hospital
Killed	407	387	211	1,005	
Admitted to hospital	460	365	131	956	
At First-aid posts	687	510	167	1,364	
Totals	1,554	1,262	509	3,325	54

THE WORK OF THE CASUALTY SERVICES

Central Control. Until the end of March 1941, the Medical Officer of Health or the Deputy Medical Officer of Health were on duty at Control Centre, and Dr. Diamond, the Deputy Medical Officer of Health, was killed when on duty there on March 31, 1941. One assistant medical officer of health was on duty at each of the four report centres and when necessary acted as incident medical officer. Owing to the serious shortage of medical staff, the arrangements then had to be revised. Control centre duty was taken on a weekly rota by the Deputy Medical Officer of Health, the Clinical Tuberculosis Officer and the C.D. Medical Officer, with the Medical Officer of Health on second call for each. Experienced lay staff of the grade of Depot Superintendents took duty at report centres.

The control centre was able to keep watch on the situation over the whole city, to transfer services from the area of one Report Centre to another, to distribute as evenly as possible the load of work at first-aid posts and hospitals, to send out mobile units or individual doctors to incidents, to arrange for the mortuary service to be expanded to meet needs and to co-operate with the Welfare Service, the Canteen Service, the Blood Transfusion Service and the Casualty Information Bureau Service.

As a general rule a doctor was not sent to an incident unless people were trapped. Party leaders had instructions to see that at incidents first aid was limited to what was necessary to secure the speedy removal of the patient in safety and comfort to aid post or hospital. At night in cold and wet weather elaborate first aid was impossible and even harmful.

Telephone communications in limited areas were occasionally cut off from Report and Control centre—here the cyclist messenger service proved its worth.

The First-aid Services. The difficulties encountered in organising and staffing the casualty services have already been referred to, but in due course the personnel of these services settled down to their job of succouring the wounded and gave a good account of themselves. Casualties amongst the personnel were more common than honours and awards, but the men and women in the services had the satisfaction of knowing that they did a grand job and that they deserved and received the gratitude of those whom it had been their privilege to help.

The work of the first-aid parties and of the girl ambulance drivers was beyond all praise. These men and women carried out their difficult work in conditions of extreme danger with a fine spirit. Fatigue and nervous strain failed to affect their cheerful devotion to duty.

During the heavy raids, help was obtained from other authorities under the Regional Scheme, but such help was only used during hours of daylight to let as many as possible of the local personnel have a much needed rest in preparation for whatever duty the following night might require of them. Co-operation with the other civil defence and public utility services was close and effective.

First-aid parties vied with each other in getting speedily to incidents and on many occasions they were the first of the services to arrive.

The numbers of vehicles as at June 1940, and August 1941, were:

	Ambulance (first line)	Trailer ambulance (second line)	Bus ambulances	F.A. Party cars	Volunteer cars	Sitting case cars
June 1940	53	40	8	10	approximately 50	—
August 1941	63	39	8	32	approximately 50 available	33

The first-aid party cars, the sitting case cars, and most of the volunteer cars were fitted with towing bars for use with the trailer ambulance if required.

Five large mobile units were originally mobilised, but these proved to be too unwieldy, although they were convenient for getting staff and equipment to a new site if a first-aid post was knocked out. The most practical unit was found to be a doctor and an orderly in a car. A rota was drawn up of mobile units and of medical officers on first call, with the remainder ready to be called on if required. The staff was drawn from the first-aid post at the hospital where the mobile unit was stationed. Dispersal was thus secured.

Damage in the Casualty Services. Seven first-aid posts were damaged during raids, and two were temporarily put out of action. On April 16, 1941 a first-aid post at one of the hospitals received a direct hit and the staff had to be transferred to another part of the hospital until extensive repairs were carried out. Six posts were damaged during heavy raids on May 8 and 9, 1941, and July 18, 1941. One of these posts was seriously damaged, but the staff continued to treat casualties till the following day, when the post had to be abandoned.

Between March 28 and July 18, 1941, twelve first-aid party depots were damaged, five of them so badly as to be put out of action, one depot received a direct hit from a heavy calibre bomb and six first-aid party men and one cyclist messenger were killed and four men were wounded.

On May 8, 1941, two ambulance garages were destroyed, with the loss of five ambulances, one trailer ambulance, two sitting case cars and two other vehicles. On the same night three bus ambulances were destroyed in the Corporation bus station, which was completely wrecked.

Of the personnel of the casualty services eleven were killed including Dr. D. Diamond, the Deputy Medical Officer of Health, and twenty injured on duty.

THE WORK OF THE HOSPITALS

When the scheme for the reception of air raid casualties requiring hospital treatment was being prepared the existing accommodation in Hull and the East Riding was surveyed by Dr. C. F. Good, of the Ministry of Health, and the Medical Officer of Health in collaboration with Dr. R. L. Thornley, Medical Officer of Health of the East Riding County Council and representatives of the voluntary hospitals in the area. The primary difficulty was that all five hospitals in the city to which casualties would be taken from incidents lay in the more vulnerable parts of the city. Four of the hospitals, the Hull Royal Infirmary and Victoria Children's Hospital (Voluntary) and the Anlaby Road and Beverley Road Hospitals (Municipal) were all within a short distance of the principal railway station and the fifth—previously the Hedon Road Maternity Hospital—was close to the main dock. Arrangements were accordingly made for rapid transfers, should the necessity arise, by bus ambulances and ambulances to hospitals outside the city.

Two inner base hospitals—Sutton Annexe of the Hull Royal Infirmary situated three miles from the centre of the city and part of the City Hospital for Infectious Diseases, and Cottingham, five miles from the city centre—were eventually used to receive casualties direct from incidents and first-aid posts outside a radius of one mile from the centre of the city. Risk of exposure of the patients to further bombing was thus reduced.

Two base hospitals—Beverley, eight miles and Driffield, fifteen miles from the city—were used for transfers from the inner hospitals. Transfers were so arranged that on the night after a raid approximately the same number of empty beds were available as before the raid. Transfers were decided upon by the Group Officer, Mr. T. Ritchie Rodger, O.B.E., F.R.C.S.Ed., in consultation with the Surgical Adviser and Medical Superintendents, and bus ambulances were used for these journeys.

The staffs at the various hospitals carried out their onerous duties in a highly efficient manner; and the members of the nursing staffs, many of whom were very young, by their courage and devotion to duty during the raids, played an important part in comforting and sustaining their patients. Two surgical teams and one resuscitation team were allocated to each receiving hospital for work during raids and the services rendered by the doctors were all that could be desired.

Supplies of blood and plasma were maintained at all the hospitals and were replenished without delay under arrangements made by the Regional Blood Transfusion Officer.

DAMAGE TO HOSPITALS

The five casualty receiving hospitals within the city boundary were all damaged more or less severely, but no patients or members of the staff were seriously injured. The application of muslin to the windows prevented injury to patients and staff by flying glass.

The more serious incidents were:

Anlaby Road Institution and Hospital: On the night of July 10–11, 1941, H.E. bombs damaged wards, the operating theatre block, X-ray department, etc., and 330 beds were temporarily put out of use.

Beverley Road Institution and Hospital: On the night of March 18–19, 1941, an H.E. bomb demolished part of the boundary wall and part of the female house and greenhouse; 75 beds were permanently rendered useless.

Hedon Road Hospital: On the night of May 8–9, 1941, severe damage was sustained and except for 30 beds for emergency purposes, this hospital of 174 beds ceased to function. The first-aid post continued in operation.

Hull Royal Infirmary: On the night of March 31, 1941, a parachute mine exploded near the end of the Victoria Wing of the Infirmary damaging three wards and putting 157 beds out of action. 107 patients were transferred (44 to their own homes, 47 to base hospitals and 16 to a convalescent home). After repairs had been executed, 95 beds were restored and brought into use.

On the night of May 8–9, 1941, the hospital buildings were extensively damaged by fires from incendiary bombs and blast from H.E. bombs. The 60 patients in the hospital were transferred to other hospitals and the hospital was out of commission.

Later, two small wards with accommodation for 28 patients were repaired and reopened for the reception of cases, e.g. urgent emergencies and air raid casualties. The out-patients' department, first-aid post and orthopaedic department continued to function.

Post Raid Conferences

Several of these meetings were held in the city during the days following heavy raids and were presided over by the Regional Commissioner, or by one of his deputies. They were attended by Regional departmental chiefs, the heads of the local services and the members of the Emergency Committee. Though he admitted the necessity of having some means of checking the results of raiding upon the various services and of ensuring assistance from Regional reserves, the Medical Officer of Health was of the opinion that those who had been up all night guiding, directing and supervising the services—and the work to be done for many hours after a heavy raid—were not at their best at such conferences. The Regional Commissioner and the senior members of his staff appreciated the position and released the heads of the local services from the conferences, as soon as they had made their reports.

WATER SUPPLIES

The water supply service was damaged during 27 raids in 335 places and 15,182 feet of piping from 2 in. to 25 in. were required for repairs. The damage during the nights of May 7–8 and 8–9 and July 18, 1941, was the most extensive. In the raid on July 18, 73 mains were fractured, including 14 trunk mains, but fortunately the mains previously damaged had all been repaired before this raid. In areas subjected to concentrated damage in the heavy raids, it was necessary to supply some domestic consumers and a limited number of trade consumers with water from water carts and standpipes fixed on the nearest available hydrants.

In spite of frequent raids the Water Department maintained the city's water supplies with commendable efficiency and the speed with which they carried out repairs to water mains, etc., deserves high praise. The safety of the public was not forgotten. When the mains were repaired whether contaminated or not, a solution of stabilised bleach at a strength of 50 parts per million was applied through hydrants, to make sure that the whole of the isolated section of the main was sterile. The mains were then flushed out and put into service.

SEWERAGE

The City Engineer's report stated that almost all the sewers in the city were interconnected and that no section of the sewerage system ever ceased to function, in spite of extensive damage from air raids. If it was not possible to clear a channel through the damaged sewer immediately, the sewerage was diverted along other sewers, but the aim was to maintain the flow through the damaged section and this was usually done within twenty-four hours. Temporary dams were constructed in the sewers to direct the flow, but there was no flooding nor any serious inconvenience to householders.

SANITATION

The availability of water and the maintenance of sewerage as described above enabled the Medical Officer of Health and his staff of sanitary inspectors to advise householders to continue to use W.C.s that were not damaged. Resort had not to be made to the digging of trench latrines, etc.

Amongst the many problems which had to be faced by the Chief Sanitary Inspector and his staff after raids, were such diverse matters as water supplies, drainage of individual houses, adequacy of sanitary arrangements at reception centres, fly breeding among debris, while the Chief Food Inspector and his staff dealt with foodstuffs damaged in shops, warehouses, etc., and gave valuable assistance to the Salvage Officer in dealing with foodstuffs.

The demands made upon the staff were heavy; they had to shoulder the responsibilities of civil defence work in addition to their normal duties, to lose much sleep during the nights of long alerts, to be constantly in difficult and dangerous conditions, with ranks seriously depleted by the demands of the fighting services, but they responded willingly to all calls made upon them.

CHAPTER 12

SOUTH WALES

1940 to 1941

Contributed by the Welsh Board of Health

ADMINISTRATION

WALES, which constituted Region 8, differed from other regions in that the Welsh Board of Health already existed as an executive machine of Government specially concerned with the problems of the principality and intimately acquainted with the existing hospital, health and other facilities. In other regions a new organisation to administer the hospital and first-aid services had to be set up, but in Region 8 the work could be and was conveniently discharged by the Welsh Board of Health without more than an internal reorganisation and augmentation of its medical and administrative staff. Apart from this difference the regional organisation of the Emergency Medical Services in Wales was the same as for other regions.

PREPARATORY WORK

At the time of the Munich crisis in 1938 some useful spade work in preparing the framework of an emergency hospital scheme had been done. It had shown that a number of deficiencies would have to be made good if there was to be an efficient emergency service capable of dealing with war-time needs. It was necessary to protect the hospitals, to provide extra accommodation, to increase hospital staffs and to provide much additional equipment.

Between September 1938, and the outbreak of war in September 1939, intensive preparatory work was done in two main directions. Firstly, hospitals, by means of visits by the Hospital Officer and his staff and by circulars and memoranda, had to be informed and instructed in the duties and responsibilities which they would have to face in the event of war; secondly, local authorities needed guidance and assistance in organising and equipping their first-aid post and ambulance services. In those days it was commonly supposed that Wales would probably not be subjected to continuous or intense attack from the air, and as a consequence the expansion of hospital services was restricted, particularly in respect of new hutted hospitals and wards, so that work in more vulnerable regions could be undertaken. The only new building work approved before the outbreak of war was the addition of accommodation for new beds for casualties at the North Wales Tuberculosis Sanatorium and a new 600-bed hutted hospital at Chepstow (just within the Welsh border), which was promised to the Welsh National Memorial

Association for use for tuberculous patients if war requirements did not prevent it.

WAR CONDITIONS

Later on, under the actual stress of war, experience was to prove that vulnerability or non-vulnerability, even if it could be determined in advance, was not a proper guide in deciding upon regional needs. Non-vulnerable regions had to bear the load of transferred sick and the sick from transferred populations (e.g. workers and evacuees) normally borne by the vulnerable areas. Moreover, Wales had throughout the war a large army population in process of training for whom hospital accommodation had to be found. Thus the original expectation that an extension of hospital services would be necessary on account only of air raid casualties was partly erroneous, for the dominant need was for more beds to cater for an abnormally large temporary increase in population and for the reception of sick persons from other regions. In the earlier months of the war the extra hospital beds held in readiness for air raid casualties were idle, the expected air attacks not having come, and it was decided to use them for Service casualties. During the period covering the battle of France, rail-borne convoys of service sick and wounded were sent to hospitals controlled by the Emergency Medical Service, and the Civil Defence Casualty Services were used to convey them by stretcher bearers and ambulances.

THE POSITION AFTER THE FALL OF FRANCE

With the fall of France there arose a new situation which closely affected Wales. The ports of South Wales, which had hitherto been considered unlikely targets for enemy aircraft because of their distance from enemy airfields, became vulnerable when new airfields were established in Normandy and Brittany and, in fact, some of the first bombs to fall in the United Kingdom fell in South Wales just before the intense air attacks on Southern England during the Battle of Britain. So far as Wales was concerned, it was then too late to deal adequately with the new situation by the erection of large hutted hospitals; the rate of building would have to be slow because labour and materials were wanted for more urgent works of defence. Moreover, the problem of augmenting hospital staffs was acute. The hutted hospital at Chepstow was not completed at this time and the situation was met by an extensive emptying of hospital beds in public assistance institutions and mental hospitals. Sites for new temporary hospitals were found at Cardiff, Newport and Swansea but eventually it was only at Swansea that the building of a new hospital was allowed to proceed. Not until two years later was a new hutted hospital of 600 beds completed at Morriston, Swansea.

SOUTH WALES

In the interval of 1940 and 1941, however, the existing hospitals in Wales managed to cope with the demand by crowding and by using make-shift annexes in buildings such as church halls, etc.

AIR ATTACKS ON WALES

As was to be expected, the area attacked was almost wholly confined to Cardiff and Swansea—Newport and Pembroke Dock were the only other important centres attacked, the latter twice and the former once.

The story of the air raids on Wales is based on reports to the Welsh Board of Health by W. G. Richards, M.D., Assistant Hospital Officer, Region 8.

1940, EARLY RAIDS

The South Wales casualty services were among the first in the country to come into action. This area was little affected by the daylight raids during the Battle of Britain, although a few 'planes paid early visits in daylight, Llanelly and Cardiff being attacked on July 9 and a rural area in Carmarthenshire and Swansea on July 10. Thirty H.E. bombs were dropped and caused a small number of casualties, of which 24 were killed, 29 admitted to hospital and 43 treated at first-aid posts. The hospitals and first-aid posts had no difficulty in dealing with this small number of casualties, but it was sufficient to give the civil defence personnel an opportunity of testing and improving their organisation.

After an interval of a month Swansea was attacked at night on August 10 and Neath at night on August 12, and during the day on August 20. Forty-eight H.E. bombs were dropped during these raids causing 84 casualties, of which 23 were fatal, 16 seriously injured and 45 slightly injured. In these raids also the emergency services promptly and efficiently dealt with the casualties.

SWANSEA, SEPTEMBER 1

The first real test of these services came on the night of September 1, when Swansea was heavily attacked, 164 H.E. bombs being dropped causing 154 casualties, of which 34 were fatal, 38 were admitted to hospital and 82 were treated at first-aid posts. The work of the hospitals and of the first-aid post personnel was highly commended by the Mayor and Corporation and the general public. It was considered, however, that better arrangements might have been made for the relief of the staff of the first-aid posts as they showed signs of fatigue after a long night of strenuous work. Apparently also, anti-tetanic serum was not administered, in accordance with instructions, to all the injured cases attending the first-aid posts. No reason for this omission has been given.

No damage was caused to hospitals or first-aid posts and no more raids of any kind occurred in this area during the next four months.

CARDIFF, JANUARY 2, 1941

The enemy returned to the charge with a heavy attack on Cardiff on the night of January 2–3, 1941. The raid began at 8.40 p.m. and went on for over six hours continuously and, after an interval, two more short attacks were made. 150 H.E. bombs were dropped and also 14 paramines, which caused widespread damage and 619 casualties. Of these 144 were fatal, 168 admitted to hospital and 307 treated at first-aid posts, but it is known that there were many more slightly injured who did not go to the posts or hospitals for treatment. The larger number of casualties as compared with the last raid on Swansea was entirely due to the greater number of houses that were demolished. Many people were trapped and hours were spent in getting out the seriously injured and the dead.

The casualties were spread over a large area and there was no single major incident with a large number. This facilitated the work of the ambulance service which established a shuttle service between the incidents and the first-aid posts and hospitals, one ambulance usually being found sufficient for each incident. At most of the incidents one first-aid party was also found to be sufficient. As a reserve, however, the Anglo-American Ambulances (Great Britain) were called out and did exceedingly valuable work as reliefs. Five ambulances were also summoned from Newport to act as additional reserves; each of these only came into action as a relief for one journey.

In Cardiff a 'panel' system had been organised which provided for the calling out of a general practitioner to each incident by the wardens. This system worked very well and ensured that all the cases had early expert treatment and were distributed direct from the incidents to hospitals or first-aid posts in accordance with the type of injury and in priority according to its severity. This system undoubtedly saved many lives.

The numerous paramines which were dropped made the evacuation of several areas imperative, and the Ambulance Transport Officer of the city arranged to transfer the evacuated population to certain earmarked centres. There were a number of bed-ridden, sick, aged and crippled people living in the evacuation area and a number of cases of measles, whooping cough, cerebrospinal meningitis, etc., who could not be evacuated to the rest centres, and special arrangements were made to use the isolation hospital. This hospital had suffered some damage, windows having been blown in and the lighting system wrecked, but it was habitable. Moving these cases kept the ambulance transport on duty for many hours after the raid had ended and threw extra strain on the personnel. To add to the difficulties, although a panel of undertakers had been organised to remove the dead, their arrangements were so inadequate that the ambulances had to carry out these duties, which prolonged the very considerable time they were on duty.

All ten first-aid posts were used for the treatment of casualties but the great majority were dealt with at the posts attached to the City Lodge Hospital and at the Cardiff Royal Infirmary. The work at the former, which is situated in a thickly populated central area, was much hampered by upwards of 2,500 homeless people who congregated there for shelter. The result was that the smooth and progressive disposal of casualties could not be maintained. The electric light plant was out of action, which increased the general confusion, and it is probable that many slightly injured persons who were treated at this post were not recorded. It was obvious that better police arrangements for shepherding the homeless to the rest centres were essential.

At the Cardiff Royal Infirmary this interference with the normal work of the first-aid post did not occur. Perfect order prevailed and the casualties were rapidly and efficiently dealt with.

The only hospital put out of action was the Llandough Hospital which is situated well out of Cardiff. It suffered extensive damage from paramines dropped in the grounds, several wards were rendered untenable and only three were usable on the following day; 164 patients had to be evacuated from this hospital to other areas.

Slight damage was caused to the City Lodge Hospital, the lighting was cut off and no operations were done until the following morning. In accordance with the Emergency Medical Services' instructions, every hospital should have installed an emergency lighting set of one of the types recommended and should also have provided a sufficient number of hurricane lamps in order to permit of urgent operations and of the general work of the hospitals being carried on; no explanation has been given why this had not been done at this hospital.

Further difficulties were caused in this hospital, which was of a very old type, by the presence of a large number of chronic cases, many of whom were accommodated in upper wards, the only access to which was by narrow twisting staircases. The Regional Authorities rightly came to the conclusion that these chronic cases must be moved as a precaution against further heavy attacks and 254 of these patients were therefore transferred to more suitable accommodation outside Cardiff on January 3 and the succeeding days. It was decided that in future only ambulant patients should be admitted to the upper floors of the hospital. The difficulty of getting these stretcher cases removed from the upper wards by the narrow staircases would have led to a serious state of affairs had these wards been damaged during the raid.

The Civil Defence Services worked exceedingly well under great strain, and there was very little delay in reporting at the incidents. The chief delay was due to many of the main roads being blocked by fallen debris. This could have been avoided had the arrangements for routing the ambulances and first-aid parties been properly attended to.

SWANSEA, JANUARY 17, FEBRUARY 19 AND 22

A heavy attack, lasting from 7 p.m. on January 17 to 5 a.m. on the 18th, was made on Swansea and caused considerable damage to property, but a comparatively small number of casualties considering the intensity and duration of the attack, in which 178 H.E. bombs were dropped. The casualties were 35 killed, 38 admitted to hospital and 59 slightly wounded. Nearly all were admitted to the Swansea General Hospital. Three patients died from multiple injuries after admission.

As the result of the experience gained from previous raids every section of the Civil Defence Services worked smoothly; incidents were promptly dealt with and the patients were rapidly dressed at the first-aid posts and disposed of either to hospital for further treatment or to their homes. Although the telephone system was extensively damaged, all staff detailed for duty reported without being summoned.

This raid was followed by another which continued for three nights from February 19 to 22. This proved to be the heaviest attack yet experienced in South Wales, no less than 896 H.E. bombs being dropped. The attacks started between 7 p.m. and 8 p.m. each night and went on until the early hours of the morning, the heaviest attack being on the third night. The total casualties were not as heavy as might have been expected: 219 were killed, 256 admitted to hospital and 146 slightly injured and treated at first-aid posts. The attack was widespread but the main target was the heart of the town. All three hospitals were fully used and all the fixed and mobile first-aid posts were in action. Ten extra practitioners were called out by the Control Centre to give assistance and act as reliefs to the hard-worked regular staffs.

The Swansea General Hospital received some damage which resulted in the Princess Royal Hospital admitting more cases than could adequately be dealt with, and a breakdown of communications prevented any diversion of the stream of patients. Ambulances found great difficulty in making a speedy passage through the streets filled with fallen debris. As the result of a direct hit on the Swansea General Hospital, 99 patients had to be evacuated during the raid to outlying hospitals, but 86 beds could still be used. The Trinity Place first-aid post also received a direct hit on the third night and was partly out of action.

Two mobile surgical teams from Cardiff had to be called in on the second night to release surgeons who had been working continuously, and on the third night more teams were summoned from Cardiff and Newport. On the 22nd another team from Cardiff was sent and on the 23rd the R.A.F. provided a team which remained on duty until the 25th. Resuscitation teams were also sent from Cardiff and worked throughout the second and third nights.

A feature of these attacks was the very low proportion of first-aid post cases compared with hospital cases, but there is evidence that a large number of slightly injured never attended the posts at all.

It was noticeable that there was no proper system of messengers to replace the telephones when communications broke down, in spite of the experience gained from previous raids.

The 'saturation' point at each hospital was passed on each night and neither the Control Centre nor the hospitals seemed to understand that saturation point can be reached before the bed capacity is exhausted if the operating facilities of the hospital are exhausted. The Control Centre did not seem to realise that the proper action was to call in the reinforcing ambulances arranged for by the Regional Hospital Officer, to transfer the excess cases who could be moved to hospitals outside the attacked area.

The proportion of one operating theatre to each 200 to 300 beds in hospital was found to be quite insufficient for heavy attacks of this kind.

CARDIFF, MARCH 3, APRIL 29

On March 3 Cardiff was again attacked and the raid lasted for five hours. A large number of incendiary bombs was dropped but only 60 H.E. bombs. These, however, were of heavy calibre, resulting in higher casualties than usual, there being 57 killed, 119 admitted to hospital and 124 treated at the first-aid posts. As might be expected from the large number of incendiary bombs which had to be dealt with, about 25 per cent. of the casualties treated at the first-aid posts were due to burns. Most of these walked to the first-aid posts for treatment. The Cardiff Royal Infirmary suffered some damage from fire.

On April 29 four paramines, one oil bomb and a heavy load of incendiaries were dropped on Cardiff, but the latter nearly all fell in fields to the west of the city. Only three of the paramines falling in residential areas caused casualties; 33 persons were killed, 65 seriously injured and 55 slightly injured. Most of the severe casualties were trapped cases, as was usual when paramines were dropped, and several times during the night doctors visited the incidents and administered morphia to accessible casualties who were being released by the rescue parties. At City Lodge Hospital, where 47 cases were admitted, a surgical team worked all night.

PEMBROKE DOCK

On May 12 the Pembroke Dock area was attacked and 60 H.E. bombs were dropped, which resulted in 36 deaths, 22 admissions to hospital and 18 slightly injured casualties treated at first-aid posts. The raid lasted about two hours.

The civil defence arrangements apparently failed in many respects; the warden service broke down, because many wardens slept out of the dock area at night, and only one ambulance was able to function. The mobile unit was sent out by the chief warden and was used as an ambulance. If the military authorities had not come to the rescue and provided Service ambulances, stretcher bearers and R.A.M.C. officers, many casualties would have been unattended.

Another attack was made on this area on June 11 when, although 91 H.E. bombs were dropped, only three civilians and four R.A.F. personnel were killed, three cases were admitted to hospital and six treated at first-aid posts. This small number of casualties threw no strain on the civil defence arrangements, but it was apparent from the first raid that the arrangements of Pembroke Dock left much to be desired. The total population living in the dock area was now less than three hundred.

NEWPORT

On July 1, eight paramines were dropped in Newport in about twenty minutes, resulting in much damage to property. The casualties were 29 killed, 47 admitted to hospital and 60 treated at first-aid posts. The work of the medical and first-aid services was, on the whole, satisfactory.

ROGERSTONE

At Rogerstone, which is in a rural area, two paramines were dropped on October 7 near the aluminium factory; 11 persons were killed, 14 admitted to hospital and 24 treated at first-aid posts. The fixed post, the mobile unit and the first-aid post in the factory were all called into action, and as this was their first raid, there was some confusion at the start, but a doctor who was not summoned arrived at the incident within ten minutes, an ambulance within twenty minutes and the mobile unit within twenty-five minutes. Two more doctors arrived shortly after and the first casualties left for hospital forty-five minutes after the bombs had dropped, so that little fault can be found with the services in this small place.

GENERAL COMMENTARY

Dr. Trevor Jones, Welsh Board of Health, Regional Hospital Officer for Wales, expressed the opinion that the hospital and first-aid services on the whole worked well but that some confusion was caused by uninjured persons collecting at the hospitals and posts instead of at the rest centres. The system of calling out practitioners as 'incident doctors' and in 'light units' proved invaluable and the surgeons' reports on treatment were generally satisfactory. The problem of dealing with the chronic sick and helpless patients in the upper wards of hospitals would have been insurmountable if any city hospitals housing these patients had been badly damaged before these patients had been evacuated to the rural areas.

South Wales

No.	Date	Duration of attack	Locality attacked	Approximate number and type of bombs	Killed	Admitted to hospital	Treated at first-aid posts	Damage to property
	1940:							
1	July 9	A few minutes	Llanelly	11 H.E.	—	—	6	Slight
2	9	A few minutes	Cardiff	2 H.E.	7	1	5	Slight
3	10	Half an hour	Carmarthenshire rural areas	13 H.E.	7	10	16	Slight
4	August 10	A few minutes	Swansea	4 H.E.	10	12	16	Slight
5	10	Half an hour	Swansea	16 H.E. (30 lb.)	15	4	—	Slight
6	12	Half an hour	Neath	20 H.E.	3	5	2	Slight
7	20	A few minutes	Neath	4 H.E.	5	7	43	Slight
8	September 1	Six hours	Swansea	164 H.E.	34	38	82	Fairly extensive; no hospitals or F.A.P.s hit
	1941:							
9	January 2	Seven hours	Cardiff	150 H.E., 14 paramines	144	168	307	Widespread: one hospital badly damaged, one slightly damaged
10	17	Ten hours	Swansea	178 H.E.	55	38	59	Widespread
11	February 19–21	Eight to ten hours on each night	Swansea	896 H.E.	219	256	146	One hospital and one F.A.P. damaged. Widespread damage to property
12	March 3	Five hours	Cardiff	60 H.E.	57	119	124	Fairly extensive damage
13	April 29	Two hours	Cardiff	4 paramines	33	65	56	Much damage
14	May 12	Two hours	Pembroke Dock	60 H.E.	36	22	18	Fairly extensive damage
15	June 11	Three hours	Pembroke Dock	91 H.E.	7	3	6	Slight
16	July 1	Twenty minutes	Newport	Eight paramines	29	47	66	Slight
17	October 7	A few minutes	Rogerstone	Two paramines	11	14	18	Slight

The table on previous page contains particulars of the enemy attacks on South Wales and of the casualties and damage caused.

Dr. W. G. Richards summed up his impression of the work of the casualty services as follows:

> 'Much has been learnt and many changes carried out in the Casualty Services, changes that were collateral rather than fundamental. A new tradition, a new comradeship and a quality of leadership was born in the bombed areas of Wales—a "threefold cord which is not quickly broken." Much is owing to the old ambulance men of pre-war days as well as to the new recruits, whose knowledge is no longer limited to the abstract pages of the "black-book", for they have become practitioners of the art of first-aid.'

CHAPTER 13
BELFAST
April to May 1941

Contributed by the Department of Health and Local Government, Northern Ireland

As there was no separate Ministry of Health in Northern Ireland, civil defence services worked under the supreme authority of one Minister, the Minister of Public Security, and in the casualty services particularly this was of great advantage. It served to eliminate the divided control, overlapping of effort and other disadvantages with which the services in Great Britain had to contend.

Another factor which made for ease of working in the casualty service was that as early as December 1940, the then Minister of Public Security transferred the administration of civil defence in Belfast from the local authority to a small, active body of three members, the Belfast Civil Defence Authority.

Added to these there was another advantage in Belfast in that service heads could keep in close touch with ministerial officers and matters of importance could be decided without delay, and, where necessary, put into operation immediately. This was of particular value in the period immediately following the air raids on Belfast.

ADMINISTRATION OF THE CASUALTY SERVICES

The comparative isolation of Northern Ireland and the special nature of some of its civil defence problems led to specialised arrangements for administration in Belfast. All the major services were placed under the supreme control of part-time volunteer officers. In the casualty service, however, the titular head throughout the war was the Medical Superintendent Officer of Health for Belfast. In effect, owing to other duties, this officer early in the war delegated the administration to Dr. R. C. MacMillan. When Dr. MacMillan resigned in 1941, the administration of the service was vested in a chief casualty officer, Professor T. T. Flynn, a voluntary officer. It remained in his hands till the service was disbanded in 1945.

In order to maintain liaison between the lay side of the administration and the medical side, the Civil Defence Authority, in August 1941, appointed as medical liaison officer, a doctor who had distinguished himself by the excellence of his work in the air raids as medical officer of the mobile casualty service in 'G' district, Belfast.

For civil defence, Belfast was divided into eight districts (A–H) corresponding to the police districts. In addition, it was arranged that the Harbour area (I district) should be included in the general scheme for Belfast, thus making nine districts in all.

General control of each district was placed in the hands of voluntary district officers. Thus there were eight district casualty officers (H and I districts were combined), each having a deputy where possible.

PROVISION OF FIRST-AID POSTS, FIXED AND MOBILE

The earliest scheme provided for twenty-seven fixed aid posts. The number actually created was fifteen, arranged as follows: one in each of the following districts: A (city proper), D, H and I; two in each of the following: B, C, F and G and three in E district. One of the fixed posts in G district was afterwards abandoned. Closely associated with each fixed post was a mobile post, consisting of a single decker omnibus, fitted out and equipped according to ministerial specifications. Medical officers and deputies were in charge of these posts. The medical officer for the mobile aid posts also had charge in the initial stages of the training of first-aid parties and ambulance attendants. In effect the arrangement was that of a casualty depot in which were included a fixed post and a mobile post. Three of these were situated in the externs of hospitals and some others at schools.

In order to cope with the demands of the public for more adequate protection, certain elementary types of fixed posts were established. These were known respectively as first-aid points and auxiliary first-aid points. The latter were mostly situated in dwelling houses, wardens' posts, etc., and usually no doctors were attached to them.

Mobile Aid Posts. Experience showed that omnibuses were too unwieldy for this purpose and their place was taken by much lighter vehicles. Some mobile aid posts were replaced by mobile medical units, consisting of a doctor with a nurse and a first-aider, with the most urgently needed equipment. These were intended to attend at incidents with the utmost speed to treat emergency cases.

The introduction of full-time manning on the fall of France in 1940 and the need to find extra space for storage, sleeping, eating, etc., led to the establishment of separate depots in large houses or other premises.

DEPOT SYSTEM

The decision to have the larger depots of this type was made early in 1941. Besides these main depots (one to each district) there were numbers of dispersal depots to which services were dispersed on alerts. The establishment of depots, each with a trained superintendent in charge, relieved the medical practitioners of a great deal of responsibility and work. At none of the depots were there any rescue squads. Although later the relationship between this service and the rescue service became closer they were never combined as they were in England. As far as possible, all male personnel in the casualty service were trained in rescue methods at the Rescue School at Felden, near Belfast.

TRAINING

Medical officers were responsible for the training, discipline, health and recreation of the personnel in all posts and depots. Their duties and powers were much greater than in Great Britain. It was found in general that the interest taken by the volunteers depended to a large extent on the personality of the doctor.

It was soon obvious, however, that part-time medical officers could not give the necessary time to this work, especially as the civilian medical services had been much depleted by war needs, nor had they the specialised knowledge for the operational training of first-aid parties and of the ambulance service. This led to a fundamental change in training methods. As soon as possible, also, the system by which all doctors were called out on alerts or raids was changed to a rota system.

In 1940, a roster of daily duties and training had been drawn up by the medical practitioners and district casualty officers, and, in October 1940, two inspectors were appointed to see that these duties were carried out and, in particular, to supervise the training of first-aid parties. It had been incumbent upon all members of the personnel to possess on appointment a certificate of the St. John Ambulance Brigade or British Red Cross Society or to obtain the certificate as soon as reasonably possible. As far as possible, the Conjoint Board arranged to use medical officers from the casualty service for instruction in such certificate classes.

In order to see that knowledge of first-aid and of gas precautions was kept up to date, proficiency examinations for all members of the personnel were arranged. The task of examining nearly 2,000 members of the service was shouldered by the medical officers themselves. Cups were presented to be competed for each year, and awarded to the post or point showing the greatest efficiency for the year.

Arrangements were made with the Fire Service late in 1940 to allow nurses of the casualty service to assist in the city ambulance service. This training undoubtedly contributed largely to the efficiency of the service in the air raids of 1941. When the Fire Service was nationalised, the city ambulance service was handed over *in toto* to the casualty service and a new system of calling up was established. The medical officers of the service took a great interest in seeing that the ambulance service was efficiently trained. The number of cases handled by the city ambulances increased from 3,000 in 1941 to nearly 7,000 in 1944. Medical practitioners generally took increasing advantage of this service. The service provided transport for the obstetrical flying squads instituted by the city.

In July 1942 a Casualty Training School at Glencairn House, Belfast, was opened. The medical side of the syllabus of this school was given into the hands of two part-time medical officers. A large proportion of the full-time personnel of the service passed through this school and many qualified for its certificate. The school was comparable in standard to similar schools in England. It was not residential and was not lavishly furnished, but was reasonably well equipped. It was used by the Ministry of Public Security for week-end courses for country doctors, representatives of local authorities and country personnel. The school closed down when the services were reduced in November 1944.

GAS CLEANSING

Fixed gas cleansing stations were associated with most fixed aid posts and some first-aid points. The first stations constructed were very primitive but by modifying in some details the plan of the British Ministry some most efficient combined stations were built. In addition some eighteen mobile stations were acquired.

Training in gas precaution methods was begun as early as May 1939, and continued until 1944 for doctors and members of the A.R.P. services.

THE RAIDS

Belfast experienced four air attacks, two of minor and two of major importance.

The First Raid. The earliest opportunity for the casualty organisation to go into action came on April 8, 1941, when German aircraft first appeared over the city. The raid, a small one in comparison with two that were to follow, began at 0010 hours and lasted until 0359 hours. It is estimated that six planes took part.

The first casualty in the city was a warden who was going to his post. He was injured by shrapnel during the first burst of gunfire, which preceded the sounding of the siren. A number of posts were brought into action during the night, particularly those situated at Mersey Street and Grove School. First-aid parties and the ambulance service dealt with casualties from incidents at Queen's Island and in the Harbour area, the seriously injured being conveyed to the Royal Victoria Hospital. During the raid a stick of bombs fell in the vicinity of Grove Post which was damaged by blast and had to be evacuated. The casualties in this raid were:

Killed	13
Injured and detained	34
Injured but not detained	47
Total	94

The damage to property was light.

The Second Raid. This, the heaviest raid on the city, occurred at 2240 hours on April 15, 1941 and lasted until 0445 hours the next morning. If the previous raid was the first opportunity of action, this one provided a good test. The services came through successfully, the personnel carrying out their duties with the utmost courage, calmness, efficiency and speed, and even under the most difficult and dangerous circumstances morale was exceptionally high.

During this raid, bombs of many calibres, weighing approximately 83 tons were dropped. The damage to property all over the city was extensive but was overshadowed by the heavy death roll, which was out of all proportion to the number of persons seriously injured. That the raid accounted for 745 deaths must in part be ascribed to the fact that the citizens had not yet become shelter conscious and that the raid came soon after the Easter holiday, and caught many returning holidaymakers in the city.

Intense activity prevailed at many of the city's fixed posts and points. Posts were dealing with up to 150 cases and one had as many as 40 being dealt with at the same time. Many of the injured were policemen, firemen and firewatchers who returned to their duties after treatment and a cup of tea. The first-aid point at Woodvale was in the centre of a heavily bombed area, and early in the raid telephone and electric light failed. A large number of casualties was treated at incidents and at the point, but in the conditions that prevailed it was impossible to keep a proper record of them. Neither was it possible to remove the seriously injured to hospital until the raid was over, and it also became necessary to accommodate dead bodies in a room of the building.

Two hours after the raid began, the post in Cliftonpark Avenue received heavy damage and the upper part of the walls collapsed. Casualties then undergoing treatment were taken to the adjacent rescue depot, and other personnel set up a temporary post in Belfast Model School and salvaged a good deal of essential equipment. As it was found impossible to obtain an ambulance, one of the men commandeered a cleansing department lorry and in this made several trips to hospital with stretcher cases. In his earlier journeys he unwittingly passed over an unexploded bomb in the street. Later, the area was roped off.

Mobile teams rendered great service in various parts of the city. The Mater Hospital's five first-aid parties, complete with ambulances and cars, were employed to the limit of their capacity. Early in the raid one hospital reported its inability to accept any more stretcher cases for some time and arrangements had to be improvised to retain the more seriously injured at the post. These circumstances forced the medical officer-in-charge to perform at the post an amputation on a warden, both of whose legs had been badly smashed. One leg was almost completely severed but so little did the patient realise the extent of his injuries that he urged the staff to hurry as he had work to do. He was also most anxious to find his helmet which had been blown away.

The number of persons treated in the various fixed posts and points throughout the city cannot be given accurately. Apart from those officially given there were many who, once their injuries had been dressed, could not be restrained from rushing off to make enquiries about their relatives and friends before any record of them could be made.

The casualties caused by this raid were:

Killed	745
Injured and detained	420
Injured but not detained	1,091
Total	2,256

The casualties caused in this raid were, therefore, heavier than those caused on any one day in any part of the United Kingdom outside of London. Damage to property was fairly extensive.

The Third Raid. This raid occurred on May 5, 1941, the alert sounding at 0014 hours and the "raiders passed" being signalled at 0450 hours. This caused the heaviest damage to property. Fortunately the death roll was only about a quarter of that experienced in the previous raid. This may be attributed in part to extensive evacuation that had occurred and to a better use of shelters. Posts which had worked feverishly on the night of April 15 were again in the thick of events, and others which had not previously been heavily engaged were now busy.

Electricity and gas failed at Woodvale and the telephone was also out of order. Communications depended on messenger boys, whose work commanded general admiration. The point, as in the previous raid, was a scene of much activity.

The Mersey Street post was destroyed by blast damage and a shower of incendiaries. The latter were extinguished but a further fall came, the post was completely gutted and its staff, no longer able to fight the fires, had to withdraw to a nearby church hall after entering the burning building to rescue valuable medical equipment.

Throughout the raid mobile units were kept extremely busy and proved their worth once again.

Casualties on this occasion were:

Killed	178
Injured and detained	154
Injured but not detained	615
Total	947

The raid caused a great deal of material destruction to property. Throughout the raid the personnel of the casualty services stood up to the test well and all showed a high sense of public duty.

The Fourth Raid. This, the last, came on May 7, 1941. It caused the least damage and the smallest number of casualties. The alert sounded at 0044 hours, and the all clear at 0315 hours. There was only one incident, caused by a parachute mine which fell on an air raid shelter which, together with surrounding buildings, was demolished. The casualties caused by this one incident were:

Killed	14
Injured and detained	32
Injured but not detained	No definite information

As a result of these four raids, the depot at Holywood Road known as Barnardo's Home was demolished and the first-aid post at Mersey Street Public Elementary School was burnt out by an incendiary bomb attack. A number of first-aid posts and depots had to be evacuated because blast had destroyed windows and caused other damage. Some also had to be evacuated, because there were unexploded bombs in the vicinity.

The casualty service was fortunate in that very few of its personnel were injured and none was killed. Less than twelve were injured, none seriously. Eight decorations were awarded for gallantry shown during the air raids. Of these, two were given to the members of the casualty services, one, the British Empire Medal, being awarded to Nurse Denise Forster and the other to S. J. Campbell, a first-aid worker. Many doctors showed great courage and resource during the raids.

Damage to Property. The following table gives particulars of the numbers of houses (including premises of all kinds) destroyed or damaged in the four air raids on Belfast:

Number of houses destroyed	3,205
Number of houses seriously damaged	3,996
Number of houses slightly damaged	49,684
Total	56,885

THE LESSONS LEARNED FROM THE RAIDS IN BELFAST

Central Control. In the larger raids, the mistake made by control centre was the overcalling of resources from outside areas. At one time more than 120 first-aid parties and ambulances were in a most vulnerable area in the centre of the city. Most country parties who were called in had nothing to do.

Fixed Aid Posts. Experience showed that it was a mistake to put first-aid posts in the externs of hospitals. The idea of first-aid posts was really to prevent overcrowding in hospital externs. Nevertheless, in Belfast three such externs were taken over for this purpose. The result was that during the raids these externs became filled with the wounded, the dying and the dead and the actual work for which the post was intended could not be carried out with the efficiency desirable. Converted first-aid posts were often found to be unsatisfactory. The most satisfactory type of building was one specially constructed for the work.

Mobile Aid Posts. These were found to be of less value than expected. There were altogether too many and as they were at first in single decker buses they were unwieldy in operation and most unsatisfactory. Further, they were not called for even when necessary, so that doctors in charge of them, in sheer desperation, took them out during the raids on a roving commission. Four would have been enough for the city, placed under the orders of a central control. On the other hand, mobile medical units would probably have been of the greatest value; but they had not been established at the time of the raids.

Gas Precautions. Mobile gas cleansing units and fixed gas cleansing stations were not regarded as being of much value to the public but were useful as personnel gas cleansing stations. A well developed household gas cleansing scheme, it is believed, would have served the public interests much better, as by this means the time lag would have been eliminated.

Depots. At one time Belfast had fifteen casualty depots, altogether too many. Four properly constructed depots strategically situated at the outskirts of the city, combined with rescue and including the local report centre, would have been ample.

Mortuary arrangements suffered some dislocation during the raids. It was found that wardens were much more interested in helping the wounded than in keeping communications intact. In this way, for example, one point was entirely isolated during the two heavy raids, but though the wardens said that they were unable to get through, a doctor who needed more equipment was able to arrive at the height of the raid at the A.R.P. stores and load a car with materials for the point.

Had there been subsequent raids on Belfast, these experiences and lessons would have been put to good account, but fortunately no more raids came and Belfast enjoyed freedom from air attack until the end of the war.

CHAPTER 14
THE "BAEDEKER" RAIDS

IN the latter half of April 1942, the enemy started a series of comparatively heavy attacks on the Cathedral Cities of Exeter, Bath, Norwich, York and Canterbury, which was said by the enemy to be a reprisal for the bombing of Hanseatic towns on the Baltic. Hitler stigmatised these raids as acts of vandalism directed at objects of 'kultur' in these ancient and historic cities. He therefore threatened to lay in ruins every cathedral city in Britain mentioned in 'Baedeker'.

The first of these raids was directed against the City of Exeter on April 23, 1942. This raid apparently went astray, as a considerable number of H.E. bombs and incendiaries fell in open country, in the village of Ide to the south-west and at Exminster; only six bombs fell in the city. On the early morning of April 25, however, there was a very heavy attack on Exeter, followed by heavy attacks on Bath on the nights of April 25–26 and 26–27, Norwich on April 27–28, York on the morning of 29, Norwich again on the night of 29–30, and Exeter again on May 4. A further heavy attack on Norwich was attempted on the night of May 8–9, but, since the previous raids on this city, extensive provisions had been made for defence, such as a balloon barrage, mobile A.A. guns and night fighters. The result was that the raiders were driven off and unloaded large numbers of bombs in the rural areas around the city. In the city itself, only one H.E. bomb fell. After an interval of three weeks, on June 1, a short sharp attack was made on Canterbury, followed by smaller ones on June 2, 3 and 7. Norwich sustained another fairly heavy raid on the night of June 26–27, during which thousands of incendiaries were dropped. This was the end of this series of raids.

The following description of the raids on these five cities from the medical point of view has been compiled from special contributions made by the medical officers of health and others for the purpose of this History:

EXETER

The area of the city in 1938 was 4,718 acres and the population 69,240, but at the time of the raids Exeter was a 'reception' area and the population was estimated to have increased to about 81,700 owing to the influx of evacuees. Thus the density of the population was about seventeen persons per acre.

EMERGENCY MEDICAL SERVICES

Hospitals. The three casualty receiving hospitals in Exeter were the Royal Devon and Exeter Hospital, with an expanded capacity of 510 beds, of which 235 were estimated to be available for casualties, the Exeter City Hospital, and its annexe the Exeter Children's Home, with a total of 303 beds which included 91 casualty beds, and the Princess Elizabeth Orthopaedic Hospital, with a normal capacity of 138 beds and 67 reserve beds. There was also the St. Thomas Public Assistance Institution, a Class II hospital which could have taken a few casualties. There were, therefore, approximately 400 beds for the reception of casualties direct from incidents. The nearest base hospital, the Exminster Emergency Hospital, about five miles south of the city, with 320 beds and 66 reserve 'A' beds, provided first-class accommodation for the evacuation of cases fit for transfer.

Casualty Services. There were four fixed first-aid posts, three of which were normally used as clinics, and a fleet of ten C.D. local ambulances and seventeen sitting case cars. In addition to A.R.P. ambulances there were also available in emergency one police ambulance, three St. John and five American Red Cross ambulances, as well as the E.M.S. bus-ambulance transport stationed locally. The number of A.R.P. ambulances was subsequently increased to fourteen. Twenty-one first-aid parties had been organised and trained, only five of which were wholetime. Before the first raid in April 1942, there had been nine sporadic attacks by single planes, some of which had caused damage and casualties of varying severity. These, together with numerous 'alerts' without incidents, gave the Civil Defence Services much realistic practice which taught them very valuable lessons, especially the necessity for 'independent action' and 'scouting', at incidents near first-aid posts, or when telephone communications had broken down. The scheme introduced and practised for exercising independent action proved invaluable during the heaviest raid on May 4 when the telephone system was put out of action at an early stage.

THE RAIDS

G. B. Page, M.D., D.P.H., the Medical Officer of Health, supplied the material for the account of the raids given below:

The First Raid. During the raid on April 23, when six 250-kg. bombs fell, there were five fatal, two seriously injured and 19 slightly injured casualties; but the damage to water mains and sewers was severe, entailing the provision of a temporary water supply and measures to ensure the purity of the water when the mains were again brought into use. Neither on this occasion nor subsequently did any illness occur as the result of damage to the public water supply.

The Second Raid. This sharp attack began early on the morning of April 25, and incidents occurred at widely separated points, dive bombing being used in many places. In all, 65 H.E. bombs, weighing approximately 30 metric tons, and large numbers of incendiaries were dropped, resulting in 74 fatal casualties, 20 seriously injured and 36 slightly injured treated at hospitals and 44 persons treated at the first-aid posts. The principal mortuary was put out of action and No. 2 first-aid post was slightly damaged. Reinforcements of 15 first-aid parties, 12 ambulances and 11 casualty cars were called in from surrounding districts and these greatly facilitated the rapid removal of the casualties in this short, sharp raid which lasted little more than an hour. On the 26th a lone raider, possibly a stray from the raid on Bath that morning, dropped a single H.E. bomb and a shower of incendiaries, some of which fell in the grounds of the City Hospital. The H.E. bomb caused four fatal casualties, one seriously injured and 14 slightly injured.

The Third Raid. After a lapse of eight days a heavy raid started in the early morning of May 4 and lasted about an hour, during which 160 H.E. bombs, six paramines and thousands of incendiaries were dropped. The weight of the H.E. bombs was estimated to be about 75 metric tons. In addition to dive bombing, the streets were machine gunned. Widespread damage was caused, chiefly in the centre of the city, but the casualty list was not unduly high: 164 persons were killed, 70 seriously injured, 77 slightly injured but admitted to hospital, and 408 casualties were treated at the out-patient departments of hospitals and first-aid posts. Amongst those treated at the first-aid posts were 41 seriously injured casualties subsequently transferred to hospital, the total seriously injured was therefore 111.

THE WEIGHT OF ATTACK AND CASUALTIES

During all these raids 237 bombs weighing about 105 metric tons were dropped and 247 persons were killed, 207 admitted to hospital and 476 treated at out-patient departments and first-aid posts—an average of 8·9 casualties per ton, of whom 2·4 per ton were killed.

DAMAGE TO HOSPITALS

Many buildings of historic interest, including the Cathedral, were badly damaged, but the work of the Emergency Medical Service was only seriously interfered with when the 'House' portion of the City Hospital was destroyed. It contained no casualty beds, but the kitchen, laundry, administrative offices and the nurses' home were wiped out, and it became difficult to run the hospital. (See Plates XXXVII and XXXVIII.) The staff of the institution and hospital showed great courage and determination in rescuing the aged and bedridden patients from the burning buildings, which were on fire in several places. Their courage and devotion to duty were subsequently recognised by the award of the George Medal to Nurse Knee, and British Empire Medals and a number of Commendations to other members of the staff. Eighteen lives were unfortunately lost in this building. As it was temporarily deprived of its utility services, the City Hospital was no longer available for casualties and had to be completely evacuated after the raid. The Princess Elizabeth Hospital was damaged, entailing a partial temporary evacuation, and was also partly isolated by blocked roads; the Royal Devon Hospital escaped damage but fallen masonry and other debris made it difficult of access.

THE AMBULANCE SERVICES

Curiously enough, not a single vehicle of the ambulance service suffered damage, the only breakdown being due to a burst tyre. This service with its outside reinforcements, which consisted of twenty ambulances and eleven casualty cars, did magnificent work in getting the seriously injured from the incidents and first-aid posts to the hospitals in spite of the blocked roads, which entailed long detours.

FIRST-AID POSTS

No post suffered damage of any consequence, but the staff of No. 2 post had much extra work thrown on them by blocked roads, 110 cases being treated there, including many serious cases.

THE AFTERMATH

Outside assistance of every kind was quickly given by the Regional authorities. The British Red Cross Society and St. John Organisation sent a 'flying column' which did yeoman service, visiting the numerous rest centres which were opened in the surrounding rural area. Later, mobile bathing and laundry units were supplied which were of great value in places where damage to water mains interrupted the water supply for several days. The officer commanding the Twelfth Field Hygiene Section, R.A.M.C., stationed at Okehampton, put his unit at the disposal of the Medical Officer of Health from May 9; their services were invaluable in clearing up the mortuary, a very necessary and unpleasant task, many of the remains recovered from burnt or demolished buildings being no more than fragments, from which identification had to be attempted. Some of the remains were found to be those of animals, of which considerable numbers were killed; these were disposed of by a mobile team from the R.S.P.C.A.

The measures to be taken during the aftermath had been carefully planned, even rehearsed, and an efficiently staffed Information Centre, on which all departments of the local authority were represented, was soon functioning. By notices and loud speaker vans, information and instructions were given to the public from time to time about improvised arrangements for carrying on the public services, and as to the precautions which citizens should take.

By the end of the week, most of the public services were again working: closed schools were reopened, and the maternity and child welfare clinics, situated in three of the first-aid posts, were in operation. The gas supply, however, was interrupted for about three weeks in a large area of the city. The water supply in a huge housing estate and its neighbourhood was partly out of action until May 17.

The following are some impressions contributed by Mr. A. L. Candler, F.R.C.S., Senior Surgeon, Royal Devon and Exeter Hospital, on the work of the hospital during the raids:

Clinical Points. The dead and admissions to hospitals were, as in other raids, not unequal in numbers and, excluding those dying or dead on admission, only a few injuries proved to be really serious to life or limb, though on admission this was difficult to assess.

Only three cases of burns were admitted to hospital, which is remarkable when there were so many fires.

Glass injuries caused total blindness in two people, and three others lost one eye, otherwise the innumerable glass cuts were of little consequence except for disfigurement. There was no need to try to remove buried glass; it was rarely found.

No one can estimate wounds in an air raid until the patient is fully undressed; for example, one man was lying fully clothed on a bed with an overcoat on. He was shocked and his pulse was just palpable. He was talking and showed no signs of gross bleeding; he was in no apparent pain. I asked for a blood transfusion before fully undressing him, in order to be on the safe side. This was done, but he died in an hour. On undressing him I found that the whole of the back of his pelvis and buttocks were missing; there was little bleeding. I felt rather foolish, particularly as I had dealt with numerous casualties in the last war. The transfusion was just a waste of blood.

Transfusions were found to be needed less than was expected and although several were given, I saw only one case where it was certainly of great value; the others would probably have recovered without transfusion. My view is that transfusions are of great help to raise the resistance of septic persons.

I saw no uraemia from crushed limbs, nor even the suspicion of any.

Administrative Points. Looking back after the big raids, I felt how easy the work of the hospital had been in spite of apprehensions I had at the time, such as approaching fires, the overcrowding of the admission hall, want of bearers and foresight for a possible raid on the following night.

The ambulances did their work well.

Twenty soldiers were completely played out by unloading and dispersing 80 stretcher cases to the various parts of the hospital at different levels. The need for fit men as stretcher bearers was very obvious.

It is essential for the proper working of a hospital that one of the visiting staff must be in supreme command and that one surgeon of experience should receive casualties, sort out the cases and assess the treatment required.

Comparison with Casualties of the last War. In the last war I was a surgical specialist dealing with casualties sent to this country from Flanders, when I learned of appalling sepsis, tetanus and gas gangrene. I was also a surgical specialist in Salonica, Mesopotamia and the N. W. Frontier of India during the Afghan War. Casualties from Dunkirk and France also came my way in this war.

There is not the slightest doubt that sepsis from air raids in England is trivial in comparison with that in Flanders and much less than in Salonica and Mesopotomia. In my opinion the reasons are as follows:

(a) No fixed trenches in heavily manured and fouled soil;
(b) No tetanus, which is usually due to surface contamination from manured soil;
(c) Debridement, leaving wounds open, fixation in plaster, all done within a few hours of the wound, which has given astonishing results in comparison to the last war.

Miss Knapp, Matron of the Princess Elizabeth Orthopaedic Hospital, has given her impressions as follows:

The psychological value of air raid shelters was very great. Young nurses, maids and walking cases felt much safer there—partly because the sounds were deadened—and one did not feel so much at the mercy of the awful screaming dive bombers as in the nurses' home or in the large hall and under the stairs, previously considered the safest places.

Some of the young probationers who had never heard a siren before coming to hospital showed amazing courage and discipline.

The patients behaved splendidly. As many of them as possible were placed under their beds on the floor, with a spare mattress put on the wires over them as a protection against splinters. The women and children seemed less anxious than the men.

The value of the mental and physical help given by the members of Toc H who arrived within a few minutes of the alert, and also of the voluntary wardens could not be over-estimated. Several had lost their own homes while helping at the hospitals.

The prompt control of incendiary bombs saved what might have been a disastrous fire.

The stunned feeling which followed the 'raiders passed', as though the appalling fires and crashing buildings seen and heard so close must have been a bad dream and not even remotely connected with Exeter.

There was a remarkable smoothness in the work of the ambulances and of the organisation dealing with casualties, most of which were very severe.

The co-operation of everyone during the evacuation of the patients to other hospitals, homes, etc. during the eight hours following the last raid was splendid. Seventy patients had to be evacuated owing to the damage to the roof of the hospital, lack of gas and water and the presence of an unexploded bomb in the garden.

The need for the immediate treatment of shock for as long as possible before surgical or nursing treatment is attempted was fully shown.

GENERAL COMMENTS

It may be said that the medical organisation provided to deal with attacks from the air functioned most efficiently, as did the arrangements for the supply of assistance under the mutual aid plans.

The shortage of stretcher bearers was a difficulty which has been stressed in many towns, and in Exeter, as elsewhere, was wholly due to the complete mobilisation of all fit men for the Fighting Services, the munition factories, etc.

BATH

The area of Bath in 1938 was 5,152 acres and the population 68,801, but, like Exeter, it was a 'reception' area and the population in the spring of 1942 was estimated to have reached about 83,000.

EMERGENCY MEDICAL SERVICES

Hospitals. Bath, owing to its popularity as a spa, was fortunate in being well provided with hospitals, the smaller of which were chiefly for the treatment of special diseases. These were originally included in the E.M.S. and afterwards 'suspended', so they were not required to make bedstate returns; but they were still liable to be called upon to admit casualties in emergencies. Five Class 1A hospitals were functioning as casualty receiving hospitals. These were:

Class IA hospitals	Normal bed capacity	Expanded reserve
Royal National	156	64
St. Martin's E.M.S.	332	126
Bath and Wessex Orthopaedic	126	30
Forbes Fraser	72	24
Royal United	197	67

The Royal National Hospital in normal times was a special hospital for the treatment of rheumatic diseases, but was expanded and equipped to accommodate casualties. The Royal United Hospital had a specially equipped 'Fracture A' department. The St. Martin's Hospital was a Public Assistance Institution with a normal capacity of 444 beds. These were not used by the E.M.S., as a hutted hospital containing 420 beds had been built in the grounds for this purpose. This hospital also contained a 'Fracture A' department.

Suspended hospitals	Normal bed capacity	Expanded reserve
Eye Infirmary	30	—
Ear, Nose and Throat	25	25
Lansdown Hospital	50	—

No special number of beds was either reserved for or excluded from occupation by casualties, since it was intended to evacuate ordinary cases from the various institutions as necessary. As it happened, practically all the April casualties were dealt with at St. Martin's and the Royal United Hospitals.

There were immediately available about 600 first-class beds with a reserve of 200 beds, excluding the suspended hospitals.

Casualty Services. Four fully staffed and equipped first-aid posts and five ambulance depots housing twenty-six ambulances and a number of casualty cars were suitably distributed in the city.

THE RAIDS

J. F. Blackett, M.D. (Lond.), Medical Officer of Health, and Dr. B. A. Astley Weston, M.B., Ch.B., Deputy Medical Officer of Health, contributed the story of the raids from which the account below has been compiled.

The Baedeker raids on Bath began at 2259 hours on April 25, and ended at 0245 hours on the 27th. They consisted of four attacks, the first of which lasted for an hour and twelve minutes and was followed, after an interval of only thirty-five minutes, by one of twenty-four minutes' duration. About three and a half hours later, a third and longer attack was made. It was maintained for an hour and twenty-seven minutes and ended at 0602 hours on April 26. At 0115 hours on the 27th came the fourth and final attack, which lasted 90 minutes. During this series of four raids, which took place within a period of about twenty-eight hours, an estimated total of 360 H.E. bombs and several thousands of incendiary bombs were dropped, resulting in 1,272 casualties, of whom 400 were killed. The seriously injured cases admitted to hospital amounted to 357, and 515 slightly injured casualties were treated at first-aid posts. The casualties in relation to weight of attack were higher at Bath than in the Baedeker raids elsewhere, and were given by the Ministry of Home Security as 3·0 killed, and 9·2 total casualties per ton.

Although the total damage and loss of life was less than in many larger towns, few places suffered so much in so short a time. Damage to houses was very extensive; many churches and schools and the well known Assembly Rooms were ruined, but the main shopping centres were largely unaffected and no important industry was seriously disturbed. The special features, architectural and historical, which gave Bath its unique place among English cities, suffered no great or irreparable damage. There were no objects of military importance in the city. Bath was entirely undefended, which engendered in the inhabitants a peculiar sense of fear and helplessness not felt in defended areas.

THE WORKING OF THE CASUALTY SERVICES

When the raids started on April 25, the regular 'stand by' personnel of the casualty services were at their posts. One ambulance, one casualty car and one first-aid party were on duty at each of the five ambulance depots and a party of first-aiders with their leader at each of the four first-aid posts. When the siren sounded the remainder of the personnel reported for duty and, in spite of the intensity of the attack, within an hour all were on duty, and at no time during the raids was the work hampered by lack of staff. As many of those concerned were young men and women, few of whom had had actual experience in dealing with injuries, or of the harrowing situation under fire, it was a source of satisfaction that there was no record of any abstentions from duty or refusal or hesitation to undertake even the most unpleasant and dangerous of tasks.

The attack was in three waves with short intervals, terminating at 0602 hours on the 26th. By 0300 hours 310 casualties had been collected and taken to the hospitals and first-aid posts—a notable achievement. All the ambulances were in full use and in addition six vans with emergency stretcher fittings were supplied by the Admiralty Security Office. Other ambulances were also supplied by the Regional Authorities, the maximum in use being 36.

By 0700 hours all the dead and wounded had been dealt with except those dead and living casualties continually being discovered by the rescue and demolition squads. Half the Civil Defence personnel were therefore released for rest and refreshment. The ambulances, in addition to dealing with casualties, removed many old and infirm persons from damaged houses to accommodation arranged for them by the Social Welfare Department of the city.

All the ambulance depots and first-aid posts were damaged to some extent. Temporary ambulance depots were set up on the outskirts of the city and the first-aid posts were repaired as far as possible.

By nightfall the casualty services had been reorganised and the entire personnel who had been working the previous night reported for further duty.

The experience of Exeter led to a general expectation of further raids and a considerable number of people left the town to spend the night in the open fields and in the underground workings in the surrounding hills. At 0115 hours on the 27th the enemy launched another severe attack which lasted until 0245 hours. The attack on the first night had followed a line roughly east and west along the railway and the river, the second ran north and south through the shopping centres and residential areas. After this raid a number of 500 kg. bombs were dug up in the shopping centres, which accounted for their escape from serious damage; but much damage was done in working class and middle class residential areas. Among the small two-storied houses in the working class areas the inhabitants as a rule suffered minor injuries and were not trapped by debris, but in the large four or five-storied Georgian houses many of the inhabitants were trapped and killed or seriously injured.

THE HOSPITAL SERVICES

Most of the 357 seriously injured patients went to one or other of the two large hospitals in the city, and the admission of so many in so short a time naturally put a very heavy strain on their resources. No effort was spared by the staffs and as a result they were able to cope with the situation in a way which deserves the greatest credit. Resuscitation and blood transfusion procedures, for which ample facilities were available, were used immediately on arrival with very satisfactory results. It was considered undesirable to operate during the actual raid and better in the patient's own interest to delay such active treatment until there had been some recovery from shock. For this reason a large medical staff was not required. A surgical unit from Bristol rendered great assistance during the first day or two. It can be said with confidence that no patient suffered permanent harm from any defect in the hospital services, which functioned admirably, though not always in precise accord with pre-arranged plans.

Types of Injury. Large numbers of the dead appeared to have been killed instantly by blast, while others were so seriously injured by flying fragments that they must have died quickly from shock and haemorrhage. Of the cases treated at first-aid posts or hospitals, the majority had flesh wounds and fractures with varying degrees of shock. Serious haemorrhage was not much in evidence among those still living. Tourniquets were never used. Very few gunshot wounds were seen although there was much machine gunning of streets. As in other places, it was found that owing to the darkness, dirt and general confusion, the first-aid methods as taught could seldom be used. All that was done or necessary was to reduce shock, temporarily immobilise fractures and arrange for rapid transport to hospital for expert active treatment. Morphia was used, but not always in sufficient doses. Few cases of hysteria had to be dealt with during the raids; such as were found were more common as part of the aftermath. Children and young persons behaved remarkably well and there was no evidence subsequently that their nerves were seriously affected.

One hospital was partially destroyed, viz. the Royal National Hospital for Rheumatic Diseases; the Lansdown Hospital and Nursing Home and the Ear, Nose and Throat Hospital received some damage.

Mortuary Arrangements. These were found to be quite inadequate and additional arrangements had to be improvised. The staff was also augmented by experienced men from Bristol, whose help was invaluable.

GENERAL COMMENTS

The organised scheme for Air Raid Precautions had of course, been under preparation for years, and although some of the pre-arranged plans broke down and unforeseen circumstances had to be met by rapid improvisations, on the whole the scheme worked very well indeed.

The problem of finding accommodation for thousands of homeless people was much greater than had been expected. Many found accommodation with friends in Bath or farther afield. Large numbers had to be provided with temporary day and night accommodation in the rest centres in the city and in the surrounding villages. Public feeding stations had to be established and mobile canteens, largely provided by voluntary effort, constantly toured the city.

The food and water supply presented urgent health problems. More than a hundred tons of food, perishable and otherwise, in bombed shops, were promptly examined by the sanitary inspectors and by the immediate steps taken, the loss of food, which might have been serious, kept down to about four per cent. The public were advised to drink only boiled water or water sterilised by tablets issued by the Health Department. An adequate supply of these had been obtained beforehand, but the demand was limited to a few thousands. No food or water borne diseases were reported or discovered after the raids.

The School Medical Department perforce became an information bureau on a large scale, as parents in the habit of consulting the staff about their children's ailments felt they could obtain help from them, and help was forthcoming as a general rule.

The work of the Casualty Bureau in ensuring the rapid distribution of information regarding casualties was much hampered by the telephones being out of order and by the inadequacy of the messenger service. This caused delays in the receipt of information from the mortuaries and hospitals and thus in the preparation of lists for posting up at regular intervals. The stream of personal enquiries also greatly hampered the work of the staff of the bureau. In the light of experience a large centrally situated Information Bureau was organised after the raids to give information on all matters likely to arise during and after future attacks. To this bureau the public would be directed for information of every possible kind instead of to the various departmental offices of the corporation.

After this raid no further attack in this series was made on Bath.

NORWICH

The area of the city in 1938 was 7,923 acres and the estimated population about 126,000, but, owing to the proximity of the east coast (18 miles) and the removal of industries of military importance, the population had fallen to about 112,000 by the spring of 1942.

EMERGENCY MEDICAL SERVICES

Hospitals. Norwich was particularly well served by hospitals. There were in the city three Class 1A hospitals:

Hospital	Total beds	Casualty beds
Norfolk and Norwich (voluntary)	396	136
Woodlands Hospital (municipal)	286	156
Jenny Lind Children's Hospital (voluntary)	68	35

In addition to these, there were two advanced base hospitals: the Thorpe Emergency Hospital with 300 casualty beds and the Drayton Emergency Hospital with 100 beds, each four miles from the city. These had been set up in blocks of the County and City Mental Hospitals respectively. There were also several annexes and auxiliary hospitals in the adjacent rural areas.

These hospitals formed the Norwich Group, with Mr. C. Noon, O.B.E., F.R.C.S., as Group Adviser to the Regional Hospital Officer. All these hospitals had the advantage of the services of the consultants of the honorary staff of the Norfolk and Norwich Hospital, all specialists of high professional standing, from amongst whom no less than six mobile surgical teams had been formed. The Norfolk and Norwich Hospital was also a depot for anti-tetanic and anti-gas-gangrene sera and an oxygen depot, and the Jenny Lind was an ether depot. In addition to these, a 'key reserve' hospital of 145 beds had been partially equipped in the Wymondham Senior School, seven miles from the city.

First-aid Posts. At the time of the Baedeker Raids there were four fixed first-aid posts and two heavy mobile units situated half north and half south of the river Wensum, which divides the city into two approximately equal parts.

Ambulances. There were thirty-two whole-time local service ambulances and sixty-two part-time sitting casualty cars, owner driven, dispersed in four ambulance depots and in addition twenty eight-stretcher inter-hospital ambulances stationed in the city. Ten whole-time and twenty-eight part-time first-aid parties, with adequate reserves, had been trained and equipped.

THE RAIDS

The account below was compiled from a contribution by Dr. G. L. Leggat, O.B.E., M.B., D.P.H., Deputy Medical Officer of Health, who was in charge of the casualty services of the Civil Defence organisation.

The first heavy raid occurred on the night of April 27–28, 1942, immediately after the last raid on Bath. Before this raid, between July 9, 1940 and August 8, 1941, Norwich had experienced thirty-one attacks by enemy aircraft. These were of the 'tip and run' order, usually carried out by a single plane and mainly at night. During these raids the casualties were 81 killed, 102 admitted to hospital and 192 slightly injured. The heaviest casualties occurred on July 9, 1940, when Messrs. Boulton and Paul's factory received four direct hits during the afternoon when it was full of workmen; 26 were killed and 48 were seriously injured and admitted to the Norfolk and Norwich Hospital. Between August 9, 1941 and April 27, 1942, the city was raid free.

These preliminary raids provided most of the Civil Defence Services with realistic practice which stood them in good stead during the later heavy raids.

PLATE XXXVII. The wrecked City Hospital.

PLATE. XXXVIII The wrecked City Hospital.

Planet News

PLATE XXXIX. The Woodlands Hospital, April 29, 1942.

Eastern Daily Press

PLATE XL. The Norfolk and Norwich Hospital on fire, April 28, 1942.

On the night of April 27–28, between twenty-five and thirty planes delivered the first of the 'Baedeker' raids on Norwich, a short, sharp attack which lasted less than an hour. Many incendiaries, and 185 H.E. bombs were dropped; the H.Es. were estimated to weigh about 52 metric tons. There were 585 casualties, of which 162 were killed, 160 seriously injured and 263 slightly injured. After an interval of forty-eight hours another attack with about the same number of planes was made on the night of 29–30, which lasted about forty minutes; 112 H.E. bombs, weighing about 45 metric tons, fell on the city. The casualties were 270 of which 69 were killed, 89 seriously injured and 112 slightly injured. This was succeeded by a small incendiary raid on the night of April 30—May 1, resulting in a few minor fires. The raid that went astray, already referred to, followed on the night of May 8–9. Unfortunately, the one bomb that fell in the city, a large H.E. bomb, caused much damage at Woodlands Hospital, putting out of action the main boiler house and the kitchens, so that the hospital had to be temporarily evacuated (see Plate XXXIX).

On June 26–27, a very heavy incendiary attack was made, accompanied by thirty-four H.E. bombs weighing about 11 metric tons. This raid caused 86 casualties: 16 killed, 15 seriously injured and 55 slightly injured. This may be considered to have been the last of the Baedeker Raids on Norwich, but there was another less severe incendiary raid, accompanied by seven H.E. bombs on the night of August 2–3, causing 33 casualties, of which 5 were killed, 13 seriously injured and 15 slightly injured. Most of these casualties were caused by incendiary bombs of the explosive nose type.

The total casualties in these raids from April to August 1942, were: 252 killed, 277 seriously injured and 445 slightly injured. There were subsequently other minor raids of the 'tip and run' type to which all the coast towns in East Anglia were subjected during the whole period of the raids, subsequent to the fall of France.

The casualty rates per metric ton of H.E. bombs dropped in the Baedeker raids on Norwich were: killed 2·3, seriously injured 2·4 and slightly injured 3·9; these were about the same rates as those in other Cathedral cities, but as the result of the incendiary raid in June 1942, the damage to property in Norwich was greater.

The cumulative effect of these constant raids and the destruction caused by fires gave Norwich the appearance of one of the most damaged towns in the country.

DAMAGED HOSPITALS

The two large hospitals in the city suffered very heavily. On April 27–28 one ward block of the Norfolk and Norwich Hospital was damaged by blast, and, after 80 casualties had been admitted, further severely wounded casualties had to be diverted to the Woodlands

Hospital. The 'institutional' portion of this hospital had received direct hits on this night by H.E. bombs and incendiaries which caused extensive damage. Twelve inmates were killed and eight seriously injured; the remaining 411 inmates all had to be evacuated to institutions in the county on April 28. (See Plate XL.) The hospital blocks, however, could continue to admit patients as they had only suffered minor damage to windows and roofs. On the night of April 29–30, when the Norfolk and Norwich Hospital was threatened by large fires in adjacent buildings the Woodlands Hospital again had to deal with most of the casualties. The staff of the hospital were therefore more or less continually on duty from the evening of April 27 until the evening of May 1, treating casualties and transferring patients to institutions and hospitals outside the city. These duties were carried out under very considerable difficulties, telephonic communications being cut off and the electric supply having failed. Casualties had to be admitted by the light of hand torches and hurricane lamps. Fortunately the emergency lighting set for the operating theatre remained intact and essential surgical work was not interfered with. When the boiler house and kitchens were destroyed on the night of May 8–9, the hospital had to be temporarily evacuated, but as patients could still be admitted for short periods no permanent loss of beds resulted.

The position after the heavy incendiary raid on June 26–27 was materially altered as on that night the Norfolk and Norwich Hospital was extensively damaged by fire. Two first floor wards were completely gutted and the ground floor wards in the same block were rendered quite unusable. The nurses' home, the domestic staff's quarters, the main operating theatre and linen store also were gutted and 124 beds were lost as a result of this damage.

In addition to the casualty clearing hospitals, the municipal Maternity Home was completely put out of action by a direct hit on June 27. None of the staff or patients was seriously injured. The patients were evacuated on the following day to a temporary home at Earlham Hall outside the city. The Matron received the M.B.E. for her devotion to duty and good work. The Isolation Hospital opposite the Woodlands Hospital was also extensively damaged by blast.

Despite the extensive damage to the different hospitals not a single patient nor member of the staff was injured.

The work of the staff at all hospitals was of a very high order, and it would be impossible to speak too highly of the courage and self sacrificing endurance of the medical, nursing and ancillary staffs. Minor difficulties were experienced—occasional delays in transfers, slips in ensuring that interchange of ambulance equipment was complete and so on; but these were but trivialities when balanced against the really excellent work that was done.

THE WORK OF THE HOSPITALS

The following tables show the admissions to hospitals and the numbers of patients transferred as the result of the various raids:

Admissions to Hospitals

Date of raid, 1942	Hospitals						Totals
	Norfolk and Norwich	Wood-lands	Jenny Lind	Isolation	Thorpe	Drayton	
April 27–28	87 (9)	77 (8)	5	4 (1)	1	4	178 (18)
29–30	20 (1)	68 (5)	–	–	6	1	95 (6)
June 26–27	15 (2)	3 (2)	–	–	1	–	19 (4)
August 2–3	8 (1)	6	–	–	–	–	14 (1)
Other raids	15	1	–	–	–	–	16
Totals	145 (13)	155 (15)	5	4 (1)	8	5	322 (29)

Note. The bracketed figures show the numbers who died after admission.

Transfer of Patients

Date of transfers 1942	From Norfolk and Norwich Hospital to:—			From Woodlands Hospital to:—		
	Other hospitals	Own homes	Total	Other hospitals	Own homes	Totals
April 28	122	115	237	68	8	76
29	21	–	21	–	–	–
30	48	14	62	54	23	77
May 1–2	26	–	26	33	–	33
9	–	–	–	51	14	65
June 27	207	–	207	–	–	–
Totals	424	129	553	206	45	251

The following notes on the work of the hospitals have been extracted from contributions to the Medical History by Mr. A. J. Blaxland, F.R.C.S., Senior Surgeon, Norfolk and Norwich Hospital and Dr. Emrys Williams, Senior Medical Officer, Woodlands Hospital:

Norfolk and Norwich Hospital. The number of beds in this hospital was not sufficient to meet the demands of the civilian population and there was usually a waiting list of about 700. From the outbreak of the war the normal work of the hospital was further hampered because the beds for civilians had to be reduced by 25 per cent. to provide immediate accommodation for possible casualties and Service patients.

On the night of April 27, there were 343 patients (of whom 26 were in the private block) in the hospital, including Service patients.

In view of the vulnerable situation of the hospital, with extensive window space, close to a railway station and a large factory, arrangements had been made whereby all patients from the upper wards were to be transferred to a commodious basement below ground level, which could house 100 patients, immediately it became obvious that a major air raid was commencing. Provision was also made to cut off the circulation of hot water and superheated steam in the large pipes in this basement. In addition, an operating suite with four operating tables was set up in the basement—a provision which proved invaluable when the main operating suite was destroyed in a later raid. These arrangements were at once put into effect when the dropping of many flares presaged a heavy raid. This work fell almost entirely on the staff of the hospital, including the nurses and the residential house officers, as no outside stretcher bearers were immediately available. It was a tedious business, made very difficult by having to be done almost in darkness, as very early in the raid many windows and blinds were blown out. The transfer was not completed until the raid was half over.

Casualties began to arrive shortly after the raid: 87 were admitted, of whom nine were moribund and died soon afterwards; 95 others who were lightly wounded were treated at the first-aid post attached to the hospital and then sent home or to rest centres. Of the admissions, 20 per cent. required intravenous serum or blood. Operations were performed on 73; 25 had more than one wound and 27 had fractures, mostly compound. Three compound fractures of the skull required craniotomy. There was one severe case of crush syndrome, both lower limbs being involved without an open wound or fracture; the patient died five days later.

As two members of the surgical staff, with anaesthetists and nurses, were working at the Woodlands Hospital, a surgical team was sent over from Cambridge. This team arrived at noon on April 28, and gave much appreciated relief. The operations were all finished by 7 p.m., i.e. within nineteen hours of the receipt of injury.

On April 28, 115 patients considered fit enough were sent to their homes; 122 were transferred to E.M.S. hospitals outside Norwich; 6 to Bury St. Edmunds; 36 to Attleborough and 80 to White Lodge Emergency Hospital, Newmarket. Thus ample bed accommodation was provided for further casualties. During the two following days, 29 further transfers were made to Attleborough and 40 to Newmarket. All these transfers were made in the inter-hospital ambulances and transport.

When the second raid occurred on the night of April 29–30, a few patients from the first floor wards had already been moved to the basement and the patients from the ground floor were also transferred there at the beginning of the raid. As large fires were near, after 20 casualties had been admitted and 42 treated at the first-aid post in the out-patient department, further casualties were diverted to the Woodlands Hospital. On June 26–27, the hospital was much damaged by fire; four large wards, the operating theatre and certain other parts of the hospital were gutted. When the fires broke out the patients in the basement were brought up and laid on the lawns, after which the hospital staff, aided by 100 soldiers billeted close by and many civilian volunteers, salvaged as much material from the burning building as possible, including the valuable equipment of the operating theatres. Meanwhile, inter-hospital transport had arrived and 101 patients were transferred to the Emergency Hospital at Thorpe, four miles from the city, 60 to the Woodlands Hospital, 3 to the Drayton Emergency Hospital and 5 to Attleborough. All the patients had been removed shortly after dawn. The absence of panic, in spite of awe-inspiring experiences was remarkable.

After the raids, by temporary expedients and temporary roofing and repairs to the damaged hospital wards, etc., the hospital was able to function fully early in 1943.

The Woodlands Hospital. The damage to this hospital and the attached institution and the evacuation of the inmates have already been referred to.

After the raid on April 27–28, 77 casualties were admitted, including 18 injured inmates from the institution. On April 29–30, 75 casualties were admitted, seven of which were found to be dead on arrival. From 12.43 a.m. on April 30, all casualties in Norwich were diverted to this hospital, as the Norfolk and Norwich Hospital, in danger from nearby fires, was no longer available.

On April 28, 57 patients were transferred to White Lodge Emergency Hospital, Newmarket and 11 Service patients to an auxiliary hospital. On April 30, 54 patients were transferred to White Lodge, Newmarket, and 39 children to the Little Plumstead Hall Institution. On May 2, 33 more patients were sent to Newmarket.

The injuries of the casualties admitted during the two heavy raids are summarised below:

Eye injury		Shock			Flesh wounds		Contusions		Crush injury	Penetrating wounds		Burns	Fractures	Dislocations
Both eyes	Loss of one eye	Slight	Moderate	Severe	Superficial	Deep	Superficial	Deep		Chest	Abdomen			
2	1	41	3	8	53	10	3	7	5	3	1	1	39	2

Fractures: Bones Involved

	Humerus	Radius	Ulna	Metacarpal	Phalangeal	Femur	Tibia	Fibula	Rib	Spinal Column	Clavicle	Skull	Pelvis	Grand Total
Male	1	4	5	1	1	5	6	1	4	1	–	1	1	31
Female	1	–	–	2	–	–	1	1	2	–	1	–	–	8
Total	2	4	5	3	1	5	7	2	6	1	1	1	1	39

Types of Fractures

	Simple	Compound	Comminuted
Male	15	6	4
Female	4	3	1
Total	19	9	5

By improvisations made while the destroyed boilers and kitchens were being replaced, the hospital continued to function as a casualty clearing hospital. This work was completed by June 27.

Dr. Williams acknowledged with gratitude the assistance given by the surgeons and nurses of the Norfolk and Norwich Hospital after the two severe raids in April and also the help received from one R.A.M.C. and two R.A.F. medical officers. The work of the surgeon and house surgeon sent from Addenbrooke's, Cambridge, by the Regional Hospital Officer was also greatly appreciated.

The help and co-operation of Dr. Leggat, the Deputy Medical Officer of Health, was also acknowledged and the loyal service of the medical, nursing and other staff of the hospital under most trying conditions during the raids and for several days following the raids, was described as magnificent.

THE WORK OF THE CIVIL DEFENCE CASUALTY SERVICES

First-aid Posts. All the fixed posts were brought fully into use during the two heavy raids, but the heavy mobile units were not used as definite post units. The doctors and staff, however, did much valuable work at incidents in assisting the first-aid parties; they therefore really functioned as light mobile units, to which they were afterwards converted.

The fixed posts other than those attached to the hospital fully justified their maintenance, even if they were never to be used again.

The loss of rest centres led to a certain amount of congestion at the first-aid posts. The damage to posts was luckily negligible during the heavy raids, but in the incendiary raid in June one post was completely gutted; most of the equipment was saved and transferred to a nearby Infant Welfare Clinic where the post was able to function fully by the same evening.

Ambulance Services and First-aid Parties. These two services worked from combined depots and most of the personnel were part-time, but in spite of the heavy raids there were always sufficient part-time workers on duty at the depots and many, during this difficult period, remained more or less on continuous duty. The work of the first-aid parties was favourably commented on by the hospital authorities. Of the 395 persons treated at first-aid posts only 27 had to be transferred to hospital.

Two ambulances became a total loss, one from direct bomb damage and the other by being driven into an unmarked crater full of water. Others were damaged by splinters, broken glass, etc., and a few had mechanical breakdowns; these were in use again in a few hours. No ambulance depot was put out of action in the heavy raids, but two of the four depots were destroyed by fire during the incendiary raid; all the ambulances and much of the equipment were salvaged and temporary depots were set up.

Reinforcements and Mutual Aid. As a precautionary measure, when it was evident that heavy attacks were impending, an early call was sent to neighbouring authorities and to the Region for outside assistance. This help was not required on the first night, but it was extensively used on the second night, and in post-raid work. From neighbouring authorities, 13 ambulances, 12 first-aid parties and 7 casualty cars were supplied on April 27–28 and 16 ambulances, 14 first-aid parties and 9 casualty cars on the 29–30. In addition the Regional authorities supplied 9 ambulances, 19 first-aid parties and 3 casualty cars. Ample reliefs were therefore available.

Personnel Casualties. The following casualties occurred among the Civil Defence Casualty Service personnel:

	On duty		In their own homes	
	Male	Female	Male	Female
Killed	2	–	–	2
Seriously injured	3	1	–	–
Slightly injured	3	–	3	–

Mortuaries. Two mortuaries had been provided, one of which was put out of action on the evening of the first raid. The second was gutted by fire during the incendiary raid. An improvised mortuary was set up in marquees in a public park and mobile gas cleansing units were used to supply water. The number of bodies dealt with was 178.

Rest Centres. In all, ten were opened; two were rendered unusable and two damaged in the first raid; and in the second raid these two latter were put out of action and two others in addition. 3,460 persons were accommodated in the rest centres, in which many thousands more had meals.

Damaged Houses. The total number of houses damaged was 28,594, of which 3,132 were either beyond repair or had to be evacuated pending repairs. Many of these were destroyed by fire during the incendiary raid in June.

Damage to Water Supply and Sewerage. There was fairly extensive damage to water mains and sewers, but the usual precautions were taken to ensure that pure water only was drunk until the mains were repaired. The thorough cleansing of the mains by chlorination before they were put into use prevented the outbreak of any waterborne diseases.

GENERAL COMMENTS

The Hospital Organisation in Norwich was put to a very severe test by these raids, which, although they did not cause many casualties, threw a heavy strain on the hospitals' staffs by putting portions of the two hospitals temporarily out of action. When medical officers and nurses are fully engaged with the treatment of serious casualties and have to select and prepare large numbers of patients for transfer to other hospitals, while at the same time parts of the hospital are on fire and being subjected to a heavy bombardment, it would not be surprising if a certain amount of confusion were to occur. In the Norwich hospitals, however, there was no such confusion and, with the help of surgeons and nurses from other hospitals under the mutual aid arrangements, whose arrival afforded much needed relief and permitted some of the staff to obtain short periods of rest, the work continued day and night.

An equal strain was thrown on the local ambulance services which, after having conveyed the seriously wounded patients to the hospitals, had to continue with the work of transferring large numbers of aged and infirm patients from the institution section of the Woodlands Hospital to other institutions in the county.

The work of transporting the casualties and patients from the two hospitals was mostly carried out by the inter-hospital transport. Here again mutual aid, in the shape of relief ambulances from outside the area, played a great part in carrying through these strenuous duties without delay and it cannot be said that any section of the organisation failed to fulfil its obligations.

The city authorities dealt rapidly and efficiently with the many problems which arose from the large number of homeless persons requiring to be fed and housed.

YORK

In December 1938, the area of York was 6,456 acres and the population 98,210. The population rose very slightly and in December 1940, was estimated to be 100,800 or just over seventeen persons per acre.

THE EMERGENCY MEDICAL SERVICES

Hospitals. There was only one first-class hospital in York at the beginning of the war, the York County Hospital with a normal capacity of 222 beds. Extra beds and equipment were issued to this hospital by the Ministry of Health, thus increasing its capacity by crowding to 278 beds. Of these 170 were normally occupied. The remaining 108 beds were therefore available for casualties, but 25 of these were classed as Reserve "A" beds. There was also the City Infirmary, a Public Assistance Institution with a normal hospital capacity of 191 beds. This hospital was upgraded by the Ministry and equipped to deal with 229 patients but, owing to shortage of staff and a normal occupancy of about 165, only five beds and 59 reserve beds were on the average available for casualties. This hospital had two annexes, Poppleton Gate and Poppleton Hall, containing accommodation for 98 convalescents. These were transferred to the new City of York General Hospital, which was under construction and was intended eventually to accommodate 360 patients; but only half the scheme was in hand when it opened. It was partially opened for 90 beds on January 1, 1942, and could provide about 45 beds for casualties. There were thus only slightly over 200 Class I beds immediately available when the first heavy raid occurred, of which only about 130 were adequately staffed. It was fortunate, therefore, that the city was only subjected to one fairly heavy raid and that during this period the hospitals escaped. Had heavy and repeated raids occurred and the hospitals been put out of action, the situation would have been very serious.

Civil Defence Casualty Services. Four first-aid posts were in use when the heavy raid occurred. One of the original posts, in the Lendal Horse Repository had been found unsuitable and replaced by a newly-built post adjoining it. A post in this area near the railway station, a probable target for the enemy's bombs, was rightly considered necessary, which it proved to be. In addition, two first-aid points were established on the outskirts of the city at Clifton and Dringhouses. Two mobile first-aid units were also available.

Ambulances and First-aid Parties. These were based on three depots in which seventeen whole-time ambulances and eight whole-time casualty cars were housed; twenty part-time cars had also been arranged for.

THE RAIDS

P. R. McNaught, M.D., D.P.H., the Medical Officer of Health, supplied information on which the following account is based.

Between August 11, 1940, and April 3, 1942, York experienced eight minor raids during which 10 H.E. bombs and a few incendiaries fell in the city. Two persons were killed, five admitted to hospital, four treated as out-patients and three at first-aid posts. Each of these raids only lasted a few minutes and occurred usually when Hull and other adjoining areas were being attacked. There were also raids in August, September and December 1942, with a small number of casualties.

On April 29, 1942, the only heavy raid began at 0242 hours and lasted eighty minutes. Seventy-nine H.E. bombs, of which ten did not explode, fell within the city and others fell outside the city boundary. Nearly all these were heavy bombs, very few of small calibre being dropped. Large numbers of I.Bs. were also dropped. Nearly all the heavy damage occurred outside the city walls. The weight of attack in the 'Baedeker' raids on York was estimated by the Ministry of Home Security at 47 tons of H.E., the casualty rates per ton being: killed, 1·6; total casualties, 6·1.

THE WORK OF THE CASUALTY SERVICES

The Central Control for the city was situated in the Council Offices adjacent to the Guildhall and when the Guildhall took fire the control room was evacuated and a temporary control set up in the Mansion House.

At 0330 hours the telephone service was interrupted and messengers and despatch riders were used to maintain communication. Apart from the delays in conveying instructions to the ambulance depots and first-aid posts and in receiving reports, this service worked most satisfactorily.

First-aid Posts. All the four first-aid posts came into action, as did the Clifton first-aid point, which was damaged by blast but carried on and dealt with 22 casualties; 62 casualties were dealt with at the first-aid posts.

Ambulances. Within a few minutes of the first bombs dropping, all the ambulances were ready for duty and the 'off duty' drivers and attendants had reported. Army and R.A.F. vehicles also gave assistance in conveying cases to the hospitals and later twelve ambulances from adjoining areas were despatched to the city as reliefs. Among the Civil Defence personnel four persons were killed and three seriously injured.

Hospitals. One hundred and one cases were admitted to hospitals, 52 to the City General Hospital and 49 to the County Hospital, which also dealt with 58 slightly injured casualties as out-patients. Seventy-nine civilians were killed and there was in addition a number of fatal Service casualties. Outside the city in the adjoining Flaxton Rural District 15 persons were killed and 6 seriously injured.

Mr. D. V. Marshall, F.R.C.S.Ed., Medical Superintendent of the City Hospital, reported that in this hospital all the cases arrived after 0500 hours, principally because the first cases were taken to the County Hospital until it was full. The operating theatre's two tables were used continuously until 0900 hours dealing with minor injuries, mostly due to glass. The most serious cases, after resuscitation therapy, were then taken in hand and operating continued till 1600 hours. Four cases of crush syndrome were admitted, and 1 other, apparently less seriously injured, was transferred to Meanwood Park E.M.S. Hospital, Leeds, with 19 other cases of minor injury. There the usual renal symptoms associated with crush injury supervened and the patient died. The 4 remaining cases were treated as soon as possible by intermittent pulsation, the Morris Lung being used at a frequency of about fifteen changes per minute. The pulsation treatment was carried out for about twenty minutes every two or three hours and continued for two or three days until the patients seemed quite well and had no urinary symptoms. Intravenous transfusions were also given to these patients. All 4 cases recovered, although the crush injuries were so severe that at first Mr. Marshall, from previous experience of such cases in Hull, had not had much hope of their recovery.

Mortuaries. Two mortuaries had been provided, the staffs of which effectively carried out their duties. There were no unidentified bodies.

AFTER THE RAID

On the following morning the Regional Hospital Officer arranged to evacuate all patients fit to be moved and for reliefs of nursing personnel.

The City Corporation opened an Administrative and Information Centre which remained open for three days and dealt with 4,663 persons.

Of the twenty rest centres seventeen were brought into use including the two medical rest centres. Two centres were unusable owing to severe damage; seven received minor damage. All but seven centres were closed again by noon on April 30. Over 2,000 homeless persons were dealt with in these rest centres. The three British Restaurants were fully used and served food to all requiring it as well as sending out cooked food in mobile canteens.

DAMAGE TO PUBLIC SERVICES

Five H.E. bombs and a number of I.Bs. fell on the waterworks: the roof of the main engine house was shattered, a filter house was entirely demolished and two large mains were broken, and there was further damage to the distribution system in various parts of the city. Temporary supplies of water were made available and the usual safeguards were adopted to prevent water-borne diseases, of which no cases occurred.

GENERAL COMMENTS

Reviewing the experiences of the raid, it may be said that all the services did all that was required of them. Any small defects in the organisation which became apparent, and which were subsequently remedied, did not in any way detract from the general efficiency of the services.

The arrangements by which only one hospital at a time received casualties does not seem to have anything to recommend it; the practice in most towns was to use the nearest hospital staffed and equipped to deal with the cases.

CANTERBURY

The peace-time population of Canterbury was about 25,000 and the acreage approximately 5,000. At the beginning of the war Canterbury was a reception area, and the influx of evacuees from the crowded Medway towns resulted in a considerable rise in the population. After the fall of France, under threat of invasion, the city was declared an evacuation area and the population rapidly fell to about 11,000. The greater part of the centre of Canterbury, which was the most thickly populated, consisted of narrow streets of old timbered buildings which made it very vulnerable to fire from incendiaries. It was only about five minutes' flying time from the nearest enemy airfield and, as it was a traffic centre from which roads radiated to the chief coast towns, it was an obvious object of enemy attack. For this reason, adequate shelter was provided for the whole population in reinforced basements, standard surface shelters, 'Nissen', 'Anderson' and 'Morrison' shelters.

EMERGENCY MEDICAL SERVICES

The only Class I hospital in the city was the Kent and Canterbury Hospital, a well equipped voluntary hospital, the capacity of which had been expanded from its normal of 181 beds to 333. The normal civilian bed occupancy was about 154, and 105 beds were available for casualties, with a reserve of 74 beds which, however, could only be used in a grave emergency without additional staff. There was also a Class II municipal hospital which could accommodate 76 patients with a reserve of 114 beds. This provision of casualty beds was considered sufficient in view of the scale on which shelters had been provided.

Casualty Services. Two first-aid posts, one of which was attached to the Kent and Canterbury Hospital, and one mobile first-aid post, had been provided.

Twelve four-stretcher ambulances were available, of which two were only part-time, and eleven first-aid parties, of which four were part-time; all located in two depots.

THE RAIDS

This account, the fifth and last in the series, is compiled from a report contributed by the Medical Officer of Health, Dr. W. G. Evans, M.R.C.S., D.P.H.

Before the first 'Baedeker' raid, bombs were dropped on the city on twenty-six occasions between August 12, 1940, and April 20, 1941, i.e. during the 'Battle of Britain' and the subsequent heavy raids on London. The number of H.E. bombs was 214 and casualties were 30 killed, 16 seriously injured and 104 slightly injured, a very low casualty rate. Most of these raids occurred during daylight, the only night raid causing casualties being the last on April 20, when one H.E. bomb caused six casualties, of which one was fatal. After this date there were no more incidents until June 1942.

On June 1, 1942, just before 0100, the sirens sounded. Ten minutes later the local 'imminent danger' signal was given and two minutes later flares were dropped over the city, showing that Canterbury was on this occasion the enemy's objective. Warning had already been received from the Regional Commissioner's office that reprisal raids were to be expected as the result of the 1,000-bomber raid on Cologne on May 30. Soon afterwards the bombs began to drop, and the attack continued until 0210. One hundred and thirty H.E. bombs, including one of at least two tons in weight, five delayed action and twelve unexploded bombs fell during this period. In addition it was estimated that about 3,600 incendiary bombs were scattered all over the inhabited area. The H.E. bombs all fell in an area of little more than half a square mile. As a result of this scattered raid many fires were caused and the narrow streets of the city were in several places completely blocked by debris. One bomb caused considerable damage in the Cathedral precincts. On the following night about 1,300 incendiaries were dropped and on June 3 a few H.E. bombs and 2,000 incendiaries. After an interval of three days, 22 H.E. bombs and 1,000 incendiaries fell on June 7. There were no further incidents until the daylight raid on October 31, 1942. The casualties caused by the raids in June were as follows:

Date	Killed	Seriously injured	Slightly injured
June 1	42	47	51
2	—		
3	5	6	18
7	1	4	4
Totals	48	57	73

Early in the raid on June 1, a bomb hit the main trunk telephone line and the whole telephone system was temporarily useless; a little later the water main, a main sewer and the gas and electricity mains were badly damaged and these services were also put out of action. The Controller of the Civil Defence Services, Mr. G. W. Marks, O.B.E., was killed by a direct hit on his house.

In these circumstances it is not surprising that communications broke down and no information was received from the Control Room until some time after the raid was over. Not only was information lacking regarding casualties, but also regarding blocked roads, with the result that messengers were unable to find their way to the hospitals and first-aid posts except by a system of trial and error, the longest way round often being the quickest.

This chapter of accidents threw the whole organisation out of gear and the initiative fell to the leaders of the first-aid parties. In the absence of information they organised units consisting of one first-aid party and one ambulance and sent them out to separate sections of the city to reconnoitre and deal with any incidents which could be found and, in the circumstances, no other action seemed possible. This plan worked reasonably well in the small area attacked and these parties were soon able to contact the wardens and get to work at the incidents. The regular parties were also reinforced by ample and unsolicited assistance from the neighbouring authorities under the Kent County Mobile Reserve Organisation. The R.A.M.C. and other military units also sent parties to the stricken area to render what assistance they could. It was found that most of the serious cases were those that had been trapped in basements under heaps of debris and all were accounted for in a surprisingly short time and disposed of to the hospitals or the first-aid posts.

The subsequent attacks were much lighter and seemed to be half-hearted, possibly because the A.A. defence had been considerably strengthened and a balloon barrage put up. At no time were the services at the hospitals or the first-aid posts put to any strain as the casualties came in a slow and steady stream from the incidents. In view of the concentration of the attack, the casualties were small in number, which was doubtless due to the quality of the shelters. As an example, the 2-ton bomb previously referred to burst a few yards from a 'Nissen' type shelter and made a crater 75 ft. in diameter and 45 ft. in depth; the earth covering the shelter was blown away, the steel roof was dented, the concrete floor cracked and the whole shelter moved about 18 in., but only one of the seven occupants of this shelter was hurt, he having sustained a few fractured ribs by being thrown against the shelter wall.

The mobile unit was only called out on two occasions, but it was unable to operate as such units were intended to. A grave disadvantage was the restriction on mobility and access to incidents owing to the narrowness of many of the streets of the city. As in many other places the mobile unit was later replaced by two light units.

It was fortunate that the only casualty receiving hospital in the city escaped being hit, otherwise serious difficulties would have arisen as casualties would have had to have been conveyed considerable distances to hospitals in other districts. In Kent a mutual aid system was in operation whereby each casualty receiving hospital had six or more hospitals to which cases could be transferred should the need arise.

POST-RAID PROBLEMS

As two of the biggest rest centres had been completely destroyed by fire, 2,500 homeless people had to be accommodated and were dispersed to the Kent Public Assistance Committee's centres in the surrounding rural area.

Because of the lack of water it took a considerable time to get the fires under control, and, as water mains and sewers had been fractured and the water supply was thus polluted in certain areas, nothing but boiled water could be used until the necessary repairs were made and the supply chlorinated. No epidemic of water-borne diseases of any kind occurred.

INDEX

Air attacks on Scotland, 108
Air-raid casualties in London, 210–220
Air-raid casualties, Scottish, 78
Air Raid Precautions Act, N. Ireland, 153
Air Raid Precautions Advisory Committee, N. Ireland, 152
Air Raid Precautions, Clyde Estuary, 87
Air raid shelters, amenity in, Scotland, 85
Air raids, period of intensive, London, 208
Air raids on Bath, 468
    Belfast, 136, 456
        lessons learnt from, 142, 459
    Bermondsey, 286
    Birmingham, 360
    Bristol (Plates XXXV, XXXVI), 415
    Bromley (Plates IV, V), 266
    Canterbury, 485
    Cardiff, 446, 449
    City of London, 278
    Croydon, 272
    Exeter, 462
    Hackney, 301, 304
    Hull, 435
    industrial centres, 193–460
    London (Plates I–XIX), 208–315
        lessons of, 307, 313
    Manchester Group, 346
    Merseyside, 322
    Norwich (Plates XXXIX, XL), 472
    Pembroke Dock, 449
    Plymouth (Plate XXXIV), 406
    Port of London, 306
    Portsmouth (Plates XXXI, XXXII), 399
    St. Marylebone, 291
    Sheffield, 424
    Southampton, 385
    Swansea, 445, 448
    Wales, 445, 451
    York, 482
Ambulance and Civil Defence Services, N. Ireland, 152–162
Ambulance services, Birmingham, 359
    Bristol, 415, 419
    Coventry, 375, 376
    Exeter, 464
    London, 203
    Manchester Group, 345, 351
    Merseyside, 321, 336
    N. Ireland, 157
    Norwich, 472, 479
    Scotland, 82
    Sheffield, 423, 427
    York, 481, 482
Ambulances, bus, N. Ireland, 128
    City of London, 277, 280
    inter-hospital, Scotland, 77
American Ambulance, 79
Amputations, Scotland, 32
Ancillary Hospital Services, Scotland, 63
Ancillary Services, Scotland, 49–86

Anti-gas arrangements, Coventry, 371
Anti-typhoid inoculation, Coventry, 381
Assistant Hospital Officer, N. Ireland, appointment of, 148
Auxiliary hospitals, Scotland, 39

Bacteriological Service, Scotland, 68
'Baedeker' raids, 461–487
Bath, 467
Bedstate, Scottish, 98, 101, 102, 103
Belfast, 453–460
    air raids on, 136, 456
    lessons learnt from raids on, 142, 459
    Emergency Hospital, establishment of, 145
    transferred to Musgrave Park, 149
Bermondsey, work of Civil Defence Services in, 285
Birkenhead, damaged hospitals in (Plate XXXII), 331
Birmingham, 358–369
    air raids on (Plate XXIV–XXVI), 360
Blood Transfusion Service, N. Ireland, 186, 188
    Scotland, 68
Bootle, damaged hospitals in, 334
Brain injuries, Scotland, 35
Bristol, 414–422
    air raids on (Plates XXXV, XXXVI), 415
    casualties in, 418
    doctors' experiences in raids on, 420
British Red Cross Society, 78
Bromley, work of Civil Defence Services in (Plates IV, V), 265
Building hospitals, Scotland, 24, 100
Bus ambulances, N. Ireland, 128

Canadian Orthopaedic Unit, 32
Canterbury, 484
Cardiff, air raids on, 446, 449
Car pool, volunteer, N. Ireland, 147
Casualties, admission to hospital, N. Ireland, 131
    at Hull, nature of, 435
    in London air raids, statistics, 210–220
    clearance of, at perimeter, Coventry (Plate XXVIII), 377
    discharge from hospital, N. Ireland, 131
    disposal of, Manchester Group, 350
    marine, Clyde Estuary, 88
    treated in N. Ireland hospitals, 150
Casualty bureau, Birmingham, 360
    bureaux, Manchester Group, 355
    hospitals, organisation of, London, 197, 202
    recording organisation, 205
Casualty Service, N. Ireland, pre-war, 125

INDEX

Casualty Services, Bath, 468
    Belfast, administration, 453
        training, 455
    Canterbury, 484
    Exeter, 462
    Hull, 434, 437
    Southampton, 383
    Scotland, organisation, 5–19
    working of, during raids, 279
Casualty trains, civilian, Scotland, 76
Central Casualty Bureau, New Scotland Yard, 206
Central Middlesex County Hospital, 237
Charing Cross Hospital, 233
City planning, Coventry, 382
Civil Defence Ambulance Service, London, 203
    Scotland, 82
    N. Ireland, 152–162
Civil Defence Casualty Services, Birmingham, composition, 358
    Birmingham, in action (Plates XXIV–XXVI), 365
    Bristol (Plate XXXVI), 414, 419
    London, 202
    Norwich, 478
    Plymouth, 406
    Portsmouth, 397
    Scottish, 79
    Sheffield, 423, 426
    York, 481, 482
Civil Defence exercises, N. Ireland, 146
Civil Defence functions, N. Ireland, new Ministry for, 132
    Bermondsey, 285
    Bromley (Plates IV, V), 265
    City of London, 275
    Croydon, 272
    Hackney, 299
    Port of London Authority, 304
    St. Marylebone, 289
    London, personnel of, 310
    London, work of (Plates V–XVII), 265–315
    Merseyside, 319, 336
Civil Nursing Reserve, N. Ireland, 176
    Scotland, 54
Civilian casualty trains, Scotland, 76
Civilian Hospital Medical Service, N. Ireland, 163
Civilian sick at Emergency Hospital, N. Ireland, 145
Conscription of doctors, N. Ireland, 169
Consultant advisers, honorary, N. Ireland, 135, 164
    in medicine and surgery, N. Ireland, 149
Coventry, 370–382
    air raids on (Plates XXIX, XXX), 372
    distinguished visitors to, 379
    scheme of Emergency Medical Services (Plates XXVII, XXVIII) 372
    weight of attack and casualties, 372
Clinical laboratories, Scotland, 64
Clyde anchorages, 87–96
Crash hospitals, Scotland, 44
Croydon, work of Civil Defence Services in, 271

Decentralisation of Hospital Officer control, N. Ireland, 133, 147
Depot system, Belfast, 454, 460
District Nursing Service, Scotland, 59
Domestic staffs, Scotland, 62
Domiciliary medical attendance, N. Ireland, 132

Emergency Bacteriological Service, Scotland, 68
Emergency Hospital, Belfast, 145, 149
Emergency Hospital Scheme, N. Ireland, 127
    N. Ireland, headquarters administration, 142
Emergency Hospital Service, Scotland, long-term policy, 20–48
    short term policy, 10
Emergency Hospitals Blood Transfusion Service, N. Ireland, 188
Emergency Medical Service patients, admissions of, Scotland, 117
    categories of, Scotland, 104
Emergency Medical Services, Bath, 467
    Canterbury, 484
    Coventry (Plates XXVII, XXVIII), 370
    Exeter, 461
    N. Ireland, 123–191
    Norwich, 471
    London, organisation of, 197
    Scotland, 1–121
        in action, 97–120
    York, 481
Emergency organisation, Merseyside, in action, 326
Emergency Pathological Laboratory Services, Scotland, 64
Evacuation, Plymouth, 412
Evacuations from Merseyside, 338
Exeter, 461

First-aid parties, Birmingham, 359
    City of London, 276, 279
    Manchester Group, 349
    Merseyside, 321, 337
    N. Ireland, 154
    Norwich, 479
    Sheffield, 423, 427
    York, 481
First-aid points, N. Ireland, 157
    Scotland, 82
First-aid Post organisation, Scotland, 79
First-aid posts, Birmingham, 358, 368
    Belfast, 454, 459
    Bermondsey, 285
    Bristol, 414, 419
    Croydon, 274
    Exeter, 464
    Hackney, 299
    London, 203, 308, 311
    Manchester Group, 346, 351
    Merseyside, 321 (Plate XXIII), 336
    N. Ireland, 156
    Norwich, 472, 478
    Plymouth, 412
    St. Marylebone, 289, 291, 296, 298
    Sheffield, 423, 427
    York, 482

First-aid posts and depots, City of London, 275, 280, 281, 282
First-aid services, Hull, 438
Fracture clinic, special centre for, N. Ireland, 146

Gas casualties, Scotland, 38
Gas cleansing arrangements, N. Ireland, 161
Gas cleansing, Belfast, 456, 460
Gas-cleansing units at hospitals, N. Ireland, 134, 139
Gas officers, N. Ireland, courses of instruction for, 165
General Nursing Council, 59
Gleneagles Fitness Centres, 75
Group Officers, London, 201
Guy's Hospital, 261

Hackney, work of Civil Defence Services in, 299
Health and Local Government, Ministry of, N. Ireland, 147
Hill End Emergency Hospital, St. Albans, 229
Home Affairs, Ministry of, N. Ireland, 154
Home Guard, Ulster, co-operation with, 158
Horton Hospital, 254
Hospital accommodation, N. Ireland, 135
    Scotland, 8, 121
Hospital adaptation, Scotland, 26
Hospital administration, Scotland, 21
Hospital building, Scotland, 24, 100
Hospital clearance policy, Scotland, amended, 101
Hospital equipment, Scotland, 16, 27
Hospital expansion, N. Ireland, 130–137
Hospital hutments, N. Ireland, 145, 151
Hospital Medical Service, Civilian, N. Ireland, 163
Hospital occupancy statistics, Scotland, 117
Hospital Officer, N. Ireland, appointment of, 126
    duties, 130
Hospital Officer control, N. Ireland, decentralisation of, 133, 147
Hospital Officers, Scotland, 16
Hospital policy, Coventry, 381
Hospital protection, Scotland, 27
Hospital Services, Bermondsey, 285
    Bristol (Plate XXXV), 414, 416
    Croydon, 272
Hospital survey, Scotland, 10
Hospital treatment, N. Ireland, priority for key workers, 147
Hospital waiting lists, Scotland, 106
Hospitals, auxiliary, Scotland, 39
    Bath, 467, 469
    Birmingham, 358
    casualty receiving, in N. Ireland, 140
    crash, Scotland, 44
    damage to, Coventry (Plates XXIX, XXX), 375, 378
    Exeter (Plates XXXVII, XXXVIII), 463
    Hull, 440
    Manchester Group, 351
    Merseyside (Plates XVIII–XX, XXII), 330
    in Norwich (Plates XXXIX, XL), 473
    London (Plates I–III), 222, 223, 230, 233, 237, 243, 247, 252, 257, 259, 261
Exeter, 461, 465
for admission of evacuees, N. Ireland, 141
Hull, 439
London, evacuation to Scotland, 114
    organisation of casualty, 197, 202
Manchester Group, 342, 354
Merseyside, 319, 327
N. Ireland, additional whole-time medical officers at, 165
    casualties treated in, 150
    gas-cleansing units at, 134, 139
    honorary medical staff to, 164
    restriction on admissions, 132
    work of, 1939–41, 130–137
    work of, 1941–46, 142–151
Norwich, 471, 475
pathological services in, N. Ireland, 182
Plymouth (Plate XXXIII), 405
Portsmouth, 398
Scotland, expansion by construction, 100
    in action, 97
    restriction of admissions, 98
Scottish, E.M.S. bed complements of, 121
shadow, Scotland, 44
Sheffield, 423, 428
work of, in London raids, 220–264
York, 481, 482
Houses, damage to, Coventry, 381
    Norwich, 480
    damaged, Manchester Group, 356
Hull, 433–442
Hull, air raids on, 435

Incident Medical Officers, Birmingham, 359, 365
Inter-hospital ambulance transport, London, 204, 238
    Scotland, 77
Inter-hospital transport, Manchester Group, 345
    Merseyside, 318

Laboratory Services, N. Ireland, 182–191
Lay Services, Scotland, 49, 61
Liverpool, damaged hospitals in (Plates XVIII–XX), 330
London, air-raid casualties in, 210–220
    air raids on (Plates I–XIX), 208–315
    general review, 307
    lessons of, 307, 313
    area of, 194, 195
    City of, casualties in, 282
    heavy raids on, 278
    lesson of raids on, 283
    organisation of Civil Defence in, 275, 277
    distribution of attacks on, 213, 259

INDEX

London, organisation of Emergency Medical Services in, 197
   period of intensive raids on, 208
   population of, 196
   weight of attack on, 216
   work of Civil Defence Services in (Plates V–XVII), 265–315
London Hospital, 224
London hospitals, evacuation of, to Scotland, 114
   work of, 220–264
Lung irritant cases, Scotland, 38

Manchester, damage to hospitals in, 351
Manchester Group, 341–357
   air raids on, 346
   area and population, 341
   emergency service in action, 349
   medical organisation, 342
   scale of attacks and casualties, 346
Marine casualties, Clyde Estuary, 88
Maxillo-facial Unit, Scotland, 33
Medical attendance, domiciliary, N. Ireland, 132
Medical Officers of Health, London region, 315
Medical personnel of casualty hospitals, London, 200
   N. Ireland, classification of, 180
   163–176
   ratio to population, 181
   supply to Services, 168
Medical Personnel (Priority) Committee for N. Ireland, 170
Medical Services, Scotland, 49
Medical War Committee, N. Ireland, 125, 166
Mental disorders, units for, Scotland, 37
Merchant seamen, welfare of, 93
Merseyside, 317–340
   air raids on (Plates XVIII–XXIII), 322
   area and population, 317
   medical organisation, 318
   scale of attacks and casualties, 322
Middlesex Hospital (Plate III), 237
Mobile aid posts, Belfast, 454, 460
   N. Ireland, 156
Mobile first-aid posts, City of London, 276
   London, 308
   Scotland, 82
Mobile first-aid units, St. Marylebone, 289, 293, 296, 298
Mobile medical units, N. Ireland, 157
Mobile Nursing Unit, N. Ireland, 178
Mobile surgical teams, Manchester Group, 345
   N. Ireland, 135
Mobile units, Birmingham, 359, 366
Mobile X-ray vans, N. Ireland, 144
Mobilisation, preliminary, Scottish, 97
Mortuaries, Birmingham, 359
   Bristol, 420
   City of London, 280
   Coventry, 375
   Manchester Group, 355
   Merseyside, 321, 338
   Norwich, 479
   St. Marylebone, 290, 295
   Scotland, 84

Mortuary Service, N. Ireland, 160
Musgrave Park, transfer of Emergency Hospital to, 149

National Register of medical profession, N. Ireland, 180
Nerve injury and disease units, Scotland, 38
Nerve injuries, special centre for, N. Ireland, 146
Neurosis, special centre for, N. Ireland, 144
Newport, air raid on, 450
Northern Ireland, Emergency Medical Services in, 123–191
Northern Ireland Medical War Committee, 125, 166
Northern Ireland, ratio of practitioners to population in, 181
Norwich, 471
Nurses Act, 1945, 61
Nurses (Scotland) Act, 1943, 61
Nursing auxiliaries, N. Ireland, intensive course for, 178
Nursing Officer, N. Ireland, appointment of, 178
Nursing personnel of casualty hospitals, London, 201
Nursing personnel, N. Ireland, 176
Nursing Services, Scotland, 49, 54
Nursing Unit, mobile, N. Ireland, 178

Operational control, Merseyside, 319
Ophthalmic Units, Scotland, 35
Orthopaedic Nursing, Scotland, 61
Orthopaedic surgery, special centre for, N. Ireland, 146
Orthopaedic units, Scotland, 31

Park Prewett Hospital, Basingstoke, 241
Pathological Laboratory Services, Scotland, 64
Pathological services at hospitals, N. Ireland, 182
Pembroke Dock, air raids on, 449
Penicillin, use of, N. Ireland, 190
Plastic Unit, Scotland, 33
Plymouth, 405–413
   air raids on (Plate XXXIV), 406
   control and communications, 408, 410
   medical organisation, 405
   scale of attacks and casualties, 412
Police, duties of station, London, 205
Port of London Authority, work of Civil Defence Services in, 304
Portsmouth, 396–404
   air raids on (Plates XXXI, XXXII), 399
   medical organisation, 396
Psychoneurosis, units for, Scotland, 37
Public cleansing centres, Scotland, 82
Public health considerations, post-raid, Coventry, 380
Public Health Laboratory Services, N. Ireland, 182

Raigmore Hospital, 67
Refugees and repatriates, Scotland, 90

INDEX

Regional Resuscitation Officers, N. Ireland, 143
Rehabilitation, Scotland, 72
Rescue Service, 298
Rest centres, N. Ireland, medical aspects, 159
    Norwich, 480
    Sheffield, 432
Resuscitation in shock, 131, 143
Resuscitation, London, 247
Resuscitation officers, N. Ireland, courses of instruction for, 165
Resusitation wards, Manchester Group, 354
River Ambulance Service (Plates VI–IX), 306
Rogerstone, air raid on, 450

Salford, damage to hospitals in, 352
Sanitation, Hull, 442
Sanitation problem, Coventry, 380
Scotland, administrative responsibility, 5
    air attacks on, 108
    Emergency Medical Services in, 1–121
    evacuation of London hospitals to, 114
    ratio of practitioners to population in, 181
    Regional organisation, 6
    special units, 27
Sector I, work of hospitals in, 220
    II, work of hospitals in, 222
    III, work of hospitals in, 227
    IV, work of hospitals in, 231
    V, work of hospitals in, 236
    VI, work of hospitals in, 238
    VII, work of hospitals in, 242
    VIII, work of hospitals in, 246
    IX, work of hospitals in, 251
    X, work of hospitals in, 257
    organisation, London, 197
Services, supply of doctors to, N. Ireland, 168
Sewerage, Hull, 442
Sewerage in Norwich, 480
Sewerage, Sheffield, 432
Shadow hospitals, Scotland, 44
'Shadow' scheme, N. Ireland, 128
Sheffield, 423–432
    air raids on, 424
Shelters, medical services in, 359
Shocked casualties, resuscitation of, 131, 142
Southampton, 383–395
    air raids on, 385
    casualty service of, 383

South Wales, 443–452
    administration in, 443
    air raids on, 445, 451
Specialist advisers, honorary, N. Ireland, 164
St. Andrew's Ambulance Association, 78
St. Bartholomew's Hospital, 228
St. George's Hospital, 244
St. Marylebone, work of Civil Defence Services in, 289
St. Mary's Hospital, 240
St. Thomas's Hospital, 248
    Hydestile, Surrey, 249
Stores and equipment, Manchester Group, 356
Stretcher bearers, Manchester Group, 354
Stretcher parties, Hackney, 302
    St. Marylebone, 290, 293, 296
Surgical teams, mobile, N. Ireland, 135
Sutton Emergency Hospital, 255
Swansea, air raids on, 445, 448

Technical staffs, Scotland, 61
Thoracic Units, Scotland, 36
Transport arrangements, Scotland, 17
    St. Marylebone, 290
Transport Services, Scotland, 76
Typhoid hazard, Coventry, 380

Ulster Home Guard, co-operation with, 158

Volunteer car pool, N. Ireland, 147

Waiting lists, hospital, Scotland, 106
Wallasey, damaged hospitals in, 333
Wales, ratio of practitioners to population in, 181
    South (see South Wales)
Water supplies, damage to, Sheffield, 431
    Hull, 441
Water-supply, Canterbury, 487
    in Norwich, 480
    Plymouth, 409
    post-raid, Coventry, 380, 381
    York, 483
Welfare services, Scotland, 63, 74

X-ray vans, mobile, N. Ireland, 144

York, 481

www.ingramcontent.com/pod-product-compliance
Lightning Source LLC
Chambersburg PA
CBHW060452300426
44113CB00016B/2566